THE GREENWOOD ENCYCLOPEDIA OF

African American Literature

ADVISORY BOARD

THE GREENWOOD ENCYCLOPEDIA OF
African American Literature

VOLUME I

A–C

Edited by

Hans Ostrom and J. David Macey, Jr.

GREENWOOD PRESS
Westport, Connecticut • London

Library of Congress Cataloging-in-Publication Data

The Greenwood encyclopedia of African American literature / edited by Hans Ostrom and J. David Macey, Jr.
    p. cm.
    Includes bibliographical references.
    ISBN 0–313–32972–9 (set : alk. paper)—ISBN 0–313–32973–7 (v. 1 : alk. paper)—
    ISBN 0–313–32974–5 (v. 2 : alk. paper)—ISBN 0–313–32975–3 (v. 3 : alk. paper)—
    ISBN 0–313–32976–1 (v. 4 : alk. paper)—ISBN 0–313–32977–X (v. 5 : alk. paper) 1. American
    literature—African American authors—Encyclopedias. 2. African Americans—Intellectual life—
    Encyclopedias. 3. African Americans in literature—Encyclopedias. I. Ostrom, Hans A.
    II. Macey, J. David.
    PS153.N5G73 2005
    810.9'896073—dc22   2005013679

British Library Cataloguing in Publication Data is available.

This book is included in the *African American Experience* database from Greenwood Electronic Media.
For more information, visit www.africanamericanexperience.com.

Library of Congress Catalog Card Number: 2005013679
ISBN: 0–313–32972–9 (set)
       0–313–32973–7 (vol. I)
       0–313–32974–5 (vol. II)
       0–313–32975–3 (vol. III)
       0–313–32976–1 (vol. IV)
       0–313–32977–X (vol. V)

First published in 2005

Greenwood Press, 88 Post Road West, Westport, CT 06881
An imprint of Greenwood Publishing Group, Inc.
www.greenwood.com

Printed in the United States of America

The paper used in this book complies with the
Permanent Paper Standard issued by the National
Information Standards Organization (Z39.48–1984).

10 9 8 7 6 5 4 3 2 1

CONTENTS

List of Entries   vii

Topical List of Entries   xxiii

Preface   xli

Introduction   xlvii

Chronology   liii

The Encyclopedia   1

General Bibliography and Resources   1809

Index   1819

About the Editors   1959

About the Advisory Board   1961

About the Contributors   1963

LIST OF ENTRIES

Abernathy, Ralph David (1926–1990)

Abolitionist Movement (c. 1820–1865)

Adams, Jenoyne (born 1972)

Adoff, Arnold (born 1935)

Affirmative Action

Affrilachian Poets (1991–present)

Afrocentricity

Ai (born 1947)

Albert, Octavia Victoria Rogers
    (1853–1889)

Aldridge, Ira (1807–1867)

Alers, Rochelle (born 1943)

Alexander, Elizabeth (born 1962)

Alexander, Lewis (1900–1945)

Ali, Muhammad (born 1942)

Allen, Jeffrey Renard (born 1962)

Allen, Richard (1760–1831)

Allen, Samuel Washington (born 1917)

Allison, Hughes (1908–c. 1974)

Als, Hilton (born 1961)

Amos, Robyn (born 1971)

Amsterdam News (1909–present)

Anderson, Garland (1886–1939)

Anderson, Mignon Holland (born 1945)

Anderson, Stanice (born 1950)

Anderson-Thompkins, Sibby (born 1966)

Andrews, Raymond (1934–1991)

Andrews, Regina M. (1901–1993)

Andrews, William L. (born 1946)

Angelou, Maya (born 1928)

Ansa, Tina McElroy (born 1949)

Anthony, Sterling (born 1949)

Apess, William (1798–183?)

Archives and Collections: 1828–Present

Archives and Collections: Notable
    Collections

Armstrong, William H[oward] (1914–1999)

Asim, Jabari (born 1962)

Assimilation

Atkins, Russell (born 1926)

Atlanta, Georgia

Attaway, William (1911–1986)

Aubert, Alvin (born 1930)

Auset, Kupenda. *See* Harland-Watts, Joette

Austin, Doris Jean (1949–1994)

Autobiography

Back-to-Africa Movement

Baisden, Michael (born 1963)

Baker, Houston A., Jr. (born 1943)

Baker, Josephine (1906–1975)

Baker, Nikki (born 1962)

Baldwin, James (1924–1987)

Ballad

Ballard, Allen B. (born 1933)

Baltimore, Maryland

Baltimore Afro-American (1892–present)

Bambara, Toni Cade (1939–1995)

Bandele, Asha (born 1968)

Banks, Leslie Esdaile (born 1959)

Banneker, Benjamin (1731–1806)

Baraka, Amiri (born 1934)

Baraka, Ras (born 1970)

Barnes, Steven Emory (born 1952)

Barnett, LaShonda Katrice (born 1974)

Barrax, Gerald W. (born 1933)

Basie, William "Count" (1904–1984)

Basketball

Beadle, Samuel A. (1857–1932)

Beals, Melba Patillo (born 1941)

Beam, Joseph (1954–1988)

Bearden, Romare (1912–1988)

Beat Movement, The (1945–1965)

Beatty, Paul (born 1962)

Beckham, Barry (born 1944)

Beckwourth, James (1798–c. 1867)

Bell, Derrick (born 1930)

Bell, James Madison (1826–1902)

Benjamin, Robert C. O. (1855–1900)

Bennett, Gwendolyn (1902–1981)

Bennett, Hal [George Harold] (born 1930)

Benson, Leticia (born 1963)

Bernal, Martin (born 1937)

Berry, Bertice (born 1961)

Berry, Charlene A. (born 1967)

Bibb, Henry Walton (1815–1854)

Birtha, Becky (born 1948)

Black American Literature Forum (1976–1991)

Black Arts Movement (1960–1970)

Black Arts Repertory Theatre/School

Black Athena Controversy (1987–present)

Black Atlantic

Black Dialogue (1965–1972)

Black Family

Black Nationalism (c. 1827–present)

Black Panther Party (for Self-Defense) (1966–c. 1980)

Black Power (1960–present)

Black Studies

Bland, Eleanor Tayor (born 1944)

Blank Verse

Blaxploitation

Blues, The

Blues Poetry

Bond, Julian (born 1940)

Bonner, Marita (1899–1971)

Bontemps, Arna (1902–1973)

Boston, Massachusetts

Bowen, Michele Andrea (born 1961)

Boyd, Melba (born 1950)

Boyd, Valerie (born 1963)

Boyer, Jill Witherspoon (born 1947)

Bradley, David Henry, Jr. (born 1950)

Braithwaite, William Stanley Beaumont (1878–1962)

Brawley, Benjamin Griffith (1882–1939)

Bridgforth, Sharon (born c. 1960)

Briscoe, Connie (born 1952)

Broadside Press (1965–present)

Brooklyn, New York

Brooks, Gwendolyn (1917–2000)

Broughton, Virginia W. (c. 1856–1934)

Brown, Cecil (born 1943)

Brown, Claude (1937–2002)

Brown, Elaine (born 1943)

Brown, Fahamisha Patricia (born 1942)

Brown, Frank London (1927–1962)

Brown, Hallie Quinn (1845–1949)

Brown, Henry "Box" (c. 1815–?)

Brown, John (1800–1859)

Brown, Linda Beatrice (born 1939)

Brown, Lloyd (1913–2003)

Brown, Sterling A. (1901–1989)

Brown, Wesley (born 1945)

Brown, William Wells (1815–1884)

Browne, Theodore (c. 1910–1979)

Brownies' Book, The (1920–1921)

Bryan, Ashley (born 1923)

Buchanan, Shonda (born 1968)

Buckley, Gail Lumet (born 1937)

Bullins, Ed (born 1935)

Bunkley, Anita Richmond (born 1944)

Burrill, Mary ("Mamie") Powell (c. 1882–1946)

Burroughs, Margaret Taylor Goss (born 1917)

Burton, Annie Louise (1860–?)

Burton, LeVar (born 1957)

Bush-Banks, Olivia Ward (1869–1944)

Busia, Akosua (born 1966)

Bussey, Louré (born c. 1971)

Butcher, Philip (born 1918)

Butler, Octavia E. (born 1947)

Butler, Tajuana "TJ" (born 1971)

Byrd, Adrianne (born c. 1976)

Cain, George (born 1943)

Caldwell, Ben (born 1937)

Callaloo (1976–present)

Campanella, Roy (1921–1993)

Campbell, Bebe Moore (born 1950)

Campbell, James Edwin (1867–1896)

Carby, Hazel V. (born 1948)

Carmichael, Stokely (1941–1998)

Carroll, Vinnette (1922–2003)

Carter, Charlotte (born 1943)

Carter, Rubin "Hurricane" (born 1937)

Carter, Stephen L. (born 1954)

Cartiér, Xam Wilson (born 1949)

Cary, Lorene (born 1956)

Cary, Mary Ann Camberton Shadd (1823–1893)

Cassells, Cyrus (born 1957)

Censorship

Chambers, Veronica (born 1971)

Chancy, Myriam J. A. (born 1970)

Charles, Kraal (Kayo) Y. (born 1975)

Chase-Riboud, Barbara (born 1939)

Chennault, Stephen D. (born 1940)

Chesnutt, Charles Waddell (1858–1932)

Chicago, Illinois

Chicago Defender (1905–present)

Chicago Renaissance (c. 1930–1950)

Children's Literature

Childress, Alice (1916–1994)

Chisholm, Shirley Anita St. Hill (1924–2005)

Christian, Barbara T. (1943–2000)

Christian, Marcus Bruce (1900–1976)

Civil Rights Movement

Civil War, American (1861–1865)

Clair, Maxine (born 1939)

Clarke, Breena

Cleage [Lomax], Pearl Michelle (born 1948)

Cleaver, Eldridge (1935–1998)

Cleaver, Kathleen Neal (born 1946)

Cliff, Michelle (born 1946)

Clifton, Lucille (born 1936)

Clinton, Michelle T. (born 1954)

Cobb, Ned (1885–1973)

Cobb, William Jelani (born c. 1972)

Coffin, Frank B[arbour] (1871–1951)

Cold War, The (c. 1947–1960)

Cole, Harriette (born c. 1963)

Coleman, Anita Scott (1890–1960)

Coleman, Evelyn (born 1948)

Coleman, Wanda (born 1946)

College Language Association

Collier, Eugenia (born 1928)

Colonialism

Color of Skin

Colter, Cyrus (1910–2002)

Columbian Orator, The (c. 1797)

Combahee River Collective (c. 1974–1980)

Comic Books. See CQ Comics Group; Graphic Novels; Milestone Comics/ Milestone Media

Coming-of-Age Fiction

Cone, James H. (born 1939)

Conjuring

Cook, William W. (born 1933)

Cooking

Cooper, Anna Julia Haywood (1858/ 1859–1964)

Cooper, Clarence, Jr. (1934–1978)

Cooper, J[oan] California (born 193?)

Coppin, Fanny Marion Jackson (c. 1837–1913)

Corbin, Steven (1953–1995)

Cornish, Sam[uel] James (born 1935)

Cornish, Samuel Eli (c. 1790–1858)

Corrothers, James (1869–1917)

Cortez, Jayne (born 1936)

Cosby, William (Bill) (born 1937)

Cose, Ellis (born 1950)

Cotter, Joseph Seamon, Jr. (1895–1919)

Cotter, Joseph Seamon, Sr. (1861–1949)

Cowdery, Mae V. (1909–1953)

CQ Comics Group (1997–present)

Craft, William (1824–1900) and Ellen Smith Craft (1826–1891)

Crafts, Hannah

Creole

Crime and Mystery Fiction

Crisis, The (1910–present)

Cross-Dressing

Crouch, Stanley (born 1945)

Crummell, Alexander (1819–1898)

Cruse, Harold Wright (born 1916)

Cullen, Countee (1903–1946)

Cuney-Hare, Maud (1874–1936)

Dandridge, Raymond Garfield (1882–1930)

Danner, Margaret Esse Taylor (1915–1984)

Danticat, Edwidge (born 1969)

Darden, Christopher (born 1957)

Dasein Literary Society (1958–1960)

Dash, Julie (born 1952)

davenport, doris (born 1949)

Davis, Angela Y. (born 1944)

Davis, Arthur P. (1904–1996)

Davis, Bridgett M. (born 1960)

Davis, Daniel Webster (1862–1913)

Davis, Frank Marshall (1905–1987)

Davis, Ossie (1917–2005)

Davis, Thulani N. (born 1949)

Dean, Phillip Hayes (born 1937)

DeBerry, Virginia (born c. 1962) and Donna Grant (born c. 1963)

Deconstruction

Delaney, Lucy A. (c. 1828–?)

Delany, Martin R. (1812–1885)

Delany, Samuel R. (born 1942)

DeLoach, Nora (1940–2001)

Demby, William (born 1922)

Dent, Thomas Covington (1932–1998)

Derricotte, Toi (born 1941)

Detroit, Michigan

Dett, R[obert] Nathaniel (1882–1943)

Detter, Thomas P. (c. 1826–?)

DeVeaux, Alexis (born 1948)

Dialect Poetry

Diaspora

Dickerson, Debra J. (born 1959)

Dickey, Eric Jerome (born 1961)

Dillon, Leo (born 1933) and Diane Dillon (born 1933)

Dixon, Melvin (1950–1992)

Dodson, Howard (born 1939)

Dodson, Owen (1914–1983)

Dorr, David F. (1827/1828–1872)

Douglass, Frederick (1818–1895)

Dove, Rita (born 1952)

Drake, David (c. 1800–c. 1870)

Drama

Drumgoold, Kate (c. 1858–?)

Du Bois, W.E.B. (1868–1963)

Duckett, Larry (1953–2001)

Due, Tananarive (born 1966)

Duke, Lynne (born 1956)

Dumas, Henry (1934–1968)

Dunbar, Paul Laurence (1872–1906)

Dunbar-Nelson, Alice Moore (1875–1935)

Duncan, Thelma Myrtle (born 1902)

Dunham, Katherine (born 1909)

Durem, Ray (1915–1963)

Durham, David Anthony (born 1969)

Dyson, Michael Eric (born 1958)

Dystopian Literature

Eady, Cornelius (born 1954)

Early, Gerald Lyn (born 1952)

Ebony (1945–present)

Edmonds, S[heppard] Randolph (1900–1983)

Edwards, Grace F[rederica] (born c. 1943)

Edwards, Junius (born 1929)

Edwards, Louis (born 1962)

Elam, Patricia (born c. 1971)

Elaw, Zilpha (c. 1790–?)

Elder, Lonne, III (1927–1996)

Elizabeth (1766–1866)

Ellington, Edward Kennedy "Duke" (1899–1974)

Ellis, Erika (born 1965)

Ellis, Thomas Sayers (born 1965)

Ellis, Trey (born 1962)

Ellison, Ralph (1914–1994)

Emanuel, James A. (born 1921)

Epic Poetry/The Long Poem

Epistolary Novel

Equiano, Olaudah (1745–1797)

Erotica

Essay

Evans, Mari (born 1923)

Everett, Percival (born 1956)

Evers, Medgar (1925–1963)

Exoticism

Expatriate Writers

E-Zines, E-News, E-Journals, and E-Collections

Fabio, Sarah Webster (1928–1979)

Fair, Ronald L. (born 1932)

Fales-Hill, Susan (born 1962)

Farmer, Nancy (born 1941)

Fauset, Jessie Redmon (1882–1961)

Federal Writers' Project (c. 1936–1941)

Feminism/Black Feminism

Feminist/Black Feminist Literary Criticism

Ferrell, Carolyn (born 1962)

Fiction. See Coming-of-Age Fiction; Crime and Mystery Fiction; Epistolary Novel; Graphic Novels; Historical Fiction; Horror Fiction; Novel; Romance Novel; Science Fiction; Short Fiction

Finney, Nikky (born 1957)

Fire!! (1926)

Fisher, Rudolph John Chauncey (1897–1934)

Fleming, Sarah Lee Brown (1876–1963)

Flowers, Arthur Rickydoc (born 1950)

Folklore

Folktales

Food. See Cooking

Foote, Julia (1823–1900)

Forbes, Calvin (born 1945)

Ford, Nick Aaron (1904–1982)

Formal Verse

Forman, Ruth (born 1968)

Forrest, Leon (1937–1997)

Forster, Gwynne (born c. 1966)

Fortune, T[imothy] Thomas (1856–1928)

Foster, Frances Smith (born 1944)

Foster, Sharon Ewell (born 1957)

Franklin, C. L. (1915–1984)

Franklin, J. E. (born 1937)

Franklin, John Hope (born 1915)

Frazier, Edward Franklin (1894–1962)

Free Southern Theater (1963–1979)

Free Verse

Fuller, Charles H., Jr. (born 1939)

Fuller, Hoyt (1923–1981)

Fullilove, Eric James (born 1954)

Fulton, David Bryant (1863–1941)

Furious Flower Conference (1994, 2004)

Gaines, Ernest James (born 1933)

Gaines, Patrice (born 1949)

Garnet, Henry Highland (1815–1882)

Garvey, Marcus (1887–1940)

Gates, Henry Louis, Jr. (born 1950)

Gay Literature

Gayle, Addison, Jr. (1932–1991)

Gayle, Roberta (born 1963)

Gender

Genesis Press (1993–present)

George, Nelson (born 1957)

Gibson, Patricia Joann (born 1952)

Gilbert, Mercedes (1889–1952)

Gillespie, Dizzy (1917–1993), Charlie Parker (1920–1955), and Thelonious Monk (1917–1982)

Gilmore, Brian (born 1962)

Gilmore-Scott, Monique (born c. 1967)

Gilpin Players

Gilroy, Paul (born 1956)

Giovanni, Nikki (born 1943)

Glave, Thomas (born 1964)

Goines, Donald (1937–1974)

Goldberg, Whoopi (born 1955)

Golden, Marita (born 1950)

Gomez, Jewelle (born 1948)

Gordone, Charles (1925–1995)

Gospel Music

Gossett, Hattie (born 1942)

Gothic Literature

Gould, Sandra Lee (born 1949)

Graham, Lorenz [Bell] (1902–1989)

Graham, Ottie B. (1900–1982)

Graham, Shirley (1896–1977)

Graphic Novels

Great Depression (1929–1939)

Great Migration

Green, Carmen (born 1963)

Green, John Patterson (1845–1940)

Greenfield, Eloise (born 1929)

Greenlee, Sam (born 1930)

Gregory, Dick [Richard] (born 1932)

Griggs, Sutton E. (1872–1933)

Grimes, Terris McMahan (born 1952)

Grimké, Angelina Emily (1805–1879)

Grimké, Angelina Weld (1880–1958)

Grimké, Archibald Henry (1849–1930)

Grimké, Charlotte Forten (1837–1914)

Grimké, Francis James (1850–1937)

Grimké, Sarah Moore (1792–1873)

Gronniosaw, James Albert Ukawsaw (c. 1710–?)

Grooms, Anthony (born 1955)

Gulf War (1991)

Gumby, Levi-Sandy Alexander (1885–1961)

Gunn, Bill (1934–1989)

Gunn, Gay G. (born 1947)

Guy, Rosa (born 1925)

Haiku

Hailstock, Shirley (born 1948)

Hair

Haiti

Haley, Alex (1921–1992)

Hall, Prince (c. 1735–1807)

Hambone (1974–present)

Hamilton, Virginia (1936–2002)

Hammon, Briton (flourished 1760)

Hammon, Jupiter (1711–c. 1806)

Hansberry, Lorraine (1930–1965)

Hansen, Joyce (born 1942)

Hardy, James Earl (born c. 1972)

Harland-Watts, Joette [Kupenda Auset] (born 1967)

Harlem, New York

Harlem Renaissance (c. 1920–1932)

Harper, Frances Ellen Watkins (1825–1911)

Harper, Michael S. (born 1938)

Harper, Phillip Brian (born 1961)

Harrington, Oliver (Ollie) (1912–1995)

Harris, Bill (born 1941)

Harris, E[verette] Lynn (born 1955)

Harris, Eddy L. (born 1956)

Harris, Peter J. (born 1955)

Harris, Trudier (born 1948)

Harrison, Hubert Henry (1883–1927)

Haskins, James S. (born 1941)

Hassan, Umar Bin (born 1948)

Hawkins, Walter Everette (1883–?)

Hayden, Robert (1913–1980)

Hayes, Terrance (born 1971)

Haynes, David (born 1955)

Haynes, Lemuel (1753–1833)

Haywood, Gar Anthony (born 1954)

Hazzard, Alvira (1899–1953)

Heard, Nathan (1936–2004)

Hemans, Donna (born 1970)

Hemings, Sally (1773–1835)

Hemphill, Essex (1957–1995)

Henderson, David (born 1942)

Henderson, George Wylie (1904–1965)

Henry, John (c. 1870–present)

Henson, Josiah (1789–1883)

Hercules, Frank (1911–1996)

Hernton, Calvin Coolidge (1932–2001)

Herron, Carolivia (born 1947)

Heyward, [Edwin] DuBose (1885–1940) and Dorothy [Hartzell Kuhns] Heyward (1890–1961)

Hill, Abram (1910–1986)

Hill, Donna (born 1955)

Hill, Ernest (born 1961)

Himes, Chester (1909–1984)

Hip-Hop

Historical Fiction

Hoagland, Everett H., III (born 1942)

Holder, Laurence (born 1939)

Holiday, Billie (1915–1959)

Holton, Hugh (1946–2001)

Holtzclaw, William Henry (1870–1943)

hooks, bell (born 1952)

Hopkins, Pauline Elizabeth (1859–1930)

Hopkinson, Nalo (born 1960)

Horne, Frank Smith (1899–1974)

Horror Fiction

Horton, George Moses (c. 1797–c. 1883)

Howard University Press (1972–present)

Hubbard, Dolan (born 1949)

Hudson-Smith, Linda (born 1950)

Hughes, Langston (1902–1967)

Hull, Akasha [Gloria T.] (born 1944)

Humor

Hunt, Marsha (born 1946)

Hunter, Travis (born 1969)

Hurston, Zora Neale (1891–1960)

Iceberg Slim (1918–1992)

Internet. See E-Zines, E-News, E-Journals, and E-Collections

Jackson, Angela (born 1951)

Jackson, Brian Keith (born 1967)

Jackson, Elaine (born 1943)

Jackson, George Lester (1941–1971)

Jackson, Jesse L[ouis] (born 1941)

Jackson, Mae (born 1946)

Jackson, Mattie J. (c. 1846–?)

Jackson, Monica

Jackson, Murray E. (1926–2002)

Jackson, Rebecca Cox (1796–1871)

Jackson, Sheneska (born 1970)

Jackson-Opoku, Sandra (born 1953)

Jacobs, Harriet Ann (1813–1897)

James, Darius (born c. 1969)

James, Kelvin Christopher (born c. 1945)

Jazz

Jazz in Literature

Jeffers, Lance (1919–1985)

Jefferson, (Blind) Lemon (1893–1929)

Jefferson, Roland S. (born 1939)

Jeffries, Tamara Yvette (born 1964)

Jenkins, Beverly Hunter (born 1951)

Joans, Ted (1928–2003)

Joe, Yolanda (born 1962)

John the Conqueror

Johnson, Amelia E. (1859–1922)

Johnson, Angela (born 1961)

Johnson, Charles R. (born 1948)

Johnson, Charles Spurgeon (1893–1956)

Johnson, Doris (born 1937)

Johnson, Fenton (1888–1958)

Johnson, Freddie Lee, III (born 1958)

Johnson, Georgia Douglas (1886–1966)

Johnson, Guy (born 1945)

Johnson, Helene (1906–1995)

Johnson, Jack (1878–1946)

Johnson, James P[rice] (1894–1955)

Johnson, James Weldon (1871–1938)

Johnson, Mat (born 1970)

Johnson Publishing Company (1942–present)

Johnson-Coleman, Lorraine (born 1962)

Johnson-Hodge, Margaret

Jones, Edward P. (born 1950)

Jones, Edward Smyth (1881–?)

Jones, Gayl (born 1949)

Jones, Laurence C. (1884–1975)

Jones, Patricia Spears (born 1955)

Jones, Sarah (born 1974)

Jones, Solomon (born 1967)

Jones-Meadows, Karen

Jordan, Barbara Charline (1936–1996)

Jordan, June (1936–2002)

Jordan, Michael Jeffrey (born 1963)

Journal of Black Poetry (1966–1973)

Joyce, Joyce Ann (born 1949)

Just Us Books (1988–present)

Kai, Nubia (born 1948)

Karenga, Maulana (born 1941)

Kaufman, Bob (1926–1986)

Keats, Ezra Jack (1919–1983)

Keckley, Elizabeth (c. 1818–1907)

Keene, John R., Jr. (born 1965)

Kelley, Norman (born 1954)

Kelley, William Melvin (born 1937)

Kelley-Hawkins, Emma Dunham (1863–1938)

Kenan, Randall Garrett (born 1963)

Kennedy, Adrienne (born 1931)

Killens, John Oliver (1916–1987)

Kincaid, Jamaica (born 1949)

King, Martin Luther, Jr. (1929–1968)

King, Woodie, Jr. (born 1937)

Kitchen Table: Women of Color Press (1981–present)

Kitt, Sandra (born 1947)

Knight, Etheridge (1931–1991)

Knopf, Alfred A. (1892–1984)

Kocher, Ruth Ellen (born 1965)

Komunyakaa, Yusef (born 1947)

Kool Moe Dee (born 1963)

Kweli, Talib (born 1975)

Labor

Ladd, Florence (born 1932)

Lamar, Jake (born 1961)

Lane, Pinkie Gordon (born 1923)

Langston, John Mercer (1829–1897)

Langston Hughes Society (1981–present)

Lanusse, Armand (1812–1867)

Larsen, Nella (1891–1964)

Last Poets, The

Lattany, Kristin Hunter (born 1931)

LaValle, Victor (born 1972)

Lawrence, Jacob (1917–2000)

Leadbelly [Ledbetter, Huddie] (1889–1949)

Lee, Andrea (born 1953)

Lee, Helen Elaine (born 1959)

Lee, Jarena (1783–?)

Lee, Spike (born 1957)

Lesbian Literature

Lester, Julius (born 1939)

Lewis, Theophilus (1891–1974)

Lincoln, C[harles] Eric (1924–2000)

Literary Canon

Literary Societies

Livingston, Myrtle Smith (1902–1973)

Location Theory

Locke, Alain LeRoy (1886–1954)

Lorde, Audre (1934–1992)

Los Angeles, California

Lotus Press (1972–present)

Louis, Joe (1914–1981)

Love, Monifa A. (born 1955)

Love, Nat (1854–1921)

Lynching

Lynching, History of

Lyric Poetry

Mackey, Nathaniel (born 1947)

Madgett, Naomi Long (born 1923)

Madhubuti, Haki R. (Don L[uther] Lee) (born 1942)

Magazines, Literary

Major, Clarence (born 1936)

Major, Marcus (born c. 1972)

Malcolm X (1925–1965)

Mallette, Gloria (born 1953)

Margetson, George Reginald (1877–?)

Marrant, John (1755–1791)

Marriage

Marshall, Paule (born 1929)

Marxism

Mataka, Laini (born c. 1951)

Matheus, John F. (1887–1983)

Mathis, Sharon Bell (born 1937)

Matthews, Victoria Earle (1861–1907)

Mayfield, Julian (1928–1984)

Mays, Benjamin Elijah (1894–1984)

Mays, Willie Howard, Jr. (born 1931)

McBride, James (born 1957)

McCall, Nathan (born 1955)

McCarthyism (1950–1954)

McCauley, Robbie (born 1947)

McClellan, George Marion (1860–1934)

McCluskey, John Ashbery, Jr. (born 1944)

McDonald, Janet A. (born 1953)

McDowell, Deborah E. (born 1951)

McElroy, Colleen (born 1935)

McFadden, Bernice (born 1965)

McKay, Claude (1889–1948)

McKay, Nellie Yvonne (born 1947)

McKinney-Whetstone, Diane (born 1953)

McKissack, Patrica (born 1944)

McKnight, Reginald (born 1956)

McLarin, Kim (born c. 1964)

McMillan, Terry (born 1951)

McPherson, James Alan (born 1943)

Memphis, Tennessee

Menard, John Willis (1838–1893)

Meriwether, Louise (born 1923)

Messenger, The (1917–1928)

Metaphor

Micheaux, Oscar (1884–1951)

Middle Passage, The (c. 1540–1855)

Milestone Comics/Milestone Media (1992–present)

Miller, E. Ethelbert (born 1950)

Miller, May (1899–1995)

Miller, R. Baxter (born 1948)

Millican, Arthenia Jackson Bates (born 1920)

Milner, Ron (1938–2004)

Minstrelsy

Misogyny

Mississippi Delta

Mitchell, Loften (1919–2001)

Modernism (c. 1890–1940)

Mojo

Monk, Thelonious. *See* Gillespie, Dizzy, Charlie Parker, and Thelonious Monk

Monroe, Mary (born 1951)

Monteilh, Marissa (born c. 1974)

Moody, Anne (born 1940)

Moore, Charles Michael (1948–2003)

Moore, Jessica Care (born 1971)

Moore, Lenard D. (born 1958)

Moore, Opal (born 1953)

Morrison, Toni (born 1931)

Mosley, Walter (born 1952)

Moss, Thylias (born 1954)

Mossell, Gertrude Bustill (1855–1948)

Motley, Willard (1909–1965)

Mowry, Jess (born 1960)

Mulatto

Mullen, Harryette (born 1954)

Multicultural Theory

Murray, Albert (born 1916)

Murray, Pauli (1910–1985)

Musical Theater

Myers, Walter Dean (born 1937)

Mystery Fiction. *See* Crime and Mystery Fiction

Myth

NAACP

Nadir (1877–1915)

Naming

Narrative Poetry

Nashville, Tennessee

Nation of Islam

Nature

Naylor, Gloria (born 1950)

Neal, Larry (1937–1981)

Neely, Barbara (born 1941)

Neff, Heather (born 1958)

Négritude (c. 1930–1960)

Negro

Negro Digest (1942–1951, 1961–1970)

Negro Units, Federal Theatre Project (1935–1939)

Negro World (1918–1933)

Nell, William Cooper (1816–1874)

Nelson, Annie Greene (1902–1993)

Nelson, Jill (born 1952)

Nelson, Marilyn (born 1946)

New Criticism (1930–1970)

New Negro (1920s)

New Negro, The (1925)

New Orleans, Louisiana

New York City. *See* Brooklyn, New York; Harlem, New York; Harlem Renaissance

Newsome, Effie Lee (1885–1979)

Newspapers, African American

Newton, Huey Percy (1942–1989)

Newton, Lionel (born 1961)

Nichols, Nichelle (born 1933)

Njeri, Itabari (born 1955)

Nkombo (1968–1974)

NOMMO (1969–1976)

Northup, Solomon (1808–1863)

Novel

Nugent, Richard Bruce (1906–1987)

Núñez, Elizabeth (born c. 1950)

Nuyorican Poets Café

OBAC

O'Daniel, Therman B. (1908–1986)

Oklahoma

Opportunity (1923–1949)

OyamO (born 1943)

Oyewole, Abiodun (born c. 1946)

Packer, ZZ (born 1973)

Paris, France

Parker, Charlie. *See* Gillespie, Dizzy, Charlie Parker, and Thelonious Monk

Parker, Pat (1944–1989)

Parks, Gordon (born 1912)

Parks, Suzan-Lori (born 1963)

Parody

Passing

Pate, Alexs D. (born 1950)

Patterson, Raymond R. (1929–2001)

Pennington, James William Charles (1807–1870)

Penny, Rob[ert] Lee (1941–2003)

Perdomo, Willie (born 1967)

Performance Poetry

Perkins, Useni Eugene (born 1932)

Perrin, Kayla (born 1969)

Perry, Charles (1924–1969)

Perry, Phyllis Alesia (born 1961)

Petry, Ann Lane (1908–1997)

Pharr, Robert Deane (1916–1989)

Philadelphia, Pennsylvania

Phillips, Carl (born 1959)

Phillips, Gary (born 1955)

Photography

Phylon (1940–1987; 1992–present)

Pinckney, Darryl (born 1953)

Pinkney, Sandra (born 1971) and Myles Pinkney (born 1971)

Pittsburgh, Pennsylvania

Pittsburgh Courier (1907–1965)

Plato, Ann (c. 1820–?)

Plumpp, Sterling D. (born 1940)

Poetics

Poetry. *See* Ballad; Blank Verse; Blues Poetry; Dialect Poetry; Epic Poetry/The Long Poem; Formal Verse; Free Verse; Haiku; Lyric Poetry; Narrative Poetry; Performance Poetry; Poetics; Prose Poem; Sonnet; Surrealism; Villanelle

Polite, Carlene Hatcher (born 1932)

Popel [Shaw], Esther A. B. (1896–1958)

Porter, Connie Rose (born 1959)

Postmodernism

Poststructuralism

Powell, Kevin (born 1969)

Prison Literature

Prose Poem

Protest Literature

Publishers and Publishing

Queer Theory

Ra, Sun (1914–1993)

Race

Race Riots

Race Uplift Movement

Racial Discovery Plot

Ragtime

Rahman, Aishah (born 1936)

Rampersad, Arnold (born 1941)

Randall, Dudley Felker (1914–2000)

Randolph, Asa Philip (1889–1979)

Rap

Rastafarian

Ray, Henrietta Cordelia (c. 1852–1916)

Raymond, Linda (born 1952)

Realism

Reconstruction

Redbone Press (1995–present)

Redding, J. Saunders (1906–1988)

Redmond, Eugene B. (born 1937)

Reed, Ishmael (born 1938)

Reggae

Reid-Pharr, Robert F. (born 1965)

Remond, Charles Lenox (1810–1873)

Remond, Sarah Parker (1824–1894)

Research Resources: Electronic Works

Research Resources: Reference Works

Rhodes, Jewell Parker (born 1954)

Rice, Patty (born c. 1976)

Richardson, Willis (1889–1977)

Ridley, John (born 1965)

Riley, Len

Ringgold, Faith (born 1930)

Rivers, Conrad Kent (1933–1968)

Robeson, Paul (1898–1976)

Robinson, C. Kelly (born 1970)

Robinson, Jackie [Jack Roosevelt] (1919–1972)

Robotham, Rosemarie Angela (born 1957)

Roby, Kimberla Lawson (born 1965)

Rodgers, Carolyn M[arie] (born c. 1945)

Romance Novel

Rose, Tricia (born 1962)

Rowe, George Clinton (1853–1903)

Roy, Lucinda (born 1955)

Rushin, [Donna K.] Kate (born 1951)

Rux, Carl Hancock (born c. 1968)

Sage: A Scholarly Journal on Black Women (1984–1995)

Salaam, Kalamu ya (born 1947)

Sambo

San Francisco Bay Area, California

Sanchez, Sonia (born 1934)

Sanders, Dori (born 1930)

Sapphire [Lofton, Ramona] (born 1950)

Satire

Scarborough, William Sanders (1852–1926)

Schomburg, Arthur A. (1874–1938)

Schuyler, George Samuel (1895–1977)

Science Fiction

Scott-Heron, Gil (born 1949)

Scottsboro Boys, The

Scruggs, Afi-Odelia E. (born 1954)

Seacole, Mary (1805–1881)

Séjour, Victor (1817–1874)

Senna, Danzy (born 1970)

Sermons

Sexual Revolution (c. 1960–1980)

Shackelford, Theodore Henry (1888–1923)

Shaik, Fatima (born 1952)

Shakur, Tupac (1971–1996)

Shange, Ntozake (born 1948)

Shannon, Angela (born 1964)

Shannon, Ray (pseudonym of Gar Anthony Haywood)

Sheffey, Ruthe T. (born c. 1926)

Shepherd, Reginald (born 1963)

Sherman, Charlotte Watson (born 1958)

Shine, Ted [Theodis] (born 1931)

Shockley, Ann Allen (born 1927)

Short Fiction

Signifying

Simmons, Herbert (born 1930)

Simmons, Russell (born 1957)

Sinclair, April (born 1955)

Sister Souljah (born 1964)

Slang

Slave Narrative

Slavery

Smiley, Tavis (born 1964)

Smith, Amanda Berry (1837–1915)

Smith, Anna Deavere (born 1950)

Smith, Barbara (born 1946)

Smith, Bessie (1894–1937)

Smith, Effie Waller (1879–1960)

Smith, Mary Burnett (born 1931)

Smith, Venture (1728/1729–1805)

Smith, William Gardner (1927–1974)

Smitherman, Geneva (born 1940)

Snoe, Eboni (born 1955)

Sonnet

Soul

South, The

Southerland, Ellease (born 1943)

Southern Studies

Spellman, A. B. (born 1935)

Spence, Eulalie (1894–1981)

Spencer, Anne (1882–1975)

Spillers, Hortense J. (born 1942)

Spirituals

St. John, Primus (born 1939)

St. Louis, Missouri

Stepto, Robert Burns (born 1944)

Steptoe, John (1950–1989)

Stetson, Jeff (born 1949)

Steward, Theophilus Gould (1843–1924)

Stewart, Maria W. (1803–1879)

Still, William (1821–1902)

Still, William Grant (1895–1978)

Stowe, Harriet Beecher (1811–1896)

Strange, Sharan (born 1959)

Surrealism

Survey Graphic (1921–1948)

Swindle, Renée

Swing

Tademy, Lalita (born 1948)

Talented Tenth (c. 1900–1930)

Tanner, Benjamin Tucker (1835–1923)

Tarpley, Natasha (born 1971)

Tarry, Ellen (born 1906)

Tate, Eleanora Elaine (born 1948)

Tate, Greg (born 1957)

Taulbert, Clifton LeMoure (born 1945)

Taylor, Mel (born 1939)

Taylor, Mildred D. (born 1943)

Taylor, Regina (born 1959)

Taylor, Susie King (1848–1912)

Terrell, Mary Eliza Church (1863–1954)

Terry [Prince], Lucy (c. 1730–1821)

Tervalon, Jervey (born 1958)

Texas

Theater. See Drama

Thelwell, Michael (born 1939)

Theology, Black and Womanist

Third World Press (1967–present)

Thomas, Joyce Carol (born 1938)

Thomas, Lorenzo (born 1944)

Thomas, Piri (born 1928)

Thomas-Graham, Pamela (born 1963)

Thompson, Era Bell (1905–1986)

Thompson, Robert Farris (born 1932)

Thurman, Howard (1900–1981)

Thurman, Wallace (1902–1934)

Till, Emmett (1941–1955)

Tillman, Katherine Davis Chapman (1870–c. 1946)

Tokenism

Tolson, Melvin B. (1898–1966)

Toomer, Jean (1894–1967)

Touré, Askia Muhammad Abu Bakr el (born 1938)

Travel Writing

Trethewey, Natasha (born 1966)

Trice, Dawn Turner (born 1965)

Trickster

Troupe, Quincy Thomas, Jr. (born 1943)

Truth, Sojourner (1797–1883)

Tubbee, Okah (1810–?)

Tubman, Harriet Ross (c. 1820–1913)

Turner, Darwin T. (1931–1991)

Turner, Henry McNeal (1834–1915)

Turner, Nat (1800–1831)

Turpin, Waters E. (1910–1968)

Twain, Mark (1835–1910)

Tyree, Omar (born 1969)

Ulen, Eisa Nefertari (born 1968)

Umbra Workshop (1962–1963)

Uncle Tom

Underground Railroad

Utopian Literature

Van Der Zee, James (1886–1983)

Van Peebles, Melvin (born 1932)

Van Vechten, Carl (1880–1964)

Vashon, George Boyer (1824–1878)

Verdelle, A. J. (born 1960)

Vernacular

Vernon, Olympia (born 1973)

Vietnam War (1961–1975)

Villanelle

Voice of the Negro, The (1904–1907)

Voodoo/Vodoun

Vroman, Mary Elizabeth (1923–1967)

Wade-Gayles, Gloria Jean (born 1938)

Walker, Alice (born 1944)

Walker, Blair S. (born 1955)

Walker, David (1785–1830)

Walker, Joseph A. (1935–2003)

Walker, Margaret Abigail (1915–1998)

Walker, Persia (born 1957)

Walker, Rebecca (born 1969)

Wallace, Michele Faith (born 1952)

Walrond, Eric D[erwent] (1898–1966)

Walter, Mildred Pitts (born 1922)

Walton, Anthony (born 1960)

Waniek, Marilyn Nelson. See Nelson, Marilyn

Ward, Douglas Turner (born 1930)

Ward, Jerry Washington, Jr. (born 1943)

Ward, [James] Theodore (Ted) (1902–1983)

Washington, Booker T. (1856–1915)

Washington, Mary Helen (born 1941)

Washington, Teresa N. (born 1971)

Washington, D.C.

Waters, Ethel (1896–1977)

Weatherly, Tom (born 1942)

Weaver, Afaa Michael (born 1951)

Webb, Frank J. (c. 1828–c. 1894)

Webb, Mary (1828–1859)

Weber, Carl (born 1970)

Wells-Barnett, Ida B. (1862–1931)

Wesley, Dorothy Burnett Porter (1905–1995)

Wesley, Valerie Wilson (born 1947)

West, Cheryl L. (born 1965)

West, Cornel (born 1953)

West, Dorothy (1907–1998)

Wheatley, Phillis (c. 1753–1784)

Whipper, William (1804–1876)

White (Racial Designation)

White, Edgar Nkosi (born 1947)

White, Paulette Childress (born 1948)

White, Walter Francis (1893–1955)

Whitehead, Colson (born 1969)

Whitfield, James Monroe (1822–1871)

Whitfield, Van (born c. 1964)

Whitman, Albery Allson (1851–1901)

Wideman, John Edgar (born 1941)

Wilkins, Roy (1901–1981)

Wilks, Talvin Winston (born 1961)

Williams, Bert (1874–1922)

Williams, Billy Dee (born 1937)

Williams, Crystal (born 1970)

Williams, Edward Christopher (1871–1929)

Williams, George Washington (1849–1891)

Williams, John A. (born 1925)

Williams, Patricia J. (born 1951)

Williams, Samm-Art (born 1946)

Williams, Sherley Anne (1944–1999)

Williams-Garcia, Rita (born 1957)

Wilson, August (born 1945)

Wilson, Edward Everett (1867–1952)

Wilson, Ernest James, Jr. (1920–1990)

Wilson, Francis H. (Frank) (1886–1956)

Wilson, Harriet E. (c. 1827–c. 1863)

Winbush, Raymond (born 1948)

Winfrey, Oprah (born 1954)

Wolfe, George C. (born 1954)

Women's Clubs

Woods, Paula L. (born 1953)

Woodson, Carter G. (1875–1950)

Woodson, Jacqueline (born 1964)

World War I (1914–1918)

World War II (1939–1945)

Wright, Bil (born c. 1974)

Wright, Charles H. (born 1918)

Wright, Charles S. (born 1932)

Wright, Courtni Crump (born 1950)

Wright, Jay (born 1935)

Wright, Richard (1908–1960)

Wright, Sarah Elizabeth (born 1928)

Wright, Zara (flourished 1920s)

Yarbrough, Camille (born 1934)

Yerby, Frank Garvin (1916–1991)

Young, Al (born 1939)

Young, Andrew (born 1932)

Young, Kevin (born 1970)

Youngblood, Shay (born 1959)

Zane (born 1967)

Zu-Bolton, Ahmos, II (born 1935)

TOPICAL LIST OF ENTRIES

The following list of entries, organized according to topical categories, includes a complete list of author entries and provides a comprehensive overview of the *Encyclopdedia*'s coverage of the literary, critical, historical, cultural, and regional contexts of African American literature. Please consult the Index for assistance in locating discussions of specific literary texts and other topics.

Athletes and Sports

Ali, Muhammad (born 1942)

Basketball

Campanella, Roy (1921–1993)

Carter, Rubin "Hurricane" (born 1937)

Johnson, Jack (1878–1946)

Jordan, Michael Jeffrey (born 1963)

Louis, Joe (1914–1981)

Mays, Willie Howard, Jr. (born 1931)

Robinson, Jackie [Jack Roosevelt] (1919–1972)

Authors

Abernathy, Ralph David (1926–1990)

Adams, Jenoyne (born 1972)

Adoff, Arnold (born 1935)

Ai (born 1947)

Albert, Octavia Victoria Rogers (1853–1889)

Aldridge, Ira (1807–1867)

Alers, Rochelle (born 1943)

Alexander, Elizabeth (born 1962)

Alexander, Lewis (1900–1945)

Allen, Jeffrey Renard (born 1962)

Allen, Richard (1760–1831)

Allen, Samuel Washington (born 1917)

Allison, Hughes (1908–c. 1974)

Als, Hilton (born 1961)

Amos, Robyn (born 1971)

Anderson, Garland (1886–1939)

Anderson, Mignon Holland (born 1945)

Anderson, Stanice (born 1950)

Anderson-Thompkins, Sibby (born 1966)

Andrews, Raymond (1934–1991)

Andrews, Regina M. (1901–1993)

Andrews, William L. (born 1946)

Angelou, Maya (born 1928)

Ansa, Tina McElroy (born 1949)

Anthony, Sterling (born 1949)

Apess, William (1798–183?)

Armstrong, William H[oward] (1914–1999)

Asim, Jabari (born 1962)

Atkins, Russell (born 1926)

Attaway, William (1911–1986)

Aubert, Alvin (born 1930)

Austin, Doris Jean (1949–1994)

Baisden, Michael (born 1963)

Baker, Nikki (born 1962)

Baldwin, James (1924–1987)

Ballard, Allen B. (born 1933)

Bambara, Toni Cade (1939–1995)

Bandele, Asha (born 1968)

Banks, Leslie Esdaile (born 1959)

Banneker, Benjamin (1731–1806)

Baraka, Amiri (born 1934)

Baraka, Ras (born 1970)

Barnes, Steven Emory (born 1952)

Barnett, LaShonda Katrice (born 1974)

Barrax, Gerald W. (born 1933)

Basie, William "Count" (1904–1984)

Beadle, Samuel A. (1857–1932)

Beals, Melba Patillo (born 1941)

Beam, Joseph (1954–1988)

Beatty, Paul (born 1962)

Beckham, Barry (born 1944)

Beckwourth, James (1798–c. 1867)

Bell, James Madison (1826–1902)

Benjamin, Robert C. O. (1855–1900)

Bennett, Gwendolyn (1902–1981)

Bennett, Hal [George Harold] (born 1930)

Benson, Leticia (born 1963)

Bernal, Martin (born 1937)

Berry, Bertice (born 1961)

Berry, Charlene A. (born 1967)

Bibb, Henry Walton (1815–1854)

Birtha, Becky (born 1948)

Bland, Eleanor Taylor (born 1944)

Bonner, Marita (1899–1971)

Bontemps, Arna (1902–1973)

Bowen, Michele Andrea (born 1961)

Boyd, Melba (born 1950)

Boyd, Valerie (born 1963)

Boyer, Jill Witherspoon (born 1947)

Bradley, David Henry, Jr. (born 1950)

Braithwaite, William Stanley Beaumont (1878–1962)

Brawley, Benjamin Griffith (1882–1939)

Bridgforth, Sharon (born c. 1960)

Briscoe, Connie (born 1952)

Brooks, Gwendolyn (1917–2000)

Broughton, Virginia W. (c. 1856–1934)

Brown, Cecil (born 1943)

Brown, Claude (1937–2002)

Brown, Elaine (born 1943)

Brown, Fahamisha Patricia (born 1942)

Brown, Frank London (1927–1962)

Brown, Hallie Quinn (1845–1949)

Brown, Henry "Box" (c. 1815–?)

Brown, Linda Beatrice (born 1939)

Brown, Lloyd (1913–2003)

Brown, Sterling A. (1901–1989)

Brown, Wesley (born 1945)

Brown, William Wells (1815–1884)

Browne, Theodore (c. 1910–1979)

Bryan, Ashley (born 1923)

Buchanan, Shonda (born 1968)

Buckley, Gail Lumet (born 1937)

Bullins, Ed (born 1935)

Bunkley, Anita Richmond (born 1944)

Burrill, Mary ("Mamie") Powell (c. 1882–1946)

Burroughs, Margaret Taylor Goss (born 1917)

Burton, Annie Louise (1860–?)

Bush-Banks, Olivia Ward (1869–1944)

Busia, Akosua (born 1966)

Bussey, Louré (born c. 1971)

Butcher, Philip (born 1918)

Butler, Octavia E. (born 1947)

Butler, Tajuana "TJ" (born 1971)

Byrd, Adrianne (born c. 1976)

Cain, George (born 1943)

Caldwell, Ben (born 1937)

Campbell, Bebe Moore (born 1950)

Campbell, James Edwin (1867–1896)

Carmichael, Stokely (1941–1998)

Carroll, Vinnette (1922–2003)

Carter, Charlotte (born 1943)

Carter, Stephen L. (born 1954)

Cartiér, Xam Wilson (born 1949)

Cary, Lorene (born 1956)

Cary, Mary Ann Camberton Shadd (1823–1893)

Cassells, Cyrus (born 1957)

Chambers, Veronica (born 1971)

Charles, Kraal (Kayo) Y. (born 1975)

Chase-Riboud, Barbara (born 1939)

Chennault, Stephen D. (born 1940)

Chesnutt, Charles Waddell (1858–1932)

Childress, Alice (1916–1994)

Christian, Marcus Bruce (1900–1976)

Clair, Maxine (born 1939)

Clarke, Breena

Cleage [Lomax], Pearl Michelle (born 1948)

Cleaver, Eldridge (1935–1998)

Cleaver, Kathleen Neal (born 1946)

Cliff, Michelle (born 1946)

Clifton, Lucille (born 1936)

Clinton, Michelle T. (born 1954)

Cobb, Ned (1885–1973)

Cobb, William Jelani (born c. 1972)

Coffin, Frank B[arbour] (1871–1951)

Cole, Harriette (born c. 1963)

Coleman, Anita Scott (1890–1960)

Coleman, Evelyn (born 1948)

Coleman, Wanda (born 1946)

Collier, Eugenia (born 1928)

Colter, Cyrus (1910–2002)

Cone, James H. (born 1939)

Cooper, Anna Julia Haywood (1858/1859–1964)

Cooper, Clarence, Jr. (1934–1978)

Cooper, J[oan] California (born 193?)

Coppin, Fanny Marion Jackson (c. 1837–1913)

Corbin, Steven (1953–1995)

Cornish, Sam[uel] James (born 1935)

Cornish, Samuel Eli (c. 1790–1858)

Corrothers, James (1869–1917)

Cortez, Jayne (born 1936)

Cose, Ellis (born 1950)

Cotter, Joseph Seamon, Jr. (1895–1919)

Cotter, Joseph Seamon, Sr. (1861–1949)

Cowdery, Mae V. (1909–1953)

Craft, William (1824–1900) and Ellen Smith Craft (1826–1891)

Crafts, Hannah

Crouch, Stanley (born 1945)

Crummell, Alexander (1819–1898)

Cruse, Harold Wright (born 1916)

Cullen, Countee (1903–1946)

Cuney-Hare, Maud (1874–1936)

Dandridge, Raymond Garfield (1882–1930)

Danner, Margaret Esse Taylor (1915–1984)

Danticat, Edwidge (born 1969)

Darden, Christopher (born 1957)

Dash, Julie (born 1952)

davenport, doris (born 1949)

Davis, Angela Y. (born 1944)

Davis, Bridgett M. (born 1960)

Davis, Daniel Webster (1862–1913)

Davis, Frank Marshall (1905–1987)

Davis, Thulani N. (born 1949)

Dean, Phillip Hayes (born 1937)

DeBerry, Virginia (born c. 1962) and Donna Grant (born c. 1963)

Delaney, Lucy A. (c. 1828–?)

Delany, Martin R. (1812–1885)

Delany, Samuel R. (born 1942)

DeLoach, Nora (1940–2001)

Demby, William (born 1922)

Dent, Thomas Covington (1932–1998)

Derricotte, Toi (born 1941)

Dett, R[obert] Nathaniel (1882–1943)

Detter, Thomas P. (c. 1826–?)

DeVeaux, Alexis (born 1948)

Dickerson, Debra J. (born 1959)

Dickey, Eric Jerome (born 1961)

Dillon, Leo (born 1933) and Diane Dillon (born 1933)

Dixon, Melvin (1950–1992)

Dodson, Howard (born 1939)

Dodson, Owen (1914–1983)

Dorr, David F. (1827/1828–1872)

Douglass, Frederick (1818–1895)

Dove, Rita (born 1952)

Drake, David (c. 1800–c. 1870)

Drumgoold, Kate (c. 1858–?)

Du Bois, W.E.B. (1868–1963)

Duckett, Larry (1953–2001)

Due, Tananarive (born 1966)

Duke, Lynne (born 1956)

Dumas, Henry (1934–1968)

Dunbar, Paul Laurence (1872–1906)

Dunbar-Nelson, Alice Moore (1875–1935)

Duncan, Thelma Myrtle (born 1902)

Dunham, Katherine (born 1909)

Durem, Ray (1915–1963)

Durham, David Anthony (born 1969)

Dyson, Michael Eric (born 1958)

Eady, Cornelius (born 1954)

Edmonds, S[heppard] Randolph (1900–1983)

Edwards, Grace F[rederica] (born c. 1943)

Edwards, Junius (born 1929)

Edwards, Louis (born 1962)

Elam, Patricia (born c. 1971)

Elaw, Zilpha (c. 1790–?)

Elder, Lonne, III (1927–1996)

Elizabeth (1766–1866)

Ellis, Erika (born 1965)

Ellis, Thomas Sayers (born 1965)

Ellis, Trey (born 1962)

Ellison, Ralph (1914–1994)

Equiano, Olaudah (1745–1797)

Evans, Mari (born 1923)

Everett, Percival (born 1956)

Fabio, Sarah Webster (1928–1979)

Fair, Ronald L. (born 1932)

Fales-Hill, Susan (born 1962)

Farmer, Nancy (born 1941)

Fauset, Jessie Redmon (1882–1961)

Ferrell, Carolyn (born 1962)

Finney, Nikky (born 1957)

Fisher, Rudolph John Chauncey (1897–1934)

Fleming, Sarah Lee Brown (1876–1963)

Flowers, Arthur Rickydoc (born 1950)

Foote, Julia (1823–1900)

Forbes, Calvin (born 1945)

Ford, Nick Aaron (1904–1982)

Forman, Ruth (born 1968)

Forrest, Leon (1937–1997)

Forster, Gwynne (born c. 1966)

Fortune, T[imothy] Thomas (1856–1928)

Foster, Frances Smith (born 1944)

Foster, Sharon Ewell (born 1957)

Franklin, C. L. (1915–1984)

Franklin, J. E. (born 1937)

Fuller, Charles H., Jr. (born 1939)

Fuller, Hoyt (1923–1981)

Fullilove, Eric James (born 1954)

Fulton, David Bryant (1863–1941)

Gaines, Ernest James (born 1933)

Gaines, Patrice (born 1949)

Garnet, Henry Highland (1815–1882)

Gayle, Roberta (born 1963)

George, Nelson (born 1957)

Gibson, Patricia Joann (born 1952)

Gilbert, Mercedes (1889–1952)

Gilmore, Brian (born 1962)

Gilmore-Scott, Monique (born c. 1967)

Giovanni, Nikki (born 1943)

Glave, Thomas (born 1964)

Goines, Donald (1937–1974)

Golden, Marita (born 1950)

Gomez, Jewelle (born 1948)

Gordone, Charles (1925–1995)

Gossett, Hattie (born 1942)

Gould, Sandra Lee (born 1949)

Graham, Lorenz [Bell] (1902–1989)

Graham, Ottie B. (1900–1982)

Graham, Shirley (1896–1977)

Green, Carmen (born 1963)

Green, John Patterson (1845–1940)

Greenfield, Eloise (born 1929)

Greenlee, Sam (born 1930)

Griggs, Sutton E. (1872–1933)

Grimes, Terris McMahan (born 1952)

Grimké, Angelina Emily (1805–1879)

Grimké, Angelina Weld (1880–1958)

Grimké, Archibald Henry (1849–1930)

Grimké, Charlotte Forten (1837–1914)

Grimké, Francis James (1850–1937)

Grimké, Sarah Moore (1792–1873)

Gronniosaw, James Albert Ukawsaw (c. 1710–?)

Grooms, Anthony (born 1955)

Gunn, Bill (1934–1989)

Gunn, Gay G. (born 1947)

Guy, Rosa (born 1925)

Hailstock, Shirley (born 1948)

Haley, Alex (1921–1992)

Hamilton, Virginia (1936–2002)

Hammon, Briton (flourished 1760)

Hammon, Jupiter (1711–c. 1806)

Hansberry, Lorraine (1930–1965)

Hansen, Joyce (born 1942)

Hardy, James Earl (born c. 1972)

Harland-Watts, Joette [Kupenda Auset] (born 1967)

Harper, Frances Ellen Watkins (1825–1911)

Harper, Michael S. (born 1938)

Harper, Phillip Brian (born 1961)

Harrington, Oliver (Ollie) (1912–1995)

Harris, Bill (born 1941)

Harris, E[verette] Lynn (born 1955)

Harris, Eddy L. (born 1956)

Harris, Peter J. (born 1955)

Harrison, Hubert Henry (1883–1927)

Haskins, James S. (born 1941)

Hassan, Umar Bin (born 1948)

Hawkins, Walter Everette (1883–?)

Hayden, Robert (1913–1980)

Hayes, Terrance (born 1971)

Haynes, David (born 1955)

Haynes, Lemuel (1753–1833)

Haywood, Gar Anthony (born 1954)

Hazzard, Alvira (1899–1953)

Heard, Nathan (1936–2004)

Hemans, Donna (born 1970)

Hemphill, Essex (1957–1995)

Henderson, David (born 1942)

Henderson, George Wylie (1904–1965)

Henson, Josiah (1789–1883)

Hercules, Frank (1911–1996)

Hernton, Calvin Coolidge (1932–2001)

Herron, Carolivia (born 1947)

Heyward, [Edwin] DuBose (1885–1940) and Dorothy [Hartzell Kuhns] Heyward (1890–1961)

Hill, Abram (1910–1986)

Hill, Donna (born 1955)

Hill, Ernest (born 1961)

Himes, Chester (1909–1984)

Hoagland, Everett H., III (born 1942)

Holder, Laurence (born 1939)

Holton, Hugh (1946–2001)

Holtzclaw, William Henry (1870–1943)

Hopkins, Pauline Elizabeth (1859–1930)

Hopkinson, Nalo (born 1960)

Horne, Frank Smith (1899–1974)

Horton, George Moses (c. 1797–c. 1883)

Hudson-Smith, Linda (born 1950)

Hughes, Langston (1902–1967)

Hull, Akasha [Gloria T.] (born 1944)

Hunt, Marsha (born 1946)

Hunter, Travis (born 1969)

Hurston, Zora Neale (1891–1960)

Iceberg Slim (1918–1992)

Jackson, Angela (born 1951)

Jackson, Brian Keith (born 1967)

Jackson, Elaine (born 1943)

Jackson, George Lester (1941–1971)

Jackson, Mae (born 1946)

Jackson, Mattie J. (c. 1846–?)

Jackson, Monica

Jackson, Murray E. (1926–2002)

Jackson, Rebecca Cox (1796–1871)

Jackson, Sheneska (born 1970)

Jackson-Opoku, Sandra (born 1953)

Jacobs, Harriet Ann (1813–1897)

James, Darius (born c. 1969)

James, Kelvin Christopher (born c. 1945)

Jeffers, Lance (1919–1985)

Jefferson, Roland S. (born 1939)

Jeffries, Tamara Yvette (born 1964)

Jenkins, Beverly Hunter (born 1951)

Joans, Ted (1928–2003)

Joe, Yolanda (born 1962)

Johnson, Amelia E. (1859–1922)

Johnson, Angela (born 1961)

Johnson, Charles R. (born 1948)

Johnson, Charles Spurgeon (1893–1956)

Johnson, Doris (born 1937)

Johnson, Fenton (1888–1958)

Johnson, Freddie Lee, III (born 1958)

Johnson, Georgia Douglas (1886–1966)

Johnson, Guy (born 1945)

Johnson, Helene (1906–1995)

Johnson, James P[rice] (1894–1955)

Johnson, James Weldon (1871–1938)

Johnson, Mat (born 1970)

Johnson-Coleman, Lorraine (born 1962)

Johnson-Hodge, Margaret

Jones, Edward P. (born 1950)

Jones, Edward Smyth (1881–?)

Jones, Gayl (born 1949)

Jones, Laurence C. (1884–1975)

Jones, Patricia Spears (born 1955)

Jones, Sarah (born 1974)

Jones, Solomon (born 1967)

Jones-Meadows, Karen

Jordan, June (1936–2002)

Joyce, Joyce Anne (born 1949)

Kai, Nubia (born 1948)

Karenga, Maulana (born 1941)

Kaufman, Bob (1926–1986)

Keats, Ezra Jack (1919–1983)

Keckley, Elizabeth (c. 1818–1907)

Keene, John R., Jr. (born 1965)

Kelley, Norman (born 1954)

Kelley, William Melvin (born 1937)

Kelley-Hawkins, Emma Dunham (1863–1938)

Kenan, Randall Garrett (born 1963)

Kennedy, Adrienne (born 1931)

Killens, John Oliver (1916–1987)

Kincaid, Jamaica (born 1949)

King, Woodie, Jr. (born 1937)

Kitt, Sandra (born 1947)

Knight, Etheridge (1931–1991)

Kocher, Ruth Ellen (born 1965)

Komunyakaa, Yusef (born 1947)

Kool Moe Dee (born 1963)

Kweli, Talib (born 1975)

Ladd, Florence (born 1932)

Lamar, Jake (born 1961)

Lane, Pinkie Gordon (born 1923)

Langston, John Mercer (1829–1897)

Lanusse, Armand (1812–1867)

Larsen, Nella (1891–1964)

Lattany, Kristin Hunter (born 1931)

LaValle, Victor (born 1972)

Lee, Andrea (born 1953)

Lee, Helen Elaine (born 1959)

Lee, Jarena (1783–?)

Lester, Julius (born 1939)

Lewis, Theophilus (1891–1974)

Lincoln, C[harles] Eric (1924–2000)

Livingston, Myrtle Smith (1902–1973)

Lorde, Audre (1934–1992)

Love, Monifa A. (born 1955)

Love, Nat (1854–1921)

Mackey, Nathaniel (born 1947)

Madgett, Naomi Long (born 1923)

Madhubuti, Haki R. (Don L[uther] Lee) (born 1942)

Major, Marcus (born c. 1972)

Mallette, Gloria (born 1953)

Margetson, George Reginald (1877–?)

Marrant, John (1755–1791)

Marshall, Paule (born 1929)

Mataka, Laini (born c. 1951)

Matheus, John F. (1887–1983)

Mathis, Sharon Bell (born 1937)

Matthews, Victoria Earle (1861–1907)

Mayfield, Julian (1928–1984)

Mays, Benjamin Elijah (1894–1984)

McBride, James (born 1957)

McCall, Nathan (born 1955)

McCauley, Robbie (born 1947)

McClellan, George Marion (1860–1934)

McCluskey, John Ashbery, Jr. (born 1944)

McDonald, Janet A. (born 1953)

McDowell, Deborah E. (born 1951)

McElroy, Colleen (born 1935)

McFadden, Bernice (born 1965)

McKay, Claude (1889–1948)

McKay, Nellie Yvonne (born 1947)

McKinney-Whetstone, Diane (born 1953)

McKissack, Patrica (born 1944)

McKnight, Reginald (born 1956)

McLarin, Kim (born c. 1964)

McMillan, Terry (born 1951)

McPherson, James Alan (born 1943)

Menard, John Willis (1838–1893)

Meriwether, Louise (born 1923)

Micheaux, Oscar (1884–1951)

Miller, E. Ethelbert (born 1950)

Miller, May (1899–1995)

Millican, Arthenia Jackson Bates (born 1920)

Milner, Ron (1938–2004)

Mitchell, Loften (1919–2001)

Monroe, Mary (born 1951)

Monteilh, Marissa (born c. 1974)

Moody, Anne (born 1940)

Moore, Charles Michael (1948–2003)

Moore, Jessica Care (born 1971)

Moore, Lenard D. (born 1958)

Moore, Opal (born 1953)

Morrison, Toni (born 1931)

Mosley, Walter (born 1952)

Moss, Thylias (born 1954)

Mossell, Gertrude Bustill (1855–1948)

Motley, Willard (1909–1965)

Mowry, Jess (born 1960)

Mullen, Harryette (born 1954)

Murray, Albert (born 1916)

Murray, Pauli (1910–1985)

Myers, Walter Dean (born 1937)

Naylor, Gloria (born 1950)

Neal, Larry (1937–1981)

Neely, Barbara (born 1941)

Neff, Heather (born 1958)

Nell, William Cooper (1816–1874)

Nelson, Annie Greene (1902–1993)

Nelson, Jill (born 1952)

Nelson, Marilyn (born 1946)

Newsome, Effie Lee (1885–1979)

Newton, Lionel (born 1961)

Njeri, Itabari (born 1955)

Northup, Solomon (1808–1863)

Nugent, Richard Bruce (1906–1987)

Núñez, Elizabeth (born c. 1950)

OyamO (born 1943)

Oyewole, Abiodun (born c. 1946)

Packer, ZZ (born 1973)

Parker, Pat (1944–1989)

Parks, Gordon (born 1912)

Parks, Suzan-Lori (born 1963)

Pate, Alexs D. (born 1950)

Patterson, Raymond R. (1929–2001)

Pennington, James William Charles
    (1807–1870)

Penny, Rob[ert] Lee (1941–2003)

Perdomo, Willie (born 1967)

Perkins, Useni Eugene (born 1932)

Perrin, Kayla (born 1969)

Perry, Charles (1924–1969)

Perry, Phyllis Alesia (born 1961)

Petry, Ann Lane (1908–1997)

Pharr, Robert Deane (1916–1989)

Phillips, Carl (born 1959)

Phillips, Gary (born 1955)

Pinckney, Darryl (born 1953)

Pinkney, Sandra (born 1971) and Myles
    Pinkney (born 1971)

Plato, Ann (c. 1820–?)

Plumpp, Sterling D. (born 1940)

Polite, Carlene Hatcher (born 1932)

Popel [Shaw], Esther A. B. (1896–1958)

Porter, Connie Rose (born 1959)

Powell, Kevin (born 1969)

Ra, Sun (1914–1993)

Rahman, Aishah (born 1936)

Randall, Dudley Felker (1914–2000)

Randolph, Asa Philip (1889–1979)

Ray, Henrietta Cordelia (c. 1852–1916)

Raymond, Linda (born 1952)

Reed, Ishmael (born 1938)

Reid-Pharr, Robert F. (born 1965)

Remond, Charles Lenox (1810–1873)

Remond, Sarah Parker (1824–1894)

Rhodes, Jewell Parker (born 1954)

Rice, Patty (born c. 1976)

Richardson, Willis (1889–1977)

Ridley, John (born 1965)

Riley, Len

Ringgold, Faith (born 1930)

Rivers, Conrad Kent (1933–1968)

Robinson, C. Kelly (born 1970)

Robotham, Rosemarie Angela (born
    1957)

Roby, Kimberla Lawson (born 1965)

Rodgers, Carolyn M[arie] (born c. 1945)

Rose, Tricia (born 1962)

Rowe, George Clinton (1853–1903)

Roy, Lucinda (born 1955)

Rushin, [Donna K.] Kate (born 1951)

Rux, Carl Hancock (born c. 1968)

Salaam, Kalamu ya (born 1947)

Sanchez, Sonia (born 1934)

Sanders, Dori (born 1930)

Sapphire [Lofton, Ramona] (born 1950)

Scarborough, William Sanders (1852–
    1926)

Schuyler, George Samuel (1895–1977)

Scott-Heron, Gil (born 1949)

Scruggs, Afi-Odelia E. (born 1954)

Seacole, Mary (1805–1881)

Séjour, Victor (1817–1874)

Senna, Danzy (born 1970)

Shackelford, Theodore Henry (1888–
    1923)

Shaik, Fatima (born 1952)

Shakur, Tupac (1971–1996)

Shange, Ntozake (born 1948)

Shannon, Angela (born 1964)

Shannon, Ray (pseudonym of Gar Anthony Haywood)

Sheffey, Ruthe T. (born c. 1926)

Shepherd, Reginald (born 1963)

Sherman, Charlotte Watson (born 1958)

Shine, Ted [Theodis] (born 1931)

Shockley, Ann Allen (born 1927)

Simmons, Herbert (born 1930)

Simmons, Russell (born 1957)

Sinclair, April (born 1955)

Sister Souljah (born 1964)

Smiley, Tavis (born 1964)

Smith, Amanda Berry (1837–1915)

Smith, Anna Deavere (born 1950)

Smith, Barbara (born 1946)

Smith, Effie Waller (1879–1960)

Smith, Mary Burnett (born 1931)

Smith, Venture (1728/1729–1805)

Smith, William Gardner (1927–1974)

Smitherman, Geneva (born 1940)

Snoe, Eboni (born 1955)

Southerland, Ellease (born 1943)

Spellman, A. B. (born 1935)

Spence, Eulalie (1894–1981)

Spencer, Anne (1882–1975)

St. John, Primus (born 1939)

Steptoe, John (1950–1989)

Stetson, Jeff (born 1949)

Steward, Theophilus Gould (1843–1924)

Stewart, Maria W. (1803–1879)

Still, William (1821–1902)

Still, William Grant (1895–1978)

Stowe, Harriet Beecher (1811–1896)

Strange, Sharan (born 1959)

Swindle, Renée

Tademy, Lalita (born 1948)

Tanner, Benjamin Tucker (1835–1923)

Tarpley, Natasha (born 1971)

Tarry, Ellen (born 1906)

Tate, Eleanora Elaine (born 1948)

Tate, Greg (born 1957)

Taulbert, Clifton LeMoure (born 1945)

Taylor, Mel (born 1939)

Taylor, Mildred D. (born 1943)

Taylor, Regina (born 1959)

Taylor, Susie King (1848–1912)

Terrell, Mary Eliza Church (1863–1954)

Terry [Prince], Lucy (c. 1730–1821)

Tervalon, Jervey (born 1958)

Thelwell, Michael (born 1939)

Thomas, Joyce Carol (born 1938)

Thomas, Lorenzo (born 1944)

Thomas, Piri (born 1928)

Thomas-Graham, Pamela (born 1963)

Thompson, Era Bell (1905–1986)

Thurman, Howard (1900–1981)

Thurman, Wallace (1902–1934)

Tillman, Katherine Davis Chapman (1870–c. 1946)

Tolson, Melvin B. (1898–1966)

Toomer, Jean (1894–1967)

Touré, Askia Muhammad Abu Bakr el (born 1938)

Trethewey, Natasha (born 1966)

Trice, Dawn Turner (born 1965)

Troupe, Quincy Thomas, Jr. (born 1943)

Truth, Sojourner (1797–1883)

Tubbee, Okah (1810–?)

Tubman, Harriet Ross (c. 1820–1913)

Turner, Henry McNeal (1834–1915)

Turpin, Waters E. (1910–1968)

Twain, Mark (1835–1910)

Tyree, Omar (born 1969)

Ulen, Eisa Nefertari (born 1968)

Van Der Zee, James (1886–1983)

Vashon, George Boyer (1824–1878)

Verdelle, A. J. (born 1960)

Vernon, Olympia (born 1973)

Vroman, Mary Elizabeth (1923–1967)

Wade-Gayles, Gloria Jean (born 1938)

Walker, Alice (born 1944)

Walker, Blair S. (born 1955)

Walker, David (1785–1830)

Walker, Joseph A. (1935–2003)

Walker, Margaret Abigail (1915–1998)

Walker, Persia (born 1957)

Walker, Rebecca (born 1969)

Wallace, Michele Faith (born 1952)

Walrond, Eric D[erwent] (1898–1966)

Walter, Mildred Pitts (born 1922)

Walton, Anthony (born 1960)

Waniek, Marilyn Nelson. *See* Nelson, Marilyn

Ward, Douglas Turner (born 1930)

Ward, Jerry Washington, Jr. (born 1943)

Ward, [James] Theodore (Ted) (1902–1983)

Washington, Booker T. (1856–1915)

Washington, Mary Helen (born 1941)

Washington, Teresa N. (born 1971)

Waters, Ethel (1896–1977)

Weatherly, Tom (born 1942)

Weaver, Afaa Michael (born 1951)

Webb, Frank J. (c. 1828–c. 1894)

Webb, Mary (1828–1859)

Weber, Carl (born 1970)

Wesley, Dorothy Burnett Porter (1905–1995)

Wesley, Valerie Wilson (born 1947)

West, Cheryl L. (born 1965)

West, Dorothy (1907–1998)

Wheatley, Phillis (c. 1753–1784)

Whipper, William (1804–1876)

White, Edgar Nkosi (born 1947)

White, Paulette Childress (born 1948)

Whitehead, Colson (born 1969)

Whitfield, James Monroe (1822–1871)

Whitfield, Van (born c. 1964)

Whitman, Albery Allson (1851–1901)

Wideman, John Edgar (born 1941)

Wilkins, Roy (1901–1981)

Wilks, Talvin Winston (born 1961)

Williams, Bert (1874–1922)

Williams, Crystal (born 1970)

Williams, Edward Christopher (1871–1929)

Williams, George Washington (1849–1891)

Williams, John A. (born 1925)

Williams, Samm-Art (born 1946)

Williams, Sherley Anne (1944–1999)

Williams-Garcia, Rita (born 1957)

Wilson, August (born 1945)

Wilson, Edward Everett (1867–1952)

Wilson, Ernest James, Jr. (1920–1990)

Wilson, Francis H. (Frank) (1886–1956)

Wilson, Harriet E. (c. 1827–c. 1863)

Winbush, Raymond (born 1948)

Wolfe, George C. (born 1954)

Woods, Paula L. (born 1953)

Woodson, Jacqueline (born 1964)

Wright, Bil (born c. 1974)

Wright, Charles H. (born 1918)

Wright, Charles S. (born 1932)

Wright, Courtni Crump (born 1950)

Wright, Jay (born 1935)
Wright, Richard (1908–1960)
Wright, Sarah Elizabeth (born 1928)
Wright, Zara (flourished 1920s)
Yarbrough, Camille (born 1934)
Yerby, Frank Garvin (1916–1991)
Young, Al (born 1939)
Young, Andrew (born 1932)
Young, Kevin (born 1970)
Youngblood, Shay (born 1959)
Zane (born 1967)
Zu-Bolton, Ahmos, II (born 1935)

Critical Movements and Terms

Black Arts Movement (1960–1970)
Black Athena Controversy (1987–
    present)
Black Atlantic
Black Studies
Deconstruction
Feminist/Black Feminist Literary
    Criticism
Harlem Renaissance (c. 1920–1932)
Last Poets, The
Literary Canon
Location Theory
Marxism
Metaphor
Modernism (c. 1890–1940)
Multicultural Theory
Myth
New Criticism (1930–1970)
Poetics
Postmodernism
Poststructuralism
Queer Theory
Realism
Signifying

Southern Studies
Surrealism
Vernacular

Critics and Scholars

Andrews, William L. (born 1946)
Baker, Houston A., Jr. (born 1943)
Bell, Derrick (born 1930)
Bernal, Martin (born 1937)
Carby, Hazel V. (born 1948)
Chancy, Myriam J. A. (born 1970)
Christian, Barbara T. (1943–2000)
Cook, William W. (born 1933)
Davis, Arthur P. (1904–1996)
Du Bois, W.E.B. (1868–1963)
Early, Gerald Lyn (born 1952)
Emanuel, James A. (born 1921)
Franklin, John Hope (born 1915)
Frazier, Edward Franklin (1894–1962)
Gates, Henry Louis, Jr. (born 1950)
Gayle, Addison, Jr. (1932–1991)
Gilroy, Paul (born 1956)
Harris, Trudier (born 1948)
Herron, Carolivia (born 1947)
hooks, bell (born 1952)
Hubbard, Dolan (born 1949)
Locke, Alain LeRoy (1886–1954)
Love, Monifa A. (born 1955)
Major, Clarence (born 1936)
McKay, Nellie Yvonne (born 1947)
Miller, R. Baxter (born 1948)
Murray, Pauli (1910–1985)
O'Daniel, Therman B. (1908–1986)
Rampersad, Arnold (born 1941)
Redding, J. Saunders (1906–1988)
Redmond, Eugene B. (born 1937)
Reid-Pharr, Robert F. (born 1965)

Rose, Tricia (born 1962)

Schomburg, Arthur A. (1874–1938)

Schuyler, George Samuel (1895–1977)

Smith, Barbara (born 1946)

Smitherman, Geneva (born 1940)

Spillers, Hortense J. (born 1942)

Stepto, Robert Burns (born 1944)

Thompson, Robert Farris (born 1932)

Thurman, Howard (1900–1981)

Turner, Darwin T. (1931–1991)

Van Vechten, Carl (1880–1964)

West, Cornel (born 1953)

White, Walter Francis (1893–1955)

Williams, Patricia J. (born 1951)

Woodson, Carter G. (1875–1950)

Wright, Charles H. (born 1918)

Historical and Social Issues

Abolitionist Movement (c. 1820–1865)

Affirmative Action

Afrocentricity

Assimilation

Back-to-Africa Movement

Black Athena Controversy (1987–present)

Black Atlantic

Black Family

Black Nationalism (c. 1827–present)

Black Panther Party (for Self-Defense) (1966–c. 1980)

Black Power (1960–present)

Black Studies

Blaxploitation

Censorship

Civil Rights Movement

Civil War, American (1861–1865)

Cold War, The (c. 1947–1960)

Colonialism

Color of Skin

Cooking

Creole

Cross-Dressing

Diaspora

Exoticism

Feminism/Black Feminism

Gender

Great Depression (1929–1939)

Great Migration

Gulf War (1991)

Hair

Haiti

Hip-Hop

Labor

Lynching

Lynching, History of

Marriage

Marxism

McCarthyism (1950–1954)

Middle Passage, The (c. 1540–1855)

Minstrelsy

Misogyny

Modernism (c. 1890–1940)

Mojo

Mulatto

NAACP

Nadir (1877–1915)

Naming

Nation of Islam

Nature

Négritude (c. 1930–1960)

Negro

New Negro (1920s)

New Negro, The (1925)

Passing

Protest Literature

Race

Race Riots

Race Uplift Movement

Rap

Reconstruction

Sambo

Scottsboro Boys, The

Sexual Revolution (c. 1960–1980)

Slang

Slavery

Talented Tenth (c. 1900–1930)

Till, Emmett (1941–1955)

Tokenism

Uncle Tom

Underground Railroad

Vietnam War (1961–1975)

White (Racial Designation)

World War I (1914–1918)

World War II (1939–1945)

Historical and Cultural Figures

Abernathy, Ralph David (1926–1990)

Ali, Muhammad (born 1942)

Bearden, Romare (1912–1988)

Bell, Derrick (born 1930)

Bond, Julian (born 1940)

Brown, Elaine (born 1943)

Brown, John (1800–1859)

Burton, LeVar (born 1957)

Campanella, Roy (1921–1993)

Carmichael, Stokely (1941–1998)

Carter, Rubin "Hurricane" (born 1937)

Chisholm, Shirley Anita St. Hill (1924–2005)

Cleaver, Eldridge (1935–1998)

Cosby, William (Bill) (born 1937)

Davis, Angela Y. (born 1944)

Davis, Ossie (1917–2005)

Douglass, Frederick (1818–1895)

Evers, Medgar (1925–1963)

Garvey, Marcus (1887–1940)

Gilpin Players

Goldberg, Whoopi (born 1955)

Gregory, Dick [Richard] (born 1932)

Gumby, Levi-Sandy Alexander (1885–1961)

Haley, Alex (1921–1992)

Hall, Prince (c. 1735–1807)

Hemings, Sally (1773–1835)

Henry, John (c. 1870–present)

Holiday, Billie (1915–1959)

Jackson, George Lester (1941–1971)

Jackson, Jesse L[ouis] (born 1941)

John the Conqueror

Jordan, Barbara Charline (1936–1996)

Jordan, Michael Jeffrey (born 1963)

King, Martin Luther, Jr. (1929–1968)

Kool Moe Dee (born 1963)

Lawrence, Jacob (1917–2000)

Leadbelly [Ledbetter, Huddie] (1889–1949)

Lee, Spike (born 1957)

Louis, Joe (1914–1981)

Malcolm X (1925–1965)

Mays, Willie Howard, Jr. (born 1931)

Newton, Huey Percy (1942–1989)

Nichols, Nichelle (born 1933)

Randolph, Asa Philip (1889–1979)

Robeson, Paul (1898–1976)

Robinson, Jackie [Jack Roosevelt] (1919–1972)

Shakur, Tupac (1971–1996)

Smith, Bessie (1894–1937)

Stowe, Harriet Beecher (1811–1896)

Truth, Sojourner (1797–1883)

Turner, Nat (1800–1831)

Twain, Mark (1835–1910)

Van Der Zee, James (1886–1983)

Van Peebles, Melvin (born 1932)

Wells-Barnett, Ida B. (1862–1931)

Wilkins, Roy (1901–1981)

Williams, Bert (1874–1922)

Williams, Billy Dee (born 1937)

Winfrey, Oprah (born 1954)

Young, Andrew (born 1932)

Journals, Magazines, and Newspapers

Amsterdam News (1909–present)

Baltimore Afro-American (1892–present)

Black American Literature Forum (1976–1991)

Black Dialogue (1965–1972)

Brownies' Book, The (1920–1921)

Callaloo (1976–present)

Chicago Defender (1905–present)

Columbian Orator, The (c. 1797)

Crisis, The (1910–present)

Ebony (1945–present)

E-Zines, E-News, E-Journals, and E-Collections

Fire!! (1926)

Hambone (1974–present)

Journal of Black Poetry (1966–1973)

Magazines, Literary

Messenger, The (1917–1928)

Negro Digest (1942–1951, 1961–1970)

Negro World (1918–1933)

Newspapers, African American

Nkombo (1968–1974)

NOMMO (1969–1976)

Opportunity (1923–1949)

Phylon (1940–1987; 1992–present)

Pittsburgh Courier (1907–1965)

Sage: A Scholarly Journal on Black Women (1984–1995)

Survey Graphic (1921–1948)

Voice of the Negro, The (1904–1907)

Literary Forms and Genres

Autobiography

Ballad

Blank Verse

Blues Poetry

Children's Literature

Coming-of-Age Fiction

Crime and Mystery Fiction

Dialect Poetry

Drama

Dystopian Literature

Epic Poetry/The Long Poem

Epistolary Novel

Erotica

Essay

Folklore

Folktales

Formal Verse

Free Verse

Gay Literature

Gothic Literature

Graphic Novels

Haiku

Hip-Hop

Historical Fiction

Horror Fiction

Humor

Jazz in Literature

Lesbian Literature

Lyric Poetry

Marxism

Minstrelsy

Musical Theater

Mystery Fiction. *See* Crime and Mystery
Fiction

Myth

Narrative Poetry

Novel

Parody

Performance Poetry

Poetry. *See* Ballad; Blank Verse; Blues
Poetry; Dialect Poetry; Epic Poetry/The
Long Poem; Formal Verse; Free Verse;
Haiku; Lyric Poetry; Narrative Poetry;
Performance Poetry; Poetics; Prose
Poem; Sonnet; Surrealism; Villanelle

Prison Literature

Prose Poem

Protest Literature

Racial Discovery Plot

Rap

Realism

Romance Novel

Satire

Science Fiction

Sermons

Short Fiction

Signifying

Slave Narrative

Sonnet

Spirituals

Surrealism

Travel Writing

Trickster

Utopian Literature

Villanelle

Literary Movements, Schools, and Organizations

Affrilachian Poets (1991–present)

Beat Movement, The (1945–1965)

Black Arts Movement (1960–1970)

Black Arts Repertory Theater/School

Broadside Press (1965–present)

Chicago Renaissance (c. 1930–1950)

College Language Association

Combahee River Collective (c. 1974–
1980)

CQ Comics Group (1997–present)

Dasein Literary Society (1958–1960)

Expatriate Writers

Federal Writers' Project (c. 1936–1941)

Free Southern Theater (1963–1979)

Furious Flower Conference (1994, 2004)

Harlem Renaissance (c. 1920–1932)

Kitchen Table: Women of Color Press
(1981–present)

Langston Hughes Society (1981–
present)

Last Poets, The

Literary Societies

Lotus Press (1972–present)

Negro Units, Federal Theater Project
(1935–1939)

Nuyorican Poets Café

OBAC

Third World Press (1967–present)

Umbra Workshop (1962–1963)

Women's Clubs

Music and Musicians

Baker, Josephine (1906–1975)

Basie, William "Count" (1904–1984)

Blues, The

Blues Poetry

Cuney-Hare, Maud (1874–1936)

Dett, R[obert] Nathaniel (1882–1943)

Ellington, Edward Kennedy "Duke" (1899–1974)

Gillespie, Dizzy (1917–1993), Charlie Parker (1920–1955), and Thelonious Monk (1917–1982)

Gospel Music

Hip-Hop

Holiday, Billie (1915–1959)

Jazz

Jazz in Literature

Jefferson, (Blind) Lemon (1893–1929)

Johnson, James P[rice] (1894–1955)

Leadbelly [Ledbetter, Huddie] (1889–1949)

Monk, Thelonious. *See* Gillespie, Dizzy, Charlie Parker, and Thelonious Monk

Musical Theater

Parker, Charlie. *See* Gillespie, Dizzy, Charlie Parker, and Thelonious Monk

Ra, Sun (1914–1993)

Ragtime

Rap

Reggae

Robeson, Paul (1898–1976)

Shakur, Tupac (1971–1996)

Smith, Bessie (1894–1937)

Soul

Spirituals

Swing

Waters, Ethel (1896–1977)

Publishers

Broadside Press (1965–present)

CQ Comics Group (1997–present)

Federal Writers' Project (c. 1936–1941)

Genesis Press (1993–present)

Howard University Press (1972–present)

Johnson Publishing Company (1942–present)

Just Us Books (1988–present)

Kitchen Table: Women of Color Press (1981–present)

Knopf, Alfred A. (1892–1984)

Lotus Press (1972–present)

Milestone Comics/Milestone Media (1992–present)

Publishers and Publishing

Redbone Press (1995–present)

Third World Press (1967–present)

Regions and Regionalisms

Affrilachian Poets (1991–present)

Atlanta, Georgia

Baltimore, Maryland

Boston, Massachusetts

Brooklyn, New York

Chicago, Illinois

Chicago Renaissance (c. 1930–1950)

Detroit, Michigan

Great Migration

Haiti

Harlem, New York

Harlem Renaissance (c. 1920–1932)

Los Angeles, California

Memphis, Tennessee

Mississippi Delta

Nashville, Tennessee

New Orleans, Louisiana

New York City. *See* Brooklyn, New York; Harlem, New York; Harlem Renaissance

Oklahoma

Paris, France

Philadelphia, Pennsylvania
Pittsburgh, Pennsylvania
San Francisco Bay Area, California
South, The
Southern Studies
St. Louis, Missouri
Texas
Washington, D.C.

Religion and Spirituality
Abolitionist Movement (c. 1820–1865)
Conjuring
Folklore
Gospel Music
Mojo

Nation of Islam
Rastafarian
Sermons
Slave Narrative
Soul
Spirituals
Theology, Black and Womanist
Voodoo/Vodoun

Research Resources
Archives and Collections: 1828–Present
Archives and Collections: Notable
    Collections
Research Resources: Electronic Works
Research Resources: Reference Works

PREFACE

The five volumes of *The Greenwood Encyclopedia of African American Literature* offer an inclusive overview of African American literature from its origins in the colonial period through the present day. As a uniquely comprehensive reference tool, the *Encyclopedia* gathers in one place information about African American writers, the genres and the geographical and cultural environments within which they have worked, and the social, political, and aesthetic movements in which they have participated. The *Encyclopedia* functions both as a source of information about African American literature and as a gateway to further reading and research. Entries are, for example, extensively cross-referenced to emphasize relationships among writers, literary forms, and social and historical events; to signal a cross-reference, a name, term, or phrase appears in **bold**. Each entry includes a list of resources for in-depth research.

The *Encyclopedia* will meet the needs of a wide range of readers, including middle and high school students and their teachers, college students and their professors, and general readers interested in learning more about the history and the range, richness, and vitality of African American literature over the past three centuries. Each entry has been written to be accessible to readers with little or no previous knowledge of African American literature or literary criticism and, at the same time, to provide critical and bibliographic information that will be of use to students and scholars who already possess significant expertise in African American and literary studies.

SCOPE

The *Encyclopedia* includes 1,029 entries, written by more than 200 scholars from around the world. These entries are arranged alphabetically, from **Abernathy, Ralph David**, in Volume 1 to **Zu-Bolton, Ahmos, II**, in Volume 5. The majority of entries, biographical in nature, provide details about the lives and literary works of African American authors from the eighteenth century through the present day. Most entries include an overview of the critical reception of the author's work. All entries have a selected bibliography of significant primary and secondary texts; longer bibliographies are divided into separate lists of primary sources and secondary sources. Each section of each bibliography is arranged alphabetically, according to the last name of author, artist, or editor. Videographies and discographies are included whenever appropriate.

A second group of entries addresses genres such as the **novel** and the **prose poem** or specific literary forms or techniques such as the **ballad**, the **sonnet**, and **surrealism**. Other entries explore the literary histories of specific African American communities, whether in wide geographical regions such as **the South** or in specific cities or neighborhoods such as **Chicago, Illinois**, or **Harlem, New York**. Entries on topics such as **Black Power**, the **Civil Rights Movement**, **Négritude**, **Reconstruction**, and **reggae** provide historical and cultural information essential for interpreting African American literature. Finally, a number of entries explore techniques of literary analysis such as **multicultural theory**, **feminist criticism**, and **deconstruction**, or the work of specific literary critics and scholars, including **James Emanuel**, **bell hooks**, and **Arnold Rampersad**, whose work has significantly influenced the development and trajectory of African American studies. Each entry emphasizes its topic's literary dimensions, referring readers to specific works and writers.

One of our primary goals in editing this *Encyclopedia* was to include as many writers as we could within the scope of five volumes. We recognized immediately that even in five volumes it would be necessary to exclude many writers; this is yet another illustration of how much African American literature has grown in less than 300 years. The rationale for an author-centered encyclopedia is straightforward: African American authors have been responsible for creating African American literature. They are its sine qua non, and a comprehensive reference work should include as many author entries as possible. At the same time, we have taken care that each author entry focuses on literary works and does not overemphasize the author's biography. Topical entries, we realized, would be essential in order to provide the wider contexts essential to interpreting African American literature. We have therefore included a generous number of entries on topics ranging from **Afrocentricity** and the **blues** to **literary societies**, **prison literature**, the **Talented Tenth**, and **women's clubs**.

Roughly 80 percent of the *Encyclopedia*'s entries are devoted to individual writers, and the remaining 20 percent focus on more general topics. The *Encyclopedia* thus provides two main avenues of approach to African American literature. Readers may begin by considering the works of a single writer and then proceed to a consideration of works by the author's contemporaries, as well as his or her literary debts and legacies. Other readers may begin by learning about a genre, category, topic, movement, concept, or event, then move on to a consideration of specific authors and works. Generous cross-referencing will enable readers to make countless connections among authors, events, and ideas in the history of African American literature. The *Encyclopedia* does not include entries on individual works, such as *Invisible Man* or *The Color Purple*; as valuable as such entries might be, and as useful as they are in other kinds of reference works, we concluded early on that such entries would swell the size of this work to unmanageable proportions. Readers seeking information on a particular work should consult the entry on the work's author or the index, which will identify each of the entries that discusses the work in question. Readers interested in specific genres will also want to consult the more general entries devoted to genres (e.g., **drama**) or, in the case of particularly expansive genres such as poetry or fiction, to subgeneric categories (e.g., **novel** or **horror fiction**). Thousands of individual works by African American writers receive attention in the *Encyclopedia*, most from more than one perspective and many in multiple historical, critical, and theoretical contexts.

CREATING THIS *ENCYCLOPEDIA*

We began our work on the *Encyclopedia* by making lists. We consulted anthologies new and old; we looked at other kinds of reference works; we consulted library catalogs; we took stock of the African American works that we and our colleagues read, write about, and teach; we spent time in new, used, and virtual bookstores; we viewed documentaries on African American literature; and we searched the Internet for checklists, bibliographies, and tables of contents. We shared the lists that emerged from our research with an advisory board of distinguished scholars of African American literature and with our colleagues at institutions across the country. We also eagerly solicited suggestions for entries from contributors and other visitors to the *Encyclopedia* Web site, where we posted our lists of proposed entries for over a year. The final list of entries in the *Encyclopedia*, while unprecedented in its inclusivity, is by no means exhaustive, and the editors regret the many omissions that were necessary in order to keep the *Encyclopedia* to a reasonable length. The process of selection was a difficult one, due to the breadth and depth of the field. We worked closely with our advisory board to produce a list of entries that, if not all-encompassing, is broadly representative of the forms that African American literature has taken and of the projects that African American writers have undertaken during the past three centuries.

WHAT IS INCLUDED

In addition to more than a thousand entries on African American writers and topics in African American literature, the *Encyclopedia* has a critical introduction that provides an overview of the history of African American literature. The *Encyclopedia* also includes, at the beginning of each volume, a topical list of entries, organized by category. In addition, the *Encyclopedia* offers a detailed chronology, 117 illustrations, a general index of entries, and a general bibliography. Readers interested in further bibliographical information will want to consult the entries devoted to **Archives and Collections**, **Literary Magazines**, **Newspapers**, and **Reference Works**.

First-time readers of the *Encyclopedia* may wish, in addition to reading this preface, to begin with the introduction, which provides a brief history of African American literature. Readers interested in specific authors, texts, or topics will do well to consult the general and topical indexes. All readers will want to thumb through the volumes one at a time, visiting old friends, making new acquaintances, and (re)discovering the richness, the variety, and the profound power of the African American literary tradition.

ACKNOWLEDGMENTS

The list of acknowledgments for a project of this scale, like the list of entries, must necessarily be long but will inevitably be incomplete. As determined as we, the advisory board, and our contributors have been to make this *Encyclopedia* as comprehensive as possible, we know that African American literature is simply too extensive to be represented by any single reference work. After nearly three years of work, we are glad to see *The Greenwood Encyclopedia of African American Literature* join the family of reference works on the subject, not just because we believe that it will enrich the family, but also because we know that reference works past, present, and future are most useful when used in concert, complementing each other. Our first acknowledgment, then, comes in the form of sincere homage to the authors and editors of other reference works in the field of African American literature, including bibliographies and bio-bibliographies, companions to literature, databases, dictionaries of biography, and reference guides. We also offer our admiration and thanks to librarians worldwide who help their libraries' patrons make the best use of reference works.

The editors of *The Greenwood Encyclopedia of African American Literature* are deeply grateful for the hard work of each and every one of our more than 200 contributors, whose work is both the heart and the soul of these volumes and whose brief biographies appear at the end of Volume 5. We are also grateful for the advice and guidance provided by the members of our advisory board: Dr. Houston Baker, Jr., of Duke University; Dr. Emily Bernard of the University of Vermont; Dr. Michele Elam of Stanford University; Dr. Dolan Hubbard of Morgan State University; and Dr. Sheila Smith McKoy of North Carolina State University. Our editors at Greenwood Press—George Butler, Shana Grob, and Anne Thompson—have been of inestimable assistance in the development and completion of this project. Finally, we are grateful to the University of Puget Sound and the University of Central Oklahoma, which have provided resources and facilities without which the *Encyclopedia* could not have been completed.

We also wish to express our sincere thanks to John Donohue and his colleagues at Westchester Book Group.

We have been blessed to have the support and advice of Jackie Bacon Ostrom, Spencer Ostrom, David and Joan Macey, Nick Yasinski, Kevin Hicks, and Blaire Notrica, whose encouragement and insight have sustained us throughout the three years we have worked on this project.

INTRODUCTION

I've known rivers ancient as the world and older than the flow of human
blood in human veins.
                              —*Langston Hughes, "The Negro Speaks of Rivers"*

Like the great rivers in **Langston Hughes**'s famous poem, African American
literature has no single starting point but many headwaters and tributaries. It
flows, in part, from the songs, tales, lore, knowledge, and beliefs that Africans
brought with them to North America. Channeled through the determina-
tion of African Americans to acquire literacy and to begin to wield the written
word, the river that represents this literature courses through the American
national experience and has transformed the social, cultural, and political
landscape of American history. From poets of the eighteenth century and the
autobiographies of nineteenth-century slave narrators to the heady days of the
Harlem Renaissance and the political and aesthetic struggles of the **Civil
Rights** and **Black Power** movements, African American literature has continued to expand and gather strength. At the beginning of the twenty-first
century, this rich and varied tradition, already encompassing thousands of
texts in every genre, continues its explosive growth as writers experiment with
new forms, techniques, and genres. Scholars and teachers have been at work
for over a century collecting, editing, and interpreting the works of African
American writers from every period and from every quarter of the United
States, and their work, in turn, has provided a new impetus both for the study
of African American literature of the past three centuries and for every sort of
innovation in the emerging literature of the twenty-first century.

EARLY AFRICAN AMERICAN LITERATURE

To begin telling the story of African American literature at the beginning is, in some ways, an impossibility. African American literature began at different moments, and from its earliest days it has reflected the wide variety of lived experiences and artistic techniques that have continued to distinguish the African American literary tradition. One might argue that African American literature "began" when **Lucy Terry** wrote the poem "Bars Fight" in 1746, or when **Phillis Wheatley** published *Poems on Various Subjects* in 1773, or when the poet **George Moses Horton** published *The Hope of Liberty* in 1829. Again and again, African American literature has been reborn in new forms, responding to the experiences, desires, and needs of writers and readers in different places and at different times. **Henry Bibb, William Wells Brown, Frederick Douglass, Olaudah Equiano, Harriet Ann Jacobs, Sojourner Truth**, and other eighteenth- and nineteenth-century writers, for example, wove together memoir, politics, and spirituality to create a rich and complex new form of literature, the **slave narrative**, which both responded to and transcended inhumane circumstances.

African American literature expanded as work songs, **gospel** songs, and **folktales** found their way into written form, and it grew again as African American writers published works of poetry, **autobiography**, and fiction, as well as pamphlets, **sermons**, and tracts, during the late nineteenth and early twentieth centuries. In the works of writers including **Frances E. W. Harper, Booker T. Washington, Charles Chesnutt, W.E.B. Du Bois, Sutton Griggs**, and **Alice Moore Dunbar-Nelson**, African American literature acquired new forms of expression, originality, and vision. Works such as Washington's *Up from Slavery* (1901), Chesnutt's *The Marrow of Tradition* (1901), and Du Bois's *The Souls of Black Folk* (1903), like Frederick Douglass's *Narrative of the Life of an American Slave* (1845), changed not only African American literature but America itself.

THE HARLEM RENAISSANCE

African American literature became increasingly protean in the twentieth century. In roughly ten years (c. 1920–1932), the Harlem Renaissance produced an astonishingly innovative and diverse body of literature. The literary culture of the Harlem Renaissance encouraged productive disagreements about the literary aspirations of African Americans, and it laid an indestructible cultural and conceptual foundation on which later writers would build. Perhaps no other movement in American literary history has been as productive, as vibrant, or as influential. Examining the first (1922) and second (1931) editions of **James Weldon Johnson**'s landmark anthology, *The Book of American Negro Poetry*, is one way to measure the astounding difference that this single decade made in the shape and the scope of African American literature.

In this brief period, **Gwendolyn Bennett, Arna Bontemps, Sterling Brown, Countee Cullen, Jessie Redmon Fauset**, Langston Hughes, **Zora Neale**

Hurston, **Nella Larsen**, **Claude McKay**, **Rudolph Fisher**, **George Schuyler**, **Wallace Thurman**, **Jean Toomer**, and **Dorothy West**, to name but a few writers, began their careers. At the same time, established writers and editors, including **Charles Spurgeon Johnson**, Du Bois, James Weldon Johnson, **Walter White**, and **Alain Locke**, discovered new contexts and purposes for their ideals, energy, and literary work. Readers continue to rediscover the literature of the Harlem Renaissance, which dramatizes a host of crucial issues connected to sexuality and **gender**, economics and social class (*see* **Marxism**), racist violence, **passing**, **Modernism**, and the conflict between **assimilation** and **Black Nationalism**, while students, teachers, critics, and scholars continue to explore the Harlem Renaissance's wide-reaching influence and implications.

THE BLACK ARTS MOVEMENT

While the Harlem Renaissance itself drew to a close with the onset of the **Great Depression**, African American literature continued to develop and expand. The writers working during the decades between the end of the Harlem Renaissance and the beginning of the **Black Arts Movement** in the 1960s are difficult to categorize. Scholar and critic **R. Baxter Miller**, for example, refers to some of these writers as being "between worlds" (*Black American Poets Between Worlds, 1940–1960*, University of Tennessee Press, 1986). **Chester Himes** symbolizes this period well. Known best for his work in **crime fiction**, Himes was also an important writer of **protest literature**, an **expatriate**, and an immensely prolific and versatile author. His contemporaries, including **Melvin B. Tolson**, **Richard Wright**, **Robert Hayden**, **Ralph Ellison**, **Margaret Walker**, **Gwendolyn Brooks**, and, slightly later, **James Baldwin** and **Lorraine Hansberry**, are as different from each other as each is from Himes, but like him, they created literature that asserts authority, independence, and originality. The gravity and durability of their work are unmistakable.

The Black Arts Movement opened the way to an explosion of African American literature that has made it, ironically, perhaps the last great African American literary movement; African American literature after the Black Arts Movement may be too abundant and varied ever again to be characterized in terms of a single movement. The Black Arts Movement rekindled old debates from the Harlem Renaissance about literature and art, and it also began new ones. Reacting to implacable racism and reflecting the resolve of the indefatigable **Civil Rights Movement**, the writers of the Black Arts Movement spoke with the urgency demanded by the **Cold War**, the **Vietnam War**, and other political crises, giving voice to **Black Nationalism**, **Black Power**, and "Black Is Beautiful." As responsive as writers such as **Amiri Baraka**, **Sonia Sanchez**, **Haki R. Madhubuti**, **Nikki Giovanni**, and **Quincy Troupe** were to contemporary political and social crises, their ideas and their works have had tremendous staying power and have exerted a significant influence on the development of African American literature since the 1970s.

CONTEMPORARY AFRICAN AMERICAN LITERATURE

African American literature has continued to flourish since the period of the Black Arts Movement. Working in a wide variety of genres, writers including **Maya Angelou, Ernest J. Gaines, Audre Lorde, Ishmael Reed, Toni Cade Bambara, Alice Walker, John Edgar Wideman, Michael S. Harper, Octavia Butler, Gloria Naylor, August Wilson**, and **Terry McMillan** have expanded the audience for African American literature and have pushed that literature in countless new directions. This, however, is to name only a few of the most visible and celebrated contemporary African American writers, those likely to be represented in such texts as the *Norton Anthology of African American Literature* (2nd ed., 2004), edited by **Henry Louis Gates, Jr.**, and **Nellie Y. McKay**. Such anthologies show the extent to which African American literature has grown, and they make representative works by crucial authors accessible to readers from a variety of backgrounds, both inside and outside of the academy. There is, of course, much more to African American literature than the work of its most highly acclaimed or historically important writers, as influential as those writers have been.

The African American literary tradition is a complex and pluralistic one, and many important contributors to this tradition remain little known outside of academic circles. Critic Joan Sherman characterizes such writers as invisible, even as she and other scholars engage in the valuable work of "recovering" their writings for new generations of readers (*Invisible Poets: Afro-Americans of the Nineteenth Century*, University of Illinois Press, 1974). These "invisible" writers have laid the groundwork for many of the most important movements and developments in the history of African American literature, and their work richly rewards revisiting. **Gertrude Mossell**, for example, was an important feminist, suffragist, and visionary journalist; **Lewis Alexander**, a little-known writer of the Harlem Renaissance, was the author of a number of remarkable poems; and **Rob Penny**, a participant in the Black Arts Movement, was a potent force in contemporary **drama**, in academia, and most of all in his community. The works of these and other lesser-known African American writers can be found in libraries, bookstores, and **archives and collections**, waiting to challenge the preconceptions and expand the horizons of readers in a new century. At the same time, thousands of African American writers are producing poems and stories, **romance** and mystery novels, **science fiction, performance poetry**, creative nonfiction, and **essays**. The river of African American literature has become an ocean.

AFRICAN AMERICAN STUDIES

While the African American literary tradition is a long one, the study of African American literature has developed as a distinct academic field only within the relatively recent past. The first **Black Studies** programs, which emerged alongside and to some extent out of the Black Arts Movement, were established at San Francisco State University and at the University of California at Berkeley in 1968. In the same year, just before she retired from teaching, Margaret Walker helped to establish a similar program at Jackson State University. Black Studies programs were established at many other colleges and universities within the next few years; they were created at Boston College and at the State University of New York at Binghamton (now Binghamton University), for example, in 1969. Black Studies, of course, has a rich and complex history of its own, seeds of which were planted in earlier generations, including that of the Harlem Renaissance. Visionaries such as Arna Bontemps, **Arthur Schomburg**, and **Carl Van Vechten** preserved books, manuscripts, documents, photographs, and other materials in libraries, so that they would be ready when something like Black Studies eventually took shape. The Civil Rights Movement, the Free Speech Movement, the **Vietnam War**, and the assassinations and violence that characterized the turbulent decade of the 1960s helped to shape the intellectual and cultural contexts of Black Studies, as did the experiences, choices, and courage of individual students, teachers, and writers.

Over thirty years after the initiation of the first Black Studies programs, the journalist Amy Alexander, writing about a nationally publicized conflict within the African American Studies program at Harvard University, observed that, in spite of the conflict, "mainstream news organizations seemed to take it for granted that black studies programs have at last arrived" ("Reading Between the Lines," *Blackworld*, January 24, 2002: http://www.africana.com/columns/alexander/bl_lines_35.asp). Well established by 2002, Black Studies has helped to transform not just the study but the very definition of American literature. Black Studies has effected fundamental changes in how we study, teach, publish, and read all forms of literature. African American Studies—one of Black Studies' newer names—has recovered ignored writers, discovered lost writers, published previously unpublished writings, developed new strategies for reading and interpretation, and brought African American magazines, journals, and anthologies to bookstores and college classrooms. In the process, the discipline has become an intellectual meeting place as students and scholars working in a variety disciplines, including English, history, philosophy, communication, sociology, and religious studies, interact in unprecedentedly productive ways.

Perhaps most important, African American Studies has begun to tell the story, or stories, of African American literature. It has begun to identify traditions, trace lineages, and take inventory. By reclaiming a literary past and asserting the validity of the *Black* American literary present, African American Studies has changed the future of African American literature. Black Studies is not solely responsible, of course, for the abundance, variety, accessibility, and stature of African American literature today, but its influence on the perception and the reception of African American literature would be difficult to overestimate. Where African American Studies now intersects with **feminist criticism**, women studies, and sexuality and gender studies, its influence is even more various.

REFERENCE WORKS IN AFRICAN AMERICAN LITERATURE

The Greenwood Encyclopedia of African American Literature joins a burgeoning family of literary reference works within the dynamic and evolving field of African American Studies. The works that constitute that family are too numerous to name here. Outstanding among them, however, are the dictionaries of biography (1984–1987) edited by **Trudier Harris** and Thadious M. Davis; *The Oxford Companion to African American Literature* (1997), edited by **William L. Andrews, Frances Smith Foster**, and Trudier Harris; the series *Modern African American Writers* (1994), edited by Matthew J. Bruccoli and Judith S. Baughman; *Afro-American Fiction, 1853–1976: A Guide to Information Sources* (1979), by Edward Margolies and David Bakish; *Black American Fiction: A Bibliography* (1978), by Carol Fairbanks and Eugene A. Engeldinger; Maryemma Graham's *Cambridge Companion to the African American Novel* (2004); and Preston M. Yancey's *The Afro-American Short Story: A Comprehensive, Annotated Index with Selected Commentaries* (1986). This list omits numerous fine reference works on African American literature, and it neglects entirely the many excellent bibliographies, bio-bibliographies, encyclopedias, and reference guides on individual authors, an area of scholarship that has expanded greatly since the 1980s. Readers are invited to consult both the entry on **reference works** and the section devoted to reference works in the general bibliography at the end of this *Encyclopedia* for a more complete account of the resources available in this area. To all the other tillers in the field of reference scholarship, we express our thanks, our respect, and our admiration.

Hans Ostrom, Tacoma, Washington
J. David Macey, Jr., Edmond, Oklahoma

CHRONOLOGY

1517	Slave trade to the New World begins.
1526	Spanish ships bring slaves to North America.
1543	*On the Revolutions of the Heavenly Spheres*, by Copernicus, is published.
1564	William Shakespeare is born. Galileo Galilei is born.
c. 1602	William Shakespeare writes *Hamlet*.
1605	*Don Quixote*, by Miguel de Cervantes, is published.
1616	William Shakespeare dies.
1619	A Dutch ship brings the first Africans to Jamestown, Virginia.
1620	The *Mayflower* docks at Cape Cod, Massachusetts.
1641	The Colony of Massachusetts legally recognizes **slavery**. *Discourse on Method*, by René Descartes, is published.
1652	Rhode Island adopts a law prohibiting slavery.
1667	*Paradise Lost*, by John Milton, is published.
1689	The Japanese poet Basho writes *The Narrow Road to the Deep North*.
1712	Pennsylvania adopts a law against slavery. A slave revolt occurs in New York City.
1726	*Gulliver's Travels*, by Jonathan Swift, is published.

c. 1730	**Lucy Terry [Prince]** is born in Africa.
1732	George Washington is born.
1734	Daniel Boone is born.
1743	Thomas Jefferson is born.
1746	Lucy Terry writes the poem "Bars Fight."
c. 1753	**Phillis Wheatley** is born.
1755	Samuel Johnson's *Dictionary of the English Language* is published in England.
1769	Napoleon Bonaparte is born.
1770	Crispus Attucks, an African American, is killed in the **Boston** Massacre.
1773	*Poems on Various Subjects, Religious and Moral*, by Phillis Wheatley, is published. **Sally Hemings** is born.
1775–1783	The Revolutionary War.
1776	The Declaration of Independence is written.
1779	Articles of Confederation are ratified.
1789	George Washington is elected president. The French Revolution begins. *The Interesting Narrative of the Life of Olaudah Equiano; or, Gustavus Vassa, the African*, by **Olaudah Equiano**, is published.
1791	*The Private Life of the Late Benjamin Franklin* (later known as the *Autobiography of Benjamin Franklin*) is published.
1791–1792	*The Rights of Man*, by Thomas Paine, is published.
1797	**Sojourner Truth** is born.
1798	*Lyrical Ballads*, by William Wordsworth and Samuel Taylor Coleridge, is published.
1799	In France, Napoleon's coup d'état succeeds.
1803	Louisiana Territory is purchased from France by the United States; the land mass of the United States thereby doubles.
1812	Charles Dickens is born. Napoleon invades Russia. The War of 1812, in which both slaves and free Blacks fight, begins.
1815	Napoleon's army is defeated at the Battle of Waterloo.
1818	**Frederick Douglass** is born.
1819	Queen Victoria is born. Walt Whitman is born.

1820	George III, King of England, dies.
1822	Denmark Vesey organizes a slave revolt in Charleston, South Carolina, but he is betrayed, and it fails.
1826	Thomas Jefferson dies.
1827	*Tamerlane and Other Poems*, by Edgar Allan Poe, is published.
1829	*The Hope of Liberty*, a collection of poems by **George Moses Horton**, is published. *David Walker's Appeal*, by **David Walker**, is published.
1829–1837	Native American tribes are driven from their homelands to "Indian Territories," including what is now **Oklahoma**.
1831	**Nat Turner** leads a slave rebellion in Virginia. He is subsequently captured and executed.
1835	Sally Hemings dies.
1845	*Narrative of the Life of Frederick Douglass, an American Slave, Written by Himself*, is published.
1849–1850	*David Copperfield*, by Charles Dickens, is published.
1851	"Ain't I a Woman?," a speech by Sojourner Truth, is delivered in Akron, Ohio.
1853	*Clotel; Or, the President's Daughter: A Narrative of Slave Life in the United States*, a novel by **William Wells Brown**, is published.
1854	*Poems on Miscellaneous Subjects*, by **Frances Ellen Watkins Harper**, is published.
1855	*Leaves of Grass*, by Walt Whitman, is published.
1857	The U.S. Supreme Court reaches its decision in the *Dred Scott* case. *Madame Bovary*, by Gustave Flaubert, is published.
1859	*On the Origin of Species*, by Charles Darwin, is published. **John Brown**'s raid on Harpers Ferry occurs.
1860	The total population of African American slaves is roughly 4 million. South Carolina secedes from the United States; it is the first state to do so.
1861	*Incidents in the Life of a Slave Girl*, by **Harriet Ann Jacobs**, is published.
1861–1865	The American **Civil War**.
1863	The Emancipation Proclamation is issued by President Abraham Lincoln.
1864	The Fugitive Slave Laws are repealed.

1865	April 9: General Robert E. Lee surrenders to General Ulysses S. Grant. The Civil War ends. April 15: Abraham Lincoln dies from gunshot wounds suffered the night before at Ford's Theatre in **Washington, D.C.**
1867	The period of **Reconstruction** begins in **the South**.
1868	The U.S. Congress passes the Fourteenth Amendment to the U.S. Constitution, granting African Americans equal citizenship and civil rights. The Meiji Restoration begins in Japan. **W.E.B. Du Bois** is born.
1869	The National Woman Suffrage Association is established. *War and Peace*, by Leo Tolstoy, is published.
1872	**Paul Laurence Dunbar** is born.
1874	Robert Frost is born.
1876	Alexander Graham Bell invents the telephone.
1877	The U.S. military withdraws from the South, and Reconstruction ends.
1881	The Tuskegee Institute is founded, under the leadership of **Booker T. Washington**.
1884	*The Adventures of Huckleberry Finn*, by **Mark Twain**, is published.
1892	The **Baltimore Afro-American** is established. Walt Whitman dies.
1893	*Oak and Ivy*, by **Paul Laurence Dunbar**, is published.
1894	**Jean Toomer** is born.
1895	Frederick Douglass dies in Washington, D.C. Booker T. Washington speaks at the Atlanta Exposition. *Violets and Other Tales*, by **Alice Moore Dunbar-Nelson**, is published.
1896	The U.S. Supreme Court issues its decision in *Plessy v. Ferguson*.
1897	William Faulkner is born.
1898	The Spanish-American War. **Melvin B. Tolson** is born.
1899	*The Conjure Woman*, by **Charles Waddell Chesnutt**, is published. Ernest Hemingway is born. **Edward Kennedy "Duke" Ellington** is born.
1901	Queen Victoria dies. *Up from Slavery*, by Booker T. Washington, is published.
1902	**Langston Hughes** is born. **Arna Bontemps** is born.
1903	*The Souls of Black Folk*, by W.E.B. Du Bois, is published.
1904	*Lyrics of Life and Love*, by **William Stanley Braithwaite**, is published.
1905	The **Chicago Defender** is founded.

1906	Paul Laurence Dunbar dies.
1908	**Richard Wright** is born.
1909	The National Association for the Advancement of Colored People (**NAACP**) is founded, led by W.E.B. Du Bois.
1910	Mark Twain dies. *The Crisis* is established.
1913	The First International Exhibit of Modern Art, also known as the Armory Show, takes place in New York City.
1914	**World War I** begins. **Ralph Ellison** is born.
1915	Booker T. Washington dies.
1916	*Rachel*, a play by **Angelina Weld Grimké**, is performed. **Frank Yerby** is born. *The General Theory of Relativity*, by Albert Einstein, is published.
1917	The United States enters World War I. Over 365,000 African Americans are drafted into military service during this war. The Russian Revolution begins.
1918	World War I ends. *The Heart of a Woman*, by **Georgia Douglas Johnson**, is published.
1919	The Volstead Act is passed, beginning the era of Prohibition. *Ten Days That Shook the World*, by John Reed, is published.
1920	The beginning of the **Harlem Renaissance** is often linked to this year.
1922	The *Book of American Negro Poetry*, edited by **James Weldon Johnson**, is published. *Harlem Shadows*, by **Claude McKay**, is published. *The Waste Land*, by T. S. Eliot, is published.
1923	*Cane*, by Jean Toomer, is published.
1924	**James Baldwin** is born. *The Fire in the Flint*, by **Walter White**, is published.
1925	*The Great Gatsby*, by F. Scott Fitzgerald, is published. **The New Negro**, an anthology edited by **Alain Locke**, is published.
1926	*The Sun Also Rises*, by Ernest Hemingway, is published. *The Weary Blues*, by Langston Hughes, is published. The single issue of the magazine *Fire!!*, edited by **Wallace Thurman** and others, is published.
1927	*Caroling at Dusk*, edited by **Countee Cullen**, is published. *Ebony and Topaz*, edited by **Charles Spurgeon Johnson**, is published.
1928	**Maya Angelou** is born.
1929	*The Sound and the Fury*, by William Faulkner, is published. Walter White's *Rope & Faggot*, a landmark study of **lynching**, is published. *Plum*

Bun, by **Jessie Redmon Fauset**, is published. The U.S. stock market crashes. The **Great Depression** begins. **Martin Luther King, Jr.**, is born.

1930   *Not Without Laughter*, a novel by Langston Hughes, is published. The **Nation of Islam** is established.

1931   The case of the **Scottsboro Boys** begins in Alabama. *Black No More*, by **George Samuel Schuyler**, is published. **Toni Morrison** is born.

1932   *The Southern Road*, by **Sterling A. Brown**, is published. *The Conjure-Man Dies*, by **Rudolph Fisher**, is published.

1933   Adolf Hitler becomes Chancellor in Germany. National Prohibition ends in the United States. President Franklin Roosevelt institutes New Deal policies.

1934   *The Ways of White Folks*, by Langston Hughes, is published. Rudolph Fisher dies.

1935   *Mulatto*, a play by Langston Hughes, is produced in New York.

1936   *Black Thunder*, by Arna Bontemps, is published.

1937   The **College Language Association** is established. *Their Eyes Were Watching God*, by **Zora Neale Hurston**, is published. Langston Hughes writes articles about the Spanish Civil War for *The Baltimore Afro-American*.

1939   **World War II** begins. *The Grapes of Wrath*, by John Steinbeck, is published.

1940   *The Big Sea*, by Langston Hughes, is published. *Native Son*, by Richard Wright, is published.

1941   The Japanese air force attacks Pearl Harbor, Hawaii, in December. The United States enters World War II. The first commercial television broadcast occurs.

1942   *Dust Tracks on a Road*, by Zora Neale Hurston, is published. *For My People*, by **Margaret Walker**, is published.

1944   *Rendezvous with America*, by **Melvin B. Tolson**, is published. The short story "King of the Bingo Game," by Ralph Ellison, is published.

1945   *Black Boy*, by Richard Wright, is published. *If He Hollers Let Him Go*, by **Chester Himes**, is published. *A Street in Bronzeville*, by **Gwendolyn Brooks**, is published. The United States drops two atomic bombs on Japan. World War II ends. The United Nations is established.

1946   *The Street*, by **Ann Petry**, is published. Countee Cullen dies. *The Stranger*, by Albert Camus, is published. *The Foxes of Harrow*, by Frank Yerby, is published.

1947	**Jackie Robinson** breaks the color line in professional baseball, playing for the **Brooklyn** Dodgers.
1948	Claude McKay dies. *The Living Is Easy*, by **Dorothy West**, is published. *Death of a Salesman*, by Arthur Miller, is produced.
1949	The Chinese Revolution occurs.
1950	Gwendolyn Brooks wins the Pulitzer Prize for her book of poetry, *Annie Allen*, published in 1949.
1950–1953	The Korean War.
1951	*Montage of a Dream Deferred*, by Langston Hughes, is published.
1952	*The Old Man and the Sea*, by Ernest Hemingway, is published. *Invisible Man*, by Ralph Ellison, is published. Dwight Eisenhower is elected president.
1953	*Go Tell It on the Mountain*, by James Baldwin, is published. Langston Hughes is called to testify before Senator Joseph McCarthy's Permanent Subcommittee on Investigations (*see* **McCarthysim**).
1954	The U.S. Supreme Court issues its two landmark decisions in *Brown v. Board of Education, Topeka, Kansas*.
1955	*Notes of a Native Son*, by James Baldwin, is published. Walter White dies.
1957–1958	The desegregation of public schools in Little Rock, Arkansas, occurs. *On the Road*, by Jack Kerouac, is published.
1958	*The Book of Negro Folklore*, edited by Langston Hughes and Arna Bontemps, is published.
1959	*A Raisin in the Sun*, by **Lorraine Hansberry**, is produced on Broadway. *Brown Girl, Brownstones*, by **Paule Marshall**, is published.
1960	Zora Neale Hurston dies. Students in North Carolina stage a sit-in at lunch counters to protest Jim Crow laws ("separate but equal accommodations"). Richard Wright dies.
1961	*Preface to a Twenty Volume Suicide Note* and *Dutchman*, both by LeRoi Jones (**Amiri Baraka**), are published. Ernest Hemingway dies.
1962	*Ballad of Remembrance*, by **Robert Hayden**, is published. James Meredith enrolls at the University of Mississippi. William Faulkner dies.
1963	Martin Luther King, Jr., writes "Letter from Birmingham Jail." *The Fire Next Time*, by James Baldwin, is published. John F. Kennedy is assassinated. W.E.B. Du Bois dies. **Medgar Evers** is assassinated. Robert Frost dies.
1964	Martin Luther King, Jr., wins the Nobel Peace Prize. The Free Speech Movement begins at the University of California, Berkeley. *The Dead Lecturer*, by Amiri Baraka, is published.

1965   *Harlem Gallery*, by Melvin B. Tolson, is published. *The Autobiography of Malcolm X*, which **Alex Haley** helps to write, is published. The **Vietnam War** begins. Malcolm X is assassinated. Winston Churchill dies. Lorraine Hansberry dies.

1966   The **Black Panther Party** is established. *Jubilee*, by Margaret Walker, is published. *The Book of Negro Humor*, edited by Langston Hughes, is published. Melvin B. Tolson dies.

1967   Thurgood Marshall becomes a Justice of the U.S. Supreme Court. *The Best Short Stories by Negro Writers*, edited by Langston Hughes, is published. Langston Hughes dies. *Think Black*, by **Haki R. Madhubuti**, is published. Jean Toomer dies. *Soul on Ice*, by **Eldridge Cleaver**, is published.

1968   *Poems from Prison*, by **Etheridge Knight**, is published. *The First Cities*, by **Audre Lorde**, is published. Richard M. Nixon is elected president. Martin Luther King, Jr., is assassinated. Robert F. Kennedy is assassinated. **Shirley Chisholm** is elected to Congress.

1969   The first **Black Studies** program at a four-year university is established at San Francisco State College. *home coming*, by **Sonia Sanchez**, is published. *Black Pow-Wow: Jazz Poems*, by **Ted Joans**, is published. The U.S. agency NASA lands a man on the moon. A riot breaks out after the Stonewall Inn is raided by police in Manhattan; the event is associated with the beginning of the Gay Pride movement. *Black Boogaloo: Notes on Black Liberation*, by **Larry Neal**, is published.

1970   *I Know Why the Caged Bird Sings*, by Maya Angelou, is published. *Dear John, Dear Coltrane*, by **Michael S. Harper**, is published. *I Am a Black Woman*, by **Mari Evans**, is published.

1971   *The Black Aesthetic*, by **Addison Gayle**, is published. *The Black Poets*, edited by **Dudley Randall**, is published. *The Autobiography of Miss Jane Pittman*, by **Ernest James Gaines**, is published.

1972   *Mumbo Jumbo*, by **Ishmael Reed**, is published.

1973   A treaty between the United States and North Vietnam is signed in **Paris, France**, ending the Vietnam War. *The Lynchers*, by **John Edgar Wideman**, is published. Arna Bontemps dies.

1974   President Nixon resigns because of the Watergate scandal. Duke Ellington dies.

1975   *for colored girls who have considered suicide/when the rainbow is enuf*, by **Ntozake Shange**, is produced in New York City. *Corregidora*, by **Gayl Jones**, is published.

1976   *Roots*, by Alex Haley, is published. It is turned into a television miniseries in 1977.

1977   *Elbow Room*, by **James Alan McPherson**, is published. *Dhalgren*, by **Samuel R. Delany**, is published.

1978   James Alan McPherson wins the Pulitzer Prize for *Elbow Room*.

1979   *Kindred*, by **Octavia E. Butler**, is published.

1980   *The Salt Eaters*, by **Toni Cade Bambara**, is published. Ronald Reagan is elected president.

1981   *The Chaneysville Incident*, by **David Bradley**, is published. *A Soldier's Play*, by **Charles Fuller**, is published. *Ain't I a Woman: Black Women and Feminism*, by **bell hooks**, is published. *Women, Race, and Class*, by **Angela Davis**, is published.

1982   *The Color Purple*, by **Alice Walker**, is published. *The Women of Brewster Place*, by **Gloria Naylor**, is published. Charles Fuller wins the Pulitzer Prize for *A Soldier's Play*. *Ma Rainey's Black Bottom*, by **August Wilson**, is produced.

1983   Alice Walker wins the Pulitzer Prize for *The Color Purple*.

1984   *Sister Outsider: Essays and Speeches*, by Audre Lorde, is published. The human immunodeficiency virus (HIV) is identified as the cause of AIDS.

1985   *Linden Hills*, by Gloria Naylor, is published. *Afro-American Folktales: Stories from Black Traditions*, edited by Roger D. Abrahams, is published. *Annie John*, by **Jamaica Kincaid**, is published.

1986   *Thomas and Beulah*, by **Rita Dove**, is published. *Our Dead Behind Us*, by Audre Lorde, is published. *In the Life: A Black Gay Anthology*, edited by **Joseph Beam**, is published. *The **Oprah Winfrey** Show* debuts on televison.

1987   Rita Dove wins the Pulitzer Prize. James Baldwin dies. *Heavy Daughter Blues*, by **Wanda Coleman**, is published.

1988   *The Signifying Monkey*, by **Henry Louis Gates, Jr.**, is published.

1989   The Berlin Wall is torn down, signaling the dissolution of Communist regimes in the Soviet Union and Eastern Europe.

1990   August Wilson wins the Pulitzer Prize for the play *The Piano Lesson*. **Charles R. Johnson** wins the National Book Award for the novel *Middle Passage*. *Devil in a Blue Dress*, by **Walter Mosley**, is published.

1991   Frank Yerby dies.

1992   William Jefferson Clinton is elected president. *Technical Difficulties*, by **June Jordan**, is published. *Waiting to Exhale*, by **Terry McMillan**, is published. *Jazz*, by Toni Morrison, is published. *Through the Ivory Gate*, by Rita Dove, is published.

1993   Toni Morrison wins the Nobel Prize for Literature. Rita Dove is named Poet Laureate.

1994   *Race Matters*, by **Cornel West**, is published. *The Portable Harlem Renaissance Reader*, edited by David Levering Lewis, is published. *Juba to Jive: A Dictionary of African American Slang*, by **Clarence Major**, is published. Ralph Ellison dies. **Yusef Komunyakaa** wins the Pulitzer Prize for his book *Neon Vernacular*.

1996   *The Norton Anthology of African American Literature*, edited by Henry Louis Gates, Jr., and **Nellie Y. McKay**, is published.

1998   Margaret Walker dies.

2000   *Step into a World: A Global Anthology of the New Black Literature*, edited by **Kevin Powell**, is published. Gwendolyn Brooks dies. *In the Blood*, by **Suzan-Lori Parks**, is published.

2001   *Giant Steps: The New Generation of African American Writers*, edited by **Kevin Young**, is published. The University of Missouri Press begins to publish *The Complete Works of Langston Hughes* in 16 volumes.

2002   *Transcircularities: New and Selected Poems*, by **Quincy Troupe**, is published. *Black Like Us: A Century of Lesbian, Gay, and Bisexual African American Fiction*, edited by Devon W. Carbado, Dwight A. McBride, and Donald Weise, is published. *The Bondwoman's Narrative*, by **Hannah Crafts**, is published.

2003   *Love*, by Toni Morrison, is published. *The Other Woman*, by **Eric Jerome Dickey**, is published.

2004   *American Smooth*, by Rita Dove, is published.

A

Abernathy, Ralph David (1926–1990). Pastor, civil rights leader, and autobiographer. Abernathy was a founder of the Southern Christian Leadership Conference (SCLC) with **Martin Luther King, Jr.**, Bayard Rustin, and Fred Shuttlesworth. The SCLC was an instrumental organization in the **Civil Rights Movement**, advocating persistent but nonviolent direct action. Before the SCLC was founded (1957), Abernathy and King helped to organize a boycott of the Montgomery, Alabama, bus system (1955) to protest "separate but equal" laws and practices that, for example, forced African Americans to sit at the back of municipal buses. Abernathy was born in Linden, Alabama, attended Alabama State University, and earned an M.A. in sociology from Atlanta University in 1951. He then became pastor of the First Baptist Church in Montgomery. Although Abernathy was a key figure in the SCLC and the Civil Rights Movement, he was less well known than the charismatic King. After King was assassinated in **Memphis, Tennessee (1968)**, Abernathy became president of the SCLC, and for almost a decade he guided the organization during a difficult political time (Douglas;

Rev. Ralph David Abernathy speaks at a National Press Club luncheon, 1968. Courtesy of the Library of Congress.

1

Huggins). He resigned from the post in 1977 and became pastor of a Baptist church once more, this time in **Atlanta, Georgia**. In 1989, Abernathy published his autobiography, *And the Walls Came Tumbling Down*, which includes his perspectives on his friendship with King and their involvement in the Civil Rights Movement. His daughter, Donzaleigh, published a study of her father and King, and of the two friends' involvement in the movement (2003).

Resources: Donzaleigh Abernathy, *Partners to History: Martin Luther King Jr., Ralph David Abernathy, and the Civil Rights Movement* (New York: Crown, 2003); Ralph Abernathy, *And the Walls Came Tumbling Down* (New York: Harper & Row, 1989); Carlyle C. Douglas, "Ralph Abernathy: The Man Who Fights to Keep King's Dream Alive," *Ebony* 25 (Jan. 1970), 40+; Nathan Huggins, *Ralph Abernathy: Civil Rights Leader* (New York: Chelsea House, 1995).

Hans Ostrom

Abolitionist Movement (c. 1820–1865). "Give me liberty, or give me death." These were the words of one of the Founding Fathers of the United States, Patrick Henry, and by the nineteenth century they had become the rallying cry of fighters for the rights of the "poor African bondsman." Subject to ridicule in the early 1820s as a despised band of crackpots, antislavery activists had, by the 1850s, gained national recognition. The beginnings of antislavery activism lay in America's War of Independence, which liberated the country from British colonial rule. Thomas Jefferson's rhetoric, "All men are created equal," not only had an impact upon contemporary politics but also formed the bedrock of antislavery thought. Legislation was passed that not only prohibited **slavery** in the northern states by 1787 but also placed a ban on the international slave trade from Africa in 1808. (The slave trade continued illegally well into the nineteenth century.) However, such laws represented small measures; over 3 million slaves were still left in bondage, the majority of them living on the plantations of the American South.

The earliest antislavery leaders were Quakers who attacked slavery as a moral evil and argued for the equality of all men before God. However, it was the religious movement of the 1830s known as the Second Great Awakening that provided the main impetus for organized antislavery efforts. The Second Great Awakening's belief that evangelical preaching possessed the power to transform the individual and his or her role in society inspired activists to believe they could effect change. Early antislavery activists ran meetings, organized petitions, and distributed literature dramatizing the plight of the poor slave in order to convert audiences by tactics of moral suasion. Amid a whirlpool of controversy, the American Colonization Society was founded in 1817, with the purpose of sending freed slaves **back to Africa** and to establish Monrovia (present-day Liberia) in 1822. This scheme was supported by Henry Clay, James Monroe, Thomas Jefferson, and even the noted abolitionist William Lloyd Garrison early in his career. The movement also attracted support from African American men such as **Martin Delany** and Paul Cuffee, who saw this as an opportunity to recapture the lost glory of Africa. Historians estimate

Individual portraits of Charles Sumner, Henry Ward Beecher, Wendell Phillips, William Lloyd Garrison, Gerrit Smith, Horace Greeley, and Henry Wilson, c. 1866. Courtesy of the Library of Congress.

that by 1860 as many as 12,000 Africans had returned to Africa. However, by the 1850s, the black abolitionist wing of the movement had strengthened, and men such as **Frederick Douglass**, **Henry Highland Garnet**, and **William Wells Brown** voiced their disgust with colonization. Douglass in particular argued that African Americans were living and had lived in the United States, had a right to do so, and intended to stay.

Prior to the publication of **Harriet Beecher Stowe**'s novel *Uncle Tom's Cabin* in 1852, abolitionists held very little sway in the North. However, in the South, they provoked widespread and entrenched opposition that made itself manifest in anti-abolitionist propaganda. Throughout the nineteenth century, fugitive slaves played a powerful role in swaying public opinion as they published their narratives of suffering and redemption and gave dramatic performances in packed auditoriums. On the abolitionist podium, men and women such as Frederick Douglass, William Wells Brown and **Sojourner Truth** bared their souls and exhibited their bodies as proofs of the violence of slavery and White depredations. The antislavery movement gave birth to a rich literary renaissance that included the publication of newspapers and periodicals such as *The Antislavery Almanac* and *The Slave's Friend* (for children); the circulation of medallions, petitions, and gift books (*The Liberty Bell* and *Autographs for Freedom*); the performances of songs such as "The Fugitive's Song" (dedicated to Frederick Douglass); the widespread printing of slave narratives, poetry, and plays; and the spectacular theatrical reenactments of escape and presentations of antislavery tableaux.

By the late 1820s, the movement had gathered considerable support in the North. While smaller societies took root in New York and **Boston, Massachusetts**, founded by Lewis and Arthur Tappan and William Lloyd Garrison, Theodore Dwight Weld organized the national American Anti-Slavery Society in 1833. Garrison and his supporters soon gained control of this society by voicing their commitment to nonresistance and an end to "union with slaveholders." By 1830, abolitionists had replaced the notion of gradual reform with that of immediate abolition as Southern defenses of slavery became more pronounced. In 1831, Garrison founded *The Liberator* and organized lecture tours that included fugitive slave women such as Sojourner Truth and Ellen Craft as well as the free white women Lydia Maria Child, Lucretia Mott, and **Sarah** and **Angelina Grimké**. The dissemination of propaganda led to attacks by mobs in the North, the murder of abolitionist editor Elijah P. Lovejoy in 1837, and the passing of the gag rule prohibiting discussions on abolition. By the 1840s, fissures appeared in the movement between those who believed the American Constitution was a pro-slavery document fit only for burning in the streets (Garrison et al.) and others who felt that reform was possible simply by living up to the principles set down in the American Constitution (Douglass, Gerrit Smith, et al.).

By the 1850s, the situation had become desperate: **Texas** had been annexed as a slaveholding state, the Fugitive Slave Act (1850) was passed, and the Missouri Compromise (1854) was repealed, giving slaveholders free reign in western territories. Black abolitionists lost faith in pacifist reform and began to advocate violence; Henry Highland Garnet advised audiences, "Rather die freemen than live to be slaves." Throughout the nineteenth century, slaves had been heroically committed to the use of violence in gaining their freedom; they included such men and women as Toussaint L'Ouverture in Haiti, Gabriel Prosser in Virginia, Denmark Vesey in North Carolina, **Nat Turner** in Virginia, and **Harriet** "Moses" **Tubman** on her journeys with escaped slaves from the South to the North. In 1859, the firebrand abolitionist **John Brown** attacked the arsenal at Harpers Ferry, Virginia, forcing antislavery men such as Douglass into exile and provoking the ire of pro-slavery defenders. His actions were a harbinger of what was to come as black prophecies were fulfilled: the outbreak of the **Civil War** and the Emancipation Proclamation in 1863 proved that slavery was to end only in bloodshed. Against a backdrop of black bodies swaying in trees from the 1870s on and the rise of racial hate groups such as the Ku Klux Klan, the lions of abolition and their supporters continued to press for the rights of the descendants of Africa and for "freedom to ring" finally, and at last, for all citizens in the "model Republic."

Resources: Lewis Perry and Michael Fellman, eds., *Antislavery Reconsidered: New Perspectives on the Abolitionists* (Baton Rouge: Louisiana State University Press, 1979); Benjamin Quarles, *Black Abolitionists* (Oxford: Oxford University Press, 1969); John Stauffer, *The Black Hearts of Men* (Cambridge, MA: Harvard University Press, 2002); James B. Stewart, *Holy Warriors: The Abolitionists and American Slavery* (New York: Hill and Wang, 1976); Ronald G. Walters, *The Antislavery Appeal: American Abolitionism After 1830* (New York: W. W. Norton, 1978); Jean Fagan Yellin and John C. Van Horne, eds., *The Abolitionist Sisterhood: Women's Political Culture in Antebellum America* (Ithaca, NY: Cornell University Press, 1994).

Celeste-Marie Bernier

Adams, Jenoyne (born 1972). Novelist. Raised in San Bernadino, California, Jenoyne Adams studied political science at California State University at Fullerton and spent a year abroad studying Spanish at the University of Malaga. After completing her degree, she worked as a journalist with newspapers such as the *Precinct Reporter* in San Bernardino County and the *Tri County Bulletin* in Orange County. She is currently an agent with the Levine/Greenberg Literary Agency, where she represents clients such as the novelist Cherlyn Michaels. Adams is married to the writer Michael Datcher and has read with him at venues throughout the United States. They have been particularly active supporters of the World Stage Performance Gallery in the largely African American neighborhood of Leimert Park Village in **Los Angeles, California**. Adams's comfort on stage can be traced in part to her having performed for a time with an African dance troupe.

Adams has held a PEN USA Emerging Voices fellowship, and she has been a UCLA Extension Writing Program Community Access Scholar and a writing consultant for Voices in Harmony, which helps at-risk young people write and stage plays that address current social issues. Adams's own work has been included in such anthologies as *Catch the Fire!!! A Cross-Generational*

Anthology of Contemporary African-American Poetry (1998), *Drumvoices Revue* (2000), *Role Call* (2002), and *Brown Sugar 2* (2003).

Adams's highly regarded first novel, *Resurrecting Mingus* (2001), focuses on the personal and family crises that confront Mingus Browning, a successful lawyer in her mid-thirties. The daughter of a Black father and a White mother who, after thirty-five years of marriage, are engaged in a bitter divorce, Mingus has always been closer to her father but finds she has a great deal of feminine sympathy for her mother in this circumstance. Mingus herself is torn between two men—a White police officer and a Black television producer. Already drawn into the estrangement of their parents, her lifelong competitiveness with her sister Eva is further exacerbated when Eva becomes involved with the television producer—after Mingus has talked him into giving Eva a job. The novel balances sensitive characterizations with an engagingly melodramatic plot.

Adams' less-well-received second novel, *Selah's Bed* (2003), explores the reasons for and the ramifications of the secret sexual affairs of Selah Wells, the frustrated wife of a minister. Frequent flashbacks to Selah's past expose how her upbringing has shaped her adult behavior and has caused her to associate both self-assertion and self-loathing with sexuality.

Resources: Jenoyne Adams: *Resurrecting Mingus* (New York: Free Press, 2001); *Selah's Bed* (New York: Free Press, 2003); Shirley Chevalier, review of *Resurrecting Mingus*, *Black Issues Book Review*, May/June 2001, 21; Robin Green-Cary, review of *Selah's Bed*, *Black Issues Book Review*, Jan./Feb. 2003, 35.

Martin Kich

Adoff, Arnold (born 1935). Poet, editor, and teacher. Adoff is a longtime advocate of multiculturalism in literature, especially in works for children and young adults. In his writing he often addresses African American issues and experiences. He has a reputation for using his writing as a means of activism, and several of his books, including the anthology *I Am the Darker Brother* (1968) and the picture book *black is brown is tan* (1973), have been acknowledged as groundbreaking works.

Adoff considers himself, first and foremost, a poet (White). He has made poetry a part of his life since the age of eleven. The working-class Bronx neighborhood in New York city where he grew up was ethnically diverse, and family members were concerned with social justice. Adoff was encouraged to read broadly and to feel things passionately. Perhaps it is not surprising that after enrolling at City College of New York to follow in his father's footsteps as a pharmacist, Adoff quickly changed his major and focused on writing and political activism.

While a graduate student at Columbia University, Adoff was a schoolteacher and manager of the jazz musician Charlie Mingus, Adoff's "spiritual father" (Hile and Des Chenes). As Adoff has explained, jazz first demonstrated to him that "what was called 'American culture' most often did not include black or Latino culture" (Hile and Des Chenes).

Mingus introduced Adoff to **Virginia Hamilton**, an African American novelist and writer for children, in 1958. The pair married two years later and moved to

Europe. In response to the activity of the **Civil Rights Movement**, the couple and their children returned to the United States a few years later. Back in New York City, Adoff returned to teaching. His students in **Harlem, New York**, were the inspiration for his first work as an anthologist. Adoff had a long-standing interest in Black literature and would seek out Black magazines and periodicals in bookshops. He became aware of a lack of good Black literature in the anthologies and textbooks his students used. In response to the need for better literature, Adoff compiled poems he had collected and used in his teaching. From this came *I Am the Darker Brother: An Anthology of Modern Poems by Negro Americans* (1968). Subsequent anthologies of Black poetry and prose included *Black on Black: Commentaries by Negro Americans* (1968), *City in All Directions: An Anthology of Modern Poems* (1969), *Brothers and Sisters: Modern Stories by Black Americans* (1970), *It Is the Poem Singing into Your Eyes: An Anthology of New Young Poets* (1971), *The Poetry of Black America: An Anthology of the Twentieth Century* (1973), and *Celebrations: A New Anthology of Black American Poetry* (1978).

During this time, Adoff continued to work on his own poetry. His first poetry book for young children, *MA nDA LA*, was published in 1971. Two years later Adoff introduced the first interracial family in children's literature with his seminal work *black is brown is tan* (1973). This celebration of family love, based on his own family and winner of the 1973 School Library Journal Best Children's Book award, is still in print.

Adoff often revisits multicultural themes of **race**, identity, and interracial families in his writing. He also explores common experiences of children and, most often, African American children. In recognition of his contributions to **children's literature**, Adoff received the National Council of Teachers of English Award in Excellence in Poetry for Children in 1988. Today, Adoff is primarily a poet (White).

Resources: Primary Sources: Arnold Adoff, *black is brown is tan*, illustrated by Emily Arnold McCully (1973; repr. New York: HarperCollins, 1992); Arnold Adoff, ed.: *Brothers and Sisters: Modern Stories by Black Americans* (New York: Macmillan, 1970); *Celebrations: A New Anthology of Black American Poetry* (New York: Silver Burdett, 1978); *City in All Directions: An Anthology of Modern Poems* (New York: Macmillan, 1969); *I Am the Darker Brother: An Anthology of Modern Poems by Negro Americans* (1968; repr. New York: Simon and Schuster, 1997); *It Is the Poem Singing into Your Eyes: An Anthology of New Young Poets* (New York: Harper & Row, 1971); *The Poetry of Black America: An Anthology of the Twentieth Century* (New York: Harper & Row, 1973). **Secondary Sources:** Jeffrey S. Copeland, *Arnold Adoff* (Boston: Twayne, 1997); Kevin S. Hile and E. A. Des Chenes, "Arnold Adoff," in *Authors and Artists for Young Adults* (Farmington Hills, MI: Gale Group, 2003); Mary Lou White, "Profile: Arnold Adoff," *Language Arts* 65 (1988), 584–588.

Heidi Hauser Green

Affirmative Action. Social concept. The term "affirmative action" is used to describe modern political/social programs that aim to improve the participation of members of certain groups, sometimes by granting preferential treatment, or even by attempting to ensure fair treatment, in such areas as higher education, employment, and contract and business opportunities. Affirmative action is, as it implies, *positive* action taken by the government, a private employer, or an institution in order to promote the recruitment and participation of members of certain previously ignored, excluded, or disadvantaged groups within certain fields where they are underrepresented (such as graduate schools or professional occupations, for example). Affirmative action programs were first conceived in the United States during the presidential administration of John F. Kennedy. They were seen as a means of compensating and improving opportunities for African Americans in society. The list of beneficiaries of affirmative action has grown in the twenty-first century to include women, Alaskan Natives, Native Americans, Hispanic Americans, Asian Americans, disabled Americans, and Vietnam veterans. Thus, today, the groups targeted by affirmative action are several—and usually include those groups defined by a personal characteristic, such as **race**, **gender**, ethnic heritage, or physical disability, on the basis of which the group's members have historically been subject to systematic or institutional discrimination. Typically, affirmative action involves dispensing unique benefits or allocating resources to improve the group's situation. Most often, today, affirmative action is used to refer to programs that consider the group's personal characteristic as a positive factor in determining whether an individual is entitled to the benefits of the program. Affirmative action programs also properly include outreach and recruitment programs needed to ensure that members of the targeted group are aware of certain programs and opportunities and can seek the benefits on equal terms with others, and to identify and eliminate discriminatory practices.

The first official usage of the term "affirmative action" in conjunction with providing equal opportunities for racial minorities came in 1961, when President John F. Kennedy issued Executive Order 10925, which required federal contractors to take "affirmative action" in employing workers on a nondiscriminatory basis. In 1965, President Lyndon B. Johnson advocated affirmative action for African Americans in his now famous commencement address at Howard University. In his speech, Johnson utilized the "fair race" metaphor, and argued that it is not fair for society to take a person who has been shackled for years by chains, unshackle the chains, and expect the previously hampered runner to compete equally with those who had been running unencumbered for years. Rather, according to Johnson, special compensation and consideration should be afforded to those previously hampered and hindered by discrimination, in order to make the race a truly fair one. Several months after delivering his commencement address at Howard, President Johnson issued Executive Order 11246, which set forth the policy of the federal government in providing equal opportunities in federal employment regardless of race, color, religion, or national origin, prohibited discrimination in hiring by both the government and private contractors who held government contracts and performed services on behalf of the government, and promised the "full realization of equal employment opportunity through a positive, continuing program in each department and agency."

Since the issuance of these two executive orders, a bevy of executive orders have followed, and various presidents have sought to expand or reduce the use of affirmative action to include different beneficiaries or different areas of society. Over time, numerous initiatives have been established by federal statute and state laws as well. By the 1980s and 1990s, attacks against the use of affirmative action increased. During the Reagan administration, the federal government was hostile to affirmative action. In the late 1990s and early years of the new millennium, several states, such as Washington, California, and Florida, passed laws that prohibited the use of affirmative action. As the debate over the efficacy and constitutionality of affirmative action has intensified, the state and federal judiciaries have weighed in as well. This has resulted in more than thirty years of case law addressing the legality of preferential treatment programs based on race and/or gender. Each case has defined or redefined in some way the permissibility of affirmative action programs under the Constitution, or has dictated limitations on how and when an affirmative action plan can be used, if at all. Thus, the debate in the court system (and the resulting thirty years of judicial precedent and decisions) covers not only the proper scope and role of affirmative action programs, but also the question of whether or not such programs should exist at all under the Constitution. There is also a continuing political and legal debate as to which groups (if any) should receive the benefits of affirmative action, particularly when the affirmative action program involves group-based preferences, and majority groups are denied benefits by virtue of special preferential programs.

Perhaps the most famous of all of the judicial decisions pertaining to affirmative action is the Supreme Court's 1978 decision in *Regents of the University of California v. Bakke*, a landmark affirmative action case in the area of higher education that rejected fixed racial quotas in the educational context as unconstitutional while allowing for the use of race as one factor in admissions policies. The decision ushered in a quarter-century of confusion in higher education as to whether or not the use of race-conscious or gender-conscious affirmative action plans violate the Equal Protection Clause of the Fourteenth Amendment. A bevy of lower court decisions reached conflicting results as to legitimacy and constitutionality of affirmative action programs in higher education. Finally, in June 2003, exactly a quarter-century after *Bakke*, the Supreme Court weighed into the debate again in the cases of *Gratz v. Bollinger* and *Grutter v. Bollinger*, cases heralded as the "Alamo for affirmative action." In *Gratz* (dealing with the use of affirmative action in undergraduate admissions), the Court declared the University of Michigan undergraduate admissions process unconstitutional, in violation of the Equal Protection Clause of the Fourteenth Amendment, because the university plan employed race-conscious preferences that, according to the Supreme Court, utilized race as the determinative factor for many applicants. Additionally, again according to the Court, the university plan also interfered with the individualized consideration of each applicant. In *Grutter* (dealing with the use of affirmative action in law school admissions), the Court upheld the affirmative action plan utilized at the

University of Michigan Law School, holding that the plan was narrowly tailored to achieve a compelling governmental interest because the plan adequately considered the individual merits of each candidate without relying on a rigid mathematical system of review that (in the undergraduate plan) overestimated race as a factor. In *Grutter*, the Court also famously declared that diversity in higher education is a compelling government interest, a position that was first delineated by Justice Powell (known as the diversity rationale) twenty-five years earlier in *Regents of the University of California v. Bakke*.

Thus today, taken in its totality, understanding affirmative action requires navigating through a maze of historical events, scholarly literature and research, judicial cases, constitutional restrictions, statutes, executive orders, regulations, studies, and popular writings on the subject. A whole genre of political science books and writings is dedicated to affirmative action, and an impressive body of literature and printed materials on this field exists today. Black writers and scholars such as **Cornel West, Derrick Bell, Henry Louis Gates, Jr., Stephen Carter, Lorene Cary, Nikki Giovanni**, Glenn Loury, and Christopher Edley have significantly contributed to the literature and the debates on this important topic, debates that are likely not to cease until the dream of a truly egalitarian society is achieved.

Resources: James A. Beckman, ed., *Affirmative Action: An Encyclopedia*, 2 vols. (Westport, CT: Greenwood Press, 2004); Christopher Edley, *Not All Black and White: Affirmative Action, Race, and American Values* (New York: Hill and Wang, 1996); Henry Louis Gates, Jr., and Cornel West, *The Future of the Race* (New York: Vintage Books, 1997); Glenn C. Loury, *One by One from the Inside Out: Essays and Reviews on Race and Responsibility in America* (New York: Free Press, 1995); Philip F. Rubio, *A History of Affirmative Action: 1619–2000* (Jackson: University Press of Mississippi, 2001); John David Skrentny, *The Ironies of Affirmative Action: Politics, Culture, and Justice in America* (Chicago: University of Chicago Press, 1996); Cornel West, *Race Matters* (New York: Vintage Books, 1993; repr. 1994).

James A. Beckman

Affrilachian Poets (1991–present). A group of poets and short story writers. Originating in Lexington, Kentucky, on the University of Kentucky campus, the Affrilachian Poets came into existence in 1991. Frank X Walker (born 1961), a student and poet on campus, attended a literary event that year originally titled "The Best of Appalachian Writing," at which a panel of fiction writers, four White authors from Kentucky and one African American author from South Carolina, discussed their craft. The organizers had to change the title to "The Best of Southern Writing" to accommodate the South Carolinian, **Nikky Finney**. Upon leaving the event, Walker wondered, " 'Why weren't African-American writers in Kentucky represented?' " (Newberry).

Infuriated by one of seemingly innumerable instances in which African American writers were excluded from Appalachian literature, Walker turned his frustration to creativity and coined the term "Affrilachia" to accommodate both his African American and his Appalachian heritages. Over the course of the next year, and after he coined the term, he found other emerging writers with whom to form the writers' group now known as the Affrilachian Poets. Because the group includes some individuals not born and raised in Appalachia, the concept of "Affrilachia" expands the notion of what it means to be Appalachian. The term "Affrilachia" explodes regional and even racial stereotypes while broadening the literature of the region to encompass a greater variety of writing and subject matter. When asked to define the Affrilachian aesthetic, Walker says, "I would define [it] as a collective commitment to make the invisible visible, to redefine the literary landscape of the region as one that is more diverse than mass media portrays [*sic*] it as" (Burriss).

Born in Danville, Kentucky, a town near the Dix River, Walker eventually made his way to Lexington to attend the University of Kentucky. He considers his upbringing "very urban because I grew up in the housing projects most of my life versus the farm. That's the one image you don't get when you think of Appalachia. You think mostly rural" (Burriss; Ledford).

These urban images and sounds can be found in Walker's collection of poetry, *Affrilachia*, published in 2000 by Old Cove Press. From scenes of asphalt basketball courts to riffs of **hip-hop** street language, Walker dispels the rural stereotypes of Appalachia to show that another side exists. Just as he illustrates this Appalachian rural/urban duality, Walker exhibits another duality when he draws from both traditional Appalachian and African American values. Typical of Appalachians' respect for family, he honors his own family members throughout his poetry. And, inspired by the **Harlem Renaissance** and the **Black Arts Movement**, Walker employs a political poetics to express outrage over the social injustices that oppress all people of color.

Responding to a question about the traditions the Affrilachian Poets work from or are inspired by, Walker reflects, "The Affrilachian Poets were started by a group of writers, mostly English majors, who have read and are familiar with both the Harlem Renaissance and the Black Arts movement of the '60s. Our/my influential literary role models are out of these traditions. We can't help but be shaped and influenced and acknowledge a connection to the continuum of literature that preceded us" (Burriss).

Coincidentally, Nikky Finney, the South Carolinian writer at the conference Walker had attended, accepted a teaching position at the University of Kentucky and helped form the Affrilachian Poets. Though she was born and raised in the Low Country of Carolina, Finney spent much of her girlhood on her grandfather's farm in the foothills of Appalachia, where she "could see the tips of the Great Smoky Mountains way off in the distance" (Finney). In all her works, she carries the political torch of the Harlem Renaissance and the Black Arts Movement. Often drawing from actual historical atrocities, Finney imbues her poetry with clear political sentiments that demand accountability from those she perceives to be perpetrators.

Crystal Wilkinson (born 1962), poet, short story writer, and teacher, eventually joined the group. Unlike Walker, Wilkinson was born and raised on a sixty-acre farm on Indian Creek in rural Casey County, Kentucky, thus typifying the rural central Appalachian experience. After Wilkinson graduated from Eastern Kentucky University and moved to Lexington, a friend introduced her to Walker, who invited her to read at a local restaurant's open mic night. Thereafter, she became a constant presence at area literary events and joined the Affrilachian Poets.

In her first collection of short stories, *Blackberries, Blackberries*, published in 2000 by Toby Press, Wilkinson presents characters who are all Black and all Appalachian country. As a result, she dispels the stereotype that "hillbillies" are not Black. In her second short story collection, *Water Street*, released in 2002 by Toby Press, Wilkinson invites readers into the interior lives of Water Street residents who face the intricacies of negotiating this human life, with all its suffering and all its joy.

Kelly Norman Ellis (born 1964), poet and teacher, was born in Illinois but was raised in Mississippi and Tennessee. She came to Lexington to obtain her doctoral degree in English from the University of Kentucky. After Walker invited her to read before an audience at the university, she became the second woman (after Finney) to join the Affrilachian Poets. Ellis published her first compilation of poems, *Tougaloo Blues*, in 2003 with Third World Press. In this work she pays homage to her ancestors, in both the Appalachian and the African traditions, reflecting on the paths they paved for her. Echoing Walker's sentiments, Ellis illustrates that the continuum of African American culture and literature will not be interrupted, only advanced. Truly, all of the Affrilachian Poets have positioned themselves within a long and enduring African American literary tradition.

Resources: Theresa Burriss, E-mail correspondence with Frank X Walker (Mar. 3, 2003); Jean Donahue and Fred Johnson, *Coal Black Voices: A Documentary*, VHS format (Covington, KY: Media Working Group, 2001); Nikky Finney, "Salt-Water Geechee Mounds," in *Bloodroot: Reflections on Place by Appalachian Women Writers*, ed. Joyce Dyer (Lexington: University Press of Kentucky, 1998); Katherine Ledford, unpublished interview with Frank X Walker, University of Kentucky, 1996; Elizabeth Newberry, "Poets Turned Prophets: Affrilachian Poets Claim the Space Between Two Worlds," Sojourners/SojoNet, http://www.sojo.net/magazine/index.cfm/action/sojourners/issue/soj00009/article/000931.html (Sept.–Oct. 2000); Crystal Wilkinson, "On Being 'Country': One Affrilachian Woman's Return Home," in *Confronting Appalachian Stereotypes: Back Talk from an American Region*, ed. Dwight B. Billings et al. (Lexington: University Press of Kentucky, 1999).

Theresa L. Burriss

Afrocentricity. A highly postmodern and controversial philosophy placing African history, culture, ideas, and interests in the center of African/African American Studies. Afrocentricity attempts to counteract both white racism and a defeatist self-image among Blacks. It denounces Eurocentric education for portraying Africa as a primitive continent and perpetuating the idea of Africans as an uncivilized and inferior race. Afrocentricity is based on the belief that the African continent is the cradle of humankind and that Africans have richer historical and cultural resources than their European counterparts. It is also a Pan-African ideology seeking liberation of diasporan Blacks, as well as of Blacks on the African continent. Afrocentrists are generally anti-White, are religiously dedicated to the triumph of Black culture, and reject the accommodationist approach to race relations earlier adopted by such figures as **Harriet Tubman** and **Booker T. Washington**.

A number of African/African American intellectuals are credited with sowing the seeds of Afrocentric thought in the early and mid-twentieth century. According to **Marcus Garvey**, leader of a **"back-to-Africa"** movement, black empowerment was a prerequisite for liberating—and elevating the status of—Africans around the globe. Such an empowerment would come from recognizing the Black cultural heritage. Elijah Muhammad, a leader of the **Nation of Islam**, appealed Blacks to discard the slave mentality and regain their self-esteem as people from the cradle of civilization. Blacks would not be free, he believed, until they learned to consider themselves as subjects rather than objects. In *The Mis-Education of the Negro* (1933), **Carter Godwin Woodson** contended that White-centered education was not conducive to Black Americans' upward mobility and self-image. **W.E.B. Du Bois**, in *The World and Africa: An Inquiry into the Part Which Africa Has Played in World History* (1947), demonstrated how African civilization was superior to that of Europe and how Europeans historically victimized Africans. Another Afrocentric thinker, **Malcolm X**, encouraged fellow Blacks to stop thinking Eurocentrically and to affirm that "black is beautiful."

It was Cheikh Anta Diop, a Senegalese scholar and activist, who provided the most significant influence on the development of Afrocentric philosophy. In such well-known books as *The African Origin of Civilization: Myth or Reality* (1974) and *Civilization or Barbarism: An Authentic Anthropology* (1991), Diop rewrote world history by highlighting the superiority of Africans. According to him, Africa was the home of all civilizations and ancient Egyptian culture exemplified the glory of African civilization.

Scholarly debate of Afrocentric philosophy has intensified since the 1970s. In *They Came Before Columbus* (1976), for example, Ivan Van Sertima argues that Africans settled on the American continent before Columbus arrived. Like earlier Afrocentrists, he reconstructs world history by shifting the center of ancient civilization from Europe to Africa, especially Egypt.

A prolific writer, Molefi Kete Asante is perhaps the most visible theorist of Afrocentricity today. He is credited with coining and popularizing the term "Afrocentricity." In *Afrocentricity* (3rd ed., 1988), *The Afrocentric Idea* (rev. ed., 1998), *Afrocentricity, the Theory of Social Change* (2nd ed., 2003), and other books, he promotes a radical paradigmatic and pedagogical shift in **Black Studies**. In *Afrocentricity*, for example, he surveys the development of Afro-centrism, justifies Afrocentric ideology, and offers a specific course of action to perpetuate the progress and prosperity of Blacks. According to Asante, Black empowerment necessitates liberating oneself from Eurocentric language, acquiring intellectual vigilance, and adopting a self-affirming ideology that views Blackness as its ultimate reality. In his view, Afrologists must analyze their subject competently, possess clarity of Afrocentric purpose, and understand the interrelationship between their subject and the world at large. Asante proposes various tactics and strategies for reconstructing Afrocentric lives; they include thinking Afrocentrically, pursuing the common good of Blacks, reclaiming the central position of African history, and replacing self-defeating symbols and actions with decolonizing, self-liberating symbols and actions. Other prominent Afrocentric scholars today include Maulana Karenga, author of *Introduction to Black Studies* (1982); Chancellor Williams, who advocates that African history belongs to Africans, not to Arabs and Europeans; and **Martin Bernal**, who in *Black Athena: The Afroasiatic Roots of Classical Civilization* (1987–1991), claims that Eurocentric scholars have thoroughly overlooked, denied, or suppressed the Hamito-Semitic origins of ancient civilization (*see* **Black Athena Controversy**).

Afrocentricity has caused significant controversy among scholars. Its opponents—who include a significant number of Blacks—point to the nationalistic, chauvinistic, and race-specific elements as its fundamental weakness; they assert that it is as exclusivist and oppressive as Eurocentrism is. They also raise questions about the objectivity of scientific and historical evidence that Afrocentrists use to support their claims. According to **Gerald Early**, Merle Kling Professor of Modern Letters at Washington University in **St. Louis, Missouri**, the Afrocentric claim that Blacks are more spiritual, family- and community-oriented, natural, rhythmic, and peace-loving than Whites is nonsense—an idea based more on wishful thinking than on fact. Some critics view the Afrocentric movement as a romantic endeavor to create a glorious past that did not really exist.

Resources: Molefi Kete Asante: *The Afrocentric Idea*, rev. ed. (Philadelphia: Temple University Press, 1998); *Afrocentricity*, 3rd ed. (Trenton, NJ: Africa World Press, 1988); *Afrocentricity, the Theory of Social Change*, 2nd ed. (Chicago: African American Images, 2003); Martin Bernal, *Black Athena: The Afroasiatic Roots of Classical Civilization*, 2 vols. (New Brunswick, NJ: Rutgers University Press, 1987–1991); Cheikh Anta Diop: *The African Origin of Civilization: Myth or Reality*, trans. Mercer Cook (New York: Lawrence Hill, 1974); *Civilization or Barbarism: An Authentic Anthropology*, trans. Yaa-Lengi Meema Ngemi, ed. Harold J. Salemson and Marjolijn de Jager (Brooklyn, NY: Lawrence Hill, 1991); W.E.B. Du Bois, *The World and Africa: An Inquiry into the Part Which Africa Has Played in World History* (New York: Viking Press, 1947); Gerald Early, "Understanding Afrocentricity," *Civilization*, July/Aug. 1995, pp. 31–39; Maulana Karenga, *Introduction to Black Studies* (Inglewood, CA: Kawaida, 1982); Ivan Van Sertima, *They Came Before Columbus* (New York: Random House, 1976); Chancellor Williams, *The Destruction of Black Civilization: Great Issues of a Race from 4500 B.C. to 2000 A.D.*, rev. ed. (Chicago: Third World Press, 1987); Carter Godwin Woodson, *The Mis-Education of the Negro* (Washington, DC: Associated Publishers, 1933).

John J. Han

Ai (born 1947). Poet. Ai is a modern master of the dramatic monologue, a poetic form perfected by Robert Browning in the nineteenth century, in which a fictional or historical person created by, but usually unrelated to, the poet speaks the entire lyric poem and thus reveals significant aspects of her or his life and personality. Sometimes the effect created is one of unwitting revelation on the part of the speaker. Ai has assumed the voice or idiosyncratic characteristics of, among others, a female police officer who lost her brother in the September 11 terrorist attacks on the World Trade Center ("Dread," 2003), a psychopathic drifter ("The Hitchhiker," 1973), a protofeminist Peruvian immigrant ("The Mother's Tale," 1986), a missing union leader ("Jimmy Hoffa's Odyssey," 1991), a paranoid, cross-dressing version of the notorious head of the Federal Bureau of Investigation ("Hoover, J. Edgar," 1993), and an adolescent Tutsi girl ("Rwanda," 1999). In a 1990 interview, Ai explained her grounds for inhabiting these personae: "I always try to be true to the character, that's the thing about me. Whatever character, I set up what I like to think are the keys to the character at the beginning of the poem, and then I proceed to go back over and enlarge, throughout the poem.... I like to think that as long as I'm true to my vision of the character, it's all right" (Erb, 30).

Born in Albany, **Texas**, Ai spent most of her childhood in Tucson, Arizona, and **Los Angeles, California**. Her original given name was Florence Anthony. She earned a bachelor's degree in Japanese from the University of Arizona, where she also studied Buddhism, and a master of fine arts degree from the University of California, Irvine. While at Arizona, Ai met Galway Kinnell, an established poet and professor of English at New York University, who became her mentor and friend. Kinnell submitted Ai's master's thesis, written in her second year at Irvine, to Houghton Mifflin for publication; this work eventually became her first published book of poems, *Cruelty* (1973).

Ai has published six more books of poetry since then: *Killing Floor* (1979), winner of a Lamont Poetry Award from the Academy of American Poets; *Sin* (1986), winner of an American Book Award from the Before Columbus Foundation; *Fate* (1991); *Greed* (1993); *Vice: New and Selected Poems* (1999), winner of a National Book Award; and *Dread* (2003). Other honors include a Guggenheim fellowship (1975), a Bunting Institute fellowship at Radcliffe College (1975–1976), and a grant from the National Endowment for the Arts. In 2000 Oklahoma State University, Stillwater, granted her tenure and a full professorship of poetry and fiction.

At age twenty-six Ai learned that she was the product of an affair between her mother—a woman of Dutch, Black, Irish, Choctaw, and southern Cheyenne ancestry—and a Japanese man she had met at a streetcar stop. Just a few years before this discovery, in 1969, Ai had stopped using her given name, Florence Anthony, and had begun using the Japanese word for "love" (*ai*) as a pseudonym; later she legally adopted the appellation. These two biographical facts come to bear on her poetry. As several critics have noted, the word *ai* sounds like a personal pronoun ("I") and the bodily organ used for sight ("eye"). Her unique ethnic identity allows her both to see and to speak from a diverse range of perspectives, and she envisions her role as poet as one who witnesses, then writes.

Finding a language capable of depicting violence and victimhood has been an ongoing quest within Ai's work. In this way she aligns herself with her literary forebear **Langston Hughes**, who also believed that literature and other types of high culture should verbalize the experiences of those who might not otherwise find themselves represented therein. Her personae speak "with a slight sense of dislocation," as she writes in "Greetings Friend" (*Dread*, 57), favoring slang over lyrical diction, realism over aestheticism, common idioms over metaphors. "The Testimony of J. Robert Oppenheimer" remarks upon Ai's poetic project: to teach us to "accept the worst in ourselves" (*Vice*, 77), thus liberating the wounded from suffering in silence or uttering inarticulately to those who cannot or will not heed their cries. Ai's work includes, rather than excludes, and tells truths that are difficult but nevertheless necessary to hear.

Resources: Ai: *Cruelty* (Boston: Houghton Mifflin, 1973); *Dread* (New York: W. W. Norton, 2003); *Fate: New Poems* (Boston: Houghton Mifflin, 1991); *Greed* (New York: W. W. Norton, 1993); *Killing Floor* (Boston: Houghton Mifflin, 1979); *Sin* (Boston: Houghton Mifflin, 1986); *Vice: New and Selected Poems* (New York: W. W. Norton, 1999); Lisa Erb, "Dancing with the Madness: An Interview with Ai," *Mānoa: A Pacific Journal of International Writing* 2, no. 2 (Fall 1990), 22–40; Cary Nelson, ed., "Ai," *Modern American Poetry* (Nov. 2003), http://www.english.uiuc.edu/maps/poets/a_f/ai/ai.htm; Rob Wilson, "The Will to Transcendence in Contemporary American Poet Ai," *Canadian Review of American Studies* 17, no. 4 (1986), 437–448.

Jessica Allen

Albert, Octavia Victoria Rogers (1853–1889). Historian. Albert's most notable contribution to African American literature was her posthumously published account of her interviews with former slaves, *The House of Bondage; or, Charlotte Brooks and Other Slaves.*

Albert was born to slave parents in Oglethorpe, Georgia. The details of her childhood remain largely a matter of conjecture. She reportedly attended Atlanta University in 1870, although the 1870 census shows her boarding with a family in Sumter County, Georgia, and working as a teacher; she may have done both. In 1873 she was teaching in Montezuma, Georgia; there, she met Aristide Elphonso Peter Albert, a fellow teacher three years her senior; they were married on October 21, 1874, in Macon, Georgia. They seem to have had two daughters—Laura Albert and Sarah Albert are listed with them in the 1880 census—but some published accounts refer to Laura as their "only daughter" (Ravi).

In 1878, Aristide Albert was ordained in the Methodist Episcopal Church, and the Alberts moved to Houma (Terrebonne Parish), Louisiana. Evidence suggests that it was here that Octavia began researching what would later become *The House of Bondage*. Consisting of her first-person reports of interviews with former slaves about the hardships they faced, the excitement and challenge of freedom in a still racist society, and their faith, *The House of Bondage* is a valuable piece of oral history. It also implicitly challenges the chivalric representation of slaveholders common in the popular literature and culture of the time.

In late 1879, the Alberts moved to **New Orleans, Louisiana**, and Aristide Albert continued his rise among the Methodist Episcopal clergy. In 1881, he was appointed assistant editor of *Southwestern Christian Advocate*, a major regional Methodist Episcopal newspaper. He spoke at the New Orleans World Exposition in 1885, and in 1887 he was named editor of the *Advocate*. Given most school systems' restrictions against married women teachers and her responsibilities as the spouse of an up-and-coming minister, it is doubtful that Albert taught again, although she probably assisted her husband with the *Advocate*. She also seems to have been active in parish work.

Albert died on August 19, 1889, and soon afterward, Aristide Albert decided to publish his wife's work serially in the *Advocate*. The accounts of former slaves—along with Octavia Albert's direct and thoughtful narration—fit neatly with the *Advocate*'s dual focus on strengthening readers' faith and families. The *Advocate* regularly, for example, published a column called "Lost Friends," in which former slaves looking for family members could place notices. According to the preface that Aristide and his daughter Laura wrote for the book version of *The House of Bondage*, "letters poured in . . . urging him" to publish the work as a book, which he did in 1890. (*See* **Slave Narrative**; **Slavery**.)

Resources: Octavia V. R. Albert, *The House of Bondage*, ed. Frances Smith Foster (New York: Oxford University Press, 1988); Geetha Ravi, "Octavia Victoria Rogers Albert," in *African American Authors 1745–1945: A Bio-Bibliographical Critical Sourcebook*, ed. Emmanuel S. Nelson (Westport, CT: Greenwood Press, 2000); Vital Records and Censuses of Georgia and Louisiana.

Eric Gardner

Aldridge, Ira (1807–1867). Actor. Aldridge was a pioneering actor who took roles no other African American actor had taken before, and consequently changed the perception of Black actors with regard to classic **drama**, including that of Shakespeare. Born in New York City in 1807, Aldridge attended the African Free School between 1820 and 1824. The school, established by the Manumission Society in 1787, sought to educate African Americans, with the aim of creating a group of intelligent alumni who would participate in the **abolitionist movement**. During his years at the African Free School, Aldridge discovered the theater—a passion that would drive him for the rest of his life and would define his legacy after his death. In 1822 he joined the African Company, William Brown's New York black theater company, and learned the craft of acting from lead actor James Hewlett. Although the closing of the African Company in the following year would permanently end Aldridge's association with New York theater and American theater, it would serve as the catalyst for the start of his distinguished European stage career. In 1824 Aldridge traveled to London and joined the acting ensemble at the Royal Coburg Theatre. During that year, he consistently appeared in plays about men and women of color. He assumed the roles of Oroonoko in the stage play *The Revolt of Surinam; or A Slave's Revenge*, Gambie in *The Slave*, Cristophe in *The Death* *of Cristophe*, the king in *King of Haiti*, and, most famously, the title role in *Othello*. The following year, Aldridge continued his education by attending Glasgow University before returning to the London stage. Among the many roles he performed over the next three years, his 1827 performance of Lear in *King Lear* stands out. It marked the first time that a major Shakespearean character other than Othello had been played by a nonWhite actor in London.

As Aldridge's fame swelled, he was invited to perform in 1833 at London's famed Covent Garden, thus becoming the first American actor to perform on its stage. Aldridge, who appeared in a series of plays at Covent Garden, received a mixed response from audiences. He was applauded by some audience members and was the subject of racial epithets from others. Over the next twenty years, Aldridge continued to perform in London but increasingly found that the major theaters in the city, including Covent Garden, refused to cast him. With limited opportunities, he left London in 1853 and began a tour of continental Europe. Aldridge was celebrated in every country he visited, and embraced by the ruling monarchs of Austria, Finland, Prussia, and Russia, among other countries.

Although Aldridge is chiefly remembered for his work in the London theater, his legacy rests on his performances of Shakespearean characters (such as Othello, Shylock, and Macbeth) across continental Europe. Whereas racism and prejudice ultimately limited the roles that he could embody on the London stage, they did not function as limiting factors on the Continent. Aldridge died on tour in Lodz, Poland, in 1867. Throughout his lifetime, he remained committed to the abolitionist cause. Aldridge frequently gave speeches against Black enslavement and donated money to abolitionist organizations. He was buried in Lodz's Evangelical Cemetery with state honors. His grave is a national shrine of Poland.

Resources: Samuel A. Hay, *African American Theatre: An Historical and Critical Analysis* (New York: Cambridge University Press, 1994); Errol Hill, *Shakespeare in Sable: A History of Black Shakespearean Actors* (Amherst: University of Massachusetts Press, 1984); Errol Hill, ed., *The Theatre of Black Americans: A Collection of Critical Essays* (New York: Applause Theatre Book Publishers, 1980, 1987); Herbert Marshall and Mildred Stock, *Ira Aldridge: The Negro Tragedian* (London: Rockliff, 1958).

Harvey Young

Alers, Rochelle (born 1943). Novelist. Rochelle Alers is the author of several best-selling **romance novels** that speak to a growing number of educated, professional, and financially well-to-do African American women. Although romance novels in general have their beginnings in 1949, with the introduction of Harlequin Romances, romance novels written by African Americans for African Americans did not begin to appear until the 1980s. The advent of the African American romance novel provided fresh material to the African American literary tradition of stories about alienation, poverty, **slavery**, and segregation that no longer reflected the economic, social, and cultural changes occurring in the lives of modern African Americans. Building upon the legacy of the early pioneers of African American romance novelists, Alers published *Careless Whispers* (1988) and launched a full-time writing career.

Alers has published numerous novels that contain characters and issues that mirror the lives of her readers. Like her readers, Alers's heroines are professional and accomplished women. Her protagonists include Zahara Jenkins, a banking executive, in the short story "Special Delivery," published in the anthology *Rosies Curl and Weave* (1999); Sara, a high-powered New York City attorney, in *Just Before Dawn* (2000); Hope Sutton, a psychologist, in *Lessons of a Lowcountry Summer* (2004); and Aimee Frasier, a historian, in *Island Bliss* (2002). Alers presents issues such as infertility, divorce, single parenting, and domestic violence, that arise in the lives of African American women ("Biography"). She enlivens some of her stories, such as *Homecoming* (2002), *Renegade* (2003), and *Hidden Agenda* (1997), with mystery and adventure. Her novels take place in an assortment of locales, from urban and Southern settings to tropical islands. At the heart of her stories are men and women who overcome painful pasts and embrace positive and healing relationships. Her positive images overshadow the real-life obstacles that have historically affected African American couples.

Resources: Rochelle Alers: *Careless Whispers* (New York: Doubleday, 1988); *Hidden Agenda* (Washington, DC: Arabesque, 1997); *Homecoming* (Washington, DC: BET Publications, 2002); *Just Before Dawn* (Washington, DC: Arabesque, 2000); *Lessons of a Lowcountry Summer* (New York: Pocket Books, 2004); *Renegade* (Washington, DC: Arabesque, 2003); Rochelle Alers, Donna Hill, Felicia Mason, and Frances Ray, *Rosies Curl and Weave* (New York: St. Martin's Press, 1999); Rochelle Alers, Marcia King-Gamble, Carmen Green, and Felicia Mason, *Island Bliss* (New York: St. Martin's Press, 2002); "Rochelle Alers," *Biography*, Nov. 1, 2004, http://www.rochellealers.com/bio.asp; Monica Jackson, "Romance in Black and White," *Monica Jackson Online*, Nov. 24, 2004, http://monicajackson.com/blackwhite-mj.htm; Gwendolyn Osborne, "How Black Romance—Novels, That Is—Came to Be," *Black Issues Book Review* 4 (2002), 50; Elsie B. Washington, *Uncivil War: The Struggle Between Black Men and Women* (Chicago: Noble Press, 1996); Elonda R. Wilder-Hamilton, "Uncovering the Truth: Understanding the Impact of American Culture on the Black Male–Black Female Relationship," paper presented at the Black Family Conference, Louisville, KY, Mar. 15, 2002; Sherri Winston, "Black Voices in Prose: Take a Deep Breath, Exhale," *Fort Lauderdale Sun-Sentinel*, Aug. 8, 2001, p. E1.

Gladys L. Knight

Alexander, Elizabeth (born 1962). Poet, playwright, and critic. Alexander's body of work is committed to complex negotiations with and representations of Black life, particularly of Black women. Born in **Harlem, New York**, and raised in **Washington, D.C.**, Alexander is from a middle-class, college-educated background. She received her B.A. from Yale University, her M.A. from Boston University (where she worked with Derek Walcott), and her Ph.D. in English from the University of Pennsylvania. In 1990, she published her first book of poetry, *The Venus Hottentot*, in the *Callaloo* Poetry Series (University Press of Virginia), which thematically deals with class, sexuality, and Black cultural history. *Body of Life*, her second collection, appeared in 1996 from Tia Chucha Press and continued Alexander's exploration of Black women's sexuality and subjectivity. Her third poetry collection, *Antebellum Dream Book*, came out in 2001 from Graywolf Press. Inspired by a series of dreams Alexander had while pregnant, her third book builds on the earlier themes of her work and includes two longer cycle poems, "Narrative: Ali" and "Neonatology." Her drama, poetry, and critical prose have appeared in **Callaloo**, *Signs, The Paris Review,* the *Village Voice,* and the *Women's Review of Books,* among numerous others. Her poetry has been widely anthologized, including in **Clarence Major**'s *The Garden Thrives: Twentieth-century African-American Poetry* (1996).

Among Alexander's numerous awards for writing are an NEA fellowship, a Pushcart Prize, and the George Kent Award, presented to her by the poet **Gwendolyn Brooks**. Alexander has taught at Smith College, where she was the Grace Hazard Conkling poet-in-residence and the director of the college's poetry center; Haverford College; the University of Chicago, where she received the highest teaching award, the Quantrell Award for excellence in undergraduate teaching; and at Yale University, where she is a fellow at the Whitney Humanities Center and a professor in the African American Studies Department. Alexander also participates in the Cave Canem poetry workshops as a faculty member. She has lectured and read internationally, on her own work and on African American literature and culture. She also has published a collection of essays on African American literature and history, *The Black Interior* (2004), and produced her play, *Diva Studies,* at the Yale School of Drama (1996). She served as dramaturge on the original production of **Anna Deavere Smith**'s *Twilight: Los Angeles, 1992.* Alexander's work stems from a deep engagement in African American culture, both popular and avant-garde, from **Michael Jordan** to **Toni Morrison**. Her poetry in particular is often noted for its use of wit, its lyric quality, and its ability to intelligently surprise even when covering familiar territory. Alexander is a leading poet and critic who engages African American popular culture and historical events with an intellectual but humorous approach.

Resources: Academy of American Poets, "Elizabeth Alexander," 2001, www.poets.org/poets; Elizabeth Alexander: *Antebellum Dream Book* (St. Paul, MN: Graywolf Press, 2001); *The Black Interior* (St. Paul, MN: Graywolf Press, 2004); *Body of Life* (Chicago: Tia Chucha Press, 1996); *The Venus Hottentot* (Charlottesville: University Press of Virginia, 1990); Jane Clayton, "Color Everywhere," *Washington Post,* Oct. 21, 2001, p. 13; Clarence Major, ed., *The Garden Thrives: Twentieth-century African-American Poetry* (New York: HarperCollins, 1996); Christine Phillip, "An Interview with Elizabeth Alexander," *Callaloo* 19, no. 2 (1996), 493–507.

Samantha Pinto

Alexander, Lewis (1900–1945). Poet, actor and director, and editor. Alexander was one of the lesser known but more versatile poets associated with the **Harlem Renaissance** and with the African American literary scene of **Washington, D.C.**, where he was born, grew up, and attended public schools

(Martin, "Lewis Grandison Alexander"). Although apparently he never published a book of poems, his poetry appeared in some of the most influential anthologies and magazines of the period. He was well acquainted with the writers **Gwendolyn Bennett**, **Georgia Douglas Johnson**, **Angelina Grimké**, **Marita Bonner**, and **Countee Cullen**, as well as with the librarian and scholar E. C. Williams (Martin, "Georgia Douglas Johnson"). Alexander graduated from Howard University, where he was active in theater productions. As both a director and an actor, he continued to be involved with theater in Washington in the early 1920s. As an actor in the Ethiopian Art Theatre, he performed in productions of *Salome* and *A Comedy of Errors* in New York City (Martin, "Lewis Grandison Alexander"). As a poet, Alexander worked in both traditional Anglo-American forms, including the **sonnet**, and the Japanese **haiku** form. He published his poetry in three magazines that were important to the Harlem Renaissance: *The Messenger*, *Opportunity*, and *Fire!!* (Watson). His sonnet "Africa" appeared in *Opportunity* in May 1924, and his poem "Enchantment" appeared in **Alain Locke**'s influential anthology, *The New Negro* (1925). Alexander also contributed work to a special issue of the Mexican journal *Palms* that was edited by Countee Cullen in 1926. In 1927 Cullen included work by Alexander in the anthology *Caroling Dusk*. Also in 1927, Alexander helped students at the University of North Carolina to gather material for a special "Negro" issue of *The Carolina Magazine*. Similar special issues of the magazine were published in 1928 and 1929, again with Alexander's assistance (Martin, "Lewis Grandison Alexander"). At this writing, very little is known about the last decade or more of Alexander's life.

Resources: Lewis Alexander: "Africa," *Opportunity*, May 1924; "Enchantment," in *The New Negro*, ed. Alain Locke (New York: Boni, 1925); poems in *Caroling Dusk: An Anthology of Verse by Negro Poets*, ed. Countee Cullen (New York: Harper & Brothers, 1927); George-McKinley Martin: "Georgia Douglas Johnson," in *The Black Renaissance in Washington*, Public Library of Washington, DC, http://www.dclibrary.org/blkren/bios/johnsongd.html (July 2004); "Lewis Grandison Alexander," in *The Black Renaissance in Washington*, Public Library of Washington, DC, http://www.dclibrary.org/blkren/bios/alexanderlg.html (July 2004), which reprints several poems by Alexander; Wallace Thurman, et al., eds., *Fire!!: A Quarterly Devoted to the Younger Negro Artists* (1926; facs. repr. New York: Fire Press, 1985); Steven Watson, *The Harlem Renaissance: Hub of African-American Culture, 1920–1930* (New York: Pantheon, 1995), 91.

Hans Ostrom

Ali, Muhammad (born 1942). Boxer and poet. Though this three-time heavyweight champion, born Cassius Clay, was a featured player in several classic fights (including 1974's "Rumble in the Jungle" with George Foreman and 1975's "Thrilla in Manila" with Joe Frazier), Ali's importance to the African American literary community stems from his willingness to fuse his personal politics with his public persona. From his membership in the **Nation of Islam**, to his refusal to serve in the American military during the **Vietnam War** (which led to his being stripped of the title and banned from boxing from

Muhammad Ali, 1967. Courtesy of the Library of Congress.

1967 to 1971), to his efforts for global peace, few athletes have so consistently risked their reputations on behalf of social issues. Countless African American writers (among them **Gerald Early**, **Spike Lee**, and Richard Durham) have discussed Ali's social significance in great detail; White writers such as George Plimpton, Norman Mailer, and Hunter Thompson also have written extensively about Ali's cultural importance.

To discuss Ali is to discuss a complex, conflicted man whose words and actions were full of paradox: he repeatedly opposed the pacifist ideologies of the **Civil Rights Movement** of the 1960s, yet he became a symbol of the antiwar movement by refusing to serve in Vietnam; he spoke about the evils of racism but often referred to other fighters in explicitly racist terms; he was often critical of America's sociopolitical realities, but accepted the honor of lighting the opening flame at the 1996 Summer Olympics in **Atlanta, Georgia**.

Perhaps the only aspect of Ali's person that is not open to debate is his rhetorical brilliance, which foreshadowed the advent of **rap** music as a dominant cultural force in the 1980s. Though he has published a handful of poems and an "autobiography" (which he later admitted he had not read, let alone written), the most important of Ali's rhetorical exploits were captured orally. The boasts and short poems that he performed before and after many of his fights were some of the most engaging, clever flights of verbal fancy the sporting world has been witness to. (The most famous is his description of his fighting style; he said he could "float like a butterfly and sting like a bee.")

What is most impressive about Ali's speechifying is the playful manner in which he was able to frame his braggadocio in sociopolitical terms, as when he insisted (in the months leading up to his 1974 bout with George Foreman), "If you think the world was shocked when Nixon resigned, wait until you see me kick Foreman's behind." Though his statements were often unrepentantly cruel, there is no denying the rhetorical power that Ali's spirited soliloquies possessed. What is equally without question is the sense of social empowerment and cultural identity that Ali's words helped to forge for the African American community at large, as he unapologetically carried himself as a confident, independent man who was unwilling to adhere to anyone else's beliefs as to how an African American athlete should behave.

Resources: Muhammad Ali and Hana Yasmeen Ali, *The Soul of a Butterfly: Reflections on Life's Journey* (New York: Simon and Schuster, 2004); Gerald Early, *This Is Where I Came In: Black America in the 1960s* (Lincoln: University of Nebraska Press, 2003); Gerald Early, ed., *The Muhammad Ali Reader* (New York: Quill Press, 1999); Thomas Hauser, *Muhammad Ali: His Life and Times* (New York: Simon and Schuster,

1991); Mark Kram, *Ghosts of Manila: The Fateful Blood Feud Between Muhammad Ali and Joe Frazier* (New York: HarperCollins, 2001); David Remnick, *King of the World: Muhammad Ali and the Rise of an American Hero* (New York: Vintage Books, 1999).

Paul Tayyar

Allen, Jeffrey Renard (born 1962). Poet, essayist, fiction writer, and professor. Allen is a native of **Chicago, Illinois**, and at this writing is associate professor of English at Queens College of the City University of New York. Allen earned a Ph.D. in English with an emphasis in creative writing from the University of Illinois at Chicago. He has published two books of poetry, *Harbors and Spirits* and *Rails Under My Back*. His work is also included in *Bum Rush the Page: A Def Poetry Jam*, and his essays and poems have appeared in *Antioch Review*, **Callaloo**, *Notre Dame Review*, *Ploughshares*, and other journals.

Resources: Jeffrey Renard Allen: *Harbors and Spirits* (Wakefield, RI: Asphodel, 1998); *Rails Under My Back* (New York: Farrar, Straus, Giroux, 2000); Louis Reyes Rivera and Tony Medina, eds., *Bum Rush the Page: A Def Poetry Jam* (New York: Three Rivers Press, 2001).

Hans Ostrom

Allen, Richard (1760–1831). American preacher, religious reformer, and nonfiction writer. Allen was born into a family of domestic slaves in **Philadelphia, Pennsylvania**, who were owned by Benjamin Chew, the chief justice of Pennsylvania. He and his family were sold around his sixth birthday to a farmer near Dover, Delaware. When his owner converted to Methodism, Allen and his brother were offered the opportunity to purchase their freedom; about the age of twenty he was free. Allen had become a devoted Methodist, and he traveled the United States, spreading his faith and honing his oratorical skills. In February 1786 Allen accepted an invitation to come to Philadelphia to speak. Settling there in what was then a haven from slavery and home to more free Blacks than any other city, he played a vital role in the city's religious life until his death. In Philadelphia, Allen first preached for the mixed-race Methodist congregation of St. George's Church, but by late 1786 he had assembled a group of Black Methodists who met together for worship; this group later formed the core of the Free African Society. When St. George's began to restrict the seating of Black churchgoers in 1792 (Nash, 118–119), Allen participated in a protest and he and Absalom Jones redoubled their efforts to form an independent Black church.

By 1794, with help from Declaration of Independence signer Benjamin Rush, Jones and the Society had sufficient support to form their own church, the African Church of Philadelphia, which aligned itself with the Episcopal Church. Allen remained loyal to Methodism, however, and founded Bethel African Church the same year. Though the prominent presence of freed Blacks in Methodism remained controversial, Allen was made the church's first Black deacon in 1799. In 1806 he was seized by a Southern slave catcher; Allen had the local influence and renown to have the man arrested for kidnapping. In

1807 Bethel Church added an "African Supplement" to its charter that increased its autonomy from the Methodist Church, and in 1816, with four other Black Methodist congregations in the Northeast, Bethel formed the independent African Methodist Episcopal Church. Allen was its first bishop.

Allen was active in helping treat Philadelphians struck by a yellow fever epidemic in 1793, in the **Underground Railroad**, and in promoting Black schools in the city. He opposed efforts to deport Blacks to American colonies in an 1827 letter to *Freedom's Journal*, and organized the first National Negro Convention in Philadelphia in 1830, largely to address concerns of anticolonialism. Allen wrote a brief autobiography, *The Life, Experience, and Gospel Labours of the Rt. Rev. Richard Allen* (published 1833), a narrative defending the heroic actions of African Americans during the plague (1794, with Absalom Jones), an explanation of the A.M.E. Church's doctrines (1817, with Jacob Tapsico), and various sermons and addresses. Allen appears in two works by **John Edgar Wideman**: as a character in "Fever" (1992), and in *The Cattle Killing* (1996), in which the fictional protagonist's story follows Allen's biography.

Resources: Richard Allen, "The Life, Experience, and Gospel Labours of the Rt. Rev. Richard Allen," in *My Soul Has Grown Deep, Classics of Early African-American Literature*, ed. John Edgar Wideman (New York: One World–Ballantine, 2002), 6–20; Richard Allen and Jacob Tapsico, *Doctrines and Discipline of the A.M.E. Church* (Philadelphia: Cunningham, 1817); Carol V. R. George, *Segregated Sabbaths: Richard Allen and the Emergence of Black Churches 1760–1840* (New York: Oxford University Press, 1973); Absalom Jones and Richard Allen, "A Narrative of the Proceedings of the Black People During the Awful Calamity in Philadelphia, in the Year 1793," in *My Soul Has Grown Deep: Classics of Early African-American Literature*, ed. John Edgar Wideman (New York: One World–Ballantine, 2002), 26–39; Gary Nash, *Forging Freedom: The Formation of Philadelphia's Black Community, 1720–1840* (Cambridge, MA: Harvard University Press, 1988); John Edgar Wideman: *The Cattle Killing* (Boston: Houghton Mifflin, 1996); "Fever," in *The Stories of John Edgar Wideman* (New York: Pantheon, 1992), 239–265; "Richard Allen," in *My Soul Has Grown Deep: Classics of Early African-American Literature*, ed. John Edgar Wideman (New York: One World–Ballantine, 2002), 1–5.

Ian W. Wilson

Allen, Samuel Washington (born 1917). Poet, editor, educator, and critic. Under his legal name, as well as under the pseudonym Paul Vesey, Samuel W. Allen has written significant poems and essays that span the second half of the twentieth century. Allen's long career and often anthologized work have earned him a place among the most respected contemporary African American writers.

Allen was born into a minister's family in Columbus, Ohio, and later attended Fisk University, where he participated in a writing workshop led by **James Weldon Johnson**. After he received his J.D. from Harvard Law School in 1941, Allen's formal literary career began in France following his service in the U.S. Army during **World War II**. While studying in **Paris**, Allen became involved with the **Négritude** movement, a group of Caribbean and African poets writing in French, and with the help of **Richard Wright**, he became an important part of *Présence Africaine* in 1949, contributing poems and essays to the magazine as well as serving as an editor and translator. Because of his active career in law, Allen published his first volume of poetry under the name Paul Vesey; he eventually abandoned the legal profession, in 1968, to dedicate more time to literature. Allen taught at Tuskegee Institute, Wesleyan University, and Boston University before retiring in 1981. His early European experiences helped to shape the distinctive Pan-African quality of his works throughout his life, and his later writings continue to stress the shared heritage of Africans and African Americans.

Allen's poetry has graced the pages of more than 100 anthologies, including **Arna Bontemps**'s *American Negro Poetry* (1963), **Langston Hughes**'s *New Negro Poets, U.S.A.* (1964), and **Arthur P. Davis** and **J. Saunders Redding**'s *Cavalcade* (1971). His first volume of poems was *Elfenbein Zähne* (1956), which was published in Germany. Subsequent collections—*Ivory Tusks and Other Poems* (1968), *Paul Vesey's Ledger* (1975), and *Every Round and Other Poems* (1987)—further established his reputation as an important African American poet. Many of these poems lament the tragic legacy of **slavery** and draw upon the church, oral traditions, and African heritage as a means of liberation and empowerment. "To Satch (American Gothic)" and "A Moment Please" remain two of Allen's most acclaimed poems, and "Harriet Tubman, aka Moses" has been permanently mounted for display in the **Boston, Massachusetts**, subway's Ruggles station. Noteworthy essays by Allen include "Negritude and Its Relevance to the American Negro Writer" and his more recent "Recollections of Sterling Allen Brown: Wit and Wisdom," as well as his translation of Jean-Paul Sartre's "Black Orpheus." Allen also edited the collection *Poems from Africa* (1973), which was illustrated by **Romare Bearden**. The 1998 video anthology *Furious Flower* includes Allen in its first volume, *Elders*, which is dedicated to the voices that inspired the **Black Arts Movement** and later African American writers, and captures Allen reading and discussing his poetry.

Resources: Samuel W. Allen: *Elfenbein Zähne* (Heidelberg, Germany: Wolfgang Rothe, 1956); *Every Round and Other Poems* (Detroit: Lotus Press, 1987); *Ivory Tusks and Other Poems* (New York: Poets Press, 1968); "Negritude and Its Relevance to the American Negro Writer," in *The American Negro Writer and His Roots* (New York: American Society of African Culture, 1960); *Paul Vesey's Ledger* (Detroit: Broadside Press, 1975); "Recollections of Sterling Allen Brown: Wit and Wisdom," *Callaloo* 21, no. 4 (1998), 852–859; Samuel W. Allen, ed., *Poems from Africa* (New York: Crowell, 1973); Samuel W. Allen, contrib.: *American Negro Poetry*, ed. Arna Bontemps (New York: Hill and Wang, 1963); *Cavalcade*, ed. Arthur P. Davis and Saunders Redding (Boston: Houghton Mifflin, 1971); *The Forerunners*, ed. Woodie King, Jr. (Washington, DC: Howard University Press, 1981); *New Negro Poets*, ed. Langston Hughes (Bloomington: Indiana University Press, 1964); Samuel W. Allen, trans., Jean-Paul Sartre, *Black Orpheus* (Paris: Présence Africaine, 1963); Ruth L. Brittin, "Samuel Allen," in *Dictionary of Literary Biography*, vol. 41, *Afro-American Poets Since 1955*, ed. Trudier Harris and Thadious M. Davis (Detroit: Gale, 1985), 8–17; George Dickenberger, "Paul Vesey," *Black*

Orpheus 4 (1958), 5–8; *Furious Flower*, vol. 1, *Elders* (San Francisco: California Newsreel, 1998), video; Edward A. Scott, "Bardic Memory and Witness in the Poetry of Samuel Allen," in *The Furious Flowering of African American Poetry*, ed. Joanne Gabbin (Charlottesville: University Press of Virginia, 1999).

Esther Godfrey

Allison, Hughes (1908–c. 1974). Playwright. Allison was a socially conscious African American playwright during a time when many African American playwrights were accused of pandering to White ideals. He is best known for *The Trial of Dr. Beck* (1937), and he is credited with educating audiences of both races regarding the need to challenge racism throughout American society.

Born in New Jersey, Allison spent much of his childhood traveling with his mother, a concert pianist. His grandfather was a **Reconstruction** era judge. He attended Upsala College, where he majored in English and history, and then found employment with the Federal Theatre Project (FTP; Craig, 24).

Allison's association with the FTP was troubled. Though the FTP produced only one of his plays, *The Trial of Dr. Beck*, its national director, Hallie Flanagan, described Allison's work as "more mature in dramatic technique than any Negro playwright to date" (Ross, 150). *The Trial of Dr. Beck* opened in New Jersey to rave reviews, then moved to Broadway, **Harlem, New York**, and New Jersey again. The courtroom melodrama follows the trial of Dr. Beck, an African American man accused of murdering his wife. It also provides a forum for a discussion of the myth of White superiority in American society, as well as color discrimination privileging lighter skin over dark skin within the African American community (Fraden, 108–110).

Allison then began work on a trilogy of plays that would document the African American experience from about 1800 to the 1930s. Only one of the plays, *Panyared* (1938), was completed; and it was never produced. *Panyared*, meaning "kidnapped" or "man seized," is based on the history of the slave trade, and follows several Africans who are captured, transported to the United States, and sold into **slavery**. It illustrated the violently deleterious effects of the slave trade, both physically and spiritually, for all involved.

Though the circumstances surrounding Allison's final year as an FTP employee are uncertain, he did write at least one more play. *It's Midnight over Newark* (1941) was produced by the Mosque Theatre in Newark. Allison then became disenchanted with theater, and stopped writing drama (Fraden, 110). (*See* **Federal Writers' Project; Negro Units Federal Theatre Project**.)

Resources: Hughes Allison: *It's Midnight over Newark*, electronic ed. (Alexandria, VA: Alexander Street Press, 2002); *The Trial of Dr. Beck*, electronic ed. (Alexandria, VA: Alexander Street Press, 2002); E. Quita Craig, *Black Drama of the Federal Theatre Era: Beyond the Formal Horizons* (Amherst: University of Massachusetts Press, 1980); Rena Fraden, *Blueprints for a Black Federal Theatre, 1935–1939* (New York: Cambridge University Press, 1994); Bernard L. Peterson, Jr., *Early Black American Playwrights and Dramatic Writers* (Westport, CT: Greenwood Press, 1990); Ronald Patrick

Ross, "Black Drama in the Federal Theatre, 1935–1939," Ph.D. dissertation, University of Southern California, 1972.

Elizabeth A. Osborne

Als, Hilton (born 1961). Journalist, art critic, and author of literary nonfiction. Hilton Als was raised in **Brooklyn, New York,** by his mother, Marie, who had emigrated from Barbados before he was born. Growing up in a working-class family in a predominantly minority neighborhood, Als realized that he was gay from a young age. He attended Brown University, but upon graduation, jobs seemed scarce. As Als often notes with good humor, despite some close calls at entering into screenwriting, he remained in the secretarial profession until the age of thirty-two, when Jonathan Van Meter picked him as an editor-at-large for the magazine *VIBE*. From there, Als's career in journalism started to take off with contributions to such periodicals as *Essence, New York Times Magazine, Out,* and *VIBE.* He was an advisory editor of the art quarterly *Grand Street,* which ceased publication in 2004. Currently, he is a staff writer for *The New Yorker* and *The Village Voice,* focusing on gay issues. He is largely known as an art critic, and received the George Jean Nathan Award for Drama Criticism in 2004. His witty writing style is a highly versatile mix of memoir, investigative journalism, art criticism, and cultural commentary in which issues of pop culture, **race,** sexuality, and **gender** are foregrounded. Nowhere are all these thematic threads so artfully combined as in his only published full-length book, *The Women* (1996), praised widely for Als's astute psychological and sociopolitical insight into his own sexual and racial alterity as he identifies himself with the problematic "negress." His second book, *The Group,* is scheduled for release in 2005 and presents a nuanced interpretation of author **James Baldwin**'s conflicting moral and intellectual identity. (*See* **Gay Literature**.)

Resources: Hilton Als: *Diary: A Weeklong Electronic Journal,* http://slate.msn.com/id/2095547/entry/2095566/, 2004; foreword, in David Margolick, *Strange Fruit: The Biography of a Song,* intro. Ellis Marsalis (New York: Ecco Press, 2001); *The Group* (New York: Farrar, Straus, Giroux, 2005); *The Women* (New York: Farrar, Straus, Giroux, 1996); Hilton Als, with James Allen, John Lewis, and Leon F. Litwack, *Without Sanctuary: Lynching Photography in America* (Santa Fe, NM: Twin Palms, 2000).

Alicia D. Williamson

Amos, Robyn (born 1971). Romance novelist. Amos developed an interest in **romance novels** in high school; "happy endings" and "strong women taking control of their lives" became her self-proclaimed "addiction" (*Robyn Amos*). A year after she graduated from college with a degree in psychology, she decided she wanted to pursue writing romance novels instead of a Ph.D. as a psychologist.

Despite her vast knowledge of the genre, Amos struggled with writing her first novel for a year before it was finished. She sold her first book, *Promise Me* (1997), three months after completing it, and was offered a two-book contract with Arabesque Pinnacle Books in 1995, at the age of twenty-five. Amos sold a two more books, *Private Lies* (1998) and *Into the Night* (1998) to Arabesque, and her following two romances, *Bachelorette Blues* (1999) and *Hero at Large* (2000), to Silhouette Books. *Bring Me a Dream* (2001) and *Wedding Bell Blues* (2004) were published on a two-book contract with Harper/Torch. Amos's works focus on African American characters, and they develop romantic narratives that sometimes incorporate suspenseful subplots. As a writer, Amos struggles with mediating Black stereotypes in creating real and believable characters to whom her audience will relate. She believes romance novels can be a powerful medium for conveying ethnic experiences and female empowerment (*Robyn Amos*).

At this writing, Amos works as an assistant editor for the National Club Association. She maintains a personal Web site, which contains advice for beginning writers.

Resources: Robyn Amos: "After Midnight," in *I Do!* (New York: Pinnacle Books/Arabesque, 1998), a novella; *Bachelorette Blues* (New York: Silhouette Books, 1999); *Bring Me a Dream* (New York: HarperTorch, 2001); *Hero at Large* (New York: Silhouette Intimate Moments, 2000); *Into the Night* (New York: Pinnacle Books/Arabesque, 1998); *Private Lies* (New York: Pinnacle Books/Arabesque, 1998); *Promise Me* (New York: Pinnacle Books/Arabesque, 1997); *Robyn Amos*, http://www.robynamos.com; *True Blue* (Washington, DC: BET Books, 1999); *Wedding Bell Blues* (New York: HarperTorch, 2004); Phylicia Oppelt, "Writing in Living Color: Romance Novelist Robyn Amos and the Stuff of Dreams," *Washington Post*, Aug. 15, 1998, p. B1.

Allison Bennett

Amsterdam News **(1909–present).** African American political newspaper. Despite a financially turbulent history, the *Amsterdam News* has remained a prominent, politically alert African American newspaper since its founding in 1909 by James H. Anderson with an initial investment of $10 (*New York Amsterdam News*). Named for the avenue where Anderson lived (and edited the paper in its first year), the paper focused on local concerns and events, and Black social organizations. It was printed weekly and sold for 2 cents per copy. In 1910, the *Amsterdam News* offices relocated to **Harlem, New York**, and Anderson took on business partner, Edward A. Warren, who served as publisher until his death in 1921.

George W. Harris, J. E. Robinson, and William Kelly were among the first editors of the paper; West Indian immigrant Cyril V. Briggs, later editor of the *Colored American Review*, contributed to the paper from 1912 to 1919, when he was fired for radicalism in his editorials. Other contributors included **T. Thomas Fortune**, Marvel Cooke, **W.E.B. Du Bois**, **Langston Hughes**, **Roy Wilkins**, and Adam Clayton Powell, Jr.

The ownership of the paper has changed numerous times. Anderson sold his interest to Sadie Warren, the widow of publisher Edward Warren, in 1926. Warren sold the paper for $5,000 in 1936 to C. B. Powell and P.M.H. Savory, two physicians originally from the West Indies, a year after a six-week employee strike (one of the first involving Black workers and a Black employer) and further financial difficulties. Powell, who served as editor and publisher, and Savory, who served as secretary and treasurer, established a union contract for employees, and renamed the paper the *New York Amsterdam Star-News* in 1941;

they returned to the original title in 1943. The *Amsterdam News* rose from a circulation of 35,841 in 1940 to become the largest community weekly for Blacks in the United States. Following **World War II**, the newspaper began publishing a second issue every week, and circulation exceeded 100,000 (as high as 111,427 in 1947). The paper's success continued through the 1950s and 1960s, when it firmly supported the **Civil Rights Movement** and the work of **Martin Luther King, Jr.**, Elijah Muhammad, and **Malcolm X**. By 1964, however, circulation had dropped to 75,500, and in 1971, after the death of Savory and the illness of Powell, the newspaper was sold for $2.3 million to businessmen and politicians, among them Percy Sutton, M. Carl McCall, and Clarence Jones. A second strike occurred in 1983, due to financial problems; Wilbert Tatum became the publisher, editor, and principal stockholder in 1984. Tatum's personal position against the American legal system and the New York City police force was the subject of much criticism from both White and Black subscribers over the next decade. In 1993, circulation dropped to 32,701, the staff numbered fewer than fifty, and Tatum's attempt to revive the paper and merge the *Amsterdam News* with the *New York Post* failed. Tatum's daughter Elinor currently owns the paper, which is still believed to significantly impact political controversies within the Black community.

The *Amsterdam News*, often criticized for its sensational headlines, traditionally focuses on political and social issues affecting the African American community. During Franklin Delano Roosevelt's New Deal, the newspaper's political affiliation switched from the Republican to the Democratic Party, and it supported democratic reforms as its readership grew in the 1930s. During World War II, the *Amsterdam News* became a public platform for political debate, and advocated collaboration between Jews and Blacks in 1942 for gaining civil rights and equal opportunity in the U.S. armed forces and industries (*see* Simmons).

In the mid-1970s, the newspaper's political activism, this time militantly voicing a demand for civil rights, was attacked by the public. Shifting its focus to more moderate and less provocative concerns of the African American community, the paper thereafter discussed social events and promoted political triumphs, and changed from a broadsheet to a tabloid size in 1979. Though it presently competes against other New York and national publications, the *Amsterdam News* remains a prominent publication devoted to African American social and political issues.

Resources: David R. Jones, *The Urban Agenda: A Selection of Columns Reprinted from the New York Amsterdam News* (New York: Community Service Society of New York, 1994); *New York Amsterdam News*, http://www.amsterdamnews.org/News/aboutus.asp?sID=30; Charlene B. Regester, *Black Entertainers in African American Newspaper Articles* (Jefferson, NC: McFarland, 2002); Jack Salzman et al., *Encyclopedia of African-American Culture and History* (New York: Macmillan Library Reference, 1996); Charles A. Simmons, *The African American Press: A History of News Coverage During National Crises, with Special Reference to Four Black Newspapers, 1827–1965* (Jefferson, NC: McFarland, 1998).

Allison Bennett

Anderson, Garland (1886–1939). Playwright, entrepreneur, and minister. Anderson's play *Appearances*, which opened at the Frolic Theater on October 13, 1925, was the first full-length play by an African American dramatist to be produced on Broadway, and the first to have a racially diverse cast. With only four years formal education, Anderson's success came from his strong belief in God and his philosophy of self-determination and optimism. He was born in Kansas and later moved to California, where he worked as a newspaper boy, and later as a bellhop and switchboard operator at a hotel in San Francisco (1917). In 1924, after seeing Channing Pollock's play *The Fool*, Anderson decided to become a playwright so he could share his beliefs about the power of positive thinking with a large audience. In three weeks, Anderson wrote his only produced play, *Appearances*. He sent it to the famous performer Al Jolson, who gave Anderson money to travel to New York to find a producer. While in New York, Anderson generated free publicity for his play by giving interviews to local newspapers, including the **Amsterdam News**, the noted African American newspaper. Eventually, his perseverance led him to **Washington, D.C.**, where he was granted a meeting with President Calvin Coolidge, who accepted a copy of the script. On April 5, 1925, Anderson had a public reading of his play performed by the popular Black actor Richard B. Harrison at the Waldorf-Astoria hotel in New York that was attended by more than 600 prominent New Yorkers. Months later a producer bought *Appearances*.

After it premiered in New York, *Appearances* opened in **Los Angeles, California** (1927), **San Francisco, California** (1928), and other U.S. cities and in several European cities (1930). While Anderson was in London, he became the first African American member of the esteemed literary organization PEN (International Association of Poets, Playwrights, Editors, Essayists, and Novelists); had a BBC program *The Voice of Uncommon Sense*, on which he delivered inspirational messages to listeners; and started a business called Andy's NuShack, which introduced malted drinks to England. For the remainder of his life, Anderson traveled extensively throughout the United States and Canada giving lectures on his Christian faith, and became a minister for the Center of Constructive Thinking (1935). Although Anderson's play "marked the beginning of an integrated Broadway stage" (Hatch, 456) during the **Harlem Renaissance**, Kreizenbeck (69) states that "For whatever reasons, Anderson never became a leader or a role model in the African American community." Anderson's other works include the play *Extortion* (1929); an autobiography, *From Newsboy to Bellhop to Playwright* (1925); and the play *Uncommon Sense: The Law of Life in Action* (1933).

Resources: Garland Anderson: *From Newsboy to Bellhop to Playwright* (San Francisco: [publisher unknown], 1925); *Uncommon Sense: The Law of Life in Action* (London: L. N. Fowler, 1933); James V. Hatch, "Anderson, Garland," in *American National Biography*, vol. 1 (New York: Oxford University Press, 1999), 455–456; Alan Kreizenbeck, "Garland Anderson and *Appearances*: The Playwright and His Play," in *Experimenters, Rebels, and Disparate Voices*, ed. Arthur Gerwirtz and James J. Kolb (Westport, CT: Praeger, 2003), 55–70.

Brande Nicole Martin

Anderson, Mignon Holland (born 1945). Novelist and short story writer. Anderson's contribution to African American literature includes her compelling sense of place, revealed, for example, in her short story collection *Mostly Womenfolk and a Man or Two* (1976) and in her novel *The End of Dying* (2001). She writes about Virginia's Eastern Shore, a small strip of land wedged between the Atlantic Ocean on the east and Chesapeake Bay on the west, and home to her. Born in Northampton County, Virginia, Anderson grew up in Cheriton, the daughter of Frank Bernard Holland, Cheriton's only mortician, and Ruby Vivian Treherne Holland. In both works noted above, Anderson presents the oppressive spirit of Virginia's Eastern Shore, an oppression paralleling that in Sarah E. Wright's *This Child's Gonna Live* (1969), a novel of Blacks' experiences on Maryland's Eastern Shore.

Anderson received her B.A. in English and comparative literature from Fisk University (1966), where she studied fiction under Fisk University's writer-in-residence, the novelist **John Oliver Killens**. In 1970, she received the M.F.A. from Columbia University (1970). From 1963–1973, Anderson penned more than thirty stories, a few of which were published in *The Black Communicator*, *Black World*, *Freedomways*, and **Negro Digest**. Following the advice of Grace Killens, wife of John Oliver Killens, Holland collected and published twelve stories as *Mostly Womenfolk and a Man or Two*. After rearing two children, Holland published *The End of Dying*, which fleshes out the character Carrie Allen from *Mostly Womenfolk*. Currently, Anderson teaches creative writing at the University of Maryland, Eastern Shore.

Resources: Mignon Holland Anderson: *The End of Dying* (Baltimore: AmErica House, 2001); *Mostly Womenfolk and a Man or Two* (Detroit: Third World Press, 1976); George Kent, "*Mostly Womenfolk and a Man or Two*" [review], *Black Books Bulletin* 4, no. 4 (Winter 1976), 52–53.

Rita B. Dandridge

Anderson, Stanice (born 1950). Author, freelance writer, motivational speaker, and life coach. Born into the fourth generation of Andersons to live in **Washington, D.C.**, Anderson had a privileged upbringing. The first part of her life was filled with tragedy—rape at age thirteen, abusive relationships, and eighteen years of drug and alcohol addiction. With the help of a drug abuse treatment program, Alcoholics Anonymous, and friends and family, Anderson was able to break the hold drugs and alcohol had on her life. Since receiving treatment, Anderson has worked as an editorial assistant for USAToday.com and written two nonfiction books: *12-Step Programs: A Resource Guide for Helping Professionals* (1999) and *I Say a Prayer for Me: One Woman's Life of Faith and Triumph* (2002). *I Say a Prayer for Me* gives an account of Anderson's struggles and the healing power she found in God. She got a contract to write the book with the help of **Patrice Gaines**, author of *Laughing in the Dark: From Colored Girl to Woman of Color—A Journey from Prison to Power*, who saw the online column ("Sharing the Hope") and E-mail series ("Food for the Spirit" and "Power Moments with God") Anderson developed to promote her work. The column and E-mail series are one component of her Web site, www.stanice.com.

Since writing the book, Anderson has served as a life coach to women trying to break free from abusive relationships and addictions. With Gaines, she developed and now teaches a writing workshop, "The Book Within: How to Get Your Writing Out onto the Page and into the World." Anderson has delivered speeches to audiences at graduations, conferences, churches, hospitals, and prisons in the United States and the Caribbean. In addition to leading writing workshops, she is serving as the 2004–2005 guest author for the University of the District of Columbia's Claude Brown Writers & Readers Series. Anderson presently resides in Maryland with her son. She is working with Patrice Gaines on a four-woman play.

Resources: Stanice Anderson: *I Say a Prayer for Me: One Woman's Life of Faith and Triumph* (New York: Walk Worthy Press/Warner, 2002); official Stanice Anderson Web site, www.stanice.com; *12-Step Programs: A Resource Guide for Helping Professionals* (Holmes Beach, FL: Learning Publications, 1999); The Sistah Circle Book Club: An African American Women's Book Club, "An Interview with Stanice Anderson," http://www.thesistahcircle.com/interview-sanderson.htm; Writers Net, "Stanice Anderson," http://www.writers.net/writers/4338.

Melissa Couchon

Anderson-Thompkins, Sibby (born 1966). Writer, poet, actor, and activist. Born in Winterville, North Carolina, to a family of educators, Sibby Anderson-Thompkins graduated with a B.A. (1987) and M.A. (1990) in communication from the University of North Carolina, at Chapel Hill. While a student, she used theater to address social and political issues such as violence against women, educational access for African Americans, and apartheid in South Africa.

Two individuals have influenced Anderson-Thompkins's work. Like the African American poet **Ntozake Shange**, Anderson-Thompkins uses an almost rambling free association, rhythmically punctuated by silence and interruptions of thought. The work of **Zora Neale Hurston**, a trained anthropologist who used her status and ability as a storyteller to document the everyday language and culture of Black people, also has influenced Anderson-Thompkins. For example, in her poem "Interlude," she documents the dialect and vernacular of the rural North Carolina where she grew up.

In all of Anderson-Thompkins's work there are traces of her own life. Autobiographical in nature, it focuses on the ordinary and the mundane—revealing the unspoken notions we have about race and identity. By casting a light upon specific people or events or emotions, she illuminates the uniqueness of each story she tells.

Among the poets featured in *In the Tradition: An Anthology of Young Black Writers*, edited by **Kevin Powell** and **Ras Baraka**, Anderson-Thompkins's contributions are unique. Unlike much of the writing of the 1990s that focused on the Black urban **hip-hop** experience, she tells intimate, personal stories that search for meaning in the particulars of the human condition rather than commenting on larger political and social issues.

After working as an educator in the 1990s, Anderson-Thompkins pursued a master's degree in educational research at Georgia State University, graduating in 2001. During this time she traveled nationally to conduct workshops on youth culture, hip-hop, and rape. She is currently pursuing a Ph.D. in educational research.

Anderson-Thompkins has distilled the many strains of her work into a form that is both scholarly and artistic. As an ethnographer, she combines the power of storytelling and qualitative research methodology. Two of her most recent publications, *Fund Raising from Black-College Alumni* and "Developing Trust, Negotiating Power: Transgressing Race and Status in the Academy," exemplify this combination. In each study, Anderson-Thompkins listens to the voices of the participants and uses narrative to share these voices with the reader. Issues of voice, representation, and power are common themes in her work and in her life's passions.

Resources: Sibby Anderson-Thompkins, Kelleye Blackburn, and Jasmine Williams, "Using Youth Culture to Reach the Hip-hop Generation," in *Reclaiming Our Youth: Building a Nonviolent Society*, ed. Robert Warkentin and Dan Rea (New York: McGraw-Hill, 2001); Joanne Dowdy, Narcel Reedus, Sibby Anderson-Thompkins, and Patricia Heim, "The Making of Griots: One Black Film Maker's Journey with Six Teenagers," *The High School Journal* 86, no. 4 (Spring 2003); Marybeth Gasman and Sibby Anderson-Thompkins: *Fund Raising from Black-College Alumni: Successful Strategies for Supporting Alma Mater* (Washington, DC: CASE Books, 2003); "A Renaissance on the Eastside: Motivating Inner-City Youth Through Art," *Journal of Education for Students at Risk* 8, no. 4 (Fall 2003); Marybeth Gasman, Cynthia Gerstl-Pepin, Sibby Anderson-Thompkins, Lisa Rasheed, and Karry Hathaway, "Developing Trust, Negotiating Power: Transgressing Race and Status in the Academy," *Teachers College Record* 106, no. 4 (Spring 2004); Kevin Powell and Ras Baraka, eds., *In the Tradition: An Anthology of Young Black Writers* (New York: Harlem River Press, 1992).

Marybeth Gasman

Andrews, Raymond (1934–1991). Novelist and memoirist. In a style influenced by the Black oral tradition, Andrews's writing chronicles and satirizes rural Georgia life from **World War I** through the 1960s.

Appalachee, Georgia, where Andrews grew up, became the fictional Muskhogean County, the setting and subject of his novels *Appalachee Red* (1978), *Rosiebelle Lee Wildcat Tennessee* (1980), and *Baby Sweet's* (1983). The lives of his family and three others are fictionalized in the trilogy, as are the segregated South's interracial and economic relations. Andrews relates in his autobiography, *The Last Radio Baby* (1990), that he worked from age nine to age fifteen as a sharecropper, attending—when work allowed—the Black country elementary school and then the town school. At fifteen, he left to live in **Atlanta, Georgia**, at the YMCA, attend Booker T. Washington High School, and work at various jobs. Andrews later served in the U.S. Air Force, attended

Michigan State University, and worked in New York City for KLM Airlines before quitting at age thirty-two, to begin the writing career about which he had dreamed. He also worked as a photograph librarian and courier. He returned to Georgia in 1984 and died in 1991 from a self-inflicted gunshot wound.

The trilogy's characters are legendary in size, strength, skill, and cleverness, and their exploits are greater than life, portrayed in heroic tales with satiric commentary by an omniscient narrator. In the first book, for example, Appalachee Red is the son of a local White man, John Morgan, and Little Bit Thompson, his Native American and Black mistress. Appalachee Red, who was sent north as a child to escape danger, returns to awe the Black residents with his style, to operate a popular café, and to challenge the White police chief, "Boots" White. The trilogy's female protagonists, Little Bit, Rosiebelle Lee Wildcat Tennessee, and Appalachee Red's lover, Baby Sweet, are sexually provocative but tough, shrewd, and loving as well.

The hallmark of Andrews's fiction is that it entertains with affectionate humor and storytelling virtuosity, yet unflinchingly depicts the racial and economic oppression Black people experienced and their struggles for education and material success. Andrews says, "I knew we were victims . . . yet I knew we were much more. And this 'more' is what I wanted to write about" ("The Necessity of Blacks' Writing Fiction," 297). Andrews won the James Baldwin Prize for Fiction in 1978 for *Appalachee Red*, and in 1992 he won the American Book Award of the Before Columbus Foundation for *Jessie and Jesus; and Cousin Claire*.

Resources: Ray Andrews: *Appalachee Red* (New York: Dial, 1978); *Baby Sweet's* (New York: Dial, 1983); *Jessie and Jesus; and Cousin Claire* (Atlanta: Peachtree, 1991); *The Last Radio Baby: A Memoir* (Atlanta: Peachtree, 1990); "The Necessity of Blacks' Writing Fiction About the South," *African American Review* 27 (1993), 297–299; *Rosiebelle Lee Wildcat Tennessee* (New York: Dial, 1980); Onita Estes-Hicks, "The Way We Were: Precious Memories of the Black Segregated South," *African American Review* 27 (1993), 9–18; Jeffrey J. Folks, " 'Trouble' in Muskhogean County: The Social History of a Southern Community in the Fiction of Raymond Andrews," *Southern Literary Journal* 30, no. 2 (1998), 66–76; "Raymond Andrews," in *Contemporary Authors*, New Revision Series (Farmington Hills, MI: Gale Group, 1999), 15: 31–32.

Anna R. Holloway

Andrews, Regina M. (1901–1993). Playwright, theater founder, and librarian. Andrews may be better known now as a socially active member of the **Harlem Renaissance**, a librarian, and a theater founder than as a playwright. She was born Regina M. Anderson, in **Chicago, Illinois**. She attended Wilberforce University in Ohio, the University of Chicago, and Columbia University. She earned a master's degree in library science from Columbia. Starting in the 1920s, she was employed by the New York Public Library System and remained with the system until she retired in 1967. In 1924 she worked with **W.E.B. Du Bois** and others to establish an African American drama company in **Harlem, New York**; it was named the Krigwa Players, and its home was the library branch on 135th Street ("Anderson"). The Krigwa Players later become the Negro Experimental Theatre and the Harlem Experimental Theatre; it anticipated the work of the Harlem Suitcase Theatre, with which **Langston Hughes** was associated. Andrews knew Hughes, **Jean Toomer**, **Countee Cullen**, and other notables in the Harlem Renaissance, and her apartment was one of many sites where artists, intellectuals, and others met during that vibrant era ("Anderson"). As a playwright, Andrews is known for three plays: the one-act *Climbing Jacob's Ladder*, which concerns **lynching** and which was produced by the Negro Experimental Theatre; *Underground*, which concerns the **Underground Railroad**; and *The Man Who Passed*. She wrote *Climbing Jacob's Ladder* and *Underground* under the pseudonym Ursula Trelling ("Anderson").

Resources: "Anderson [*sic*], Regina M," *Britannica Online*, http://www.britannica.com/blackhistory/micro/725/90.html; Regina M. Andrews: *Climbing Jacob's Ladder*, in *Strange Fruit: Plays on Lynching by American Women*, ed. Kathy A. Perkins and Judith L. Stephens (Bloomington: Indiana University Press, 1998); *The Man Who Passed*, in *Harlem's Glory: Black Women Writing, 1900–1950*, ed. Lorraine Elena Roses and Ruth Elizabeth Randolph (Cambridge, MA: Harvard University Press, 1996).

Hans Ostrom

Andrews, William L. (born 1946). Scholar, editor, and professor. Andrews is an eminent scholar of African American literature, with particular expertise in African American **autobiography** in general and **slave narratives** in particular. At this writing, he is E. Maynard Adams Professor of English at the University of North Carolina at Chapel Hill, where he received his M.A. in 1970 and his Ph.D. in 1973. Andrews's first book, *The Literary Career of Charles W. Chesnutt* (1980), was followed by *To Tell a Free Story* (1986), which surveys African American autobiography through 1865. Andrews has edited *Three Classic African American Novels*, which brings together in one volume *Clotel*, by **William Wells Brown**; *Iola Leroy*, by **Frances E. W. Harper**; and *The Marrow of Tradition*, by **Charles Waddell Chesnutt**. More recently, Andrews has coedited two crucial works in the field of African American literature: *The Norton Anthology of African American Literature* (1996) and *The Oxford Companion to African American Literature* (1999). He also has written introductions to reprints of important works of literature, including **James Weldon Johnson**'s *The Autobiography of an Ex-Colored Man*, and he has edited a casebook for the study of the novel *Beloved*, by **Toni Morrison**. On his academic home page, Andrews writes, "I'm now series editor of *North American Slave Narratives, Beginnings to 1920*, a complete digitized library of autobiographies and biographies of North American slaves and ex-slaves, funded by the National Endowment for the Humanities, Ameritech, and the University of North Carolina at Chapel Hill. I continue to study the historical linkages between white and black writers in the formation of American literature, African American literature, and southern literature."

Resources: William L. Andrews: home page, http://www.english.unc.edu/faculty/andrewsw.html; *The Literary Career of Charles W. Chesnutt* (Baton Rouge: Louisiana State University Press, 1980); *To Tell a Free Story* (Urbana: University of Illinois

Press, 1986); William L. Andrews, ed.: *Three Classic African American Novels* (New York: Vintage, 1990); *Toni Morrison's "Beloved": A Casebook* (New York: Oxford University Press, 1999); William L. Andrews, Frances Smith Foster, and Trudier Harris, *The Oxford Companion to African American Literature* (New York: Oxford University Press, 1997); William L. Andrews, Henry Louis Gates, Jr., and Nellie Y. McKay, eds., *The Norton Anthology of African American Literature* (New York: W. W. Norton, 1996); James Weldon Johnson, *The Autobiography of an Ex–Colored Man*, intro. William L. Andrews (New York: Penguin, 1990).

Hans Ostrom

Angelou, Maya (born 1928). Autobiographer, poet, actress, producer, director, scriptwriter, political activist, and editor. Angelou, having overcome exceptional adversity, has emerged as one of the most remarkable self-affirming literary and cultural voices in contemporary American literature.

Angelou was born Marguerite Johnson on April 4, 1928, in **St. Louis, Missouri**. At the age of three, she was sent to Stamps, Arkansas, with her brother, Bailey, to live with their grandmother, Momma, after her parents' divorce. Momma was the owner of a small convenience store and managed to scrape by during the **Great Depression**.

Five years later, her father took Maya back to her mother in St. Louis. In 1936 she was raped by her mother's boyfriend, Mr. Freeman. This event was confusing to Maya, because Freeman had made prior sexual advances toward her that were unrecognized or misinterpreted as love. Angelou writes, "He held me so softly that I wished he would never let go. I felt at home. From the way he was holding me I knew he'd never let me go or let anything bad happen to me. This was probably my real father and we had found each other at last" (*I Know Why the Caged Bird Sings*, 71). After his ensuing trial, Freeman was murdered. Angelou felt responsible for his death and became mute for a period of about five years, and was sent back to Stamps to live with her grandmother.

Angelou's muteness was finally broken by Bertha Flowers, a woman who not only brought speech back into her life, but also initiated a new romance with literature and a profound sense of self. Angelou writes, "I was liked, and what a difference it made. I was respected not as Mrs. Henderson's grandchild or Bailey's sister, but just for being Marguerite Johnson" (*I Know Why the Caged Bird Sings*, 98). This sense of self-awareness and pride, in turn, brought Angelou literary fame.

Angelou was reunited with her mother in **San Francisco, California**, in 1940. She became the first female streetcar conductor in San Francisco and gave birth, at sixteen, to her son, Guy. To support her family, she held a variety of jobs, such as working as a cook, a waitress, and even a madam. She finally settled into performing as a professional dancer.

Angelou spent most of the early 1950s performing at the Purple Onion and touring with the musical *Porgy and Bess*. During this time she adopted the name Maya Angelou. Maya is derived from her childhood nickname, "My," given to her by her brother Bailey. Angelou was the last name of her first husband, Tosh Angelou, a white former sailor to whom she was married for two and a half years.

After touring for several years, Angelou moved with her son to New York, where she became actively involved with the Harlem Writer's Guild. Her association with such respected authors as **James Baldwin**, John Henrik Clarke, and **Paule Marshall** led to the beginnings of her writing career. Baldwin introduced Angelou to Judy Feiffer. Feiffer and one of her friends at Random House encouraged Maya to write not only poetry but also her autobiography.

During this time Angelou became a social activist. She was asked by **Martin Luther King, Jr.**, to serve as the northern coordinator for the Southern Christian Leadership Conference after *Cabaret for Freedom* with Godfrey Cambridge, a comedian. In 1961 she wrote (with Ethel Ayer) and acted in an off-Broadway production, *The Blacks*, with Louis Gossett, Jr., Cicely Tyson, and James Earl Jones. The production was highly successful, but Angelou stayed for only a short time due to the director's refusal to pay for music she had written for the show with Ayer.

As her writing accelerated, Angelou met and moved to Africa with Vusumzi Make, a South African freedom fighter, in 1961. The relationship did not last, and Angelou moved with her son to Ghana, where she wrote articles for the *Ghana Times* and was features editor of *The African Review*. She also taught courses at the University of Ghana before returning to the United States in 1966.

In 1969, Angelou's first autobiography, *I Know Why the Caged Bird Sings*, was published. The book was a best-seller and was nominated for the National Book Award. However, Angelou's talents did not stop there. In 1971 she became the first Black woman to have a screenplay produced. *Georgia, Georgia* was well received by critics. Angelou's *I Know Why the Caged Bird Sings* was followed by other autobiographies that continued to narrate the extraordinary circumstances of her life: *Gather Together in My Name* (1975), *Singin' and Swingin' and Gettin' Merry Like Christmas* (1976), *The Heart of a Woman* (1981), *All God's Children Need Traveling Shoes* (1986), and *A Song Flung Up to Heaven* (2002). These autobiographies catalog her extraordinary life experiences and have been lauded by critics as a significant contribution to African American literature because of Angelou's profound sense of self and her environment. Her work has been compared to that of **Frederick Douglass** and **Richard Wright** in its emphasis on the effect of the external environment, including the culture and the people, on the narrator. In 1979 she wrote the script and composed the music for the television movie *I Know Why the Caged Bird Sings*.

Angelou has written several volumes of poetry, including *Just Give Me a Cool Drink of Water 'fore I Diiie* (1971), which was nominated for the Pulitzer Prize; *Oh Pray My Wings Are Gonna Fit Me Well* (1975); *And Still I Rise* (1978); *I Shall Not Be Moved* (1990); and *Phenomenal Woman: Four Poems Celebrating Women* (1994). She received a Tony Award nomination for her role as Mrs. Keckley in *Look Away* in 1973 and an Emmy nomination for her role as Nyo Boto in the *Roots* miniseries in 1977. She appeared in the film *How to Make An American Quilt* (1995) and directed *Down in the Delta* (1998). She was appointed to the

Bicentennial Commission by President Gerald Ford, and to the Commission of International Women's Year by President Jimmy Carter, and recited her poem "On the Pulse of Morning" at the inauguration of President Bill Clinton, for which she won a Grammy Award for Best Spoken Word Album in 1994. She is currently the Reynolds professor of American Studies at Wake Forest University in Winston-Salem, North Carolina, where she received a lifetime appointment in 1981. In 2002 she was elected to the National Women's Hall of Fame. She has received honorary degrees from institutions such as Boston College (1983), the University of Southern California (1989), the American Film Institute (1994), Brown University (1994), and Columbia University (2003).

Resources: Maya Angelou: *All God's Children Need Traveling Shoes* (New York: Random House, 1986); *And Still I Rise* (New York: Random House, 1978); *Gather Together in My Name* (New York: Random House, 1975); *The Heart of a Woman* (New York: Random House, 1981); *I Know Why the Caged Bird Sings* (New York: Random House, 1969); *I Shall Not Be Moved* (New York: Random House, 1990); *Just Give Me a Cool Drink of Water 'fore I Diiie* (New York: Random House, 1971); *Oh Pray My Wings Are Gonna Fit Me Well* (New York: Random House, 1975); *Phenomenal Woman: Four Poems Celebrating Women* (New York: Random House, 1994); *Singin' and Swingin' and Gettin' Merry Like Christmas* (New York: Random House, 1976); *A Song Flung Up to Heaven* (New York: Random House, 2002); Joanne M. Braxton, *Black Women Writing Autobiography: A Tradition Within a Tradition* (Philadelphia: Temple University Press, 1989); "Maya Angelou," in *Black Women in America*, ed. Darlene Clark Hine, vol. 1 (Brooklyn, NY: Carlson Publishing, 1993); "Maya Angelou," in *Notable Black American Women*, ed. Jessie Carney Smith, vol. 1 (Detroit: Gale Research, 1992); Karen O'Connor, *Contribution of Women, Literature* (Minneapolis: Dillon Press, 1984).

Lindsey Renuard

Ansa, Tina McElroy (born 1949). Novelist, journalist, essayist, and teacher. Ansa is best known for writing novels that concern the African American family and include significant spiritual and supernatural elements. She was born in Macon, Georgia, and graduated from Spelman College in 1971. The first job she took after graduating was at the *Atlanta Constitution*, where she was the first Black woman to hold a position. Over the course of eight years, she served as copy editor, makeup editor, layout editor, entertainment writer, features editor, and news reporter. Since 1982, Ansa has been a freelance journalist, newspaper columnist, and writing workshop instructor at Brunswick College, Emory University, and Spelman College. To date, she has written four novels: *Baby of the Family* (1989), *Ugly Ways* (1993), *The Hand I Fan With* (1996), and *You Know Better* (2002). In each of her novels, characters have a direct line of communication with the spiritual realm. *Baby of the Family* discusses the life of a young Black girl who (like Ansa) was born with a caul, a thin layer of skin covering her face. In Southern tradition, babies who are born with cauls are special. They have a unique connection to the supernatural world and are in many cases able to communicate with ancestral spirits. In addition to her creative writing and journalism, Ansa has written essays including "Women and the Movement" (1988), "A Shower Massage, Phone Sex and Separation" (1993), and "Confessions" (2000). Ansa resides on St. Simons Island, Georgia, with her husband, videographer Jonee Ansa. At this writing, they are working on a film adaptation of her first novel, *Baby of the Family*.

Resources: Tina McElroy Ansa: *Baby of the Family* (San Diego: Harcourt Brace Jovanovich, 1989); *The Hand I Fan With* (New York: Doubleday, 1996); *Ugly Ways* (New York: Harcourt Brace, 1993); *You Know Better* (New York: William Morrow, 2002); Rebecca Carroll, "Tina McElroy Ansa," in her *I Know What the Red Clay Looks Like: The Voices and Vision of Black Women Writers* (New York: Carol Southern, 1994); Donna Olendorf, "[Tina] Ansa," in *Contemporary Authors*, vol. 142 (Detroit: Gale Research, 1994), 11–12.

Gail L. Upchurch

Anthony, Sterling (born 1949). Novelist. Born and raised in **Detroit, Michigan**, Sterling Anthony earned a B.S. in packaging engineering from Michigan State University and an M.B.A. in marketing and finance from Roosevelt University in **Chicago, Illinois**. He worked for several Fortune 500 firms in the food, medical, and automotive industries. Next he taught courses in packaging engineering as an adjunct professor at Michigan State. Currently, he is an industry consultant specializing in packaging and marketing, and is an expert witness in product liability cases.

Anthony describes himself as "simply a longtime aficionado of the genre, who conceived a story, wrote it, and got lucky." His first, and thus far only, novel, *Cookie Cutter* (1999), centers on a serial killer of prominent African Americans whose signature is the Oreo cookies that he leaves in their hands after he has murdered them. The killer is a light-skinned, upwardly mobile, and politically ambitious African American funeral director named Isaac Shaw. It becomes clear that he is seeking to compensate for his own dissimulations about his race by violently eliminating others who have seemingly sold out to the White establishment.

The investigation of Shaw's crimes is conducted by homicide detective "Bloody Mary" Cunningham of the Detroit Police Department. Not only has Cunningham had to come to terms with what it means to be African American and female on a police force in a racially divided city with more than its share of violent crime, but she is also haunted by her memories of the major **race riots** that almost wrecked the city and cost her brother's life. Killer and cop converge in a manner that suggests that the novel is less about the causes of criminality than about the profound psychological tensions that have defined, and that continue to define, African American consciousness.

Resources: Sterling Anthony, *Cookie Cutter* (New York: Ballantine, 1999); Sybil Steinberg, "Forecasts: Fiction," *Publishers' Weekly*, Oct. 4, 1999, p. 63.

Martin Kich

Apess, William (1798–183?). Minister and autobiographer. Apess, a Pequot, wrote *A Son of the Forest* (1829, 1831) and *The Experiences of Five Christian*

Indians of the Pequod Tribe (1833). The works were published together in 1992. *The Experiences* begins with the narration of Apess's religious conversion and includes four of his converts' dictated conversion stories. The more radical *A Son* begins by claiming his descent from King Philip, king of the Pequots. Both works are conversion narratives in the tradition of the jeremiad, a work styled on the lamentations of Jeremiah, intended to create change by listing doleful complaints. This kind of narrative became a powerful tool for African American writers **Maria W. Stewart** and **David Walker**, who convinced audiences of the immorality of **slavery** by testifying to their experiences as free Blacks and testifying for their people held in slavery (*see* **Abolitionist Movement**). Using this form, Apess linked abolitionism to the struggle for Native American sovereignty, stating his claims for the humanity of Native Americans and Africans in biblical rhetoric.

Born in Colrain, Massachusetts, and abandoned by his mother, Apess was raised by an alcoholic grandmother who beat him so severely that he was taken from her and placed into service at the age of five. He converted to Christianity at age fifteen. Compelled to preach, he sought ordination from the Methodist Episcopal Church. He was refused, and later was ordained by the Protestant Methodist Church (1829–1830). Despite preaching in predominantly White churches, Apess spoke out against Whites' racism and colonialism, asking Whites if they "are the only beloved images of God?...Can you charge the Indians with robbing a nation almost of their whole continent?" Apess condemned alcohol; he died of liver problems and extreme poverty shortly after publication of his works. He wished "in the sincerity of [his] soul, that it were banished from our land," claiming Whites introduced alcohol to seduce Native Americans of both land and virtue, resulting in poverty, hunger, and child abuse. Apess preached Christianity for all, asserting that Whites should be made to pay for the sinfulness of their crimes against other nations.

Resource: William Apess, *On Our Own Ground: The Complete Writings of William Apess, a Pequot*, ed. Barry O'Connell (Amherst: University of Massachusetts Press, 1992).

Pamela Ralston

Archives and Collections: 1828–Present. African American literature is a relatively new category with a limited number of archives and collections dedicated solely to this area of study. Public, private, and academic institutions are seeking to enlarge their libraries' archives and collections to include African American history, culture, and literature. Archives and collections are important to the vitality of African American literature. They help to preserve works, documents related to writers' lives, and material connected to literary movements. To aid research and accessibility, many institutions are working to digitize parts of their archives and collections so that they can be viewed via the Internet.

Many public, private, and academic libraries have collections of African American literature. The size of the library and the needs of its users will partly determine the scope of a given library's African American literature holdings. Some small public circulating libraries may choose to purchase a selection of African American literary classics along with works by contemporary, popular African American authors. An academic institution, such as a college or university, may acquire rare first editions of novels or manuscripts for their archive or collection; however, relatively few libraries have a comprehensive archive or collection of African American literature.

The history of African American literature's archives and collections is twofold in that before academic and public archives and collections came into being, private collections existed. The first collection of circulating materials was started by and for African American men on March 20, 1828, in **Philadelphia, Pennsylvania**. It is thought that the first African American book collector, who was also an abolitionist and pamphleteer, was David Ruggles (1810–1849), who started collecting in the 1830s (Sinnette et al., 5). Other notable Black bibliophiles and collectors were **Arthur Alfonso Schomburg**, **Langston Hughes**, **W.E.B. Du Bois**, and **Carl Van Vechten**. Many of these private collections were the foundations for the academic and public archives and collections that developed during the twentieth century (Sinnette et al., 59).

Some of the prominent archives and collections of African American literature are found in large urban areas such as **Harlem, New York**, **Washington, D.C.**, **Chicago, Illinois**, and **Atlanta, Georgia**. The New York Public Library's Schomburg Center for Research in Black Culture (1972), the Moorland-Spingarn Research Center in Washington D.C. (1973), the Chicago Public Library's Vivian G. Harsh Research Collection of Afro-American History and Literature (1975), and the Atlanta-Fulton Public Library's Auburn Avenue Research Library on African-American Culture and History (1994) are some of the notable institutions with archives or collections relating to African American literature. The location of these archives and collections mirrors some of the main eras of African American literary, artistic, and political activity during the twentieth century: the **Harlem Renaissance** in New York City (1920s to mid-1930s), the **Chicago Renaissance** (1930s and 1940s), and the **Civil Rights Movement** (in which Washington, D.C., and Atlanta played crucial roles in the 1960s).

Digital collections of African American literature are developing out of major archives and collections in order to promote further research in African American studies. This recent technological development, which started in the mid-to-late 1990s, allows users to view parts of an archive or collection through the Internet. By selectively digitizing an institution's archives or collections, the institution's library may raise the public's awareness of the institution's holdings. Ironically, the arrival of digital collections has raised concern over providing too much access; that is, as more people become aware of a collection, the overall use of materials increases both physically and electronically. While the main purpose of many institutions is to have their archives and collections utilized, too much physical use can lead to the deterioration of materials.

One important digital collection is "North American Slave Narratives, Beginnings to 1920," at the University of North Carolina at Chapel Hill. This

Poster encouraging citizens to use the resources at the Schomburg Collection of the New York Public Library to learn more about African and African American history and culture, c. 1942. Courtesy of the Library of Congress.

collection of primary documents features individual and collective stories of African American slaves during the eighteenth, nineteenth, and twentieth centuries.

African American women have played an important role in the development of African American literature, and their work is available for all to read from the New York Public Library's digital collection "Digital Schomburg African American Women Writers of the 19th Century."

"Voices from the Gaps: Women Writers of Color," from the University of Minnesota, is an index that allows users to perform a variety of searches. When a writer is selected from the list, an entry appears; the entry includes a biography, criticism of the writer's work, a selected bibliography, a list of works by the author, and some related links.

The Chicago Public Library has created the digital collection, "Chicago Renaissance 1932–1950: Images and Documents from the Vivian G. Harsh Research Collection," which provides an overview of the literary accomplishments during this period. These are just a few examples of digital collections; as technology continues to improve, the number of digital collections on the Internet will most likely increase, as will the breadth of current digital collections. (*See* **Archives and Collections: Notable Collections**.)

Resources: *Auburn Avenue Research Library on African-American Culture and History*, Atlanta-Fulton Public Library, http://www.af.public.lib.ga.us/aarl/hours_directions_phones.html; *Chicago Renaissance 1932–1950: A Flowering of Afro-American Culture*, "Images and Documents from the Vivian G. Harsh Research Collection," Chicago Public Library, http://www.chipublib.org/digital/chiren/literature.html; *Digital Schomburg African American Women Writers of the 19th Century*, Schomburg Center for Research in Black Culture, New York Public Library, http://digital.nypl.org/schomburg/writers_aa19/toc.html; *The Moorland-Spingarn Research Center*, Howard University, http://www.founders.howard.edu/moorland-spingarn/default/html; *North American Slave Narratives, Beginnings to 1920*, ed. William L. Andrews (University of North Carolina, Chapel Hill, 2003), http://docsouth.unc.edu/neh/neh.html; *Schomburg Center for Research in Black Culture*, New York Public Library, http://www.nypl.org/research/sc/sc.html; Elinor Des Verney Sinnette, W. Paul Coates, and Thomas C. Battle, eds., *Black Bibliophiles and Collectors: Preservers of Black History* (Washington, DC: Howard University Press, 1990); *The Vivian G. Harsh Research Collection of Afro-American History and Literature* (2001), Carter G. Woodson Regional Library, Chicago Public Library, http://www.chipublib.org/002branches/woodson/wnharsh.html; *Voices from the Gaps: Women Writers of Color* (English Department, University of Minnesota), http://voices.cla.umn.edu/newsite/index.htm.

Heather L. Althoff

Archives and Collections: Notable Collections. There are a number of African American archives throughout the county, many of them focusing on specific authors and regions. The Northeast is home to the larger research institutions for **Black Studies**. The Schomburg Center for Research in Black Culture of the Research Libraries of the New York Public Library has more than 125,000 volumes and more than 1,000 periodicals pertaining to African and African American history, literature, and culture. It holds rare manuscripts, oral histories, playbills, letters, videotapes, and other materials. In **Washington, D.C.**, the Library of Congress has extensive holdings in Black history, literature, and culture throughout its collection. Its archival materials include Black folktales and the Daniel A. P. Murray Pamphlet Collection. Howard University's Moorland-Spingarn Research Center has the largest African American collection in a university, with more than 175,000 volumes and comprehensive and in-depth manuscript and archival collections.

The James Weldon Johnson Collection in Yale University's Beinecke Library focuses on African American writers from the **Harlem Renaissance** to the present. Among its original manuscripts are writings by **Langston Hughes**, **Zora Neal Hurston**, and **Richard Wright**. The papers of Richard Wright, **Jean Toomer** and others are also available. Suffolk University offers an African American Literature Collection in the Mildred F. Sawyer Library in **Boston, Massachusetts**, which is a combined project of Suffolk, the Boston Museum of Afro-American History, and the National Park Service's African American National Historic Site. Founded in the 1971, the collection focuses on Black fiction and poetry, with an emphasis on New England authors. In **Philadelphia, Pennsylvania**, the Charles L. Blockson Afro-American Collection at Temple University contains many first editions, among them works by **Phillis Wheatley**, Johannes Capitein, **Frances Ellen Watkins Harper**, **Paul Laurence Dunbar**, and **Carter G. Woodson**. The Samuel Holmes section of the archive centers on Philadelphia and includes **slave narratives**. Among the authors are **Olaudah Equiano**, **Sojourner Truth**, and **Frederick Douglass**. The Harris Collection at Brown University's John Hay Library in Providence, Rhode Island, covers the broad range of African American literature from the early eighteenth century to the present.

In the South, the Auburn Avenue Research Library of the Atlanta-Fulton Public Library specializes in African and African American materials, with more than 35,000 books and a large microformat collection. The University of Virginia's Electronic Text Center: African American provides online access to poems, letters, and slave narratives. The Augusta Baker Collection of African-American Children's Literature and Folklore at the University of South Carolina holds more than 1,600 children's books, papers, and illustrations. Fisk University Library in **Nashville, Tennessee**, includes special collections of Langston Hughes, **W.E.B. Du Bois**, and **Charles Chesnutt**, and Black oral histories.

The largest African American collection in the Midwest is the Vivian G. Harsh Research Collection of Afro-American History and Literature. It contains more than 70,000 books (including rare titles), 500 magazine and journal titles, and more than 5,000 microfilm reels. It has an extensive manuscript collection, including the Illinois Writers Project "Negro in Illinois" papers from the **Federal Writers' Project**, which focuses on Illinois African American history and culture from 1779 to 1942 and is accessible through an online index. The University of Minnesota Libraries hosts a large

Black literature archive in its Givens Collection. There are approximately 8,000 items covering novels, plays, short stories, and essays by African American authors, as well as author biographies and literary criticism. One section of the archive emphasizes the history of Black literature and includes correspondence, playbills, photographs, and newspaper clippings documenting eras such as the Harlem Renaissance and the **Black Arts Movement**. The Wisconsin Historical Society houses an African American newspapers and periodicals collection and has digitized all issues of the nineteenth-century *Freedman's Journal*, which is freely accessible via the Internet.

West of the Mississippi, the Robert James Terry Library at Texas Southern University in Houston has more than 22,000 items in the Heartman Collection, including books, pamphlets, journals, and slave narratives. The Bancroft Library at the University of California, Berkeley, has thousands of books, manuscripts, and correspondence ranging from the 1790s to the present in its African American Writers Collection, and a range of sources comprising its African Americans in California collection. One of the larger public library collections on the West Coast is at the Douglass-Truth branch of the Seattle Public Library. More than 9,000 books, periodicals, videos, clippings, picture files, and books are available in its African American collection. In **Los Angeles, California**, the Clayton Library of the Western Black States Research and Cultural Center has a large literature, film, music, and photograph collection, and is in the process of cataloging its materials at this writing.

Resources: *African-American Newspapers and Periodicals*, Wisconsin Historical Society, http://www.wisconsinhistory.org/libraryarchives/aanp; *African Americans in California*, Bancroft Library, University of California, http://bancroft.berkeley.edu/reference/africanamerican; *American Slave Narratives: An Online Anthology*, http://xroads.virginia.edu/~HYPER/wpa/wpahome.html; *Augusta Baker Collection of African-American Children's Literature and Folklore*, Dept. of Rare Books and Special Collections, University of South Carolina, http://www.sc.edu/library/spcoll/kidlit/baker.htm; *Charles L. Blockson Afro-American Collection*, ed. Aslaku Berhanu, Temple University, http://www.library.temple.edu/blockson/speccol.htm; *Collection of African American Literature*, Sawyer Library, Suffolk University, http://www.suffolk.edu/sawlib/speccoll/SpeccollAfroam.htm; *Collection of American Literature: The James Weldon Johnson Collection*, ed. Patricia C. Willis, Beinecke Library, Yale University, http://www.library.yale.edu/beinecke/ycaljwj.htm; Douglass-Truth Branch, Seattle Public Library, http://www.spl.org/default.asp?pageID=branch_open&branchID=9?; *Electronic Text Center: African American*, University of Virginia Library, http://etext.lib.virginia.edu/subjects/African-American.html; Kenneth Estell, ed., *African American Information Directory 1998–1999* (Detroit: Gale, 1998); *Givens Collection of African American Literature*, University of Minnesota Library, http://special.lib.umn.edu/rare/givens/aboutgivens.html; *Harris Collection of Poetry and Plays: African American Literature*, John Hay Library, Brown University, http://www.brown.edu/Facilities/University_Library/collections/harris/Harris.AALit.html; Ernest Kaiser, "Library Holdings on African Americans," in *Handbook of Black Librarianship*, ed. E. J. Josey and Marva L. DeLoach (Lanham, MD: Scarecrow, 2000), 247–276; Special Collections, Franklin

Library, Fisk University, http://www.fisk.edu/index.asp?cat=7&pid=257; Special Collections, Robert James Terry Library, Texas Southern University, http://www.tsu.edu/about/library/special.asp; Western Black States Research and Cultural Center, Clayton Library, http://www.wsbrec.org/index.html.

Maureen A. Kelly

Armstrong, William H[oward] (1914–1999). Novelist. The author of a number of highly regarded **novels** for young adults, Armstrong was born in Lexington, Virginia, and grew up on a nearby farm. After several traumatic events in his childhood left him with a stutter, he received a dramatic boost in his self-esteem when one of his teachers selected one of his essays for a prize. This event would be a watershed in his life, convincing him of the immeasurable value of both teaching and writing. Armstrong's parents were fairly strict Presbyterians, and he attended high school at Augusta Military Academy. As a teacher, he would emphasize the merits of bringing a disciplined attitude to one's studies, and in the study guides that were his first published books and that he continued to produce throughout his career, he would more formally promote the efficacy of this approach to academic success. A graduate of Hampden-Sydney College, Armstrong did graduate work at the University of Virginia. He taught history at the Kent School for fifty-two years.

Sounder (1969) is the novel for which Armstrong will be most remembered. The title character is a coon dog that demonstrates its remarkable loyalty to the family of poor African American sharecroppers who own him. Although the race of the characters is significant, the ramifications of their material poverty and the counterbalance in their rich sense of family have given the story an almost universal appeal. Since its initial publication, *Sounder* has been translated into almost thirty languages. For the novel, Armstrong received many awards—most notably, the John Newbery Medal from American Library Association, the Lewis Carroll Book Shelf Award, the Mark Twain Award from the Missouri Association of School Librarians, and the Nene Award from the Hawaii Association of School Librarians and Hawaii Library Association. In addition, the film adaptation of the novel was nominated for an Academy Award. The novel and its sequel, *Sour Land* (1971), were loosely based on the stories shared by an elderly African American teacher who worked part-time on the farm on which Armstrong grew up.

Resources: William H. Armstrong: *Barefoot in the Grass: The Story of Grandma Moses* (Garden City, NY: Doubleday, 1970); *The Education of Abraham Lincoln* (New York: Coward, McCann, and Geoghegan, 1974); *Hadassah: Esther the Orphan Queen* (Garden City, NY: Doubleday, 1972); *Joanna's Miracle* (Nashville, TN: Broadman, 1977); *The MacLeod Place* (New York: Coward, McCann, and Geoghegan, 1972); *The Mills of God* (Garden City, NY: Doubleday, 1973); *My Animals* (Garden City, NY: Doubleday, 1974); *Sounder* (New York: Harper & Row, 1969); *Sour Land* (New York: Harper & Row, 1971); *The Tale of Tawny and Dingo* (New York: Harper & Row, 1979); *Through Troubled Waters* (New York: Harper & Row, 1957); Michelle Latimer Farmer, "The Black Experience and the Human Experience: The Two *Sounder* Texts," in *The Antic Art: Enhancing*

Children's Literary Experiences Through Film and Video, ed. Lucy Rollin (Fort Atkinson, WI: Highsmith, 1993), 93–109; Nancy Huse, "*Sounder* and Its Readers: Learning to Observe," *Children's Literature Association Quarterly* 12 (Summer 1987), 66–69; Charles S. Rutherford, "A New Dog with an Old Trick: Archetypal Patterns in *Sounder*," in *Movies as Artifacts: Cultural Criticism of Popular Film*, ed. Michael T. Marsden, John G. Nachbar, and Sam L. Grogg, Jr. (Chicago: Nelson-Hall, 1982), 223–229.

Martin Kich

Asim, Jabari (born 1962). Editor, critic, poet, and playwright. Asim draws on his varied writing and life experiences to craft views on wide-ranging issues as a senior editor for the *Washington Post Book World* and a syndicated columnist for the *Washington Post* Writers Group. He says, "I'm fond of looking backward for guidance on how to move forward on various social issues from parenting to police brutality" ("Jabari Asim"). Prior to joining the *Post*, Asim worked for the *St. Louis Post-Dispatch* as a book editor, copy editor of the editorial and commentary pages, and arts editor of the weekend section. He grew up and attended schools in **St. Louis, Missouri**, and he earned a degree from Northwestern University.

Asim is an accomplished writer whose works have appeared in a variety of publications, including fiction and poetry in the anthology *In the Tradition: An Anthology of Young Black Writers* (1992), edited by **Kevin Powell** and **Ras Baraka**, and a short story, "Two Fools," in the anthology *Brotherman: The Odyssey of Black Men in America* (1996), edited by Herb Boyd and Robert Allen. His poems and a play, *Peace, Dog*, were published in *Soulfires: Young Black Men on Love and Violence* (1996), edited by Daniel J. Wideman and Rohan B. Preston. The *Los Angeles Times Book Review* and *Step into a World: A Global Anthology of the New Black Literature* (2000), edited by Kevin Powell, have featured his reviews and cultural criticism. He has published *The Road to Freedom* (2000), a novel for young adults, and *Not Guilty: Twelve Black Men Speak Out on Law, Justice and Life* (2001), an essay collection. His work as a poet and cultural critic has afforded him opportunities to participate in the video series *Furious Flower: A Revolution in African American Poetry 1960–95* (1998) and to serve as a panelist for the "A World of Words: From the Midwest to Moscow," at the Langston Hughes Let America Be America Again conference at the University of Kansas (2002).

Resources: Jabari Asim: *Not Guilty: Twelve Black Men Speak Out on Law, Justice and Life* (New York: Amistad, 2001); *The Road to Freedom* (New York: Glencoe/McGraw Hill, 2001); Joanne V. Gabbin, ed., *The Furious Flowering of African American Poetry* (Charlottesville, VA: University Press of Virginia, 1999); Derrick I. M. Gilbert, ed., *Catch the Fire!!!: A Cross-Generational Anthology of Contemporary African-American Poetry* (New York: Riverhead, 1998); "Jabari Asim," *The Washington Post Writers Group*, http://www.postwritersgroup.com/asim.htm.

Rhondda R. Thomas

Assimilation. Assimilation is the integration of a minority group into the broader society they are a part of. The sociologist Milton M. Gordon has characterized assimilation as a seven-stage process: acculturation, structural assimilation, amalgamation, the development of a sense of "peoplehood" based on the host society, the disappearance of prejudice and discrimination, and absence of civic conflict. The process of assimilation for the African American community has been one fraught with tension for more than 250 years. African Americans were first brought to the United States unwillingly, as slaves, and were given few opportunities to assimilate voluntarily into White society. From the outset, the status of slaves in the new land was clear. They were expected to accommodate their White masters, not assimilate into their lives in any meaningful manner.

After the **Civil War**, as Blacks migrated north and entered the workforce, greater levels of assimilation began to occur. Blacks came to realize that perhaps the American dream might be available to them, through perseverance and hard work. Yet assimilation was neither easy nor immediate. Although Blacks were now free, segregation throughout the country, and particularly in **the South**, relegated them to second-class citizenry.

With the 1960s came the explosion of the **Civil Rights Movement** and the rise of **Black Nationalism**. It was during this time that the United States began to evolve into a multicultural environment in which the diversity of the country's population appeared. Multiculturalism emerged as a way of celebrating and preserving diversity—embracing ethnic and racial differences—emphasizing distinct cultural traits. Multiculturalism, in many ways, challenged the idea of the United States as a cohesive nation and melting pot. During the 1970s and 1980s, multiculturalism took even more definitive shape, becoming incorporated into academic programs and textbooks to reflect the changing and diverse landscape of the United States. Multiculturalism also became apparent in popular culture, with minorities appearing on television shows such as *Good Times*, *The Jeffersons*, and *CHiPS*. It was also during this time that **Alex Haley**'s novel *Roots* was adapted into a six-part miniseries that followed several generations of a **Black family** from slavery onward. Multiculturalism put forward the notion that it was acceptable to be different and challenged assimilation as an ideal toward which all Americans needed to strive.

Today, assimilation continues to take place, but multiculturalism is also alive and well. Although controversial, **affirmative action** has emerged as another form of assimilation. Through affirmative action, employers and others consciously choose qualified people who have traditionally been marginalized in the realms of employment and education. Despite its long history, assimilation can have negative implications, because a minority culture's distinctive features can be diminished as the minority is absorbed into the majority. Nonetheless, it remains the goal of many minorities within the United States.

Assimilation has often been the subject of literature. **Lorraine Hansberry**'s play *A Raisin in the Sun* is the story of the Youngers, a disintegrating Black family on Chicago's South Side. It is a Black family trying to achieve the American dream, with many social forces working against them. The family is about to receive a $10,000 insurance check, and each has hopes for the money—hopes of rising above their circumstances. As the play unfolds, each family member reveals his or her dream for how the money should be spent—but the commonality in their hopes is providing a home for the family and becoming an American success story. *A Raisin in the Sun* depicts a Black family's hopes for assimilation and how, sometimes, with those hopes comes danger.

Nella Larsen's novel *Passing* (1929) is well known for its treatment of issues surrounding assimilation. This, the second of the two novels Larsen wrote, tells the story of Irene Redfield and Clare Kendry, two Black women who are light enough to pass as White (*see* **Passing**). Clare chooses to pass, and marries a racist White man who is ignorant of her Black heritage. Irene chooses to live in Harlem, and commits herself to racial uplift, eventually marrying a Black doctor. The narrative focuses on these two childhood friends reconnecting later in life, and what follows as Irene becomes increasingly intrigued by Clare's life. In the end, the truth about her ancestry is revealed to Clare's husband, and she dies after falling from a window. It is the ambiguous nature of this ending that has made *Passing* such a renowned work of literature, because the reader is not sure whether Irene pushed Clare out of the window or Clare committed suicide. The novel reflects the historical realities of the 1920s and 1930s, as well as the complexities inherent in assimilation.

Other novels that deal with assimilation include Fannie Hurst's *Imitation of Life*, **Ralph Ellison**'s *Invisible Man*, **Charles Chesnutt**'s *The House Behind the Cedars*, **Langston Hughes**'s *Not Without Laughter*, and **James Baldwin**'s *Another Country*. In his nonfiction writing, Baldwin also extensively examines relationships between Whites and Blacks in the United States and perplexing questions surrounding the topic of assimilation. (*See* **Multicultural Theory**.)

Resources: James Baldwin: *Another Country* (New York: Dial, 1962); *The Price of the Ticket: Collected Nonfiction, 1948–1985* (New York: St. Martin's Press, 1985); Charles Chesnutt, *The House Behind the Cedars*, ed. Judith Jackson Fossett (New York: Modern Library, 2003); Gerald Early, ed., *Lure and Loathing: Essays on Race, Identity, and the Ambivalence of Assimilation* (New York: Penguin, 1993); M. Giulia Fabi, *Passing and the Rise of the African American Novel* (Urbana: University of Illinois Press, 2001); Milton M. Gordon, *Assimilation in American Life: The Role of Race, Religion, and National Origins* (New York: Oxford University Press, 1964); Langston Hughes, *Not Without Laugher* (1930; repr. New York: Scribner's, 1995); Hope Landrine and Elizabeth Klonoff, *African American Acculturation: Deconstructing Race and Reviving Culture* (Thousand Oaks, CA: Sage, 1996); Nella Larsen, *Passing* (New York: Modern Library, 2000); Beverly Tatum: *Assimilation Blues: Black Families in a White Community* (New York: Basic Books, 1999); *Why Are All the Black Kids Sitting Together in the Cafeteria?* (New York: Basic Books, 2003); Gayle Freda Wald, *Crossing the Line: Racial Passing in Twentieth-century U.S. Literature and Culture* (Durham, NC: Duke University Press, 2000).

Roxane Gay

Atkins, Russell (born 1926). Poet, dramatist, composer, and theorist. Russell Atkins is among the most fearlessly experimental and intellectually challenging writers of American literature published since **World War II**. His prolific output of poetry, drama, and music explores the overlap and friction between linguistic, visual, aural, and dramatic modes of expression, making him a significant forerunner of contemporary interest in the possibilities of multimedia art. Atkins was one of the first African American poets to employ the formal resources of aural, concrete, and visual poetry in his work, and his plays, which he prefers to describe as "poetry-dramas" or "poems-in-play-form," use highly artificial verse forms and staging techniques to engage with the volatile social content one would expect to find in works with titles like *The Abortionist* (1954) and *The Exoneration* (1973). In the field of music composition, Atkins has most notably expounded an influential theory of "psychovisualism," which argues for a conception of music as a structured cognitive space that is best comprehended through an accompanying visual form rather than merely received and heard as music.

Born and raised in Cleveland, Ohio, Atkins founded the little magazine *Free Lance* with Caspar L. Jordan in 1950 and oversaw its publication until the magazine folded in 1980. According to Ronald Henry High, *Free Lance* "is probably the oldest Black-owned literary magazine" (24), yet it published many White writers and characterized itself as a forum for avant-garde poetry and prose. Atkins has also been affiliated with the Iowa Writers Workshop and the Karamu Theatre in Cleveland.

The emphasis in Atkins's work on what he calls "conspicuous technique" is at odds with many received ideas about African American literature's mandate to communicate the lessons of historical experience to its audience. However, his commitment to undermining received forms of expression and fostering intellectual innovation has inspired critic Aldon Lynn Nielsen to compare his work's potential literary importance to the significance of Anthony Braxton's work in **jazz** and even of Jacques Derrida's work in philosophy.

Resources: Russell Atkins: *Here in The* (Cleveland, OH: Poetry Center of Cleveland State University, 1976); *Heretofore* (London: Breman, 1968); *Phenomena* (Wilberforce, OH: Free Lance Poets and Prose Workshop, 1961); "Selected Poems and Prose 1950–1991," ed. Julie Patton, *Crayon* 2 (1999), 5–43; *Two by Atkins: The Abortionist and The Corpse* (Cleveland, OH: Free Lance Press, 1963); *Whichever* (Cleveland, OH: Free Lance Press, 1978); Ronald Henry High, "Russell Atkins," in *Afro American Poets Since 1955*, ed. Trudier Harris and Thadious M. Davis (Detroit: Gale Research, 1985), 24–32; Aldon Lynn Nielsen: *Black Chant: Languages of African-American Postmodernism* (Cambridge: Cambridge University Press, 1997); "Black Deconstruction: Russell Atkins and the Reconstruction of African-American Criticism," *Diacritics* 26, no. 3–4 (1996), 86–103.

David Cuthbert

Atlanta, Georgia. Atlanta began as a village, but because of the railroad, became a bustling city in the middle of the nineteenth century. "South of the North, yet north of the South, lies the city of a Hundred Hills, peering out from the shadows of the past into the promise of the future," **W.E.B. Du Bois** wrote of Atlanta in his 1903 classic *The Souls of Black Folk* (262). Indeed, ever since Du Bois published his book, Atlanta's wealth of African American heritage has made it an urban center for Blacks in **the South**. Those raised, educated, and employed in Atlanta have played integral roles in its Black literary tradition, chronicling such historical moments as the **Civil Rights Movement** and representing such locations as Auburn Avenue (once one of the richest African American neighborhoods) and the Atlanta University Center. Black Atlantans have produced intellectual, creative, religious, and political work that reflects and sustains African American culture.

Two of Atlanta's most prominent literary figures are Du Bois and **James Weldon Johnson**, who cowrote "Lift Ev'ry Voice and Sing" in 1900 and published *The Autobiography of an Ex-Colored Man* in 1912. Johnson attended Atlanta University and served on the Atlanta chapter and national board of the **NAACP**. He also published several volumes of prose and poetry. As a sociology professor at Atlanta University from 1897 to 1910, Du Bois investigated the effects of racism. At the Paris Exposition in 1900, Du Bois presented photographs and documents on the condition of the Negro in Georgia, including Black Codes (state laws regarding race), from 1732 to 1899. After founding the Niagara Movement, which merged with the NAACP in 1909, and editing *The Crisis*, Du Bois returned to Atlanta University. From 1934 to 1944, he edited the *Encyclopedia of the Negro*, founded **Phylon**: *The Atlanta University Review of Race and Culture*, and published *Black Reconstruction* and *Dusk of Dawn*. Du Bois's major intellectual adversary, **Booker T. Washington**, also gained prominence from experience in Atlanta. The writings of both were included in **The Voice of the Negro**, a journal published in Atlanta from 1904 until 1906. At the Atlanta Exposition in 1895, Washington stated that Blacks should aim for economic success through education and industrial training instead of demands for equal rights. This "Atlanta Compromise," detailed in Washington's autobiographical narrative *Up from Slavery*, served as a major point of contention with Du Bois, who believed that racist conditions could be challenged and that a **"Talented Tenth"** of African Americans would lead other African Americans forward.

Holding true to Du Bois's view, Atlanta has had its share of talented writers throughout the nineteenth and twentieth centuries. Atlanta University student **Octavia V. Rogers Albert** set the stage for female authors with *The House of Bondage; or, Charlotte Brooks and Other Slaves* in 1890. **Georgia Douglas Johnson**, an Atlanta native and **Harlem Renaissance** poet, published poetry in **Opportunity** and *The Crisis* magazines. Her four books, including *The Heart of a Woman* (1918) and *Bronze* (1922), portray the experiences of Black women in a literary period dominated by males. Other Atlantans affiliated with New York's cultural and literary scene are civil rights activist **Walter White** (also an Atlanta University graduate), author of *The Fire in the Flint* (1924) and *Flight* (1926) and secretary of the NAACP from 1931 to 1955, and poet and fiction author Welborn V. Jenkins, whose work appeared in *The Crisis*. Poet **William Stanley Braithwaite** taught at Atlanta University from 1935 to 1945 and published several volumes of formal lyric poetry in **Harlem, New York**.

51

The extensive list of Atlanta natives who found national success includes **Abram Hill**, playwright and cofounder of the American Negro Theatre; essayist, novelist, and poet **Clarence Major**; and **Black Arts Movement** notable **Hoyt Fuller**, who established the **OBAC** Writers' Workshop in Chicago. After editing *Negro Digest* (later renamed *Black World*)—a primary magazine of the Black Arts Movement—Fuller returned to Atlanta to edit the international Black journal *First World*.

Literary reception in Atlanta was bolstered by Black media including the *Atlanta Daily World*, the city's oldest continuously published Black newspaper, founded in 1928. They also included the *Atlanta Independent*, which articulated concerns of Black Atlanta until its publication ended in 1933 (*see* **Newspapers**). Black media recorded such events as the 1906 **race riot**, which was provoked by propaganda concerning Black men menacing White women and resulted in attacks on African Americans by approximately 10,000 White men (Grant; Keating). The riot revealed tremendous racial conflict that would escalate with the resurgence of the Ku Klux Klan in the 1920s and antiintegration laws that continued through the 1960s. Throughout these trials, the city's Black residents maintained hope and promise, as is evident in their entertainment, business success, education, and literature. Annie L. McPheeter, the first Black Atlanta public librarian, indexed Atlanta newspapers in volumes of *Negro Progress in Atlanta, Georgia*. Atlanta native Herman "Skip" Mason, Jr., accentuates the city's Black culture in several books, including *African-American Entertainment in Atlanta* and *Black Atlanta in the Roaring Twenties*. Before becoming executive editor of *Ebony* magazine, Lerone Bennett, Jr., was a journalist for the *Atlanta Daily World*. The Morehouse graduate has since written *Before the Mayflower: A History of Black America*.

Morehouse, Spelman, and Morris Brown colleges, Clark Atlanta University (formerly Clark University and Atlanta University), and the Interdenominational Theological Center have been responsible for much of Atlanta's cultural production since the late nineteenth century. Their students and faculty have produced works in all genres of literature, from Civil Rights Movement memoirs to novels to plays.

Hugh Gloster, past president of Morehouse and contributing editor of *Phylon*, was educated at Morehouse and Atlanta University. Gloster wrote *Negro Voices in American Fiction* and *The Negro Novel in America* in 1948. Morehouse also produced and employed renowned ministers who published key cultural and theological texts. Poet/minister William Holmes Borders, who wrote *Thunderbolts* in 1942, attended Morehouse, as did poet/minister **Benjamin Brawley**. Brawley served on Morehouse's faculty and wrote several histories of the American Negro, as well as *History of Morehouse College* (1917). His volumes of poetry include *The Desire of the Moth for the Star* (1906) and *The Dawn and Other Poems* (1911). **Howard Thurman**, one of **Martin Luther King, Jr.**'s role models, inspired rhetoric of the Civil Rights Movement and twenty books. Thurman became active in the antilynching movement as a Morehouse student and later taught religion both there and at Spelman. **Benjamin E. Mays**, who mentored

King, served as president of Morehouse from 1940 to 1967. His **autobiography**, *Born to Rebel* (1971) is still in print.

In the tradition of these figures, King graduated from Morehouse College and gained prominence as a minister, orator, organizer, and essayist. His books include *Stride Toward Freedom* (1958) and *Why We Can't Wait* (1964). Since his death in 1968, King's family has kept his struggle for nonviolent racial progress alive through literature. Coretta Scott King authored *My Life with Martin Luther King, Jr.*, in 1969. King's father, Atlanta minister Martin Luther King, Sr., chronicled his own life in *Daddy King* (1980). King's children have also published speeches and memoirs. King's colleagues who have documented the civil rights struggle in autobiographies include former Southern Christian Leadership Conference president **Ralph David Abernathy** (*And the Walls Came Tumbling Down*) and Georgia congressman and former SNCC chairman John Lewis (*Walking with the Wind*). NAACP leader **Julian Bond** authored *A Time to Speak, a Time to Act* (1972), and Atlanta native Vernon E. Jordan, Jr., former president of the National Urban League, published his memoir, *Vernon Can Read!*, in 2001.

Spelman alumnae include **Tina McElroy Ansa**, known for her novels set in the fictional town of Mulberry, Georgia. Ansa began her career as a writer and editor at the *Atlanta Constitution*. Black feminist author and Spelman alumna and professor Beverly Guy-Sheftall founded *Sage: A Scholarly Journal on Black Women* and wrote *Gender Talk* with Johnetta B. Cole. **Pearl Cleage**, whose best-seller *What Looks like Crazy on an Ordinary Day* and subsequent novels have been received with much acclaim, is also a Spelman alumna and professor. Cleage worked in Atlanta media before writing several plays, including *Blues for an Alabama Sky* (1999). Her *Flyin' West*, which premiered in Atlanta in 1992, was one of the most frequently produced plays in America from 1992 to 1993. Cleage founded and edited *Catalyst* in 1986. The magazine's first issue featured essays and poetry by **bell hooks**, **June Jordan**, **Nikki Giovanni**, and **Audre Lorde**.

Donna Akiba Harper, Professor of English and Dean of Undergraduate Studies at Spelman, is a well-known editor and scholar of **Langston Hughes**'s writing, including his Jesse B. Simple stories.

In addition to inspiring the work of Atlanta residents, Atlanta's history has inspired the work of nationally renowned Black writers. **James Baldwin**'s *Evidence of Things Not Seen* (1986) and **Toni Cade Bambara**'s *Those Bones Are Not My Child* (1999) are based on the Atlanta child murders (1979–1981). More than forty African American children were killed before Wayne Williams, a Black man, was convicted. The murders sparked political and racial controversy, and both texts question its resolution with the suspect's arrest. Since Bambara's death in 1995, Tayari Jones has followed Bambara's lead, so to speak, with *Leaving Atlanta* (2002), a novel based on the child murders. In *The Condemnation of Little B* (2002), former **Black Panther Party** leader **Elaine Brown** (now an Atlanta resident) discusses racial and economic implications in the trial of Michael "Little B" Lewis, who was convicted of murder in Atlanta and sentenced to life in jail at the age of fourteen. A popular fictional account of Atlanta history, Alice Randall's *The Wind Done Gone*, revisits Margaret Mitchell's *Gone with the Wind*. Georgia-born **Raymond Andrews** published regional fiction and wrote a memoir, *Once upon a Time in Atlanta*, before his death in 1991. Novelist **Travis Hunter**, author of *The Hearts of Men, Married But Still Looking,* and *Trouble Man*, resides in Atlanta, as does poet **Joette Harland Watts** (Kupenda Auset).

Through the literature of Atlantans, themes of African American life have been revealed, challenged, and celebrated. The city's annual National Black Arts Festival, Black bookstores, and Black publishing companies circulate and produce work that continues that of Atlanta University's earliest graduates and professors. The Auburn Avenue Research Library maintains records of Black Atlanta history. *EightRock*, a magazine of music, dance, film, and literature, was printed in Atlanta from 1990 to 1994. Magazines currently produced in the city include *Upscale* (fashion, society, and entertainment), *Venus* (which highlights the Black gay lifestyle), *Atlanta Tribune: The Magazine,* and *Booking Matters*. As Atlanta builds upon the progress generated in recent years by the late mayor Maynard Jackson, Jr., its literature will continue, as Du Bois foresaw, to document past and future growth.

Resources: George Cantor, *Historic Black Landmarks* (Detroit: Visible Ink, 1991); W.E.B. Du Bois, *The Souls of Black Folk,* in *Three Negro Classics* (New York: Avon Books, 1965); Mamie Marie Booth Foster, comp., *Southern Black Creative Writers, 1829–1953* (Westport, CT: Greenwood Press, 1988); Donald L. Grant, *The Way It Was in the South: The Black Experience in Georgia* (New York: Birch Lane Press, 1930); Larry Keating, *Atlanta: Race, Class, and Urban Expansion* (Philadelphia: Temple University Press, 2001); Deidre Mullane, ed., *Crossing the Danger Water: Three Hundred Years of African-American Writing* (New York: Anchor, 1993).

Janaka N. Bowman

Attaway, William (1911–1986). Novelist. Though he has faded almost completely from the literary memory of the twentieth century, William Attaway was an active and militant Communist writer who remained loyal to **Marxism** even at the height of the **Cold War**. Yet Attaway's fiction, especially his major novel, *Blood on the Forge* (1941), did not comply with the ideological directives of the Communist Party, and the book received mixed reviews from left-wing literary critics (Foley).

Attaway was born in Mississippi, but his family moved to **Chicago, Illinois**, when he was five. His father, William S. Attaway, was a medical doctor, and his mother, Florence P. Attaway, was a teacher. His relationship with his parents was never easy, and after graduating from high school, Attaway refused to attend the University of Illinois Medical School, which his parents had chosen for the continuation of his studies. He held a variety of jobs while he traveled throughout the United States, but he finally enrolled at the University of Illinois in 1933. While studying there, he wrote his first literary work, a play called *Carnival*. The years at the University of Illinois were also marked by his encounter with **Richard Wright** and the South Side Writers Club, as well as by his participation in the **Federal Writers Project**. In 1936, he graduated, and his short story "Tale of the Blackamoor" was published in *Challenge*.

Subsequently, Attaway moved to New York City, where he worked as a labor organizer and as an actor; he performed in the touring production of *You Can't Take It with You*, by Moss Hart and George S. Kaufman (Draper; Odom). He then moved to **Philadelphia, Pennsylvania**, where he completed his first novel, *Let Me Breathe Thunder* (1939), partially modeled on Steinbeck's *Of Mice and Men*. The novel concerns the relationship between two White migrant workers and a Mexican American youth. Attaway secured a two-year grant from the Julius Rosenwald Foundation and worked full-time on his next novel, *Blood on the Forge*. Its plot focuses on the plight of Southern African American workers in the Pennsylvania steel strikes of 1919, but the novel also investigates the tensions between White and Black workers, pessimistically envisaging no unity between the two working-class groups. As Alan Wald has pointed out, some ideas in the novel, which was published just before the entrance of the United States into **World War II**, clashed with the Communist Party's call for a popular front against fascism. The *Daily Worker* condemned what it characterized as the novel's divisive message.

Attaway apparently continued his political militancy. For example, Wald points to evidence suggesting that Attaway helped to hide Black Communist Party leaders who went underground during the Cold War. However, Attaway's literary career declined, and he turned to writing screenplays, radio scripts, teleplays, and music, including songs that Harry Belafonte recorded (Cox). His songs are published in *Calypso Song Book* (1957) and *Hear America Singing* (1967). Belafonte wrote an introduction to the latter. After living in Barbados for ten years (1966–1976), Attaway returned to the United States, where he died of cancer.

Resources: William Attaway: *Blood on the Forge* (Garden City, NY: Doubleday, Doran, 1941); *Calypso Song Book* (New York: McGraw-Hill, 1957); *Hear America Singing* (New York: Lion Press, 1967); *Let Me Breathe Thunder* (Garden City, NY: Doubleday, Doran, 1939; repr. Chatham, NJ: Chatham House Bookseller, 1969); James L. Cox, *Mississippi Almanac 1997–1998* (Yazoo City, MS: Computer Search & Research, 1997), 107; James P. Draper, ed., *Black Literature Criticism*, vol. 1 (Detroit: Gale Research, 1992), 56–74; Barbara Foley, *Radical Representations: Politics and Form in U.S. Proletarian Fiction, 1929–1941* (Durham, NC: Duke University Press, 1993); William J. Maxwell, *New Negro, Old Left: African American Writing and Communism Between the Wars* (New York: Columbia University Press, 1999); Ashley Shrez Odom, "William Attaway," *Mississippi Writers and Musicians Project*, http://www.shs.starkville .k12.ms.us/mswm/MSWritersAndMusicians/writers/AttawayWilliam/WilliamAttaway .html; Alan Wald, *Exiles from a Future Time: The Forging of the Mid-Twentieth-Century Literary Left* (Chapel Hill: University of North Carolina Press, 2002).

Luca Prono

Aubert, Alvin (born 1930). Poet, playwright, short story writer, editor, publisher, literary critic, and educator. A native of Louisiana, Aubert has established himself as an innovative poet, often centering his work on his childhood and adolescence in Louisiana. As the founder and editor of a literary journal, he has provided an avenue for many scholars and creative writers to contribute to African American literature and criticism. In 1975, while teaching at the State University of New York at Fredonia, Aubert founded *Obsidian: Black Literature in Review*, which moved to Wayne State University in 1979. The first issue included contributions by poet **Lorenzo Thomas**, novelist **Leon Forrest**, and literary critic **Houston A. Baker, Jr.** Aubert received support from editorial board members Kofi Awooner, **Ernest J. Gaines**, Blyden Jackson**, J. Saunders Redding**, and **Darwin T. Turner**. He was awarded an Editor's Fellowship grant in 1979 by the Coordinating Council of Literary Magazines for its publication. After it ceased publication in 1982, the journal was reissued as *Obsidian II* in 1986, housed at North Carolina State University, where it is presently *Obsidian III: Literature in the African Diaspora*.

As a poet, Aubert rejected the idea of artistic compromise and regarded the poet as one belonging and committed to poetry (Vander, 31). Although he was criticized in the 1970s for not responding to the **Black Arts Movement**, his poetry is nevertheless distinguished by his attention to craft and his focus on personal experiences and reflections on specific events, rich in the use of Louisiana folk culture and diction. His poetry collections include *Against the Blues* (1972); *Feeling Through* (1975); *South Louisiana: New and Selected Poems* (1985); *If Winter Come: Collected Poems 1967–1992* (1994); and *Harlem Wrestler, and Other Poems* (1995). In 2004, Aubert received the **Furious Flower** Poetry Lifetime Achievement Award, acknowledging him as a chronicler and a pioneer of the Black literary experience.

Resources: Alvin Aubert: *Against the Blues: Poems* (Detroit: Broadside Press, 1972); *Harlem Wrestler; and Other Poems* (East Lansing: Michigan State University Press, 1995); *If Winter Comes: Collected Poems 1967–1992* (Pittsburgh, PA: Carnegie Mellon University Press, 1994); *South Louisiana: New and Selected Poems* (New Orleans, LA: Lunchroom Press, 1985); Tom Dent, "Alvin Aubert: *South Louisiana: New and Selected Poems*," *Black American Literature Forum* 22, no. 1 (Spring 1988), 127–129; Norman Harris, "Alvin Aubert," in *Dictionary of Literary Biography*, vol. 41, *Afro-American Poets Since 1955*, ed. Trudier Harris and Thadious M. Davis (Detroit: Gale, 1985), 32–36; Herbert Woodward Martin, "Alvin Aubert: *South Louisiana: New and Selected Poems*," *Black American Literature Forum* 21, no. 3 (Fall 1987), 343–348; R. Goldman Vander, "Aubert, Alvin," in *Oxford Companion to African American Literature*, ed. William L. Andrews, Frances Smith Foster, and Trudier Harris (New York: Oxford University Press, 1997), 31; Jerry W. Ward, Jr., "Alvin Aubert: Literature, History, Ethnicity," *Xavier Review* 7, no. 2 (1987), 1–12.

Loretta G. Woodard

Auset, Kupenda. *See* **Harland-Watts, Joette.**

Austin, Doris Jean (1949–1994). Essayist and novelist. In her work, Austin explored the psychological and social dynamics of the class divide between rich and poor in the African American community.

Austin was born in Mobile, Alabama, in 1949, and grew up in Jersey City, New Jersey, in a close, multigenerational household. She began writing in high school and later was a member of the Harlem Writer's Guild, a Mac-Dowell Colony fellow, and a recipient of the DeWitt Wallace/Reader's Digest Award for Literary Excellence. Austin wrote one novel, *After the Garden*, which was published in 1987. She also wrote short stories; edited an anthology of short stories, *Streetlights*, which was published in 1996; and wrote articles for *Essence* magazine and the **Amsterdam News**.

Austin's most significant work, *After the Garden*, examines broader issues of conflicts between class and religion within the context of a relationship between two individuals and their families. Class conflict between the bourgeoisie and the working class is presented symbolically as a distinction between "gardens" and "weeds," and geographically in the settings of the middle class, suburban Astor Place, and the working-class, urban Kearney Avenue. The protagonist in this coming-of-age story is Elzina, a young woman raised by her strict, middle-class, puritanical grandmother. Jesse, a popular classmate from a socially liberal, working-class family that lives on Kearney Avenue, impregnates Elzina while they are in high school. Despite serious differences in worldview and life experience, the pair marries. Elzina must reconcile the overt disapproval of her grandmother with her love for Jesse. Jesse struggles with unemployment and is eventually convicted of armed robbery, for which he receives a harsh sentence. Her grandmother dies, and Elzina develops poor health; eventually she moves in with Jesse's family, where she experiences and grows to understand a different set of social expectations. After several traumatic events, she is eventually able to reconcile the conflicting social forces.

Austin died of liver cancer in 1994.

Resources: Doris Jean Austin, *After the Garden: A Novel* (New York: New American Library, 1987); Doris Jean Austin and Martin Simmons, eds., *Streetlights* (New York: Penguin Books, 1996); Phiefer L. Browne, "Austin, Doris Jean," in *The Oxford Companion to African American Literature*, ed. William L. Andrews, Frances Smith Foster, and Trudier Harris (New York: Oxford University Press, 1997); Evora Jones, "Doris Jean Austin," in *Contemporary African American Novelists*, ed. Emmanuel S. Nelson (Westport, CT: Greenwood Press, 1999), 6–11.

Kimberly Black-Parker

Autobiography. As the etymological roots of the word (*auto*/self, *bios*/life, and *graphe*/writing) indicate, autobiography is the art and practice of writing the story of one's own life. An autobiography is a written or spoken narrative in which an individual tells the story of how he or she came over time to be an independent, often original, agent.

In *The Oxford Companion to African American Literature*, **William L. Andrews**, arguably the preeminent scholar of African American autobiography, explains that during its evolutionary phase African American autobiography "held and continues to hold a position of priority, if not preeminence, among the narrative traditions of black America . . . [and] has testified since the late eighteenth century to the commitment of people of color to realize the promise of their American birthright and to articulate their achievements as individuals and as persons of African descent" (Andrews and Bassard, "Autobiography," 34).

Briton Hammon's spiritual autobiography, *Narrative of the Uncommon Sufferings, and Surprizing Deliverance of Briton Hammon, a Negro Man*, published in **Boston, Massachusetts,** in 1760, was the first work by a Black author published in North America. It is also a good example of the journey/quest motif and the theme of atonement. In 1747 Hammon left his Boston employer and sailed to Jamaica. His narrative describes his kidnapping, his imprisonment, and finally a reunion with his master more than ten years later. Other important autobiographies of this era include those by **James Gronniosaw** and **Venture Smith**.

It was almost fifty years after the publication of Hamon's *Narrative*, according to Andrews, before African American autobiographers began to prove to readers that they were best qualified to tell their own stories. From these beginnings until the proclamation of full emancipation in 1865, Black American autobiography evolved into a complex "oratorical" mode springing from narratives of ex-slaves who spoke on the antislavery lecture circuit (Andrews, *To Tell a Free Story*, 1; Emmanuel Nelson, ed., *African American Autobiographers*).

Between 1760, the year of the first African American autobiography, and 1831, the year of the **Nat Turner** insurrection, narratives written by former slaves seemed less concerned with **slavery** itself as a primary topic and concentrated more on issues of self-fulfillment and spiritual growth. Notable African American spiritual autobiographies include those by **John Marrant, Sojourner Truth,** George White, **Richard Allen, Zilpha Elaw, Lucy A. Delaney, Elizabeth** (also known as Old Elizabeth), **Jarena Lee,** and John Jea (Nelson).

Andrews argues that perhaps more than any other form of literary discourse, autobiography has been chosen by African Americans to articulate ideals of selfhood integral to an African American sense of identity, both individual and communal. More important, "autobiography has helped African Americans bear witness to an evolving tradition of liberated and empowered individuality" (Andrews and Bassard, "Autobiography," 34).

Besides providing a forum for sociopolitical and cultural concerns, African American autobiography established a tradition of powerful personal writing. Early African American autobiography influenced writing by Black American writers from **William Wells Brown** to **Charles W. Chesnutt,** from **W.E.B. Du Bois** to **Richard Wright, Ralph Ellison,** and **James Baldwin,** as well as **Frances E. W. Harper, Pauline Hopkins, Zora Neale Hurston, Margaret Walker,** and **Toni Morrison.**

Andrews, in *African American Autobiography*, concludes that African Americans had been dictating and writing first-person accounts of their lives for almost a century before the first Black American novel appeared in 1853: "It is significant that this novel, William Wells Brown's *Clotel*, was subtitled *A*

Narrative of Slave Life in the United States and was written by a man who had made his initial literary fame as a fugitive slave autobiographer. Ever since, the history of African American narrative has been informed by a call-and-response relationship between autobiography and its successor, the novel" (Andrews, *African American Autobiography*, 1). From this perspective, then, one genre, the **novel**, can be said to have grown out of another genre, autobiography, in African American literature.

Many themes arise in the evolution of the African American autobiography. In *To Tell a Free Story*, Andrews identifies several "organizing principles and moral issues" that were also popular in white autobiographical genres. He cites "the captivity narrative, the conversion account, the criminal confession, the spiritual autobiography, and the journal of ministerial labors" (Andrews, *To Tell a Free Story*, 38). In *The Oxford Companion to African American Literature*, however, Andrews uses two controlling categories, "Secular Autobiography" (34) and "Spiritual Autobiography" (37), to help organize the potentially endless list of themes and moral and political issues (Andrews and Bassard, "Autobiography"). The best-known secular autobiographies were written by fugitives who documented the brutality of **slavery**.

The most effective narratives focused as much on the individual as on the institution of slavery, placing special emphasis on how slaves escaped and/or fought against brutality. Classic autobiographies of this kind include **Frederick Douglass**'s *Narrative of the Life of Frederick Douglass, an American Slave* (1845), William Wells Brown's *Narrative of William Wells Brown, a Fugitive Slave* (1847), and **Harriet Jacobs**'s *Incidents in the Life of a Slave Girl* (1861). **William and Ellen Craft**, **Solomon Northup**, **Henry Bibb**, Mary Prince, and Moses Roper also wrote autobiographies that fall into the "secular" category.

After emancipation, African Americans, led by **Booker T. Washington** (*Up from Slavery*, 1901), continued the autobiographical tradition. In the first part of the twentieth century, W.E.B. Du Bois, Zora Neale Hurston, **Langston Hughes**, and Richard Wright produced important autobiographical writing. Since **World War II**, autobiography in the hands of individuals as different as **Malcolm X**, **Ned Cobb**, James Baldwin, **Amiri Baraka**, **Samuel Delany**, **Angela Davis**, **Claude Brown**, and **Audre Lorde** has taken on a wide spectrum of topics, including sexuality, religion, class, and the **black family**. **Maya Angelou** and **John Edgar Wideman** have produced prize-winning autobiographies, confirming the continuing literary vitality of African American first-person narrative. Even more recently, **Anne Moody**, **Patrice Gaines**, **Itabari Njeri**, **Janet McDonald**, **Nathan McCall**, **Gloria Wade-Gayles**, and **Lorene Cary** have produced acclaimed autobiographies, continuing the tradition that began over two centuries earlier.

Resources: Frederick Luis Aldama, "Re-Visioning African American Autobiography," *MFS: Modern Fiction Studies* 46, no. 4 (Winter 2000), 1004–1007; William L. Andrews, *To Tell a Free Story: The First Century of Afro-American Autobiography, 1760-1865* (Urbana: University of Illinois Press, 1988); William L. Andrews, ed., *African American Autobiography: A Collection of Critical Essays* (Englewood Cliffs, NJ:

Prentice-Hall, 1993); William L. Andrews and Katherine Clay Bassard, "Autobiography," in *The Oxford Companion to African American Literature*, ed. William L. Andrews, Francis Smith Foster, and Trudier Harris (New York: Oxford University Press, 1997), 34–39; Maya Angelou, *I Know Why the Caged Bird Sings* (New York: Bantam, 1983); James Baldwin, *Collected Essays* (New York: Library of America, 1998); Jonathan Bradford Brennan, "Speaking Cross Boundaries: A Nineteenth-Century African/Native American Autobiography," *A/B: Auto/Biography Studies* 7, no. 2 (Fall 1992), 219–238; William Wells Brown: *Clotel; or, The President's Daughter*, ed. Hilton Als (New York: Modern Library, 2001), also in *Three Classic African-American Novels*, ed. William Andrews et al. (New York: Signet, 1990); *Narrative of William Wells Brown, a Fugitive Slave, Written by Himself* (Boston: American Anti-Slavery Society, 1847); Lorene Cary, *Black Ice* (New York: Knopf, 1991); Frederick Douglass, *Narrative of the Life of Frederick Douglass, an American Slave, Written by Himself* (New York: W. W. Norton, 1997); Patrice Gaines, *Laughing in the Dark: From Colored Girl to Woman of Color—A Journey from Prison to Power* (New York: Crown, 1994); Henry Louis Gates, Jr., and William Andrews, eds., *Slave Narratives* (New York: Library of America, 2000); James Albert Ukawsaw Gronniosaw, *A Narrative of the Most Remarkable Particulars in the Life of James Albert Ukawsaw Gronniosaw, an African Prince*, ed. W. Shirley (Bath, UK: S. Hazzard, 1770); Briton Hammon, *A Narrative of the Uncommon Sufferings, and Surprizing Deliverance of Briton Hammon, a Negro Man* (Boston: Green & Russell, 1760); Langston Hughes: *The Big Sea* (New York: Knopf, 1940); *I Wonder as I Wander* (New York: Rinehart, 1956); Zora Neale Hurston, *Dust Tracks on a Road: An Autobiography* (New York: HarperPerennial, 1996); Harriet A. Jacobs, *Incidents in the Life of a Slave Girl, Written by Herself* (Cambridge, MA: Harvard University Press, 1987); George E. Kent, "Maya Angelou's *I Know Why the Caged Bird Sings* and Black Autobiographical Tradition," in *African American Autobiography: A Collection of Critical Essays*, ed. William L. Andrews (Englewood Cliffs, NJ: Prentice-Hall, 1993); Jeff Loeb, "MIA: African American Autobiography of the Vietnam War," *African American Review* 31, no. 1 (Spring 1997), 105–123; Audre Lorde, *The Cancer Journals* (San Francisco: Aunt Lute Books, 1997); Malcolm X, *The Autobiography of Malcolm X*, written with Alex Haley (New York: Ballantine, 1987); R. Baxter Miller, "The Rewritten Self in African American Autobiography," in *Alternative Identities: The Self in Literature, History, Theory*, ed. Linda Marie Brooks (New York: Garland, 1995), 87–104; Emmanuel S. Nelson, ed., *African American Autobiographers: A Sourcebook* (Westport, CT: Greenwood Press, 2002); Itabari Njeri, *Every Good-bye Ain't Gone* (New York: Vintage, 1991); Crispin Sartwell, *Act Like You Know: African American Autobiography and White Identity* (Chicago: University of Chicago Press, 1998); Johnnie M. Stover, "Nineteenth-Century African American Women's Autobiography as Social Discourse: The Example of Harriet Ann Jacobs," *College English* 66, no. 2 (Nov. 2003), 133–154; Maurice Wallace, "Constructing the Black Masculine: Frederick Douglass, Booker T. Washington, and the Sublimits of African American Autobiography," in *Subjects and Citizens: Nation, Race, and Gender from Oroonoko to Anita Hill*, ed. Michael Moon and Cathy N. Davidson (Durham, NC: Duke University Press, 1995); Booker T. Washington, *Up from Slavery*, ed. William L. Andrews (New York: Oxford University

Press, 1995); John Edgar Wideman, *Brothers and Keepers* (New York: Vintage, 1995); Roland L. Williams, Jr., *African American Autobiography and the Quest for Freedom* (Westport, CT: Greenwood Press, 2000); Richard Wright, *Black Boy* (New York: Perennial Classics, 1998).

John Greer Hall

B

Back-to-Africa Movement. The desire to go back to Africa began as the impassioned hope of enslaved Africans in America and swelled into various movements, producing along the way a mass of writings that contributed greatly to the African American literary tradition. Slaves openly expressed their longing to return to Africa in folk songs and other **folklore, slave narratives**, letters, and addresses. Examples of early literature include tales about slaves who fled back to Africa, as well as the following excerpt from a folk song:

> Run, nigger, run;
> de patter-roller catch you;
> Run, nigger, run,
> and try to get away
>
> ("Run to Rz," *Folk Music Index*)

A patter-roller is a runaway slave hunter. In the 1700s, many free blacks petitioned the government to establish settlements for them in Africa. Other proponents of the concept "back to Africa" include Paul Cuffee (1759–1817), a wealthy merchant and ship captain, who paid for African Americans to settle in what is now Sierra Leone; the American Colonization Society, which founded Liberia in 1822; and **Martin Delany**, who published his back-to-Africa philosophy in his newspaper, *The Mystery* (1843–1847), and in *The Condition, Elevation, Emigration and Destiny of the Colored People of the United States, Politically Considered* (1852). Delaney also edited, with **Frederick Douglass**, the *North Star*. Although Abraham Lincoln's views concerning what to do about the predicament of African Americans evolved, at one point in his political career he found the idea of African Americans returning to Africa appealing (Donald).

African Americans continued to feel oppressed after emancipation (1865), as evidenced by letters sent to the American Colonization Society. One man wrote, "We have little or no voice here & our wages are so small we scarcely have enough means to subsist upon . . . we feel like children away from home and are anxious to get home [Africa]" (Redkey, 8). Another man wrote, "they run the Negroes with hound dogs now days and times as did before 1865. Oh may God help us to get out from here to Africa" (Redkey, 10). Bishop **Henry M. Turner**, an advocate for the emigration of impoverished rural Blacks, edited a monthly African Methodist Episcopal newspaper, *Voice of Missions*. He wrote fearlessly against the condition of Blacks in America. In the 1900s, **Marcus Garvey** led the largest back-to-Africa movement in America's history and used the **Negro World**, which "became one of the most popular African American newspapers in the U.S." (Altman, "Marcus Garvey," 99), to promote self-determination.

Literature concerning a return to Africa went through a relatively dormant period in the mid-to-late 1900s until Louis Farrakhan, leader of the **Nation of Islam**, addressed African Americans in the "Million Man March" on **Washington, D.C.**, in 1995. In his speech, Farrakhan asserted that African Americans still suffered from "inferiority," "powerlessness," and other ills as a result of White domination, and that the only reasonable course was to pursue economic power, not a return to Africa (Van Deburg, 315–327). Farrakhan provides another illustration of how African Americans have utilized literature, whether in the form of letters, journals, or addresses, to express their grievances, promote their ideals, and expand a growing consciousness in the pursuit of equality, self-empowerment, and resistance to oppression.

Resources: Susan Altman: "American Colonization Society," in *The Encyclopedia of African-American Heritage* (New York: Facts on File, 1997); "Autobiography of Abou Bekir Sadiki, Alias Edward Doulan," *Journal of Negro History* 21 (1936), 52–55; "The Autobiography of Omar ibn Said, Slave in North Carolina," *American Historical Review* 30 (1925), 787–795; "Marcus Garvey," in *The Encyclopedia of African-American Heritage* (New York: Facts on File, 1997); "Martin Robinson Delany," in *The Encyclopedia of African-American Heritage* (New York: Facts on File, 1997); "Paul Cuffee," in *The Encyclopedia of African-American Heritage* (New York: Facts on File, 1997); Martin R. Delany, *Condition, Elevation, Emigration and Destiny of Colored People of the United States Politically Considered* (New York: Arno Press, 1968); David Herbert Donald, *Lincoln* (New York: Simon and Schuster, 1995); Virginia Hamilton, *The People Could Fly: American Black Folktales* (New York: Knopf, 1985); Darlene Clark Hine, William C. Hine, and Stanley Harrold, *The African-American Odyssey* (Upper Saddle River, NJ: Prentice-Hall, 2000); Edwin S. Redkey, *Black Exodus: Black Nationalist and Back-to-Africa Movements, 1890–1910* (New Haven, CT: Yale University Press, 1969); "Run to Rz," *Folk Music Index*, http://folkindex.mse.jhu.edu/R11.htm#Runboru; William L. Van Deburg, ed., *Modern Black Nationalism: From Marcus Garvey to Louis Farrakhan* (New York: New York University Press, 1997).

Gladys L. Knight

Baisden, Michael (born 1963). Novelist, playwright, publisher, and radio and television talk show host. A native of **Chicago**, and a former driver for the Chicago Transit Authority, Michael Baisden wrote and self-published his first book, *Never Satisfied: How/Why Men Cheat* (1995), which went on to sell more than 300,000 copies. Not one to shy away from controversy, Baisden took on, with this collection of interviews, the role of social commentator on the subject of infidelity. In 1996 he formed Love, Lust, and Lies, a series of relationship seminars. His radio show of the same name became popular in New York City, where he was known as "The Bad Boy of Kiss." He penned his first novel, *Men Cry in the Dark* (1997), as a rebuttal to novelist **Terry McMillan**'s best-seller *Waiting to Exhale*. Baisden has published two more novels, *The Maintenance Man* (1999) and *God's Gift to Women* (2002). Baisden had a short stint as the host of the television talk show *Talk or Walk* in 2001. Continuing to expand his repertoire, Baisden became a playwright as *Men Cry in the Dark* began a national tour in 2002 featuring Richard Roundtree and Alan Payne, followed by a production of *The Maintenance Man* featuring Billy Dee Williams. Baisden is involved with several ventures, including the Happily Single Web site, and is the chief executive officer of Legacy Publishing.

Resources: *Contemporary Black Biography*, vol. 25 (Detroit: Gale, 2000); Michael Baisden: *God's Gift to Women* (New York: Touchstone, 2002); *Maintenance Man: It's Midnight, Do You Know Where Your Woman Is* (Atlanta: Legacy, 1999); *Men Cry in the Dark* (Irving, TX: Legacy, 1997); *Never Satisfied: How/Why Men Cheat* (Schaumburg, IL: Legacy, 1995); Web site, www.michaelbaisden.com.

Dera R. Williams

Baker, Houston A., Jr. (born 1943). Theorist, professor, and poet. A product of what he described as "racist, stultifying" Louisville, Kentucky, Baker is one of the most respected and multifaceted scholars of African American and other ethnic literatures. His work focuses on the dynamics of literary representation of twentieth-century race relations.

Along with editing scholarly collections—including *Black Literature in America* (1971), one of the first African American literature anthologies—Baker has published numerous books on critical theory, scores of scholarly essays, and several collections of his own poetry. In 1992, he became the first Black president of the Modern Language Association of America. Baker has been a vocal advocate for well-trained teachers at the high school and college levels, and has made available an in-depth study of ethnic literatures at all educational levels. Currently a Professor of English and of African and African American Studies at Duke University (since 1999), he has been on the faculties of Yale University (1968–1970), the University of Virginia (1970–1974), and the University of Pennsylvania (1974–1998).

While working on his doctoral research as a Victorianist, Baker shifted his focus to begin writing about what he termed "vernacular literatures," works defined by aesthetic and political elements not found in so-called canonical works of literature (*Blues, Ideology, and Afro-American Literature*). For Baker,

African American literary production, like other noncanonical literatures, needs to be studied through principles embedded in its own set of aesthetic experiences, and judged, criticized, and elucidated on its own terms. *Blues, Ideology, and Afro-American Literature: A Vernacular Theory* (1984), one of Baker's most influential texts, grounds this theory in the American **blues** form. For Baker, the metaphor of the "crossroads," made famous by the likes of blues guitarist Robert Johnson (1911–1938), offers a matrix for understanding African American literature.

These "impulses" have informed Baker's more recent studies on such genres of **vernacular** literature as **rap** music, modernism, the **Harlem Renaissance**, and the writings of **Booker T. Washington**. Foregrounded in this work are the cross-cultural and cross-linguistic contacts that erupt in meetings of dominant and nondominant Americana. Such meetings are often overtly politically charged. For example, *Turning South Again* (2001) offers a reading of Washington's conception of citizenship on Southern plantations at the turn of the twentieth century and sees striking parallels in the constraints on Black economic and social mobility in the "prison-industrial complex" existing at century's end.

Resources: Houston A. Baker: *Black Studies, Rap, and the Academy* (Chicago: University of Chicago Press, 1993); *Modernism and the Harlem Renaissance* (Chicago: University of Chicago Press, 1987); *Blues, Ideology, and Afro-American Literature: A Vernacular Theory* (Chicago: University of Chicago Press, 1984); *Blues Journeys Home* (Detroit: Lotus Press, 1985); *Turning South Again: Re-Thinking Modernism/Re-Reading Booker T.* (Durham, NC: Duke University Press, 2001); *Workings of the Spirit: The Poetics of Afro-American Women's Writing* (Chicago: University of Chicago Press, 1991); Houston A. Baker, ed., *Black Literature in America* (New York: McGraw-Hill, 1971).

Keith Feldman

Baker, Josephine (1906–1975). Entertainer and author. Baker performed in Revue Negre, the Black vaudeville show that transported the spirit of the **Harlem Renaissance** to **Paris**, in 1925. There, Baker gained international stardom, dancing nude to African rhythms and wearing her famous banana skirt. While Picasso adopted "cubist" forms from exotic artifacts brought to Europe as a result of Napoleon's invasion of Egypt, Baker transformed herself into an exotic figure who appealed to a predominantly White masculine public. By 1927, expatriate Baker became a celebrated French citizen and had published an **autobiography**, *Les Mémoires de Joséphine Baker*, written with Marcell Sauvage. Baker became active in the French Resistance during **World War II**, and in the **Civil Rights Movement** in the 1950s and 1960s in the United States.

Robert Hayden's poem "Aunt Jemima of the Ocean Wave" portrays Jemima/Baker as that displaced "Sepia High Stepper in Europe...that fake mammy to God's mistakes." Jean Claude Baker and Chris Chase's *Josephine: The Hungry Heart* and Phyllis Rose's *Jazz Cleopatra*, among other books, have remade Baker into a world-class icon of beauty and brawn. **Shay Youngblood**'s novel *Black Girl in Paris* depicts a heroic woman's escape from **the South** to

Josephine Baker, 1927. Courtesy of the Yale Collection of American Literature, Beinecke Rare Book and Manuscript Library.

find artistic liberation in Paris. In the satire "The Rear End Exists," playwright **Suzan-Lori Parks** describes the ample buttocks of both "Hottentot and Black Venus": she "just wiggled her fanny and all the French fell in love." In **bell hooks**'s *Black Looks: Race and Representation*, Baker is presented as the new and improved African amazon. (*See* **Exoticism**.)

Resources: Jean-Claude Baker and Chris Chase, *Josephine: The Hungry Heart* (New York: Random House, 1993); Josephine Baker and Jo Bouillon, *Josephine*, trans. Mariana Fitzpatrick (New York: Harper & Row, 1977); Josephine Baker with Marcel Sauvage, *Les Mémoires de Joséphine Baker* (Paris: Kra, 1927); Bryan Hammond and Patrick O'Connor, *Josephine Baker* (Boston: Little, Brown, 1991); Lynn Haney, *Naked at the Feast: A Biography of Josephine Baker* (New York: Dodd, Mead, 1981); Arlen Hansen, *Expatriate Paris: A Cultural and Literary Guide to Paris of the 1920's* (New York: Arcade, 1990); Robert Hayden, *Collected Poems* (New York: Liveright, 1985); bell hooks, *Black Looks: Race and Representation* (Boston: South End Books, 1992); Janet McDonald, "A Sister in Paris," *Essence*, May 1994; Suzan-Lori Parks, "The Rear End Exists," *Grand Street* 14, no. 3 (Winter 1996), 11–17; Phyllis Rose, *Jazz Cleopatra: The Story of Josephine Baker* (New York: Vintage, 1991); Tyler Stovall, *Paris Noir: African Americans in the City of Light* (Boston: Houghton Mifflin, 1996); Petrine Archer Straw, *Negrophilia: Avant-Garde Paris and Black Culture in the 1920s* (London: Thames and Hudson, 2000); Shay Youngblood, *Black Girl in Paris* (New York: Riverhead Books, 2000).

Renee Kemp-Rotan

Baker, Nikki (born 1962). Novelist. A native of Greene County in southwestern Ohio, Nikki Baker received a B.S. from Purdue University and an M.B.A. from the University of Chicago. A successful financial analyst, she has volunteered at community agencies providing services to gay and lesbian young people. Drawing on her professional and personal experiences, she has written mystery novels exploring lesbian themes. The central character is Virginia Kelly, an African-American lesbian who works in investment firms and must confront the complications that arise from the misperception that she may be a "double **token**" employee.

The first three Virginia Kelly novels were published by Naiad Press. *In the Game* (1991) introduces Virginia Kelly as she investigates the murder of a friend's lover, who is found dead outside the bar in which the friend had confided her suspicions about her lover's infidelity. Virginia's personal life becomes unsettled as a new acquaintance, a lawyer, increasingly creates conflict in her existing relationship.

The Lavender House Murder (1992) is set in Provincetown, Massachusetts. While vacationing, Virginia investigates the shooting death of a lesbian reporter who had a reputation for "outing" prominent women who had kept their lesbianism private.

Although the title acknowledges Baker's adaptation of a Chandleresque style to a very different milieu, *Long Goodbyes* (1993) is set in Virginia's midwestern hometown, where continuing hypocrisies about **race** and sexual preference ultimately connect to several unsolved murders.

In *The Ultimate Exit Strategy* (2001), the first of the Virginia Kelly mysteries to be published by Bella Books, the focal situation involves the proposed sale of the firm for which Virginia works and the murder of the firm's president, which may threaten the sale. Issues in Virginia's personal life are equally unresolved, as she must make some decisions about her new relationship with a punkish younger woman while dealing with the renewed interest of a former lover—who just happens to be in charge of the murder investigation.

Resources: Nikki Baker: *In the Game* (Tallahassee, FL: Naiad, 1991); *The Lavender House Murder* (Tallahassee, FL: Naiad, 1992); *Long Goodbyes* (Tallahassee, FL: Naiad, 1993); *The Ultimate Exit Strategy* (Tallahassee, FL: Bella Books, 2001); Katherine Kizilos, "Women Who Stalk the Mean Streets," interview, *The Age* (Melbourne) June 8, 1994, p. 15.

Martin Kich

Baldwin, James (1924–1987). Novelist, essayist, playwright, poet, and activist. James Baldwin was one of the most influential and widely respected voices in American literature of the twentieth century, the heir to **W.E.B. Du Bois**'s intellectual fervor and **Richard Wright**'s anger, and the predecessor of **Toni Morrison**'s challenging aesthetics. Baldwin was born in **Harlem, New York**, on August 2, 1924, the oldest of nine children. His mother, Emma Berdis Jones, married his stepfather, the preacher David Baldwin. One of Baldwin's public-school teachers in Harlem was **Countee Cullen**. James never knew his biological father, and his relationship with his stepfather was antagonistic. Yet James became a preacher when he turned fourteen, having undergone a religious conversion similar to the one that John Grimes, the protagonist of Baldwin's first novel, *Go Tell It on the Mountain* (1953), experiences. He describes this experience in *The Fire Next Time* (1963). Before he was twenty, Baldwin had left the church, and this painful decision is reflected in many of his works.

Baldwin's writing career began after he graduated from high school in 1942. He reviewed books, and in 1948 he published his first essay and his first short story, "Previous Condition," about the torment of a young actor who leaves Harlem, and then is evicted from an apartment in a White neighborhood, leaving him with nowhere to go. Reacting to similar instances of racist persecution, Baldwin left for **Paris** soon thereafter, the first of many periods of exile. Paris gave Baldwin the opportunity to confront a number of pasts that related to his own identity. As he describes in "Encounter on the Seine" (1950), his African past exists in Paris in the form of Frenchmen of African descent and Algerian immigrants. Baldwin discovers his kinship with these people who are connected to him by the color of his skin, yet the French Africans are different because of their status as colonial subjects rather than as American tourists or expatriates. "Encounter on the Seine" demonstrates Baldwin's awareness of the complex connection between **race** and his identity. The murderous anger he felt toward American racists could only tear him apart or land him in jail, so he left his native country. He would come to realize in Paris that racism was going to follow him. He went from Paris to a village in Switzerland, where he completed his first novel.

Go Tell It on the Mountain is a familiar attempt to examine the author's younger self in fiction, but it takes an unusual form, with the **coming-of-age** story of fourteen-year-old John Grimes framing the stories of John's aunt, stepfather, mother, and biological father. The middle section of the book, the stories of John's parents and aunt, broadens the scope of the novel to include the struggles of African Americans who left their homes in the early twentieth century. John's story takes place on his fourteenth birthday. Like Baldwin, who underwent a violent conversion experience at the age of fourteen, John is surprised to find himself on the "threshing floor" in front of the altar of his church. Also like Baldwin, who went to Paris partially to escape the racial persecution of his home country, John attempts to escape the filth and low station of his home. But dirt follows John just as racism followed Baldwin. John attempts to transcend his circumstances in solitude, first by mounting a hill in Central Park, then by entering a movie theater. In both cases he is attracted to fame and wealth, the very sins that his stepfather Gabriel denounces from the pulpit. John's individual identity quest is diverted by guilt over his obligations to family. He reenters Gabriel's church and, fulfilling everyone's expectations that he will become a minister to compensate for his brother's misbehavior, he prepares himself for conversion. John's journey continues in Baldwin's 1955 play *The Amen Corner*. In this play, David Alexander is caught between the ways of the church, represented by his mother, who is a pastor, and the ways of the world, represented by his father, who is a jazz musician. In contrast to John Grimes, David runs off to explore himself not through religion, but through art.

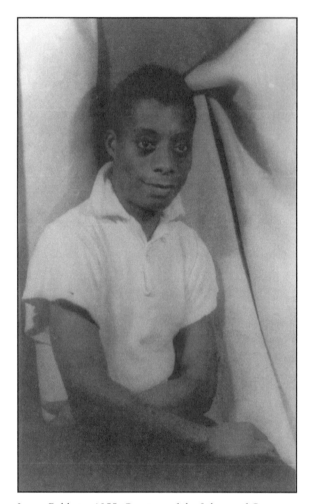

James Baldwin, 1955. Courtesy of the Library of Congress.

Whereas in *Go Tell It on the Mountain*, the sexual attraction between male characters is suggested subtly, Baldwin's second novel, *Giovanni's Room* (1956), addresses the subject of homosexuality in such a direct way that it shocked publishers and readers alike. Although homosexuality is not incidental in *Giovanni's Room*, the novel is really about something broader: the refusal to accept oneself, which leads to the impossibility of loving another. Though he acknowledged his own bisexuality, Baldwin spent much of his career arguing with labels, and would never accept being called "gay." Yet *Giovanni's Room* is widely considered Baldwin's "gay novel," perhaps because it was so unusual in 1956 to read fiction about homosexual experiences described so candidly, and perhaps because the narrator David's homosexual experiences pointedly frame the dilemma of the novel. In contrast to his other novels, *Giovanni's Room* is not about race relations or racism: David is White. Baldwin did not want to overburden the book's central message with too many issues.

Baldwin again attempted to create a deeply affecting psychological narrative about facing reality and about the responsibility of the individual to care for others in his most famous short story, "Sonny's Blues" (1957), published the year after *Giovanni's Room* appeared. The narrator of "Sonny's Blues" attempts to lead an upright, middle-class existence in order to avoid suffering. Just as Giovanni causes David to see life from another point of view, so the narrator's brother, Sonny, causes him to revise his own safe viewpoint. Because of the healing power of music, "Sonny's Blues" ends in transcendence rather than tragedy.

Baldwin's message took on a more political and racially charged context during the turbulent 1960s. The **Civil Rights Movement** had begun, and it needed guidance. Baldwin returned from Europe and journeyed to **the South** to witness firsthand how the promise of America was failing, and to provide hope for its renewal. His essays in *Nobody Knows My Name* (1961) and *The Fire Next Time* (1963) gained him fame as the rising star in the American literary scene, and he was invited to the White House to meet President John Kennedy and Attorney General Robert Kennedy, who consulted him on American race relations. The long essay "Down at the Cross," from *The Fire Next Time*, is considered by many to be Baldwin's best work: a combination of reportage, personal history, and historic commentary that provides an important perspective and offers a vision of the anger exploding throughout America. From this point on, the tone of his essays became apocalyptic, and Baldwin's increasing militancy can be seen in the last short story he published, "Going to Meet the Man" (1965), which gave the title to his only collection of stories. "Going to Meet the Man" is a vicious story filtered through the viewpoint of a racist White sheriff who as a youth had witnessed the lynching and castration of a Black man and is permanently damaged as a result.

Baldwin's perspective changed as a result of his political involvement in the South in the early 1960s. His 1964 play *Blues for Mister Charlie* coincided with the onset of the **Black Arts Movement**. Inspired by the infamous 1955 murder of **Emmett Till**, *Blues for Mister Charlie* illustrates the connection Baldwin perceived between racial violence and sexual mythology. It also dramatizes the possibilities for violent or nonviolent reactions to racial injustice. Richard Henry, who is murdered at the outset of the play, had given a gun to his father, Meridian, and although Meridian does not fire it in the third act, he is carrying it under his Bible at the play's conclusion, as if to signal the potential danger to come. Baldwin's novels *Another Country* (1962) and *Tell Me How Long the Train's Been Gone* (1968) are notable departures. They are sprawling narratives that range over time and space in a way that his earlier works do not. Baldwin's readers had to revise their preconceived notions of Baldwin if they were to follow these challenging books. Many readers were not willing to do so, and although *Another Country* was successful in terms of sales and received some good reviews, its publication marked a turning point in Baldwin's reputation, especially as a novelist (Campbell).

Although its reviews were not universally laudatory, *Another Country* pleased many readers and critics, and it remains one of Baldwin's greatest literary achievements in terms of its daring experimentation and its engagement with human despair, American identity, and the complexity of sexual and racial relationships. It begins with the final, desperate days of Rufus Scott, a despondent Black New Yorker who has been emotionally damaged and marginalized by society. He has no outlet for the bitterness and poison that fill him, though he attempts to take them out on Leona, a Southern White woman. When he realizes the futility of this attempt either to love or to hate, Rufus feels that he has no alternative but to commit suicide. The bulk of the novel concerns the way Rufus's friends and family continue their lives in the aftermath of the tragedy.

Like *Another Country*, *Tell Me How Long the Train's Been Gone* explores nearly all of the themes associated with Baldwin's work: the conflicted role of the artist, the tense relationship between brothers, the church's oppression, the difficulty of self-acceptance, and the failure of contemporary America to deal with its race problems. The novel is the story of Leo Proudhammer, a stage and film actor who suffers a heart attack and who uses his convalescence to reflect upon his life. Weary of his role as a spokesman, Baldwin was clearly projecting a side of himself in the character of Leo. Leo helps himself recuperate by telling his story, making himself vulnerable in a way actors typically do not. From the public's perspective, his story is the classic rags-to-riches tale, made more poignant because he grew up poor and Black. In the novel's final pages a White character holds Leo up as an example of how anyone of any race can succeed in America. At the same time, a militant Black character named Christopher presents a persuasive case for the type of righteous anger evident in groups such as the **Black Panther Party** in the late 1960s. Like *Blues for Mister Charlie*, this novel ends with the potential for future violence, yet it does not endorse violence as the solution to America's racial strife.

The anger that characterizes the play and two novels Baldwin published in the 1960s can be seen in his essays of the same period, which also tended to be longer and more ambitious than his earlier efforts. To be Black during that decade invariably meant that one was asked to choose between two distinct forces: the radical militancy associated with **Malcolm X** and the Black Muslims, and the peaceful nonviolence associated with **Martin Luther King, Jr.** As someone who resisted labels and who never stayed in America long, Baldwin found himself left behind or left out of the debates that he had contributed to so frequently in the early 1960s. In Baldwin's celebrated essay on Elijam Mohammed, "Down at the Cross" (1962), he had already distanced himself from the Black Muslims, though not from Malcolm X. His book-length essay *No Name in the Street* (1972) was a comprehensive attempt to come to terms with the turbulence of race relations in contemporary America.

In this ambitious and wide-ranging essay, he tried to demonstrate his anger in the aftermath of the assassinations of **Medgar Evers**, Malcolm X, and King.

No Name in the Street ends on a typical Baldwinian note of prophecy: "I think black people have always felt this about America, and Americans, and have always seen, spinning above the thoughtless American head, the shape of the wrath to come" (195). This wrath derives at least partially from one of the most pervasive injustices in contemporary America, the systematic police brutality and wrongful imprisonment that defined African American experience in the post–Civil Rights era. Baldwin addressed this situation in *If Beale Street Could Talk* (1974), a novel markedly different from Baldwin's earlier work in terms of its **vernacular** voice. Tish Rivers, the novel's narrator, is a streetwise nineteen-year-old Black girl, a character type less prominent in Baldwin's previous novels (with the exception of Ida in *Another Country*). Tish and her family seek to prove the innocence of her boyfriend, Fonny, who has been wrongfully charged with rape. The situation is urgent, for she is carrying Fonny's baby. Baldwin turns his attention to injustice on the street in this novel, which is another **blues** story, as the title indicates.

Baldwin's health was beginning to deteriorate when his final novel, *Just Above My Head* (1979), was published. *Just Above My Head* has a huge cast of characters and covers the range of Baldwin's travels, from New York City to Paris to the American South. Readers are introduced to characters who are confused by their sexual attractions in the face of society's taboos. As in *Beale Street*, Baldwin sees a tremendous need for strong, functional families as supports for the individual. Among all of these familiar Baldwin motifs is the central struggle of Hall, the narrator, who is a witness to his brother's life.

In Baldwin's final years he published his collected poems in a slim volume titled *Jimmy's Blues*, which appeared first in England in 1983. The volume did not receive much attention; no one seemed prepared to think of Baldwin as a poet at this point in his career. The poems, written at various times throughout his life, are distilled versions of the blues theme that he had been trying to communicate all along, and the themes of blindness, invisibility, the burden of the witness, and the difficulties of loving are once again evident. His last work, *The Evidence of Things Not Seen* (1985), was similarly neglected and is similarly important, a counterpart to his most famous essay, "Down at the Cross," and an exploration of the post-Civil Rights South paralleling his earlier explorations in *Nobody Knows My Name*. During this trip south Baldwin was investigating a series of child murders that began in **Atlanta, Georgia**, in 1979. He ended up writing about the murders as evidence of something more widespread in America: the racism, lack of faith, and lack of vision that plagues our nation and prevents its dream. The book exposes the truth beneath the surface of American society. The Atlanta murders provided Baldwin with a final opportunity to meditate on his nation, to expose its shortcomings, and to predict its future.

Baldwin died in southern France in 1987 from cancer of the esophagus. His death was marked by a tremendous celebration of his life at the Cathedral of St. John the Divine in New York, and celebrations thereafter have focused on his literary achievements and his wisdom. There has been a resurgence in recent years of criticism about Baldwin's life and writing; five books of criticism and one biography have been published on his writings since the mid-1990s. Although there is always healthy debate over what Baldwin should be remembered for, there is no doubt that he will be remembered as one of the most important American writers of the latter twentieth century.

Resources: Primary Sources: James Baldwin: *The Amen Corner* (New York: Dial, 1968; first produced 1955); *Another Country* (New York: Dial, 1962); *Blues for Mister Charlie* (New York: Dial, 1964); *The Evidence of Things Not Seen* (New York: Holt, Rinehart, and Winston, 1985); *The Fire Next Time* (New York: Dial, 1963); *Giovanni's Room* (New York: Dial, 1956); *Go Tell It on the Mountain* (New York: Knopf, 1953); *Going to Meet the Man* (New York: Dial, 1965); *If Beale Street Could Talk* (New York: Dial, 1974); *James Baldwin: Collected Essays*, ed. Toni Morrison (New York: Library of America, 1998); *James Baldwin: Early Novels and Stories*, ed. Toni Morrison (New York: Library of America, 1998); *Jimmy's Blues* (London: Michael Joseph, 1983); *Just Above My Head* (New York: Dial, 1979); *No Name in the Street* (New York: Dial, 1972); *Nobody Knows My Name* (New York: Dial, 1961); *Notes of a Native Son* (Boston: Beacon, 1955); *The Price of the Ticket: Collected Nonfiction 1948–1985* (New York: St. Martin's Press, 1985); *Tell Me How Long the Train's Been Gone* (New York: Dial, 1968). **Secondary Sources:** Katherine L. Balfour, *The Evidence of Things Not Said: James Baldwin and the Promise of American Democracy* (Ithaca, NY: Cornell University Press, 2001); Harold Bloom, ed., *James Baldwin* (New York: Chelsea House, 1986); Donald Bogle, "A Look at the Movies by Baldwin," *Freedomways* 16, no. 2 (Spring 1976), 103–108 [review of *The Devil Finds Work*]; James Campbell, *Talking at the Gates: A Life of James Baldwin* (Berkeley: University of California Press, 2002); Trudier Harris, *Black Women in the Fiction of James Baldwin* (New York: Cambridge University Press, 1996); Trudier Harris, ed., *New Essays on "Go Tell It on the Mountain"* (New York: Cambridge University Press, 1996); David Leeming, *James Baldwin* (New York: Knopf, 1994); Dwight A. McBride, ed., *James Baldwin Now* (New York: New York University Press, 1999); D. Quentin Miller, ed., *Reviewing James Baldwin: Things Not Seen* (Philadelphia: Temple University Press, 2000); Horace A. Porter, *Stealing the Fire: The Art and Protest of James Baldwin* (Middletown, CT: Wesleyan University Press, 1989); Lynn Orilla Scott, *Witness to the Journey: James Baldwin's Later Fiction* (East Lansing: Michigan State University Press, 2002); Fred L. Standley and Nancy V. Burt, eds., *Critical Essays on James Baldwin* (Boston: G. K. Hall, 1988); Fred L. Standley and Louis H. Pratt, eds., *Conversations with James Baldwin* (Jackson: University Press of Mississippi, 1989); W. J. Weatherby, *James Baldwin: Artist on Fire* (New York: D. I. Fine, 1989).

D. Quentin Miller

Ballad. Both a form of song and a form of lyric poetry, the ballad emerged first as a form of song. Subsequently, literary writers based poetry on that particular song form. One example is the English poet William Wordsworth, who, with Samuel Taylor Coleridge, published *Lyrical Ballads*, a book of poems, in 1798.

It is widely assumed that ballad traditions in the United States are traceable to the nation's Anglo-Celtic cultural heritage. However, African American culture, which emerged from the interaction between blacks and whites, produced its own ballads. Folklorists and other scholars in the United States have tended to focus on British and Irish balladry and, at least by comparison, have neglected African American balladry, which, despite sharing features with Anglo-Celtic balladry, possesses distinctive attributes.

Ballads of both traditions are characterized by a strophic (stanzaic) narrative text. (In Greek poetry and drama, a strophe is a unit or series of lines.) That is, both types of ballads are structured according to a melody line that is consistently repeated through a series of verses; often, this series of verses is interrupted by a repeated chorus or refrain. Typically, ballads tell a story and thus can be considered narrative songs. The verses in ballads that are narrative songs, as well as the corresponding stanzas in poems based on the ballad form, often contain four lines (a quatrain). Different patterns of rhyme occur in both types of ballads, but most often in a given quatrain every other line rhymes, the notation for which is ABAB (Padgett).

Most of the ballads from both the Anglo-Celtic-American tradition and the African American tradition originally were anonymously composed and orally transmitted, the major exception being "broadsides," a subcategory of ballads that feature a lyric printed on a single sheet of paper intended for commercial sale. Anonymous ballads from both traditions were committed to written form by ballad collectors, who often printed the lyrics on a single sheet and sold the sheets to other people, which spread ballads into new localities.

The most easily identifiable distinction between the two ballad traditions is the difference in performance style. White singers historically accentuated a conservative approach when performing ballads. That is, the audiences of White singers—mostly members of their home communities—expected ballads to be sung impersonally and unemotionally, and to feature lyrics and melodies that were familiar within those communities. African American culture, on the other hand, traditionally favored the singing of ballads from a first-person perspective, with singers frequently altering the texts and tunes to reflect their own emotions and sense of aesthetics, and to respond to the particular dynamics of the social environments in which they were singing.

The traditional African American ballad repertoire included some of the Anglo-Celtic ballads categorized during the late nineteenth century by scholar Francis James Child. Folklorist Dorothy Scarborough, in her book *On the Trail of Negro Folk-Songs* (1925), documented Black singers performing a number of these British ballads, including "The Hangman's Tree" (Child ballad #95), "The Cherry Tree Carol" (Child ballad #54), and "Barbara Allen" (Child ballad #84). Illustrating the tolerance for individualized interpretations of ballads among African Americans, Scarborough noted that she had witnessed one Black ballad singer, in a performance of "Lady Isabel and the Elf Knight" (Child ballad #4), freely and unself-consciously substituting the phrase "apple bay" for the stock ballad epithet "dapple gray." Historically, African Americans sang Anglo-Celtic ballads mostly within their own communities, yet before emancipation, black singers (mostly women) sang certain ballads to White children on plantations, including "Old Bangum" (derived from "Sir Lionel," Child ballad #18), "Froggie Went a-Courtin'," and the Irish ballad "Skewball" (also known as "Stewball").

Additionally, African Americans adopted ballads that had been created entirely in the New World (folklorists have named these "native American ballads," but the term is unrelated to "Native American" in the sense of North American Indians). Many such ballads (including "Old Blue") emerged during the nineteenth century within White communities in the American **South**. Blacks also sang commercial ballads (for instance, "Blue-Tailed Fly") originally composed by Whites for minstrel shows and vaudeville, forms of nineteenth-century popular entertainment (*see* **Minstrelsy**).

Two widely popular American ballads about disasters likely originated among Blacks. Historian and author Harold Courlander, in *A Treasury of Afro-American Folklore* (1976), speculated that "Casey Jones" is one of these ballads. Courlander asserted that the ballad—which chronicled a 1900 trainwreck in Vaughn, Mississippi, and the death of that train's engineer—was composed by a Black railroad worker who had worked for Jones. Folklorist Newman I. White, in his 1928 book *American Negro Folk-Songs*, maintained that the ballad about the 1912 sinking of the *Titanic* probably emerged among Blacks, in that "[o]ne or two unusually accurate details in the various versions [of the ballad] may be due to an illustrated book on the *Titanic* which enjoyed extensive sales among the Negroes soon after the disaster" (347).

Unquestionably of African American origin were the "blues-ballads," so named for their blending of Black and White musical and lyrical elements. Most blues-ballads focused on a dramatic event and concerned the exploits of a central protagonist; some of these protagonists were heroes (as in the famous blues-ballad "John Henry"), but many were antiheroes (killers, "badmen") whose violent behavior sometimes was judged as excessive (for example, in the ballad "Stagger Lee" or "Stagolee"), and at other times was rationalized as having been necessary under specific situations ("Po Lazarus"). Several blues-ballads, including "John Henry" and "John Hardy," were popular among Southern whites before the **Great Depression**. Other blues-ballads, including "Frankie and Johnny" (or "Frankie and Albert"), "Betty and Dupree," and "Delia," were seldom sung by Whites until becoming incorporated into the repertoires of musicians during the urban folk revival of the 1950s and 1960s. Recordings documenting Anglo-Celtic-American and African American balladry traditions are preserved at the Library of Congress in **Washington, D.C.**

The African American blues-ballad can be distinguished from other genres of secular African American music that contain verbal components—the lyric folk song and the blues—in that a blues-ballad emphasizes narrative, while the other genres accentuate emotion. The blues-ballad also differs from the toast, another traditional narrative form of lyrical expression within African American culture. Generally describing a strong character in an extreme situation, such as the popular toast titled "Shine and the *Titanic*" (which concerned a

Black man who swam safely to shore after the ship sank), a toast was spoken or chanted rather than sung; also, a toast was generally performed with a greater degree of improvisation than a blues-ballad.

Many works by African American authors reinterpreted the ballad form, and some of these employed literary approximations of colloquial Black speech. **Countee Cullen**'s 1923 poem "The Ballad of the Brown Girl: An Old Ballad Retold" won second prize in the prestigious nationwide Witter Bynner Poetry Contest and helped launch Cullen as a major literary figure in the **Harlem Renaissance**. Other poets associated with that cultural movement likewise borrowed from the African American ballad tradition, including **Sterling Brown**, whose 1932 poem "The Ballad of Joe Meek" depicted the plight of a law-abiding African American who is transformed into a militant after being physically attacked by White policemen. Brown's poem "Odyssey of Big Boy" is also in ballad form, using five-line stanzas in which the fifth line repeats the fourth. Brown also wrote his own version of "Frankie and Johnny."

Langston Hughes used the ballad form in numerous poems, often to deliver political and social messages, but also for other purposes. In "Ballad of Booker T." (1941), for instance, Hughes praised the African American leader, while in "Ballad of Roosevelt" (1934) the poet satirized the renowned White political figure—who was generally respected by Depression-era African Americans— for not substantially improving the economic conditions in which Blacks lived. As Ostrom notes, Hughes's *Collected Poems* contains twenty-five poems with "ballad" in the title, and features other poems in the ballad form. Hughes's 1938 poem "Ballad of Ozie Powell" concerned one of the **Scottsboro Boys**, and Hughes' 1949 poem "The Ballad of Margie Polite" chronicled a **race riot** in Harlem. Most of Hughes's "Madam" poems were composed in ballad form, including the "Ballad of the Fortune Teller" (1942). Hughes also wrote "The Ballad of Walter White" in homage to the civil rights leader and writer (*see* **White, Walter**).

Dudley Randall's poem "Ballad of Birmingham," one of the most widely read literary ballads in the period since the 1950, was written in reaction to the 1963 killing of four African American girls in the bombing of the 16th Street Baptist Church in Birmingham, Alabama, by White supremacists. Deploying dramatic license by changing the story to depict the death of just one girl, Randall reflected the influence of British balladry in advancing the story's action through a conversation between that girl and her mother. To protect his copyright after a folk singer had set "Ballad of Birmingham" to music, Randall distributed the poem as a broadside, reinvigorating a practice once common in Britain (and in colonial America).

Other literary works by African American authors to draw upon the ballad legacy include a 1970 poem by **Margaret Walker**, "The Ballad of the Free," which lauded the heroism of a revolutionary Black leader, Haitian patriot Toussaint L'Ouverture, whom Walker associated with other African American leaders of slave insurrections. **Loften Mitchell** utilized the ballad tradition to provide narrative structure for two plays about war: *Ballad for Bimshire*

(1962) and *Ballad of the Winter Soldiers* (1964). The former was staged as a musical in 1963 in collaboration with Irving Burgie, and the latter was written with **John Oliver Killens**.

The traditional African American blues-ballad "John Henry" inspired numerous works in various literary genres by Black authors. For example, the acclaimed novel *John Henry Days* (2001) by **Colson Whitehead** reassessed the John Henry legend (and African American identity generally) from a contemporary middle-class Black perspective.

African Americans working in arts other than literature have likewise been influenced by the ballad. Visual artists, for example, have long attempted to illustrate subjects originally depicted in ballads. In his 1943 painting *Old Black Joe*, Horace Pippin interpreted a sentimental Civil War-era ballad of the same name composed by White songwriter Stephen Foster. Black visual artists have represented the folk hero John Henry in drawings, paintings, and sculpture. Predictably, African American musicians have long found inspiration in balladry traditions. Since the 1950s, Black musicians ranging from Harry Belafonte and Odetta, to Lloyd Price, Brook Benton, Taj Mahal, and the duo Cephas and Wiggins, have recorded and performed blues-ballads (as have many White musicians). Similarly, the recording group Arrested Development in 1994 cited one of Langston Hughes's literary ballads, "Ballad of the Landlord" (1951), as having inspired their popular **rap** song "Mister Landlord."

Resources: *Afro-American Spirituals, Work Songs, and Ballads* (New York: Rounder Select, 1994), CD; Arrested Development, *Zingalamaduni* (Los Angeles: Capitol Records, 1994), CD [includes "Mister Landlord"]; Alan Norman Bold, *The Ballad* (New York: Methuen, 1979); David Levering Lewis, ed., *The Portable Harlem Renaissance Reader* (New York: Viking, 1994), 229–232; John A. Lomax and Alan Lomax, comps., *American Ballads and Folk Songs* (New York: Macmillan, 1935); Hans Ostrom, *A Langston Hughes Encyclopedia* (Westport, CT: Greenwood Press, 2002), esp. 19–20, 229–230; Ron Padgett, ed., *A Handbook of Poetic Forms* (New York: Teachers & Writers Collaborative, 1987), esp. 17–20; Alex Preminger, Frank J. Warnke, and O. B. Hardison, eds., *Princeton Encyclopedia of Poetry and Poetics*, enl. ed. (Princeton, NJ: Princeton University Press, 1974); Reed Smith, *South Carolina Ballads: With a Study of the Traditional Ballad Today* (New York: Ayer, 1974); Newman Ivey White, *American Negro Folk Songs* (Cambridge, MA: Harvard University Press, 1928); William Wordsworth and Samuel Taylor Coleridge, *Lyrical Ballads*, ed. W.J.B. Owen (1798; repr. Oxford: Oxford University Press, 1969).

Ted Olson

Ballard, Allen B. (born 1933). Professor, scholar, and novelist. In 2000 Ballard published *Where I'm Bound*, a historical novel based on the experiences of the 3rd U.S. Colored Cavalry in the **Civil War**. The protagonist is Joe Duckett, an African American scout for a Black army unit from Mississippi who must not only survive the war but also try to get back to the plantation from which he was liberated and find his wife and daughter. The book won the First Novelist Award from the Black Caucus of the American Library Association, and the *Washington Post* named it a Notable Book of the Year. Ballard attended Central High School in **Philadelphia, Pennsylvania**, and earned a B.A. from Kenyon College. He earned a Ph.D. in government from Harvard University and taught government for twenty-five years at the City College of New York. He also served as dean of the faculty at New York University, and at this writing he is Professor of History and Africana Studies at the State University of New York in Albany. Ballard has contributed to the *New York Times Magazine* and is the author of the nonfiction books *The Education of Black Folk* and *One More Day's Journey: The Story of a Family and a People*.

Resources: Allen B. Ballard: "Biography," *Allen B. Ballard*, http://www.allenballard.com/index.htm; *The Education of Black Folk* (New York: Harper & Row, 1973); *One More Day's Journey: The Story of a Family and a People* (New York: McGraw-Hill, 1984); *Where I'm Bound* (New York: Simon and Schuster, 2000).

Hans Ostrom

Baltimore, Maryland. An argument can be made that African Americans have played a more extended and prominent role in the development of Baltimore than in that of any other American city. Although Maryland was a state that permitted slavery, from its beginnings Baltimore attracted free African Americans from throughout **the South**, including a number of former slaves who were emancipated as a result of their service with the American and British armies during the Revolutionary War. By 1850, more than 25,000 free African Americans lived in Baltimore, constituting about 15 percent of the city's population.

After the **Civil War**, the African American community continued to develop as an economic, educational, social, and cultural force within the city. Until the 1890s, the African American population was spread fairly evenly throughout the city's districts. But the industrial development of the city—in particular, the development of the great steel mills at Sparrows Point—made the city a prime destination for the **Great Migration** of African Americans out of the Deep South. In response, the city government instituted Jim Crow laws that segregated African Americans into certain districts, schools, and social associations. These laws would remain in force for the first half of the twentieth century.

Between 1950 and 1970, the decline of heavy manufacturing and "White flight" to the suburbs combined to make African Americans the majority population in the city. The decline in the city's population and the consequent erosion of its economic, commercial, and tax bases has meant that life in Baltimore has increasingly been defined by economic, rather than strictly racial, issues. Jerome Dyson Wright's novel *Poor Black and in Real Trouble* (1976) provides a vividly personal chronicle of the racial tensions and endemic violence that have defined Baltimore's transition from an industrial community with a White majority to an economically marginalized community with a Black majority.

In 1895, the Mutual United Brotherhood of Liberty was established in Baltimore to defend the rights of African Americans in the city and beyond, in particular against racially motivated criminal charges. By the time of the

Great Depression, Baltimore had the second largest **NAACP** chapter in the United States. In the 1980s, the national headquarters of the NAACP was relocated to the city. Moreover, Baltimore is home to three historic Black colleges and universities: Morgan State University, Coppin State University, and Sojourner Douglass College. Three Baltimore museums have noteworthy collections of African American art: the Baltimore Museum of Art, the James E. Lewis Museum of Art, and the Walters Art Museum. The African American art historian James A. Porter was a Baltimore native.

The Baltimore Afro-American, a weekly established in 1892, remains the longest continuously published African American newspaper in the United States. **Langston Hughes** covered the Spanish Civil War for *The Afro-American*. Another reporter for the newspaper, Elizabeth Murphy Moss, became the first female African American war correspondent of **World War II**. Other alumni of *The Afro-American* have included sports journalist Joe Bostic. Michael Datcher has reported for the *Baltimore Sun*. Howard University librarian W. Paul Coates has directed Black Classic Press in Baltimore since 1978.

In 1922, the Douglass Theater, the first theater in the United States wholly owned and operated by African Americans, opened in Baltimore. Founded in 1953, the Arena Players is the oldest African American community theater group in the United States. Each year, the Arena Players stage five productions, ranging from classic works to contemporary African American plays. The playwright **Shirley Graham** taught at Morgan College in the late 1920s and early 1930s, and her first two plays, *Tom-Tom* (1929) and *Coal Dust* (1930), were initially produced there. The playwright **Anna Deavere Smith**, whose works include *On Black Identity and Black Theater* (1990), *Fires in the Mirror* (1992), *Twilight: Los Angeles, 1992* (1993), *House Arrest First Edition* (1997), and *Piano* (2000), is a Baltimore native.

Several of the most prominent figures in African American literary history have lived in Baltimore. As a young man, **Frederick Douglass** worked on the docks at Fells Point in east Baltimore. **Frances E. W. Harper**, perhaps the most prominent African American poet of the **Reconstruction** era, was a Baltimore native and much influenced by her early acquaintance with Douglass. Her best-known collections of poems include *Autumn Leaves* (1845), *Poems on Miscellaneous Subjects* (1854), and *Moses: A Story of the Nile* (1869). An outspoken supporter of racial and gender equality, Harper eventually became more widely recognized for her public speaking tours than for her verse. An interesting footnote is that her short story "The Two Offers" (1859) may be the first short story published by an African American in an American periodical.

The poet **Countee Cullen** may have been born in Baltimore, but Louisville, Kentucky, and New York City have also been identified as his birthplace. His poem "Incident" treats a traumatic exposure to racism during a childhood visit to Baltimore. After leaving home to travel with a theatrical troupe, **Zora Neale Hurston** completed her secondary education at the Morgan Academy in Baltimore. A half-century later, New York native **Tupac Shakur** attended the Baltimore School for the Arts.

The poet and critic **Eugenia Collier** began her teaching career at Baltimore Community College but has subsequently taught at the University of Maryland, Baltimore County (UMBC), at Howard University, at Coppin State University, and at Morgan State University. Critic and editor **Dolan Hubbard** chairs the Department of English and Language Arts at Morgan State, while the critic and editor Miriam DeCosta-Willis has directed the African Studies program at UMBC since 1991. The poet Gloria Oden has taught at UMBC since 1971; her collections include *The Naked Frame* (1952), *Resurrections* (1978), and *The Tie That Binds* (1980). Some of **Z. Z. Packer**'s experiences while teaching English and creative writing in Baltimore have been depicted in the stories of her collection, *Drinking Coffee Elsewhere* (2003).

Candian Lawrence Hill has set his novel *Any Known Blood* (1997) largely in Baltimore, where his mixed-race protagonist searches for information about his African American ancestors and a deeper sense of his African American heritage.

African American novelists with Baltimore connections have been even more broadly represented among the genres of popular fiction. **Blair S. Walker** has written a mystery-detective novel *Don't Believe Your Lying Eyes* (2002) featuring Baltimore journalist Darryl Billups. A multicultural take on the Western, **David Anthony Durham**'s *Gabriel's Story* follows the adventures of a young African American who flees the deepening racism in post–Civil War Baltimore for the opportunities seemingly available in the new African American communities on the Kansas frontier. African Caribbean by ancestry and quite peripatetic himself, Durham worked for a time in a sushi restaurant in Baltimore. Among African American children's authors who have been born or have lived in Baltimore, the most prominent have been Augusta Baker and Elizabeth Fitzgerald Howard.

Resources: Ralph Clayton: *Black Baltimore, 1820–1870* (Bowie, MD: Heritage, 1987); *Slavery, Slaveholding and the Free Black Population of Baltimore* (Bowie, MD: Heritage, 1993); Kenneth D. Durr, *Behind the Backlash: White Working Class Politics in Baltimore, 1940–1980* (Chapel Hill: University of North Carolina Press, 2003); Harold A. McDougall, *Black Baltimore: A New Theory of Community* (Philadelphia: Temple University Press, 1993); Sherry H. Olson, *Baltimore: The Building of an American City*, rev. ed. (Baltimore: Johns Hopkins University Press, 1997); W. Edward Orser, *Blockbusting in Baltimore: The Edmondson Village Story* (Lexington: University Press of Kentucky, 1994); Christopher Phillips, *Freedom's Port: The African-American Community of Baltimore, 1790–1860* (Urbana: University of Illinois Press, 1997).

Martin Kich

Baltimore Afro-American (1892–present). Newspaper. The *Baltimore Afro-American* (popularly referred to as the *Afro*) is one of the country's largest circulation African American newspapers, reporting regional, national, and international news. Currently owned and operated by the fourth generation of members of the Murphy family, the weekly has led the way in quality journalism, covering African American life from the late nineteenth century through the **Harlem Renaissance** to racial equality and economic advancement.

The first issue of the *Afro-American* was published in Baltimore on August 13, 1892 (Farrar, 1); it was edited by Rev. William Alexander of the Sharon Baptist Church. A political activist, Alexander used the weekly to campaign for civil rights at a time when there was a rising tide of racist sentiment in the nation. In 1897, the paper's parent company, Northwestern Family Supply, filed for bankruptcy, and the *Afro-American*'s presses were sold at a public auction to John Henry Murphy, Sr. A former slave set free by the Maryland Emancipation Act of 1863, Murphy had been manager of the paper's printing department. At the time of the sale, he was fifty-two years old and was already publishing *The Sunday School Helper* from the basement of his home. He ran the *Afro-American* for twenty-five years and said it was "the one thing I didn't fail in" (Farrar, 4).

In 1900 the *Afro-American* merged with the *Ledger*, a paper published by Rev. George F. Bragg of St. James Episcopal Church, and became the *Afro-American Ledger*. The early years were filled with hardship as the newspaper struggled to survive in a highly competitive and narrow Black newspaper market. To strengthen its financial resources, the *Afro-American Ledger* re-incorporated as the Afro-American Company of Baltimore in 1907. Eight years later the newspaper changed its name again, to the *Afro-American*. During that time, its reputation steadily grew along with its readership. African Americans sought the newspaper by any means; it was read aloud to illiterates and passed around to those who couldn't afford to buy an issue (Farrar, 6). While continuing to cover the usual news stories, the newspaper abandoned its conservative format and adopted a more sensationalist layout. Stories about sex and crime dominated the front page, accompanied by tabloid headlines and pictures. One of the most notorious sex scandals reported by the newspaper involved the novelist and folklorist **Zora Neale Hurston**. In 1948 she was arrested and charged with molesting a ten-year-old boy. The newspaper covered the story extensively and erroneously reported that Hurston molested three young children (Farrar, 12). Eventually the accusations against Hurston were found to be groundless, and the case was eventually dropped. Hurston suffered from the negative publicity in the Black press, and never recovered her reputation.

In addition to its reports of news and scandals, the *Afro-American* brought literary and scholarly expression to a wider audience. It published poems, serials, and essays by both major and less-known artists. **Langston Hughes**, **Claude McKay**, William Worthy, and **J. Saunders Redding** were among the many talented African Americans whose works were showcased in the newspaper. Hughes published poems in the *Afro* and covered the Spanish Civil War for it. Between 1925 and 1950, almost 1,000 short stories appeared in the magazine section (Ford and Faggett, 10). Drawn from everyday life, they underscored an increasing national consciousness regarding equality (Ford and Faggett, 14). In an introduction to an anthology compiled from the *Afro-American*, Carl Murphy noted that the purpose of these stories had been to increase racial understanding and "present Negro characters outside of their familiar stereotypes . . . [and] portray them in their normal activities as American citizens . . . laughing, weeping, singing, struggling, achieving, failing, praying, sinning, and dreaming, dreaming of things his whiter brothers have dared to dream also" (10–11).

At the time of John Murphy's death in 1922, the *Afro-American* had become an important voice in the Black community. It was transformed from a local Baltimore paper to a nationally recognized publication, with news bureaus and distribution offices in other cities. Murphy was succeeded by one of his five sons, Carl Murphy, who was editor and publisher for the next forty-five years. He followed the course set by his father and further expanded the newspaper's circulation and distribution, with regional editions in **Washington, D.C.**, **Philadelphia, Pennsylvania**, Richmond, and Newark. During his tenure, Murphy used the *Afro-American*'s national status to actively campaign for Black equality in the United States Foremost was the issue of education, including equal pay for teachers, the appointment of Black administrators, and the desegregation of higher education. The newspaper also called for improvements in employment and housing opportunities as well as in criminal justice. The themes of capital punishment, police brutality, and unfair trials figured prominently in that effort. The paper's success was mixed. Sometimes its crusades effected social change, as in its constant news and editorial coverage of the **NAACP** desegregation lawsuit against the state-run University of Maryland School of Law (Farrar, 47–48). At other times the paper's efforts were frustrated because it lacked the political clout to influence government officials.

Carl Murphy died in 1967, and his daughter, Frances L. Murphy II, became chairperson and publisher of the newspaper. During her tenure, the newspaper received an award in 1969 from the American Society of Journalism School Administration "in recognition of the distinguished record of a newspaper which has served a predominantly black community and which has actively engaged in community service" (Wolseley, 100). The newspaper continues to be managed by family members. In an effort to accommodate the needs of the Black reader, the *Afro-American* gives strong coverage of news from Africa, supplemented with regional news and stories from cities with large African American communities. In addition, the paper devotes generous space to editorials, opinion columns, and letters. One of the oldest Black-run and -operated newspapers, the *Afro-American* remains true to its original mission "to present to the world that side of the African American [people] that can be had in no other way, and . . . as far as possible assist in the great uplift of the people it represents" (Farrar, xii). (*See* **Newspapers**.)

Resources: "About Us," *The Afro-American Newspaper*, http://www.afro.com/aboutus.htm; Hayward Farrar, *The "Baltimore Afro-American," 1892–1950* (Westport, CT: Greenwood Press, 1998); Nick Aaron Ford and H. L. Faggett, "Introduction," in *Best Short Stories by Afro-American Writers, 1925–1950*, ed. Nick Aaron Ford and H. L. Faggett (Boston: Meador, 1950; Millwood, NY: Kraus Reprint, 1977), 13–14; Carl Murphy, "Foreword," in *Best Short Stories by Afro-American Writers, 1925–1950*, ed. Nick Aaron Ford and H. L. Faggett (Boston: Meador, 1950; Millwood, NY: Kraus

Reprint, 1977); Hans Ostrom, *A Langston Hughes Encyclopedia* (Westport, CT: Greenwood Press, 2002), 25–28, 298–300; Robert E. Wolseley, *The Black Press, U.S.A.*, 2nd ed. (Ames: Iowa State University Press, 1990).

Lori Ricigliano

Bambara, Toni Cade (1939–1995). Novelist, short story writer, essayist, screenwriter, editor, and activist. Bambara is best known for her well-crafted short stories and novels, and for being among a vibrant group of younger African American women writers that emerged in the late 1960s and early 1970s. Bambara was born in New York City; her original name was Toni Cade, under which she first published short stories. She later adopted a family name she discovered in her great-grandmother's attic trunk, and thereafter she was known as Toni Cade Bambara (Bambara, *Deep Sightings*). Bambara's fiction often contains nonlinear plots and includes multiple narrators; some of the short stories have simpler structures. Her writing addresses community struggles, political movements, and environmental concerns, as well as personal conflicts and problems faced by ordinary people.

According to Bambara, her mother, Helen Brent Henderson Cade, created an environment of respect for thought and privacy in their home; she also instilled in Bambara an awareness of social and political struggles (Bambara, *Deep Sightings*).

Bambara earned her B.A. in 1959 from Queens College, and soon thereafter she worked for a year in a psychiatric hospital (Stanford, 47). She earned an M.A. in American literature in 1965 from City College of New York, where she subsequently became an instructor. Through her studies, Bambara became acquainted with writings of **Zora Neale Hurston** and **Langston Hughes** (among others), whose work seems to have influenced Bambara's language and style. In her literary antecedents, Bambara seemed to find strength rather than constraint (Bambara, *Deep Sightings*; Guy-Sheftall).

In the 1970s she taught in several educational settings, including Spelman College, the Neighborhood Arts Center, Stephens College, and Livingston College of Rutgers University. She was also active in both the **Civil Rights Movement** and the women's movement. Bambara populates her fiction with characters who struggle with recognizable situations and realize that they do not have all the answers. This approach invites the reader to empathize with their predicaments. Bambara grounds her writing firmly in the historical moment and its crises. The struggles of her fictional characters correspond with those of surrounding contemporary communities.

Gorilla, My Love (1972) contains fifteen short stories, was well received by reviewers and critics, and was reprinted many times. A second collection, *The Sea Birds Are Still Alive* (1977), was less well received (Stanford, 47). Bambara's first novel, *The Salt Eaters*, appeared in 1980 and includes numerous settings, characters, and shifts of time. The novel won both the American Book Award and the Langston Hughes Society Award in 1981, as well as a Zora Neale Hurston Society Award several years later.

Many readers have seen an activist element in Bambara's writing. Tate suggests that Bambara's work "examine[s] philosophical, historical, political, metaphysical truths, or rather assumptions" (Tate, 23). Bambara's texts often appear to work from the implied premise that the personal is political. Much of Bambara's fiction, including *The Salt Eaters* and stories in *Gorilla, My Love*, is written in relatively plain language and focuses on ordinary people and common situations. One of her most anthologized stories, from *Gorilla, My Love*, is "Raymond's Run"; the narrator is a young woman whose affection for her disabled brother, Raymond, is revealed in the story, which concludes with a kind of triumph for Raymond. Bambara also edited anthologies of African American women's writing and of tales and stories in the folk tradition. She was general editor, for Wayne State University Press, of a series of African American literature and biography. She also published essays on writing, the African American cinema, and other topics.

In the 1980s Bambara was heavily involved in making films. For example, she helped write the script for a documentary film by Louis Massiah, *The Bombing of Osage Avenue* (1986), which she also narrated. She won an Academy Award for this work (Stanford, 48). She also worked on and appeared in the documentary *More Than Property*, and she worked on another documentary by Massiah, *W.E.B. Dubois—A Biography in Four Voices* (1995). Her second novel, *Those Bones Are Not My Child*, was published posthumously. (*See* **Black Arts Movement**; **Gender**; **Short Fiction**.)

Resources: Primary Sources: Toni Cade Bambara: *The Black Woman: An Anthology* (New York: New American Library, 1970); *Deep Sightings and Rescue Missions: Fiction, Essays, and Conversations*, ed. Toni Morrison (New York: Vintage, 1999); *Gorilla, My Love* (New York: Random House, 1972); *The Salt Eaters* (New York: Vintage, 1981); *The Seabirds Are Still Alive: Stories* (New York: Random House, 1977); *Tales and Stories for Black Folks* (Garden City, NY: Zenith Books, 1971); *Those Bones Are Not My Child* (New York: Pantheon, 1999). **Secondary Sources:** Elliott Butler-Evans, *Race, Gender, and Desire: Narrative Strategies in the Fiction of Toni Cade Bambara, Toni Morrison, and Alice Walker* (Philadelphia: Temple University Press, 1989); Keith Byerman, *Fingering the Jagged Grain: Tradition and Form in Recent Black Fiction* (Athens: University of Georgia Press, 1985); Mari Evans, ed., *Black Women Writers (1950–1980): A Critical Evaluation* (Garden City, NY: Anchor-Doubleday, 1984); Beverly Guy-Sheftall, "Commitment: Toni Cade Bambara Speaks," in *Sturdy Black Bridges: Vision of Black Women in Literature*, ed. Roseann Bell, Bettye Parker, and Beverly Guy-Sheftall (Garden City, NY: Anchor, Doubleday, 1979); Louis Massiah, dir. and prod.: *The Bombing of Osage Avenue* (Philadelphia: Scribe Video, 1986), VHS format; *W.E.B. Dubois: A Biography in Four Voices* (San Francisco: California Newsreel, 1995), VHS format; Mickey Pearlman, ed., *American Women Writing Fiction: Memory, Identity, Family, Space* (Lexington: University Press of Kentucky, 1989); Marjorie Pryse and Hortense J. Spillers, eds., *Conjuring: Black Women, Fiction, and Literary Tradition* (Bloomington: Indiana University Press, 1985); Barbara Smith, ed., *Home Girls: A Black Feminist Anthology* (New Brunswick, NJ: Rutgers University Press, 2000); Ann Folwell Stanford, "Toni Cade Bambara," in *The Oxford Companion to African American*

Literature, ed. William L. Andrews, Frances Smith Foster, and Trudier Harris (New York: Oxford University Press, 1997); Janet Sternberg, ed., *The Writer on Her Work: Contemporary Women Writers Reflect on Their Art and Situation*, vol. 1 (New York: W. W. Norton, 1980); Claudia Tate, ed., *Black Women Writers at Work* (New York: Continuum, 1983); Susan Willis, *Specifying. Black Women Writing the American Experience* (Madison: University of Wisconsin Press, 1987).

Michael Cook and Linda S. Watts

Bandele, Asha (born 1968). Journalist, poet, memoirist, novelist, and editor. Born in the Bronx and raised in Manhattan, Bandele completed a B.A. at the New School for Social Research and an M.F.A. at Bennington College. Features editor, then editor-at-large, and most recently community editor at *Essence*, Bandele has interviewed a number of prominent individuals for the magazine, including Kofi Annan, Harry Belafonte, Kadiatou Diallo, and Winne Madikizela-Mandela. In a very short period, Bandele has also established herself as a poet, a memoirist, and a novelist.

Bandele's first collection of poems, *Absence in the Palm of My Hands* (1996), demonstrates why she is well-known as a "spoken-word" poet. The poems are emotionally complex, unflinchingly honest, often deeply angry, and yet, at their center, grounded in genuine sympathy. Carefully crafted but accessible, they have struck a deep chord with many of her contemporaries.

Bandele's much-acclaimed memoir, *The Prisoner's Wife* (1999), recounts how she met, developed a friendship with, and ultimately married her husband, Rashid, an inmate serving a long sentence for murder.

Inspired by the police shooting of Amadou Diallo, Bandele's first novel, *Daughter* (2003), treats two "accidental" killings by the police. The central character is a single mother named Miriam. When her daughter Aya is mistaken for a robbery suspect and shot by police, Miriam flashes back to the period before Aya's birth. Against her own mother's wishes, she had fallen in love with a janitor named Bird. A Vietnam vet equally troubled by his memories of the war and angered by his treatment since his return to civilian life, Bird had been killed by the police shortly before Aya's birth. The novel is an exploration of the corrosive effects of anger left unexpressed.

Resources: Asha Bandele: *Absence in the Palm of My Hands* (New York: Writers & Readers, 1996); *Daughter: A Novel* (New York: Scribner's, 2003); *The Prisoner's Wife: A Memoir* (New York: Scribner's, 1999); Susan Straight, "Collateral Damage: A Traumatic Shooting Produces New Reckonings with a Family's Past," *Washington Post*, Jan. 4, 2004, p. F8.

Martin Kich

Banks, Leslie Esdaile (born 1959). Novelist. Banks is a remarkably prolific writer of fiction. She has written more than sixteen novels and five novellas in a variety of genres, including **romance**, women's fiction, **crime fiction**, and **horror fiction**, under the pen names L. A. Banks, Leslie Esdaile, Leslie E. Banks, and, most recently, Leslie Esdaile Banks. Banks's agent, Manie Barron of the William Morris Agency, believes Banks is the first African American woman to have written commercial fiction for five major publishing houses simultaneously: St. Martin's Press, Simon and Schuster, Kensington, BET/Arabesque, and Genesis Press (Web site). Much of Banks's fiction has a paranormal element. Her dark fiction is noteworthy for her use of strong African American heroines and heroes, realistic urban settings, and humorous contemporary slang. Her romances often include characters of mixed heritage and diverse socioeconomic backgrounds who must face the true-to-life difficulties that Banks herself has faced: divorce, job loss, and blended families.

A native of West **Philadelphia, Pennsylvania**, Leslie Esdaile Banks graduated with a degree in business in 1980 from the Wharton School of the University of Pennsylvania. She began a career in corporate marketing and executive management, for the following ten years occupying high-level positions in Fortune 100 companies and large corporations, including Xerox and Hewlett Packard. Her entrepreneurship later led her to become a marketing and economic development consultant for small businesses, nonprofits, and community-based organizations, before striking out into publishing.

Banks first considered writing in 1992 after an accident left her daughter's arm and hand severely burned—an injury that would require seventeen surgeries. Caring for her daughter while also getting a divorce from her first husband, she began to consider writing as a flexible alternative to employment. Encouraged by a small group of close friends turned enthusiastic readers, Banks began writing in earnest. She published her first novel, *Sundance*, in 1996 with Pinnacle. This book was the first of a two-book contract offered by the publishing house and was followed by *Slow Burn* in 1997.

Banks's other works include The Vampire Huntress series (2003–2005, published under the pen name L. A. Banks), *Sister Got Game* (2004), and a novel series based on the ShowTime/Paramount television series *Soul Food*, as well as romances, women's fiction, mysteries, and horror novels (published under the name L. A. Banks). More information about Banks, her novels, and her fiction career can be found at her Web sites, esdailebooks.com and vampirehuntress.com.

Resources: L. A. Banks (pseudonym): *The Awakening: A Vampire Huntress Legend* (New York: St. Martin's Press, 2004); *The Hunted: A Vampire Huntress Legend* (New York: St. Martin's Press, 2004); *Minion: A Vampire Huntress Legend* (New York: St. Martin's Press, 2003); Leslie E. Banks: *Sister Got Game* (New York: Dafina, 2004); *Soul Food: Through Thick and Thin* (New York: Pocket Stars, 2003); Leslie Esdaile Banks, Web sites, esdailebooks.com and vampirehuntress.com; Leslie Esdaile (pseudonym): *Slow Burn* (New York: Pinnacle, 1997); *Sundance* (New York: Pinnacle, 1996).

Michelle LaFrance

Banneker, Benjamin (1731–1806). Almanac writer, surveyor, and natural historian. Banneker, the first Black scientist of note in America, was born a free man in Maryland, even though his father and grandfather had been slaves. His grandmother, an Englishwoman deported as an indentured servant, started her own farm after seven years of bondage. She taught him to read and write, and for several winters he attended a small interracial Quaker school. When he was twenty-two, with only a pocket watch as a model, he made a clock, carving the cogwheels out of wood. By all accounts this was the first striking clock manufactured completely in America. Banneker's mechanical, inventive abilities brought him renown, and he was encouraged in his endeavors by Joseph Ellicott, who operated gristmills in the area. One of Ellicott's sons, George, an amateur astronomer, lent Banneker scientific books and instruments, including a telescope. Already an avid observer of the stars, and now in possession of the right tools, Banneker taught himself the principles of calculus and enough spherical trigonometry to chart out the ephemeris, a table showing the positions of the sun, moon, and planets during the course of a year, as well as information concerning eclipses and astronomical constants.

In connection with his observations and calculations, Banneker began work on an almanac that combined tide tables and moon phases with epigrams and homespun wisdom. Traditionally almanacs were relatively inexpensive pamphlets, and from their first appearance in English, they appealed to common readers interested in the world around them. According to Bernard Capp, almanacs were successful because they fulfilled a wide variety of roles, "cheaply and concisely" (23). Dating back to the origins of European printing in the fifteenth century, almanacs remained a popular and widely practiced form of writing in eighteenth-century America. Moreover, as Charles Cerami has pointed out, at the time when Banneker was writing, almanacs "were a leading form of publication," and for many families "these annual editions were the only form of printed material in the house" (76).

Banneker's manifest skill with precision instruments brought him to the attention of Maj. Andrew Ellicott, George's cousin, who invited him to join the team that had been commissioned by George Washington to survey the "Federal Territory" that would eventually to become the new capital. After spending three months along the banks of the Potomac, Banneker was eager to resume work on an almanac, and he sent a manuscript of this work to Secretary of State Thomas Jefferson. In the cover letter, Banneker pointed out the logical and moral inconsistency of freethinkers, such as Jefferson, remaining slaveholders, even quoting back to him words Jefferson had penned in the Declaration of Independence: "All men are created equal." He called for an end to slavery and for measures to be taken to help Blacks become educated. His almanac was itself a testimony to the fallacy of the then-popular belief in the intellectual inferiority of Blacks. Within four days of receiving Banneker's packet, Jefferson replied in a letter, dated August 30, 1791. (The original letter is in the Manuscript Division at the Library of Congress and is often reprinted in connection with Banneker's letter—among other places, in volume 1 of In Their Own Words [Melzer].) Jefferson said he was impressed with Banneker's accomplishment and would forward the almanac to the Marquis de Condorcet, Secretary of the Academy of Sciences at Paris. Jefferson wrote in his letter to Banneker that he considered the almanac "a document to which your whole colour had a right for their justification against the doubts which have been entertained of them."

Since there is no record of receipt, it remains an open question whether Jefferson actually sent the almanac to France. Despite the importance of Banneker's book, both as evidence of what Blacks could accomplish and as a compendium of accurate, useful information, Banneker had difficulty getting it published. However, with the aid of abolitionist societies, primarily in Maryland and Pennsylvania, his almanacs were published for the years 1792 through 1797, and these six books went through twenty-eight editions. *Benjamin Banneker's Almanac* sold widely, and it was purchased in states as far away as Kentucky. Each issue included commentaries, literature, and fillers that, more often than not, had political and humanitarian content. Banneker's almanacs thus can be seen as being among the first public documents to promote racial equality. But they represented first-rate scientific methodology as well, for even though his last published almanac appeared in 1797, Banneker correctly predicted an eclipse for October 1800 that no other astronomer had calculated. His decision to discontinue his almanac series sprang in part from poor sales, which may have resulted from a lull in antislavery activism, abolitionist groups having helped with the distribution of Banneker's almanacs from the beginning.

Undated portrait of Benjamin Banneker. Courtesy of the North Wind Picture Archives.

In his remaining years Banneker entertained visitors at his farm, wrote a treatise on bees, studied the cycle of the seventeen-year locust, and remained a pamphleteer for the antislavery movement. At the time of his death, the clock he had built fifty-three years before was still ticking and regularly striking the hour. Banneker's diary and notes, as well as miscellaneous publications, are available through the Historical Society of **Washington, D.C.**; the Maryland Historical Society has copies of his almanacs. The Library Company and the Union Library Catalog of Pennsylvania, both in **Philadelphia** (where Banneker's almanacs originally were printed by Joseph Crukshank), are available for the years 1792–1794. Complete texts of letters and select ephemera of Banneker can be found through the Resource Bank, "Africans in America": www.pbs.org.wgbh .aia/part2. A reprint of *Banneker's Almanac* was undertaken in the mid-1950s by Rhistoric Publications in Philadelphia ("Afro-American History Series"). Although there are, at present, no facsimile reproductions or authoritative editions of Banneker's almanacs and incidental writings, such as his treatise on bees, selections can be found in Bedini's biography of Banneker. There are many secondary resources available at the Banneker Museum and Historical Park, located at the site of his former home in Oella, Maryland, which opened in 1998.

Resources: Silvio A. Bedini, *The Life of Benjamin Banneker: The First African-American Man of Science*, 2nd ed., rev. and enl. (Baltimore: Maryland Historical Society, 1999); Bernard Capp, *English Almanacs, 1500–1800: Astrology and the Popular Press* (Ithaca, NY: Cornell University Press, 1979); Charles Cerami, *Benjamin Banneker: Surveyor, Astronomer, Publisher, Patriot* (New York: John Wiley, 2002); Laura Baskes Litwin, *Benjamin Banneker: Astronomer and Mathematician* (Berkeley Heights, NJ: Enslow, 1999); Milton Meltzer, ed., *In Their Own Words: A History of the American Negro 1916–1966*, vol. 1 (New York: Thomas Y. Crowell, 1964).

Bill Engel

Baraka, Amiri (born 1934). Poet, playwright, essayist, editor, novelist, and political activist. Baraka is a controversial and prolific writer who has transformed his name, philosophy, and political stance throughout his career, yet has maintained a consistently rebellious and contentious tone, never relenting in his attacks on the status quo. He first changed his name from LeRoy to LeRoi Jones and then began using the Islamic name Imamu Amiri Baraka (1968) before finally using just Amiri Baraka (1974). From his early involvement in the **Beat Movement**, he went on to become a leading figure in **Black Nationalism** and the **Black Arts Movement**, and is now most often regarded as a spokesperson for Third World **Marxism**. Baraka has been accused by some critics of unevenness in the quality of his work, of being racist, and of sacrificing aesthetics to his leftist political views; others see him as an authentic voice of and leader for African Americans and as one whose innovations and wide-ranging talents mark him as among the greatest African American authors, comparable in influence with **W.E.B. Du Bois** and **Richard Wright**.

Baraka was born Everett Leroy Jones in Newark, New Jersey, to Coyette "Coit" LeRoy Jones, a postal supervisor, and Anna Lois Jones, a social worker. After graduating from high school with honors in 1951, he attended Rutgers University on a scholarship, then transferred to Howard University in 1952. At Howard, he changed the spelling of his name to LeRoi. After dropping out of Howard University (1954), Baraka joined the Air Force (what he calls the "Error Farce" in his *Autobiography*), from which he received an undesirable discharge (1957). He settled in Greenwich Village, where he met and married a Jewish woman, Hettie Cohen (1958). Baraka and his wife (who took the name Hettie Jones) published the Beat literary journal *Yugen*, and he interacted with and was influenced by such authors as Allen Ginsberg, Charles Olson, and Frank O'Hara.

In 1960, following the Cuban revolution, Baraka traveled to Cuba with a group of African American authors and intellectuals, and met Fidel Castro and a group of Latin American intellectuals. Baraka's essay "Cuba Libre" is based on these meetings and is divided into two sections: "What I Brought to the Revolution" and "What I Brought Back Here." In 1961, he published his first collection of poems, *Preface to a Twenty Volume Suicide Note*. In it, according to one critic, Baraka "probes into the realms of autobiography and identity, high art and avant-gardist artists, Black music, American popular culture, and the heroes and anti-heroes of the Western world" (Sollors, 37). Baraka later wrote *Blues People: Negro Music in White America* (1963), a nonfiction book in which he discusses **jazz** and **blues** as expressions of African American social history; he also published a second collection of poetry, *The Dead Lecturer* (1964). During this period, Baraka further developed his dramatic technique by writing such plays as *The Slave* (1964) and *Dutchman* (1964), an absurdist drama focusing on racial stereotyping and identity. *Dutchman* is about Clay, a well-dressed young Black man who is taunted by Lula, a flirtatious white woman, for acting white while they are riding together on the subway. When the incessant taunting enrages Clay, Lula stabs him to death. *Dutchman*, which received an Obie for the best Off-Broadway production, greatly enhanced Baraka's visibility and reputation.

In 1965, the year **Malcolm X** was assassinated, Baraka divorced Hettie and moved to **Harlem, New York**, where he started the short-lived **Black Arts Repertory Theatre/School**, beginning a period during which he focused on Black Nationalism, Black arts, and other African American issues, and increasingly began to use Black English in his writing. Baraka then returned to Newark, where in 1966 he married an African American woman, Sylvia Robinson (now Amina Baraka); founded Jihad Productions (1966), which published the works of such African American authors as **Ben Caldwell**, Yusef Iman, and Clarence Reed; and founded Spirit House (1967), an African American community theater and center for arts and culture. He also became active in politics, Black Nationalism, and the **Nation of Islam**, even helping arrange a national **Black Power** conference (1967). During the 1967 **race riots** in Newark, Baraka was arrested and convicted of unlawfully carrying firearms and resisting arrest, but his conviction was overturned

Amiri Baraka, 1965. Courtesy of the Library of Congress.

on appeal. Baraka was also instrumental in electing Kenneth Gibson, Newark's first African American mayor (1970) and one of the first African American mayors of a major U.S. city; in organizing the Congress of African People (1970), a national Pan-African organization; and in arranging the National Black Political Convention (1972), which met in Gary, Indiana.

By 1974, Baraka was shifting his focus from Black Nationalism and Islam to Third World Marxism and had dropped the title Imamu (Swahili for spiritual leader) from his name. In his poetry collection *Hard Facts* (1976), Baraka's focus is on class struggles, and he is highly critical of the African American middle class and many African American authors and intellectuals, such as **Nikki Giovanni**, for selling out to White ideals. He also wrote several plays, including *The Motion of History* (1977), *What Was the Relationship of the Lone Ranger to the Means of Production* (1979), and *Dim'Cracker Party Convention* (1980). For two decades (1980–2000) Baraka was a professor of African Studies at the State University of New York at Stony Brook while continuing his prolific writing career, penning plays, essays, and poetry, including *Wise, Why's, Y's* (1996), an epic poem in which Baraka uses the narrative persona of a griot (an African storyteller) to discuss the history of oppression and struggle of African Americans.

Baraka was named poet laureate of New Jersey by Governor James E. McGreevey, but just one month after he became poet laureate (2002), Baraka was asked to resign after an outcry following a public reading of his "Somebody Blew Up America" (2001), a poem about the 9/11 terrorist attacks. Baraka was accused of anti-Semitism, primarily on the basis of the lines "Who knew the World Trade Center was gonna get bombed/Who told 4000 Israeli workers at the Twin Towers/To stay home that day/Why did Sharon stay away?" Ultimately, since there was no way to rescind the award and Baraka refused to give it up, the position of poet laureate was abolished in New Jersey (2003), effectively stripping Baraka of the title before his term was completed.

Resources: Primary Sources: Amiri Baraka: *The Autobiography of LeRoi Jones* (New York: Freundlich Books, 1984; repr. Chicago: Lawrence Hill Books, 1997); *The LeRoi Jones/Amiri Baraka Reader*, ed. William J. Harris (New York: Thunder's Mouth, 1991); *Selected Plays and Prose of Amiri Baraka/LeRoi Jones* (New York: William Morrow, 1979); *Somebody Blew Up America and Other Poems* (Albany, NY: House of Nehesi, 2004); *Transbluesency: The Selected Poems of Amiri Baraka/LeRoi Jones (1961–1995)*, ed. Paul Vangelisi (St. Paul, MN: Marsilio, 1995); *Wise, Why's, Y's: The Griot's Tale* (Chicago: Third World Press, 1995); LeRoi Jones, *Blues People: Negro Music in White America* (New York: William Morrow, 1963). **Secondary Sources:** Bob Bernotas, *Amiri Baraka: Poet and Playwright*, ed. Nathan I. Huggins (New York: Chelsea House, 1991); Cecil Brown, "About LeRoi Jones," *Evergreen Review* 75 (Feb. 1970), 65–70; Ralph Ellison, "The Blues," *New York Times Review of Books*, Feb. 6, 1964, pp. 5–7; Suzy Hansen, "Amiri Baraka Stands by His Words," *Salon.com*; William J. Harris, "The Transformed Poem," in *Poetry and Poetics of Amiri Baraka: The Jazz Aesthetic* (Columbia: University of Missouri Press, 1985), 91–121; Theodore Hudson, *From LeRoi Jones to Amiri Baraka: The Literary Works* (Durham, NC: Duke University Press, 1973); Werner Sollors, *Amiri Baraka/LeRoi Jones: The Quest for a "Populist Modernism"* (New York: Columbia University Press, 1978); Jerry Gafio Watts, *Amiri Baraka: The Politics and Art of a Black Intellectual* (New York: New York University Press, 2001).

David Carrell

Baraka, Ras (born 1970). Poet, activist, teacher, politician, writer. The son of **Amiri Baraka**, he has contributed to African American literature through poetry, rhythm and blues, and **rap**. With **Kevin Powell** he edited *In the Tradition: An Anthology of Young Black Writers*, featuring the works of Black poets (1993). He did vocals for the Fugee's album *The Score* (1996), which won the Grammy for Best Rap Album (1997). He released his own spoken-word album, *Shorty for Mayor*, to favorable reviews (1998). This album features pensive poetry set to music, and its highlight is the single "Hot Beverage in Winter," featuring Lauryn Hill. Baraka later appeared on Hill's album *The Miseducation of Lauryn Hill*, which won numerous music awards (1998). His poem "For the Brothers Who Ain't Here" appeared in *Poetry Nation: The North American Anthology of Fusion Poetry* (1998); it forms a poetics of fusion eliminating distinctions between oral and written traditions. He is one of the founders of Verse 4 Verse, a literary series that promotes poetry, in Newark, New Jersey. His dialogue "Black Youth Black Art Black Face—An Address" appeared in *Step into a World: A Global Anthology of the New Black Literature* (2000). His "*An American* Poem" appeared on the CD *Jazz Poetry Kafe: The BlackWords Compilation*, a collection of poetry, spoken work, acid jazz, and world rhythms (2000).

Resources: Regie Cabica and Todd Swift, *Poetry Nation: The North American Anthology of Fusion Poetry* (Montreal: Vehicle Press, 1998); Kevin Powell, ed., *Step into a World: A Global Anthology of the New Black Literature* (New York: John Wiley, 2000).

Aaron Peron Ogletree

Barnes, Steven Emory (born 1952). Science fiction novelist, short story writer, and screenwriter. Steven Barnes is a writer with a deeply spiritual outlook whose books trace the importance of human growth and the struggle of well-meaning individuals to do good in a harsh environment.

Born in **Los Angeles, California**, to Emory and Eva Mae Barnes, he attended Los Angeles High School, Los Angeles City College, and Pepperdine University before withdrawing to turn his energies toward commercial fiction, something he felt the university could not teach him. Contacts with Ray Bradbury led to two encouraging letters from the established science fiction master, but it was his collaboration with Larry Niven on a novel set in a near future theme park—*Dream Park* (1981)—that launched his career. This novel led to two sequels: *The Barsoom Project* (1989) and *The California Voodoo Game* (1992). Further collaborations followed—with Niven on *The Descent of Anansi* (1982) and *Achilles' Choice* (1991), and with Niven and Jerry Pournelle on *The Legacy of Heorot* (1987) and *Beowulf's Children* (1995).

An accomplished martial artist who has used his expertise to write articles for *Blackbelt* magazine, Barnes created a trilogy of novels featuring Aubry Knight, an assassin in the near future who tries to use his lethal skill for good. In this trilogy—*Streetlethal* (1982), *Gorgon Child* (1989), and *Firedance* (1994), Knight fends off drug dealers, religious cultists, and hired killers, respectively, but also undergoes a transformation from a killer trying to do good to a builder trying to be fully human. Barnes's Web site, www.lifewrite.com, details a complete approach to fitness, living, and writing that has grown out of his lifelong fascination with martial arts.

Though Barnes has never made it a goal to be seen specifically as the great African American novelist, he deals with race effectively, in part by drawing three-dimensional African American characters. His alternate-history series,

Lion's Blood (2002) and *Zulu Heart* (2003), imagines an America of the 1800s that is dominated by Africans who have Europeans as their slaves. Set as the country is moving toward civil war, these novels focus on an Irish ex-slave and an Ethiopian nobleman who are caught between the two sides. Widely praised, these novels provide for the possibility of new ways of looking at **race**.

Resources: Primary Works: Steven Barnes: *Blood Brothers* (New York: TOR Books, 1996); *Charisma* (New York: TOR Books, 2002); *Firedance* (New York: TOR Books, 1994); *Five Minute Miracle and Lifewriting*, Web site, http://www.lifewrite.com; *Gorgon Child* (New York: TOR Books, 1989); *Iron Shadows* (New York: TOR Books, 1998); *The Kundalini Equation* (New York: TOR Books, 1986); *Lion's Blood: A Novel of Slavery and Freedom in an Alternate America* (New York: Aspect/Warner Books, 2002); *Streetlethal* (New York: Ace Books, 1982); *Zulu Heart* (New York: Warner Books, 2003); Steven Barnes and Larry Niven: *Achilles' Choice* (New York: TOR Books, 1991); *The Barsoom Project* (New York: Ace Books, 1989); *The California Voodoo Game* (New York: Ballantine, 1992); *The Descent of Anansi* (New York: TOR Books, 1982); *Dream Park* (New York: Ace Books, 1981); *Saturn's Race* (New York: TOR Books, 2000); Steven Barnes, Larry Niven, and Jerry Pournelle: *Beowulf's Children* (New York: TOR Books, 1995); *The Legacy of Heorot* (New York: Simon and Schuster, 1987). **Secondary Sources:** "Barnes, Steven Emory," *Contemporary Authors Online*, http://galenet.galegroup.com; Sandra Y. Govan, "Barnes, Steven," in *The Oxford Companion to African American Literature*, ed. William L. Andrews, Frances Smith Foster, and Trudier Harris (New York: Oxford University Press, 1997), 52; Frances Hamit, "The Self Evolution of Steven Barnes," *Players* 14, no. 9 (Feb. 1988), 36–40; Jay P. Pedeson, ed., *St. James Guide to Science-Fiction Writers* (Detroit: St. James Press, 1996); Jessie Carnie Smith, ed., *Notable Black American Men* (Detroit: Gale, 1998).

Thomas J. Cassidy

Barnett, LaShonda Katrice (born 1974). Short story writer and scholar. Barnett is best known for her *Callaloo & Other Lesbian Love Tales* (1999), a collection of sixteen short stories that focus on lesbian relationships, particularly among women of color, in eras other than the twentieth century. Barnett has contributed short stories to numerous anthologies, including *Hot and Bothered: Short, Short Fiction of Lesbian Desire* and *Hot and Bothered 2: Short, Short Fiction of Lesbian Desire*, both edited by Karen X. Tulchinksky; *Does Your Mama Know? An Anthology of Black Lesbian Coming Out Stories*, edited by Lisa C. Moore; and *Chasing the American Dyke Dream: Homestretch*, edited by Susan Fox Rogers. She has also presented at numerous workshops and participated in symposiums in African American Studies.

Barnett is currently a doctoral student in the American Studies program at the College of William and Mary. Her dissertation, tentatively titled "I Got Thunder (and It Rings): Afrodiasporic Voicing in the Music of Abbey Lincoln, Cassandra Wilson and Nina Simone," examines the political representations and cultural contributions of three preeminent singers whose work pushes the boundaries of categorization and musical disciplines. Barnett reviewed, for Amazon.com, Abbey Lincoln's "Wholly Earth," a 1999 CD that showcases Lincoln's unique vocal style. Barnett presented a paper at the 2001 symposium "For Love of Abbey: A Symposium," sponsored by the Institute for Research in African-American Studies at Columbia University.

Barnett grew up in Park Forest, Illinois. She began writing as a child and turned to writing lesbian literature because she was unable to find stories that reflected her own experiences. She has a B.A. in English literature and language studies from the University of Missouri and an M.A. in women's history from Sarah Lawrence College. (*See* **Lesbian Literature**.)

Resources: LaShonda K. Barnett, *Callaloo & Other Lesbian Love Tales* (Norwich, VT: New Victoria, 1999); Lisa C. Moore, ed., *Does Your Mama Know: An Anthology of Black Lesbian Stories* (Decatur, GA: Redbone Press, 1997); Susan Fox Rogers, ed., *Chasing the American Dyke Dream* (San Francisco: Cleis Press, 1998); Karen X. Tulchinsky, ed., *Hot and Bothered* (Vancouver, BC: Arsenal Pulp Press, 1998–2003).

Patricia L T Camp

Barrax, Gerald W. (born 1933). Poet. Born in Attala, Alabama, Barrax moved with his family to **Pittsburgh, Pennsylvania**, when he was eleven years old. After graduating from high school, he served in the U.S. Air Force from 1953 to 1957. For a decade after his discharge, he worked as a mail carrier while completing a B.A. degree at Dusquesne University in 1963 and a master's degree at the University of Pittsburgh in 1969. For two years, he was an instructor at North Carolina Central University. Since 1970, he has served as a special instructor in the English Department at North Carolina State University. Barrax has been married twice, and his relationships with his wives and with his children from both marriages have provided a touchstone for his treatment of broader issues confronting African American society and culture. The combination of confessional and topical elements in his choice of subjects is reflected in his integration of radically experimental poetic techniques into fairly accessible, traditional lyrical forms.

In Barrax's first book, *Another Kind of Rain* (1970), he focuses in some poems on his strained relationships with his sons from his first marriage, and in other poems on the broader social forces transforming the African American family. On their surfaces, the poems are strikingly unusual, juxtaposing urban slang expressions with conventional references to literary figures and works. In *An Audience of One* (1980), Barrax explores the ways in which the deep sense of renewal that he has found in his second marriage might connect to the need for a renewed sense of focus and purpose in African American society. His third collection, *Leaning Against the Sun* (1992), is pointedly transcendental, searching out intimations of the divine in both personal relationships and social arrangements. In 1998, Louisiana State University Press published *From a Person Sitting in Darkness: New and Selected Poems*, a collection that permits an appreciation of the persistent elements in Barrax's considerable evolution as a poet.

Resources: Gerald Barrax: *Another Kind of Rain* (Pittsburgh, PA: University of Pittsburgh Press, 1970); *An Audience of One* (Athens: University of Georgia Press, 1980); *From a Person Sitting in Darkness: New and Selected Poems* (Baton Rouge:

Louisiana State University Press, 1998); *Leaning Against the Sun* (Fayetteville: University of Arkansas Press, 1992); Michael McFee, " 'Dazzle Gradually': The Poetry of Gerald Barrax," *Callaloo* 20, no. 2 (Spring 1997), 327–340; Lenard D. Moore, "On Hearing Gerald W. Barrax," *Black American Literature Forum* 21 (Fall 1987), 241–242; Joyce Pettis, "An Interview with Gerald Barrax," *Callaloo* 20, no. 2 (Spring 1997), 312–326.

Martin Kich

Basie, William "Count" (1904–1984). Big-band leader, pianist, and arranger. Ever the entertainer, Basie popularized big-band **swing** and stayed in the limelight of popular African American entertainment for more than sixty years. His meticulous symphonic arrangements broadened the definition of what it meant to be a **jazz** composer, and his interest in representing through dance music the quick-paced and dynamic interventions of urban life turned his compositional techniques into a kind of literary jazz.

Born in Redbank, New Jersey, young Bill Basie went to New York City to study stride piano with established **Harlem Renaissance** performers. While accompanying a touring group on the vaudeville circuit in 1927, Basie was hospitalized for spinal meningitis in Kansas City, Missouri; while recovering, he became a part of the vibrant Kansas City jazz community, working with such seminal swing groups as Walter Page's Blue Devils and Bennie Moten's Kansas City Orchestra. By the end of the 1930s, Basie had made a name for himself—literally and figuratively—he changed his moniker to "Count," moved back to New York with some of the most talented performers he'd met in Kansas City, and began recording some of the tunes popular with dance audiences across the country. Signature Basie compositions such as "One O'Clock Jump" (1937), "Jumpin' at the Woodside" (1938), and "Taxi War Dance" (1939), all dance tunes representing the pace of urban life, ensured the popularity and prominence of what became known as the Count Basie Orchestra. Capitalizing on the growing international popularity of jazz, Basie (along with **Duke Ellington** and Louis Armstrong) worked for decades as an unofficial cultural diplomat, bringing to foreign locales a picture of American musical precision, improvisational ingenuity, and freedom. His orchestra kept the vibrancy of precisely scored big-band swing music in the public eye, even as musical styles and the broader context of American racial politics changed dramatically.

Basie's **autobiography**, published posthumously, documents his travels through these dramatic changes. Originally recorded as an audio document by jazz writer **Albert Murray**, this entertaining collection of personal anecdotes locate Basie's life within the dynamics of these fluctuating worlds. The wider field of jazz aesthetics evolved dramatically from the 1930s through the early 1980s, moving from large swing groups such as Basie's to smaller four- and five-piece combos, from the compositional precision of dance music to "free jazz" improvisation. At the same time, America's racial politics shifted in ways that, while broadening the accessibility of larger venues and bringing better pay and more exposure to African American musicians, also radicalized the music in ways that continually challenged mainstream America to listen and take notice. Although Basie was not overtly political, his story expresses some of the major debates in the complex struggles of 20th-century African American culture.

Resources: Count Basie, *Good Morning Blues: The Autobiography of Count Basie* (1985; repr. New York: Da Capo, 2002); Stanley Dance, *The World of Count Basie* (New York: Da Capo, 1985).

Keith Feldman

Basketball. Basketball was developed in the United States at the end of the nineteenth century. James Naismith is credited with inventing the game in the 1890, in Springfield, Massachusetts. Since then it has achieved worldwide popularity. Alongside **jazz**, **blues**, **rap**, and various types of dance, basketball has begun to be considered not just a sport but also part of African American popular cultural expression, a link to understanding innovation and experimentation in other aspects of culture, such as literature. Although basketball began as a White sport played at YMCAs and its first short-lived professional leagues were all White, Black club teams in the New York area were well established by 1910. By then, Howard, Lincoln, and Union universities had teams, as did Hampton Institute. **Paul Robeson**, a four-year varsity football player for Rutgers University, also played basketball until his graduation in 1919. By the late 1920s Black players began to appear on the rosters of the teams for Columbia University, the University of Southern California, and Western Illinois State Teachers College. African Americans played important roles in the early days of professional basketball, the two most important teams being the New York Renaissance Five ("The Rens") and the Harlem Globetrotters. Both were organized in the 1920s and were among the most dominant teams of the 1930s. Chuck Cooper, Nat "Sweetwater" Clifton, and Earl Lloyd were, respectively, the first Black players to be drafted by, to sign with, and to play for an NBA team (all during the 1950–1951 season). The last gasp for racially segregated basketball came when the team of Texas Western College (now the University of Texas-El Paso), which featured five African American starters, defeated the University of Kentucky's all-White team for the 1966 NCAA championship.

Basketball plays a role in works by a number of American writers, including John Updike's "Ex-Basketball Player" and his four "Rabbit" novels, as well as books of poems by a former player in the National Basketball Association, Tom Meschery. **Quincy Troupe**'s basketball poem, "A Poem for 'Magic,'" in his *Avalanche: Poems* (1996), celebrates how Earvin "Magic" Johnson "wiled [his] way to glory" and his "reverse hoodoo gem/off the spin," suggesting the connections that African American writers see between basketball, ingenuity, creativity, and African culture. **John Edgar Wideman**, who played basketball for the University of Pennsylvania from 1959 to 1963, has written most substantially about the game from a literary perspective: basketball features prominently in "Doc's Story" in *Fever* (1989) and in portions of the novels *Reuben* (1987) and *Philadephia Fire* (1990). In "Doc's Story" a group of men trading basketball stories at a park turn to the topic of Doc, so attuned to the game that he was able to play even when blind; the narrator weaves this story into that of his collapsed relationship with a woman who lacks faith in their interracial relationship. In *Philadelphia Fire* the playground basketball the narrator engages in leaves him in pain but feeling alive, and it helps him reframe his search for answers about the bombing of the MOVE-like house that serves as the impetus for the story. In *Reuben*, a supporting character is a recruiter for a college team and must deal with mind-numbing travel and the troubling economics of college basketball, which grants young men an opportunity to go to college but carries with it a whiff of the minstrel show and calls for payoffs and falsified expense reports. His lifestyle disturbs his psyche to the extent that he murders a stranger in a public bathroom.

Wideman's most developed treatment of the game and its relationship to literature comes in *Hoop Roots: Playground Basketball, Love, and Race* (2001). There he links basketball to his own writing practice, discerning in both a creativity and a tie with the past that relates to the communal creation of meaning and the sharing of history. Call-and-response and the ring shout are two examples of African American folk culture that Wideman finds within the sport. Recognizing the game's origins in White culture, Wideman focuses his attention on the specific practice of playground basketball. This variety of the game (also called "street") encourages a type of play often criticized by commentators when it makes its way into the college or professional game; Allen Iverson has perhaps most often been the subject of such comments for his type of play, his tattoos, and his lifestyle off the court. Wideman, however, values this type of basketball for its place outside normal time, and he locates in it a tapping of the strength of African ancestors. He calls the temporal transformation in playground basketball "Great Time," a notion developed from John Mbiti's 1969 book *African Religions and Philosophy* (Wideman, "Storytelling," 267). Wideman writes, connecting the sport to playing jazz: "Playground hoop is doing it. Participating in the action. *Being there.* The chance to be out there flying up and down the court. Its duration finite. Its time only time, yet so intimate, inalienable, saturated, whole, it's all time, Great Time. Each isolated moment briefer than brief . . . also provides continuity, the novel, constantly evolving, improvised context allowing the solo, the move to happen one more time because the players share lore—assumptions, standards, common memories (an aesthetic) about making music, playing the game" (*Hoop Roots*, 49; italics in original).

For Wideman, playground basketball is a folk art not unlike the blues or the sermons in African American churches, all providing inspiration and material for literature (*Hoop Roots*, 172–173): affirming the communal, everyday, and popular form of basketball forms a crucial part of his aesthetic vision of the source and power of his own writing. Wideman's description of the game is echoed by Michael Eric Dyson's description of **Michael Jordan**'s game: he senses in it a "will to spontaneity" (67), "stylization of the performed self" (68), and "edifying deception" (68–69). In an interview with Wideman, Jordan recognized this aspect of his game: "The defense alters many of my shots, so I create. I've always been able to create in those situations, and I guess it's the Afro-American game I have, that's just natural to me. And even though it may not be the traditional game that Americans have been taught, it works for me" ("Michael Jordan," 141).

Resources: Mike Douchant, *Encyclopedia of College Basketball* (New York: Gale Research, 1995); Michael Eric Dyson, "Be Like Mike? Michael Jordan and the Pedagogy of Desire," in his *Reflecting Black: African-American Cultural Criticism* (Minneapolis: University of Minnesota Press, 1993), 64–75; John S. Mbiti, *African Religions and Philosophy* (London: Heinemann, 1969); Alex Sechare, ed., *The Official NBA Basketball Encyclopedia*, 2nd ed. (New York: Villard Books, 1994); Quincy Troupe, "A Poem for 'Magic,'" in his *Avalanche: Poems* (Minneapolis, MN: Coffee House Press, 1996), 40–42; John Edgar Wideman: *Hoop Roots: Playground Basketball, Love, and Race* (Boston: Houghton Mifflin, 2001); "Michael Jordan Leaps the Great Divide," *Esquire*, Nov. 1990, pp. 138+; *Reuben* (New York: Henry Holt, 1987); "Storytelling and Democracy (in the Radical Sense): A Conversation with John Edgar Wideman," *African American Review* 34 (2000), 263–272.

Ian W. Wilson

Beadle, Samuel A. (1857–1932). Poet, novelist, and lawyer. Although Beadle never gained the national prominence enjoyed by some of his literary contemporaries, his work remains a watershed achievement in African American literature because it addresses the oppression and dehumanization endured by Blacks in America, especially in **the South**.

Born in **Atlanta**, Beadle moved with his family to Jackson, Mississippi, at the close of the **Civil War**. He completed undergraduate work at Atlanta University and Tougaloo College and received some legal training in the prominent law firm of Patrick Henry. Admitted to the Mississippi bar in 1884 after a grueling examination by both African American and White lawyers, Beadle received harsh treatment from some judges who refused to allow him to practice in their courtrooms because of his race. Nevertheless, he enjoyed a successful civil practice; among his clients were J. B. Hart, a prominent cotton merchant, several banking institutions, and several fraternal orders, including the Gideons and the Odd Fellows.

Beadle initially composed verses for the amusement of friends; he published his first volume, *Sketches from a Life in Dixie* (1899), at their request. Of the seven stories and fifty-three poems included in *Sketches*, only three addressed the precariousness of African American life in America. In "Lines," Beadle addresses the mistreatment that African American soldiers experienced upon their return from America's war with Spain in 1898. His second effort was *Adam Shuffler* (1901), a collection of short prose pieces delineating African American life. His second poetry collection and last creative offering, *Lyrics of the Under World* (1912), is the most heralded both stylistically and thematically. Included in this collection is a preface by the author in which he professes his novice status as a poet; however, most important, he addresses why he has chosen such a title. The title expresses his angst as an African American, one of a group that is consistently "treated as alien enemies in the land of their nativity."

Beadle moved to **Chicago, Illinois**, in 1930 and continued to practice law until his death in 1937.

Resources: Samuel A. Beadle: *Adam Shuffler* (Jackson, MS: Harmon Publishing, 1901); *Lyrics of the Under World* (Jackson, MS: W. A. Scott, 1912); *Sketches from a Life in Dixie* (Chicago: Scroll Publishing & Literary Syndicate, 1899); James B. Lloyd, ed., *Lives of Mississippi Authors, 1817–1967* (Jackson: University Press of Mississippi, 1981); Irvin C. Mollison, "Negro Lawyers in Mississippi," *Journal of Negro History* 15, no. 1 (Jan. 1930), 38–71; Randall Patterson, "Black Mississippi Poet of the Early Twentieth Century," *POMPA: Publication of the Mississippi Philological Association* (1992), 131–136; Theressa G. Rush, Carol F. Myers, and Ester S. Arata, eds., *Black American Writers Past and Present: A Biographical and Bibliographical Dictionary* (Metuchen, NJ: Scarecrow, 1975).

Candice Love Jackson

Beals, Melba Patillo (born 1941). Memoirist and journalist. A native of Arkansas, Beals (then Melba Patillo) was among nine African American high school students who were chosen to integrate Central High School in Little Rock, Arkansas, in 1957. She joined Elizabeth Eckford, Ernest Green, Gloria Ray, Carlotta Walls, Minnijean Brown, Terrence Roberts, Jefferson Thomas, and Thelma Mothershed in what quickly became an event of national importance. The governor of Arkansas, Orval Faubus, defied the federal order to integrate Little Rock's public schools, an order preceded by the two U.S. Supreme Court decisions under *Brown v. Board of Education of Topeka, Kansas*. President Dwight Eisenhower responded by sending federal troops to enforce the law and ensure that the nine students would be admitted to Central High School. The integration was televised and reported nationally. During the ordeal, the nine students were taunted, cursed, threatened, assaulted, and shunned by White students and townspeople, and their teachers were often less than supportive. Although the soldiers kept order, most of them were not sympathetic to the nine young African Americans. Beals kept a diary at the time but did not write the full story of her experience until she published *Warriors Don't Cry* (1995), which gives a detailed account of the days leading up to and following the forced integration, and shows how much courage was asked of the nine students, whose families' lives and homes were threatened. Beals also wrote *White Is a State of Mind: A Memoir* (1999). She earned a B.A. from San Francisco State University and an M.A. in journalism from Columbia University. She has worked as a television news reporter for the National Broadcasting Company and as a consultant in public relations and marketing, subjects about which she has also written, including the book *Expose Yourself: Using the Power of Public Relations to Promote Your Business and Yourself* (1990). At this writing, Beals lives in **San Francisco, California**.

Resources: Melba Patillo Beals: *Expose Yourself: Using the Power of Public Relations to Promote Your Business and Yourself* (San Francisco: Chronicle Books, 1990); *Warriors Don't Cry: A Searing Memoir of the Battle to Integrate Little Rock's Central High* (New York: Pocket Books, 1995; abridged ed. for young readers, New York: Simon and Schuster/Pulse Books, 2002); *White Is a State of Mind: A Memoir* (New York: Putnam, 1999); Eric Laneuville, director, *The Ernest Green Story* (Hollywood: Disney Studios, 1993), VHS format.

Hans Ostrom

Beam, Joseph (1954–1988). Essayist, editor, and activist. Joseph Beam is primarily remembered as the editor of *In the Life: A Black Gay Anthology*. This text was one of the first works—and is often heralded as *the* first work—to gather the voices and experiences of Black gay men into one representative volume.

Published in 1986, *In the Life* features entries from twenty-nine self-identified Black gay men. The book's title echoes a slang expression for these men and the gay life. The work includes poetry, short stories, and art. Several of the contributors, such as poet **Essex Hemphill** and Beam himself, have more than one entry. Although many of the contributors to *In the Life* have faded from cultural memory, others readily spring to mind when the topic of Black gay men comes up (**Melvin Dixon**, Essex Hemphill, and, certainly, **Samuel Delany**). Drawing on the title of one of the text's six sections, *In the Life* offered a previously unavailable opportunity for Black gay men to "Speak for Ourselves."

In his introduction, "Leaving the Shadows Behind," Beam laments the dearth of texts that feature Black gay male voices: "By mid-1983 I had grown weary of reading literature by white gay men who fell, quite easily, into three camps: the incestuous literati of Manhattan and Fire Island, the San Francisco cropped-moustache-clones, and the Boston-to-Cambridge politically correct radical faggots. None of them spoke to me as a Black gay man" (13). Feeling disinvited from the narratives constructed by these and other white gay men, and wanting to create a visible representation of Black gay subjectivity, Beam issued a call that eventually resulted in *In the Life*.

In his essay "Brother to Brother: Words from the Heart," Beam asserts, "Black men loving Black men is [a] revolutionary act" (240). This is a famous statement that was picked up and explicated by Essex Hemphill, and also rejected by more recent Black gay writers, such as **James Earl Hardy**. Beam continues, "Black men loving Black men is a call to action, an acknowledgment of responsibility" (242). To an extent, *In the Life* is a similar call to action, a call to Black gay men to represent their lives in the face of silence and disregard. Although race is foregrounded in the subtitle of the text, the majority of the included works speak to the coalescence of race and sexuality, resulting in a queer reading of the Du Boisian concept of double consciousness (*see* **W.E.B. Du Bois**).

In addition to editing *In the Life*, Beam worked at Giovanni's Room, a gay, lesbian, and feminist bookstore in **Philadelphia, Pennsylvania**. He was a contributing editor for *Blacklight*, a Black gay publication edited and published by *In the Life* contributor Sidney Brinkley. Beam's writing appeared in New

York's *Native*, Philadelphia's *Gay News*, and the *Advocate*. *Brother to Brother* is the companion text to Beam's *In the Life*. Essex Hemphill edited *Brother to Brother* after Beam's death from AIDS in 1988. The title *Brother to Brother* is taken from Beam's *In the Life* essay. (*See* **Gay Literature**.)

Resources: Joseph Beam, ed., *In the Life: A Black Gay Anthology* (Boston: Alyson, 1986); Essex Hemphill, ed., *Brother to Brother: New Writings by Black Gay Men* (Boston: Alyson, 1991).

Chris Bell

Bearden, Romare (1912–1988). Visual artist. Romare Bearden's visual art has both influenced and complemented the work of numerous twentieth-century Black American writers, including **Ralph Ellison, Albert Murray, August Wilson**, and **Michael S. Harper**. In some cases, specific Bearden pieces have inspired literary works with their suggestions of story or dramatic scene. August Wilson recalls, for instance, that he was compelled to write his 1988 play, *Joe Turner's Come and Gone*, after seeing Bearden's 1978 collage *Mill Hand's Lunch Bucket*, which shows three somber Black figures seated around a dining table, with industrial **Pittsburgh, Pennsylvania**, looming through the window behind them (Rocha, 11). Similarly, Wilson's Pulitzer Prize-winning *The Piano Lesson* (1990) was inspired by a 1983 Bearden silk screen of the same title: a domestic scene revealing a Black mother and daughter seated at the family piano.

While the narrative aspect of Bearden's work lends itself to dramatic or fictional exploration, perhaps the artist's broader influence on African American literature comes through his capacity for stylizing the diverse specifics of Black American life in ritual terms. Bearden's body of work offers an iconographic survey of African American experience that encompasses the folk **vernacular** and the urban contemporary. His comprehensive range of representation spans history and geography in its depiction of conjure women, quilting families, Northern factory workers, **Harlem, New York**, children, and uptown jazz musicians. Bearden's visualizations of African American life are diverse in subject matter but unified in their ceremonial intentions, always rendering the "everyday" moments of Black American experience in a self-consciously visionary manner. It is this stylized quality, in particular, that makes Bearden's work a fitting visual complement to the modernist-influenced writing of figures like Ellison and Murray.

In 1995 collages by Bearden and poems by **Langston Hughes** were combined into a children's book, *The Block*, with an introduction by **Bill Cosby**.

Resources: Alvin Ailey, James Baldwin, Romare Bearden, and Albert Murray, "To Hear Another Language," *Callaloo* 12, no. 3 (1989), 431–452; Romare Bearden, *Romare Bearden: Narrations* (Purchase, NY: Neuberger Museum of Art, 2002); Romare Bearden and Carl Holty, *The Painter's Mind* (New York: Crown, 1969); Romare Bearden and Langston Hughes, *The Block: Collage by Romare Bearden/Poems by Langston Hughes* (New York: Viking Press/Metropolitan Museum of Art, 1995); Mary Schmidt Campbell and Sharon F. Patton, *Memory and Metaphor: The Work of Romare Bearden, 1940–1987* (New York: Oxford University Press, 1991); Ralph Ellison: "The

Art of Romare Bearden," in *The Collected Essays of Ralph Ellison*, ed. John Callahan (New York: Modern Library, 1995), 684–693; "Bearden," in *The Collected Essays of Ralph Ellison*, ed. John Callahan (New York: Modern Library, 1995), 831–835; Joan Fishman, "Romare Bearden, August Wilson, and the Traditions of African Performance," in *May All Your Fences Have Gates: Essays on the Drama of August Wilson*, ed. Alan Nadel (Iowa City: University of Iowa Press, 1994), 133–149; Gail Gelburd and Thelma Golden, *Romare Bearden in Black-and-White: Photomontage Projections 1964* (New York: Whitney Museum of American Art, 1997); Michael S. Harper, "Songlines from a Tessera(e) Journal: Romare Bearden, 1912–88," in his *Songlines in Michaeltree: New and Collected Poems* (Urbana: University of Illinois Press, 2000), 200–209; Kimberly Lamm, "Visuality and Black Masculinity in Ralph Ellison's *Invisible Man* and Romare Bearden's Photomontages," *Callaloo* 26, no. 3 (2003), 813–835; Albert Murray, "The Visual Equivalent to Blues Composition: Bearden Plays Bearden," in his *The Blue Devils of Nada: A Contemporary American Approach to Aesthetic Statement* (New York: Pantheon, 1996), 117–140; Mark Rocha, "August Wilson and the Four B's: Influences," in *August Wilson: A Casebook*, ed. Marilyn Elkins (New York: Garland, 1994), 3–16; Myron Schwartzman, *Romare Bearden: His Life and Art* (New York: Harry N. Abrams, 1990); M. Bunch Washington, *The Art of Romare Bearden: The Prevalence of Ritual* (New York: Harry N. Abrams, 1973).

Michael Borshuk

Beat Movement, The (1945–1965). This countercultural explosion, erupting seemingly simultaneously in New York and **San Francisco, California**, after **World War II**, inextricably linked the worlds of **jazz**, political resistance, and literature in ways that have reverberated for decades.

A cadre of writers, including most notably Jack Kerouac, Allen Ginsberg, and William Burroughs, but extending beyond this tight-knit circle to encompass dozens of others (including African American poets LeRoi Jones/ **Amiri Baraka**, **Bob Kaufman**, and **Ted Joans**), found inspiration in what Ginsberg called the "Secret Heroes" who lurked on the outskirts of mainstream cultural acceptability. These included the bebop musicians **Dizzy Gillespie**, **Charlie Parker**, and **Thelonious Monk**; the French poet Arthur Rimbaud; the Welsh performance poet Dylan Thomas; and the American poet Walt Whitman. What grew out of this cultural explosion was a definition of "hip," of having an acute awareness of the dominant paradigms of cultural production and the ability to utilize that awareness to construct resistant forms of art in the face of consolidating American norms. Whether addressing the need to "drop out" of American society, the visionary possibilities of narcotics and alcohol, the powers of homosocial relations, or the complex position of African Americans in American culture, the Beat Movement carved a broader space in the American literary imagination through which to forward critiques from the margins for a whole generation of artists.

Poet Gary Snyder often noted that the term "Beat Generation" really referred only to four close friends living in New York City. In 1944, Ginsberg and Lucien Carr were undergraduates at Columbia University searching for a "new vision" in literature. They were soon joined by Harvard graduate Burroughs and his Columbia dropout friend Kerouac. This "new vision," according to Carr, "was trying to look at the world in a new light, trying to look at the world in a way that gave it some meaning. Trying to find values . . . that were valid. And it was through literature all this was supposed to be done." In order to reconceptualize what it meant to be valid in the postwar era, this small contingent looked to the artistic product being created outside the ivory towers in which they had been indoctrinated to find alternative forms.

Along with French surrealism and nineteenth-century American transcendentalism, central to these forms was the growth of bebop jazz music, especially what was being produced in the tight urban spaces of New York City. Kerouac in particular found deep inspiration in such young jazz musicians as Parker and Gillespie, who were rearticulating standard show tunes in order to construct something deeply personal, deeply individual, in their improvised solos. They were, in Kerouac's terms, "musically as important as Beethoven/Yet not regarded as such at all." Kerouac's classic *On the Road* (1957) captured this spirit, whereby an individual could traverse the American landscape, and his own motion, the quick impulse-driven choices he made, could drive an entire narrative, and be encapsulated in the jazz solo. "Here were the children of the American bop night . . . and you had to look around to see where the solo was coming from, for it came from angelic smiling lips upon the mouthpiece and it was a soft, sweet, fairy tale solo on an alto. Lonely as America, a throatpierced sound in the night."

Kerouac and many others utilized this jazz-inspired literary form in both poetry and prose. A fairly common critique of this practice has been that these primarily White middle-class authors appropriated a romanticized vision of Blackness such that the "otherness" of being Black in America was exoticized and essentialized without any concern for material difference or racism. Black was something these authors sought to become. For example, Ginsberg's "Howl" (1955–1956), one of the Beat Movement's touchstone poems, sees "the best minds of my generation . . . dragging themselves through the negro streets at dawn." Kerouac's narrator in *The Subterraneans* (1958) wishes he "were a Negro" when he is in Denver's "colored section." And perhaps the most controversial—and lasting—appropriation of Blackness in conceptualizing what it meant to be "hip" is found in Norman Mailer's *The White Negro* (1957). While Mailer saw the politically powerful position of African Americans as "living on the margin between totalitarianism and democracy for two centuries," he grounded his vision of a White "Beat philosophy" in what many have seen as a degrading and simplistic stereotype of sexualized and racialized violence.

Several African American poets grew out of the Beat Movement. Kaufman, like Kerouac and others, saw revolutionary potential in the use of the jazz idiom, whereby the Beat poet could "blow African jazz in Alabama jungles and wail/ savage lovesongs of unchained fire." (**Langston Hughes**, of an older generation, had brought elements of blues and jazz into his poetry decades earlier and anticipated some features of Beat poetry.) Joans, a multimedia performance artist, mixed trumpet-playing with painting and spoken-word poetry. Having lived in much of the United States, Europe, and Africa, Joans located his jazz-inflected language in a variety of politically charged scenes. *Black Pow-Wow: Jazz Poems* (1969), an early collection of Joans's poetry, moves from the streets of Paris, to the Belgian Congo, to New York City and San Francisco.

One of the most illustrative shifts to come out of the Beat Movement was its particular evolution into the **Black Arts Movement** in the late 1960s, led primarily by Jones/Baraka. Jones/Baraka saw in the Beats' new engagement with popularized form "the language of this multinational land, of mixed ancestry, where war dances and salsa combine with country and Western, all framed by African rhythm-and-blues confessional." *Preface to a Twenty-Volume Suicide Note* (1961), *The Moderns* (1963), and *Blues People* (1963) all utilize the position of the marginalized poet to see, in popular culture, modes to critique the nation. While this earlier work was more interested in exploring the aesthetic possibilities of these forms, after the assassination of **Malcolm X** in 1965, Baraka's work became far more politically inflected. He distanced himself from the White community and founded the **Black Arts Repertory Theatre/School** in **Harlem, New York**, through which he was an activist for Black cultural nationalism and became tightly involved with the **Civil Rights Movement**.

The Beat Movement, often derided in high literary circles, regained some of its aesthetic clout in the 1990s as scholars and general readers alike clamored to find a quintessentially American twentieth-century literary tradition. However, while the works of Kerouac, Ginsberg, and Burroughs have been rightfully canonized, the important politically charged efforts of African Americans who utilized Beat forms have yet to receive the scholarly attention they deserve.

Resources: Lee Bartlett, ed., *The Beats: Essays in Criticism* (Jefferson, NC: McFarland, 1981); William S. Burroughs, *Naked Lunch* (1959; repr. New York: Grove Weidenfeld, 1992); Gregory Corso, *The Happy Birthday of Death* (New York: J. Laughlin, 1960); Michael Davidson, *The San Francisco Renaissance: Poetics and Community at Mid-Century* (New York: Cambridge University Press, 1989); Lawrence Ferlinghetti, *A Coney Island of the Mind: Poems* (New York: J. Laughlin, 1974); Allen Ginsberg, *Collected Poems 1947–1980* (New York: HarperPerennial, 1988); Ted Joans, *Teducation* (Minneapolis, MN: Coffee House Press, 1999); Leroy Jones/Amiri Baraka, *Transbluency: The Selected Poetry of Amiri Baraka/Leroi Jones* (St. Paul, MN: Marsilio, 1995); Bob Kaufman, *Cranial Guitar: Selected Poems* (Minneapolis, MN: Coffee House Press, 1996); Jack Kerouac, *On the Road* (1957; repr. New York: Penguin, 1991); A. Robert Lee, ed., *The Beat Generation Writers* (East Haven, CT: Pluto, 1996); Norman Mailer, *The White Negro* (San Francisco: City Lights, 1957); Kostas Myrsiades, ed., *The Beat Generation: Critical Essays* (New York: Peter Lang, 2002); John Tytell, *Naked Angels: The Lives and Literature of the Beat Generation* (New York: McGraw-Hill, 1976).

Keith Feldman

Beatty, Paul (born 1962). Novelist and poet. Beatty is known in part for his satiric writing. He was born in **Los Angeles**. After high school, he attended Brooklyn College, where he received an M.F.A. in creative writing. Later, he received an M.A. in psychology from Boston University. Beatty's passion for writing led to two volumes of poetry and two novels. His first volume of poems, *Big Bank Take Little Bank*, published by the **Nuyorican Poets Café** in 1991, was deemed one of the best collections of the year by *The Village Voice* and made the *Los Angeles Times* best-seller list. Three years later, his second, *Joker, Joker, Deuce* was published as part of Penguin Poets collection. He later ventured into the novel genre, producing *White Boy Shuffle* (1996) and *Tuff* (2001).

Beatty's hilarious and scathing first novel, *White Boy Shuffle*, embraces the verbal tradition of **satire** within the parameters of a tale about a Black surfer bum who undergoes a transformation from local outcast to basketball icon, and then accepts his calling as messiah of a "divided, down-trodden people." Critics have said that *WBS* is "a blast of satirical heat from the talented heart of Black American Life," and that Beatty is as "much in the tradition of Richard Pryor [as] Ralph Ellison" (Pratt). His follow-up book, *Tuff*, explores an inner-city young man who has both addictions and goals, and strives to release one and embrace the other. Beatty continues to receive praise from his contemporaries, one of whom observes: "Beatty's brusque and profane writing style doesn't detract at all from the validity of the book, in fact, it adds to it" (Jordan).

Beatty has made the successful transition from slam poet to writer. His first book of poems announced his arrival, and his second has solidified his residence within the borders of American literature. He currently lives and works in New York.

Resources: Paul Beatty: *Big Bank Take Little Bank* (New York: Nuyorican Café Press, 1991); *Joker, Joker, Deuce* (New York: Penguin, 1994); *Tuff: A Novel* (New York: Anchor Books, 2001); *The White Boy Shuffle: A Novel* (Boston: Houghton Mifflin, 1996); Barbara Hoffert, "The Auter Allure," *Library Journal* 121 (Oct. 1996), 46; Jennifer Jordan, "The New Literary Black Face," *Black Issues Book Review* 4 (Mar./Apr. 2002), 26–29; Sam Pratt, "Big Book," *Esquire*, July 1996, p. 24; Tom Tammaro, "Book Reviews: Arts and Humanities," *Library Journal* 116 (Jan. 1991), 107.

Melvin G. Hill

Beckham, Barry (born 1944). Novelist, biographer, nonfiction writer, and publisher. Beckham's best-known work is the novel *Runner Mack* (1972), which satirizes the **Vietnam War**, dramatizes issues connected to **Black Power**, and parodies conventions of **slave narratives** and rags-to-riches tales. Beckham had published his first novel, *My Main Mother*, in 1969, while he was still enrolled at Brown University. He is a native of New Jersey, where *My Main Mother* is set. In 1982, Dutton published Beckham's nonfiction book, *The Black Student's Guide to College*. Beckham himself published a revised edition of this book (1995) and, at this writing, operates Beckham House Publishing in Providence, Rhode Island. He has written a biography of a legendary playground basketball player in **Harlem**, Earl Manigault; it is titled *Double Dunk* and has been reissued by Beckham House Publishing. (*See* **Basketball**.)

Resources: Barry Beckham: *The Black Student's Guide to College* (New York: Dutton, 1982; rev. ed., Providence, RI: Beckham House, 1995, and Lanham, MD:

Madison Books, 1999); *Double Dunk: The Inspiring Story of a Harlem Basketball Legend* (1981; repr. Providence, RI: Beckham House, 1993); *My Main Mother* (New York: Walker, 1969; repr. Providence, RI: Beckham House, 2004); *Runner Mack* (New York: William Morrow, 1972); Jeff Loeb, "Beckham, Barry," in *The Oxford Companion to African American Literature*, ed. William L. Andrews, Frances Smith Foster, and Trudier Harris (New York: Oxford University Press, 1997), 55; Sanford Pinsker: "About *Runner Mack*: An Interview with Barry Beckham," *Black Images: A Critical Quarterly on Black Arts and Culture* 3, no. 3 (1974), 35–41; "A Conversation with Barry Beckham," *Studies in Black Literature* 5, no. 3 (1974), 17–20; Wiley Lee Umphlett, "The Black Man as Fictional Athlete: *Runner Mack*, the Sporting Myth, and the Failure of the American Dream," *MFS: Modern Fiction Studies* 33, no. 1 (Spring 1987), 73–83; Joe Weixlmann, "Barry Beckham: A Bibliography," *College Language Association Journal* 24, no. 4 (June 1981), 522–528; Loretta G. Woodard, "Barry Beckham (1944–)," in *Contemporary African American Novelists: A Bio-Bibliographical Critical Sourcebook*, ed. Emmanuel S. Nelson (Westport, CT: Greenwood Press, 1999), 29–35.

Hans Ostrom

Beckwourth, James (1798–c. 1867). Autobiographical writer, explorer, mountain man, and Crow chief. Author of *The Life and Adventures of James P. Beckwourth, Mountaineer, Scout, and Pioneer, and Chief of the Crow Nation of Indians* (1856), Beckwourth played a major role in the exploration and settling of the West. He was born in Virginia to a slave mother and an English father but spent most of his childhood in Missouri. He left for the West as a young adult, going on various trapping expeditions and gaining fame as a highly capable mountain man. Beckwourth was captured by the Crow in 1828, eventually became a chief, and married numerous Crow women. Persistently adventurous, he discovered a pass through the Sierra Nevada Mountains that now bears his name and that became a route for gold hunters and others headed to California. At an advanced age, he served as a guide to Col. John Chivington in the horrific Sand Creek massacre of the Cheyenne. Not long after the massacre he returned to the Crow and died near the Bighorn River.

Beckwourth dictated his highly colorful memoir to Thomas Bonner, an itinerant California justice of the peace, in 1854–1855. He was the only African American to publish a book about his experiences as an early frontiersman. The book achieved some success; however, because of Beckwourth's reputation as the teller of wild tales, what is truth and what is fiction is difficult to establish at this point. Bill Hotchkiss wrote a historical novel based on Beckwourth's life, *Medicine Calf* (1981).

Resources: James P. Beckwourth, *The Life and Adventures of James P. Beckwourth as Told to Thomas D. Bonner* (Lincoln: University of Nebraska Press, 1972); Bill Hotchkiss, *Medicine Calf* (New York: W. W. Norton, 1981).

Stephanie Gordon

Bell, Derrick (born 1930). Legal scholar and short story writer. An influential professor of law, Derrick Bell uses parables and short stories to explore the role of race and racism in American law and culture. His work formed the intellectual foundation of the area of legal thought known as critical race theory.

Bell's career has been both distinguished and controversial. Born in **Pittsburgh, Pennsylvania**, Bell entered the University of Pittsburgh School of Law in 1954, the same year as the Supreme Court's *Brown v. Board of Education* decision, and graduated in 1957. Soon afterward, he joined the **NAACP** Legal Defense Fund at the invitation of Thurgood Marshall. From 1960 to 1965, he litigated for Southern school desegregation. In 1971, Bell became the first African American tenured professor at Harvard Law School and, in 1973, published his seminal book, *Race, Racism and American Law*. Through a detailed study of case law, Bell argued that racial subordination and the protection of White social and economic interests were central to American jurisprudence. Drawing upon his arguments, Bell's students, from the 1980s on, expanded his work into critical race theory. He became dean of the University of Oregon School of Law in 1980. After five years, he departed when the school refused to offer a faculty position to an Asian American woman who had been a short-list candidate. Returning to Harvard, Bell continued to be an influential teacher. In 1992, he resigned to protest Harvard's unwillingness to hire women of color for the faculty. At present, he is a visiting professor of law at New York University.

After Bell had established himself as an attorney and scholar, his work took a literary direction with four books: *And We Are Not Yet Saved: The Elusive Quest for Racial Justice* (1987), *Faces at the Bottom of the Well: The Permanence of Racism* (1992), *Gospel Choirs: Psalms of Survival in an Alien Land Called Home* (1996), and *Afrolantica Legacies* (1998). For these works, he has written parables and short story sequences that explore racism's relationship to the law and provoke thought about the possibilities for social change. His best-known and recurring character is the fictional Geneva Crenshaw, a powerful legal mind who often engages in dialogue with Bell. Their dialogues explore why traditional jurisprudence often opposes substantive economic and social equality for African Americans.

The hypothetical situations offered by Bell's parables throw American racial ideologies into sharp relief. Among his most vivid stories is "The Space Traders," published in *Faces at the Bottom of the Well*, in which space aliens offer American leaders tremendous technological advances in exchange for African American citizens. After considerable debate, African Americans are indeed sold to the alien visitors. Bell's parable meditates on the willingness of white America to sacrifice the interests of African Americans in exchange for economic and social advantages.

In subsequent works, Bell has continued to expand his literary scope, reflecting on his own role as an activist and intellectual through both memoir and scholarly writing.

Resources: Derrick Bell: *Afrolantica Legacies* (Chicago: Third World Press, 1998); *And We Are Not Saved: The Elusive Quest for Racial Justice* (New York: Basic Books, 1987); *Confronting Authority: Reflections of an Ardent Protester* (Boston: Beacon Press, 1996); *Ethical Ambition: Living a Life of Meaning and Worth* (New York: Bloomsbury

Press, 2002); *Faces at the Bottom of the Well: The Permanence of Racism* (New York: Basic Books, 1992); *Gospel Choirs: Psalms of Survival in an Alien Land Called Home* (New York: Basic Books, 1996); *Race, Racism and American Law*, 5th ed. (New York: Aspen, 2004); *Silent Covenants: Brown v. Board of Education and the Unfulfilled Hopes for Racial Reform* (New York: Oxford University Press, 2004).

Richard M. Juang

Bell, James Madison (1826–1902). Abolitionist, poet, and lecturer. Bell was born in Gallipolis, Ohio. His parents' identities are unknown. At the age of sixteen, he moved to his brother-in-law's home in Cincinnati to learn plastering, the trade that would support him for most of his life. While there, in 1848, he married Louisiana Sanderlin (or Sanderline). Bell worked as a plasterer during the day and attended Cincinnati High School for Colored People at night. Through his studies, Bell was indoctrinated into the principles of the radical **abolitionist movement**.

In 1854, Bell moved his family to Chatham, Ontario, where he thought he would have more freedom. In Canada, he was involved in political activities, eventually meeting **John Brown** and developing a close political and personal association with him. Bell raised money and recruited men to help Brown organize the 1859 attack on the federal arsenal at Harpers Ferry, Virginia. In 1860, Bell moved to **San Francisco, California**, where he engaged in the struggle to ensure equal education for Black children. He also played a leading role in campaigns against legal discrimination, and during the **Civil War**, he worked as a crusader for abolition.

While in California, Bell composed verse orations on historical subjects, writing some of his most rousing poems, including "Emancipation" (1862), "The Day and the War" (1864), "Lincoln" (1865), "Valedictory on Leaving San Francisco" (1866), "The Progress of Liberty" (1866), "The Dawn of Freedom" (1868), and "The Triumph of Liberty" (1870). His poems consistently address the themes of **slavery**, the Civil War, and **Reconstruction**. A number of them celebrate anniversaries of Abraham Lincoln's Emancipation Proclamation. His long poems, some containing as many as 950 lines, were meant to be recited, and have been compared to following a stream whose source is unknown. Although Bell is best known today as a poet, his poetry took second place to activism during his lifetime. While his imagery and phrasing are considered conventional, his intent is often political rather than aesthetic.

In 1865, Bell left California for Toledo, Ohio. In Ohio, he was elected a delegate to the Republican National Conventions of 1868 and 1872. He traveled frequently, espousing doctrines on human freedom and often reciting his long poems as the method of instruction. Bishop B. W. Arnett, a friend who worked with Bell in the church and often accompanied him as he gave public readings of his poetry, claimed that no one instructed people better or had a more imposing manner than Bell (Locke, "James Madison Bell," in *American National Biography*, 507).

His poems, eventually compiled in *The Poetical Works of James Madison Bell* (1901), have been described as "almost identical and dull," and "without any distinctive literary quality," although some critics, such as Joan R. Sherman, call Bell's work "inventive and readable" because of its "shrewd humor and irony, concrete topicality and personal emotion" (Locke, "James Madison Bell," in *American National Biography*, 507).

In 1870, to commemorate the Fifteenth Amendment, Bell read his ode "The Triumph of Liberty" at the Detroit Opera House. His recitations inspired his listeners, and Sherman has portrayed him as "the verse propagandist for Afro-Americans in his century." Bell, who died in Toledo in 1902, is considered the last Black poet who was able to optimistically celebrate the liberty of post–Civil War years.

Resources: James Madison Bell, *The Poetical Works of James Madison Bell* (Freeport, NY: Books for Libraries, 1970); Shari Dorantes Hatch and Michael E. Strickland, "James Madison Bell," in *African American Writers: A Dictionary*, ed. Shari Dorantes Hatch and Michael R. Strickland (Santa Barbara, CA: ABC-CLIO, 2000), 20; Qadri Ismail, "James Madison Bell," in *Encyclopedia of African American Culture and History*, vol. 1, ed. Jack Salzman, David Lionel Smith, and Cornel West (New York: Macmillan Library Reference, 1996), 301–302; Mamie E. Locke: "James Madison Bell," in *African American Lives*, ed. Henry Louis Gates, Jr. and Evelyn Brooks Higginbotham (New York: Oxford University Press, 2004), 68–69; "James Madison Bell," in *American National Biography*, vol. 2, ed. John A. Garraty and Mark C. Carnes (New York: Oxford University Press, 1999), 507–508; Robert L. Milde, "James Madison Bell," in *African American Authors, 1745–1945: A Bio-Bibliographical Critical Sourcebook*, ed. Emmanuel S. Nelson (Westport, CT: Greenwood Press, 2000), 13–16.

Truong Le

Benjamin, Robert C. O. (1855–1900). Journalist, poet, attorney, writer, and historian. Benjamin's commitment to racial uplift informed his writing career. His motto for the San Francisco *Sentinel*, a Black newspaper that he began editing in 1890, epitomized his commitment: "My race first, and my friends next." According to Simmons's *Men of Mark*, Benjamin was born in St. Kitts and attended Trinity College of Oxford University. However, there is no record of Benjamin enrolling in the college, according to the archivist; he would have been too young to gain admittance. The biographical account also asserts that he traveled widely before settling in New York and becoming a U.S. citizen.

Benjamin's writing career helps document his life. His work took him through much of the United States, where he taught, edited newspapers, practiced law after passing the bar in Tennessee in 1880, and published pamphlets, often in support of the Black community. In New York, he worked as a soliciting agent for the *New York Star* and city editor of the *Progressive American*. He also made the acquaintance of the prominent abolitionist **Henry Highland Garnet**. Benjamin edited Black newspapers in several Southern states, including Kentucky and Alabama. He continued his journalism career in California, working for such Black newspapers as the *Los Angeles Observer*, and serving as the only Black editor of the *Los Angeles Sun*, a white newspaper. Benjamin published writings that include *Poetic Gems* (1883), a poetry collection; *Don't: A Book for Girls* (1891), an etiquette book; *Southern Outrages: A Statistical Record of Lawless Doings* (1894), one of the first studies of **lynching**s; and *Light After Darkness: Being an Up-to-Date History of the American Negro* (1896).

In the late 1800s, Benjamin returned to Kentucky. He was murdered during a voter registration drive in Lexington in 1900, according to the *Mt. Vernon Signal*.

Resources: Robert C. O. Benjamin: *Life of Toussaint L'Ouverture* (Los Angeles: Evening Express Publishing, 1888); *Light After Darkness: Being an Up-to-Date History of the American Negro* (Xenia, OH: Marshall & Beveridge, 1896); *Poetic Gems* (Charlottesville, VA: Peck & Allan, 1883); *Southern Outrages* (Los Angeles: Evening Express Publishing, 1894); Mamie Marie Booth Foster, "Benjamin, Robert C. O.," in *Southern Black Creative Writers, 1829–1953* (Westport, CT: Greenwood Press, 1988), 4; James D. Hart, "Benjamin, Robert Charles O'Hara," in his *A Companion to California*, new ed. (Berkeley: University of California Press, 1987), 43–44; I. Garland Penn, *The Afro-American Press and Its Editors* (New York: Arno Press, 1969), 320–324; "Personal and Otherwise," *Mt. Vernon Signal*, Oct. 5, 1900; William J. Simmons, "R.C.O. Benjamin Esq.," in his *Men of Mark: Eminent, Progressive and Rising* (Cleveland, OH: George M. Rewell, 1887), 991–995; Arnold H. Taylor, "Benjamin, R[obert] C[harles] O['Hara]," in *Dictionary of American Negro Biography*, ed. Rayford W. Logan and Michael R. Winston (New York: Norton, 1982), 39–40.

Rhondda R. Thomas

Bennett, Gwendolyn (1902–1981). Poet and short story writer. Although she never published a book of poetry or short fiction, Gwendolyn Bennett was an important figure in the **Harlem Renaissance**, one who worked to keep its spirit alive in later times. Born to Joshua and Maime Bennett in Giddings, **Texas**, in 1902, she subsequently lived in Nevada, **Washington, D.C.**, and New York City. In New York City, she attended high school and college at a time when the Harlem Renaissance was beginning to blossom. In 1923, she published what would prove to be one of her best-known poems, "Heritage," in the Urban League's magazine, **Opportunity**. The following year, she graduated from Pratt Institute with an art degree, and moved to Howard University to teach art. In 1925, she went to **Paris, France**, to study art, all the while keeping in touch with her friends involved in the Harlem Renaissance, such as **Langston Hughes** and **Countee Cullen**. When she returned to New York in 1926, she was a member, with Hughes, Cullen, **Wallace Thurman**, and **Zora Neale Hurston**, of the editorial committee that put together the single-issue journal *Fire!!*, in which her short story "Wedding Day" appeared. The next year, she returned to Howard to teach art, and used her Harlem connections for information she used in an arts column she wrote for *Opportunity*, "Ebony Flute." This column has proved to be a rich resource for cultural historians trying to reconstruct the Harlem Renaissance through the eyes of someone who was living it.

Though her artwork was used for covers of both *Opportunity* and **The Crisis**, it is through her twenty-two poems published between 1923 and 1931 that

Bennett is best known, particularly the poems "Heritage," "To a Dark Girl," and "To Usward." Unlike Countee Cullen's poem "Heritage," which ends by asking his Lord for forgiveness for wanting to see God as Black, Bennet's poem of the same title unambiguously states a desire to connect to Africa and the "surging/Of my sad people's soul." Similarly, her poem "For a Dark Girl" says that she loves a dark girl for the "something of old forgotten queens" that lurks in her walk, and urges the girl to keep her "queenliness," forget slavery, and "laugh at fate." Similarly, "To Usward," which was written to celebrate **Jessie Redmon Fauset**'s publication of the novel *There Is Confusion*, urges "all Negro Youth" to "break the seal of years/With pungent thrusts of song"—to use art to break free of the past. Taken together, these poems express an optimistic, modernist aesthetic, urging Black creative artists to go forward by embracing a deep connection to all African history, not the narrow recent history of African American **slavery** and discrimination.

In 1928 she married Alfred Jackson, who died in 1936. By this time, the Harlem Renaissance had largely played itself out, but Bennett became active in nurturing the creative arts in others. She joined the Harlem Arts Guild, and for three years directed the Harlem Community Arts Center, a Depression era Federal Arts Project. In these and other capacities, she played a crucial role in nurturing future generations of African American artists.

Resources: Walter C. Daniel and Sandra Y. Govan, "Gwendolyn Bennett," in *The Dictionary of Literary Biography*, vol. 51, *Afro-American Writers from the Harlem Renaissance to 1940*, ed. Trudier Harris (Detroit: Gale, 1987), 3–7; Sandra Y. Govan: "After the Renaissance: Gwendolyn Bennett and the WPA Years," *The Middle Atlantic Writers Association Review* 3, no. 2 (Dec. 1988), 227–231; "Bennett, Gwendolyn," in *The Oxford Companion to African American Literature*, ed. William L. Andrews, Frances Smith Foster, and Trudier Harris (New York: Oxford University Press, 1997), 57; Maureen Honey, ed., *Shadowed Dreams: Women's Poetry of the Harlem Renaissance* (New Brunswick, NJ: Rutgers University Press, 1989); Margaret Perry, *Silence to the Drums: A Survey of the Literature of the Harlem Renaissance* (Westport, CT: Greenwood Press, 1976); Ronald Primeau, "Frank Horne and the Second Echelon Poets of the Harlem Renaissance," in *The Harlem Renaissance Remembered*, ed. Arna Bontemps (New York: Dodd, Mead, 1972), 247–267; Cheryl A. Wall, *Women of the Harlem Renaissance* (Bloomington: Indiana University Press, 1995).

Thomas J. Cassidy

Bennett, Hal [George Harold] (born 1930). Novelist. Although Bennett published one volume of poetry, *The Mexico City Poems* (1961), he is primarily known as a satirical novelist on the order of **Charles Chesnutt** and **Wallace Thurman**. Bennett's novels, set in fictional Burnside and Cousinville, trace the lives of Black Americans who are seeking a new life by moving from the South to the North. Common characters and themes are played out against a backdrop reminiscent of William Faulkner's Yoknapatawpha County.

Born in Virginia and educated in New Jersey, Bennett moved to Mexico City to attend college after a newspaper publishing venture folded. There he completed most of *A Wilderness of Vines*, which was published in 1966. Reviews of both *A Wilderness of Vines* and *The Black Wine* (1968) praised the almost mythical universe Bennett was creating in his settings of Burnside and Cousinville. However, his immaturity as a writer was noted in criticisms of his emerging style.

In *Lord of Dark Places* (1970), Bennett comes into his own as a satirical writer. The story takes the character Joe Market from 1951 to his execution in 1968. In the book, Bennett explores American racial and sexual myths. *Lord of Dark Places* has been described variously as a bildungsroman, a detective story, and a black comedy.

Death, specifically murder, is the means of gaining a true identity in *Wait Until the Evening* (1974), and sexual servitude and the power of love provide freedom in *Seventh Heaven* (1976).

Bennett's collection of short stories, *Insanity Runs in Our Family* (1977), includes "Dotson Gerber Revisited," a piece that won him recognition by *Playboy* as the most promising writer of the year. This story of a Black man who is trying to achieve recognition for his murder of a White man is set squarely in the nightmarish world of Bennett's novels. Equally nightmarish is "The Day My Sister Hid the Ham," in which the narrator turns to murder to prove his manhood.

In his outrageous and sometimes fantastical books, Bennett states his desire to "explain what [he] thinks the Negro is and to do it in the terms of fiction" (Walcott, *DLB*, 22).

Resources: Hal Bennett: *The Black Wine* (Garden City, NY: Doubleday, 1968); *Insanity Runs in Our Family* (Garden City, NY: Doubleday, 1977); *Lord of Dark Places* (New York: Norton, 1970); *The Mexico City Poems* [and] *House on Hay* (Chicago: Obsidian Press, 1961); *Seventh Heaven* (Garden City, NY: Doubleday, 1976); *Wait Until the Evening* (Garden City, NY: Doubleday, 1974); *A Wilderness of Vines* (Garden City, NY: Doubleday, 1966); Ronald Walcott: "Hal Bennett," *Dictionary of Literary Biography*, vol. 33, *Afro-American Fiction Writers After 1955* (Detroit: Thomason-Gale, 1984), 20–33; "The Novels of Hal Bennett," part 1, *Black World* 23, no. 8 (June 1974), 36–48, 89–97, and part 2, *Black World* 23, no. 9 (July 1974), 78–96.

Patricia Kennedy Bostian

Benson, Leticia (born 1963). Poet and playwright. Benson, born in Houston, Texas, has produced poems and plays that reflect the passion and energy of modern Black culture. Her poetry is included in *In the Tradition: An Anthology of Young Black Writers* (1992), edited by **Kevin Powell** and **Ras Baraka**. Her work has also appeared in other anthologies and in magazines, including *Verses that Hurt: Pleasure and Pain from the Poemfone Poets*, *Listen Up!*, and *Long Shot* magazine. Benson has also written screenplays, including one for *Thick Heat*, which was broadcast in May 2001 on the Lifetime Network, and one for *Hairstory*, which also was broadcast on the Lifetime Network, and which won the Jurors Choice Award from the Links Film Festival and Best Narrative Award from Reel Sisters of the Diaspora Film Festival.

Benson wrote the novel *When Butterflies Kiss* (2001) with nine other rising literary stars. Conceived and edited by Sékou, the novel features chapters by individual authors that collectively narrate the quest of a young Black man named Dante to discover who he is as a writer, a lover, and a friend. Benson's contribution, the penultimate chaper, "On Top of the Game," highlights her talent for poetry and dramatic narrative. Benson presents Dante's journal as he clears his head of the baggage from former relationships and begins to write again. A romantic encounter gone awry and the loss of his best friend, Malik, bring Dante to the realization that he must rethink his entire life to get beyond the mask he finally realizes he wears. In this innovative concept, where authors do not know the outcome until the end, Benson elevates the eroticism established by the chapters preceding hers and prepares Dante for his breakthrough of identity that comes in the end.

Benson received her B.A. in anthropology from the University of Oklahoma and her M.F.A. in dramatic writing from New York University in 1999. She was awarded a fellowship in playwriting by the New York Foundation for the Arts, and her verses have been installed at the Aldrich Museum's "NO DOUBT" exhibition. Benson is also a **Nuyorican Poets Café** Grand Slam Champion. At this writing, she lives in **Brooklyn, New York**. (*See* **Performance Poetry**.)

Resources: Zoë Anglesey, ed., *Listen Up!: Spoken Word Poetry* (New York: Ballantine–One World, 1999); Ras Baraka and Kevin Powell, eds., *In the Tradition: An Anthology of Young Black Writers* (New York: Harlem River Press, 1992); Sékou, ed., *When Butterflies Kiss* (Atlanta: Silver Lion Press, 2001); Jordan Trachtenberg and Amy Trachtenberg, eds., *Verses That Hurt: Pleasure and Pain from the Poemfone Poets* (New York: St. Martin's Press, 1997).

Janaka N. Bowman

Bernal, Martin (born 1937). Historian, classicist, and cultural theorist. Now professor emeritus of government and Near Eastern studies at Cornell University, Martin Bernal had been a politically committed, though largely unassuming, historian of modern China before the first volume of his *Black Athena* appeared in the United States in 1987 (*see* **Black Athena Controversy**). The provocative thesis of that book—the "origins" of ancient Greek culture being more Egypto-Semitic, perceptually "Black," than Indo-European or "**White**"—was alternately reviled and lauded in academic circles as well as the popular media. Bernal's work surfaced in the midst of the post-Reagan "culture wars," and the controversy surrounding its reception resulted from his decentering Eurocentrist belief from much-hyped discussion of "Western civilization" core curricula and cultural literacy (*see* **Literary Canon**).

Perhaps it should not have come as a complete surprise that Bernal's scholarship aroused passionate ideological sentiment. Born in the Hampstead district of London in 1937, Bernal descends from a famous line of intellectual agitators. His grandfather Alan Gardiner was a renowned Egyptologist whose introduction of Ferdinand de Saussure's structuralist linguistics to the British academy was met with smug hostility. His father, John Desmond Bernal, was a visionary sociologist of science and knowledge, a decorated wartime physicist, and a prominent Communist activist and sometime Soviet ideologue. Institutionally speaking, Gardiner and the Bernals present a pedigree of intellectual dissent. Even Martin Bernal's early work on Chinese socialism was coupled with his involvement in antiwar protest throughout the 1960s.

What Bernal could not have anticipated was the way in which Afrocentrists such as Molefi Kete Asanti and John Henrik Clarke took up the Black Athena thesis to assail cultural conservatives defending a Eurocentric bias in the study of Western philosophy, history, and art (*see* **Afrocentricity**). Derived from Bernal's analysis of historical, archaeological, and linguistic records and documents, the thesis ostensibly discounts such bias: because the ancient Greeks themselves understood their culture to be profoundly and primarily influenced by peoples from Egypt and Phoenicia, not invaders from the north, modern Eurocentric classicism only repeats the Aryan whitewashing of the origins of the West by German classicists in the eighteenth and nineteenth centuries. While irreducible to Asante's theory of Afrocentricity, the Black Athena thesis does seek to ground the very idea of the West in a more "multicultural" or "Afroasiatic" milieu than has been previously acknowledged by modern scholars (*see* **Multicultural Theory**).

Whether or not this milieu could or should be called "Black" motivated a large part of the popular debate; on paper, Bernal was frequently mistaken for being Black. Wellesley classicist Mary R. Lefkowitz was perhaps the most vocal objector to the Black Athena thesis, and her scathing *Not Out of Africa* (1996) criticizes Bernal for neglecting the archival evidence by kowtowing to fashionable identity politics. Though many colleagues joined Lefkowitz in identifying Bernal's lack of credentials in their field, classicists in general have conceded at least a notable Egypto-Semitic influence on ancient Greek culture. In that regard, Bernal's work may go down as having been more valuable for the methodological and disciplinary questions it raised than for the intricate particularities of its supporting data.

Resources: Martin Bernal: *Black Athena: The Afroasiatic Roots of Classical Civilization*, vol. 1: *The Fabrication of Ancient Greece, 1785–1985* (New Brunswick, NJ: Rutgers University Press, 1987); *Black Athena: The Afroasiatic Roots of Classical Civilization*, vol. 2: *The Archaeological and Documentary Evidence* (New Brunswick, NJ: Rutgers University Press, 1991); *Black Athena Writes Back: Martin Bernal Responds to His Critics*, ed. David Chioni Moore (Durham, NC: Duke University Press, 2001); Robert S. Boynton, "The Bernaliad: A Scholar-Warrior's Long Journey to Ithaca," *Lingua Franca* 6, no. 7 (1996), 43–50; Mary R. Lefkowitz, *Not Out of Africa: How Afrocentrism Became an Excuse to Teach Myth as History* (New York: Basic Books, 1996); Mary R. Lefkowitz and Guy MacLean Rogers, eds., *Black Athena Revisited* (Chapel Hill: University of North Carolina Press, 1996).

Kinohi Nishikawa

Berry, Bertice (born 1961). Sociologist, writer, lecturer, teacher, and television personality. Berry was born in Wilmington, Delaware, the sixth of seven children. She overcame an impoverished background to earn success in both academics and popular media. She attended Jacksonville University in Florida, graduating magna cum laude. Berry received a Ph.D. in sociology from Kent State University, where she later taught sociology and statistics. Berry's method of using humor to address difficult and complex subjects such as racism and sexism made her classes quite popular among students. She left teaching to become a comedian and went on to host her own nationally syndicated TV talk show, *The Bertice Berry Show*, in the late 1990s. Berry's writing reflects her wide-ranging interests and crosses many genres. She has written a best-selling memoir, books of humor that tackle serious social issues, and, recently, fiction. She is also a popular motivational speaker and has published a motivational book on audio compact disc. Writing satisfaction aside, Berry is "most proud of becoming an instant mother to her sister's four young children" (Web site). A recent newlywed, she lives in Savannah, Georgia. A recently completed novel, *When Love Calls, You Better Answer*, is scheduled to be released in 2005.

Resources: Bertice Berry: *Bertice: The World According to Me* (New York: Scribner's, 1996); *The Haunting of Hip-Hop* (New York: Doubleday, 2001); *I'm on My Way, but Your Foot Is on My Head: A Black Woman's Story of Getting over Life's Hurdles* (New York: Simon and Schuster, 1997); *It's Time to Change: The Art of Transformation, in Life, Love & Work* (Solana Beach, CA: Berry Productions, 2002), book on CD; *Jim and Louella's Homemade Heart-Fix Remedy* (New York: Doubleday, 2002); *Redemption Song* (New York: Ballantine, 2000); Web site, http://www.berticeberry.com/auto.html; *You Still Ghetto* (New York: St. Martin's Press, 1998); Bertice Berry and Joan Coker, *Sckraight from the Ghetto: You Know You're Ghetto If—* (New York: St. Martin's Press, 1996).

Wilma Jean Emanuel Randle

Berry, Charlene A. (born 1967). Novelist. Berry, a native of Irvington, New Jersey, is the author of three romance novels featuring African American protagonists: *Secret Obsession*, *Love's Deceptions*, and *Cajun Heat*.

Resources: Charlene A. Berry: *Cajun Heat* (New York: Genesis, 2000); *Love's Deceptions* (New York: Ballantine, 1998); *Secret Obsession* (New York: Genesis, 1997).

Hans Ostrom

Bibb, Henry Walton (1815–1854). Activist and editor. Noted in the **abolitionist movement** for his lectures and **slave narrative**, Bibb also founded the first Black newspaper in Canada, the *Voice of the Fugitive*. He was separated early from his slave mother, Mildred Jackson; his father was rumored to be a Kentucky state senator, James Bibb. Bibb's youth was filled with disruption and pain; sold at least six times before 1840, he was moved throughout the South and early developed the desire to escape.

Bibb married a slave named Malinda in 1833, and, in 1834 they had a daughter, Mary Frances. Bibb escaped in 1837 and attempted to rescue his wife and child the next year—he was captured, nearly sold in Louisville, and escaped again. He repeated his attempt at rescue in 1839, but this time Bibb, his wife, and his daughter were sold to a Louisiana slaveholder, Francis Whitfield. Whitfield was extraordinarily cruel, and Bibb repeatedly attempted to escape; finally, late in 1840, Whitfield separated the family and sold Bibb to a pair of gamblers who took him through **Texas** and Arkansas before finally selling him to a Cherokee slaveholder. After his Cherokee owner died, he once again escaped—this time, for good (Blassingame).

He eventually settled in **Detroit, Michigan**, and began lecturing against **slavery** in 1844. In 1845, Bibb again attempted to rescue his family, but found that his wife "was living in a state of adultery with her master" (Bibb, 188) and gave up hope of ever reuniting the family. Bibb's narrative, in the gendered language of the time, hints at his great personal conflict over this discovery; it suggests both that Malinda was likely forced into this role and that, given the evil of slavery, she may have reconciled herself to it. He returned north and never saw his wife or daughter again. In 1847, Bibb met Black Bostonian Mary E. Miles, and they were married in June of the next year.

Bibb's speeches, often given under the auspices of the Michigan Liberty Party, proved both popular and effective—so much so that the Detroit Liberty Association appointed a committee to verify the details of his life. Their positive conclusions were eventually printed as prefatory documents to Bibb's *Narrative of the Life and Adventures of Henry Bibb* (1849). Stunning in its descriptions of slaveholders' cruelty, Bibb's narrative became quite popular.

The Fugitive Slave Law drove the Bibbs to Canada in 1850. Here, Bibb advocated for Black emigration to Canada and continued his fight against slavery. In January 1851, the couple began a biweekly journal, *Voice of the Fugitive*, which published—among other items—narratives of fugitives. Eventually, the paper became the official journal of the Refugee Home Society, a corporation Bibb set up to purchase Canadian land for Black emigrants. Bibb became a leader among Ontario Blacks who favored self-segregating; this brought him into a now infamous conflict with **Mary Shadd Cary**. The Refugee Home Society floundered, the newspaper's circulation was a

Henry Bibb, 1875. Courtesy of the Yale Collection of American Literature, Beinecke Rare Book and Manuscript Library.

constant worry, and Bibb's health suffered after years of abuse, but he did live to see three of his brothers escape slavery and emigrate to Canada.

Resources: John W. Blassingame, "Henry Walton Bibb," in *Dictionary of American Negro Biography*, ed. Rayford W. Logan and Michael R. Winston (New York: W. W.

Norton, 1982); Charles Heglar, "Introduction," in *The Life and Adventures of Henry Bibb: An American Slave* (Madison: University of Wisconsin Press, 2001); Jason H. Silverman, *Unwelcome Guests: Canada West's Response to American Fugitive Slaves* (Millwood, NY: Associated Faculty Press, 1985).

Eric Gardner

Birtha, Becky (born 1948). Short story writer, poet, and adoption activist. Becky Birtha was born in Hampton, Virginia, and at this writing, resides in **Philadelphia, Pennsylvania**, where she spent most of her childhood. She earned an M.F.A. in creative writing from Vermont College in 1984 and was awarded a Pennsylvania Council on the Arts individual fellowship in 1985, a National Endowment for the Arts creative writing fellowship in 1988, and a Pew Fellowship in the Arts in 1993. Besides being a writer, Birtha is the Web site coordinator for a program that helps find adoptive families for older children in foster care.

In the two books of short stories and one collection of poems that Birtha has published to date, she offers vivid, nuanced depictions of Black women, particularly Black lesbians. Her fiction, included in *For Nights Like This One: Stories of Loving Women* (1983) and *Lover's Choice* (1987), describes the experiences of lesbians at a variety of life stages, from a young woman first recognizing her love for her best friend, to a middle-aged woman helping a teenager begin her own life journey, to an older woman who finds that her deceased longtime partner is never far away. Birtha's *The Forbidden Poems* (1991) expresses powerful insights about being "in the life" (that is, being lesbian, gay, or bisexual) and about life in general through poems that explore the loss of relationships, the value of supportive communities, and, as described in the title of one of her poems, "Coming to Terms with Myself."

Birtha's work is informed by her experiences as an African American, lesbian, feminist, Quaker, *and* mother. For example, in "Johnnieruth," one of her most widely reprinted stories, the fourteen-year-old narrator is elated to discover adults like herself when she witnesses two women furtively kissing in a city park. Not all of Birtha's work focuses on explicitly lesbian characters. In "The Saint and Sinners Run," a bus driver has her world turned upside down when the church ladies on her route begin to act like teenagers, and in "Route 23: 10th and Bigler to Bethlehem Pike," a poor woman takes her children to live on a city bus to keep them warm during a particularly cold winter.

Resources: Becky Birtha: *For Nights Like This One: Stories of Loving Women* (East Palo Alto, CA: Frog in the Well, 1983); *The Forbidden Poems* (Seattle: Seal Press, 1991); *Lovers' Choice* (Seattle: Seal Press, 1987); "Becky Birtha," *FemmeNoir Online*, ed. A. D. Odom, http://www.femmenoir.net/weblogonlinediary/id147.html; "Pew Fellows, 1993: Becky Birtha," *Pew Fellowships in the Arts*, http://www.pewarts.org/93/Birtha/bio.html.

Brett Beemyn

Black American Literature Forum (1976–1991). Journal. Originally the *Negro American Literature Forum* (vols. 1–10), published from 1967 to 1976, the publication became *Black American Literature Forum* when the Modern Language Association (MLA) Discussion Group on Afro-American Literature was created in 1977 with *BALF* its official publication. The discussion group requested permanent MLA division status in 1983, renaming itself Black American Literature and Culture, and becoming the only MLA English-language division focused on broader cultural concerns as well as literature. In the years from 1976 through 1991, the title of the journal remained *Literature Forum*, despite the division's broader emphasis on culture. *Black American Literature Forum* continued for fifteen volumes (vols. 10–25) as one of the most consistent, regularly published, and prominent venues for scholarly publication on African American literature. Many of the founders remained with the journal throughout and beyond these years, providing unusually stable commitment and attention—while providing for an increasingly diverse constituency and agenda. (Editor Joe Weixlmann served for twenty-eight years, handing the task to Jocelyn Moody in 2004.)

A different vision for *Black American Literature Forum* came out of advisory board discussions that limiting the journal to literature in the narrowest sense of the term was not being true to the range of Black cultural expression. The beginnings of change were marked by special issues on Black art, increasing publication on film, and members added to the editorial board to attract manuscripts in fresh areas. Looking to represent a serious voice for Black culture far beyond the confines of the Modern Language Association, the advisory board searched for a new name to reflect the journal's enhanced range of cultural expression, as well as to attract new interest from a broader range of scholar-contributors and readers. After much discussion, in 1992 the journal was renamed *African American Review* (AAR), developed a new format, and searched for wider readership—positioning a public intellectual voice. With a Lila Wallace Reader's Digest grant to increase circulation, the board took on the enormous—and perhaps impossible—task of making an academic journal with popular appeal. With a "more friendly look and feel and a color cover" to accompany the new content and editorial direction, circulation through subscription and independent bookstore chains went from 1,200 to 2,000 and peaked with press runs of 3,500–5,000 (Weixlmann). However, with the loss of independent bookstore sales in the United States, reasonable retail distribution channels have evaporated, leaving this journal, like many others, with huge economic costs and risks and dependence on subscription sales. In 2001, *AAR* moved to St. Louis University along with its editor, Joe Weixlmann.

Still a flagship African American journal and with an all-star cast of associate editors—**Houston A. Baker, Henry Louis Gates, Jr., Nellie Y. McKay,** Keith Byerman—*AAR* publishes creative writing as well as interviews, book reviews, and "essays on African American literature, theater, film, art, and culture generally" (http://aar.slu.edu/submsinf.html). Stellar contributors—including **Amiri Baraka, Trudier Harris, Toni Morrison,** and **Ishmael Reed**—assure that the journal continues to play a major role in African American studies.

Resources: *AAR: African American Review*, "Submission Guidelines for *African American Review*," http://aar.slu.edu; Joe Weixlmann, telephone interview, July 8, 2004; Carol Zuses, "Re: Divisions—Black American Literature and Culture," E-mail to the author, July 6, 2004.

Carol Klimick Cyganowski

Black Arts Movement (1960–1970). The Black Arts Movement grew out of the rebellion of the 1960s and cannot be separated from the political and social upheavals of the time. The creative component of the **Black Power** movement, this artistic revolution was shaped by a Black Nationalist agenda as the artists fought for social justice and black empowerment. While the Black Power movement, the foundation of this creative collaborative, focused on the political and social directions that African Americans should take in their demand for liberation, the Black Arts Movement simultaneously defined the direction and purpose of the creative arts, especially literature. In "The Black Arts Movement," **Larry Neal**, one of the literary theorists of the period, delineates the objectives of the movement, and explains its vision: "The Black Arts Movement is radically opposed to any concept of the artist that alienates him from his community. Black Art is the aesthetic and spiritual sister of the Black Power concept. As such, it envisions an art that speaks directly to the needs and aspirations of Black America. In order to perform this task, the Black Arts Movement proposes a radical reordering of the western cultural aesthetic. It proposes a separate symbolism, mythology, critique, and iconology" (Neal, 2039). As part of the nationalist thrust of the 1960s, the Black Arts writers looked at their art as inseparable from the people, and therefore turned their attention to the community. While Black Power sought to redirect the social, political, and economic goals for African American people, the Black Arts Movement worked for a radical change in what art should be and do.

As far back as the 1920's, **Langston Hughes** noted in his essay, "The Negro Artist and the Racial Mountain," "We younger Negro artists who create now intend to express our individual dark-skinned selves without fear or shame. . . . We know we are beautiful" (36). In Richard Wright's 1937 essay "Blueprint for Negro Writing," his idea was that the writer should function as an agent of change, and in order to do so, it was necessary to develop and use a "complex consciousness" (1407). Both Hughes and Wright were prophetic as they discussed the roles of the African American writer in presenting a certain vision of African American life and experiences.

The Black Arts writers wanted to take the positions of Hughes and Wright to another level as they sought to incorporate nationalism into their art. Although marginalized by many Blacks and most Whites, the Black Arts writers created an aesthetic that was their own. In "Toward a Black Aesthetic" (1968), **Hoyt Fuller** comments on his Chicago organization, the Organization of Black American Culture, and its definition of the Black aesthetic: "In the writers' workshop sponsored by the group, the writers are deliberatively striving to invest their work with the distinctive styles and rhythms and colors of the ghetto, with those peculiar qualities which, for example, characterize the music of a John Coltrane or a Charlie Parker or a Ray Charles" (1858). The Black Arts writers realized that rather than looking outside themselves to find material appeasing to White critics, who would relegate the Black writer to oblivion anyway, they would turn to their community for its cultural resources.

The Black Arts writers believed that since their art drew on the resources of the community, they would make it political, purposeful, and dedicated to the people. No longer were they concerned about reaching a White audience or appealing to the artistic sensibilities of the European. Committed to a literature by the people, about the people, and in the interests of the people, they wanted their material accessible to the average person in the community. To that end, they participated in community readings, workshops, forums, and council gatherings, and held creative writing contests for interested people in the community. Even theater, an artistic venue usually prohibitive to many people, found an eager young audience with their minds and hearts ripe for this new Black consciousness.

In their duty and dedication to the audience, and their rebellious approach to creativity, the artists believed their work should be instructional and consciousness-raising. With a commitment to the people's liberation, they worked with the themes of the Black Power movement—Black is beautiful, Black pride, black self-identification, revolution, **Black Nationalism**, art as a tool of liberation, racism, praise of cultural icons such as **Malcolm X** and **Martin Luther King, Jr.**, attacks against Blacks who emulated bourgeois White values, and, of course, the purpose of art. Imamu **Amiri Baraka**, a key figure in the development of the Black Arts movement, writes in his poem "Black Art" (1969), "We want 'poems that kill.' / Assassin poems, Poems that shoot / guns," declaring that if art does not destroy and rebuild, it has no purpose. He concludes the poem:

> We want a black poem. And a
> Black World.
> Let the world be a Black Poem
> And Let All Black People Speak This Poem
> Silently
> Or LOUD
>
> (*Selected Poetry*, 106–107)

Poetry was the main genre of Black Arts writing. Largely influenced by Black Nationalism and the Black Power rhetoric of some of the more vocal activists, it flourished in anthologies, broadsides, pamphlets, and books in community bookstores, workshops, and forums, at conferences, and on street corners. Many young people—activists, revolutionaries-in-the-making, artists, Black Power sympathizers, even White radicals—were content to listen to poets delivering their work against a background of conga drums. Of course not all of the poets acquired name recognition, but seeking celebrity status and recognition were considered European, and therefore discouraged. The Black Arts poets wanted a revolution.

Nikki Giovanni, another key figure of the Black Arts Movement, notes in her poem "For Saundra" (1968) that this was not a time for poetry writing, but for revolution, and that "maybe [she] shouldn't write at all / but clean [her] gun and check [her] kerosene supply" (*Selected Poems*, 59). Although there were signs that the revolution would occur in the streets, the poets believed the prerequisite for a transformation in the streets was a transformation of the mind. Haki Madhubuti (formerly Don L. Lee) in "a poem to complement other poems" (1969), writes, "change change your change change change / your / mind nigger" (2096).

As much as the Black Arts writers called for a revolution of the mind as the prerequisite to a revolution in the streets, there were also other important themes in their poetry. For example, some writers wanted to celebrate Black people—other artists, people in the community, political icons, and historical figures, among others. Baraka, Carolyn Rodgers, and Haki are among the poets who wrote poems celebrating Malcolm X and his legacy to Black nationhood. In "Beautiful Black Men" (1968), Nikki Giovanni pays tribute to the ordinary Black man on the streets, doing ordinary things. She also mentions some of the R&B performers who were popular during the 1960s—"jerry butler, wilson pickett, the impressions/temptations, mighty mighty sly" (*Selected Poems*, 54). The writers who reclaimed and celebrated the genius of John Coltrane include Sonia Sanchez, A. B. Spellman, Carolyn Rodgers, Michael Harper, Jayne Cortez, and Larry Neal.

Perhaps the most dominant theme in Black Arts poetry was the beauty and goodness of Blackness. Created to raise the level of Black awareness among the people and teach them to love themselves, many poems romanticized and glorified Blackness, presenting a vision of it as transformative, inspiring, and celebratory. Mari Evans's poem "I Am a Black Woman" (1964) looks at herself, the Black woman, as the embodiment of history, strength, and fortitude (Baraka and Baraka, 105–106). There was no question that many of the Black Arts writers believed that Black self-definition meant loving everything black, blackening those things that weren't already black, and believing in the possibility of a Black world. Developing a Black consciousness, however, did not occur without a process of reeducation and transformation. Typical of the rhetoric of the times, the Black Arts writers were critical of those who continued to embrace European values. Baraka addressed the self-hatred of the Black man who emulated middle-class whites in his 1969 poem "Black Bourgeoisie." A similar theme emerged in his "Poem for Half White College Students" (1969), in which the poet questions the self-definition of those preoccupied with European values. Anytime the poets referred to "colored" or "negro," they were usually making a pejorative comment about identity and self-definition, and rating each other's level of Blackness. Many of the Black Arts poets believed that it was their responsibility, both politically and artistically, to change the way black people looked at themselves.

While the Black Arts writers worked assiduously to educate the people to a liberating way of thinking about themselves, they were also working to develop their own style based on their own culture. No longer bound by the European standards of "good" art, nor concerned about moving into the American literary mainstream, the Black Arts writers looked to their own life and experiences for the metaphors, similes, symbols, and other literary devices, and found the Black world rich with resources. Carolyn Rodgers, for example, uses the rich cultural language of African American women in her poem "For Sistuhs Wearin' Straight Hair" (1969). Her references to "edges" and "kitchen" and hair that "was not supposed to *go back* home" (2126) are strong examples of the Black **vernacular**. In valuing their own experiences, the writers were experimental and often innovative in form, as illustrated in Sonia Sanchez's poem "a chant for young / brothers & sisters" (1970). With demonstrated emphasis on the spoken word, the poem makes interesting use of the performance nature of black speech.

Also characteristic of the style of Black Arts poetry was the use of popular street language, profanity, signification, references to Black music (particularly **jazz** and R&B), and the interconnection of form and theme. Although some of these stylistic practices were not necessarily new, the Black Arts writers aggressively stretched these techniques to the limits as they revolted against Western concepts of art. Redefining art, what it is and what it should do, the writers were the creative practitioners of the Black Power ideology.

While most discussions of Black Arts literature focused on poetry, since there were literally hundreds of poets, drama, fiction, and other narrative forms were also important areas of revolutionary expression. Drama was especially defining during the 1960s in that it presented Blacks and Whites in situations new to the theatergoing audience. This theater meant recognizing the enemy, making sure he reaps death and destruction so that a new value system, a new world, a new Black people can emerge heroically. In his 1969 essay "The Revolutionary Theatre," Baraka delineated the standards for this art form. "The Revolutionary Theatre should force change," he writes. "It should be change . . . must EXPOSE!" (*Selected Plays and Prose*, 130).

Other playwrights of the Black Arts era include **Alice Childress**, Sonia Sanchez, **Ed Bullins**, **Ted Shine**, **Adrienne Kennedy**, and lesser known names, but Baraka was clearly the spiritual leader and the most productive. Among his many plays, the most celebrated was *The Dutchman* (1964), which deals with a Black middle-class man who is murdered by the white woman he meets on the subway. This play, and others in the trilogy, *The Toilet* and *The Slave*, are striking examples of Baraka's vision of Black theater as an agent of social change.

There were other forms of literature that had a major impact on the Black Arts Movement. *The Autobiography of Malcolm X* (1965) was a defining work for the Black Power movement. Prior to its publication, Malcolm X's nationalist agenda helped to shape the political platform of the Black Power movement. Another important book, **Eldridge Cleaver**'s *Soul on Ice* (1967) presented the author's pent-up anger and aggression against an oppressive society. Because Cleaver was a member of the **Black Panther Party**, his widely read book became an important philosophical tool for the Black Power movement as much for its expressions of rage as in spite of it.

Like other genres, fiction tended to lurk in the literary shadows of poetry during the Black Arts Movement. Nevertheless, there were writers whose novels and short stories today prompt us to look again at the breadth and depth of the movement. While not as rebellious as the younger poets, and still somewhat influenced by European aesthetics, writers such as **John O. Killens, Margaret Walker, Paule Marshall, William Melvin Kelley**, and a few others contributed to the 1960s. However, **John A. Williams**'s novel, *The Man Who Cried I Am* (1967) and the fiction in *Black Fire: An Anthology of Afro-American Writing* (1968), edited by Baraka and Larry Neal, are good examples of more revolutionary contributions to the movement.

These young writers of the Black Arts Movement created a literature of liberation. Often militant in tone, sometimes angry, sometimes filled with rage, they distanced themselves from European aesthetics and drew on their own resources. With emphasis on Black language, black music, the Black spoken-word tradition, and Black performance techniques, these Black Arts writers helped to nurture the Black Power movement. The Black aesthetic, the literary directive emerging from the Black Arts Movement, provided future artists the freedom to explore and use their own cultural resources.

In the early-to-mid-1970s, the Black Arts Movement increasingly lost its momentum. Suffering from governmental interference, the activists' exclusivity and essentialism, and an intellectual and social burnout from efforts to make the rhetoric real, the Black Arts Movement could not sustain itself. However, readers today still look to the 1960s as a time when a Black world seemed possible. (*See* **OBAC**.)

Resources: Amiri Baraka: *Selected Plays and Prose of Amiri Baraka/LeRoi Jones* (New York: Morrow, 1979); *Selected Poetry of Amiri Baraka/LeRoi Jones* (New York: Morrow, 1979); Amiri Baraka (LeRoi Jones) and Amina Baraka, *Confirmation: An Anthology of African American Women* (New York: Quill, 1983); Hoyt Fuller, "Toward a Black Aesthetic" (1968), in *The Norton Anthology of African American Literature*, 2nd ed., Henry Louis Gates, Jr. and Nellie Y. McKay, gen. eds. (New York: W. W. Norton, 2004), 1853–1859; Addison Gayle, *The Black Aesthetic* (Garden City, NY: Doubleday, 1971); Nikki Giovanni, *The Selected Poems of Nikki Giovanni* (New York: Morrow, 1996); Langston Hughes, "The Negro Artist and the Racial Mountain" (1926), in *The Collected Works of Langston Hughes*, vol. 9, ed. Christopher De Santis (Columbia: University of Missouri Press, 2002), 31–36; LeRoi Jones (Amiri Baraka) and Larry Neal, eds., *Black Fire: An Anthology of Afro-American Writings* (New York: Morrow, 1968); Haki Madhubuti, "a poem to complement other poems" (1969), in *The Norton Anthology of African American Literature*, 2nd ed., Henry Louis Gates, Jr. and Nellie Y. McKay, gen. eds. (New York: W. W. Norton, 2004), 2094–2096; Larry Neal, "The Black Arts Movement" (1968), in *The Norton Anthology of African American Literature*, 2nd ed., Henry Louis Gates, Jr. and Nellie Y. McKay, gen. eds. (New York: W. W. Norton, 2004), 2039–2050; Carolyn Rodgers, "For Sistuhs Wearin' Straight Hair" (1969), in *The Norton Anthology of African American Literature*, 2nd ed., Henry Louis

Gates, Jr., and Nellie Y. McKay, gen. eds. (New York: W. W. Norton, 2004), 2126; Richard Wright, "Blueprint for Negro Writing" (1937), in *The Norton Anthology of African American Literature*, 2nd ed., Henry Louis Gates, Jr. and Nellie Y. McKay, gen. eds. (New York: W. W. Norton, 2004), 1403–1410.

Angelene J. Hall

Black Arts Repertory Theatre/School. Black Arts Repertory Theatre/School (BART/S), the brainchild of playwright/poet **Amiri Baraka**, was a short-lived attempt to establish a consciousness-raising theater company and school in New York City. Though it existed for barely one full year, a number of important Black theater/schools, including Black House in California and Spirit House Movers and Players in New Jersey, shared the BART/S formula. It stands as one of the most important theatrical experiments of the **Black Arts Movement**.

Interviews with Baraka and his ex-wife, Hettie, as well as a December 13, 1964, article in *U.S. News & World Report*, indicate that BART/S came into being in late 1964, while the founder was still living in New York City's Greenwich Village (Hudson, 21). However, the company did not establish a public reputation until it built its permanent home in **Harlem, New York**, in 1965; in March of that year Baraka moved BART/S into an old brownstone building on 130th Street with the support of some friends and fellow artists, among them Johnny Moore, Charles Patterson, William Patterson, and Clarence Reed. Decorated with a Black Nationalist variation on the ancient Athenian masks of comedy and tragedy (shaped like a war shield, rendered in black and gold, with spears behind each), the new location became a magnet for Black artists and intellectuals.

BART/S brought into the streets and communities of Harlem a visible presence of the radical revolutionary theater Baraka called for in his 1965 manifesto. Its goal and that of the revolutionary theater of the Black Arts Movement were essentially the same: to encourage a socially relevant African American drama that would contribute to the struggle for social justice (Effiong, 79). The company advocated African American arts of all forms, with poetry readings, dance performances, visual art shows, and new dramas. The troupe brought the community into the theater through street parades; a photograph in the June 1965 issue of *Liberator* shows Baraka leading a march on 125th street. It also brought the theater to the community by putting up improvised stages in parks, playgrounds, streets, and empty parking lots. The administrators targeted Black participants and sometimes actively discouraged White participation. An egg was hurled at a group of Black musicians who arrived at a BART/S performance with a famous White vocalist in their number.

BART/S produced a number of plays during 1965. An early benefit performance showcased Baraka's *The Toilet* and *Experimental Death Unit #1*, as well as Charles Patterson's *Black Ice* and Nat White's *The Black Tramp*. A street production of *Black Ice* gathered a Black audience by having a Black company member, carrying a pistol, chase a White character toward the stage.

The company produced Baraka's most famous play, *Dutchman*, multiple times. The play that had won him an Obie award at the Cherry Lane Theatre took on a more aggressively radical aspect when set uptown amid the more intrusive politics of street performance. Along with its many artistic endeavors, BART/S served as an active educational project for the African American community, providing classes in poetry, music, and art, as well as in history and martial arts. The theater also contributed to several antipoverty programs.

Funding from the federal Harlem-Youth Act (HARYOU) and the Office of Economic Opportunity provided much of BART/S's support later in 1965, but also contributed to its early demise. While the company enjoyed a $40,000 antipoverty grant, a controversy erupted over such use of public funds. Baraka remembers the problem beginning when he denied Sargent Shriver, the head of the HARYOU program, entry into the Black Arts building (*Autobiography*, 310). On November 30, 1965, an Associated Press release accused the group of racism, claiming that its productions supported secession and portrayed Whites as homosexuals. Several articles maintained that BART/S employed members of Black terrorist groups, the Five-Percenters and the Pakistani Muslims. The controversy culminated in an armed police raid on the brownstone building that reportedly uncovered drugs, firearms, bomb materials, and an underground practice range. Some officials of the antipoverty programs defended the company's activities, going so far as to argue that young people in danger of criminal involvement were the very individuals the programs were created to help (Hudson, 22–23). Despite these efforts, public funding disappeared, and this, coupled with internal disputes among the officers and the premature exodus of Baraka, saw the collapse of BART/S by the end of 1965.

Baraka described the overall benefit of BART/S as being an example to the world that Malcolm X's message had been heard, that people understood that art should be "a weapon in the Black Liberation Movement" (*Autobiography*, 311). It was during his tenure at the theater/school that Baraka completed or made considerable progress on some of his major works, including his dramatization of the mythological origins of "the white man," *Black Mass*; portions of *Home*, notably "STATE/MEANT"; his gloomy, introspective, psychological portrait *The System of Dante's Hell*; and the "Target Study" and "Black Art" sections of *Black Magic*. Among the notable playwrights and poets involved in the company's many projects were Larry Neal, who would go on to edit *Black Fire* with Baraka; Ronald Drayton, Clarence Franklin, Yusef Iman, and Sonia Sanchez. Baraka brought many of the lessons he learned at BART/S to his operation of Spirit House in 1968 (Hudson, 24).

While one can only partially quantify the material contributions of the Black Arts Repertory Theatre/School to the art and politics of the Black Arts Movement, it is fair to label it an important early step in articulating and circulating the movement's Pan-African nationalism and community-centered cultural goals. Furthermore, BART/S should be credited with rallying Harlem's African American community against racism and for bringing to it important cultural, economic, and educational possibilities (Effiong, 79).

Resources: Amiri Baraka, *The Autobiography of LeRoi Jones* (Chicago: Lawrence Hill Books, 1997); Kimberly W. Benston, ed., *Imamu Amiri Baraka: A Collection of Critical Essays* (Englewood Cliffs, NJ: Prentice-Hall, 1978); Lloyd Wellesley Brown, *Amiri Baraka* (Boston: Twayne, 1980); Philip Uko Effiong, *In Search of a Model for African American Drama: A Study of Selected Plays by Lorraine Hansberry, Amiri Baraka, and Ntozake Shange* (Lanham, MD: University Press of America, 2000); William J. Harris, *The Poetry and Poetics of Amiri Baraka: The Jazz Aesthetic* (Columbia: University of Missouri Press, 1985); William J. Harris, ed., *The LeRoi Jones/Amiri Baraka Reader* (New York: Thunder's Mouth Press, 1991); Theodore Hudson, *From LeRoi Jones to Amiri Baraka: The Literary Works* (Durham, NC: Duke University Press, 1973); Henry C. Lacey, *To Raise, Destroy, and Create: The Poetry, Drama, and Fiction of Imamu Amiri Baraka (LeRoi Jones)* (Troy, NY: Whitston, 1981); Alain Richard, *Theatre and Nationalism: Wole Soyinka and LeRoi Jones*, trans. Femi Osofisan (Ile-Ife, Nigeria: University of Ife Press, 1983); Werner Sollors, *Amiri Baraka/LeRoi Jones: The Quest for a "Populist Modernism"* (New York: Columbia University Press, 1978).

Ben Fisler

Black Athena **Controversy (1987–present).** Scholarly debate about the roots of classical civilization. **Martin Bernal**'s books about ancient Greece sparked a heated debate among scholars about the extent to which classical civilization was influenced by, or derived from, the cultures of ancient Africa. The first volume of *Black Athena: The Afroasiatic Roots of Classical Civilization* (1987) led to a flurry of articles and reviews, along with "special plenary sessions of the annual meetings of the American Philological Association and the American Research Center in Egypt" (Burstein, 157). Bernal is a self-described outsider in the field of classics. He was trained in Chinese history and is a professor of government and Near Eastern studies at Cornell University. His scholarship is largely based on the "ancient model in antiquity," in which the "Ancient Greeks, though proud of themselves and their recent accomplishments, did not see their political institutions, science, philosophy or religion as original. Instead they derived them—through the early colonization and later study by Greeks abroad—from the East in general and Egypt in particular" (Bernal, 1, 120). Beginning in the eighteenth century, academics challenged the influence of the Egyptians and Phoenicians on Greece. They discredited the ancient model, not for its internal inconsistencies but on the basis of four forces: "Christian reaction, the rise of the concept of 'progress,' the growth of racism, and Romantic Hellenism" (Bernal, 1, 189). Between 1830 and 1860, the "ancient model" was replaced with what Bernal calls the "Aryan model." This paradigm, largely shaped by the early nineteenth-century German philologist K. O. Müller and other scholars, has "dominated classical and Oriental studies until the present" (Trigger, 121).

Bernal claimed that Europeans could not tolerate the view that their culture had its roots in Africa and Southwest Asia. Instead, they held that ancient Greek culture evolved from the Indo-European peoples of the north who invaded Greece around the second millennium B.C. In volume 2 of *Black Athena* (1991),

127

Bernal continues his controversial work and provides archaeological and linguistic evidence that connects Egypt and the Near East with the Aegean world. He readily admits that the documentary material was slanted to support his strong political and social views. Bernal sought to replace the Aryan model with a "revised ancient model" that acknowledges the Greek language's Indo-European origin and attributes much of Greek religion, philosophy, science, and culture to Africa. *Black Athena Writes Back* (2001) is Bernal's reply to his critics.

While Bernal has received some positive reviews in the popular press, scholarly reaction has been "generally negative, ranging from amused scorn to active irritation" (Malamud, 317). One of Bernal's most outspoken critics is Mary Lefkowitz. In her book *Not Out of Africa* (1996), she addresses Afrocentrists and their sympathizers who, at times, resist "the traditional criteria of historical truth...[and] defend their views by lambasting critics as racist" (Konstan, 261). Lefkowitz also edited *Black Athena Revisited* (1996) with Guy Rogers. In this collection of essays, a broad array of scholars discusses Bernal's thesis, refuting his claims for the Black origins of Greek culture. Academics have attacked his knowledge of the subject and point to "factual errors, misstatements, citations of outdated and inappropriate sources, flimsy toponymic identifications, and a host of methodological difficulties" (Weinstein, 382).

Despite the controversy, there is a general appreciation for Bernal's critical inquiry into classical scholarship. His provocative work brings a new perspective to Greek history and "forces us to rethink what is meant by the concept of Western civilization" (Patterson, 42). He challenges the framework for understanding human history by making connections between a wide range of disciplines and areas.

Resources: Jacques Berlinerblau, *Heresy in the University: The Black Athena Controversy and the Responsibilities of American Intellectuals* (New Brunswick, NJ: Rutgers University Press, 1999); Martin Bernal: *Black Athena: The Afroasiatic Roots of Classical Civilization*, 2 vols. (New Brunswick, NJ: Rutgers University Press, 1987–1991); *Black Athena Writes Back: Martin Bernal Responds to His Critics*, ed. David Chioni Moore (Durham, NC: Duke University Press, 2001); Stanley M. Burstein, "Review of *Black Athena: The Afroasiatic Roots of Classical Civilization* by Martin Bernal, Vol. 2," *Classical Philology* 88, no. 2 (1993), 157–162; "Dialogue: Martin Bernal's *Black Athena*," *Journal of Women's History* 4, no. 3 (1993), 84–135; David Konstan, "Inventing Ancient Greece," review of *Not Out of Africa* by Mary Lefkowitz and *Black Athena Revisited*, ed. Mary R. Lefkowitz and Guy MacLean Rogers," *History and Theory* 36, no. 2 (1997), 261–269; Mary Lefkowitz, *Not Out of Africa: How Afrocentrism Became an Excuse to Teach Myth as History* (New York: Basic Books, 1996); Mary R. Lefkowitz and Guy MacLean Rogers, eds., *Black Athena Revisited* (Chapel Hill: University of North Carolina Press, 1996); Molly Myerowitz Levine, "The Use and Abuse of Black Athena," Review of *Black Athena: The Afroasiatic Roots of Classical Civilization* by Martin Bernal, vol. 1," *American Historical Review* 97, no. 2 (1992), 440–460; Martha A. Malamud, "Review of *Black Athena: The Afroasiatic Roots of Classical Civilization* by Martin Bernal, vol. 1," *Criticism* 31, no. 3 (1989), 317–323; Thomas C. Patterson, "Review of *Black Athena: The Afroasiatic Roots of Classical Civilization* by Martin

Bernal, Vol. 1," *Monthly Review* 40 (1988), 42–45; Bruce G. Trigger, "Brown Athena: A Postprocessual Goddess?," *Current Anthropology* 33, no. 2 (1992), 121–123; James M. Weinstein, "Review of *Black Athena: The Afroasiatic Roots of Classical Civilization* by Martin Bernal, vol. 2," *American Journal of Archaeology* 95 (1991), 381–383.

Lori Ricigliano

Black Atlantic. The term "Black Atlantic" was coined by **Paul Gilroy** in a book titled *The Black Atlantic: Modernity and Double Consciousness*. Gilroy's work opposes racial essentialism's attempt to separate contemporary Black culture from modern Western Enlightenment cultures. Gilroy worries that such separatism makes Blackness and modernity stable categories when instead, he argues, they are psychological and cultural processes that are never sealed off from one another. Gilroy sets out to demonstrate that we can conceive of modernity only in relation to race: for Gilroy, modernity began with the slave trade, that is, with the moment when Europe, Africa, and America ceased to be geographically separate and started relating to each other through commercial and cultural exchange. Gilroy imagines the Atlantic as a space where different cultures come into being through their relationship with each other. In other words, we can understand the complexities of modern Western Enlightenment cultures and of Black culture only if we recognize their relationship to one another.

These ideas could remain very abstract, but Gilroy gives his readers a concrete illustration of his argument: he portrays the slave ship as a vessel that carries people and goods, and he makes that ship a metaphor for the Black Atlantic. The ship points to the horrors and injustices of the "**middle passage**" by which slaves were brought from Africa to America. But the slave ship also stands for the way in which Gilroy imagines cultural contact and change. Gilroy points out that people who were originally from different places intermingled with each other aboard a ship. They were no longer separate when they shared a space for the duration of the voyage. As people interacted, their original cultures changed, and they created a composite of the different cultures on board. Although Joan Dayan has criticized Gilroy for turning the middle passage into a metaphor that obscures the historical and ongoing reality of slave suffering, Gilroy tries to make clear that people on board did not simply resolve their differences. He does not argue that masters and slaves interacted with each other on the same terms. On the contrary, part of his argument depends on the continued difference between them: the slave's relationship to his captors remains particularly complex in Gilroy's account, which justifies his singling out the "Black" (not the "White") Atlantic as a particularly rich culture.

Gilroy tries to capture the complexity of the Black experience through the concept of "double consciousness" that he draws from **W.E.B. Du Bois**. In *The Souls of Black Folk* (1892), Du Bois coined the term to understand the psychological condition of African Americans under segregation. Because segregation prohibited Blacks from reconciling their racial and national affiliations, Du Bois argued, Blacks developed a double consciousness of themselves as Black on the one hand and as American on the other. Although Gilroy builds on this concept of an irreconcilable racial and national identification, he also treats it critically: unlike Du Bois, Gilroy does not wish to describe Black identity only in national terms; he also wants to explain what African Americans share in common with other colonized peoples and ethnicities. Yet Gilroy runs into difficulty when he searches for a way of expressing those connections. He understands the relationship among nationally different Black cultures through the concept of **"diaspora,"** a term he borrows from Jewish studies, where it means the territorial dispersal of a group of people who are, and remain, united by their shared ethnicity and religious beliefs. As Gilroy acknowledges, the term always refers back to a homeland, but such a single homeland does not exist for Blacks, whose cultural influences are not only African but also and simultaneously European and American. The term "Black Atlantic" thus comes to designate a space of cultural dispersal that cannot be explained through any one culture of origin.

Gilroy traces the development of complex cultural forms in literature as well as in music. His conception of "culture" extends from works recognized as great art to contemporary, popular forms of creative expression such as **hip-hop**. This approach makes Gilroy's book an important model for the discipline of "cultural studies," which was emerging in Britain and the United States in the 1990s and which draws on literary studies, history, sociology, film and media studies, and women and gender studies to understand social ideas and phenomena across different spaces and times. Gilroy's book has had a remarkable effect on scholarship: the term "Black Atlantic" is now a widely recognized and frequently used concept, and journals such as *Research in African Literatures* have devoted special sections or issues to it. Laura Chrisman has pointed out that critical examinations of the Atlantic as a cultural space began with Gilroy's book, and that the book's most important contribution was the antinationalist thrust of its cultural investigation.

Whereas scholarship had focused on national traditions in geographically distinct areas, Gilroy imagined a connection between different territories and a fluid process of cultural change and negotiation. Moreover, he developed a different way by which to tell cultural history: rather than relying on an account of similarities, Gilroy emphasized the importance of difference. His work has been particularly influential in "performance studies." For instance, Joseph Roach examines performances such as Mardi Gras that draw on several cultural contexts but are not limited to any one of them. By drawing on the "Black Atlantic," Roach describes New Orleans as a port where culture is multiply influenced and never achieves a sense of permanence because it is always shifting as new influences arrive, and is always creating audiences and contexts that extend beyond the local.

Responses to Gilroy have also been critical. This criticism largely addresses the geographical areas Gilroy examines and neglects in his study. Loren Kruger has pointed out that we develop a very different sense of the Black Atlantic if we focus on parts other than the North Atlantic, such as the Caribbean or

South Africa. Charles Piot has faulted Gilroy for neglecting Africa when discussing the African diaspora. Piot points out that Gilroy has nothing to say about Africa itself, which was deeply affected by the Atlantic slave trade and modernity. This criticism of Gilroy's geopolitical neglect also extends to a concern over the viability of his claims. In trying to understand what George Elliot Clarke refers to as Gilroy's "infuriating . . . 'Americocentrism'" (Clarke, 14), Herman Bennett has suggested that the concept of diaspora depends on the nation, and that diaspora therefore cannot be an alternative for the nation in explaining historical developments.

Resources: Herman L. Bennett, "The Subject in the Plot: National Boundaries and the 'History' of the Black Atlantic," *African Studies Review*, spec. iss. on the Diaspora 43, no. 1 (2000), 101–124; Laura Chrisman, "Rethinking Black Atlanticism," *Black Scholar* 30, no. 3–4 (2000), 12–17; George Elliott Clarke, "Must All Blackness Be American?: Locating Canada in Borden's 'Tightrope Time,' or Nationalizing Gilroy's Black Atlantic," *Canadian Ethnic Studies/Etudes Ethniques au Canada* 28, no. 3 (1996), 56–71; Joan Dayan, "Paul Gilroy's Slaves, Ships, and Routes: The Middle Passage as Metaphor," *Research in African Literatures* 27 (1996), 7–14; Paul Gilroy, *The Black Atlantic: Modernity and Double Consciousness* (Cambridge, MA: Harvard University Press, 1993); Loren Kruger, "Black Atlantics, White Indians, and Jews: Locations, Locutions, and Syncretic Identities in the Fiction of Achmat Dangor and Others," *South Atlantic Quarterly* 100, no. 1 (2001), 111–143; Charles Piot, "Atlantic Aporias: Africa and Gilroy's Black Atlantic," *South Atlantic Quarterly* 100, no. 1 (2001), 155–170; Joseph R. Roach, *Cities of the Dead: Circum-Atlantic Performance* (New York: Columbia University Press, 1996).

Colleen Glenney Boggs

Black Dialogue (1965–1972). Periodical. *Black Dialogue* was started as an off-campus publication by Black San Francisco State College students in 1965. A quarterly journal, the magazine remained based in **San Francisco, California**, until 1968, when it relocated to New York (1969–1972). The idea for the journal emerged from San Francisco State College's Negro Student Association, which would later be known as the Black Student Union. *Black Dialogue's* editors were Arthur A. Sheridan, Abdul Karim, Edward Spriggs, Aubrey Labrie, Dingane Joe Goncalves, and Marvin Jackmon (Marvin X). The journal addressed both national and local issues, and presented political writings, literary works, and artwork to the Black community.

The emergence of a number of "revolutionary" journals and literary magazines—including *Soulbook, Journal of Black Poetry, Freedomways, Liberator, Black Scholar*, and **Negro Digest**/*Black World*—during the 1960s was a direct reflection of the political times. According to Caroline Gerald, these journals and magazines clearly showed "the literary enactment of the crisis of the Sixties: The Break with the West" (Johnson and Johnson, 165). By 1965, the **Civil Rights Movement** was beginning to be viewed as a lost cause, and **Malcolm X** was assassinated just before *Black Dialogue* went to press. The first issue of *Black Dialogue* was dedicated to Malcolm X.

The **Black Arts Movement** also coalesced in 1965 following Malcolm X's assassination. **Amiri Baraka**, the most widely published Black writer of the time other than **James Baldwin**, moved to **Harlem, New York**, to begin the **Black Arts Repertory Theatre/School**. Though the project failed, its ideology lived on to merge with that of the **Black Power** movement. Both the Black Arts Movement and the Black Power movement were nationalistic in that they both spoke to the desire of African Americans to define their own lives and culture.

Out of the Black Arts Movement emerged Black theater groups, Black poetry performances, and Black journals. *Black Dialogue* was the first major Black arts literary publication. The political values of the Black Arts Movement were now being expressed in the works of Black artists, poets, writers, novelists, musicians, and other artists. Ironically, a major reason that the philosophy of the Black Arts Movement was so readily adopted was the development of nationally distributed magazines. These magazines circulated manifestos and provided publication sites for Black writers. Most literary publications rejected Black Arts writers, and in the early 1960s most Black Arts writers published mainly in two New York–based nationally distributed magazines, *Freedomways* and *Liberator*.

The creators of *Black Dialogue* felt the need to provide a space where Black artists and political activists could directly address Black people, and they wanted the journal to be viewed as a literary magazine by Blacks, for Blacks.

It is important to note that *Black Dialogue*, in addition to being a political and literary journal, was also noncommercial. It operated on limited funding and was primarily distributed through Black dealers and by subscription. Advertising was limited to Black publishing companies and other Black journals.

Resources: *Black Dialogue* 1, no. 3–4 (1965); 2, no. 5 (Fall 1966); 3, no. 6 (Winter 1967–1968); 4, no. 1–2 (Spring 1969–Summer 1970); Abby Arthur Johnson and Ronald Maberry Johnson, *Propaganda and Aesthetics: The Literary Politics of African-American Magazines in the Twentieth Century* (Amherst: University of Massachusetts Press, 1991); Kaluma Ya Salaam, "Historical Overviews of the Black Arts Movement," in *The Oxford Companion of African American Literature*, ed. William L. Andrews, Frances Smith Foster, and Trudier Harris (New York: Oxford University Press, 1997).

Rochell Isaac

Black Family. The Black family has been a subject of sociological and scientific investigation since the 1920s, and today is one of the most widely researched areas of study in the social sciences. Scholars have long asserted that there are problems inherent in the Black family unit—problems that have contributed to poverty, educational failures, and high levels of unemployment within the Black community. Several forces have affected the dynamics and structure of the Black family, including urbanization, discrimination, economic inequality, and the integration of cultural family practices from Africa. But to understand the Black family, one must first look to the history of **slavery** and how the Black family unit was affected.

Slave families faced precarious dilemmas. The slave trade disrupted the stability of the Black family by placing Black men and women under the direct control of slave owners. Upon arrival in the United States, families were often separated because they were not recognized as anything more than property. Because, as slaves, Black men and women were considered property, it was therefore illegal for them to marry one another. Thus, slaves were rarely able to maintain a cohesive family unit. Black men and women who lived on separate plantations would often travel at night to visit one another and preserve romantic relationships. Otherwise, they had to receive a master's permission to visit a loved one. Slaves also looked forward to Christmas, when separated family members were often able to spend a week together. When slaves were able to secure their freedom, they often worked to raise money to buy the freedom of their family members, or tried to help their enslaved family members escape to the North, where they could be free.

Some slave owners encouraged their slaves to marry, believing that this would make Black men less rebellious and inclined to run away. They also encouraged these couplings so as to increase the number of slaves under their control. Some slave women were offered incentives, such as the promise of freedom, if they bore fifteen children.

The issue of the Black family was further complicated by the sexual exploitation of Black women. Husbands were unable to protect their wives and daughters from sexual harassment or abuse at the hands of their masters. In his autobiography, *Narrative of the Life and Adventures of Henry Bibb, an American Slave* (1849), **Henry Bibb**, a slave who became an antislavery activist, wrote: "If my wife must be exposed to the insults and licentious passions of wicked slave-drivers and overseers; if she must bear the stripes of the lash laid on by an unmerciful tyrant; if this is to be done with impunity, which is frequently done by slaveholders and their abettors, Heaven forbid that I should be compelled to watch the sight."

Black men and women had no recourse when their children or partners were sold. In fact, slave owners often used the threat of sale to punish and control their slaves who had families. Because young children had to remain with their mothers, many Black families were matrilineal. Black children rarely spent significant amounts of time with their fathers in this oppressive climate, setting the stage for a future where broken homes were prevalent.

After the **Civil War**, Black families began to reconnect. Black men and women married legally, in churches, baptized their children, and gave children new family names. At the same time, the Black family continued to deal with many societal and economic pressures. Economic disparities, high unemployment and underemployment, inequality in housing and educational opportunities, and substandard health care all worked to undermine the stability of the Black family. The effects of urbanization, with fathers working long hours and mothers entering the workforce to help support their families, created family structures where Black children were not able to spend a great deal of time with either parent.

In 1965, the difficulties of the Black family were brought to the forefront in a report by Daniel Patrick Moynihan, *The Negro Family: The Case for National*

Action. In the ensuing years, the report has been both applauded and criticized for the facts and information presented. Moynihan was a sociologist and politician who became active in the Democratic Party during the 1950s. Two years before releasing his report, Moynihan had written *Beyond the Melting Pot* (1963) with Nathan Glazer—a study that examined American ethnicity. As assistant secretary of labor, Moynihan undertook an analysis of poverty within the Black community—a study that made a strong connection between poverty and the instability of the Black family structure. The Moynihan report stated: "The gap between the Negro and most other groups in American society is widening. The fundamental problem, in which this is most clearly the case, is that of family structure. The evidence—not final, but powerfully persuasive—is that the Negro family in the urban ghettos is crumbling. A middle-class group has managed to save itself, but for vast numbers of the unskilled, poorly educated city working class the fabric of conventional social relationships has all but disintegrated" (http://www.dol.gov/asp/programs/history/webid-moynihan.htm).

After the report was released, Moynihan was widely criticized as a racist although, in recent years, his analysis has been labeled prescient. While the Moynihan report offered no solutions, it had plenty to say about the state of the Black family. Black families were depicted as highly unstable, if not completely broken. The report cited such statistics as "nearly a quarter of Negro women living cities who have ever married are divorced, separated, or are living apart from their husbands." The report also stated that a number of Black families were headed by women, who were more fertile than their White counterparts, and that most Black children received public assistance at some point during their childhood. Throughout the report was the implication that responsibility for the downfall of the Black family could be placed squarely on the shoulders of the Black woman.

Since the 1960s, Black marriage rates have declined and Black single-parent households have increased significantly. Societal changes have led to an increase in unmarried couples choosing to live together. A shortage of marriageable Black men has contributed to the decline in marriage rates within the Black community. For every 100 Black women, there are only 88 men, and the Black male community has been further been depleted by the disproportionate number of Black men who are incarcerated.

Sociological studies have shown that there are many characteristics unique to the Black family. Whether or not there is a father present in the Black family, many Black children are exposed to male members of the extended family and other members of the community. Black families are more hierarchical in nature, with strict behavioral demands placed upon Black children. Grandparents are regularly involved in the lives of Black children and can, in certain cases, serve as the primary caregivers. Older siblings play an equally important role, given the increase in households where both parents work outside of the home. These older siblings are responsible for the care of younger siblings and maintenance of the household while parents are at work. Spirituality, ethnic identity, and ancestry are all driving forces in maintaining the unity of the Black family—preserving an understanding of the past and a belief in a higher power to connect families across generations.

While the effects of slavery, discrimination, and economic inequality continue to affect the Black family, the Black family is a resilient and unique unit that continues to evolve. The subject of the family has, of course, been taken up by innumerable African American writers, from the time of **slave narratives** to the most contemporary literature (*see* Billingsley, Brown, Calloway, Federmayer, Hansell, Harris, Hill-Lubin, and Rushdy in Resources).

Resources: Andrew Billingsley: "The Conception of the Black Family in the Fiction of Waters E. Turpin," in *Swords upon This Hill*, ed. Burney J. Hollis (Baltimore: Morgan State University Press, 1984), 63–72; *The Evolution of the Black Family* (New York: National Urban League, 1976); Licia Calloway, *Black Family (Dys)function in Novels by Jessie Fauset, Nella Larsen, & Fannie Hurst* (New York: Peter Lang, 2003); Eleanor Engram, *Science, Myth, Reality: The Black Family in One-Half Century of Research* (Westport, CT: Greenwood Press, 1982); Éva Federmayer, "Black Woman and the Reconstruction of the Black Family: Jessie Fauset's *There Is Confusion*," *Hungarian Journal of English and American Studies* 1 (1996), 93–102; Herbert Gutman, *The Black Family in Slavery and Freedom, 1750–1925* (New York: Pantheon, 1976); William H. Hansell, "Essences, Unifyings, and Black Militancy: Major Themes in Gwendolyn Brooks's Family Pictures and Beckonings," *Black American Literature Forum* 11, no. 2 (Summer 1977), 63–66; Trudier Harris, "'I Wish I Was a Poet': The Character as Artist in Alice Childress's *Like One of the Family*," *Black American Literature Forum* 14, no. 1 (Spring 1980), 24–30; Robert Hill, *Research on the African American Family: A Holistic Perspective* (Westport, CT: Auburn House, 1993); Mildred A. Hill-Lubin, "The Grandmother in African and African-American Literature: A Survivor of the African Extended Family," in *Ngambika: Studies of Women in African Literature*, ed. Carole Boyce Davies (Trenton, NJ: Africa World Press, 1986), 257–270; Burney J. Hollis, ed., *Swords upon This Hill: Preserving the Literary Tradition of Black Colleges and Universities* (Baltimore: Morgan State University Press, 1984); Martha Hursey, "Images of Black Women: Family Roles in Harlem Renaissance Literature," *Dissertation Abstracts International* 37 (1976), 2836A–2837A; K. Sue Jewell, *Survival of the African American Family* (Westport, CT: Praeger, 2003); Harriette P. McAdoo, ed., *Black Families*, 3rd ed. (Thousand Oaks, CA: Sage, 1997); Daniel Patrick Moynihan, *The Negro Family: The Case for National Action* (Washington, DC: U.S. Department of Labor, 1965), http://www.dol.gov/asp/programs/history/webid-moynihan.htm; Ashraf Rushdy, *Remembering Generations: Race and Family in Contemporary African American Fiction* (Chapel Hill: University of North Carolina Press, 2001); Robert Staples, *The Black Family: Essays and Studies*, 6th ed. (Belmont, CA: Wadsworth, 1999); Robert J. Taylor et al., eds., *Family Life in Black America* (Thousand Oaks, CA: Sage, 1997); M. H. Washington, ed., *Memory of Kin: Stories About Family by Black Writers* (New York: Doubleday, 1991).

Roxane Gay

Black Nationalism (c. 1827–present). Black Nationalism refers to African American sociopolitical theories, organizations, and actions that responded collectively and interactively to deep-seated institutional racism in the United States during the nineteenth and twentieth centuries and into the twenty-first century. Black Nationalism evolved in response to the fact that, as individuals and as a group, African Americans have seen their social, political, economic, and educational endeavors hindered by institutional racism. One of its premises is that instead of focusing on securing civil rights that have yet to be enjoyed or that prove to be insufficient, African Americans should create institutions independent of Whites, either within or outside the United States—in Africa, for example. Black Nationalism endeavors to oppose what it identifies as White supremacy, and it adapts both political and literary responses to this objective. Although the term did not appear in an American dictionary until 1963 (*Merriam-Webster*, 119), Black Nationalism's principles are evident in African American literature as early as the eighteenth century. Published in 1772, *The Interesting Life of Olaudah Equiano*, for instance, recognizes and connects race and nation: his text refers to fellow captives as "my countrymen" (Equiano, 56) and "Africans of all languages" (Equiano, 57). Equiano's recognition of race and nation, integral aspects of Black Nationalism, is demonstrated by his textual differentiation between Africans as his countrymen (Guineans) and "the white people" and "these white people's country" (Equiano, 55).

Scholars disagree about how best to define Black Nationalism more precisely. Sometimes it is described as being rooted in the philosophies and mobilizing activities of the **Black Power** movement of the 1960s. Ogbar, for instance, defines Black Nationalism as "the belief that Black people, acting independently of whites, should create viable Black institutions for their survival," adding that "racial pride, dignity, racial separation, and hard work are the staples of Black Nationalism" (53–57). Often Black Nationalists are described as "radicals" who choose to separate from Whites (*Merriam-Webster*, 119). In contrast, scholars in African American Studies tend to define Black Nationalism as a complex collection of theories that find expression both in writing and in reaction to racial oppression. In this definition, Black Nationalism is seen as responding to no single methodology for instituting racism, but instead as adjusting its responses to immediate modes of apparent oppression practiced within American institutions. Viewed from this perspective, Black Nationalism, by design, revises its strategies and goals, yet retains the belief that blacks are globally connected, and therefore constitute a kind of Black nation. **Richard Allen** and **David Walker** are considered to be two early proponents of Black Nationalism. In 1830, independent of one another, they wrote abolitionist prose that argued against President Jackson's cooperation with and encouragement of the American Colonization Society's (ACS) agenda.

Begun in 1817 and headed by Henry Clay, the ACS had as its central goal relocation of free blacks to Africa. On its face the policy proposed a return of free blacks to their homeland. However, Walker's 1829 *Appeal* and Allen's editorials featured in *Freedom's Journal* suggested that the ACS's aim was not to liberate free Blacks, but rather to separate them from slaves, a separation that, in theory, would discourage slave revolts and lessen the economic consequences of more subtle resistance. Such resistance might come in the form of completing one's tasks—such as picking cotton or herding cattle—slowly; or it might come in the form of losing and breaking tools required to complete one's work.

Martin Delany was one among a growing population of free African Americans to understand emigration as a way of gaining civil rights and providing opportunities for Blacks to acquire wealth. In *The Condition, Elevation, Emigration and Destiny of the Colored People of the United States* (1852), Delany urged support for the first **Back-to-Africa** movement organized by Blacks. **James M. Whitfield**, poet and social critic, reiterated Delany's Black Nationalist view in *America and Other Poems*, published in 1853. From Delany and Whitfield's position, shared by **Alexander Crummel** and **Henry Highland Garnet**, equality and integration were not forthcoming, and institutional racism appeared to be a permanent part of American society. The Emancipation Proclamation (1863) created a set of social and economic circumstances feared by white plantation owners and poor Southern Whites.

By 1870, Congress had enacted Thirteenth, Fourteenth, and Fifteenth Amendments to the U.S. Constitution, which, respectively, ended slavery, protected citizens equally, and granted voting rights to Black men. Of course, the amendments were selectively and inconsistently enforced. Consequently, Black Nationalism modified its objectives and strategies to confront racist institutions and practices that were in theory, but not in reality, outlawed by the three new amendments. Poetry, historical fiction, and nonfiction prose by African Americans, including **Phillis Wheatley**, **Harriet Wilson**, **Maria Stewart**, **George Moses Horton**, **William Wells Brown**, and **Sutton Griggs** were part of a Black Nationalist response by raising issues concerning wage labor, suffrage, and protection from Whites' organized violence against African Amerians. The implicit and explicit arguments that Black Nationalist literature contained no longer sprang chiefly from moral and religious perspectives, but from constitutional law. For example, **Charles Chesnutt**'s *Marrow of Tradition* highlights the brutal murder of Blacks attempting to vote in the 1898 elections in Wilmington, North Carolina. Although *Marrow* was not well received by a predominantly White audience, Chesnutt's response to discriminatory conditions and disregarded voting rights in the South encouraged African American literature to begin considering political action formerly deemed impractical. In contrast to Chesnutt, the Christian writer **Henry McNeal Turner** suggested that freedom would not necessarily be found in constitutional law, and sponsored Black emigration to West Africa in sermons and essays such as "The Negro and the Army" (1862) and "God Is a Negro" (1895).

At the time of Turner's death in 1915, African American literature and journalism began to proliferate. The **Harlem Renaissance** marked the first period in American literary history in which African Americans could openly debate questions of racial identity. In the Harlem Renaissance, notions of a black aesthetic, central to Black Nationalist thought, emerged. **W.E.B. Du Bois** and **Alain Locke** contributed forcefully to debates about connections between art, politics, and social activism. Locke, author of "The New Negro" (1925), attempted to reconcile what Du Bois defined as double consciousness in *The Souls of Black Folk* (1903). As a self-proclaimed **Negro** and American, Locke argued that aesthetics should be universal, not contingent upon race or history. Du Bois, on the other hand, argued that the Blackness and the experiences of African Americans were unique and that art should approach them that way. Although Locke and Du Bois were both cultural pluralists, Du Bois's prose expressed a Black Nationalist understanding of aesthetics. On a completely different front, **Marcus Garvey** organized and promoted a Back-to-Africa movement. Black newspapers, journals, and magazines, such as the ***Chicago Defender***, *The Journal of Negro History*, ***Opportunity***, and ***The Crisis***, debated issues of race, interracial heritage, and the Black aesthetic. Essays, short stories, and poetry by **Dorothy West**, **Jean Toomer**, **Claude McKay**, and **Countee Cullen** considered meanings of Black racial identity, including interracial heritage.

Black Nationalism does not distinguish between Africans and descendants of Africans. According to its principles, all Africans and their descendants are connected in lineage and political struggle. This view was a point of contention during the Harlem Renaissance, a time when Black Nationalism's stance on race and emigration was perceived to be ambiguous and ineffective. From an integrationist or biracial stance, Blacks helped build America's wealth as slaves and without reward; therefore, they should remain to claim their rights as American citizens. Although Du Bois and **Booker T. Washington** disagreed about other issues, they agreed that Blacks should continue to be American citizens. **Langston Hughes** wrote extensively on Blackness. His poem "The Negro Speaks of Rivers" (1921) is a testament to the longevity of Black culture, and his short stories collected in *The Ways of White Folks* (1934) present Blackness as an experience affecting every facet of life, in every social class, in every region of the United States (*see* Ostrom).

During the **Great Depression** and **World War II**, a Black Nationalist perspective, which consistently sees poverty to be a result of racism, was challenged by a Marxist-influenced socialist perspective. Perhaps partly influenced by ideas of socialism, much African American literature of the 1940s and 1950s did not see emigration as a viable solution, but saw labor movements as a potentially viable alternative. Socialist influence on African American literature is recognizable in texts such as **Lloyd Brown**'s *Iron City* (1951) and **Richard Wright**'s *Uncle Tom's Children* (1938) and *Native Son* (1940). It also is evident in Langston Hughes's poetry of the 1930s. In the wake of the **Great Depression**, African American literature produced works articulating the deprivation within the Black experience. **Ann Petry**'s *The Street* (1946) and **Ralph Ellison**'s *Invisible Man* (1952) provide fictional accounts of the social and political consequences for uneducated and poor African Americans.

The politically and racially charged 1960s brought the rise of the Black Power movement, the rhetoric of which heavily influenced African American literature. The **Black Arts Movement** produced **jazz** and R&B compositions;

poetry, **performance poetry**, and spoken word; critical essays, dramatic plays, and blaxploitation films; and fiction—all expressing Black power, pride, and nationalism. **Lorraine Hansberry**'s plays *A Raisin in the Sun* (1959) and *To Be Young, Gifted and Black* (published posthumously in 1969), encourage Blacks to face restrictive covenants head-on and to be proud of their Blackness. **Malcolm X**'s autobiography (1965) makes plain race's interconnected factors, while urging Blacks to respond violently if necessary. Malcolm X also became a kind of symbol for the connection between Black Nationalism and the **Nation of Islam**. Poetry and drama by **Amiri Baraka** not only attacks the White power structure but also speaks to Black accountability for perpetuating stereotypes. **Woodie King**, a theater director, and **Ron Milner**, a playwright and jazz musician, edited a volume of Black plays, *Black Drama Anthology* (1971), that presents a wide range of expression of the Black aesthetic. The African writer E. U. Essien-Udom wrote an important study, *Black Nationalism: A Search for an Identity in America* (1962).

Poetry and lyrics penned by entertainers also interweave Black Nationalist principles. James Brown's "Say It Loud, I'm Black and I'm Proud" (1969), **Gil Scott-Herron**'s "Whitey on the Moon" and "The Revolution Will Not Be Televised" (1970), and the **Last Poets**' "Niggers Are Scared of Revolution" (1970) are musical poetic contributions to the Black Nationalist voice. While arguing based on Black Nationalism's logic, not only did Black artists make significant contributions to African American literature, but they also served as predecessors to **rap** music's development in the mid-1970s. Rap artists, including Common, De La Soul, Mos Def, **Talib Kweli**, **Tupac Shakur**, and Public Enemy, to name only a few, have promoted Black Nationalist ideas and practices in their music since 1989.

Resources: Howard Brotz, ed., *African American Social and Political Thought: 1850–1920* (New Brunswick, NJ: Transaction, 1992); Olaudah Equiano, *The Interesting Narrative of the Life of Olaudah Equiano, Written by Himself*, ed. Vincent Carretta (Boston: Bedford Books, 1995); E. U. Essien-Udom, *Black Nationalism: A Search for an Identity in America* (Chicago: University of Chicago Press, 1962; New York: Dell, 1964); Joanne Grant, ed., *Black Protest: 350 Years of History, Documents, and Analyses* (New York: Fawcett Columbine, 1968); *Merriam-Webster's Collegiate Dictionary*, 10th ed. (Springfield, MA: Merriam-Webster, 2000); Jeffrey Ogbonna Green Ogbar, "Prophet Nat and God's Children of Darkness: Black Religious Nationalism," *Journal of Religious Thought* 53–54, no. 1 (1997), 51–71; Hans Ostrom, *Langston Hughes: A Study of the Short Fiction* (New York: Twayne, 1993); Dean E. Robinson, *Black Nationalism in American Politics and Thought* (Cambridge: Cambridge University Press, 2001); William L. Van Deburg, ed., *Modern Black Nationalism: From Marcus Garvey to Louis Farrakhan* (New York: New York University Press, 1997).

Ellesia Ann Blaque

Black Panther Party (for Self-Defense) (1966–c. 1980). When they were college students, **Huey Newton** and Bobby Seale founded the Black Panther Party in October 1966 in Oakland, California. They originally called the organization the Black Panther Party for Self-Defense. It was designed to challenge and stop police brutality and to address social, legal, and economic disparities in the United States specific to Black people. It was the first organization of its kind to demand a halt to police brutality and to put together a mode of operation that directly "policed the police" in Oakland, California. Newton and Seale studied law and therefore knew that they could legally carry unconcealed weapons as they patrolled streets, following the police. Newton and Seale dubbed themselves Minister of Defense and Chairman of the Black Panther Party. They put the police on notice that a new organization was monitoring their behavior. During the early years, most Panthers carried weapons.

Ending police brutality was not the only purpose of the Black Panther Party for Self-Defense. Seale and Newton drafted a ten-point program and platform that addressed many of the ills that plagued what **Eldridge Cleaver**, the Minister of Information, termed "the Black colony of Babylon America." The ten-point program and platform were at first separated into divisions titled "What We Want" and "What We Believe." "What We Want" designated specific points and "What We Believe" explained the philosophical motives for the Panthers' goals. The "What We Want" section reads: "1—We want freedom. We want the power to determine the destiny of our black community. 2—We want full employment for our people. 3—We want the white racist businessman to end the robbery and exploitation of the black community. 4—We want decent housing, fit for shelter of human beings. 5—We want decent education that teaches us about the true nature of this decadent American system, and education that teaches us about our true history and our role in present-day society. 6—We want all black men to be exempt from military service. 7—We want an immediate end to police brutality and murder of black people. 8—We want all black men and women to be released from the federal, county, state, and city jails and prisons. 9—We want every black man brought to trial to be tried in a court by a jury of his peer group as it is defined by the Constitution of this United States. 10—We want land, bread, housing, education, clothing, justice, and peace." Thinkers influencing the Panther ideology and philosophy included Mao Tse-tung, Frantz Fanon, and **Malcolm X**.

This ten-point program was distributed throughout Oakland, California, mostly to what Newton and Seale called the "brothers on the block." The Panthers opened their first office in Oakland on January 1, 1967. On May 2, 1967, Bobby Seale led thirty armed Panthers, six women and twenty-four men, to the State Capitol at Sacramento to challenge a proposed new gun law designed to remove the guns from the patrolling Panthers. For this event, the Panthers received international attention when Bobby Seale read a mandate before the press that explained why Panthers needed to carry arms. This event illustrated the historical phenomenon of police violence against Blacks, and it rivaled the nonviolent **Civil Rights Movement**. Former participants in the Student Nonviolent Coordinating Committee, such as **Stokely Carmichael**, H. Rap Brown, and **Kathleen Cleaver** either joined or were "drafted into" the Panthers.

Newton and Seale selected the name and symbol of the Panthers because of the nature and appearance of the animal. The panther is an aristocratic animal that never attacks, but if attacked, the panther fights back aggressively. The Panthers were anticapitalists, and they believed in revolutionary struggle if peaceful negotiations failed to gain the ten-point platform resolutions. The earliest member was seventeen-year-old Little Bobby Hutton (the "Little" to distinguish him from Bobby Seale), who became "the first to fall." Hutton was killed in a police shoot-out on April 4, 1968. Eldridge Cleaver was with him, but survived. This shoot-out happened after (and partly because of unrest following) the assassination of **Martin Luther King** in **Memphis, Tennessee**.

The history of the Black Panther Party has many elements. It is one of celebrated trials, police shoot-outs, incarcerations, espionage, and counterintelligence, as well as covert, underground, and aboveground operations. Another part of that history involves Black community reform, leadership, vanguard discipline, internationalism, multiculturalism, **Black Nationalism**, socialism, and resistance. The most noted and earliest trial concerned cofounder Huey P. Newton, charged with killing John Frey, a policeman, and wounding his partner, Herbert Heanes, in 1967. Newton faced the gas chamber for shooting these two White policemen. The reverberations of Newton's status as cofounder and Minister of Defense of the Panthers galvanized Blacks and White radicals across the country and around the world. Newton's legal and nonlegal defense—handled by Seale and Eldridge Cleaver and his wife, Kathleen Cleaver, communications secretary—was based on coalitions with Asians, Latinos, Whites, and Blacks. From the inception of the Black Panther Party, Seale and Newton espoused a willingness to work with non-Blacks, as long as they adhered to the tenets of the ten-point platform and program. Non-Blacks could not become Panther members, but they could join coalitions to assist the Panther mission. Newton served four years in prison before his release in 1971. He was the first Black male in American history to escape the death penalty on charges of shooting police officers.

When Newton returned to Oakland, he found a different Black Panther Party. The Panthers had increased in membership substantially. There were Panther chapters in most major American cities. Under the leadership of Bobby Seale, the Panthers had started breakfast programs for schoolchildren nationwide. The Panthers were conducting sickle cell anemia testing in Black communities. They had political education programs for the public. They started schools to educate Panther and community youth. They staged successful boycotts against the Safeway supermarket chain and other grocery stores that refused to donate food to the breakfast program. Eldridge and Kathleen Cleaver had slipped abroad to Algeria and France to avoid Eldridge's return to prison because of the 1968 shoot-out. The Panther newspaper, *The Black Panther*, now had an increased circulation and a layout as sophisticated as those of the Muslim newspaper *Muhammad Speaks*, started by Malcolm X. When Newton came out of prison, Hollywood offered him movie contracts and the Panther membership idolized him. His release was celebrated as "a victory for the

Poster promoting the Black Panther Party. "One of our main purposes is to unify our brothers and sisters in the North with our brothers and sisters in the South." Courtesy of the Library of Congress.

people," an offshoot of the Panther slogan "Power to the People." Yet Newton struggled to make a transition from prison to civilian life. Some say that a different Huey Newton returned from prison.

Previously, in 1969–1970, Seale had faced two simultaneous trials. One, the Chicago Eight trial, occurred partly because of a speech he gave outside of the Democratic National Convention in Chicago, in 1968. He was charged with traveling across state lines to give a seditious speech. Seven White male activists were also on trial: Dave Dellinger, Abbie Hoffman, Rennie Davis, Jerry Rubin, Lee Weiner, John R. Froines, and Tom Hayden. Judge Hoffman ordered the loquacious Seale to be bound and gagged in the courtroom because he refused to allow a court-appointed lawyer to defend him. His lawyer, Charles Garry, who was also Newton's lawyer, was ill. This animated event was made into a movie titled *The Chicago Eight* (1986). Seale also faced a hearing in New Haven, Connecticut. He and Erika Huggins, a **Los Angeles** Panther leader, were charged with the murder of a Panther/police informant, Alex Rackley. Members of the Black cultural nationalist US organization that battled for control of the Los Angeles area had recently killed Huggins's husband, John. Seale and Erika Huggins spent two years in jail while each charge was dismissed. In Chicago and New Haven, Seale was acquitted. During his trial, as during Newton's imprisonment, legions of people protested, held rallies, and supported his innocence.

The year 1969 also saw the Chicago murder of Panther leaders Fred Hampton and Mark Clark. Hampton, an extremely effective young leader of the Chicago chapter, met his death chiefly because of the animosity that continued between the Panthers and the police. In the 1970s, the families of both slain leaders were awarded compensation when evidence proved that the police had shot first into Panther headquarters. That year additionally saw the start of the prison sentence of Geronimo Elmer Pratt. He became leader of the Los Angeles branch of the Panthers after US members gunned down Alprentice "Bunchy" Carter, a charismatic Panther captain, and John Huggins. The Panthers and US disagreed over who should head the newly formed Black Studies program at UCLA. Geronimo Pratt was framed for the murder of a White woman unaffiliated with the Panthers. After serving twenty-seven years in prison, he proved his innocence and, in 1997, he walked out of prison an exonerated man (Olsen).

The West Coast Panthers set policy and held power over all of the branches around the country. The central committee of the Black Panther Party convened at headquarters in Berkeley, California. The first female to sit on the central committee was Kathleen Cleaver. She, along with Eldridge Cleaver, Seale, and Newton, guided the Panthers. When the Cleavers went to Algeria and then to France, they set up an international chapter of the organization. During this period an ideological separation occurred between Cleaver and Newton.

This breach between leaders caused a massive purge within the organization in the United States during the early 1970s. Loyalists to Cleaver defected or were purged from the Panthers. Loyalists to Newton remained in the Panthers. The ideological difference concerned emphasis: whether or not the organization continued its reformist programs or focused complete attention on revolutionary struggle. Cleaver preferred the latter. During this same period, in 1972, some Panthers ran for public office. Bobby Seale, no longer carrying weapons, ran for mayor of Oakland, and **Elaine Brown**, for City Council. Although they lost each race, both candidates made impressive showings, gaining 40 percent of the vote. Continuing the trend from policing the police to working within the system, the Panthers opened the Lamp Post lounge and restaurant in Oakland, and they put together many "survival programs," such as a free ambulance service, a senior citizen escort service, and dental and optometry programs. However, during Seale's mayoral campaign, the central committee ordered all chapters to close down and to send recruits to Oakland to help in the election process. This decision affected national membership of the Black Panther Party. When the election was over, Panther chapters around the country were bereft of members. Additionally, the excesses of Newton, his drug use, and his alleged violent acts against Black people destroyed the morale of the members and the Panthers' reputation.

According to Elaine Brown, Newton used Panther muscle to extort money from Black businesses in Oakland (*A Taste of Power*). This money was to keep their more than thirty survival programs in operation. In 1974, Seale resigned from or was forced out of the Panthers, and Elaine Brown took his place as chairman of the Party when Newton went to Cuba to escape brutality charges. Brown, a folk singer and one of Newton's paramours, had traveled to China and to Cuba representing the Panthers. During her time as chairman, she struggled with issues of sexism; however, she controlled the Panthers in a style similar to Newton's—forceful and charismatic. Additionally, she focused on creating liaisons between the organization and the business community. Much of the Panthers' finances bought legal talent to free incarcerated members and to defend Newton. Brown managed to bring Newton home from Cuba, but his excesses diminished the organization's purpose and goals. The Black Panther Party continued in the shadow of its glory years until around 1980, when the last issue of *The Black Panther* came off the press.

The Black Panther Party was at the hub of political activism and social strife in the 1960s; it became a symbol of Black Nationalism and African American self-preservation; and, indirectly, it produced several important works of African American writing, including books by Cleaver, Seale, Brown, and Newton, as well as Geronimo Pratt's compelling tale of survival, *Last Man Standing*, as told by Jack Olsen.

Resources: Elaine Brown, *A Taste of Power: A Black Woman's Story* (New York: Pantheon, 1992); Eldridge Cleaver, *Soul on Ice* (New York: McGraw-Hill, 1967); Billy (X) Jennings, "Personal Interview with Regina Jennings" (n.d.); Huey P. Newton and J. Herman Blake, *Revolutionary Suicide* (New York: Writers and Readers, 1995); Jack Olsen, *Last Man Standing: The Tragedy and Triumph of Geronimo Pratt* (New York: Anchor/Doubleday, 2000); Bobby Seale: "Personal Interview with Regina Jennings" (n.d.); *Seize the Time: The Story of the Black Panther Party and Huey P. Newton* (Baltimore: Black Classics Press, 1991).

Regina Jennings

Black Power (1960–present). Black Power is an extension of **Black Nationalism** and is characterized by cohesive self-determination in the midst of oppressive White power. Black Power was initially defined in 1966 by Kwame Ture (formerly known as **Stokely Carmichael**) as involving redefinition, unification, and organization; however, the aims of Black Power were heatedly debated during the 1960s and early 1970s. Manifestations of Black Power principles appear in African American literature produced during and after the **Black Arts Movement**.

To some degree, Black Power involves a sequence. African Americans first must come to terms with what **W.E.B. Du Bois**, in *The Souls of Black Folk* (1903), called double consciousness—the acute awareness of being oneself but also of being Black in a White society. From that point of awareness, African Americans may then reflect on their history (as Du Bois and others do), and they may try to counteract the subconscious devaluation of African American culture, an African heritage, the Black aesthetic, and so on. Finally, African Americans may then embrace their own history, culture, and worth, gaining "Black Power" (Ture and Hamilton).

African Americans who experience this sequence of reconciliation may then encourage self-definition and group unification in others, creating a conscious power block that is then organized to pool funds, knowledge, experience, protection, and skill for the establishment of institutions that support the needs and goals of Black people as individuals and as a group. The Black Arts Movement, for example, supported many community writers' groups, presses, theater groups, **Black Studies** programs, and so on (*see* **Broadside Press**; **Lotus Press**; **OBAC** Writers Workshop; **Rob Penny**; **Third World Press**). In other words, a sense of solidarity was part of the Black Power movement almost from the beginning.

Proponents of Black Power view it as one powerful political way to keep racism contained. An ideology heavily represented in African American literature during the Black Arts Movement, Black Power demands that African Americans obtain—"by any means necessary," in the words of **Malcolm X**—authority and control over their own identities, communities, wealth, well-being—and means of communication, including literature. This control is important in opposing the oppressive state structure, according to the reasoning behind Black Power. In addition to musicians, film directors, editors, and scholars, the 1960s saw the rise of fiery playwrights, poets, essayists, and novelists speaking the language of Black Power. Such writers include **Mari Evans**, **Amiri Baraka**, **Sonia Sanchez**, **Ed Bullins**, **Eldridge Cleaver**, **Jayne Cortez**, **Larry Neal**, **Maulana Karenga**, **Haki R. Madhubuti**, **Nikki Giovanni**, and the **Last Poets**. During this literary era, Black writing and discourse became a highly independent component of American literature. Rather than viewing and documenting the Black aesthetic through the lens and in the language of the dominant society, writers influenced by Black Power spoke from within their own experiences and often in the **vernacular** of that experience. Just as many **Harlem Renaissance** writers sought to move beyond nineteenth-century literary forms, so the Black Arts Movement moved beyond literary conventions belonging to the period of the **Great Depression** and **World War II**, even as **Richard Wright** and other writers of **protest literature** anticipated, to some extent, the Black Arts Movement. To a large degree, the tenets of Black Power discouraged writers and others from seeking relief and support from outside the Black community. Rather than arguing or pleading for equality, literature influenced by Black Power demanded equality in ways that were deemed unrefined and threatening by the mainstream.

Before his assassination in 1965, Malcolm X (El-Hajj Malik El-Shabazz) laid the foundation for the Black Power movement as a national speaker. As a leading minister for the **Nation of Islam** (NOI) in **Harlem, New York**, **Detroit, Michigan**, and **Philadelphia, Pennsylvania**, Malcolm X spearheaded the publication of *Muhammad Speaks*, the NOI's first nationally distributed publication. In 1964 he coined the phrase "by any means necessary" to describe how African Americans must liberate themselves from the forces of White oppression.

From its inception, the **Black Panther Party** (BPP) for Self Defense demonstrated Malcolm X's phrase, and through action and writing, it informed as well as contributed to African American literature. In *The Black Panther* newspaper (1967–1970), the BPP reported on the complexities and violence of American institutional racism. Keeping Bobby Seale's ten-point platform in the foreground in their speeches, poetry, and prose, party members wrote feverishly. **Elaine Brown** provided the group with a "Black Power National Anthem" in 1969. **Eldridge Cleaver**'s *Soul on Ice* (1967) and Carmichael's *Black Power: The Politics of Liberation* (1967) outlined the causes and effects of Black subjugation and revolution. **Huey Newton**'s "In Defense of Self-Defense: Executive Mandate Number One" justified the BPP's argument for self-protection against police brutality.

Black Power, however, not only was embedded in the rhetoric of the BPP, but also was entrenched in the language of much African American literature in the period. Numerous plays, books, poems, song lyrics, and essays were produced by the Black Arts Movement, addressing every aspect of the Black experience and demanding self-identification and control. From poetry by **Gwendolyn Brooks** and Nikki Giovanni to anthologies of drama edited by **Woodie King** and **Ron Milner**, Black Power had more than a voice; it had a forum. **Ben Caldwell**'s 1971 play *All White Caste* imagines an America without Blacks. *Junebug Graduates Tonight* (1971), a play by jazz saxophonist Archie Shepp, demonstrates the power of one Black man against America and Uncle Sam. It also includes metaphorical representations of sexual and economic seductions, ways in which African Americans are manipulated into giving up power. **Ishmael Reed** and **Ralph Ellison** produced works of criticism that explored African American literature from a Black perspective. **James Baldwin**'s novel

Another Country (1962) approached Black Power from a number of different perspectives and also explored connections between sexuality, **gender**, and power. It was also a searching examination of relationships between Whites and Blacks in New York City in the early 1960s.

The voice of Black Power did not go unheard. Nor did it go unanswered by White America, particularly J. Edgar Hoover. As head of the Federal Bureau of Investigation (FBI), Hoover targeted the reach of Black Power, the Black Arts Movement, and the **Civil Rights Movement**. For instance, the FBI developed a file on James Baldwin that eventually ran to more than 1,500 pages (Churchill and Vander Wal), and Hoover reportedly regarded Baldwin's novels as obscene and subversive. The FBI also constantly monitored the activities of Malcolm X, Dr. **Martin Luther King**, **Medgar Evers**, and others. Hoover's response to Black Power in general, and to the BPP specifically, was COINTELPRO, the Counterintelligence Program, whose sole objective, to infiltrate and neutralize organizations deemed as advocates or instigators of violence against the state, had come to fruition by the early 1970s.

Despite the dissolution of Black Power organizations, such as the BPP, the Student Nonviolent Coordinating Committee (SNCC), and the Congress of Racial Equality (CORE), the logic and ideological basis for Black Power has remained in the minds and actions of many African Americans, and in the rhetoric of much African American literature.

Resources: Ward Churchill and Jim Vander Wal, *The COINTELPRO Papers: Documents from the FBI's Secret Wars Against Dissent in the United States*, 2nd ed., ed. Manning Marable (Cambridge, MA: South End Press, 2002); Eldridge Cleaver, *Soul on Ice* (New York: Delta Books, 1968); Philip S. Foner, ed., *The Black Panthers Speak* (New York: Da Capo Press, 1995); Kwame Ture and Charles V. Hamilton, *Black Power: The Politics of Liberation* (New York: Vintage Books, 1992); William L. Van Deburg, *New Day in Babylon: The Black Power Movement and American Culture, 1965–1975* (Chicago: University of Chicago Press, 1992).

Ellesia Ann Blaque

Black Studies. Black Studies is an interdisciplinary academic field that encompasses the research and teaching on the African **diaspora** and the African American experience. It includes the study of literature, sociology, political science, anthropology, religious studies, philosophy, and history. The movement for Black Studies as a formal discipline began in the late 1960s and early 1970s, at the height of the **Civil Rights Movement**, when African Americans began to demand that their cultures and interests be served by academia.

The roots of Black Studies, however, can be found earlier. In 1897, **Alexander Crummell**, an Episcopal clergyman, writer, educator, and missionary, founded the American Negro Academy—an organization dedicated to encouraging Black Americans to participate in art, literature, and philosophy. **W.E.B. Du Bois, Paul Laurence Dunbar, James Weldon Johnson, Booker T. Washington, Arthur Schomburg, Alain Locke,** and **Archibald Grimké** were members of the Academy. Other members included academics, lawyers, physicians, members of the clergy, and community activists. The group published twenty-two research papers, written by members, before the Academy declined in the early 1920s.

In 1915, the Harvard-educated scholar and educator **Carter G. Woodson** founded the Association for the Study of African American Life and History (ASALH). His research was dedicated to studying the past of the African American and sharing that knowledge with a wider community. In 1916, ASALH began publishing *Journal of Negro History*, a scholarly digest, and in February 1926, Woodson inaugurated Negro History Week, which later grew to become Black History Month.

During this time, universities across the country began to incorporate courses dealing with African American concerns into their curricula, but these courses were few and far between. The University of Nebraska offered a course titled "The Negro Problem Under Slavery and Freedom." Harvard University offered a course titled "American Population Problems: Immigration and the Negro." A greater effort was made at historically Black colleges and universities, so that their curricula would better chronicle the history and progress of Black Americans.

It was a student strike at San Francisco State University in 1968 that brought Black Studies, as a formal discipline, into the academic realm. The student-led action, spearheaded by the Black Student Union and activist Ron Karenga, released a political statement, "The Justification for African American Studies," that eventually served as the foundation for African American Studies departments across the United States. Demands included specific offerings in Black history and literature that reinforced an open-minded examination of the African diaspora as well as a process for preparing Black students to participate in the Black community.

By 1975, sixty-five academic departments offered bachelor's degrees in Black Studies. In 1988, Temple University became the first university to award a doctoral degree in Black Studies. As time passed, Black Studies evolved from an activist-based phenomenon into a more scholarly institution that explored the Black experience in sociology, political science, literature, psychology, and economics. Harvard and Princeton maintain what are widely considered the preeminent programs in Black Studies. The two programs are home to the renowned scholars **Henry Louis Gates, Jr.**, Evelyn Brooks Higginbotham, Drew Faust, **Cornel West**, **Toni Morrison**, Nell Irvin Painter, and Anthony Appiah, among others.

While there was a rise in the popularity of Black Studies programs, there were also detractors, both Black and White. In fact, many Black scholars were skeptical for several reasons. Some argued that Black Studies takes a static view of history and ignores the relevance and importance of interactions between Blacks and members of other races. Others have argued that Black Studies programs are not rigorous enough, maintain lax standards, and lack qualified faculty members. Scholars have also realized that it has been nearly impossible to standardize Black Studies programs and the definition of what, precisely, Black Studies is, across universities. Programs with differing philosophical outlooks are teaching students different aspects of the Black experience. What Black Studies means at San Francisco State University may be drastically different from what Black Studies means at the University of Missouri, for example. Many Black Studies programs have been renamed African American Studies programs.

In addition to academic programs, there are research centers such as the Schomburg Center for Research in Black Culture, which is part of the New York Public Library system. The Schomburg Center devotes its energies to preserving artifacts of the African diaspora and Black experiences. It is named for Black scholar Arthur Schomburg, who served as curator between 1932 and 1938. The center's collections include 150,00 volumes and 85,000 microforms; 6,000 serials; 400 Black newspapers; 1,000 current periodicals; 390 rare books; 580 manuscript collections; 15,000 pieces of sheet music; 20,000 cultural artifacts including paintings, sculptures, textiles, and works on paper; 5,000 movies and documentaries; and more than 5,000 hours of recorded oral histories. The Schomburg Center features several exhibits annually, as well as seminars, readings, workshops, and film screenings. It is open to scholars and members of the public interested in research about the Black experience.

There are Black Studies periodicals that are dedicated to, or that frequently publish, articles related to the African American experience. The journals include the *African American Review*, *Black Scholar*, **Callaloo**, *Journal of Black Studies*, *Journal of Blacks in Higher Education*, *Journal of Negro Education*, and *Urban Affairs Review*. The National Council for Black Studies, which disseminates information about Black Studies and African American Studies programs, is at this writing hosted by Georgia State University in **Atlanta**.

The field of Black Studies continues to evolve as the needs and interests of the Black scholarly community evolve. A concept that was born out of protest has since become a mainstay at universities both within the United States and abroad.

Resources: William Exum, *Paradoxes of Protest: Black Student Activism in a White University* (Philadelphia: Temple University Press, 1985); Robert Harris, "The Intellectual and Institutional Development of African Studies," in *Three Essays: Black Studies in the United States*, ed. Robert Harris, Darlene Hine, and Nellie McKay (New York: Ford Foundation, 1990); Maulana Karenga, *Introduction to Black Studies*, 2nd ed. (Los Angeles: University of Sankore Press, 1993); Manning Marable, ed., *Dispatches from the Ebony Tower* (New York: Columbia University Press, 2000); Alfred Moss, *The American Negro Academy: Voice of the Talented Tenth* (Baton Rouge: Louisiana State University Press, 1981); National Council for Black Studies, Georgia State University, http://www.nationalcouncilforblackstudies.com/.

Roxane Gay

Bland, Eleanor Taylor (born 1944). Novelist. Bland's mystery series featuring police detective Marti MacAlister was the first to feature an African American woman protagonist. Born on December 21, 1944, in **Boston, Massachusetts,**

Bland was raised by a cab driver father and a homemaker mother. Divorced, with two sons, she attended college in Illinois and worked as a cost accountant for eighteen years, retiring in 1999.

The series of novels is set in a fictionalized area of northern **Chicago, Illinois**, called Lincoln Heights, which is closely modeled on Bland's hometown of Waukegan. The plots feature detective MacAlister, her children, and her extended family, while she and her White male partner tackle cases that involve various social issues and problems. The series is in the police procedural category of detective novels, but because of the female protagonist, it also invites comparison with the work of detective novelists **Barbara Neely**, Sarah Paretsky, and Sue Grafton.

Resources: Eleanor Taylor Bland: *Dead Time* (New York: St. Martin's Press, 1992); *Done Wrong* (New York: St. Martin's Press, 1995); *Fatal Remains* (New York: St. Martin's Press, 2003); *Gone Quiet* (New York: St. Martin's Press, 1994); *Keep Still* (New York: St. Martin's Press, 1996); *Scream in Silence* (New York: St. Martin's Press, 2000); *See No Evil* (New York: St. Martin's Press, 1998); *Slow Burn* (New York: St. Martin's Press, 1993); *Tell No Tales* (New York: St. Martin's Press, 1999); *Whispers in the Dark* (New York: St. Martin's Press, 2001); *Windy City Dying* (New York: St. Martin's Press, 2002); Jennifer Boentje and Christen Puhek, "Eleanor Taylor Bland," *Voices from the Gaps: Women Writers of Color*, http://voices.cla.umn.edu/newsite/authors/BLANDeleanor.htm; Richard Cohen, "Eleanor Taylor Bland," in *Contemporary Authors*, vol. 166 (Detroit: Gale, 1999), 28–30; Jon Jordan, "Interview with Eleanor Taylor Bland," *MysteryOne*, http://www.mysteryone.com/EleanorTaylorBlandInterview.htm.

Elizabeth Blakesley Lindsay

Blank Verse. Blank verse has been the predominant metrical form used in English from the Renaissance to the modern age. It is estimated that two-thirds of all dramatic and poetic compositions in English have been in blank verse. Marlowe, Shakespeare, and Milton are the most eminent of its early users, but its origin is Italian, with adaptations from Greek. Chaucer in late 1300's England and Trissino, Ariosto, and Pastor Fido, among others, in the next century in Italy, employed its earlier forms in their works. Henry Howard's translation of two books of Virgil's unrhymed *Aeneid* is the major historical marker of the English blank verse tradition. Of like significance is *Gorboduc*, the first tragedy in blank verse, the joint work of Thomas Sackville and Thomas Norton. Mainstream poets such as Dryden, Tennyson, the Brownings, Yeats, Pound, Frost, Eliot, and Wallace Stevens have taken the best advantage of its flexibility and might in the later centuries.

The basic norms of blank verse are the following: its lines are unrhymed, the reason the descriptor "blank" is used; each line is made up of five iambs, an iamb being a metrical unit of two syllables, the first unstressed and the second stressed, as in "to-day," "un-leash," or "a-gree." An iamb is also called a foot. (When studying formal poetry, scholars and other readers sometimes mark the syllabic stress or accent with an ["x"] or a ["u"] for the unstressed and a virgule

["/"] for the stressed.) A pentameter line has five iambs (ten syllables). All lines have the same meter, generally the iambic; blank verse is free of any stanzaic structures.

Iambic pentameter has strong ear appeal because of the cadence it lends to language in delivery. Closest to the natural order of speech, its rhythm corresponds somewhat to the beat of the human heart. The metrical beat of a decasyllabic (five-foot) iambic line, therefore, could be scanned thus:

x / x / x / x / x /

daDUM, daDUM, daDUM, daDUM, daDUM

x / x / x / x / x /

O how unlike the place from whence they fell! (*Paradise Lost*, I, 75)

This rule of scansion (division of a line according to accents) is not inflexible. Compensating accent shifts are often dictated by narrative or dramatic necessity. Polysyllabic or foreign terms may not easily yield to the scan measure. In such cases a line may contain an extra syllable instead of the exact ten of the pentameter, making it a "feminine ending." Gifted poets may intentionally use feminine endings for specific rhetorical purposes. Here is an example from the well-known soliloquy of Hamlet:

To be, or not to be: that is the ques-**tion**:
Whether 'tis nobler in the mind to suf-**fer**
The slings and arrows of outrageous for-**tune**,
Or to take arms against a sea of trou-**bles**,
And by opposing, end them.

(*Hamlet* III.i.58–62)

The boldface syllables represent an eleventh syllable, in contrast to the end-stopped line. End-stopped lines occurring in close sequence can force limits on the sense through structure, lessening the buoyancy that one iambic line can give to the next.

Sometimes pauses are needed, and are created grammatically or mechanically, anywhere in a line except at the end. Such a pause, called a caesura, is intended to involve the audience in the significance of the moment in a greater way. In contrast to caesura and the end stop, longer passages may allow run-on lines bound by a period in a later line. Such a section is called an enjambment.

Blank verse and free verse are two different forms. Blank verse requires rhythm and provides a heightened auditory framework and effect, whereas free verse has less regular, predictable metrical attributes but offers more freedom to the poet.

Numerous African American poets have used iambic pentameter in their verse. **George Moses Horton**'s poem "On Hearing of the Intention of a

Gentleman to Purchase the Poet's Freedom" (1829) is an example of the deployment of this metrical pattern in a **ballad** form. And **Phillis Wheatley** uses the pattern effectively in her verse, which is typically written in rhymed couplets. In the twentieth century, **Countee Cullen**, a master of formal verse, used iambic pentameter often, but almost always in rhymed forms, including the sonnets "Yet Do I Marvel" and "From the Dark Tower." The use of blank verse has been comparatively rare in African American poetry. Sections of **Melvin B. Tolson**'s "Libretto for the Republic of Liberia" is composed in blank verse, as are sections of **Robert Hayden**'s long poem "Middle Passage." **Gwendolyn Brooks**'s "The Sundays of Satin-Legs Smith" uses blank verse effectively, with variation and subtlety. (All of these poems are in *The Norton Anthology of African American Literature*.) Although **Langston Hughes** worked in a variety of formal verse forms, he tended to prefer shorter lines with three or four stresses.

Resources: Henry Louis Gates, Jr. and Nellie Y. McKay, eds., *The Norton Anthology of African American Literature* (New York: W. W. Norton, 1996); John Hollander, *Rhyme's Reason: A Guide to English Verse*, 3rd ed. (New Haven, CT: Yale University Press, 2001); Robert Pinsky, *Sounds of Poetry: A Brief Guide* (New York: Farrar, Straus and Giroux, 1998); Mark Strand and Eavan Boland, eds., *The Making of a Poem: A Norton Anthology of Poetic Forms* (New York: Norton, 2000).

Varghese Mathai

Blaxploitation. Type of film. Known more for its style and legacy than for its quality, blaxploitation—the word combines "Black" and "exploitation"—is a unique subgenre in the history of American cinema. (*The Oxford Dictionary of the English Language* dates the word to 1972.) Combining the street sensibilities of so much African American literature (such as works by **Chester Himes** and **Iceberg Slim**) with music from artists such as Isaac Hayes (who won an Oscar for his theme for *Shaft* in 1972), Curtis Mayfield, and James Brown, blaxploitation captured a spectrum of Black experience on celluloid. For many, it captured and defined a culture; for others, it was simply a further exploitation and misrepresentation of African Americans. Blaxploitation as a genre of cinema, one specifically associated with the lives and literature of the African American community, is often traced to the 1971 film *Sweet Sweetback's Baadasssss Song*, which was directed, written, and produced by, and starred, **Melvin Van Peebles** (who also composed the score). The independent film was an entirely African American production, organized by Van Peebles in response to the paucity of Blacks in the film industry. His earlier racially charged films include *Story of a Three Day Pass* (1968) and *Watermelon Man* (1970). It broke the mold of Black characterization in feature films. The story revolves around a pimp suddenly radicalized by aiding a young Black revolutionary who is beaten by White cops. The character's resulting disgust with the White establishment struck a resonant chord with Black audiences everywhere. The film's climactic finale, with its proclamation that "a baadasssss nigger is coming back to collect some dues," heralded the arrival of a new era in Hollywood and for African Americans in film.

As a genre, blaxploitation typically refers to films in which African American characters and their lifestyles are presented in a manner that reinforces often negative stereotypes, including those of the African American pimp. This, in turn, means that a number of critics of the genre saw these films as pandering to the lowest aspects of African American culture ("ghetto" images). At the same time, blaxploitation borrowed heavily from conventional Hollywood, usually in the forms of genres no longer present in mainstream commercial cinema. For example, there were black kung-fu films (such as the Jim Kelly film *Black Belt Jones* [1974]); slave narratives/westerns (such as Fred Williamson's *The Legend of Nigger Charley* [1972] and its sequel *The Soul of Nigger Charley* [1973]), sci-fi fantasies (such as *The Thing with Two Heads* [1972]), horror films (such as *Blacula* [1972]), tales of pimps and drug dealers (such as *The Mack* [1973] and *Superfly* [1972]), and numerous mafia-type stories (such as *Black Caesar* [1973]).

Sometimes the films suffered from low budgets and mediocre performances, but the hip street talk, the sex appeal, and the overt messages of **Black Power** made blaxploitation films instant hits with Black audiences. Also of cultural importance were the African American movie stars the genre created. Often plucked from obscurity, ex-football players such as Fred "the Hammer" Williamson (who became a prolific writer and director as well) and Jim Brown (*Slaughter* [1972]), models such as Richard Roundtree (*Shaft* [1971]), stand-up comedians such as Rudy Ray Moore (*Dolemite* [1975]), and leading ladies such as Pam Grier became heroes in the eyes of many Black moviegoers. But ultimately Black audiences realized they were being patronized and exploited, hence the subsequent referring to the movies created during this time as "black exploitation" or "blaxploitation." By 1975 viewers were leaving theaters in droves. For all intents and purposes the blaxploitation boom was over by the late 1970s. There were, however, moments in the mid-1980s when the genre seemed to be given a second life—particularly in movies made by African American filmmakers heavily influenced by the original 1970s films. Spike Lee's 1986 *She's Gotta Have It*, along with the satires *Hollywood Shuffle* (1987) and *I'm Gonna Git You Sucka* (1988), directed by Robert Townsend and Keenan Ivory Wayans, respectively, indicated an early renaissance for the African American artist in motion pictures. Since these films, in addition to Spike Lee's 1989 *Do the Right Thing*, there has been a new focus on African American films made by African Americans both within and without the traditional Hollywood studio system.

In addition to a sometimes nostalgic acknowledgment of the role of blaxploitation, many African American films of the 1990s attempted to criticize the exploitative nature of the original genre, thus distancing themselves from the term in general. However, by the early 1990s, films in the wake of John Singleton's 1991 *Boyz N the Hood*, often despite their good intentions, started to provide a new and volatile formula in Black films that studio executives wasted no time in exploiting. Dubbed "gangsploitation," "blaxploitation" had resurfaced, with Black men being portrayed as little beyond "gangbangers" and Black women often represented as "hos" and "welfare queens." One of the most successful examples of this can be found in the Hughes brothers' 1993 *Menace II Society*. It typified this new kind of Black exploitation film with a concentration on surface elements such as music and violence, with a narrative that on one level speaks to the Black experience but at the same time rehashes the latest streams of Black violence flowing from the evening news. These new films were well financed and, in some cases, critically acclaimed for their artistry and were considered desirable by audiences.

The revival of interest in "blaxploitation" may also be seen as a part of a resurgence in the overall "grindhouse" aesthetic of 1970s cinema, with filmmakers like Quentin Tarantino creating renewed interest in blaxploitation, kung-fu, and exploitation movies. Tarantino himself tailored his 1997 film *Jackie Brown* to actress Pam Grier, a mainstay of blaxploitation known for films such as *Coffy* (1973), *Foxy Brown* (1974), and *Friday Foster* (1975). *Shaft* was remade in 2000 by John Singleton. In this sense, African American cinema may be seen as having come full circle in terms of its "exploitative" past as a niche market. The current state of Black cinema does offer more than the images of domestics and mammies that spawned the first wave of blaxploitation, but there is still an apparent inequality across media culture at large.

Resources: Donald Bogle, *Toms, Coons, Mulattoes, Mammies & Bucks: An Interpretive History of Blacks in American Films*, 4th ed. (New York: Continuum, 2001); Ed Guerrero, *Framing Blackness: The African American Image in Film* (Philadelphia: Temple University Press, 1993); Darius James, *That's Blaxploitation: Roots of the Baadasssss 'Tude (Rated X by an All-Whyte Jury)* (New York: St. Martin's Press, 1995); Mikel J. Koven, *Blaxploitation Films* (London: Trafalgar Square, 2001); Gerald Martinez, Diana Martinez, and Andres Chavez, *What It Is... What It Was! The Black Film Explosion of the '70s in Words and Pictures* (New York: Hyperion, 1998); *The Oxford Dictionary of the English Language*, compact, 2nd ed. (Oxford: Oxford University Press, 1989), 144.

Marc Leverette

Blues, The. The blues tradition has had one of the strongest impacts on American, even world, culture of any musical genre of the twentieth century, and its influence on African American poetry has been widely acknowledged since the groundbreaking experiments of **Langston Hughes** and **Sterling Brown** in the 1920s and 1930s. The blues emerged in the 1880s from the syncretistic combination of African and European aesthetics and techniques that had previously manifested itself in such genres as **spirituals**, work songs, and field hollers. Reflecting the philosophies of the first generation of African Americans born and coming to majority outside of **slavery**, the blues presented ideas, attitudes, and a sense of style and creativity that were historically rooted in African American tradition while grappling with the new possibilities, challenges, and frustrations of African American life in the post-**Reconstruction** era and beyond.

Folklorists began collecting and publishing snippets of blues songs as early as 1902, and blues-influenced songs by Hart Wand, Arthur "Baby" Seals, and W. C. Handy appeared on sheet music in 1912. By the time the blues emerged on phonograph recordings by African Americans with Mamie Smith's recordings in 1920, they were well known especially across **the South**, where they were born and raised, and were being adapted to the urban setting by migrants to African American neighborhoods of the North. The tremendous popularity of recordings by Smith with African American audiences produced opportunities for other blues performers, mostly female for the first few years, and ensured the entry of the blues into mainstream American culture through a blues "craze" that produced recordings that ran the gamut from masterful (Bessie Smith and Ma Rainey) to insipid.

Although the blues is sometimes perceived as a rather limited genre, it is, in fact, marvelously diverse even as it remains faithful to certain common principles and structures—the use of common language, repetitious stanza forms, and variations of mostly eight- and twelve-bar musical structures—that were in place in the earliest extant blues transcriptions and recordings. To listen to the blues of Blind Blake, Charley Patton, **Blind Lemon Jefferson**, Ida Cox, and Memphis Minnie from the 1920s is to listen to highly distinctive stylists whose work reflects various geographical blues traditions that shared a common background but have marvelous local variations. Development of the blues in subsequent decades, influenced by advances in technology, influences of other genres, urbanization, and sociopolitical changes, also reflect the tremendous potential for variation and creativity within the blues tradition, producing performers, such as Little Esther Phillips, John Lee Hooker, Professor Longhair, and Little Walter, who reflected their individual styles through the tradition. This simultaneous manifestation of tradition and experimentation, and group orientation channeled through individual creativity and improvisation, reflects the connection of the blues to Africa on the one hand and to the unfulfilled principles of American democracy on the other, making the blues an ideal vehicle for the expression of group and individual pride and heritage, as well as an aural demonstration of the catch phrase of diversity, E Pluribus Unum.

Just as the quest for an American identity was at issue in the works of American writers, so African American writers sought to identify the salient aspects of African American identity in their artistic explorations. Given that many African American writers of the nineteenth century wrote with the burden of proving themselves to disbelieving White audiences, those writers frequently modeled conventional European forms and language, which were sometimes subtly informed or undercut by African American-nuanced meanings. At the turn of the twentieth century, as African American writers sought a usable aesthetic past to inform their own experimentation with an African American artistic tradition, they turned to **vernacular** music as a valuable repository for group style and values that were distinctively African American. In this tradition many writers also found values that countered what they considered to be vapid middle-class notions of propriety, repressive attitudes toward sexuality (of the type that Freud was exposing in his work), and a mechanized, industrialized society that brought about isolation and mass

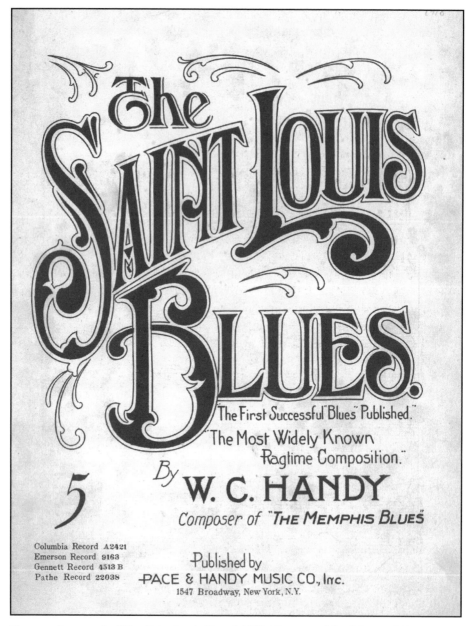

Sheet music cover for "The Saint Louis Blues," 1918. Courtesy of the Library of Congress.

dehumanization—all attitudes that were prevalent among the avant-garde writers of the so-called Jazz Age. Little wonder, then, that writers who sought to criticize the emptiness and repressiveness of contemporary American culture and to establish and champion an African American cultural heritage turned to the increasingly popular secular music of the vernacular tradition to demonstrate how African American folk practiced a healthy and creative art that was a valuable resource for "high" art.

There are various ways that the blues can influence literature, some formal and obvious, others more spiritual and impressionistic or subtle. Thus it is important to be aware of the breadth and depth of the blues tradition in order to be able to read its influence rightly. The reader must always be aware that the blues share a number of characteristics with other forms of African American vernacular music, both sacred and secular. This means that identifying a blues influence on writing must be undertaken in the broader context of all of African American vernacular music, so that what we are identifying as a blues influence is seen in the vernacular continuum. It also means that the subject must be approached with the realization that the sometimes distinct differentiations made between sacred and secular music in the academic realm are not always held as being so separate in the tradition itself. In fact, at times the melding of so-called sacred and secular elements represents an acknowledgment of the constant presence of the sacred in our daily activities, as opposed to the compartmentalizing of the sacred into a separate space of its own. Of course, there is much about the blues performance that defines its identity—you know it when you hear it, though, as always, there are those boundary benders such as the Ray Charles of "I Got a Woman" who push that line—so we can still talk about certain kinds of characteristics of blues. But we must always be mindful of the shared characteristics of Africa American vernacular musics.

There are various ways that one can identify the presence of the blues in literature. A work may be called a blues, as with **Clarence Major**'s novel *Dirty Bird Blues* or **James Baldwin**'s play *Blues for Mister Charlie*," or make use of a blues lyric in the title, as Jane Phillips did in her novel *Mojo Hand*, or use blues lyrics in the body of the text, as in Langston Hughes's short story "The Blues I'm Playing." There may be characters who perform blues or associate themselves with common blues lyrics, as in **Zora Neale Hurston**'s *Their Eyes Were Watching God* or **Alice Walker**'s *The Color Purple*. Blues performances may be a dramatic part of the text, as in **Walter Mosley**'s *R.L.'s Dream*. The traditional subject matter of the blues—though the blues is actually very diverse thematically—deals most often with loneliness and isolation stemming from difficulties in interpersonal relationships and the desire to travel or to escape from or to something, while celebrating sexuality in frank and creative language, may influence the language of a text as well.

Formally, the blues primarily use a number of lyric variations in a variety of mostly eight- and twelve-bar musical patterns. The twelve-bar, AAB pattern is most common: twelve measures of music (sometimes only approximating this length, especially in rural, folk settings or in solo performances) built with numerous stylistic variations on a basic I–IV–V chord pattern, with a single thought or "line" sung and approximately repeated (AA), followed by an end-rhyming line (B) that wraps up the thought of the stanza:

> I had me a girl, "What make you like 61 so?"
> My friends have all asked me, "What make you like 61 so?"
> I say I like it 'cause it's on the highway, and it rolls by my baby's door.

Inherent in both the musical and the lyric pattern here is a manifestation of an antiphonal or call-and-response pattern that may be traceable to work songs in the African American, and ultimately African, tradition. This antiphonal element is also present in the interaction between the singer and any instrumentalists who might respond to the singer's performance in the spaces between performed texts. Other stanza patterns include AAA (repeating the same line three times, as in Henry Thomas's "Bull Doze Blues"), ABB (singing a line, then a different line that end-rhymes, and repeating this second line), ABC (three different lines that end-rhyme), and AB refrain (singing two lines that end-rhyme in the first four bars, and then a generally constant refrain that repeats in every stanza). Ma Rainey's recorded version of "See See Rider" uses ABB, AAB, and ABC stanzas.

These formal elements offer the literary tradition identifiable structures that relate directly to African American vernacular culture and thus, when they are employed, establish a continuity between the written and oral traditions. Since the stanzas frequently only roughly approximate eight- or twelve- (or sometimes sixteen- or thirty-two-bar) stanzas, they bring a relaxed looseness to a sometimes overwrought formal literature; a feeling of immediacy, spontaneity, and improvisation; and an emphasis on the importance of performance to the artistic tradition. The page can sometimes seem a mere convenience (or inconvenience) that is a poor but sometimes necessary substitute for the artist who can't reach the audience in the best way—in person.

These lyric patterns have been employed by a variety of writers since the 1920s. Langston Hughes, who pioneered the use of blues in poetry, used the twelve-bar AAB stanza in poems such as "Out of Work," the ABB stanza in "Black Gal," and the ABC stanza in "Only Woman Blues." Sterling Brown employed the twelve-bar AAB form in "Ma Rainey"; and other poets, such as **Dudley Randall, A. B. Spellman, Ishmael Reed**, and **Sherley Anne Williams** have employed the pattern as well. Hughes also experimented using eight-bar blues stanza patterns, in poems such as "Southern Mammy Blues" and "Same in Blues," both of which employ AB refrain stanza patterns, and vaudeville blues structures in poems such as "Blue Monday." It is also likely that the call-and-response elements of these stanza forms and performance patterns find expression in poetry, prose, and drama as authors orchestrate a particular kind of verbal or thematic echoing or theme and variation in their texts, as in the developing sexuality of Janie in Zora Neale Hurston's *Their Eyes Were Watching God*, the gradual unmasking of the duplicity of human beings in **Ralph Ellison**'s *Invisible Man*, or the difference between hearing and listening in James Baldwin's "Sonny's Blues."

In terms of technique and philosophy, the blues offer a manner of expression that is rooted in African aesthetics—including percussiveness, syncopation, growling, buzzing, and straining inflections, blue notes, improvisation, and an orientation toward communal function—that serves writers as a manner of separating themselves from Western ways of approaching art and the world. These elements enliven the patter of the blueprint man in Ellison's *Invisible*

Man, and make him an attractive and ultimately heroic figure to the protagonist, who is almost hopelessly oriented toward pleasing the White community.
He is, of course, *almost* hopeless, because there is always an element of hope in
the blues, a feeling that "the sun is gonna shine in my back door someday," that
forms a central part of a "blues philosophy" of hope even with an imminent
threat of defeat and destruction. That hope even extends to the "lowest down"
in American society, the blues people of the lowest classes who created and
sustained the blues while facing the worst odds imaginable. Thus, the reference
to the blues tradition frequently helps artists challenge and overturn social and
political hierarchies by showing how the creations of the lower classes can
transcend and transform the restrictions of Western society and provide a strong
and viable alternative to "imitating the master," as Langston Hughes demonstrates in the Simple story "Jazz, Jive and Jam." And in terms of subject matter
and language, works such as **Amiri Baraka**'s "Crow Jane Poems" or "Blues
People" and **August Wilson**'s *Ma Rainey's Black Bottom* echo the language and
concerns of blues performers in a revolutionary poetic or dramatic setting.

The possibilities for using the diverse elements of the blues tradition have
been recognized by African American writers since the blues emerged into a
more popular consciousness in the first decades of the twentieth century. But
like the blues tradition itself, the uses of the blues in literature are by no means
exhausted. Rather, the blues (and **jazz**) seem to be especially central to literature since the 1950s, when disciples of Langston Hughes's blues experiments began to accept the blues as their own as well, exploring blues history,
embracing blues artistry, and championing blues performance as an inspiration
to their own aesthetics.

Resources: William Barlow, *Looking Up at Down: The Emergence of Blues Culture*
(Philadelphia: Temple University Press, 1989); Perry Bradford, *Born with the Blues*
(New York: Oak, 1965); Lawrence Cohn et al., *Nothing but the Blues* (New York:
Abbeville, 1993); Angela Y. Davis, *Blues Legacies and Black Feminism* (New York:
Pantheon, 1998); David Evans, *Big Road Blues: Tradition and Creativity in the Folk
Blues* (Berkeley: University of California Press, 1982); Robert Ford, *A Blues Bibliog-
raphy: The Literature of the Afro-American Musical Heritage* (London: RIS, 1999); W.
C. Handy, *The Father of the Blues* (New York: Macmillan, 1941); Sheldon Harris,
Blues Who's Who (New Rochelle, NY: Arlington House, 1979); Leroi Jones, *Blues
People* (New York: William Morrow, 1963); Alan Lomax, *The Land Where the Blues
Began* (New York: Pantheon, 1993); Paul Oliver, *The Meaning of the Blues* (New York:
Collier, 1963); Tony Russell, John Godrich, Howard Rye, and Robert M. W. Dixon,
Yonder Come the Blues: The Evolution of a Genre (Cambridge: Cambridge University
Press, 2001); Jeff Titon, *Early Downhome Blues* (Urbana: University of Illinois Press,
1977); Steven C. Tracy, ed., *Write Me a Few of Your Lines: A Blues Reader* (Amherst:
University of Massachusetts Press, 1999).

Steven C. Tracy

Blues Poetry. The term blues poetry can refer either to the sometimes highly
poetic lyrics of **blues** performers and composers or to poetry written by authors

who have employed some aspect or aspects of the oral blues tradition, lyrically or musically, in generating their own poetic works. In either case, a familiarity with the characteristics of the blues tradition with regard to subject matter, lyric and music structures, performance techniques, and the functions of the work as a means of entertainment, education, connection to the spirit and values of the community, and a kind of therapeutic release helps readers better understand the important network of ideas that is conjured when a creative artist evokes the blues. Since the emergence of the blues into popular culture in the 1920s, poets such as **Langston Hughes, Sterling Brown, Melvin Tolson, Robert Hayden, Gwendolyn Brooks, Margaret Walker, James Baldwin, Amiri Baraka, Sonia Sanchez, Ishmael Reed, Sterling Plumpp, Sherley Anne Williams, Al Young, Etheridge Knight**, and **Jayne Cortez**, among many others, have experimented with ways to demonstrate the centrality of the blues tradition to their aesthetics and creativity, and to their sense of the nature of the world and of the art they have created to describe, criticize, celebrate, and improve it. With the influence of the blues on other musical genres, such as rhythm and blues, rock and roll, heavy metal, pop, and **hip-hop**, and the popular resurgence of blues into mainstream American culture in television, film, commercials, blues clubs, and a burgeoning blues recording industry, the influence of the blues is certain to continue and expand in the twenty-first century.

On the one hand, the roots of the blues are in West African artistic aesthetics as reflected in the nature and function of music in that society. Such elements as call-and-response patterns, syncopation (placing an accent slightly before or after the measured beat), blue notes, and growling and buzzing inflections are all found in both African music and the blues, as is an orientation toward making the music, which is part of daily life rather than a separate element of it, reflect the needs, concerns, and values of the community through the individual voice. On the other hand, the blues did not come into existence until the enforced contact of enslaved Africans with elements of European music in America. After the African elements enumerated above helped to develop distinctive African American genres such as work songs, field hollers, and **spirituals**, the stage was set for the blues to emerge in the 1880s. The blues seem to have arisen then as a result of the historical experiences of the first generation of Blacks born outside of **slavery** coming to their majority in a world that was different from the slave world of the plantations. No longer enslaved, though experiencing many of the attitudes and restrictions endured by their slave forebears, the new generation had a greater ability to move about, seeking better times, and an expanded set of choices with regard to personal relationships—both common subjects in blues songs. By joining African aesthetic components with European elements, such as stanza patterns (especially a modified version of the **ballad** stanza that was a precursor to the most common blues lyric pattern) and English language, the blues arose to provide an artistic outlet for post-**Reconstruction** African Americans. By the time the blues were first recorded by African Americans, beginning with Mamie Smith in 1920, there were a number of strong individual blues personalities and regional blues styles that demonstrated the remarkable possibilities for the innovation that has continued to be a hallmark of the blues up to the present day.

Despite the notion that the blues is a limited genre, and thus might have a limited set of characteristics to contribute to poetry, the blues are in fact quite diverse in musical structures and stanza patterns. The most common musical pattern in the blues consists of a stanza that is roughly twelve bars or measures (the metrical division of a musical composition) long, built around a musical progression that uses a I–IV–V chord pattern, and employing a division into roughly three equal parts, each of which contains a "line" or thought. However, there are also recorded examples of eight- and sixteen-bar blues, as well as other variations, especially in the vaudeville blues tradition. Lyrically, various stanza patterns are evident as well. For the twelve-bar blues, there can be one line repeated approximately three times (AAA), as in Tommy Johnson's "Lonesome Blues"; a line sung, repeated, and then completed by a different line with an end rhyme (AAB), as in Gwendolyn Brooks's "Queen of the Blues"; a line sung, and answered by a different line with end rhyme that is then repeated (ABB), commonly used for the blues, as in "See See Rider," and employed by Langston Hughes in his play *Don't You Want to Be Free?*; a line sung followed by a different line with end rhyme answering it in the first four bars, followed by a repeating refrain from stanza to stanza (AB refrain), employed in "Jim Jackson's Kansas City Blues" and in Hughes's lyric "Tired as I Can Be"; three different lines with end rhyme (ABC), as in Lonnie Johnson's "Trust Your Husband" and Hughes's "Only Woman Blues"; and a number of other variations, such as Sterling Brown's use of the blues ballad stanza in "Strange Legacies." The eight, sixteen- and other bar variations present a variety of lyric options as well. By far the most common form is the twelve-bar AAB pattern, but other patterns occur with a fair frequency.

In performance, individual artists have the freedom to shorten or extend the length of musical stanzas (as, for example, Charley Patton does in "Pony Blues") or alter the lyric pattern (as King Solomon Hill does in "The Gone Dead Train," which mixes AB and AAB stanzas). The point is that formally the blues offer the performer and the poet a set of standard forms to use, representing a passing on of tradition from one generation to another, that have not been worn out because they are flexible enough to encompass variations and idiosyncrasies of performance that may extend a twelve-bar pattern to 13 ½ bars without any worry or strain. Thus, the frequent rigidity of formal literature is replaced in blues poetry by a spontaneous, improvisatory flexibility that suggests either resistance to externally imposed European poetic standards or a more "natural" adherence to the standards of the oral tradition. The implication is that the oral tradition is a viable vehicle for poetic sentiments that could be appreciated by society in general, not just the "folk," and that even those who may have associated themselves with mainstream American mass culture, such as the literate African American middle and upper classes, should not lose sight of the value of oral culture.

Of course, the use of formal elements and the relative freedom of oral performance from the blues tradition are not the only ways that the blues are manifested in blues poetry. Some poems use the word "blues" in the title or body of the text without using the blues form, as Derek Walcott did in "Blues." There may be references to real or fictional blues singers, as in **Bessie Smith** tributes such as **Alvin Aubert**'s "Bessie" and Robert Hayden's "Homage to the Empress of the Blues," or recorded blues songs, as in Sherley Anne Williams' "Any Woman's Blues." We may come across terms or ideas that are in some ways associated with blues culture, such as the use of Crow Jane in some poems by Amiri Baraka; riders, jelly rolls, and such sexual euphemisms; or references to relentless travel in Baraka's poem "Blues People."

Resources: Houston Baker, *Blues, Ideology, and Afro-American Literature* (Chicago: University of Chicago Press, 1984); Sterling Brown, "The Blues as Folk Poetry," in *Folk-Say*, vol. 2, ed. B. A. Botkin (Norman: University of Oklahoma Press, 1930); Samuel Charters, *The Poetry of the Blues* (New York: Oak, 1963); Sascha Feinstein, *Jazz Poetry: From the 1920s to the Present* (Westport, CT: Greenwood Press, 1997); Paul Garon, *Blues and the Poetic Spirit* (London: Eddison, 1975); Stephen Henderson, *Understanding the New Black Poetry* (New York: William Morrow, 1973); Paul Oliver, *Blues Fell This Morning: Meaning in the Blues*, 2nd ed. (Cambridge: Cambridge University Press, 1990); Steven C. Tracy, *Langston Hughes and the Blues* (Urbana: University of Illinois Press, 1988); Steven C. Tracy, ed.: *A Historical Guide to Langston Hughes* (New York: Oxford University Press, 2004); *Write Me a Few of Your Lines: A Blues Reader* (Amherst: University of Massachusetts Press, 1999); Sherley A. Williams, "The Blues Roots of Contemporary Afro-American Poetry," in *Chant of Saints: A Gathering of Afro-American Literature, Art, and Scholarship*, ed. Michael S. Harper and Robert B. Stepto (Urbana: University of Illinois Press, 1979), 123–135.

Steven C. Tracy

Bond, Julian (born 1940). Civil rights activist, politician, poet, editor, essayist, and professor. A native of **Nashville, Tennessee**, and the son of Horace Mann Bond and Julia Washington, Julian Bond grew up in Lincoln, Pennsylvania, where his father served as the first Black president of Lincoln University, the oldest historically Black college in America. In 1957, the Bond family moved to **Atlanta**. Following family tradition, he attended Morehouse College, where he became friends with **Martin Luther King** and where his charisma and eloquence began to be apparent.

Bond's expressive poetry reflects a thoughtful mind at work and has been published in various anthologies, including *New Negro Poets, U.S.A.* (1964), edited by **Langston Hughes**. In 1961, Bond married Alice Louise Clapton.

In 1964, Bond traveled to Africa, and upon his return went to work for the *Atlanta Inquirer* as a reporter; shortly thereafter he became its managing editor. He was also one of the founding members of a literary magazine called *The Pegasus*.

In 1965 Bond entered the mainstream political arena. In a series of speeches and interviews, he made his positions clear. Elected that year to the Georgia

House of Representatives, he was prevented from taking his seat because of his outspoken opposition to the **Vietnam War**. In 1968, he became one of the first African Americans elected to a state legislature, and he served in the Georgia House of Representatives until 1975. Bond was a founder and worked as communications director for the Student Nonviolent Coordinating Committee (SNCC), which contributed to the **Civil Rights Movement** by helping to coordinate the growing sit-in movement. Bond was also the editor of *Student Voice*, the newspaper of SNCC, based in Atlanta.

From the 1970s to the 1990s, Bond continued his speaking tours across the country, and he is considered an influential voice not only in politics but also in education and the media. In 1972 he published *A Time to Speak, a Time to Act*, a volume of essays on race and politics. He also narrated numerous civil rights documentaries, including *A Time for Justice* and *Eyes on the Prize* (1987), for the Public Broadcasting System. Since 1988, as a visiting professor, Bond has taught at Drexel University, Harvard University, the University of Virginia, and American University.

Bond has served since 1998 as chairman of the board of the **NAACP**. From his student days to his current chairmanship of the NAACP, he has been an activist, playing a significant role in the civil rights and economic justice movements. The National Black Justice Coalition, an ad hoc coalition of black lesbian, gay, bisexual, and transgender activists, announced on February 2, 2004, that Bond was joining with other African American leaders to call for marriage equality for gay men and lesbians.

Resources: *African American Biography*, vol. 1, ed. Carol Dekane Nagel and Amy Marcaccio (Detroit: UXL, 1994), 68–71; Michelle Norris, "African American Civil Rights Leaders Come Out for Marriage Equality," *Lesbian News* 29 (Mar. 2004), 17; Evan A. Shore and Greg Robinson, "Julian Bond" (update), in *Encyclopedia of African-American Culture and History: Supplement*, ed. Jack Sazman (New York: Macmillan Reference USA, 2001), 29; David F. Smydra, Jr., "Julian Bond," in *African American Lives*, ed. Henry Louis Gates, Jr., and Evelyn Higginbotham (New York: Oxford University Press, 2004), 89–90.

Truong Le

Bonner, Marita (1899–1971). Short story writer, playwright, and essayist. Bonner was the most prolific short story writer in **Chicago** in the 1930s. Much of her short fiction is set in the multiethnic Frye Street neighborhood, and much of it was published in important African American magazines and journals, including **The Crisis** and **Opportunity**. Part of the **New Negro** movement, Bonner was also the author of plays and essays; after 1941, her literary production ceased almost entirely. Bonner was born in **Boston, Massachusetts**, where she was also raised and educated. She attended Brookline School, and in 1918 she entered Radcliffe College, where she studied English and comparative literature. While at Radcliffe, Bonner started to work as a teacher at Cambridge High School. After graduating from Radcliffe in 1922, she moved to **Washington, D.C.**, where she met the poet, playwright, and composer **Georgia Douglas Johnson**. Johnson's "S" Street salon was attended by many of the writers and artists associated with the **Harlem Renaissance**, such as **Langston Hughes**, **Countee Cullen**, **Alain Locke**, **Jessie Redmon Fauset**, and **Jean Toomer**.

Bonner started to publish essays and short stories in 1925, and these early pieces already showed her interest in the depiction of the African American working class as well as her awareness of class differences within Black communities. She displayed an experimental style in the three plays written during the 1920s—*The Pot Maker: A Play to Be Read* (1927), *Purple Flower* (1928), and *Exit, an Illusion* (1928)—which, probably intended for reading rather than performance, were never produced during her lifetime. They are all allegories of the African American quest for freedom and dignity after emancipation, and with them Bonner seems to reject the compromise option that **Booker T. Washington** proposed for improving the economic and social conditions of African Americans. What was to become her fictional world, the neighborhood of Frye Street in Chicago, first appeared in her 1926 story "Nothing New."

In 1930, Bonner married William Almy Occomy and did not resume writing until 1933. After the marriage, the couple moved to Chicago, where Bonner lived until her death in 1971. Bonner's fictional Chicago of Frye Street is a multiethnic urban tapestry in which the lives of people from different ethnic backgrounds are interwoven. Her short fiction set in Frye Street also amounts to an extensive sociological mapping of the Chicago urban ghetto and, to suggest the complexity of her subject, she started to publish her stories in several separate parts. The themes of her fiction range from the fate of mixed-race characters to the elusive promises of prosperity with which the big city lures Southern immigrants, from the relations and tensions between the different ethnic groups to the barriers that class distinctions raise within the Black community (*see* Flynn). Bonner's map of Black Chicago was never completed, in part because she became increasingly involved in Christian Science and increasingly persuaded of the negative effect upon human personality that urban environments exerted.

Resources: Maria Balshaw, *Looking for Harlem: Urban Aesthetics in African American Literature* (London: Pluto Press, 2000); Allison Berg and Meredith Taylor, "Enacting Difference: Marita Bonner's 'Purple Flower' and the Ambiguities of Race," *African American Review* 32 (Fall 1998), 468–481; Michael Denning, *The Cultural Front: The Laboring of American Culture in the Twentieth Century* (New York: Verso, 1997); Joyce Flynn, "Introduction," in Bonner's *Frye Street and Environs: The Collected Works of Marita Bonner*, ed. Joyce Flynn and Joyce Occomy (Boston: Beacon Press, 1987); Laura Hapke, *Labor's Text: The Worker in American Fiction* (New Brunswick, NJ: Rutgers University Press, 2001); Bill V. Mullen, *Popular Fronts: Chicago and African American Cultural Politics, 1935–1946* (Urbana: University of Illinois Press, 1999).

Luca Prono

Bontemps, Arna (1902–1973). Poet, novelist, children's author, and editor. Bontemps was a major figure in the **Harlem Renaissance** who, as a librarian and editor, made vital contributions to the preservation of African American culture. His children's books are groundbreaking expressions of pride in Black history and tradition.

Arnaud Wendell Bontemps was born on October 13, 1902, in Alexandria, Louisiana. His father, Paul Bismark Bontemps, was a bricklayer, and his mother, Marie Pembroke, a schoolteacher. Increasing racial tension in Alexandria caused Paul to move the family to **Los Angeles, California**, when Arna was three years old. In Los Angeles, Paul encouraged his family to assimilate as much as possible into White society. The family left the Catholic Church and became Seventh-Day Adventists. There were conflicts, however, with Bontemps's Uncle Buddy, who embodied the family's Southern Black heritage. Paul did not want the Bontemps children looking up to Buddy as a role model. Throughout his life, Bontemps resisted his father's insistence upon assimilation and embraced his African American heritage (Jones, *Renaissance Man*).

Bontemps graduated from Pacific Union College (an Adventist school) in 1923 and began working in the U.S. Post Office in Los Angeles. In 1924, he used connections within the Seventh-Day Adventist Church to secure a teaching position at the Harlem Academy, an Adventist school in New York City. **Harlem**, of course, was the center of Black culture in America at the time. Arna began associating with many writers and artists who would form the nucleus of the **Harlem Renaissance**. In that year, he formed what would be a lifelong association and friendship with **Langston Hughes**.

Throughout the 1920s, Bontemps wrote in many genres and had success publishing poetry and short stories in magazines and journals. His poems won numerous prizes; two of his best known poems are "The Day-Breakers" and "Golgotha Is a Mountain" (Lewis). He also worked on a novel, *Chariot in the Sky*, which went unpublished until 1951. In 1931, however, he published *God Sends Sunday*, a novel based to some extent on his Uncle Buddy. The novel formed the basis for his later collaboration with **Countee Cullen** on the play *St. Louis Woman*. In 1926, Bontemps married Alberta Johnson, a former student at Harlem Academy.

As the **Great Depression** gripped America, Bontemps, like many of Harlem's brightest stars, moved away from the city to find employment, securing a teaching position at Oakwood Junior College, an Adventist school in Huntsville, Alabama. The return to **the South** was a pivotal event for Bontemps. He felt more in touch with his own cultural heritage, but he was also confronted with the hatred of racism in a way that he had never experienced in Los Angeles or New York. While in Alabama, Bontemps collaborated with Langston Hughes on *Popo and Fifina*, a children's book. It depicts events in the lives of two children in **Haiti**, as their family moves to a new village in hopes of earning a better living. The story was praised for its simplicity and stylistic charm. Other children's books followed quickly, including *You Can't Pet a Possum*, in 1934. All of Bontemps juvenile works are admired for the positive image they present to African American children.

In 1934, Bontemps parted company with Oakwood after a conflict over books about civil rights he had in his own collection. He returned to Los

Angeles to do research for a book. Published in 1936, *Black Thunder* is Bontemps's most highly regarded novel. A work of **historical fiction**, it describes an unsuccessful slave revolt in Virginia led by Gabriel Prosser in 1800.

The late 1930s and early 1940s were a very busy time for Bontemps. After writing *Black Thunder*, he moved to **Chicago, Illinois**, and began teaching at the Shiloh Academy. He held this position until 1938, when he received a

Rosenwald fellowship to finance travel in the Caribbean. He returned from these travels, continued his graduate studies in English at the University of Chicago, worked as a writer for the Works Progress Administration, and published more books for children and adults. *Drums at Dusk*, another historical novel, appeared in 1939 to less enthusiastic reviews than those received by *Black Thunder*. It recounts events of the Haitian slave revolt of 1791. *The Fast Sooner Hound* appeared in 1942. It was the first of many children's books done in collaboration with Jack Conroy. In 1941, Bontemps also worked as the ghostwriter (credited as the editor) on W. C. Handy's *Father of the Blues: An Autobiography* and published *Golden Slippers: An Anthology of Negro Poetry for Young Readers*.

Although Bontemps completed all of his coursework for a Ph.D. in English at the University of Chicago, he never took his comprehensive examinations or wrote a dissertation. Instead, he enrolled in the library science program at Chicago. He completed a master's

Arna Bontemps, 1939. Courtesy of the Library of Congress.

degree in this program in 1943 and was hired as head librarian at Fisk University in **Nashville, Tennessee**. The Fisk position offered another opportunity to return to his native South, and it proved to be a profitable relationship. Bontemps remained at Fisk for twenty years and became the preeminent authority in the United States on Black librarianship and African American bibliography.

Throughout his Fisk years, Bontemps produced many successful children's books and edited a number of significant anthologies of African American literature. His *Story of the Negro* (1948) was a Newbery honored book (runner-up to the Newbery Medal winner *King of the Wind* by Marguerite Henry). *The Poetry of the Negro, 1746–1949: An Anthology* (1949), edited in collaboration with Langston Hughes, was one of the most important compilations of Black poetry up to that time, comparable in stature with the anthology **James Weldon Johnson** had published in 1922. Hughes and Bontemps also collaborated on *The Book of Negro Folklore* in 1958. The lifelong friendship between

Bontemps and Hughes was extraordinary; selected letters between the two were published in 1980 (*see* Nichols).

Bontemps's other important anthologies included *American Negro Poetry* (1963) and *Great Slave Narratives* (1969). His many histories, such as *100 Years of Negro Freedom* (1961), and biographies (primarily for children) were also well received:

Bontemps worked in many genres throughout his life, but his work as a librarian and children's author made the most lasting contributions to African American literature. His children's books demonstrated that there was a market for works that celebrated the heritage of Black America. As a librarian, he showed that African American works were important documents in the cultural heritage of the United States, worthy of being collected, edited, and anthologized. The understanding and enjoyment of African American literature would be much less substantial without his contributions.

Resources: Primary Sources: Arna Bontemps: *Black Thunder* (New York: Macmillan, 1936); *Drums at Dusk* (New York: Macmillan, 1939); *The Fast Sooner Hound*, with Jack Conroy (Boston: Houghton Mifflin, 1942); *Father of the Blues: An Autobiography by W. C. Handy* (New York: Macmillan, 1941), as ghostwriter; *Frederick Douglass: Slave, Fighter, Freeman* (New York: Knopf, 1959); *Free at Last: The Life of Frederick Douglass* (New York: Dodd, Mead, 1971); *God Sends Sunday* (New York: Harcourt, Brace, 1931); *Lonesome Boy* (Boston: Houghton Mifflin, 1955); *The Old South: "A Summer Tragedy" and Other Stories of the Thirties* (New York: Dodd, Mead, 1973); *100 Years of Negro Freedom* (New York: Dodd, Mead, 1961); *Popo and Fifina, Children of Haiti*, with Langston Hughes (New York: Macmillan, 1932); *Sam Patch, the High, Wide, & Handsome Jumper*, with Jack Conroy (Boston: Houghton Mifflin, 1951); *The Story of George Washington Carver* (New York: Grosset & Dunlap, 1954); *Story of the Negro* (New York: Knopf, 1948; enl. ed., 1955); *Young Booker: Booker T. Washington's Early Days* (New York: Dodd, Mead, 1972); Arna Bontemps, ed.: *The Book of Negro Folklore*, with Langston Hughes (New York: Dodd, Mead, 1958); *Golden Slippers: An Anthology of Negro Poetry for Young Readers* (New York: Harper & Row, 1941); *Great Slave Narratives* (Boston: Beacon, 1969); *The Harlem Renaissance Remembered: Essays* (New York: Dodd, Mead, 1972); *The Poetry of the Negro, 1746–1949*, with Langston Hughes (Garden City, NY: Doubleday, 1949), rev. as *The Poetry of the Negro, 1746–1970* (Garden City, NY: Doubleday, 1970). **Secondary Sources:** Robert E. Fleming, *James Weldon Johnson and Arna Wendell Bontemps: A Reference Guide* (Boston: G. K. Hall, 1978); Kirkland C. Jones: "Arna Bontemps," in *Dictionary of Literary Biography*, vol. 51, *Afro-American Writers from the Harlem Renaissance to 1940*, ed. Trudier Harris and Thadious M. Davis (Detroit: Gale Research, 1987), 10–21; *Renaissance Man from Louisiana: A Biography of Arna Wendell Bontemps* (Westport, CT: Greenwood Press, 1992); David Levering Lewis, ed., *The Portable Harlem Renaissance Reader* (New York: Viking, 1994), 224–226; Charles H. Nichols, ed., *Arna Bontemps–Langston Hughes Letters, 1925–1967* (New York: Dodd, Mead, 1980).

Steven R. Harris

Boston, Massachusetts. Once heralded as the "bastion of freedom" and the "home of abolition," Boston was later to be the site of intense **race riots** in the

1970s and is still known to be simultaneously segregated and politically active; it is and has been, to say the least, a racially complex city. To understand the role that Boston plays in African American literature, one must understand the history of the literature and the culture from which it emerges. Generally, Boston served an important role as a cultural and literary center before and during the **Civil War**. Critical of **the South**'s enduring system of **slavery**, many Bostonians worked for social change, supporting the **Abolitionist Movement** and assisting escaped slaves. The conception of Boston as a center for liberation and new beginnings is historically justified. Many key abolitionists worked in and around Boston, and many important early works of African American literature were published there. To see Boston exclusively as a center of antiracist activity, though, would be inaccurate. Bostonian attitudes toward race were complex and often ambivalent. We should not forget, after all, that Boston was a part of the triangular slave trade long before it became a center for abolitionists. In order to understand the city's place in African American literature and history, we must understand Boston as an early center for liberation even as we interrogate the racism that persisted during the twentieth century.

The nineteenth century, during which most of the African American literature surveyed in this entry was published, was a time of political activism and antiracist effort in Boston. In 1854, when the escaped Virginia slave Anthony Burns was found in Boston, Blacks and Whites worked together to free him from his captors. When their collective efforts failed, it is estimated that 50,000 Bostonians lined the streets leading to Boston Harbor as he was taken away in shackles. Not long after this incident, a Black church in Boston raised the money to buy his freedom, and he returned to Boston. Another famous account of the abolitionist days in Boston is the story of Wendell Phillips's protest of Thomas Sims's arrest. Sims, a fugitive slave, was tried in Boston. During the trial, Phillips delivered an address that has made him famous as an activist, event though Sims was found guilty and returned to Savannah as a slave.

While the tales of Burns and Sims are remembered in history books, often with the focus on the White men who fought for their freedom, recent scholars remind us that racism increased over the course of the nineteenth century. As racially motivated **lynchings** escalated in the South, many Northerners' horrified judgments weakened into apathy and complacency. In *Boston Confronts Jim Crow, 1890–1920*, Mark Schneider looks at this as a period of gradual acceptance of racism. While monuments to honor African Americans were erected, little was done to better the lives of contemporary African Americans. Though Boston boasted a history of abolitionism and celebrated the memory of William Lloyd Garrison, Wendell Phillips, and **Harriet Beecher Stowe**, Schneider examines the ways that the new generation of Bostonians at the turn of the century failed to live up this legacy, forgetting to continue to work alongside Blacks after emancipation.

In her 1979 study, *Black Migration and Poverty: Boston 1865–1900*, Elizabeth Hafkin Pleck offers a comprehensive study of Black Boston during this period.

Anti-Slavery Meeting on the Boston Common. *Gleason's Pictorial Drawing Room Companion*, May 1851, p. 4. Courtesy of the North Wind Picture Archives.

The same year, James O. Horton and Lois E. Horton published *Black Bostonians: Family Life and Community Struggle in the Antebellum North*. These texts go beyond the speeches and protests to examine the everyday life of Black Boston before the Civil War.

Boston has played an important role in the history of African American literature. **Briton Hammon**'s *A Narrative of the Uncommon Sufferings, and Surprizing Deliverance of Briton Hammon*, often cited as the first published work by an African American, was published in Boston by Green & Russell in 1760. This work, in which Hammon celebrates the providence of God, who has led him to safety, is historically relevant because it set the literary standards for later **slave narratives**, many of which were published in or near Boston.

Perhaps the most famous and best-documented early African American author is **Phillis Wheatley**, whose trip to Boston to validate and authenticate herself as a capable poet has become the stuff of legend. After being kidnapped and enslaved as a child, Wheatley wrote and self-published "On the Death of Reverend Mr. George Whitefield, 1770" at age seventeen. Supported by her owner, Wheatley sought out a publisher both in the colonies and in England. She was freed, and in 1772 published her first book of poetry in Boston, but only after eighteen prominent White men had examined her and, in the obligatory preface, deemed this "young negro girl . . . qualified to write them." The legend of Wheatley tells of her undergoing an oral examination to prove her authorial integrity to a panel of prestigious and powerful Bostonians.

A generation after Wheatley, **Harriet A. Jacobs** was an important literary figure in Boston. Born into slavery, she escaped to freedom in the North, where she was encouraged to record her story. She, too, found it difficult to secure a publisher, and traveled to England in search of a more generous audience. Equipped with letters of introduction from Boston, Jacobs found no success in England, and returned to America. Lydia Marie Childs of Boston became her agent and editor, enabling her finally to publish *Incidents in the Life of a Slave Girl* in 1861.

Harriet Wilson set and published her novel *Our Nig* (1859) in Boston. She exposes the racism of the North during slavery; her story follows a young girl who is mistreated though she is a free black. Her critical account of the region, considered by many to be unquestionably generous and open to free Blacks, won few readers and attracted relatively little critical interest at the time of its publication. Boston was not, it seems, ready to confront its own racist history, as Wilson prompted Bostonian readers to do.

Pauline E. Hopkins lived and wrote in Boston, where she served as women's editor and literary editor of *Colored American Magazine*. Best known for her novels, Hopkins has been called the "dean of African-American women writers." Her most successful novel, *Contending Forces: A Romance Illustrative of Negro Life North and South*, features a mixed-race family as they travel, over generations, from nineteenth-century slavery in the West Indies to early twentieth-century Massachusetts.

In the years following and coinciding with Hopkins's literary success, the cultural center of the African American community shifted to New York City. As the **Harlem Renaissance** encouraged and praised Black art, Boston took a less prominent role, both as a publishing center and as a setting for liberation.

Since the Harlem Renaissance, Boston's place in African American writing and culture has become more complex. Texts such as *The Autobiography of Malcolm X* (1965), set in part in Boston, reveal shifting race relations in twentieth-century Boston. The *Autobiography* represents the city both as a home to Malcolm X, as he becomes the first minister of Boston Temple No. 11, and as a site of turmoil as he becomes involved in the criminal underworld of the area as a youth. Christopher Brookhouse's novel *Passing Game* (2000), reveals the duality of African American relations in Boston. Brookhouse focuses on two Harvard students who grapple with White privilege, racism, and **passing**. *Caucasia*, a 1998 novel by **Danzy Senna**, offers another complicated look at race that is set, notably, in Boston. A family with an Anglo-American mother and African American father and two daughters lives in Boston. Involved in the Black-led **Civil Rights Movement**, their family is torn apart and forced to leave its home in Boston. Both *Passing Game* and *Caucasia* interrogate the layered racial texture of Boston, without merely accepting it as either the home of abolition or as a ruinous space of segregation.

Boston also has a long tradition of African American journalism. Of the thirty-five periodicals included in Melvin R. Sylvester's "Negro Periodicals in the United States," the majority were published in New York. Among other cities, though, Boston held a key position. *Colored American Magazine* was published in Boston between 1900 and 1909. William Monroe Trotter, who has been called "perhaps the single most important figure in all of Boston's African-American history" (Schneider, 109), founded the newspaper *The Guardian*. Dedicated to the fight against racial discrimination and to the development of independent political action on the part of the Black community in the United States, the paper began in 1901. *Alexander's Magazine*, also published in Boston, ran from 1905 until 1909. Later in the century, *New Challenge* was published in Boston between 1934 and 1937. This magazine focused on writing of Black artists and included work by **James Weldon Johnson, Langston Hughes, Countee Cullen, Zora Neale Hurston, Ralph Ellison**, and others. Editor **Dorothy West** attempted, in the magazine, to rejuvenate and encourage the energy of the Harlem Renaissance.

Resources: *Boston Black History*, http://www.bostonblackhistory.com; Edward Clark, *Black Writers in New England* (Boston: National Park Service, 1985); Marita Golden and E. Lynn Harris, eds., *Gumbo: A Celebration of African American Writing* (New York: Harlem Moon, 2002); Maryemma Graham, ed., *Cambridge Companion to the African American Novel* (New York: Cambridge University Press, 2004); James Oliver Horton and Lois E. Horton, *Black Bostonians: Family Life and Community Struggle in the Antebellum North* (New York: Holmes & Meier, 1979); Donal M. Jacobs, "William Lloyd Garrison's *Liberator* and Boston's Blacks, 1830–1865," *New England Quarterly* 44 (1971), 259–277; George Levesque, *Black Boston: African American Life and Culture in Urban America, 1750–1860* (New York: Garland, 1994); Museum of Afro American History, Boston, http://www.afroammuseum.org/index.htm; Martha H. Patterson, "Kin' o'Rough Jestice fer a Parson: Pauline Hopkins's 'Winona' and the Politics of Reconstructing History," *African American Review* 32, no. 3 (1998), 445–460; Edith Hafkin Pleck, *Black Migration and Poverty: Boston 1865–1900* (New York: Academic Press, 1979); Mark R. Schneider, *Boston Confronts Jim Crow, 1890–1920* (Boston: Northeastern University Press, 1997); Ann Allen Shockley, *Afro-American Women Writers, 1746–1933: An Anthology and Critical Guide* (Boston: G. K. Hall, 1988); Carol Buchalter Stapp, *Afro-Americans in Antebellum Boston: An Analysis of Probate Records* (New York: Garland, 1993).

Meredith McCarroll

Bowen, Michele Andrea (born 1961). Novelist and short story writer. Bowen debuted as a novelist in 2001 with *Church Folk*, which tells the story of Theophilus Henry Simmons, a young African American man who has just graduated from seminary and accepted a position at a church in **Memphis**. His life is complicated by Glodean Benson, a woman who finds him irresistible. Bowen's second novel, *Second Sunday*, also concerns conflict within a church and is a historical novel set in Gesthemane Missionary Baptist Church in **St. Louis**, in 1975. Bowen's first two novels were published by Walk Worthy Press, a publisher specializing in Christian literature that is affiliated with Time/Warner Books. At this writing, Bowen is at work on a book of short stories ("Michele Andrea Bowen"). She was born and grew up in St. Louis, where she attended public schools and then graduated from Washington

University with a B.A. in psychology in 1979. She earned a master's degree in educational counseling in 1981 from the University of North Carolina at Chapel Hill. Before turning to writing full-time, Bowen was a social worker in North Carolina for Child Protective Services. She has served on the board of trustees of the **Zora Neale Hurston/Richard Wright** Foundation.

Bowen reports that when she first thought of writing a novel, she knew she wanted to "write about the black church" (Siciliano). She finds the writing of **Walter Mosley** and **J. California Cooper** to be especially worthy of emulation. Bowen is married to Harold Bowen; they and their three children live in Durham, North Carolina, and Bowen is a member of St. Joseph's African Methodist Episcopal Church there ("Michele Andrea Bowen").

Resources: Michele Andrea Bowen: *Church Folk* (West Bloomfield, MI: Walk Worthy Press, 2001); *Second Sunday* (West Bloomfield, MI: Walk Worthy Press, 2003); "Michele Andrea Bowen," http://www.micheleandreabowen.com/; Jana Siciliano, "Interview with Michele Andrea Bowen," *Bookreporter.com*, http://www.bookreporter .com/authors/au-bowen-michele-andrea.asp.

Hans Ostrom

Boyd, Melba (born 1950). Poet, biographer, essayist, and educator. Boyd's poetry has been translated into German, Italian, and Spanish, and her essays, mostly addressing issues of African American identity, have been published in numerous books and journals.

From her earliest published poetry, Boyd has been concerned with "the beauty of life, and in finding beauty that is distinct in its own being" (*Contemporary Authors*). *Cat Eyes and Dead Wood* (1978) was followed by *Song for Maya* (1983) and *Thirteen Frozen Flamingoes* (1984). *The Inventory of Black Roses* was published in 1989, and *Letters to Ché* (1996) followed. Her poetry has been described by Karen Bloom as "Sextonesque" in its use of language and as moving from individual to more social issues.

In *Discarded Legacy: Politics and Poetics in the Life of Frances E. W. Harper* (1994), which was warmly received, Boyd wrote the study of **Frances E. W. Harper** as a poet-scholar. She has received some criticism for the book's lack of engagement with critical theories. Her biography of **Dudley Randall**, *Wrestling with the Muse*, has been favorably reviewed as well. Boyd worked with Randall from 1972 to 1984 as an editor at **Broadside Press**, and is the executor of his literary estate. She also produced *The Black Unicorn: Dudley Randall and Broadside Press* (1995), a documentary film about the poet and his influential press.

In 2001 Boyd edited *Abandon Automobile: Detroit City Poetry, 2001*, an anthology of poems from the **Detroit** area. *Province of Literary Cats* was published in 2002.

A Senior Fulbright lecturer in Germany in 1982–1983, Boyd has taught in various institutions in the United States and in several German universities. She is currently professor and chair of the Department of African Studies at Wayne State University in Detroit.

Resources: Karen R. Bloom, "Melba Boyd," in *Oxford Companion to African American Literature*, ed. William L. Andrews et al. (Oxford: Oxford University Press, 1997); Melba Boyd: *Cat Eyes and Dead Wood* (Highland Park, MI: Fallen Angel Press, 1978); *Discarded Legacy: Politics and Poetics in the Life of Frances E. W. Harper, 1825–1911* (Detroit: Wayne State University Press, 1994); *The Inventory of Black Roses* (Detroit: Past Tents Press, 1989); *Letters to Ché* (Detroit: Ridgeway Press, 1996); *Province of Literary Cats* (Ferndale, MI: Past Tents Press, 2002); *Song for Maya* (Detroit: Broadside Press, 1983); *Thirteen Frozen Flamingoes* (Bremen, Germany: Die Certel, 1984); *Wrestling with the Muse* (New York: Columbia University Press, 2003); Melba Boyd and M. L. Liebler, eds., *Abandon Automobile: Detroit City Poetry 2001* (Detroit: Wayne State University Press, 2001); "Melba Boyd," *Contemporary Authors Online*, www.galenet.com.

Patricia Kennedy Bostian

Boyd, Valerie (born 1963). Journalist, biographer, and teacher. Valerie Boyd was born in **Atlanta**, where she attended public schools. She earned her bachelor's degree from Northwestern University's Medill School of Journalism and has a master's degree in creative nonfiction writing and narrative journalism from Goucher College in **Baltimore, Maryland.** Today she is an assistant professor of journalism at Grady College, the University of Georgia's School of Journalism and Mass Communications, where she teaches courses in magazine article writing, feature writing, narrative nonfiction, and immersion journalism.

Boyd has worked for nearly twenty years in various capacities in the field of journalism. She founded *EightRock* (1990), a journal of African American arts and culture. She also cofounded *HealthQuest* (1992), the first magazine dedicated to African American health issues. Boyd has also been the arts editor for the *Atlanta Journal Constitution* (2001–2004). In addition, she has published articles, essays, and reviews as a freelance writer and cultural critic in *Ms.* magazine, *The Oxford American Book Magazine*, the *Washington Post*, *Creative Nonfiction*, *African American Review*, and *Step into a World: A Global Anthology of the New Black Literature*.

Boyd's greatest achievement to date is *Wrapped in Rainbows: The Life of Zora Neale Hurston* (2003). This biography is the first book on Hurston's life and work in twenty-five years. Honors Boyd has received for *Wrapped in Rainbows* include the 2004 Georgia Author of the Year Award in nonfiction, the American Library Association Notable Book Award, and the 2003 Southern Book Award for best nonfiction of the year. Boyd has commented that the process of writing *Wrapped in Rainbows* was comparable to a spiritual journey, replete with signs pointing the way. She encountered mysterious black crows, signs that seemed to symbolize Hurston, three times—once at the Hurston Festival when she was initiating her work on the biography, once at Hurston's grave when she was asking permission to write the work, and once when she finished the work.

Boyd is currently working on a book titled *Spirits in the Dark: The Untold Story of Black Women in Hollywood*, which is due out in 2008.

Resources: Valerie Boyd, *Wrapped in Rainbows: The Life of Zora Neale Hurston* (New York: Scribner's, 2003); Alvelyn J. Sanders, "Remembering Zora," http://

www.northwestern.edu/magazine/northwestern/fall2003/features/zora; *Valerie Boyd Faculty Profile*, http://www.grady.uga.edu/jour/dept/faculty/Boyd.asp.

Kathleen Adams

Boyer, Jill Witherspoon (born 1947). Poet and short fiction writer. Boyer is the author of a book of poems, *Dream Farmer* (1975), published by **Dudley Randall**'s influential **Broadside Press**. She also has published a short story, "Blood Sisters," in *Essence* magazine. Boyer is the daughter of writer and publisher **Naomi Long Madgett**. At this writing, Boyer lives in California.

Resources: Jill Witherspoon Boyer: "Blood Sisters," *Essence*, Oct. 1978, 92–93; *Dream Farmer* (Detroit: Broadside Press, 1975).

Hans Ostrom

Bradley, David Henry, Jr. (born 1950). Novelist, essayist, and professor of creative writing. Bradley is the author of two critically acclaimed novels, *South Street* (1975) and *The Chaneysville Incident* (1981), both published before he turned thirty-five. *South Street*, a novel about Bradley's personal experiences on a famous street in the African American community in **Philadelphia, Pennsylvania**, was written while Bradley was an undergraduate at the University of Pennsylvania. His second novel, the award-winning *The Chaneysville Incident*, was inspired by a local legend about thirteen escaped slaves who, when captured, preferred death to being enslaved. In both of his published works, Bradley explores the complex experience of African American history and culture, a legacy made even more complicated for the writer and historian because of 400 years fraught with the cataclysmic forces of **race**, **gender**, and class.

David Bradley was born September 7, 1950, in Bedford, Pennsylvania. He is the only son of David Henry Bradley, a minister and historian, and of Harriette Maria Jackson Bradley, a local historian. David was descended from a long line of ministers including his father, his grandfather, and his great-grandfather.

Bradley writes eloquently and passionately about the experiences and emotions that connect him to his past: the rural Black community where he was born; Mt. Pisgah A.M.E. Zion Church, which he attended; the family that nurtured his early interest in history; and later, writing about that history. This sense of personal, family, and community history became the cornerstone of Bradley's inspiration as a writer. His novels, particularly *The Chaneysville Incident*, reflect an abiding interest in American, and especially African American, history. This interest derives partly from his father, a preacher and church historian, and partly from his mother, who in *The Kernel of Greatness: An Informal Bicentennial History of Bedford County*, published to help celebrate Bedford County's 1969 bicentennial, had described the discovery of thirteen unmarked graves of runaway slaves who died on a farm near Chaneysville.

Mt. Pisgah A.M.E. Zion Church also played a significant role in Bradley's life and in his development as a writer. In the article "Portrait of a Small Black Church," written for the *New York Times*, Bradley writes, "Three generations of his family have occupied Mt. Pisgah's pulpit and worshipped in its pews. A plaque on the wall dedicates the 1960's redecoration to his grandmother. The Bible on the lectern was an offering by his father when his mother survived a dangerous illness. In the truest sense, he, not the denomination, owns Mt. Pisgah. And owes it." All of the passion and talents of a novelist are revealed when Bradley writes about the place that has left such an indelible mark on his memory. His words and vision have the power to transport the reader, to make him or her see what Bradley sees, and feel what he feels: "The Church stands on a corner at the edge of the town, where the woods press close against the pavement. It is small, wooden, painted white. The paint is peeling a little, and if you look closely at the western wall you can see that the foundation has begun to sag. But affixed to the exterior of the vestibule, a freshly painted and carefully lettered wooden sign announces that this is Mt. Pisgah A.M.E. Zion Church and that Sunday worship is held at noon. If you know your history, you will recognize the A.M.E Zion as indicating that this church is part of the African Methodist Episcopal Zion denomination. If you know your Old Testament, you might recall that Mount Pisgah was the peak on which the prophet Balaam, gazing on the massed host of Israel, intoned: 'What hath God Wrought?'" ("Portrait," 16).

There is great tenderness in Bradley's description of a place that has played such a significant role in his life, both as an individual and as an artist. There is also an undertone of regret, a sense of loss. But, being a skillful writer, he writes poignantly about these feelings as well. "For, in a day when and a place where opportunities were restricted, Mt. Pisgah gave him a chance to speak, to lead, to learn the history of his people. When opportunities became available, it was the experience gained at Mt. Pisgah that equipped him to take advantage of them; he abandoned the church that had nurtured him. He walked from Mt. Pisgah down unto the Promised Land and never really to look back" ("Portrait," 16).

The "Promised Land" that Bradley writes about is Philadelphia, and the opportunities that became available to him were the Benjamin Franklin Scholarship, a National Achievement Scholarship, a Senatorial Scholarship, and a Presidential Scholarship that he received when he graduated from Bedford Area High School in 1968. These scholarships enabled him to attend the University of Pennsylvania, where he earned a Bachelor of Arts degree, graduating summa cum laude with a major in creative writing and English. After graduation, Bradley received a Thouron British–American Exchange Scholarship, which he used to attend the University of London, graduating from the Institute for United States Studies, King's College, with a master's degree in January 1972. During his time in London, Bradley became interested in nineteenth-century American history, which gave him the research material that went into his second novel.

Resources: David Bradley: *The Chaneysville Incident* (New York: Avon, 1981); "The Faith," in *In Praise of What Persists*, ed. Stephen Berg (New York: Harper & Row, 1983); "Portrait of a Small Black Church: A Personal View from the Third

Generation," *New York Times Sunday Magazine*, Jan. 30, 1985, p. 16; and *South Street* (New York: Grossman, 1975).

John Greer Hall

Braithwaite, William Stanley Beaumont (1878–1962). Poet, editor, literary critic, and anthologist. Braithwaite, whom **W.E.B. Du Bois** called "the most prominent critic of poetry in America" (Butcher, 1), was not only an influential critic of the emerging modern poetry of the turn of the century, but also was an astute contributor to the body of writing about "the Negro" and art produced during the **Harlem Renaissance** of the 1920s.

Braithwaite was the second child of five born to William Smith Braithwaite and Emma DeWolfe in **Boston, Massachusetts**. His father, who came from a prominent family in British Guiana, was distrustful of the American education system and chose to school young William and his older sister, Eva, at home. His father's death, when Braithwaite was just seven years old, ended his home instruction and drastically changed the family's circumstances. Braithwaite attended public schools until the age of twelve, when he had to leave school "to labor in a man's world" (Butcher, 167).

Braithwaite found employment as an errand boy for two businesses in Boston before taking a job delivering galley proofs for the publisher Ginn and Company, where he later apprenticed as a compositor. Whatever Braithwaite lost by ending his formal education, he apparently gained through reading the literary works of authors such as Keats, Wordsworth, and Burns, printed by Ginn. Braithwaite's reading of these poets, especially Keats, provided the initial inspiration for his early poetic compositions. Braithwaite further supplemented his education at the Boston Public Library, where he assiduously studied the biographies and critical works of these writers.

Braithwaite began writing in earnest around 1899. His early work appeared in two Boston newspapers, the *Courant* and the *Transcript*. His first collection of verse, *Lyrics of Life and Love*, was published in 1904. He continued to publish his creative and critical works in such leading magazines as *Century* and *Atlantic Monthly*. In 1906, Braithwaite was elected to the Boston Authors Club, and the following year his first anthology, *The Book of Elizabethan Verse*, was published. A second volume of verse, *The House of Falling Leaves*, appeared in 1908. Braithwaite sealed his reputation as poet-critic nonpareil with the publication of an annual anthology of magazine verse from 1914 to 1929. The *Anthology of Magazine Verse* featured the works of poets such as Amy Lowell, Carl Sandburg, and Wallace Stevens, as well as the works of Harlem Renaissance writers such as **Sterling Brown**, **James Weldon Johnson**, and **Countee Cullen**. In 1921, Braithwaite founded and served as editor in chief of the B. J. Brimmer Publishing Company, where he published the early works of **Georgia Douglas Johnson** (*Bronze*, 1922) and James Gould Cozzens (*Confusion*, 1924) before the company folded in 1927. Braithwaite made an important contribution to the Harlem circle of writers with his essay "The Negro in American Literature," included in **Alain Locke**'s anthology *The New Negro* (1925).

Braithwaite's awards include the **NAACP**'s Spingarn Award in 1918 for his literary achievements, and honorary degrees from Taladega College and Atlanta University, where he served as professor of creative literature from 1935 to 1945. While at Atlanta, he wrote "The House Under Arcturus," the story of his life to 1904, which appeared as a serial in *Phylon*, the university quarterly, in 1941–1942. After his retirement from teaching, Braithwaite moved to **Harlem, New York**. His final works include his *Selected Poems* (1948), *The Bewitched Parsonage: The Story of the Brontës* (1950), and *Anthology of Magazine Verse for 1958* (1959). Braithwaite died June 8, 1962.

Resources: William Stanley Braithwaite: "Alain Locke's Relationship to the Negro in American Literature," in *Remembering the Harlem Renaissance*, ed. Cary D. Wintz (New York: Garland, 1996); *The Bewitched Parsonage: The Story of the Brontës* (New York: Coward-McCann, 1950); *The Book of Elizabethan Verse* (Boston: H. B. Turner, 1907); *The House of Falling Leaves* (Boston: J. W. Luce, 1908); *Lyrics of Life and Love* (Boston: H. B. Turner, 1904); "The Negro in American Literature," in *Within the Circle: An Anthology of African American Literary Criticism from the Harlem Renaissance to the Present*, ed. Angelyn Mitchell (Durham, NC: Duke University Press, 1994); *Selected Poems* (New York: Coward-McCann, 1948); Philip Butcher, ed., *The William Stanley Braithwaite Reader* (Ann Arbor: University of Michigan Press, 1972); Emmanuel S. Nelson, ed., *African American Authors, 1745–1945: A Bio-Bibliographical Critical Sourcebook* (Westport, CT: Greenwood Press, 2000); Jack Salzman, David Lionel Smith, and Cornel West, eds., *Encyclopedia of African-American Culture and History*, vol. 1 (New York: Macmillan Library Reference, 1996); Lisa Szefel, "Encouraging Verse: William S. Braithwaite and the Poetics of Race," *New England Quarterly: A Historical Review of New England Life and Letters* 74, no. 1 (Mar. 2001), 32–61; Thomson-Gale Literature Resource Center, "William Stanley Braithwaite," http://www.galenet.com/servlet.

Patricia E. Clark

Brawley, Benjamin Griffith (1882–1939). Educator, historian, and critic. The son of Edward McKnight Brawley, Benjamin Brawley was the first Black graduate of Bucknell University. His achievements as a preacher, a professor, and a college president are examined in William Simmons's *Men of Mark*. Through his father he inherited a mandate for achievement rooted in the Victorian values of Charleston's antebellum free Black elite. Born in Columbia, South Carolina, Brawley was shielded from the worst aspects of life in **the South** by the genteel circumstances of his upbringing. At Atlanta Baptist College (later Morehouse College), he found his purpose in life when he realized that "not everyone had read Shakespeare and Hugo at home." After a year teaching in rural Florida, Brawley returned to Morehouse as an instructor of English. He spent the next eight years there rising through the professorial ranks while earning an A.B. degree from the University of Chicago and an A.M. from Harvard University. After two years at Howard University, Brawley returned to Morehouse as its first dean in 1910. As part of the Archer–Brawley–Hope triumvirate, he helped to establish the college's reputation as an important center of racial uplift. From 1923 to 1931 he taught at Shaw University in Raleigh,

North Carolina. He then returned to Howard University, and taught there until his death in 1939. Brawley was known for his dynamism in the classroom and for his lessons in gentility.

Despite the demands of his teaching and administrative duties, Brawley was a prolific writer. He is best known for *The Negro in Art and Literature* (1918), *A Short History of the American Negro* (1913; rev. ed., 1919), *Early Negro American Writers* (1935), *Paul Laurence Dunbar, a Poet of His People* (1936), and *The Negro Genius* (1937). Brawley believed that recognition of Black contributions would elevate the race in the scale of civilization. His aim in these works was to chronicle Black achievement and to explicate the distinctive genius of the race in the arts. A characteristic feature of these works is an observable tension between Herderian exaltations of "folk" culture and an admiration of classical formalism. In addition to book-length projects, Brawley published countless articles, editorials, and reviews in newspapers and periodicals. Starting in 1915, his articles on various subjects appeared regularly in *Southern Workman* for nearly twenty years. Demonstrating the range of his concerns as well as his commitment to African American civil society, he lauded Black achievement and examined the responsibilities of Black educators in the task of racial uplift.

The fundamentally conservative nature of Brawley's critical perspectives led to clashes with the younger artists and intellectuals of the **Harlem Renaissance**, who coined the term "Brawleyism" as a description of his academic gentility. Conflating the realms of literary and social criticism, he argued that the "aestheticism" of the Harlem movement denied the didactic functions of art. He criticized the "modern temper" for its "hedonism," its "paganism," and its lack of regard for standards. Though he professed admiration for tradition-based rural culture, he favored the study of the classics for training in discipline, tradition, and restraint.

Resources: Benjamin Brawley: *Early Negro American Writers: Selections with Biographical and Critical Introductions* (Chapel Hill: University of North Carolina Press, 1935); *The Negro Genius: A New Appraisal of the Achievement of the American Negro in Literature and the Fine Arts* (New York: Dodd, Mead, 1937); *The Negro in Literature and Art in the United States* (New York: Duffield, 1918); *Paul Laurence Dunbar, a Poet of His People* (Chapel Hill: University of North Carolina Press, 1936); *A Short History of the American Negro*, rev. ed. (New York: Macmillan, 1919); *A Short History of the English Drama* (New York: Harcourt, Brace, 1921); John W. Parker: "Benjamin Brawley," *Crisis* 46 (May 1939), 144; "Benjamin Brawley and the American Cultural Tradition," *Phylon* 14, no. 2 (1955), 183–194; "Benjamin Brawley, Teacher and Scholar," *Phylon* 10, no. 1 (1949), 5–24; Ira De A. Reid, "Three Negro Teachers," *Phylon* 2 (1941), 137–143; William J. Simmons, *Men of Mark: Eminent, Progressive, and Rising* (1887; Chicago: Johnson, 1970).

Jeffrey R. Williams

Bridgforth, Sharon (born c. 1960). Writer, performance artist, teacher, and theater director. A native of **Los Angeles, California**, Bridgforth is best known for *The Bull-Jean Stories*, a collection of narratives that draw on African American oral traditions and other elements of the **vernacular**, mix poetry with prose, and lend themselves to dramatic performance. A central figure in the book is Bull-Dog Jean La Rue, a lesbian African American living in rural **Texas**. Bridgforth has said that when she "moved to Austin 10 years ago [circa 1990]," she "was doing outreach and education for the health department, so I was moving around and talking to different people. I started to get these stories of black women over 60 who had lived with Miss So-and-So, who were part of the church community, who had helped raise other people. These women would not use the word *lesbian*, but they were women loving women. I wanted to celebrate them, to consider what it would be like to be a woman-loving woman who is part of the community, not separate from it, and I believe there was a time it was like that, in the Black community" (Plakcy). To some extent, the book examines and dismantles the stereotype of the "bull-dyke" homosexual woman.

Bridgforth earned a B.A. in creative writing and broadcast media in 1985 from California State University at Los Angeles. She has performed parts of *The Bull-Jean Stories* nationwide and has given numerous workshops in creative writing, storytelling, and the development of one's "voice." She has worked extensively with the Austin Latina/o Lesbian Gay Bisexual Transgender Organization (ALLGO), and she helped found the Root Wy'mn Theatre in Austin. In the late 1990s, Bridgforth developed a performance piece, *amniotic/flow*, which she presented with her daughter, Sonja Perryman, who studied theater at the Tisch School of the Arts at New York University. In 2003 Lisa Bird, of ALLGO, helped Bridgforth produce a compact disc of *amniotic/flow* ("Website"). Other performance scripts she has written are *con flama*, *geechee crossing martha's overture*, *blood pudding*, *dyke/warriors prayers*, and *no mo blues*. *The Bull-Jean Stories* won the Lambda Literary Best Small Press Book Award in 1998, and in 2001 Bridgforth was named the Austin, Texas, YWCA Woman of the Year. At this writing, Bridgforth is at work on a novel, *Big Bill's/Blues*. (*See* **Lesbian Literature**.)

Resources: Sharon Bridgforth: *amniotic/flow*, performance piece on independently produced compact disc (see "Web site"); *The Bull-Jean Stories* (Austin, TX: Redbone Press, 1998); Web site, http://www.sharonbridgforth.com; C. C. Carter, "[Review of] *The Bull-Jean Stories*," *Lambda Book Report* 7, no. 6 (Jan. 1999), 15; Neil Plakcy, "Sharon Bridgforth—National Treasure," http://www.tropic62.com/national_treasure.htm.

Hans Ostrom

Briscoe, Connie (born 1952). Novelist. Connie Briscoe maintains a fierce devotion to portraying the African American experience in her novels. Born with a hearing loss, she grew up in the **Washington, D.C.**, metropolitan area. Briscoe's early life was marked by what she calls "a wonderful upbringing, sort of like that portrayed on *The Bill Cosby* [television] *Show*." From childhood through her twenties, her hearing loss was moderate, and she was able to attend public schools and go on to college at Hampton University with few problems. During her mid-twenties, the loss worsened, and she began wearing a hearing aid. Briscoe has written the novels *Sisters and Lovers* (1994), *Big Girls Don't Cry* (1996), *A Long Way from Home* (1999), *P. G. County* (2002), and *Can't Get Enough* (2005). In her debut novel, *Sisters and Lovers*, Briscoe presents three sisters who are interconnected within a community of identities framed largely by common experiences and interests. Her skillful use of language has illuminated the pain and triumphs of African American men and women from the nineteenth century through the present. In her novels, the reinforcement of private identity and racial self conveys the truth of the African American experience while highlighting the question of who or what ultimately controls social forms and has power over history. Each of her novels features the people with whom she is most familiar, the inhabitants of Washington, D.C., and Prince Georges County, Maryland, many of whom are members of the African American elite. Among the themes that resonate in her fiction are the redemptive power of love, family devotion, the celebration of friendship, and commitment to community.

Resources: Connie Briscoe: *Big Girls Don't Cry* (New York: HarperCollins, 1996); *Can't Get Enough* (New York: Doubleday, 2005); *A Long Way from Home* (New York: HarperCollins, 1999); *P.G. County* (New York: Doubleday, 2002); *Sisters and Lovers* (New York: HarperCollins, 1994).

Teresa Gilliams

Broadside Press (1965–present). Publisher. Founded in 1965 by the poet **Dudley Randall**, Broadside Press in **Detroit, Michigan**, became one of the major forces behind the **Black Arts Movement** of the 1960s and 1970s. With ninety poetry titles published from 1965 to 1977 and with more than 500,000 copies distributed during that period, Broadside Press has been credited with changing the landscape of Black poetry and small press publishing by providing a creative and political resource at a time when there were few outlets for Black poets. Named for the process of printing on a single large sheet of paper, the press's first publications were Randall's *Ballad of Birmingham*, about the 1963 Ku Klux Klan bombing of the Sixteenth Street Baptist Church in Birmingham, Alabama, which killed four black girls, and *Dressed All in Pink*, about the assassination of John F. Kennedy. In 1965 folksinger Jerry Moore asked Randall for permission to record "Ballad of Birmingham" and "Dressed All in Pink" as songs; before agreeing, Randall published each as a broadside in order to protect his rights as the author. Randall went on to publish broadsides for other poets, and eventually expanded his publication to include anthologies, chapbooks, poetry series, and political essays. By the early 1970s, Broadside Press had become the most successful small poetry press of its time, publishing works by established figures such as **Melvin B. Tolson, Margaret Walker,** and **Gwendolyn Brooks,** as well as newcomers who included **Haki R. Madhubuti** (Don L. Lee), **Nikki Giovanni, Audre Lorde, Sonia Sanchez, Etheridge Knight, Mae Jackson, James A. Emanuel,** Keorapetse Kgositsile (a South African writer, born in 1938), **Sterling D. Plumpp, Melba Joyce Boyd,** and **Lance Jeffers.**

Broadside Press's first poetry collection, *Poem Counterpoem* (1966), featured **Margaret Danner**, poet and founder of Detroit's Boone House, a Black cultural center where Randall often publicly read his poetry. At the price of a dollar each, *Poem Counterpoem* sold more than 1,500 copies. It was a unique publication for its time in that Randall's and Danner's poems were thematically arranged on facing pages to create a conversational style. The anthology *For Malcolm. Poems on the Life and the Death of Malcolm X*, edited by Randall and **Margaret Burroughs,** was published the following year (1967). According to Julian E. Thompson's survey of the press's sales records, *For Malcolm* sold 8,000 copies by 1969 and helped to establish an eager, if not captive, audience that readily purchased each new release (38). In 1969 Randall published *Black Poetry: A Supplement to Anthologies Which Exclude Black Poets*, the title of which left no doubt about one of Randall's purposes as a publisher. In 1971 he was able to pursue the goal of representing overlooked African American poets when the mass-market publisher Bantam Books brought out his anthology *The Black Poets*; the book was widely used in college courses and remains in print. The Broadside Series was introduced in 1966, and its inaugural collection, *Poems of the Negro Revolt*, featured already published favorites by **Robert Hayden** ("Gabriel"), Melvin Tolson ("The Sea-Turtle and the Shark"), Margaret Walker ("The Ballad of the Free") and Gwendolyn Brooks ("We Real Cool"). In later interviews Randall often described this collection as containing some of the best poems published by these poets (Randall, *Broadside Memories*). The series shifted its focus in 1968 and started to give attention to previously unpublished works by relatively unknown poets. The first such work in the Broadside Series was Haki R. Madhubuti's *Assassination*, about the death of **Martin Luther King, Jr.** This new direction for the Broadside Series introduced poems by Etheridge Knight, James Emanuel, Nikki Giovanni, Sonia Sanchez, and Audre Lorde, many of whom became essential figures in the **Black Arts Movement** and literary renaissance of the 1970s.

Broadside Press's contribution to the Black Arts Movement and the **Civil Rights Movement** is most evidenced by the grassroots political perspective advanced by many of its regular contributors. These poets "became major shapers of the cultural and intellectual developments [of] the Black Arts Movement," making Detroit and the Broadside Press the major hub of Black poetry publishing of the era (Thompson, 29). Pulitzer Prize winner Gwendolyn Brooks's leaving the major publishing house Harper & Row for Broadside signaled commitment to the civil rights struggle and brought more attention to the politics of the press and its writers. Poets such as Giovanni, Madhubuti, Knight, and Sanchez, whose poetic expressions are often thought to epitomize the struggle, were now outselling publications by university or trade presses. Madhubuti's *Black Pride* (1968), *Think Black* (1968), and *Don't Cry, Scream!* (1969) sold an unprecedented 80,000 copies, and Audre Lorde's *From a Land Where Other People Live* (1973) was nominated for a National Book Award. Although the royalties from Broadside Press, approximately 10 percent of sales, were not very lucrative, the popularity of their publications helped these poets secure lecture tours and academic appointments that previously would have been unheard of.

Broadside Press was also invaluable at helping to establish some of the local poets in Detroit, such as **Jill Witherspoon Boyer** (*Dream Farmer*, 1975), **Melba Joyce Boyd** (*Song for Maya*, 1982), Aneb Kgositsile (*Blood River*, 1983) and Michelle S. Gibbs (*Sketches from Home*, 1983). Many of these poets worked for Randall at the press. Boyer, daughter of Broadside poet and **Lotus Press** founder **Naomi Long Madgett** ("Sunny," 1966), served as the editor of the *Broadside Annual*, a yearly poetry anthology published from 1972 to 1974. Boyd, professor and chair of the Department of Africana Studies at Wayne State University, was Randall's assistant editor from 1972 to 1977 and went on to direct the documentary *The Black Unicorn: Dudley Randall and the Broadside Press* (1996), which chronicles Randall's influence on the development of African American literature. Dr. Aneb Kgositsile (Gloria House), first writer-in-residence at the Dudley Randall Center for Print Culture at the University of Detroit–Mercy, was an editor from 1977 to 1980.

Although Broadside's sales figures were remarkable, Randall faced considerable financial difficulties: increasing publication expenses, unpaid distribution orders, and declining public interest. In 1977 the press was sold to the Alexander Crummell Center, which was affiliated with the Episcopal Church. Aneb Kgositsile served as its editor, although there were no new titles published at this time. In 1982 Randall resumed ownership of the press, and worked there until his retirement in 1985. His last major publication was the anthology *Homage to Hoyt W. Fuller* (1984), which paid tribute to the late editor of the *Negro Digest* (renamed *Black World* in the 1970s). In 1985 Broadside Press was sold to Hilda and Donald Vest, a Detroit couple who have kept thirty-six original Broadside titles in print and added more than ten new books to its list.

Resources: Melba Joyce Boyd, *Wrestling with the Muse: Dudley Randall and the Broadside Press* (New York: Columbia University Press, 2003); Melba Joyce Boyd, dir., *The Black Unicorn: Dudley Randall and Broadside Press* (Detroit, 1996); Melba Joyce Boyd and M. L. Liebler, eds., *Abandon Automobile: Detroit City Poetry 2001* (Detroit: Wayne State University Press, 2001); Haki R. Madhubuti, "Portrait of a Founding Father," *Black Issues Book Review* (Nov. 2000), 14–15; R. Baxter Miller, "Dudley Randall," in *Afro-American Poets Since 1955*, ed. Trudier Harris and Thadious M. Davis (Detroit: Gale, 1985), 265–273; A. X. Nicholas, "A Conversation with Dudley Randall," in *Homage to Hoyt Fuller*, ed. Dudley Randall (Detroit: Broadside Press, 1984), 266–274; Dudley Randall, ed.: *Black Poetry: A Supplement to Anthologies Which Exclude Black Poets* (Detroit: Broadside Press, 1969); *The Black Poets: A New Anthology* (1971; repr. New York: Bantam Books, 1985); *Broadside Memories: Poets I Have Known* (Detroit: Broadside Press, 1975); James Sullivan, *On the Walls and in the Streets: American Poetry Broadsides from the 1960s* (Urbana: University of Illinois Press, 1997); Julius E. Thompson, *Dudley Randall, Broadside Press, and the Black Arts Movement in Detroit, 1960–1995* (Jefferson, NC: McFarland, 1999).

Dara N. Byrne

Brooklyn, New York. Borough of New York City. Although it did not have the same reputation as a magnet for Black artists and writers as **Harlem** did in the 1920s, Brooklyn and its African American literary history are rich in their own right.

In 1646, the village of Breuckelen was authorized by the Dutch West India Company. By 1683, with the British in control, New York was organized into twelve counties, including Kings County, of which the town of Brooklyn was part. The oldest Black church in Brooklyn, Bridge Street African Methodist Episcopal Wesleyan Church, was established in 1818 (Burrows and Wallace, 400). Weeksville, consisting of a small cluster of frame houses in what is now the Crown Heights section, one of the earliest middle-class Black communities, was built in the 1830s. The emerging Black middle class was more likely to own homes in the more affordable Brooklyn than in Manhattan. Downtown Brooklyn became a Black cultural center. Black churches promoted literacy and culture: Concord Baptist, Bridge Street African Wesleyan Methodist Episcopal, and Siloam Presbyterian offered classes, lectures, and concerts.

Brooklyn was incorporated into New York City in 1898, and by 1900, its Black population had tripled to 18,367 (the entire population of Brooklyn was over 1 million), with 40 percent of those living in Bedford (Connolly, 35). However, in the 1920s Harlem, in Manhattan, became the destination for many Black artists and writers, overshadowing the growing Black population in areas of Brooklyn including Bedford Stuyvesant, Fort Greene, and Crown Heights (Connolly, 52–55).

Yet Brooklyn was home to and drew interest from several Black writers of note. **Richard Wright** began his novel *Native Son* (1941) there, writing in Fort Greene Park each morning. In Brooklyn Heights, 7 Middagh Street became a gathering place for a group of writers and artists such as Carson McCullers, W. H. Auden, Anaïs Nin, Leonard Bernstein, Gypsy Rose Lee, and Salvador Dali. Wright and his wife and child lived there briefly in 1940, but it didn't suit him. Neighbors complained, and the Black superintendent of the building quit because he refused to take care of the furnace for "another Negro." Wright said the atmosphere of "general over-stimulation and excitement" was too much for him and not a good place to raise a child (Edmiston, 349–350). Wright later moved to Bedford Stuyvesant, where he finished the novel: "Wright and his friends read the whole book aloud here" (Edmiston, 335–336). In the mid-1940s, while still in Bedford Stuyvesant, Wright organized a tenants' strike and had the rent lowered; he was writing *Black Boy* (1945) at that time (Edmiston, 336).

Paule Marshall, born in Brooklyn to parents who had recently emigrated from Barbados, lived in a West Indian community in Bedford Stuyvesant, and her works reflect the struggles that Caribbean immigrants faced. In 1959, her first novel, *Brown Girl, Brownstones*, the story of a young, first-generation Caribbean American girl growing up in a West Indian section of Brooklyn during the **Great Depression** and **World War II**, was published. Her search for an identity mirrors the community's desire to assimilate yet also to maintain its culture. Another

Aerial view at night of the Brooklyn Bridge in 1903. Courtesy of the Library of Congress.

work, published in 1961, is a collection of short fiction titled *Soul Clap Hands and Sing*; it includes "Brooklyn," one of four novellas about elderly men who have chosen greed and materialism over humanity.

Novelist, social activist, and close friend of **Martin Luther King, Jr.**, **John O. Killens** lived and died in Crown Heights. In the 1950s his house was a meeting place for the Harlem Writers Guild. Among the authors who came to discuss their work were **Rosa Guy**, **Paule Marshall**, **Louise Meriwether**, **James Baldwin**, **Maya Angelou**, and **Ossie Davis** (Edmiston, 336). Killens created the Black Writers Conferences, hosted by Medgar Evers College since 1986, and wrote several novels, including *Youngblood* (1954), the story of a family in 1900–1930s Georgia; *'Sippi* (1967), which deals with the African American experience during the 1960s; and *The Cotillion; or, One Good Bull Is Half the Herd* (1971), a satirical novel attacking assimilationist and classist African Americans.

In 1960, nearly two-thirds of Brooklyn's Blacks (14 percent of the population of Brooklyn) lived in predominantly black areas, and nearly half of the residents of low-income housing projects were Black: such segregation went unchallenged (Connolly, 132). By the 1980s, racial tension in Brooklyn, as well as the rest of New York City, exploded: in 1989, African American Yusuf Hawkins was killed by a mob of whites in predominantly Italian American Bensonhurst; there was an extended boycott of a Korean grocer by African Americans in Flatbush; and riots followed the deaths of a young African American, Gavin Cato, and Yankel Rosenbaum, an Australian Jew, in Crown Heights in 1991.

Several writers responded to these incidents. **Anna Deavere Smith**'s *Fires in the Mirror: Crown Heights, Brooklyn and Other Identities* (1993) is a one-woman play in which she portrays more than thirty characters—young, old, Black, White, male, female—embroiled in the racial conflict that erupted in Crown Heights. Spike Lee's film *Do the Right Thing* (1989), filmed in Bedford Stuyvesant in the midst of this racial tension, is about the Black underclass, a community of high unemployment, high drug use, and drug-related homicides. The major source of racial tension in Lee's film is lack of ownership by African Americans: Italian Americans own the pizzeria and a Korean couple own the grocery store, in a neighborhood home to mostly African Americans. Buggin' Out's boycott and the resulting riot stem from anger over this. Lee grew up in Brooklyn, and several of his films take place in the borough, including *Jungle Fever* (1991), which addressed the effect of interracial dating and drug addiction on the Black communities, and *Crooklyn* (1994), a nostalgic portrayal of Lee's Brooklyn childhood.

More recently, **Edwidge Danticat**, born in **Haiti** in 1969, joined her parents in Brooklyn when she was twelve. Although she was teased because of her accent, the Haitian community in Brooklyn provided support, and her Creole background was an asset in her fiction. She received her M.F.A. from Brown University, and her thesis became her first novel. *Breath, Eyes, Memory* (1994) is about four generations of Haitian women in Haiti and Brooklyn who must overcome cultural traditions, poverty, and powerlessness. In 1995 Danticat was a finalist for the National Book Award for *Krik? Krak!*, a collection of short stories about Haiti and Haitian Americans.

Resources: Edwin G. Burrows and Mike Wallace, *Gotham: A History of New York City to 1898* (New York: Oxford University Press, 1999); Harold X. Connolly, *A Ghetto Grows in Brooklyn* (New York: New York University Press, 1977); Edwidge Danticat: *Breath, Eyes, Memory* (New York: Soho Press, 1994); *Krik? Krak!* (New York: Vintage Books, 1996); Susan Edmiston and Linda D. Cirino, *Literary New York: A History and Guide* (Boston: Houghton Mifflin, 1976); Grace Glueck and Paul Gardner, *Brooklyn: People and Places, Past and Present* (NewYork: Harry N. Abrams, 1991); John O. Killens: *The Cotillion; or, One Good Bull Is Half the Herd* (1971; repr. New York: Ballantine, 1988); *'Sippi* (1967; repr. New York: Thunder's Mouth, 1988); *Youngblood* (1954; repr. Athens: University of Georgia Press, 1982); Paule Marshall: "Brooklyn," in *Souls Clap Hands and Sing* (New York: Atheneum, 1961); *Brown Girl, Brownstones* (New York: Random House, 1959; repr. Old Westbury, NY: Feminist Press, 1981); Anna Deveare Smith, *Fires in the Mirror: Crown Heights, Brooklyn and Other Identities* (New York: Anchor Books, 1993); Martin Tucker, ed., *Brooklyn and the World* (Brooklyn, NY: Long Island University Press, 1983); Wilbert Turner, "Tony, Auggie, and Mook: Race Relations in Cinematic Brooklyn," in *The Brooklyn Film: Essays in the History of Filmmaking*, ed. John B. Manbeck and Robert Singer (Jefferson, NC: McFarland, 2003), 71–81; Richard Wright: *Black Boy* (1945; repr. New York: HarperPerennial, 1993); *Native Son* (1941; repr. New York: Perennial Classics, 1998).

Stacey Lee Donohue

Brooks, Gwendolyn (1917–2000). Poet. Gwendolyn Brooks ranks among the greatest American poets of all time. Few have equaled her brilliant range in both traditional and innovative uses of the **sonnet** and **ballad** forms as well as in the use of African American **vernacular**. From her first volume, A Street in Bronzeville (1945), she explored the questions of human meaning in the postwar world. Later she sought to answer, within **epic poetry** (Annie Allen, 1949), whether the consequent rift in human alienation could ever be closed. Finally, she concluded that the great visionary, whether an imagined **Langston Hughes** (Selected Poems, 1963) or an urban tenant in a decaying apartment building (In the Mecca, 1968), represents a potential for human health in moral and social dimensions. While her images are often Eurocentric—especially those before 1967—her ironic and coy tone is distinctly African American. She places Western art forms in a Black folk perspective so as to authenticate **poetics** through African American experience (Miller, "Gwendolyn Brooks," 1164).

Brooks walked a tightrope of negotiation between the beauty of artistic forms and the human self interpreting them. She voiced the hurt and triumph of the common people. Hence, she created a poetic art that helped free such people from an easy acceptance of social limits. Her earlier verse helped save the Euro-American tradition of poetry that often ignores the way the poor are human, and her later verse helped usher in a new era of new Black poets and Black aesthetics (see **Black Arts Movement**).

Brooks was born in Topeka, Kansas, on June 7, 1917, to Keziah Corinne Wims Brooks and David Anderson Brooks. As early as first grade, the dark-skinned girl began to recognize distinctions based on color, **gender**, and class. She lacked athletic skills and many social graces, as well as straight hair. For her, the writing of poetry became a positive antidote to peer rejection. Supported in these efforts by her parents, she wrote many poems about the triumph of beauty and order in the world, but discrimination based on race–gender–class would become the focus of her later poetry.

Early on, Brooks was influenced by English and American romantic poets such as William Wordsworth, John Keats, William Cullen Bryant, and Henry Wadsworth Longfellow. In 1930, at age thirteen, she wrote "Eventide" for American Childhood magazine; four years later, she began to write poetry for a variety column, "Lights and Shadows," in the **Chicago Defender**. She graduated in 1934 from the integrated Englewood High School in Topeka, and by 1935 was well on her way in writing the traditional forms of poetry. Influenced by Sara Teasdale, she focused primarily on love as a subject and occasionally treated a theme of racial pride. Briefly, she corresponded with **James Weldon Johnson**, a **Harlem Renaissance** poet, fiction writer, and editor. Her mother had taken her to meet Johnson and hear him lecture in 1933. The same year, Langston Hughes encouraged Brooks at one of his readings to continue writing, surprising her by taking time after a performance to read some of her poems. By the late 1930s, Brooks had published seventy-five poems in the Chicago Defender.

After graduating from Wilson Junior College (today Kennedy-King) in 1936, Brooks read the works of such modern poets as T. S. Eliot, Ezra Pound, and e. e. cummings. Five years later, she began to study at **Chicago**'s South Side Community Art Center with Inez Cunningham Stark, a White socialite who was a reader for *Poetry* magazine. Brooks did odd jobs and even worked as a typist. Others who studied at the Center were Henry Blakely, Brooks's future husband; William Couch, scholar of African American drama; **Margaret Taylor Goss Burroughs**, curator of African history in a Chicago museum; and **Margaret Danner**, a fine poet. Many of the poems Brooks wrote in 1941 and 1942 appeared in her initial volume, *A Street in Bronzeville* (1945).

With "Gay Chaps at the Bar" (1944) and "The Progress" (1945), Brooks won the prize awarded by the Midwestern Writers Conference. Both of the pieces rival some by W. H. Auden as the most accomplished war poems in the twentieth century. At first Brooks tried to publish her early poetry through Emily Morrison at **Alfred A. Knopf**, but finally she gathered together nineteen pieces, mainly about African Americans, and sent them to Harper. *A Street in Bronzeville*, which was published in August 1945, received a good review from Paul Engle in the *Chicago Tribune Book Review*. It was Engle, in fact, who had helped secure prizes for Brooks at the Northwestern University Annual Writers Conference that year.

For Brooks, the 1940s was a decade of rising fame. In 1945, she received the Mademoiselle Merit Award as one of the ten outstanding women of the year. In 1946 and 1947, she was awarded Guggenheim fellowships. In 1949, she won the Eunice Tietjens Memorial Prize from *Poetry* for several pieces that would appear in *Annie Allen* (1949). As a testimony to the quality of the volume, she was awarded the 1950 Pulitzer Prize, the first time it was presented to an African American. During the 1950s, she wrote reviews for the *New York Times*, **Negro Digest**, and the *New York Herald Tribune*. She also wrote personal articles such as "How I Told My Child About Race" and "Why Negro Women Leave Home."

During the next decade, Brooks developed her commitment to nurturing young students. From 1963 to 1969, she led a poetry workshop at Columbia College in Chicago and taught at Elmhurst College in Elmhurst, Illinois. About then she completed stints as the Rennebohm Professor of English at the University of Wisconsin at Madison

Gwendolyn Brooks, c. 1948. Courtesy of the Library of Congress.

and distinguished professor of the arts at the City College of New York. Though in many ways she informally began to retreat from the academic world, in 1971 she helped establish the Illinois Poet Laureate Awards to promote creative writing.

With a startling development in stylistic complexity from 1945 to 1949, and with an abrupt shift in explicit ideology from 1967 on, Brooks's poetry has retained technical excellence. Particularly riveting is the ironic distance through which she achieves a pervasiveness of historical suffering. As early as *A Street in Bronzeville* (1945) Brooks accomplished startling shifts of tense as well as shimmering perceptions about memory, writing "The Mother," for example, a classic poem about abortion. In 1975, Brooks told a literary critic that she would never again write some of the apologetic lines in *Annie Allen* (1949) that beg Whites to accept that she was human (Kent). In *Maud Martha* (1953), an autobiographical novel in poetic sketches, she tells the story of a young black girl who grows into complete womanhood. In a version written for Herbert Hill's anthology *Soon One Morning* (1963), Brooks produced what would become a revision published as "The Life of Lincoln West" in *Family Pictures* (1970). Brooks's *Bean Eaters* (1960) contained explicitly social verse. In one of her poems, a White mother–narrator agonizes over the **lynching** in 1955 of **Emmett Till**, a fourteen-year-old Chicagoan. In "The Chicago Defender Sends a Man to Little Rock," a Northern Black narrator travels to Arkansas in 1957 to witness the uproar over school integration, only to discover that those in the mob "are like people everywhere." And in "Negro Hero" and "The Progress," Brooks continues to reveal historical irony. In her poetic world, evil is endemic to human existence. Hence, all people must eschew a barbarism that threatens human life.

In the mid-1950s, Brooks was sent by the Illinois Employment Service to work as a secretary for Dr. G.N. French, the manager of a large slum known as the Mecca Building. After exploiting the tenants by selling them useless trinkets and charms, he was eventually murdered. In 1962, Brooks wrote to her Harper's editor about plans to complete a 2,000-line poem on the subject. About the same time she completed poems about **Medgar Evers** and **Malcolm X**, martyrs of the 1960s **Civil Rights Movement**, as commemorated in *Mecca* (1968) and *The World of Gwendolyn Brooks* (1971). *Report from Part One* (1972), with prefaces by Don L. Lee (**Haki Madhubuti**) and George E. Kent, details the events that helped shape her epic vision. Besides many details about her family life, the autobiography represents through fragmented sketches her supposedly magical transformation from a conservative "**Negro**" in 1945 into a proud Black woman in 1967, following the Fisk University Writers Conference. "First Fight/Then Fiddle" (*Annie Allen*, 1949) even today remains a dazzling poem about the way that military power underlies the development of European pictorial and verbal art from the Augustan age of the first century through the Crusades of the Middle Ages.

Especially during the last third of the twentieth century, Brooks earned worldwide acclaim. Though the center of her personal renaissance was certainly African, her reach extended into the Soviet block. In the summer of 1971, she traveled alone to the East African nations of Kenya and Tanzania, and in the summer of 1974, with her husband to the West African cities of Accra and Kumasi, Ghana. In viewing the slave castle at Emina—and quite likely the infamous Door of No Return through which Africans were forced as slaves to the Americas—she rounded out her own life's quest in the African **diaspora**.

Brooks's beautifully polished sonnets, historical ballads, and highly inflected **free verse**—including works resonant and delightful with the urban idiom of "We Real Cool"—have clearly won the approval of literary history. In 1970 she began, with the brief *Family Pictures*, a steady stream of eight to ten little pamphlets that appeared during the next twenty-one years. Appointed by Librarian of Congress Daniel Boorstin as consultant in poetry to the Library of Congress in 1985, she received support from John Broderick, the assistant librarian (Brooks, *Report from Part Two*). The first female writer to be accorded such a distinction, she delivered her final lecture of the position on May 5, 1986. Later the consultancy would develop into the office of poet laureate, the first of which would be Robert Penn Warren. Brooks became one of the most celebrated American women poets in the twentieth century. And she is one of the finest writers, regardless of race or gender. Through her election to the National Institute of Arts and Letters (as the first African American woman) in 1976, she more than capably filled a racial divide that had persisted since the induction of **W.E.B. Du Bois** in 1943 (Melhem, 157).

In 1989 Brooks was awarded the Frost Medal of the Poetry Society of America, and in 1990 was the first American to receive the Society of Literature Award from the University of Thessalonica in Athens. In 1994 she received the medal of the National Book Foundation for Distinguished Contribution to American Letters. Selected as the Jefferson lecturer by the National Endowment for the Humanities in 1994—"the highest honor the federal government bestows for intellectual achievement in the humanities"— Brooks received more than seventy honorary doctorates during her lifetime. "An Old Black Woman, Homeless and Indistinct" (*Drum Voices Review*, Fall/ Winter 1992–1993) encapsulates her poetic quest: "Folks used to say, 'That child is going far.'"

Many aims informed the rich complexity of Brooks's wide-ranging poetics. Though she claimed in the last third of her life to write poetry worthy of the tavern—and sometimes she actually did so—much of her early and late craft reveals a keen eye for poetic form, a penchant for profundity. By the time of her death in Chicago, on December 3, 2000, she had become one of the greatest modern poets. (*See* **Broadside Press; Randall, Dudley Felker; Third World Press**.)

Resources: Primary Works: Gwendolyn Brooks: *Aloneness* (Detroit: Broadside Press, 1971); *Annie Allen* (New York: Harper, 1949); *The Bean Eaters* (New York: Harper, 1960); *Beckonings* (Detroit: Broadside Press, 1975); *Blacks* (Chicago: Third World Press, 1987); *A Broadside Treasury* (Detroit: Broadside Press, 1971); *Children Coming Home* (Chicago: David Co., 1991); *Family Pictures* (Detroit: Broadside Press, 1970); *In Montgomery, and Other Poems* (Chicago: Third World Press, 2003); *In the Mecca: Poems* (New York: Harper & Row, 1968); *Maud Martha* (New York: Harper, 1953); *Report from Part One* (Detroit: Broadside Press, 1972); *Report from Part Two* (Chicago:

Third World Press, 1996); *Riot* (Detroit: Broadside Press, 1969); *Selected Poems* (New York: Harper & Row, 1963); *To Disembark* (Chicago: Third World Press, 1981); *The World of Gwendolyn Brooks* (New York: Harper & Row, 1971); Gwendolyn Brooks, ed., *Jump Bad: A New Chicago Anthology* (Detroit: Broadside Press, 1971). **Secondary Sources:** Jacqueline K. Bryant, ed., *Gwendolyn Brooks' "Maud Martha": A Critical Collection* (Chicago: Third World Press, 2002); Arthur P. Davis, "The Black and Tan Motif in the Poetry of Gwendolyn Brooks," *CLAJ* 6 (1962), 90–97; Joanne V. Gabbin, "Blooming in the Whirlwind: The Early Poetry of Gwendolyn Brooks," in *The Furious Flowering of African American Poetry*, ed. Joanne V. Gabbin (Charlottesville: University Press of Virginia, 1999), 252–273; Melba Joyce, "The Cultural Activism of Margaret Danner, Margaret Burroughs, Gwendolyn Brooks, and Margaret Walker During the Black Arts Movement," *Revista Canaria de Estudios Ingleses* 37 (1998), 55–67; George E. Kent, *A Life of Gwendolyn Brooks* (Lexington: University Press of Kentucky, 1990); Haki R. Madhubuti, *Say That the River Turns: The Impact of Gwendolyn Brooks* (Chicago: Third World Press, 1987); D. H. Melhem, *Gwendolyn Brooks: Poetry and the Heroic Voice* (Lexington: University Press of Kentucky, 1987); R. Baxter Miller: "Gwendolyn Brooks," in *Call and Response: The Riverside Anthology of African American Literature*, ed. Patricia Liggins Hill et al. (Boston: Houghton Mifflin, 1998); *Langston Hughes and Gwendolyn Brooks: A Reference Guide* (Boston: G. K. Hall, 1978); R. Baxter Miller, ed.: *Black American Literature and Humanism* (Lexington: University Press of Kentucky, 1981); *Black American Poets Between Worlds, 1940–1960* (Knoxville: University of Tennessee Press, 1986); Maria Mootry and Gary Smith, eds., *A Life Distilled: Gwendolyn Brooks, Her Poetry and Fiction* (Urbana: University of Illinois Press, 1987); Stephen Caldwell Wright, *On Gwendolyn Brooks: Reliant Contemplation* (Ann Arbor: University of Michigan Press, 1996).

R. Baxter Miller

Broughton, Virginia W. (c. 1856–1934). Spiritual writer and educator. Broughton's *Twenty Year's* [sic] *Experience of a Missionary* (1907) is a spiritual **autobiography** that combines religious fervor with the work of a late nineteenth-century teacher and administrator. Written in the third person, it glorifies not the achievements of an individual but the accomplishments of a life placed in service to God. Broughton, a member of the first graduating class of Fisk University, taught for twelve years in Memphis and, in 1885, became involved in a debate with the Memphis School Board following the promotion of a less experienced male teacher over herself. After meeting Joanna Moore, a White missionary, Broughton became interested in establishing Bible Bands to promote daily study of the Bible by women, though it was not until after her mother's death and a serious illness in the mid-1880s that she committed herself fully to religious work. Broughton's missionary work took her throughout the Southern states and later into the Northeast, often requiring her to travel in discomfort. Around the turn of the century, she was elected recording secretary of the Woman's National Baptist Convention, a position she held for at least twenty years. She maintained her interest in education and, in 1899, assisted Moore in running the Fireside School, which promoted home Bible study programs. Her autobiography presents her conversion as a physical and spiritual rebirth and places her commitment to God above that to her husband and five children.

Resources: Lori Askeland, "Virginia W. Broughton," in *The Oxford Companion to African American Literature* (New York: Oxford University Press, 1997); Kathleen Berkeley, "The Politics of Black Education in Memphis, Tennessee, 1868–1881," in *Southern Cities, Southern Schools: Public Education in the Urban South*, ed. David N. Plank and Rick Ginsberg (Westport, CT: Greenwood Press, 1990), 199–236; Virginia W. Broughton: *Twenty Year's [sic] Experience of a Missionary* (1907), in *Spiritual Narratives* (New York: Oxford University Press, 1988); *Women's Work, as Gleaned from the Women of the Bible, and Bible Women of Modern Times* (Nashville, TN: National Baptist Publishing Board, 1904); Evelyn Brooks Higginbotham, *Righteous Discontent: The Women's Movement in the Black Baptist Church 1880–1920* (Cambridge, MA: Harvard University Press, 1993); Joanna P. Moore, *"In Christ's Stead": Autobiographical Sketches* (Chicago: Women's Baptist Home Mission Society, c. 1902).

Tracey S. Rosenberg

Brown, Cecil (born 1943). Author of novels, scripts, and nonfiction books known for his comic, witty, and incisive writing style. He was born on July 3, 1943, in Bolton, North Carolina, to tobacco sharecropper parents. After attending North Carolina A&T State University, he transferred to Columbia University, where he earned a B.A. degree in comparative literature in 1966. Brown received an M.A. degree in English from the University of Chicago the following year and went on to earn a Ph.D. in folklore at the University of California at Berkeley in 1993. Brown's literary fame arises chiefly from his first novel, *The Life and Loves of Mr. Jiveass Nigger* (1969), which follows George Washington, an African American who travels in Europe seeking self-identity and sexual adventures. Brown's second novel, *Days Without Weather* (1983), indicts the Hollywood film industry for its perpetuation of Black stereotypes. In *Coming Up Down Home: A Memoir of a Southern Childhood* (1993), the author records his struggle and survival in the South during the 1940s and 1950s. Brown's latest work of nonfiction, *Stagolee Shot Billy* (2003), probes the legendary story of Lee Shelton, who killed Billy Lyons in a **St. Louis** bar brawl in 1895.

Resources: Jean M. Bright, "Cecil Brown," in *Dictionary of Literary Biography*, vol. 33, *Afro-American Fiction Writers After 1955*, ed. Thadious M. Davis and Trudier Harris (Detroit: Gale, 1984), 32–35; Randall Kenan, "Review of *Coming Up Down Home*," *New York Times Book Review*, Aug. 22, 1993, p. 13; Edward Margolies, "Review of *Stagolee Shot Billy*," *African American Review* 38 (2004), 171–173.

John J. Han

Brown, Claude (1937–2002). Novelist and lecturer. In 1965 Claude Brown was propelled into literary prominence when his novel *Manchild in the Promised Land* was published. He expected to sell about 100 copies. By the year 2000 the book had sold over 4 million copies and had been published in fourteen languages. This autobiographical novel became the second best-selling book that Macmillan had ever released (AALB Web site). (The best-selling was *Gone with the Wind*.)

Brown was born in **Harlem** to Ossie Brock Brown and Henry Lee Brown, who had migrated there from South Carolina, seeking a better life for their family. Brown was caught up early in the street life of **Harlem, New York**. He describes his life in vivid, compelling detail in *Manchild in the Promised Land*, which chronicles the life of Sonny, a fictionalized version of Brown. Sonny's story is one of poverty, abuse, crime, drugs, gang violence, and time spent in a series of juvenile facilities. One of the facilities where Brown himself landed was Wiltwyck School for deprived and emotionally disturbed boys, located in up-state New York. In a twist of fate, Brown gained inspiration from the facility. In the book, Brown writes kindly about the director and psychologist of Wiltwyck, Dr. Ernest Papanek, and about dining at Eleanor Roosevelt's home. (Roosevelt had helped found the school.) *Manchild in the Promised Land* is dedicated to her.

In spite of his dismal early years, Brown turned his life around, left Harlem for Greenwich Village, completed high school at night, and finished graduate school at Howard University in **Washington, D.C.** While he was at Howard, one of his teachers was **Toni Morrison**, who provided feedback on his writing. Throughout those years, Brown attended class, worked in the post office, and wrote short stories and articles. His work appeared in such periodicals as *Dissent* and *Commentary* (Nelson).

After being encouraged by Dr. Papanek, as well as by a representative of Macmillan who was familiar with his writings in *Dissent* and *Commentary*, Brown agreed to write a book-length manuscript for publication. He received an advance of $2,000, but he spent it without writing anything. However, he found motivation to write after reading **Richard Wright**'s *Eight Men*.

Brown graduated from Howard University as the book was released in 1965. This was a time of social unrest in urban ghettos of the North. *Manchild in the Promised Land* struck a chord with readers. It told of one Black man's struggle to rise above his circumstances.

In 1976 Brown released his second and last book, *The Children of Ham*. Like the first book, it featured Harlem as a backdrop. *The Children of Ham* did not achieve nearly the acclaim received by *Manchild in the Promised Land*, which continued to sell steadily. He briefly attended law school at Rutgers University.

From the 1970s to the turn of the century, Brown lived on the West Coast, and then returned to the East Coast to settle in Newark, New Jersey. During this time, he continued to write, and his work appeared in such publications as *The Saturday Evening Post*, *Life*, *Look*, *Esquire*, the *New York Times*, and the *Los Angeles Times*. In addition, he found time to support a mentoring program for youth in Harlem and a Juvenile Court diversion program in Newark. He also taught and lectured around the country. He was committed to visiting prisons and talking with the inmates. Upon his death on February 2, 2002, Claude Brown left behind a powerful literary legacy based on what he knew best—his own life experiences. These experiences were shocking to some but familiar to others. *Manchild in the Promised Land* has become a classic of American literature.

Resources: Claude Brown: *Children of Ham* (New York: Stein and Day, 1976); *Manchild in the Promised Land* (New York: Macmillan, 1965); "Claude Brown," *African American Literature Book Club*, http://aalbc.com/authors/claudebrown.htm; Haki R. Madhubuti, "In Memoriam: Claude Brown (1937–2002)," *Black Issues in Higher Education*, Feb. 28, 2002, pp. xv, 416; Emmanuel S. Nelson, "Claude Brown (1937–)," in *African American Autobiographers: A Sourcebook*, ed. Emmanuel S. Nelson (Westport, CT: Greenwood Press, 2002), 51–55.

Betty W. Nyangoni

Brown, Elaine (born 1943). Former leader of the **Black Panther Party**. Brown replaced the exiled **Eldridge Cleaver** as minister of information and in 1974 replaced Bobby Seale as chairman. Thus she held a supreme position in the male-dominated, paramilitary organization started by **Huey P. Newton** and Seale in 1966. She became chairman when Seale resigned from the organization and Newton fled to Cuba to escape several felony charges. Her memoir, *A Taste of Power* (1993), recounts her rise to power within the organization and discusses how the party, during her time in charge, became more of a community-oriented organization.

Elaine Brown was born in **Philadelphia, Pennsylvania**. She moved to **Los Angeles, California**, and, like many during the 1960s, was in search of identity, purpose, and a place in America. Recruited into the party by John Huggins, she quickly rose to prominence through her intelligence and forming allegiances with powerful men within the organization. Brown was the only female present at the UCLA meeting where Alprentice "Bunchy" Carter and John Huggins, leaders of the Los Angeles Panthers, were shot to death by members of a rival organization in 1969. She also survived a shootout between Los Angeles Panthers and the police. Prior to becoming chairman, Brown traveled to Russia, North Korea, China, and Algeria, representing the Panthers, at the behest of the exiled Eldridge Cleaver. She was the first to learn of the breach between Cleaver and Newton and Seale because of the community-oriented programs, which Cleaver believed detracted from the Panthers' revolutionary emphasis. Brown wrote and performed songs that expressed the philosophy and culture of the Black Panther Party. An original song she wrote for Eldridge Cleaver, "The Meeting," became the Black Panthers' anthem. She titled her album with Seale's slogan and book title, *Seize the Time*.

As a member of the Central Committee of the Panthers, Brown assisted in running the Panther-operated Oakland Community School, which was commended by the state legislature for meeting the highest standard of elementary education. She also secured financial backing for the Black Panthers from progressive Hollywood artists and entertainers. When she became chairman, Brown continued her interest in Oakland politics, running for city council and rearranging leadership within the Panthers to reflect the large number of women members. Orchestrating a power shift from male to female, she attacked the male chauvinism within the organization. Brown won the endorsement of the Alameda County Labor Council, the United Auto Workers, the United Farm Workers, and the Teamsters Union when she ran for public office. She won these endorsements while saddled with an allegation of having committed murder and a narcotics charge. She won 44 percent of the vote; her opponent had less than 51 percent. While leading the organization, Brown had Panthers working for Representative Ron Dellums, Mayor Lionel Wilson of Oakland, and Governor Jerry Brown.

Brown resigned from the Black Panther Party in 1977, once she had maneuvered a way for Newton to return from exile, and he took over leadership of the organization. Because of Newton's drug addiction and mental instability, she was unable to work with him. Today, Brown is director of political affairs for the National Alliance for Radical Prison Reform, and vice president of the Huey P. Newton Foundation. In addition to *A Taste of Power*, she has written *The Condemnation of Little B* (2002), a book about the trial and conviction of thirteen-year-old Michael Lewis and about what Lewis's case suggests about American society.

Resources: Elaine Brown: *The Condemnation of Little B* (Boston: Beacon Press, 2002); *A Taste of Power: A Black Woman's Story* (New York: Random House, 1993); Dewey Johnson, personal interview with Regina Jennings (1997).

Regina Jennings

Brown, Fahamisha Patricia (born 1942). Literary critic. A prominent new voice among African American literary critics, Brown was born in **Chicago, Illinois**. She received a B.A. and an M.A. in English from Loyola University in Chicago and a Ph.D. from Boston University. Currently an associate professor at the College of Staten Island of the City University of New York, Brown previously held a full-time position at Austin Peay State University and part-time positions, as an adjunct professor or graduate fellow, at more than a dozen other institutions, including Boston College, Fordham University, Harvard University, the Massachusetts Institute of Technology, Tufts University, and the University of Massachusetts at Boston.

Brown has published a number of articles on African American literature and culture, but she has most come to attention for her book *Performing the Word: African American Poetry as Vernacular Culture* (1999). Praised for its efficient, yet very perceptive treatment of a topic of considerable scope, the book presents a survey of the intrinsic connections between African American **vernacular**, African American folk traditions and popular culture, and African American poetry. Although the book is organized topically rather than chronologically, it does provide considerable historical perspective on the evolution of African American poetry from the decades preceding the **Harlem Renaissance** to the decades following the height of the **Black Arts Movement**. It includes detailed, if selective, discussions of the works of such poets as **Paul Laurence Dunbar**, **James Weldon Johnson**, **Langston Hughes**, **Gwendolyn Brooks**, **Mari Evans**, **Amiri Baraka**, **Lucille Clifton**, Mona Lisa Saloy, Reg E. Gaines, and Saul Williams.

Brown's works-in-progress include *Black Women Poets: A Critical Study* and *African Women Writers: A Research Guide*.

Resources: Tricia Baird, "Review of *Performing the Word: African American Poetry as Vernacular Culture*," *Black Issues Book Review* 2 (Mar.–Apr. 2000), 42; Fahamisha Patricia Brown, *Performing the Word: African American Poetry as Vernacular Culture* (New Brunswick, NJ: Rutgers University Press, 1999); Louis J. Parascandola, "Review of *Performing the Word: African American Poetry as Vernacular Culture*," *Library Journal*, Dec. 1, 1999, p. 130; Lorenzo Thomas, "Review of *Performing the Word: African American Poetry as Vernacular Culture*," *African American Review* 35 (Fall 2001), 483–484.

Martin Kich

Brown, Frank London (1927–1962). Novelist, journalist, jazz musician, and union organizer. Frank London Brown was born in Kansas City, Missouri, but his family moved north to **Chicago, Illinois**, when he was twelve, looking for more opportunity and racial equality. Brown experienced a tough childhood growing up on the South Side: poverty, racism, violence, and drugs—all themes that Brown dealt with in his writing. Early on, he discovered refuge and artistic influence in Black **jazz** and **blues** musicians such as Joe Williams, Muddy Waters, and Thelonious Monk, an idol of Brown's with whom he would later perform at New York's Five Spot (*see* **Gillespie, Dizzy, Charlie Parker, and Thelonius Monk**). This early bond with music forged a creative and spiritual link with the medium that is apparent in his writing. Brown sees jazz and blues as an expression of Black unity and identity—a freeing force that allows one to transcend Black oppression. He attended Wilberforce University briefly before enlisting in the Army in January 1946. Always ambitious and committed to education, Brown received his B.A. degree from Roosevelt University in 1951 and attended the Kent College of Law. During this time, he wrote book reviews for local newspapers and short stories, which he performed over jazz music in Chicago's Gate of Horn nightclub, but did not receive much literary recognition. Instead, he focused his energy on the trade union movement, eventually becoming program coordinator for the United Packinghouse Workers of America, AFL–CIO.

In 1959, Brown made a career breakthrough with the publication of his first novel, *Trumbull Park*. The book was about a black family that moves into a predominantly White government-subsidized community, where they are harassed relentlessly with threats and violence by their White neighbors, while the police stand by. The novel received good reviews for its insight into racial tensions and the psychology of African Americans constantly faced with adversity, as well as for its hopeful ending in which the father figure stands up to the mob simply by walking through them, illustrating Brown's commitment to nonviolent protest and the evolving **Civil Rights Movement**. The same year, Brown was appointed an associate editor of the Black magazine *Ebony*. His second novel, *The Myth Maker*, arose out of the thesis for his master's degree, earned from the University of Chicago in 1960; however, the book was not published until 1969, seven years after his death, and consequently received little critical attention. Its main narrative is the inward meditations of a Black drug addict who has just strangled a homeless Black man, apparently for smiling at him. Even in this grim story, there is a hopeful ending in which the main character finds that life is essentially good: "a thing warm and moving and striving with good feeling" (Hauke, 27). Brown was notably sympathetic to women in his writing, as is seen in his inclusion of two strong female characters in his novels who help the men cope with the evils of the world and weaknesses in themselves. He also strongly admired prominent female authors of his day, penning flattering articles on Mahalia Jackson and **Gwendolyn Brooks**.

Brown's work continues to be overlooked, as Fleming points out, in favor of such contemporaries as *Native Son* author **Richard Wright**; however the messages of hope and nonviolence that permeate his stories show the great value of his work, which is prized for the ways it demonstrates the undeniable humanity of Black people and their real-life stories. Brown, who died from leukemia at the age of thirty-five, struggled to remain politically active and intellectually engaged until the end. At the time of his death, he was a Ph.D. candidate at the University of Chicago, as well as a fellow on the University's Committee on Social Thought and the director of its Union Research Center.

Resources: Frank London Brown: *The Myth Maker* (Chicago: Path Press, 1969); *Short Stories by Frank London Brown* (n.p., 1965); *Trumbull Park* (Chicago: Regnery, 1959); Robert E. Fleming, "Overshadowed by Richard Wright: Three Black Chicago Novelists," *Negro American Literature Forum* 7, no. 3 (Fall 1973), 75–79; Kathleen A. Hauke, in *Dictionary of Literary Biography*, vol. 76, *Afro-American Writers, 1940–55*, ed. Trudier Harris (Detroit: Gale, 1988), 25–29.

Alicia D. Williamson

Brown, Hallie Quinn (1845–1949). Teacher, poet, fiction writer, nonfiction writer, and orator. Brown is perhaps best known as a pioneering teacher and an advocate for equality in American education. She was born in **Pittsburgh, Pennsylvania**, the daughter of former slaves. Brown received her early education in Northern schools and in Canada before attending Wilberforce University in Ohio. Shortly after graduating in 1873, she began teaching African American youth in the South who had previously been denied access to an education. After becoming a seasoned educator, she accepted an appointment as a dean at Allen University in Columbia, South Carolina, in 1885 and, in 1892, as a dean at Tuskegee Institute in Alabama (later Tuskegee University). In 1893, Brown became a faculty member at Wilberforce University, where she remained until her death in 1949. Throughout her career as an educator, Brown engaged in professional speaking on behalf of equal rights for African Americans and women. Her writings capture important linguistic and cultural contributions of African Americans and record historical contributions of African American women. Brown produced eight books between 1880 and 1937. *Bits and Odds* (1880) and *Homespun Heroines and Other Women of Distinction* (1926) are her best-known works. The first consists of a collection of poems and short stories, and the second documents important African American women from a historical perspective. Owing in part to the era in which she lived, Brown attracts the interests of literary scholars because she was able to document the struggles of African Americans when most were being denied access to a quality education and civil rights though they were U.S. citizens.

Resources: Hallie Quinn Brown: *Bits and Odds: A Choice Selection of Recitations* (1880); *Homespun Heroines and Other Women of Distinction* (1926; repr. New York: Oxford University Press, 1988); Vivian Njeri Fisher, "Brown, Hallie Quinn," in *African American Women: A Biographical Dictionary*, ed. Dorthy C. Salem (New York: Garland, 1993); Darlene Clark Hine, ed., *Black Women in America: An Historical Encyclopedia* (Brooklyn, NY: Carlson, 1993); George Johnson, "Hallie Quinn Brown," in *Dictionary of American Negro Biography*, ed. Rayford W. Logan and Michael R. Winston (New York: W. W. Norton, 1982), 67–78.

Terry Carter

Brown, Henry "Box" (c. 1815–?). Fugitive slave, antislavery lecturer, and author of the *Narrative of the Life of Henry Box Brown, Written by Himself* (1849). Born probably in 1815 on a plantation outside of Richmond, Virginia, Brown wrote a narrative of his harrowing escape from **slavery** in a wooden crate and his subsequent "resurrection" in **Philadelphia, Pennsylvania**, that brought him instant celebrity and made an important contribution to our understanding of the **slave narrative**. Indeed, Richard Newman asserts that "[t]he whole purpose of Brown's *Narrative* was, and continues to be, the creation of a medium for him to tell his story" (xiv). Brown decided to escape after his wife and children were sold and sent to North Carolina. After making a plea to God to assist him in his efforts, Brown describes how "the idea suddenly flashed" upon his mind to flee in a box (57). A storekeeper named Samuel A. Smith, a White man, helped Brown into a wooden crate 3 feet long, 2½ feet deep, and 2 feet wide. Over the course of a twenty-seven-hour train ride, he traveled 350 miles and endured excruciating conditions before reaching Philadelphia, alive and free. In 1849, the year after his escape, Brown told his story to an amanuensis, Charles Stearns, and published his narrative in **Boston, Massachusetts**. Like his compatriot **Frederick Douglass**, Brown fled to England soon after the *Narrative*'s publication and the passage of the Fugitive Slave Act in 1850. He went on to become an enormously popular lecturer in England and the United States, giving public performances of his story and constructing a panorama of slavery that exposed all Americans' complicit participation in an institution that denied the humanity of African Americans. The date and place of Brown's death are unknown.

Brown's narrative chronicles themes characteristic of slave narratives: the destruction of the family, religious hypocrisy and sexual exploitation, and the pernicious effects on both slave and slaveholder alike. The resurrection motif in Brown's narrative is particularly striking and constitutes its most significant contribution to African American letters. Indeed, Brown compares his emergence from his tomblike box to Lazarus's rising from the dead: "then came my resurrection from the grave of slavery" (Brown, 62). He sang the Fortieth Psalm as he arose to freedom, an act that Newman contends was "an intentional

The resurrection of Henry "Box" Brown at Philadelphia, who escaped from Virginia in a box 3 feet long, 2½ feet deep, and 2 feet wide, ca. 1850. Courtesy of the Library of Congress.

and carefully planned performance . . . to which he must have given much thought" (xxii). Psalm 40 is "a public pronouncement of righteousness" and a celebration of deliverance (Newman, xxiii). Henry Louis Gates, Jr., argues that by confining himself to and then literally emerging from his box, Brown makes literal the "symbolic relation between death and life. . . . [He] unwittingly had replicated the symbolic aspect of the crucifixion of Christ" (ix). Noting that Brown was an evangelical Christian, Newman explains that Brown's focus on resurrection and Psalm 40 solidify the central place of Christianity in his narrative and his "understanding that the Bible at its deepest level tells his own existential story" (xxiii).

Not satisfied with writing an account of his thrilling escape from slavery, Brown resisted the "fetishizing proclivities" of some Northern abolitionists and created a massive panorama, a pictorial representation of the condition of African Americans that demonstrated the "lies and distortions" of the slave system, particularly the moment of the slave's "translation" during the Middle Passage from human being to commodity (Wolff). Titled *The Mirror of Slavery*, it depicted the hypocrisy of abolitionism that celebrated slaves who had *become* free, while Whites enjoyed a freedom that free Blacks would never achieve (Wolff). *The Mirror of Slavery* presented "images and views of American history as people of color perceived that history," and thus challenged White Americans' cultural assumptions about and sentimental representation of the United States (Newman, xxvii).

Resources: Henry Box Brown, *Narrative of the Life of Henry Box Brown*, ed. Richard Newman (1849; repr. New York: Oxford University Press, 2002); Henry Louis Gates, Jr., "Foreword," in *Narrative of the Life of Henry Box Brown* (New York: Oxford University Press, 2002), vii–x; Richard Newman, "Introduction," in *Narrative of the Life of Henry Box Brown* (New York: Oxford University Press, 2002), xi–xxxiii; Cynthia Griffin Wolff, "Passing Beyond the Middle Passage: Henry 'Box' Brown's Translations of Slavery," *Massachusetts Review* 37 (Spring 1996), 23–45.

Rebecca R. Saulsbury

Brown, John (1800–1859). Abolitionist, militant political leader, and businessman. John Brown, known as Captain Brown, Osawatomie Brown, Old Osawatomie, and the Old Man, was a radical abolitionist remembered best for his failed attack on the federal arsenal in Harpers Ferry, Virginia (now West Virginia), in 1859. The raid and his subsequent trial and execution by the state of Virginia have been described as one of the catalysts for the outbreak of the **Civil War**. In a speech at Harpers Ferry twenty-two years after the raid and sixteen years after the conclusion of the Civil War, **Frederick Douglass** commented, "If John Brown did not end the war that ended **slavery**, he did, at least, begin the war that ended slavery. . . . John Brown began the war that ended American slavery, and made this a free republic." Furthermore, in his 1881 book *The Life and Times of Frederick Douglas*, Douglas famously commented on Brown's efforts to destroy the institution of slavery (which Brown called "the sum of all villainies"): "His [John Brown's] zeal in the cause of freedom was infinitely superior to mine. Mine was as the taper light; his was as the burning sun. I could live for the slave; John Brown could die for him." After his death, Brown's life became the subject of a bevy of biographies and books. His legacy has impacted not only the course of American history but also literature, poetry, and the arts. Over the years, Brown's legacy and memory have been particularly strong in the African American community. In 1909, a half-century after Brown's raid and execution, **W.E.B. Du Bois**, in his biographical book titled *John Brown*, reflected on Brown's special relationship with African Americans and commented that Brown was "the man who of all Americans has perhaps come nearest to touching the real souls of black folk."

John Brown was born on May 9, 1800, and spent much of the first four decades of his life in a variety of failed business ventures. His life involved constant movement and travel. He resided in and drifted through states including Connecticut, Ohio, Pennsylvania, Massachusetts, New York, Maryland, and Kansas. He also traveled to Europe as part of his ultimately unsuccessful sheep and wool business. Brown fathered twenty children (several of whom would join in his abolitionist activities), seven by his first wife, Dianthe Lusk, and thirteen by his second wife, Mary Ann Day. From his earliest days, Brown hated slavery. In November 1837, he rose in an antislavery meeting in Hudson, Ohio, and solemnly declared, "Here, before God, in the presence of these witnesses, I consecrate my life to the destruction of slavery." However, due in large part to his failures as a businessman, he continued to spend much of his day-to-day existence tending to the needs of his family.

Though Brown had been involved in the **Underground Railroad** and the **abolitionist movement** generally, his first assault on the institution of slavery came in 1855 when he joined five of his sons (Jason, Frederick, Salmon, Owen, and John, Jr.) in "Bleeding Kansas." For the next several years, Brown and his men physically battled the pro-slavery "Border Ruffians" over the issue of whether Kansas should be a free or a slave state. Brown gained national notoriety when, in May 1856, he led a band of seven men into a pro-slavery settlement and murdered five pro-slavery settlers in the dead of night in an especially brutal fashion, hacking off the limbs and severing the heads of some of the victims. During his time in Kansas, Brown formulated his Harpers Ferry plan.

By this time, Brown, supported and funded by some of the wealthiest and best-known individuals in the North (the most active of the supporters known as the "Secret Six"), desired to strike at the institution of slavery in the heart of the South. He envisioned his raid on the town of Harpers Ferry as the first major battle in a broader war to dissolve the institution of slavery by force, arm men in bondage, and effect their liberation. He contemplated a series of attacks and raids on Southern towns, whereby slaves would be liberated and join his army. Brown chose Harpers Ferry because it was situated in Virginia (a slave state), was the site of a federal arsenal (which stored thousands of arms that Brown could seize and use for future military activities), and was in proximity to mountainous terrain (which Brown would utilize in his retreat). Brown and his band of twenty-one men seized the town and the federal arsenal by force on October 16–17, 1859, but were ultimately beaten back by several local militias and, ultimately, surrounded by a contingent of U.S. Marines commanded by Lt. Col. Robert E. Lee. Brown and his surviving men were captured on October 18, 1859. No one was liberated as a direct result of the raid and seventeen individuals were killed, including the mayor of Harpers Ferry (Fontaine Beckham) and several other citizens of the town. Ironically, the first person killed by the raiders was a freed Black man named Hayward Shepherd. The first husband of the maternal grandmother (Mary Langston) of poet **Langston Hughes**, Lewis Sheridan Leary, was also a member of Brown's raiding party and was killed during the encounter on October 16. Hughes's poem, "October 16: The Raid" (1931), celebrates Brown's raid and his courage.

Brown was tried by the state of Virginia and executed on December 2, 1859. On his way to the gallows, he passed a note to his jailer. The note, which Du Bois later claimed was "the mightiest Abolition document that America has known," stated: "I, John Brown, am quite certain that the crimes of this guilty land will never be purged away but with blood. I had, as I now think vainly, flattered myself that [by] very much bloodshed it might be done." As Brown had predicted, within a year and a half of his execution, the Civil War had commenced, and the crime of slavery would be purged from the land, with the blood of hundreds of thousands of Americans spilled upon sacred fields.

In the years that followed, Brown was the subject of countless books, essays, speeches, and poems. Poems, essays, and articles about Brown have been penned by such prominent African Americans as Frederick Douglass, W.E.B. Du Bois, **George Washington Williams**, Langston Hughes, and **Countee Cullen**. Brown has been praised and analyzed in the essays and poems of such writers as A. Bronson Alcott, Wendell Phillips, Henry David Thoreau, Herman Melville, John Whittier, Ralph Waldo Emerson, Carl Sandburg, and Stephen Vincent Benet.

Some of the earlier notable books on Brown include James Redpath's *The Public Life of Capt. John Brown* (1860), F. B. Sanborn's *Life and Letters of John Brown* (1891), W.E.B. Du Bois's *John Brown* (1909), and Oswald Garrison Villard's *John Brown, 1800–1859: A Biography Fifty Years After* (1910). Villard's book is considered to be the best early scholarly work on Brown, and Du Bois' work is unique in that it offers the reader a view of John Brown from an African American perspective. Du Bois considered his 1909 biography of Brown to be his favorite of all of the books

John Brown, 1859. Courtesy of the Library of Congress.

that he wrote. His book has been characterized not only as a book about Brown, but also as a reflection of the collective African American mind-set at the turn of the twentieth century, and as a window into the mind and philosophy of Du Bois on integration and segregation. As historian John David Smith wrote in an introductory essay to the 1997 reprint of Du Bois's book on Brown, "[a]lthough generations of writers have contributed a large corpus of important and insightful works on Brown, none reflect Du Bois's inner, almost mystical identification with Brown's obsession with equal rights for blacks." Excellent books in the modern era include Louis Ruchames's *A John Brown Reader* (1959), Stephen Oates's *To Purge This Land with Blood* (1970), Benjamin Quarles's *Allies for Freedom: Blacks and John Brown* (1974), Jules Abels's *Man on Fire: John Brown and the Cause of Liberty* (1971), Richard Boyer's *The Legend of John Brown* (1972), and Paul Finkelman's *His Soul Goes Marching On: Responses to John Brown and the Harpers Ferry Raid* (1995). It is likely that future literary works, by African American and other writers alike, will feature this important historical figure, as Old John Brown continues to inspire new generations of scholars and writers to ponder the lessons of his life, the justice of his actions, and the issue of equality for all individuals.

Resources: Jules Abels, *Man on Fire: John Brown and the Cause of Liberty* (New York: Macmillan, 1971); Frederick Douglass: *John Brown, an Address by Frederick Douglas at the Fourteenth Anniversary of Storer College, Harper's Ferry, West Virginia, May 30, 1881* (Dover, NH: Morning Star, 1881); *The Life and Times of Frederick Douglas: Written by Himself* (Hartford, CT: Park, 1881; reissued in many editions); W.E.B. Du Bois, *John Brown* (1909; repr. Armonk, NY: M. E. Sharpe, 1997); Paul Finkelman, ed., *His Soul Goes Marching On: Responses to John Brown and the Harpers Ferry Raid* (Charlottesville: University Press of Virginia, 1995); Langston Hughes, "October 16: The Raid," in *The Collected Poems of Langston Hughes*, ed. Arnold Rampersad (New York: Vintage Classics, 1994), 141; Stephen B. Oates: *Our Fiery Trial: Abraham Lincoln, John Brown, and the Civil War Era* (Amherst: University of Massachusetts Press, 1979); *To Purge This Land with Blood* (New York: Harper & Row, 1970); Benjamin Quarles, *Allies for Freedom: Blacks and John Brown* (1974; New York: DaCapo Press, 2001); Oswald Garrison Villard, *John Brown, 1800–1859: A Biography Fifty Years After* (Boston: Houghton Mifflin, 1910).

James A. Beckman

Brown, Linda Beatrice (born 1939). Poet and novelist. Linda Beatrice Brown was born in Akron, Ohio. Her first publication was a book of poetry titled *A Love Song to Black Men* (1974). Primarily a writer of **historical fiction**, Brown published her first novel, *Rainbow 'Roun' Mah Shoulder*, in 1984. The story of a Black woman in **the South** in the early 1900s, the novel examines the rich folk traditions of the South as they connect with social and cultural conditions of the time.

Crossing over Jordan, published in 1995, develops as a family saga spanning a 100-year period, following the women in the fictional McCloud family from the 1800s to the mid-twentieth century. Dealing with issues such as mother–daughter relationships, the emotional legacy of **slavery**, and the transforming power of love, the novel explores the struggles of four generations. Brown is currently working on a third historical fiction novel, centered on the **Civil War**.

In 1992, Brown was appointed the Willa B. Player Distinguished Professor of Humanities at Bennett College for Women in Greensboro, North Carolina. During her tenure, she was commissioned to write *The Long Walk* (1998), an examination of Willa B. Player's presidency of Bennett College. Player was the first African American female president of a four-year college in the United States, and served Bennett College from 1955 to 1966. Brown is Player's niece. In addition to her position as the Willa B. Player Distinguished Professor of the Humanities, Brown serves as assistant to the president, Johnetta B. Cole, conducting research and writing for Bennett College.

Resources: Linda Beatrice Brown: *Crossing over Jordan* (New York: Ballantine Books, 1995); *The Long Walk* (Greensboro, NC: Bennett College, 1998); *A Love Song to Black Men* (Detroit: Broadside Press, 1974); *Rainbow 'Roun Mah Shoulder* (Chapel Hill, NC: Carolina Wren Press, 1984).

Esther L. Jones

Brown, Lloyd (1913–2003). Novelist, short fiction writer, essayist, journalist, and editor. Despite a prolific, seventy-year career dedicated to anti-oppression and "Negro"-centered efforts, Lloyd Louis Brown is not known to many readers. In a 1995 essay, "A Closet Negro Comes Out," Brown asserts that he had not wavered from his youthful decision to identify as a **Negro**, a term considered old-fashioned but one he preferred in part because, unlike the term "Black," it did not focus on color. In the essay he also asserts that he chose to align himself with the **New Negro** Movement and with the spirit of **Marcus Garvey**'s vision of universal improvement. With its focus on the global and the personal, assertiveness, and wry humor, the essay is a prime example of Brown's contribution to African American literature.

Brown is perhaps best known for his collaborations with the artist/activist **Paul Robeson**. He helped Robeson write his autobiographical manifesto, *Here I Stand* (1958), and articles for *Freedom*, the newspaper that Robeson founded. Brown also wrote *The Young Paul Robeson: "On My Journey Now"* (1997), a text that detailed the David-like battles Robeson and his family waged against the Goliath of discrimination. In addition to magazine and newspaper articles, Brown wrote the novel *Iron City* and numerous realist short stories, including those reflecting the bigotry Brown faced while serving in the U.S. military during **World War II**.

Lloyd Louis Dight was born in 1913 in St. Paul, Minnesota, a city where union activities and Progressive politics flourished in the early twentieth century. An orphan, he spent his early life in a senior citizens' home. He fictionalized his experiences in the short story "God's Chosen People," published in 1948. At an early age, he changed his name to Lloyd Louis Brown to honor the radical abolitionist **John Brown**.

Brown joined the Young Communist League in 1929. He was an ardent member of the Community Party until 1953; much of his work was in trade union organizing. Brown began as a freelance journalist in the 1930s when he covered antifascist activity in Europe. He was interested in the symbiotic relationship between racism and fascism, and the links between protest abroad and at home. International resistance would become a lifelong focus of his work. In 1941, he was jailed on conspiracy charges for seven months. His experiences in prison led to *Iron City* (1951), a novel both revolutionary and romantic. (*See* **Prison Literature**.)

Brown was the editor of *New Masses* and *Masses and Mainstream* from 1946 to 1954. A chapter of an unpublished novel, *Year of Jubilee*, appeared in *Masses and Mainstream* in 1953. In one of Brown's best-known essays, "'The Deep Pit': A Review of Ellison's *Invisible Man*," Brown excoriates **Ralph Ellison** for an "anti-Negro" text that panders to the licentious tastes of a White readership. Brown also reprimanded expatriates **Chester Himes** and **Richard Wright** for their contempt for "the Negro masses," and their self-imposed alienation (*see* **Expatriate Writers**).

Resources: Herb Boyd: "Activist/Author/Journalist Lloyd L. Brown Passes," *Amsterdam News*, Apr. 17, 2003, p. 3; "Black New Yorkers: A Man Ahead of His Time,"

Amsterdam News, Jan. 2, 2004, p. 24; Lloyd L. Brown: "A Closet Negro Comes Out," *The Progressive*, Jan. 25, 1995, p. 33; "'The Deep Pit,' A Review of Ellison's *Invisible Man*," *Masses and Mainstream* 5 (1952), 39; *Iron City* (Boston: Northeastern University Press, 1994); *The Young Paul Robeson: "On My Journey Now"* (Boulder, CO: Westview Press, 1997); Clyde Haberman, "A Postscript to the Life of a Writer," *New York Times*, June 3, 2003, sec. 2, p. 1; Karen Ruth Kornweibel, "Lloyd Brown," in *The Oxford Companion to African American Literature*, ed. William L. Andrews et al. (New York: Oxford University Press, 1997); Bill V. Mullen and James Smethurst, eds., *Left of the Color Line: Race, Radicalism, and Twentieth Century Literature of the United States* (Chapel Hill: University of North Carolina Press, 2003); Paul Robeson, *Here I Stand* (Boston: Beacon Press, 1998); John-Christian Suggs, "*Iron City*, Race and Revolutionary Romanticism Behind Bars," *Legal Studies Forum* 25 (2001), 449–459.

Monifa Love Asante

Brown, Sterling A. (1901–1989). Poet, critic, and teacher. Brown's parents were part of **Washington, D.C.**'s established black middle class. Sterling Brown was the youngest of six children. His father, also named Sterling, was a minister and a teacher at Howard University's school of religion. Brown's mother, Adelaide Allen Brown, a Fisk University graduate, introduced her son to poetry. Growing up in segregated Washington, Brown rarely experienced the overt racism that characterized much of the country. Rather, living within a world of visible Black achievement helped young Sterling to develop a sense of racial pride. At seventeen, upon graduation from Dunbar High School, he received a scholarship to Williams College, where he completed a B.A. degree (1922). Brown then attended Harvard University and earned a master's degree in literature in 1923. While at Harvard, he discovered the poems of the imagists, including Amy Lowell and H.D. Poets such as Robert Frost and E. A. Robinson, with their emphases on regionalism and realism, had a significant impact on Brown's literary development.

Brown's writing career took shape during the years of the **Harlem Renaissance**, when he taught at several colleges and universities, including Virginia Seminary at Lynchburg, Lincoln University, and Fisk. His first public recognition as a poet came in 1927 when he won an award in a poetry contest sponsored by *Opportunity*. In that same year, **Countee Cullen** selected some of Brown's poems for the anthology *Caroling Dusk*. In 1929, following in his father's footsteps, Brown accepted a professorship at Howard University. He would teach there for the next forty years.

Brown is noteworthy for three specific contributions to Black literature and criticism. As an appointed official of the **Federal Writers Project** (FWP) from 1936 to 1940, he was directly involved in the government's massive efforts to catalog the literature of the land. In his position, he worked to change the image of Black people represented in FWP publications and documents. Most important, Brown influenced the means and methods by which FWP writers were to collect interviews from the last remaining former slaves. His efforts helped to eliminate much of the condescension expressed by White writers who felt the task of preserving **slave narratives** to be beneath them.

Brown's second contribution to Black literature was as a critic. Over the course of his long career, Brown described some of the most important trends and developments in Black writing. In books, articles, and anthologies such as *Negro Poetry and Drama* (1937), "Our Literary Audience," and *The Negro Caravan* (1941), he worked to broaden the scope of what could be said in and about Black literature. Particularly, Brown emphasized the importance of folk expression as an essential part of the Black literary aesthetic. While he was teaching at Howard, Brown's insistence on the **vernacular** as a primary component of Black writing had a tremendous influence on the critical perspectives of many of his students, including such figures as **Amiri Baraka** and **Stokely Carmichael**.

What Brown is best known for, however, are the stirring images that appear in his poetry. With *Southern Road*, first published in 1932, Brown established himself as a poet of considerable talent. Brown's poetry, like the work of **Langston Hughes** and **Zora Neale Hurston**, draws upon folk images for its inspiration and synthesizes those images with a variety of other literary traditions. In his experiments with **blues** forms and the use of vernacular culture, Brown develops a vivid and complex image of Black experience around a central metaphor of the southern road. This road, whether a river, a railroad, or a rocky path, provides the key symbol for his characters' progress and development. Brown's most memorable characters—Big Boy, Old Lem, and Slim Greer, for example—speak from positions that utilize folk culture as a base for knowledge and experience.

For his Depression era work, Brown received a great deal of critical acclaim from his peers. Brown's emphasis on folk issues was equally important to the poets of the **Black Arts Movement**. Though he could not be described as a practicing member of this group of artists, he nevertheless maintained a degree of familiarity, understanding, and influence with them. In more contemporary studies of his work, critics have discussed Brown as a primary example of a particularly African American approach to modernism.

Resources: Chuck D, reading of "Odyssey of Big Boy" [poem by Sterling Brown], on *Rhapsodies in Black: Music and Words from the Harlem Renaissance*, Shawn Amos, producer, 4 discs (Santa Monica, CA: Rhino Entertainment, 2000), disc 3; Joanne V. Gabbin, *Sterling A. Brown: Building the Black Aesthetic Tradition* (Westport, CT: Greenwood Press, 1985); Mark A. Sanders, *Afro-Modernist Aesthetics and the Poetry of Sterling A. Brown* (Athens: University of Georgia Press, 1999).

Dennis Chester

Brown, Wesley (born 1945). Novelist, playwright, editor, and professor. Brown has coedited two influential anthologies and written two highly regarded novels. He studied history and political science at the State University of New York at Oswego (1968). He received an MFA in creative writing from City College of New York in 1976. A professor of literature and creative writing at Rutgers, he is an author of the 1996 PBS documentary *Du Bois: A Biography in Four Voices* (along with **Toni Cade Bambara**, **Amiri Baraka**, and **Thulani Davis**), and theatrical pieces on James Baldwin (*A Prophet Among Them*, performed at the Blue Heron's Mainstage Theatre in Manhattan) and Michael Stewart (*Life During Wartime*, which takes a look at police brutality in New York City, circa the 1980s, through a loose narrative built upon the life of a young graffiti artist who lapsed into a coma and died soon after his arrest in 1983). Brown was at work on a biography of Dexter Gordon at the time of the jazz musician's death in 1990; it has not been completed.

Both the novel *Darktown Strutters* (1994) and the play *Boogie Woogie and Booker T*, performed in 1987 at **Woodie King**'s New Federal Theatre in New York, demonstrate the influence of jazz on Brown's work. The two works compel one to rethink the fine line between racial myths and historical fact in the antebellum and **Reconstruction** periods.

A past vice president of PEN American Center, Brown spent eighteen months in a federal prison in 1972 and 1973 for refusing to serve in Vietnam; *Tragic Magic*, his first novel, published in 1978, is based on his prison experience. Brown is coeditor with Amy Ling of the multicultural readers *Imagining America: Stories from the Promised Land* and *Visions of America: Personal Narratives from the Promised Land*. (*See* **Prison Literature**.)

Resources: Wesley Brown: *Darktown Strutters* (1994; Amherst: University of Massachusetts Press, 2000); *Tragic Magic* (New York: Random House, 1978); Wesley Brown and Amy Ling, eds.: *Imagining America: Stories from the Promised Land*, rev. ed. (New York: Persea Books, 2002); *Visions of America: Personal Narratives from the Promised Land* (New York: Persea Books, 1993); Louis J. Massiah, director, *W.E.B. Du Bois: A Biography in Four Voices* (New York: Public Broadcasting System, 1996).

Josh Gosciak

Brown, William Wells (1815–1884). Novelist, playwright, historian, and autobiographer. Author of the first African American **novel**, **drama**, and travel memoir (*see* **Travel Writing**), Brown was a tireless abolitionist and, after the **Civil War**, a tireless advocate for civil rights and temperance. Born in Lexington, Kentucky, he was the son of Elizabeth, a slave, and George Higgins, the half brother of Dr. John Young, her White master. In his youth, Brown's relationship to the Young family afforded him house servant status, but when the family relocated to Missouri and needed additional funds, Brown was hired out in various capacities. As a printer's assistant to "his best master," Elijah P. Lovejoy, he developed some literacy skills; as a waiter on a steamship, he recognized the possibility of freedom. In 1832, hired to assist the slave trader James Walker, Brown learned the extent of **slavery**'s inhumanity. He prepared slaves for auction, dyeing their hair and forcing them to appear happy. An abortive escape attempt in 1833 led to his sale to a steamship owner and the sale of his mother to a **New Orleans, Louisiana**, trader. On January 1, 1834, Brown escaped. Nearly frozen and desperately ill, he sought aid from Wells Brown, a Quaker who nursed him back to health; in gratitude, he added

"Wells Brown" to his name. Brown settled in Cleveland, married (1834), found work on a steamship, and became an important link on the **Underground Railroad**. When he moved to Buffalo, New York (1836), his career as an abolitionist and temperance speaker began; it expanded after he moved to **Boston, Massachusetts,** in the 1840s. (*See* **Abolitionist Movement**.)

Brown's first literary work, *Narrative of William Wells Brown, a Fugitive Slave, Written by Himself* (1847), quickly became one of the most popular abolitionist texts after **Frederick Douglass**'s narrative. Along with showing the physical abuses attendant to slavery, this text stresses slavery's cruel disregard for family ties, as masters separated husbands from wives, parents from children, siblings from siblings. In a poignant scene of separation, the *Narrative* depicts Walker removing a crying child from its mother's arms and offering it to a friend, despite the mother's pleas as she "clung around his legs." Only after Brown's own family was separated did he seek freedom. As Brown noted in his *Narrative* and other works, including *Lecture Delivered Before the Female Anti-Slavery Society of Salem* (1847), slavery was a moral issue "striking at the foundation of society." Brown's antislavery works also included a collection of songs, *The Anti-Slavery Harp* (1848).

Vulnerable as a fugitive slave, Brown moved to Europe in 1849 and gained renown as an antislavery lecturer in Great Britain. There he wrote *Three Years in Europe; or, Places I Have Seen and People I Have Met* (1852), the first travel memoir by an African American (expanded and republished in 1855 as *The American Fugitive in Europe*). As he detailed his travels in Great Britain and Europe, Brown repeatedly contrasted Continental and American attitudes toward race. Returning to the United States after friends purchased his freedom, Brown published the first novel by an African American, *Clotel; or, The President's Daughter* (1854). Its plot fictionalizes Thomas Jefferson's relationship with his slave **Sally Hemings** and emphasizes slavery's disregard for family ties. Over the next fourteen years, Brown published three more versions of the novel.

In 1856, Brown recorded another first for African Americans when he wrote a play, *The Doughface Baked; or, How to Give a Northern Man a Backbone* (variously titled; no extant copies), a satire featuring Rev. Nehemiah Adams of Boston and condemning the Christian church's unwillingness to denounce slavery. His second play, *The Escape; or, A Leap for Freedom* (1858), a drama in five acts, apparently was never staged, although it frequently was read in public.

After compiling an abolitionist tract, *The Anti-Slavery Lectures* (1862), Brown turned his literary talents to history, publishing *The Black Man: His Antecedents, His Genius, and His Achievements* (1863). Immensely popular, the book went through ten editions in three years; it featured fifty-four biographical sketches of African Americans and was intended to counter racist views. Brown wrote two other histories—*The Negro in the American Rebellion: His Heroism and His Fidelity* (1867) and *The Rising Son; or, the Antecedents and the Advancement of the Colored Race* (1874). The former, a carefully documented review of African American participation in the Civil War, combined first-person battle accounts, reports from commanding officers, and Brown's interpretation of these; the latter was a historical study of Blacks in the United States, Africa, and the Caribbean.

In his autobiography, *My Southern Home; or, The South and Its People* (1880), Brown recounted many experiences of slaves and illustrated the continuing prejudices against freed Blacks, asserting that Blacks must be protected "in their natural, lawful, and acquired rights." Brown recounted difficulties that Blacks, being uneducated, encountered after freedom, but maintained that "future generations will marvel at the calm forbearance, good sense, and Christian zeal of the American Negro of the nineteenth century."

Resources: William Wells Brown: *The American Fugitive in Europe* (Boston: John P. Jewett, 1855); *The Anti-Slavery Harp: A Collection of Songs for Anti-Slavery Meetings* (Boston: B. Marsh, 1848); *The Black Man: His Antecedents, His Genius, and His Achievements* (New York: Thomas Hamilton; Boston: R. F. Wallcut, 1863); *Clotel; or, The President's Daughter* (1854; Boston: Bedford-St. Martin's, 2000); *The Escape; or, A Leap for Freedom: A Drama in Five Acts* (Boston: R. F. Wallcut, 1858); *My Southern Home; or, The South and Its People* (Boston: A. G. Brown, 1880); *The Narrative of William Wells Brown, a Fugitive Slave* (Boston: Anti-Slavery Office, 1847); *The Negro in the American Rebellion: His Heroism and His Fidelity* (Boston: Lee & Shepard, 1867); *The Rising Son; or, The Antecedents and Advancement of the Colored Race* (Boston: A. G. Brown, 1874); *Three Years in Europe; or, Places I Have Seen and People I Have Met* (London: Charles Gilpin; Edinburgh, Oliver and Boyd, 1852); John Ernest, *Liberation Historigraph: African American Writers and the Challenge of History, 1794–1861* (Chapel Hill: University of North Carolina Press, 2004); Maria Giulia Fabi, *Passing and the Rise of the African American Novel* (Urbana: University of Illinois Press, 2001); William Edward Farrison, *William Wells Brown: Author and Reformer* (Chicago: University of Chicago Press, 1969); L. H. Whelchel, Jr., *My Chains Fell Off: William Wells Brown, Fugitive Abolitionist* (Lanham, MD: University Press of America, 1985).

Gloria A. Shearin

Browne, Theodore (c. 1910–1979). Playwright, actor, theater organizer, novelist, and teacher. Browne was born in Suffolk, Virginia; was educated in the New York City public schools; and in the 1930s made his way to Seattle, where he began working with the Civic Repertory Theatre, which became the Seattle Repertory Theatre and then the Seattle Negro Unit of the Federal Theatre Project (Lopez). He wrote and helped produce four plays while affiliated with this theater group. The best-known of these four is *Natural Man*, based on the real man who was behind the myth of Black folk hero John Henry and who was, in fact, a railroad worker in West Virginia in the 1870s. First produced in 1937, *Natural Man* is still being produced, including a production at Stanford University in February 2003. Browne's three other plays are *Down Moses*, *Swing, Gates, Swing*, and a revision of Aristophanes' *Lysistrata*, set in Ethiopia. Following his involvement with theater in Seattle, Browne returned to the East Coast and earned a B.A. from the City College of New York in 1941. With **Theodore Ward** and **Langston Hughes**, Browne helped to establish the Negro Playwrights Company. He later earned an M.Ed. from Northeastern University in **Boston**. He settled in Roxbury, Massachusetts, and became a public school teacher. In 1955 he published *The Band Will Not Play Dixie: A Novel of Suspense* (*See* **Negro Units**.)

Resources: Theodore Browne, *The Band Will Not Play Dixie: A Novel of Suspense* (New York: Exposition Press, 1955); Luciana Lopez, "Theodore Browne, 1910?–1979," *Black Drama Biography*, http://www.alexanderstreet2.com; Bernard L. Peterson, Jr., *Early Black American Playwrights and Dramatic Writers: A Biographical Directory and Catalog of Plays, Films, and Broadcasting Scripts* (Westport, CT: Greenwood Press, 1990); Zanthe Taylor, "Singing for Their Supper: The Negro Units of the Federal Theater Project and Their Plays," *Theater* 27, no. 2–3 (1997), 43–59; Allen Woll, *Dictionary of the Black Theatre: Broadway, Off-Broadway, and Selected Harlem Theatres* (Westport, CT: Greenwood Press, 1983).

Hans Ostrom

Brownies' Book, The **(1920–1921).** Children's periodical. The first monthly issue of *The Brownies' Book* appeared in January 1920 and sought to "imbue children with the spirit and substance of the Harlem Renaissance" (Harris, "Race Consciousness," 193). Although the periodical published only twenty-four issues, it was an "aesthetic and literary innovation" (Daniel, 106) and is generally recognized as the first children's magazine by and for African Americans (Harris, "African American," 546). The periodical began as an outgrowth of an annual children's issue published by *The Crisis*, the official organ of the **NAACP**. Created by **W.E.B. Du Bois**, it was dedicated to all children, but especially to the "Children of the Sun," whose ancestors were from Africa. Together with literary editor **Jessie Redmon Fauset** and business manager Augustus Granville Dill, Du Bois challenged existing children's textbooks, **children's literature**, and literary magazines that negatively depicted African American children as "inferior, happy-go-lucky, and childlike" (Harris, "Race Consciousness," 192). In the October 1919 issue of *The Crisis*, Du Bois outlined seven goals for the new magazine:

(a) to make colored children realise that being "colored" is a normal, beautiful thing[;] (b) to make them familiar with the history and achievements of the Negro race[;] (c) to make them know that other colored children have grown into beautiful, useful and famous persons[;] (d) to teach them delicately a code of honor and action in their relations with white children[;] (e) to turn their little hurts and resentments into emulation, ambition and love of their own homes and companions[;] (f) to point out the best amusements and joys and worthwhile things of life[;] (g) to inspire them to prepare for definite occupations and duties with a broad spirit of sacrifice. (Diggs, 391)

By achieving these goals, the editors hoped "to nurture and socialize a group of children with attributes associated with the 'New Negro'" (Harris, "Race Consciousness," 192).

Issues of *The Brownies' Book* were filled with stories, poems, plays, games, biographies, and history. All but one of the original drawings were done by Black artists. In addition, writers of the **Harlem Renaissance** published their creative work in the magazine. **Nella Larsen** and **Arna Bontemps** contributed to the publication, as did **Langston Hughes**, who was a teenager in his last year at Central High School in Cleveland at the time (Ostrom). In addition to feature articles, there were several regular columns. "As the Crow Flies," written by Du Bois, reported on current events from around the world. Jessie Fauset, who penned "The Judge," responded to questions of everyday life through instructive storytelling. "The Jury" reprinted letters from the "brownies," young readers of the magazine, who often gave poignant accounts of racial discrimination. "Little People of the Month" portrayed individual children, celebrating their intelligence and creativity. Parents had a voice, too; their letters appeared in "The Grown-ups' Corner."

By December 1921 *The Brownies' Book* had a circulation of 4,000 but needed 12,000 to become financially viable (Diggs, 392–393). Unable to attract more subscribers, the publication ceased in December 1922. In the last issue, Du Bois reiterated the need for children's literature that reflected a racially diverse world (Daniel, 106).

Resources: Walter C. Daniel, *Black Journals of the United States* (Westport, CT: Greenwood Press, 1982); Irene Diggs, "DuBois and Children," *Phylon* 37, no. 4 (1976), 370–399; Violet J. Harris: "African American Children's Literature: The First One Hundred Years," *Journal of Negro Education* 59, no. 4 (1990), 540–555; "Race Consciousness, Refinement, and Radicalism: Socialization in *The Brownies' Book*," *Children's Literature Association Quarterly* 14, no. 3 (1989), 192–196; Dianne Johnson-Feelings, *Telling Tales: The Pedagogy and Promise of African American Literature for Youth* (Westport, CT: Greenwood Press, 1990); Diane Johnson-Feelings, ed., *The Best of The Brownies' Book* (New York: Oxford University Press, 1996); Dianne Johnson and Catherine E. Lewis, "Introduction" [Children's and Young Adult Literature], *African American Review* 32, no. 1 (1998), 5–7; Hans Ostrom, *A Langston Hughes Encyclopedia* (Westport, CT: Greenwood Press, 2002), 63, 69; Courtney Vaughn-Roberson and Brenda Hill, "*The Brownies' Book* and *Ebony Jr.!*: Literature as a Mirror of the Afro-American Experience," *Journal of Negro Education* 58, no. 4 (1989), 494–510.

Lori Ricigliano

Bryan, Ashley (born 1923). Illustrator, folklorist, poet, and storyteller. Bryan is known as a prolific illustrator and writer of children's books. He finds inspiration for his work in African and West Indian oral traditions, particularly folktales, poetry, and music. Born to parents who emigrated from Antigua, Bryan grew up in the Bronx in New York City. His interest in illustrating emerged in kindergarten when he made a book of ABCs. Bryan earned degrees at Cooper Union and Columbia University, and he won a Fulbright scholarship to study art in Europe. He taught at Queens College and Lafayette College and then joined the Art Department at Dartmouth College, where he taught from 1973 to 1985 and is currently professor emeritus.

Bryan has written or edited and illustrated more than thirty children's books, most of them in print at this writing. His works have garnered national recognition, including a Coretta Scott King Award for *Beat the Story-Drum, Pum-Pum* (1980) and several Coretta Scott King Honor Book Citations for his illustrations and writing. He received the May Hill Arbuthnot Lecture Award in 1990 and won the University of Southern Mississippi Medallion in 1994, an annual award for children's literature.

Bryan is acclaimed as a master storyteller in the African griot tradition. His anthologies, such as *The Dancing Granny* (1977), *All Night, All Day: A Child's First Book of African-American Spirituals* (1991), and *The Ox of the Wonderful Horns and Other African Folktales* (1993), illustrated with his vibrant paintings and drawings, reflect his commitment to introducing oral traditions of the African **diaspora** to children. He has advanced the works of African American writers by illustrating books such as *Carol of the Brown King: Nativity Poems* by **Langston Hughes** (1998), *Aneesa Lee and the Weaver's Gift* (1999) by **Nikki Grimes**, and *Jump Back, Honey: The Poems of Paul Laurence Dunbar* (1999).

Resources: Ashley Bryan: *All Night, All Day: A Child's First Book of African-American Spirituals* (1991; repr. New York: Aladdin, 2004); *Beat the Story-Drum, Pum-Pum* (New York: Atheneum, 1980; repr. New York: Aladdin Books, 1987); *The Dancing Granny* (1977; repr. New York: Aladdin Books, 1987); *The Ox of the Wonderful Horns and Other African Folktales* (New York: Atheneum, 1993); *Sing to the Sun* (New York: Harper Trophy, 1996); Ashley Bryan Papers, de Grummond Children's Literature Collection, University of Southern Mississippi; "Bryan, Ashley," http://infotrac.galegroup.com; Ramon Royal Ross, "Bryan, Ashley," in *The Oxford Companion to African American Literature*, ed. William L. Andrews, Frances Smith Foster, and Trudier Harris (New York: Oxford University Press, 1997), 108–109; Diane Telgen, "Bryan, Ashley F.," in *Something About the Author*, vol. 72 (Detroit: Gale, 1993), 26–29.

Rhondda R. Thomas

Buchanan, Shonda (born 1968). Poet. Born in Kalamazoo, Michigan, Shonda Buchanan, who has recently taken the name Nyesha Khalfani, grew up in a large, poor family of mixed African American and Native American ancestry. She subsequently settled in **Los Angeles, California**, where she has worked as an editor and a freelance writer for a number of publications, including *L.A. Weekly*, the *Los Angeles Times*, and *Turning Point* magazine. More recently, Buchanan has taught literature at Loyola Marymount University. She has received a writing fellowship from the Sundance Institute and an Emerging Voice fellowship from the P.E.N. Center U.S.A. West.

Buchanan's first collection of poems is the chapbook *Strangefruitanickelamoon* (1994). In form, her poems are often more vertical than horizontal—that is, they are composed of very short lines of one to six words and are forty to fifty lines long. This sort of form creates the initial impression that her poems are very accessible and straightforward, but ultimately it serves to draw the reader into complex and often subtle treatments of themes related to family life, relationships between women, and racial issues. Her poetry is colloquial but reflective, straightforwardly descriptive and yet very attentive to nuances of detail.

Buchanan's ancestry has provided her with materials that she has incorporated into an unpublished novel, *Baring Cross*. She has also been working on memoirs of the women in her immediate family.

Selections of Buchanan's work have been chosen for inclusion in several anthologies, most notably **Kevin Powell**'s *Step into a World: A Global Anthology of the New Black Literature* (2000) and *Catch the Fire!!! A Cross-Generational Anthology of Contemporary African-American Poetry* (1998). Her articles, reviews, poems, and short stories have appeared in such periodicals as *Caffeine* magazine, *The Drumming Between Us*, and *Venice* magazine. In addition to establishing herself as a writer, she is a performance artist with credits on stage and screen.

Resource: Shonda Buchanan, *Strangefruitanickelamoon* (Inglewood, CA: SB Publications, 1994).

Martin Kich

Buckley, Gail Lumet (born 1937). Journalist and author. Born in **Pittsburgh, Pennsylvania**, and raised in California and New York City, Buckley comes from a long line of educators, politicians, activists, and entrepreneurs. It was probably the experiences of her mother, legendary actress and singer Lena Horne, that sparked Buckley's interest in Blacks in the military. During **World War II**, the United Service Organization (USO) sent entertainers to perform for the troops in order to keep up their morale; Horne was supposed to sing for soldiers stationed at a camp in Arkansas. The Army was segregated at the time; in the first show, she was supposed to sing to White soldiers and in the second show, to Black soldiers. But when Lena walked out for the second show, German prisoners of war were seated in the front rows—ahead of African American soldiers. "Black GIs were treated worse than the enemy by their own government," Buckley explained to a radio audience. "My mother walked out. The outcome was that she was dismissed from the USO and she then went on to entertain Black troops at camps—at her own expense." Buckley, a graduate of Radcliffe College, devoted fourteen years of her life to researching the neglected role of African Americans in the military, and her book *American Patriots: The Story of Blacks in the Military from the Revolution to Desert Storm* earned an RFK Memorial Book Award.

In her first book, Buckley stayed a little bit closer to home. *The Hornes: An American Family*, traced six generations of Buckley's family tree, from her family's "founding mother," Sinai Reynolds, a slave who sold cakes on street corners to buy her freedom, to great-grandmother Cora Horne, an early feminist, to her own mother, Lena. Buckley and her brother, Teddy, grew up in the lap of luxury; their parents, Lena Horne and Louis J. Jones, divorced in 1944. Buckley has been married twice; her marriage to director Sidney Lumet ended in divorce, and she is currently married to Kevin Buckley, an editor.

Resources: Gail Lumet Buckley: *American Patriots: The Story of Blacks in the Military from the Revolution to Desert Storm* (New York: Random House, 2001); *American Patriots: A Young People's Edition*, adapted by Tonya Bolden and Gail Lumet Buckley (New York: Crown, 2003); *The Hornes: An American Family* (New York: Knopf, 1986); *Jubilee: The Emergence of African American Culture*, with Howard Dodson, Amiri Baraka, Gayraud S. Wilmore, and John Hope Franklin (New York: Simon and Schuster, 2003).

Joy Duckett Cain

Bullins, Ed (born 1935). Playwright, novelist, poet, and journalist. Best known as a dramatist, Bullins was influenced by the work of **Amiri Baraka** and has sought to reach Black audiences through realistic dramas laced with biting social commentary and criticism. He is considered an important member of the **Black Arts Movement**.

Born on July 2, 1935, Bullins spent his childhood and adolescence in his native **Philadelphia, Pennsylvania**. In 1952, he dropped out of high school and joined the Navy, where he embarked on a "self-education program." After three years in the Navy, Bullins moved to Los Angeles, where he earned his G.E.D. and then began a course of study at Los Angeles Community College. In 1964, he moved to **San Francisco, California**, where he pursued an undergraduate degree in creative writing and comparative literature at San Francisco State College. While in California, Bullins served as minister of culture for the **Black Panther Party** for Self Defense and, with Marvin X (a.k.a. Marvin Jackmon), founded. Black House, a center for performance, theater, and poetry that served for a short time as Black Panther Party headquarters. In 1965, Bullins dropped out of college to pursue playwriting. He finally earned a B.A. at Antioch University in 1989 and an MFA in playwriting from San Francisco State University in 1994.

In August 1965, at the age of thirty, Bullins made his theatrical debut at the Firehouse Repertory Theatre in San Francisco with a bill of one-act plays that included *How Do You Do?*, *Dialect Determinism, or The Rally*, and *Clara's Ole Man*. Two years later, he joined Robert Macbeth's New Lafayette Theatre as resident playwright. Bullins remained with the New Lafayette until 1973, when the theater closed; during his tenure there, he served as associate director, edited *Black Theatre*, and headed the Black Theatre Workshop, which served as a training ground for such noteworthy playwrights as Richard Wesley, **OyamO**, and Martha Charles.

Bullins's first full-length play, *In the Wine Time*, debuted in 1968. The play concerns the limited social and political options available to poor Black people in urban centers. The play was the first in Bullins's Twentieth-Century Cycle, which deals with a group of friends growing up in the 1950s and includes *The Corner* (1968), *In New England Winter* (1969), *The Duplex* (1970), *The Fabulous Miss Marie* (1971), *Home Boy* (1976), and *Daddy* (1977).

The year 1975 witnessed the premiere of Bullins's best-known and most widely acclaimed play, *The Taking of Miss Janie*. The play, which concerns "the failed alliance of an interracial group of political idealists in the 1960s" ("Bullins, Ed"), was awarded both the New York Drama Critics' Circle Award and an Obie.

Throughout his long career, Bullins has written more than 100 plays, though the playwright regards only thirty or so of them as "real" plays. Among his other noteworthy works are *It Has No Choice* (1966), *Goin' a Buffalo* (1967), *A Son Come Home; The Electronic Nigger* (which, along with *Clara's Ole Man*, won the Vernon Rice Drama Desk Award in 1968), *Street Sounds* (1970), *The Psychic Pretenders* (1972), *The Mystery of Phillis Wheatley* (1976), *Leavings* (1980), *Steve and Velma* (1980), *American Griot* (1990), and *Salaam, Huey Newton, Salaam* (1991). Much of Bullins's work is richly naturalist and is distinguished by traces of **Black Nationalism**, street lyricism, and interracial tension ("Bullins, Ed"). For his dramatic work, Bullins has received a number of distinguished awards and fellowships, including Guggenheim fellowships; Rockefeller Foundation playwriting grants; an AUDELCO Award; and a National Endowment for the Arts playwriting grant.

At present, Bullins is distinguished artist-in-residence at Northeastern University in **Boston, Massachusetts**, where he has taught since 1995. He also participates in the Cherry Lane Theater Mentor Project in New York City.

Resources: Gerald M. Berkowitz: "Ed Bullins," in *International Dictionary of Theatre*, vol. 2, *Playwrights*, ed. Mark Hawkins-Dady (Chicago: St. James Press, 1994), 191–193; "Bullins, Ed," in *Merriam-Webster's Encyclopedia of Literature* (New York: Merriam-Webster, 1995); Ed Bullins: *Duplex* (New York: William Morrow, 1971); *The Electronic Nigger, and Other Plays* (London: Faber, 1968); *Five Plays* (Indianapolis, IN: Bobbs-Merrill, 1969); *Four Dynamite Plays* (New York: William Morrow, 1972); *New—Lost Plays by Ed Bullins: An Anthology* (Honolulu, HI: New Publishing, 1994); *The Theme Is Blackness: "The Corner" and Other Plays* (New York: William Morrow, 1973); Ed Bullins, ed.: *The New Lafayette Theatre Presents* (Garden City, NY: Anchor, 1974); *New Plays from the Black Theatre: An Anthology* (New York: Bantam, 1969); Nathan L. Grant, "Ed Bullins," in *The Oxford Companion to African American Literature*, ed. William L. Andrews et al. (New York: Oxford University Press, 1997), 109–111; "Ed Bullins," in *African-American Writers: A Dictionary*, ed. Shari Dorantes Hatch and Michael R. Strickland (Santa Barbara, CA: ABC-CLIO, 2000), 41–43; Samuel A. Hay, *Ed Bullins: A Literary Biography* (Detroit: Wayne State University Press, 1997); Terry Miller, "Ed Bullins," in *McGraw-Hill Encyclopedia of World Drama*, ed. Stanley Hochman, 2nd ed., vol. 1 (New York: McGraw-Hill, 1984), 428–429; John M. Reilly: "Ed Bullins," in *Contemporary American Dramatists*, ed. K. A. Berney (London: St. James Press, 1994), 75–81; "Ed Bullins," in *Contemporary Dramatists*, 6th ed. (London: St. James Press, 1998), 81–83.

Heath A. Diehl

Bunkley, Anita Richmond (born 1944). Novelist, short story writer, and essayist. A native of Ohio and a graduate of Mount Union College, Bunkley is one of the first contemporary African American writers of **romance novels**.

This group includes Rochelle Ayers and **Donna Hill**. After her divorce from her first husband, she moved to Texas in the early 1980s with her two daughters and launched her writing career with *Emily, the Yellow Rose* (1989). After thirty-two rejections from mainstream publishers who thought the novel would not sell, Bunkley founded Rinard Press with her second husband, Crawford B. Bunkley III. Rinard Press published and sold 10,000 paperback copies of *Emily* (Gangelkoff, E4).

When Bunkley published *Black Gold* (1994), her second novel, she negotiated a contract with mass-market publisher Signet to print the work in hardcover. For the next three years, she published a romance a year under the Signet imprint: *Wild Embers* (1996), *Starlight Passage* (1997), and *Balancing Act* (1998). Writing about social inequities, Bunkley strives for historical accuracy in her novels by traveling to various sites and researching topics she writes about.

Despite her busy schedule that keeps her writing, touring as a motivational speaker, and teaching creative writing to fourth graders in Houston's Writing in the Schools Program, Bunkley has edited two anthologies with Eva Rutland and Sandra Kitt: *Sisters* (1996), a collection of three novellas in which Bunkley's "Into Tomorrow" appears, and *Girlfriends* (1999), a short story collection in which Bunkley's "At the End of the Day" is the lead story. *Steppin' Out with Attitude* (1998), a heterogeneous mix of stories, quotations, and testimonials, offers fifteen steps for young women to succeed in business and other ventures. Bunkley's most recent novels are *Mirrored Life*, a mystery (2002), and *Relative Interest* (2003).

Resources: Anita Richmond Bunkley: *Balancing Act* (New York: Signet, 1998); *Black Gold* (New York: Signet, 1995); *Emily, the Yellow Rose* (Houston, TX: Rinard, 1989); *Mirrored Life* (New York: Dafina, 2002); *Relative Interest* (New York: Dafina, 2003); *Starlight Passage* (New York: Signet, 1997); *Steppin' Out with Attitude: Sister, Sell Your Dream* (New York: HarperPerennial, 1998); *Wild Embers* (New York: Signet, 1996); Anita R. Bunkley, Sandra Kitt, and Eva Rutland, eds.: *Girlfriends* (New York: Harper, 1999); *Sisters* (New York: Dutton, 1996); Rita B. Dandridge: *Black Women's Activism: Reading African American Women's Historical Romances* (New York: Peter Lang, 2004); "Race and Womanist Representation in Anita Richmond Bunkley's *Black Gold* and *Wild Embers*," *Journal of Intercultural Discipline* 1, no. 1 (Fall 2002), 31–40; Bonnie Gangelhoff, "Teacher–Author Turns Her Novel Idea for a History Lesson into Sweet Success," *Houston Post*, Mar. 6, 1994, p. E4.

Rita B. Dandridge

Burrill, Mary ("Mamie") Powell (c. 1882–1946). Playwright. Burill stands as a pioneering African American playwright whose dramatic work advocated social change/justice and whose educational endeavors influenced the shape and direction of African American theater in the early-to-mid-twentieth century.

Born around 1882 to John H. and Clara E. Burrill, she grew up in **Washington, D.C.** Little is known about her childhood and adolescence. She attended and graduated from the M Street School (later Dunbar High School) in 1901. Immediately following her graduation from high school, Burill began a three-year course of study at the Emerson College of Oratory (later Emerson University). She returned to Emerson in 1929 and, the following year, earned a BLI (Bachelor of Literary Interpretation).

Though Burrill is best known as a playwright, her work received only moderate attention during her lifetime. In April 1919, *Aftermath*, a realistic play about a **World War I** soldier who returns home to South Carolina to discover that his father has been lynched, was published in *The Liberator* (*see* **Lynching**). That September, the *Birth Control Review* published another of Burrill's "major" plays, *They That Sit in Darkness*, considered by some critics to be "the first feminist play written by a Black woman" (Perkins 198). *They That Sit in Darkness* was a fairly radical play for its time, considering that it "conveys the message that a woman has an inalienable right to freedom of choice in matters concerning her own body" (Roses and Randolph, 37). On May 8, 1928, *Aftermath* was produced by the Krigwa Players Little Negro Theatre in association with the Workers Drama League of New York City.

Burrill's only other major play, *Unto the Third and Fourth Generations: A One-Act Play of Negro Life* (a rewrite of *They That Sit in Darkness*), was penned around 1929. It was published in Emerson's yearbook in 1930 and was dubbed "Best Junior Play of the Year."

While Burrill achieved some success as a playwright, she devoted her life to education. Around 1905, she returned to Dunbar High School, where she taught English and drama with her companion, **Angelina Grimké**. While teaching at Dunbar, Burrill mentored students who would go on to become prominent figures in African American theater, including **Willis Richardson**, the first Black dramatist to have his work produced on Broadway; and **May Miller**, the most published Black female playwright of the 1920s and 1930s. She also directed classical plays throughout the Washington, D.C., area.

Between 1907 and 1911, Burrill served as director of the Washington, D.C., Conservatory of Music and School of Expression, where she taught elocution, public speaking, and dramatics. In 1912, she met and began a twenty-five-year companionship with Lucy Diggs Slowe, dean of women at Howard University. Slowe died in 1937.

Burrill retired from Dubar in 1944 and moved to New England. Two years later, on March 13, 1946, she died in New York City after an extended illness.

Resources: Mary Burrill, "They That Sit in Darkness," in *Black Theatre USA*, ed. James V. Hatch and Ted Shine (New York: Macmillan, 1974); Rachel France, *A Century of Plays by American Women* (New York: Richards Rosen Press, 1979); James V. Hatch and Ted Shine, eds., *Black Theatre USA* (New York: Macmillan, 1974); Gloria T. Hull, *Color, Sex and Poetry: Three Women Writers of the Harlem Renaissance* (Bloomington: Indiana University Press, 1987); Barbara Molette, "Black Women Playwrights," *Black World* 25 (Apr. 1976), 28–33; Kathy A. Perkins, "Burrill, Mary P.," in *Black Women in America: An Historical Encyclopedia*, ed. Darlene Clark Hine (Brooklyn, NY: Carlson, 1993), 198; Lorraine Elena Roses and Ruth Elizabeth

Randolph, "Burrill, Mary ('Mamie')," in *Harlem Renaissance and Beyond: Literary Biographies of 100 Black Women Writers, 1900–1945* (Boston: G. K. Hall, 1990), 36–38; Patricia A. Young, "Burrill, Mary Powell," in *African American Women: A Biographical Dictionary*, ed. Dorothy C. Salem (New York: Garland, 1993), 81–82.

Heath A. Diehl

Burroughs, Margaret Taylor Goss (born 1917). Artist, educator, writer, museum founder and director, arts organizer, and political activist. Burroughs is defined by her unswerving commitment to disseminating information about African American history and culture, especially to young people. She was born November 1, 1917, in St. Rose, Louisiana, to Christopher Alexander Taylor, a farmer, and Octavia Pierre Taylor, a domestic worker. Burroughs displays a global awareness that is informed by her international travels, including visits to African countries, the West Indies, China, Brazil, and Mexico. She is a well-known artist who taught in the **Chicago, Illinois**, public schools and colleges from 1940 to 1979.

When Burroughs was five years old, her family moved to Chicago, where she attended Doolittle, St. Elizabeth, and Carter elementary schools. After graduating from Englewood High School in 1933, she earned a teaching certificate for elementary grades from the Chicago Normal College in 1937, and an upper grade art certificate from the college (renamed Chicago Teachers College) in 1939 (it is now Chicago State University), and began substitute teaching in elementary schools (1940–1945). In her third year at Chicago Teachers College Burroughs met and married Bernard Goss (1939); they had one daughter. While teaching and working on her own art projects Burroughs continued her education, earning a B.F.A. in 1946 and an M.F.A. in art education in 1948, both from the Art Institute of Chicago. By 1947, she was divorced from Goss and teaching at DuSable High School (1946–1968), and had illustrated and published her first book, *Jasper, the Drummin' Boy*. Following her retirement from DuSable, she taught at Wilson Junior College (now Kennedy King College) until 1979.

In 1949, Burroughs married her second husband, Charles Gordon Burroughs, a museum curator; in 1961, they founded the Ebony Museum of African American History, now known as the DuSable Museum of African American History. Many of the museum's artifacts came from the Burroughs' private collection that they had gathered during their extensive international travels. As an educator and artist, Burroughs was able to infuse her works with the African American culture that is central to her sense of identity. Starting with the multicultural perspective that was a part of her **Creole** ancestry and visible in the small yet diverse community outside of Louisiana, Burroughs has maintained a deep and abiding love for her African and African American heritage. This spirit is evidenced in her first poetry collection, *What Shall I Tell My Children Who Are Black?* (1968), and in her visual art, for which she has received many awards and honors. With **Dudley Randall**, she edited the poetry anthology *For Malcolm* (1967), in honor of **Malcolm X**.

Resources: Margaret T. G. Burroughs: *Jasper, the Drummin' Boy* (New York: Viking, 1947; rev. ed., Chicago: Follett, 1970); *Life with Margaret: The Official Autobiography* (Chicago: Time Publishing and Media Group, 2003); *What Shall I Tell My Children Who Are Black?* (Chicago: The Cultural Fund, 1968; repr. 1992); Mary Jane Dickerson, "Margaret T.G. Burroughs," in *Dictionary of Literary Biography*, vol. 41, *Afro-American Poets Since 1955*, ed. Trudier Harris and Thadious Davis (Detroit: Gale, 1985), 47–54; Dudley Randall and Margaret G. Burroughs, eds., *For Malcolm: Poems on the Life and the Death of Malcolm X* (Detroit: Broadside Press, 1967).

B. J. Bolden

Burton, Annie Louise (1860–?). Autobiographer. Burton's **autobiography**, *Memories of Childhood's Slavery Days* (1909), provides a child's view of the **Civil War** and the transition to postwar Southern society. Divided into eight sections, the work combines Burton's first-person account with additional material that supplements her narrative. "Recollections of a Happy Life" and "Reminiscences" offer Burton's memories of her childhood in **slavery** and episodes from her adult life. The work opens with fragmented details about her life on a plantation. Burton's style is largely dispassionate; she reports, with an often jarring lack of interpretation, such facts as her mother's escape, the hanging of a slave who was framed for the murder of a White man, and the fact that her father, a White plantation owner, never acknowledged her as his child. The remainder of this first section illustrates Burton's ability to work hard and to earn money, which she used in further endeavors, including a restaurant and a boardinghouse. "Reminiscences" repeats some of the facts given previously but focuses more closely on the immediate repercussions of the end of slavery, including Burton's transition from playful child into plantation worker. Burton devotes five pages to the story of how her mother, with barely enough food to keep her children from starving, nevertheless shares what she has with a White woman who is traveling with her own children to find her relations; the similarities between the widows continue the theme introduced in Burton's opening paragraphs: that the White and Black children on the plantation differed only in how they were treated by others.

The remaining half of the book begins with "A Vision," Burton's account of her conversion to Christianity in 1875 following a severe illness and her attendance at an evening school. This is followed by one of her essays from that time, a short biography of Abraham Lincoln, and Dr. P. Thomas Stanford's "The Race Question in America," which rejects the stereotypical faults of Black people and urges a broader recognition of Black contributions to the United States, both in the past and in the present. Burton concludes with a selection of her favorite poems and hymns. Although the final chapters are somewhat unusual within an autobiography, they illustrate the larger social context in which Burton was writing and underscore the importance of literature and religion within antebellum society.

Resources: William L. Andrews, "The Representation of Slavery and the Rise of Afro-American Literary Realism (1865–1920)," in *Slavery and the Literary Imagination*, ed. Deborah McDowell and Arnold Rampersad (Baltimore: Johns Hopkins University Press, 1989), 62–80; Annie L. Burton, *Memories of Childhood's Slavery Days* (Boston: Ross, 1909); Gabrielle Foreman, "Annie Louise Burton," in *The Oxford Companion to African American Literature*, ed. William L. Andrews et al. (New York: Oxford University Press, 1997); *Six Women's Slave Narratives* (New York: Oxford University Press, 1988).

Tracey S. Rosenberg

Burton, LeVar (born 1957). Actor, producer, director, screenwriter, and **science fiction** writer. A versatile Hollywood figure and prominent advocate of literacy among children, LeVar Burton is one of a number of African American science fiction writers who have redefined the genre in taking up historical perspectives on **race**, identity, and national politics.

He was born Levardis Robert Burton, Jr., in Landstuhl, West Germany, into an Army family stationed overseas. Though Burton achieved international fame when he played Kunta Kinte in the television miniseries adaptation of **Alex Haley**'s *Roots* (1976) in 1977, he is perhaps best known for his role as Lieutenant Commander Geordi LaForge, chief engineer of the starship *Enterprise*, in the series *Star Trek: The Next Generation* (1987–1994) and in several films. Burton is currently the long-running host of *Reading Rainbow* (1983–present), PBS's Emmy-winning educational program.

In 1997 Burton published *Aftermath*, a dystopic fiction about the forging of national community in the wake of an apocalyptic race war that lasts from 2015 to 2018 (*see* **Dystopian Literature**). Three strangers from different parts of the country set out to rescue Dr. Rene Reynolds from conspirators who wish to profit from her medical device, which enhances human brain function so that subjects may cure themselves of disease. Inspired by universal faith in human goodness as well as the desire to heal a nation torn apart by the "disease" of racial violence, the strangers' common quest serves as a parable of the triumph of cultural diversity over bigotry, terror, and nihilism.

Resource: LeVar Burton, *Aftermath* (New York: Aspect, 1997).

Kinohi Nishikawa

Bush-Banks, Olivia Ward (1869–1944). Poet and dramatist. Olivia Ward Bush-Banks came of age as a poet in the late nineteenth century, then made her mark as a dramatist and cultural critic in the twentieth century. Born on Long Island, New York, to parents of mixed racial ancestry (African American and Montauk Indian), she maintained her ties to the Montauk community throughout her life, due in large part to the influence of her maternal aunt, who raised her and to whom Bush-Banks's best-known work, *Driftwood*, was dedicated. However, Bush-Banks also celebrated her African American heritage and wrote poetry that called attention to the humanity and nobility of the Black race.

Bush-Banks's first book of poetry, *Original Poems*, was published in 1899 in Providence, Rhode Island, and was dedicated "with profound reverence and respect to the people of [her] race, the Afro-Americans." Bush-Banks later included some of these poems in *Driftwood* (1914). Several of the poems in *Driftwood* decry social injustice and pay tribute to leaders and heroes of the African American community, such as **Paul Laurence Dunbar**, the White abolitionists Wendell Phillips and William Lloyd Garrison, and an unnamed black soldier fighting at San Juan Hill. The primary conceit of the collection, comparing the poems to pieces of driftwood, exemplifies Bush-Banks's use of natural imagery and symbolism. Her poetry earned praise from Paul Laurence Dunbar, whose poetry served as her inspiration, and the poet Ella Wheeler Wilcox.

Despite the promising reception of her work, Bush-Banks was not able to sustain a career as a poet. Her interest in drama dominated the latter part of her life, and she taught dramatic expression in public schools, for the Works Progess Administration, and at New York University. She remained active within literary communities, however, and continued to write and publish poetry, essays, and plays. Her unpublished sketches featuring a character named Aunt Viney and her humorous observations about the Black community predate, as scholar Bernice Guillaume points out, **Langston Hughes**'s Simple stories by several years.

Bush-Banks is not well known today, but she exemplifies the prevailing trends in American literary culture in her lifetime. In form and theme she was indebted to the romanticism of Dunbar and the Fireside poets, in spirituality she was influenced by her deep Christian faith, and in politics she was motivated by a strong belief in social justice.

Resources: Olivia Bush-Banks, *The Collected Works of Olivia Ward Bush-Banks*, comp. and ed. Bernice F. Guillaume (New York: Oxford University Press, 1991); Bernice F. Guillaume, "Introduction," in *The Collected Works of Olivia Ward Bush-Banks* (New York: Oxford University Press, 1991).

Wendy Wagner

Busia, Akosua (born 1966). Actress, screenwriter, and novelist. Akosua Busia is the youngest daughter of a former Ashanti chief and prime minister of Ghana, the Honorable Dr. Kofi Abrefa Busia. Deborah Gregory describes Busia as a "casualty of political exile" (52). Born into the royal house of Wenchi, she grew up in Ghana, but after her father was exiled, she and her family moved to Mexico and the Netherlands before finally settling in England. Busia was formally educated in the United Kingdom at the Central School of Drama and Speech and at Oxford University. She later moved to the United States, where she would find fame as an actress. She has appeared in many Hollywood films, including *The Final Terror* (1983); *The George McKenna Story* (1986); *Low Blow* (1986); *Native Son* (1986); *The Seventh Sign* (1988); *Brother Future* (1991); *Rosewood* (1996), directed by her former husband, John Singleton; and *Tears of the Sun* (2003). However, Busia is perhaps best known for her role as Nettie in the film adaptation of **Alice Walker**'s Pulitzer Prize-winning novel *The Color Purple* (1985). In 1998, she added screenplay writing to her list of Hollywood credits. She assisted film director Jonathan Demme in the screen adaptation of **Toni Morrison**'s Pulitzer Prize-winning novel *Beloved*. The film received an Academy Award nomination for best screenplay, a major honor for first-time collaborator Busia. Her direct involvement in the films *Native Son* (1986), a film adaptation of the **Richard Wright** novel; *The Color Purple* (1985); and *Beloved* (1998) also highlights Busia's affinity for literature. Busia is the author of a novel, *The Seasons of Beento Blackbird* (1996). The novel's protagonist is Solomon Wilberforce, an African American writer of children's books, who writes under the name Beento Blackbird. Solomon divides his life among three women and three regions—Africa, the Caribbean, and America. This geographical variety springs from Busia's apparent aim to address themes of the African **diaspora**, specifically the link between Africa and the descendants of slaves in America and in the Caribbean. In this regard, her work shares similarities with that of **Paule Marshall**, author of *Brown Girls, Brownstones* (1959), and Maryse Conde, author of *Segu* (1987) and *The Children of Segu* (1989), who also explore diasporic themes in their fiction. At this writing, Busia is working on her second novel.

Resources: Deborah Gregory, "Akosua Busia out of Africa," *Essence*, Jan. 1997, 52; Pamela J. Olubunmi Smith, "The Seasons of Beento Blackbird," *World Literature Today* 71, no. 4 (Autumn 1997), 847–848.

Gail L. Upchurch

Bussey, Louré (born c. 1971). Novelist. Bussey, an extremely popular writer in the **romance novel** genre, published her first novel, *Nightfall*, in 1996. Before that, she had published numerous short stories in the African American romance magazines *Bronze Thrills* and *Black Confessions*. She is a native of New York. Her other novels include *Most of All, Twist of Fate, Love So True, Dangerous Passions*, and *Just the Thought of You*. Bussey has said, "I try to write an exciting plot, sensual love scenes, about a hero you fall in love with and with a heroine who feels like your best friend" (LaShaunda). She regards *A Feeling like No Other* as her first "mainstream novel," one that does not fit easily into the romance novel category (Website). At this writing, Bussey, who is also a singer, is recording on compact disc a compilation of songs that are connected to this novel.

Resources: Louré Bussey: *Dangerous Passions* (Washington, DC: BET/Arabesque, 2001); *A Feeling like No Other* (Jersey City, NJ: Blue Nile, 2003); *If Loving You Is Wrong* (Washington, DC: BET/Arabesque, 2003); *Images of Ecstasy* (Washington, DC: BET/Arabesque, 2000); *Just the Thought of You* (Washington, DC: BET/Arabesque, 2002); *Love So True* (Washington, DC: BET/Arabesque, 1999); *Most of All* (Washington, DC: BET/Arabesque, 1997); *Nightfall* (New York: BET/Arabesque, 1996); *A Taste of Love* (Washington, DC: BET/Arabesque, 1999); *Twist of Fate* (Washington, DC: BET/Arabesque, 1998); Web site [lourébussey.com], http://www.lourebussey.com/webroot/default.htm; LaShaunda, "Interview with Louré Bussey," *Shades of Romance*

Magazine: A Guide for Multicultural Romance Fiction, no. 4 (2001), http://www.sormag .com/bussey4.html.

Hans Ostrom

Butcher, Philip (born 1918). Editor, literary critic, and educator. Butcher, an authority on George W. Cable, **William Stanley Braithwaite**, and ethnic American literature, was born in **Washington, D.C.** He received a B.A. from Howard University (1942), and after he served in the U.S. Army (1943–1946) as a technical sergeant, he earned an M.A. from Howard (1947) and a Ph.D. in English from Columbia University (1956). He began his teaching career at Morgan State College (now Morgan State University) as an instructor in English in 1947 and remained there for thirty-two years. Butcher was promoted to assistant professor in 1949, associate professor in 1956, and professor in 1959. During his distinguished career, Butcher, who continued to teach until 1979, also served as chair of the Division of Humanities (1960–1966) and dean of the Graduate School (1972–1975).

Butcher's contributions as editor and writer have extended his influence beyond the classroom. He served as the literary editor of **Opportunity** (1947–1948) and as an associate editor of the *CLA Journal* in the 1970s. His essays were published in the *CLA Journal*, *Journal of Negro History*, *Opportunity*, **Phylon** (which also published several of his poems), *Shakespeare Quarterly*, *American Literary Realism*, and other periodicals. Butcher, who received various fellowships and research grants as well as the **College Language Association**'s Creative Scholarship Award (1964), wrote *George W. Cable: The Northampton Years* (1959), which introduced scholars and the general public to previously unknown materials, and *George W. Cable* (1962), which was volume 24 of Twayne's United States Authors series. Butcher edited *The William Stanley Braithwaite Reader* (1972), *The Minority Presence in American Literature, 1600–1900: A Reader and Course Guide* (1977), and *The Ethnic Image in Modern American Literature, 1900–1950* (1984). The Philip Butcher Papers are located at Columbia University's Rare Book and Manuscript Library.

Resources: Philip Butcher: *George W. Cable* (New York: Twayne, 1962); *George W. Cable: The Northampton Years* (New York: Columbia University Press, 1959); Philip Butcher, ed.: *The Ethnic Image in Modern American Literature, 1900–1950*, 2 vols. (Washington, DC: Howard University Press, 1984); *The Minority Presence in American Literature, 1600–1900: A Reader and Course Guide*, 2 vols. (Washington, DC: Howard University Press, 1971); *The William Stanley Braithwaite Reader* (Ann Arbor: University of Michigan Press, 1972); James A. Emanuel and Theodore L. Gross, eds., *Dark Symphony: Negro Literature in America* (New York: Free Press, 1968), 527–528; Ann Allen Shockley and Sue P. Chandler, *Living Black American Authors: A Biographical Directory* (New York: Bowker, 1973), 24–25.

Linda M. Carter

Butler, Octavia E. (born 1947). Science fiction writer. Butler is arguably the only Black female **science fiction** writer with a national reputation and is, with

Samuel R. Delany, one of the two best-known African American writers of science fiction. Her work often features Black protagonists and often explores issues of class, race, and feminism. Butler has published more than a dozen novels and one collection of short stories, and her writing has won many awards.

Born in Pasadena, California, in 1947, Butler was raised by her mother, to whom she attributes her early love of reading (*Bloodchild and Other Stories*, 125, 128–129). When she was about ten, the film *Devil Girl from Mars* convinced her she could write better stories. She has been writing science fiction ever since. By age thirteen she was mailing manuscripts to publishers. After high school she attended Pasadena City College, California State University at Los Angeles, and the University of California at Los Angeles, but her real immersion in writing came in 1970 when she began attending writing workshops (such as the Clarion Science Fiction Writers Workshop); at these she received encouragement and support from practicing science fiction writers, most notably Theodore Sturgeon.

Butler's big break came in 1976 with the publication of *Patternmaster*. Over the following years this book became part of her Patternist series, which includes *Mind of My Mind* (1977), *Survivor* (1978), *Wild Seed* (1980), and *Clay's Ark* (1984). The series describes the evolution of a culture founded and ruled by powerful telepaths. *Wild Seed*, the first in the story line, opens in Africa in the 1600s and describes the enslavement and breeding of people with psychic powers, a process that continues for generations as psychics are sought out and brought into what becomes called "the pattern"—a society of people mentally linked to each other. Each novel in the series examines a phase in the history of the telepathic culture that evolves. Although only *Wild Seed* makes explicit connections to the American culture of **slavery**, the series as a whole examines issues of enslavement and the effects of unchecked power. In 1979 Butler published *Kindred*, her work that most explicitly focuses on slavery in the United States. The protagonist, a young Black woman named Dana, is forced to travel from the 1970s back in time to Maryland in the 1830s in order to save the lives of a young Black woman and her White master, who will become Dana's great-great-grandparents, if they live long enough. The story explores the psychology of enslavement and the legacy bequeathed to Black Americans by their nation's long acceptance of a legalized slave economy.

In the mid-1980s Butler won two Hugo Awards—for the short story "Speech Sounds" (1984) and the novella "Bloodchild" (1985). Both were included in her 1995 collection *Bloodchild and Other Stories*. "Bloodchild," which Butler calls her "pregnant man story," also won Nebula and Locus awards.

Despite the acclaim she has received for her short stories, Butler considers herself primarily a novelist, and she returned to this genre in the late 1980s with the trilogy *Dawn* (1987), *Adulthood Rites* (1988), and *Imago* (1989). Called her Xenogenesis series, these works explore the resistance of Earth's few surviving human beings to their saviors—a tentacled, three-sexed alien species who nurture the human beings they rescued from Earth's holocaust back to health. The alien Oankali put these survivors in stasis while they spend years patiently restoring an Earth all but dead from human nuclear wars and planet-threatening practices. They eventually bring the remnant of the human race out of stasis and offer to return them to Earth—the price they demand is that all future offspring be products of interbreeding between the two species, thus providing the aliens with the genetic diversity needed for their own survival. In 2000 the trilogy was published in a single volume, *Lilith's Brood*.

Butler began a new series with the publication of *Parable of the Sower* (1993) and *Parable of the Talents* (1998). These books follow the fortunes of Lauren Olamina, a young Black woman who leads a small, ethnically diverse group of people determined to survive the horrific times in which they live. The first novel opens in California in 2024, and depicts a United States on its last legs, beset by drought; famine; disease; the rise of drug-crazed gangs; the collapse of the economy; the breakdown of national communication, education, and security networks; the secession of Alaska from the Union; and the near collapse of the federal government. In this world, communities wall themselves in for protection, water costs more than food, fuel-run vehicles are seldom seen, technology-based items are abandoned when they break, and literacy is an increasingly rare accomplishment. When her walled community is razed by invaders, Lauren flees north with a small group of survivors in search of safety and self-sufficiency. She gradually converts her fellow survivors to Earthseed, a religion she has conceived to provide the hope and vision needed for the human race to reverse its descent. Earthseed recognizes Change as the only god, preaches that every person must learn to shape this god in responsible ways, and says that the destiny of the human race lies among the stars.

Lauren's story continues in *Parable of the Talents*, when conditions in the United States are at their nadir. But conditions gradually improve, and Earthseed's message spreads throughout a country desperate for direction and hope. This novel follows Lauren's rise to leadership of a large religious movement and her daughter's struggles with feelings of abandonment after her separation from her family and resentment of her famous mother.

The collection *Bloodchild and Other Stories* contains five short stories followed by two "Afterwords." In the first, "Positive Obsession," Butler explains how she came to be a writer despite being told that Blacks couldn't earn their livings by writing. Her love of reading and her passion for putting words onto paper made her persevere. Success came slowly: after selling her first two short stories (only one of which made it into print), she was unable to sell anything else for five years. The second essay, "Furor Scribendi," offers advice to would-be writers.

Butler has won many prestigious awards in her career. The most significant of these recognitions came in 1995 when she received a coveted "genius grant" from the MacArthur Foundation.

Butler's reputation rests, in part, on the important role she has played in providing high-quality science fiction featuring Black protagonists (often women). Butler, a self-proclaimed feminist, was one of the first writers to create strong female African American characters in the science fiction genre. Her fiction also highlights themes that reflect African American issues. For instance, she often explores the subject of enslavement. In the Patternist series, telepathy becomes a means to enslave others. In the Parable series, weakened governments, collapsed economies, and privatization of police and medical services lead to a resurgence of "debt labor"—a term that Lauren points out is another way to say "slavery." In *Parable of the Sower*, her book set closest to current times, she shows us just how quickly and thoroughly civil rights for minority peoples could erode. Butler's works also tend to incorporate issues involving prejudice and its consequences. Human beings' intense prejudice against the kindly but repulsive-looking Oankali of her Xenogenesis series makes many choose species extinction over interspecies breeding. *Kindred* looks at the prejudice behind and perpetuated by the legalization of slavery in the United States.

Butler's importance, then, comes from both her themes and her adding a strong African American presence to the science fiction genre. Her works remind readers that racial prejudice takes many forms and is a threat to species survival; she points out how compelling the temptation is to use extreme power to enslave others; and she illustrates the fragility of the advances we have made in creating a society more committed to racial equality. Butler's strong African American protagonists—many female—fill a void in earlier science fiction offerings, which tend to offer only token representation of Blacks. Her commercial success helped to break the color barrier in one of our most popular fiction genres.

Resources: Octavia Butler, *Bloodchild and Other Stories* (New York: Four Walls Eight Windows, 1995); Robert Crossley, "Introduction," in Octavia Butler, *Kindred* (Boston: Beacon Press, 1988), ix–xxii; Michele Osherow, "The Dawn of a New Lilith: Revisionary Mythmaking in Women's Science Fiction," *National Women's Studies Association Journal* 12, no. 1 (2000), 68–83; Catherine S. Ramirez, "Cyborg Feminism: The Science Fiction of Octavia Butler and Gloria Anzaldua," in *Reload: Rethinking Women + Cyberculture*, ed. Mary Flanagan and Austin Booth (Cambridge, MA: MIT Press, 2002); Charles H. Rowell, "An Interview with Octavia E. Butler," *Callaloo* 20, no. 1 (1997), 47–66; Gregory E. Rutledge, "Futurist Fiction & Fantasy: The Racial Establishment," *Callaloo* 24, no. 1 (2001), 236–252; Ruth Salvaggio, "Octavia Butler and the Black Science-Fiction Heroine," *Black American Literature Forum* 18, no. 2 (1984), 78–81; Peter G. Stillman, "Dystopian Critiques, Utopian Possibilities, and Human Purposes in Octavia Butler's Parables," *Utopian Studies* 14 (2003), 15–35.

Grace McEntee

Butler, Tajuana "TJ" (born 1971). Novelist and poet. Butler is among those writers in the 1990s who contributed to the growth in the popularity of **romance novels** and other fiction aimed primarily at women. Her work examines a range of social and emotional issues connected to Africans, especially younger African American women. Born in Indianapolis, Indiana, on April 2, 1971, Butler moved with her family to Hopkinsville, Kentucky, when she was quite young. She attended the University of Louisville, where she received her bachelor's degree in English. After graduation she moved to

Atlanta, Georgia, and soon began work as a freelance writer. She formed her own publishing company, Lavelle Publishing, in 1997 and released a collection of her poetry, *The Desires of a Woman: Poems Celebrating Womanhood*.

A year later she published the first novel, *Sorority Sisters*. The novel features several female characters dealing with issues in their personal and professional lives. The novel's five protagonists are from different backgrounds, but they work together as a sorority pledge class, draw on one another's strengths, and forge lasting friendships. Butler's novel shows the extent to which sororities and fraternities play a significant role in the Black college experience, especially in **the South**.

In her second novel, *Hand-Me-Down Heartache*, Butler tackles the difficult issues of domestic abuse, infidelity, and self-doubt. She paints a poignant picture of a young woman attempting to find herself as she experiences conflict with her family, in romantic relationships, and in her career. Like her first novel, Butler's second celebrates enduring relationships among women. Her third novel, *The Night Before Thirty*, was published in 2003.

Resources: Tajuana Butler: *The Desires of a Woman: Poems Celebrating Womanhood* (Atlanta: Lavelle Publishing, 1997); *Hand-Me-Down Heartache* (New York: Villard, 2001); *The Night Before Thirty* (New York: Villard/Strivers Row, 2003); *Sorority Sisters* (New York: Villard, 2000); LaMonica R. Yarbrough, "Self-Published Reviews, Sorority Sisters," *Black Issues Book Review* 1, no. 5 (Sept./Oct. 1999), 50; Jeff Zaleski, Review of *Hand-Me-Down Heartache*, *Publishers Weekly*, Sept. 17, 2001, p. 55.

Cameron Christine Clark

Byrd, Adrianne (born c. 1976). Novelist. The publication of *Unforgettable* in April 2004 brought to ten the number of novels written by Adrianne Byrd. Her first book, *Defenseless*, appeared in 1997. All ten are **romance novels**, focusing on complicated love stories involving African American women; all ten feature photographs (or drawings) of young, Black heterosexual couples; all of the novels are frank in their dwelling on women's sexual desires; and all are undemanding, but retain some charm and careful characterization and engaged, if predictable, plot development.

The most melodramatic work by Byrd is *All I've Ever Wanted* (2001). Its heroine, an Atlanta waitress named Kennedy St. James (one of Byrd's many divorced leading characters), unwittingly becomes embroiled in the assassination of an assistant district attorney. St. James suffers targeting, stalking, and the kidnapping of her small son before the novel ends with her act of heroism—and the inevitable romantic union between her and a handsome, muscular detective, Max Collier. Byrd's novels invariably conclude with a climactic union with an alluring man of substance, whose attainability has wavered throughout the novel. For example, at the end of 2003's *Comfort of a Man*, the divorced thirtysomething, Brooklyn Douglas, finally feels secure in the arms of a once remote "brother with toffee-colored skin," Isaiah Washington. Before this perfect outcome, Brooklyn endures the apparent hostility of her teenage son, the grip that Washington's ailing mother has on her son, and the desperate antics of her still infatuated ex-husband, Dr. Evan McGinnis.

Byrd's main characters tend to be role models, exemplary in their practicing of safe sex and always tolerant of other racial and sexual identities.

Resources: Adrianne Byrd: *All I've Ever Wanted* (Washington, DC: BET Books/ Arabesque, 2001); *Comfort of a Man* (Washington, DC: BET Books, 2003); *Defenseless* (New York: Pinnacle Books, 1997); *Unforgettable* (Washington, DC: Arabesque, 2004); Web site, http://www.adriannebyrd.net.

Kevin DeOrnellas

C

Cain, George (born 1943). Novelist. Cain's highly regarded novel, *Blueschild Baby*, concerns one young man's experiences of urban life in New York City in the late 1960s. Cain grew up in **Harlem** and attended Iona College on a basketball scholarship. After spending time in California, Mexico, and **Texas**, he returned to New York in 1966 and began writing *Blueschild Baby*. Published in 1970, the novel focuses on a character named George Cain at the time of the 1967 Newark riots. In the novel, Cain returns from prison, struggles to overcome his heroin addiction, and reconsiders his relationships with former friends and girlfriends. In readjusting, he must also come to terms with a Black community that once held him up as a model of achievement and had high expectations for his future. Although Cain dropped out of the literary scene after writing *Blueschild Baby*, it received enthusiastic attention from critics and scholars. **Addison Gayle, Jr.**, declared it "a major breakthrough" for the **Black Arts Movement** and "the most important work of fiction by an Afro-American since *Native Son*" (BR4). George E. Kent writes that *Blueschild Baby* is "interesting both for its subject (the terror introduced into the life of the 'bright' kid rescued from the ghetto) and its struggle for identity and more positive relations to the so-called ghetto" (308). Though Cain's novel is an often dark meditation on the lures, compromises, and ambivalent solidarities of urban life, also embedded within his narrative are what **Houston A. Baker, Jr.**, characterizes as "developmental autobiographical scenes that make one feel the weight, joy, and importance of his childhood in the city" (90). Viewing the novel as a "candid and laudatory delineation of black urban culture," Baker points to *Blueschild Baby* as embodying a significant transitional moment in the genealogy of African American literature. *Blueschild*

Baby, Baker asserts, "reflects the divided loyalties and misdirection that convulsed the black freedom struggle of the sixties" and articulates a "celebration of that new locus of black culture, the inner city...the glistening asphalt and teeming tenements of a new frontier" (91).

Resources: Houston A. Baker, Jr., *Singers of Daybreak* (Washington, DC: Howard University Press, 1974), 81–91; Edith Blicksilver, "George Cain," in *Dictionary of Literary Biography*, vol. 33, *Afro-American Writers After 1955*, ed. Thadious M. Davis and Trudier Harris (Detroit: Gale, 1984), 41–43; George Cain, *Blueschild Baby* (New York: McGraw-Hill, 1970); Addison Gayle, Jr., Review of *Blueschild Baby*, *New York Times*, Jan. 17, 1971, p. BR4; George E. Kent, "Struggle for the Image: Selected Books by or About Blacks During 1971," *Phylon* 33, no. 4 (1972), 304–323.

Alex Feerst

Caldwell, Ben (born 1937). Playwright. Caldwell is a native of **Harlem, New York**, where he briefly attended the School of Industrial Arts before having to drop out in order to help support his family after the death of his father (Wattley). In the 1960s Caldwell was mentored by **Amiri Baraka**, then known as LeRoi Jones. He began writing plays, and at the Spirit House Theatre in New Jersey, his play *Prayer Meeting: or, the First Militant Minister* was produced under the title *The Militant Preacher*. Caldwell wrote *Riot Sale, or Dollar Psyche Fake-Out* in 1968 and *Hypnotism*, in 1969, and became a bona fide member of the **Black Arts Movement**, along with Baraka, **Ron Milner**, and **Ed Bullins**, among others. In 1970 he was awarded a Guggenheim fellowship. Since then, Caldwell has written more than fifty plays, many of them one-act; most of them focus on the lives and predicaments of African Americans, particularly Harlemites (Wattley). His drama is known for its comic and satiric perspectives on societal conflicts (Ladwig).

Resources: Kenneth Bowman, "The Revolution Will Not Be Televised nor Staged: An Interview with Ben Caldwell," *Callaloo* 22, no. 4 (Fall 1999), 808–824; Ed Bullins, Ben Caldwell, LeRoi Jones, and Ron Milner, *A Black Quartet: Four New Black Plays* (New York: New American Library, 1970), which includes Caldwell's *Prayer Meeting: or, the First Militant Minister*; Ronald V. Ladwig, "The Black Comedy of Ben Caldwell," *Players: Magazine of American Theatre* 51 (1976), 88–91; Hal May, Deborah A. Straub, and Susan Trosky, eds., *Black Writers: A Selection of Sketches from Contemporary Authors* (Detroit: Gale, 1989); Ama Wattley, "Benjamin Caldwell, 1937–," *Black Drama: Biography*, http://www.alexanderstreet2.com/BLDRLive/BLDR.Showcase.html.

Hans Ostrom

Callaloo **(1976–present).** Literary journal. *Callaloo*, a literary journal of African American and African **diaspora** arts and letters, originated in 1976 at Southern University in Baton Rouge, Louisiana, founded by Charles H. Rowell, who remains its senior editor. *Callaloo*'s original mission was to publish the creative writing and scholarship of Southern Black writers and was inspired by the groundbreaking work of Black writers during the 1960s and 1970s. The title is the word for a Caribbean soup made with greens, onions, and crabmeat, and represents the diversity of the Black writing community and the Black experience throughout the world. In 1977, Rowell took the journal to the University of Kentucky, and in 1986 to the University of Virginia, where it remained until 2001. As *Callaloo* has evolved, it has broadened to include the work of Black writers and artists throughout the world: poetry, fiction, interviews, critical essays, and original artwork and photography. It is printed by the Johns Hopkins University Press.

Rowell received his Ph.D. from Ohio State University in 1972 and is a prolific writer and poet in his own right; he also has interviewed such renowned contemporary intellectuals as Chinua Achebe, **Octavia Butler**, **Ernest Gaines**, **Henry Louis Gates, Jr.**, **Audre Lorde**, and **Gloria Naylor**. He also has edited the anthologies *Ancestral House: The Black Short Story in the Americas and Europe* (1995) and *Shade: An Anthology of Fiction by Gay Men of African Descent* (1996).

Callaloo's beginnings were humble, but it quickly gained prominence as a publication that critiqued and promoted Black literary culture. Throughout the years, it has published such prominent Black writers as Octavia Butler, **Alice Walker**, **Lucille Clifton**, **Samuel Delany**, Ernest Gaines, **Edwidge Danticat**, **Rita Dove**, **John Edgar Wideman**, **Toi Derricotte**, Audre Lorde, **Ralph Ellison**, and **Yusef Komunyakaa**. It has sparked critical discussions on any number of topics relevant to the lives of Black Americans and the African disapora. The journal has also published special themed issues that focus upon a specific topic of interest to its readers. These special issues have covered jazz poetics (Winter 2002), the literature and visual art of Veracruz, Mexico (Autumn 2003), the literature and culture of the Dominican Republic (Summer 2000), Haitian literature and culture (Spring and Summer 1992) and emerging women writers (Spring 1996).

In addition to publishing four times a year, *Callaloo* hosts special events for the public, including an annual October reading at the Joseph Papp Public Theater in New York, programs at the Modern Language Association's annual convention, and creative writing workshops at historically Black colleges and universities, funded in part by a grant from the National Endowment for the Arts. In May 2001, *Callaloo* cohosted a seminar, titled "The Changing Academy in the United States," in Havana, Cuba, to discuss trends in contemporary literature and cultural studies. *Callaloo* has been honored with awards from the Council of Editors of Learned Journals and the Association of American Publishers Professional Scholarly Publishing Division, and remains highly acclaimed among its peers. During the journal's twenty-fifth year, it moved, with Rowell, to Texas A&M University. Though Rowell is quoted as saying that the decision to leave the University of Virginia was difficult, he felt there would be more opportunities for the journal to continue growing at A&M, where it would have more office space and an increased budget.

In January 2002, Rowell released *Making Callaloo: 25 Years of Black Literature*, an anthology to celebrate the journal's twenty-fifth anniversary by reprinting works representative of two and half decades of black writing and art in *Callaloo*.

Resource: Charles Rowell, *Making Callaloo: 25 Years of Black Literature, 1976–2000* (New York: St. Martin's Press, 2002).

Roxane Gay

Campanella, Roy (1921–1993). Professional baseball player and autobiographer. Campanella is a member of the Baseball Hall of Fame. He was born November 19, 1921 in **Philadelphia, Pennsylvania**. His father was an Italian immigrant and his mother was of African American heritage. The family operated a small market, and as a young man Campanella was often teased by African American classmates because of his White father. Campanella attended Simon Gratz High School in Philadelphia, but he dropped out during his junior year in order to play professional baseball.

Campanella signed with the Baltimore Elite Giants of the Negro National League in 1938. He was a power-hitting catcher whose talent warranted a tryout with the Pittsburgh Pirates, but the racial barriers enforced by baseball Commissioner Kenesaw Mountain Landis prevented his signing with the Pirates. During **World War II**, Campanella assembled tank parts and played the 1943 season in the Mexican League.

During the postwar period, Brooklyn Dodgers General Manager Branch Rickey signed **Jackie Robinson**, finally breaking baseball's color barrier. Rickey also signed Campanella to a contract, and in 1948 he was playing for the club. The catcher was a key member of the Dodger dynasty that won National League pennants in 1949, 1952, 1953, 1955, and 1957, and a World Series championship in 1955.

On January 25, 1958, while he was driving home from the liquor store which he owned, Campanella was involved in an automobile accident that left him paralyzed. In 1959 he told his life story to ghost writers Dave Camerer and Joe Reichler, who helped Campanella produce his poignant autobiography, *It's Good to Be Alive*. The best-seller was an inspirational tale of Campanella's recovery from his accident as well as his overcoming racism to become one of baseball's greatest players. The memoir, however, downplays some of the conflict between Campanella and Robinson, who did not always believe that Campanella was assertive enough on issues of racial discrimination.

It's Good to Be Alive aired as a television movie in 1974, and the book remains in print. Confined to a wheelchair since 1959, Campanella died on June 26, 1993, in Woodland Hills, California. He was elected to the Baseball Hall of Fame in 1969.

Resources: Roy Campanella, *It's Good to Be Alive* (Boston: Little, Brown, 1959); Peter Golenbock, *Bums: An Oral History of the Brooklyn Dodgers* (New York: Putnam, 1984); Roger Kahn, *The Boys of Summer* (New York: HarperPerennial, 1998); Norman L. Macht, *Roy Campanella: Baseball Star* (New York: Chelsea House, 1996); Carl Prince, *Brooklyn's Dodgers: The Bums, the Borough, and the Best of Baseball, 1947–1957* (New York: Oxford University Press, 1996); Jules Tygiel, *Baseball's Great Experiment: Jackie Robinson and His Legacy* (New York: Vintage Books, 1984).

Ron Briley

Campbell, Bebe Moore (born 1950). Novelist, essayist, journalist, freelance writer, and radio commentator. A native of **Philadelphia, Pennsylvania**, and a graduate of the Philadelphia High School for Girls, Campbell earned an elementary education degree from the University of Pittsburgh. She taught school for several years and then pursued a career in writing, taking a class from the renowned writer **Toni Cade Bambara**. She tried for five years to publish her work at a time when few publishers were interested in Black writers. Her first story was published in *Essence* magazine, and then she went on to publish articles in the *New York Times*, the *Washington Post*, and *Black Enterprise*. One of her magazine pieces turned into her first book, *Successful Women, Angry Men: Backlash in the Two-Career Marriage* (1986). Campbell took up social issues in her writing and was influenced by what she saw in summers spent with her father in Jim Crow North Carolina. The **Emmett Till lynching** was the catalyst for her first novel, *Your Blues Ain't Like Mine* (1992). She also chronicles those summers in *Sweet Summer: Growing Up with and without My Dad* (1989). The 1992 Los Angeles **race riots** were the impetus for the novel *Brothers and Sisters* (1994), which explores such topics as interracial relationships, sexual harassment, and classism. Campbell went on to publish *Singing in the Comeback Choir* (1998) and *What You Owe Me* (2001). Concerned about mental illness issues, she broke new ground in 2003 with a children's book titled *Sometimes My Mommy Gets Angry*, about a mentally ill mother and her young daughter. Campbell has been a commentator with National Public Radio, and her books have been on several best-seller lists, including those of *Essence* and the *New York Times*. Among her awards are the **NAACP** Image Award for literature (1994). She also received a National Endowment for the Arts literature grant in 1980. She is still pursuing social and political activities in **Los Angeles, California**.

Resources: African American Literature Book Club (AALBC), "About Bebe Moore Campbell," http://authors.aalbc.com/bebe.htm; Bebe Moore Campbell: *Brothers and Sisters* (New York: Putnam, 1994); *Singing in the Comeback Choir* (New York: Putnam, 1998); *Sometimes My Mommy Gets Angry* (New York: Putnam, 2003); *Sweet Summer: Growing Up with and without My Dad* (New York: Putnam, 1989); *What You Owe Me* (New York: Putnam, 2001); *Your Blues Ain't Like Mine* (New York: Putnam, 1992); *Contemporary Black Biography* (Detroit: Gale, 2004); *Voices from the Gaps: Women Writers of Color*, http://voices.cla.umn.edu/newsite/index.htm.

Dera R. Williams

Campbell, James Edwin (1867–1896). Poet. Although he died before he was thirty years old, the poet James Edwin Campbell had a remarkable life. He was born in Pomeroy, Ohio, a town listed in *Ripley's Believe It or Not* because it is located below bluffs along the Ohio River and has no cross streets. After graduating from Pomeroy High School in 1884, Campbell became a teacher and an active volunteer with the Republican Party.

In 1890, Campbell moved to West Virginia, where he had accepted a position as principal of the Langston School in Point Pleasant. In 1891, he

233

married Mary Champ, a teacher. He subsequently became the first president of the Collegiate Institute, a newly established agricultural and technical college for African Americans, located in Charleston. The Collegiate Institute is now West Virginia State College.

In 1895, Campbell moved to **Chicago, Illinois**, where he became a staff writer for the *Chicago Times-Herald*. He began to contribute articles, reviews, and poems to periodicals and to build a reputation as a dynamic new voice in African American literature. While visiting his hometown in 1896, he contracted pneumonia and died.

Campbell published his two collections of poems at his own expense. *Driftings and Gleanings* (1887) was printed by a newspaper in Charleston. Containing verses in Standard English, the collection shows Campbell's facility with poetic conventions and displays some freshness of image and sentiment.

Campbell's reputation rests on his second collection, *Echoes from the Cabin and Elsewhere* (1895), which includes a dozen or so poems written in the Gullah dialect. (*See* **Dialect Poetry**.) Printed in Chicago, the collection received some good local notices and provided Campbell with almost immediate credibility as a writer when he settled in the city. In her headnote to the selections included in the anthology *African-American Poetry of the Nineteenth Century* (1992), Joan R. Sherman asserts that Campbell's second collection contains the foremost dialect poems written by an African American in the nineteenth century. Indeed, Campbell's poems predate the better-known dialect poems of **Paul Laurence Dunbar**, who became a friend of Campbell's. Moreover, Campbell's poems are more consistent than Dunbar's in their authentic rendering of folk stories in a specific dialect, and they exhibit greater attention to the realistic detailing of African American life.

Several of Campbell's poems have been reprinted fairly often. "De Conjuh Man" focuses on a traditional conjurer who can either heal or debilitate with his spells. "The Pariah" concerns a **mulatto** who falls in love with a daughter of a factory owner. Ironically, while the young woman is a blueblood who can trace her ancestry back to the Mayflower's landing in Plymouth, the mulatto can trace his ancestry back to the first group of African slaves brought to Jamestown a year earlier. "Ol' Doc Hyar" provides a wry portrait of a physician with seemingly boundless vitality, and the speaker ultimately attributes that vitality, at least in part, to the tacitly accepted irony that the physician must be paid regardless of whether the patient is healed or dies.

Resources: Mark Balhorn, "Paper Representations of the Non-Standard Voice," *Visible Language* 32, no. 1 (1998), 56–74; James Edwin Campbell: *Driftings and Gleanings* (Charleston, WV: The State-Tribune, 1887); *Echoes from the Cabin and Elsewhere* (Chicago: Donohue and Henneberry, 1895); Joan R. Sherman, "James Edwin Campbell," in *African-American Poetry of the Nineteenth Century: An Anthology*, ed. Joan R. Sherman (Urbana: University of Illinois Press, 1992), 306; Carter G. Woodson, "James Edwin Campbell, a Forgotten Man of Letters," *Negro History Bulletin* 2 (Nov. 1938), 11.

Martin Kich

Carby, Hazel V. (born 1948). Scholar and cultural/literary critic. Carby is a prominent feminist critic of African American literature and culture. Her work expresses a broad viewpoint; she invokes both a sense of history and the wider geography of the **Black Atlantic** in her critical approach to literature and culture.

Carby was born in 1948 in Oakhampton, Devon, Great Britain. She is the child of Iris Muriel Carby, a Welsh secretary, and Carlin Colin Carby, a Jamaican municipal accounts clerk and former member of the Royal Air Force. In her early years, Carby trained to become a ballerina. Her interests changed as she grew, and she became more interested in drama and, later, literature.

Carby earned a B.A. in English literature and history from Portsmouth Polytechnic in 1970. She received a teaching certificate from London University's Institute of Education in 1972, and taught high school in a poor area of northeast London from 1972 to 1979. She earned a master's degree from the Center for Contemporary Cultural Studies at Birmingham University in 1979. In 1984, she was awarded a Ph.D. by Birmingham University's Center for Contemporary Cultural Studies; her dissertation was on **slave narratives** written by women.

Carby was a lecturer at Yale University in 1981–1982. At Wesleyan University, she was an instructor from 1982 to 1984, an assistant professor from 1985 to 1988 and an associate professor from 1988 to 1989. In 1989, Carby returned to Yale as a professor of English, American Studies, and African American Studies (1989–1994). Since 1994, she has been a professor of American Studies and African American Studies. She became chairperson of the African American Studies program at Yale in 1996. She briefly stepped down in 2000 to protest the program's not receiving departmental status despite its having the leading Ph.D. in the subject area. After department status was extended to the program, Carby resumed her role as chairperson.

Carby's first monograph, *Reconstructing Womanhood* (1987), was based on her doctoral dissertation and explored the social, cultural, political, and historic "emergence of the Afro-American woman novelist." Unlike many literary critics, Carby is less concerned about uncovering an intellectual tradition in African American women's writing than in providing a materialist account of the social and cultural milieu in which writings by African American women appeared. In the text, Carby expresses a Black feminist stance as she describes and critiques aspects of the lives and writings of nineteenth- and twentieth-century authors such as Nancy Prince, **Harriet Wilson, Harriet Jacobs, Frances E. W. Harper, Anna Julia Cooper, Ida B. Wells, Pauline Hopkins, Jessie Fauset**, and **Nella Larsen**. Carby explores, in a historical context, how these writers established a simultaneously pro-African American and pro-woman intellectual, political, and social stance in a society where the predominant African American ideology contained elements of misogyny and the predominant feminist ideology contained elements of racism.

Carby's second text, *Race Men*, published in 1998, was derived from a lecture series on race and masculinity. Again adopting a feminist stance, Carby explores representations of African American masculinity in literature, photography, film, and music by exploring aspects of the lives and work of

Samuel Delany, **Paul Robeson**, **W.E.B. Du Bois**, C.L.R. James, **Leadbelly**, Danny Glover, and Miles Davis. She explores the social and political uses to which the various and differing representations of the Black male body are applied and the implications of these representations in the social construction and maintenance of national identity.

In 1999, Carby published *Cultures in Babylon: Black Britain and African America*, a collection of her work from the last twenty years. *Cultures in Babylon* is arranged in four sections, "Women, Migration and the Formation of a Blues Culture," "Black Feminist Interventions," "Fictions of the Folk," and "Dispatches from the Multicultural Wars." (*See* **Feminism/Black Feminism; Feminist/Black Feminist Literary Criticism.**)

Resources: Hazel Carby: *Cultures in Babylon: Black Britain and African America* (New York: Verso, 1999); *Race Men* (Cambridge, MA: Harvard University Press, 1998); *Reconstructing Womanhood: The Emergence of the Afro-American Woman Novelist* (New York: Oxford University Press, 1987); "Hazel Carby," in *Contemporary Black Biography*, vol. 27, ed. Ashyia Henderson (Detroit: Gale, 2001); "Hazel V. Carby," in *Contemporary Authors*, vol. 154 (Detroit: Gale, 2000).

Kimberly Black-Parker

Carmichael, Stokely (also known as Kwame Ture) (1941–1998). Civil rights activist and author. Stokely Carmichael coauthored the seminal civil rights book *Black Power: The Politics of Liberation in America* (1967). He popularized **Black Power** and, through his writings and political behavior, advocated Black pride and self-determination.

Carmichael was born in Trinidad to parents who did not finish high school. In 1952, his family moved to New York. During his high school years, he was drawn to **Black Nationalism**, participating in Bayard Rustin's Youth Marches in 1958 and 1959. He began his freshman year at Howard University in 1960 with his political values firmly in place (Cobb). While at Howard, he participated in the Nonviolent Action Group, a campus group that promoted activism on racial issues. According to *A Literary Tribute to Sterling A. Brown*, Carmichael was a protégé of Brown, a Howard professor, author, and literary and social critic whose students also included actor/playwright **Ossie Davis** and the novelist **Toni Morrison**.

Carmichael went south in the summer of 1961 as a freedom rider and was incarcerated in the infamous Parchman Penitentiary in Mississippi for forty-nine days. After graduating from college, he became chair of the Student Nonviolent Coordinating Committee (SNCC) in 1966. At a rally in 1966, he echoed the words of Willie Ricks, an SCLC organizer, and shouted "Black Power" (Cobb). Carmichael wrote *Black Power* with Charles Hamilton. He used the media to share his ideas with the wider Black community, in the United States and around the world.

Carmichael moved to Guinea in 1967; there he wrote *Stokely Speaks: Black Power Back to Pan-Africanism* (1971). He adopted the name Kwame Ture and worked to establish the All-African People's Revolutionary Party. In 1987,

Carmichael met Ekwueme **Michael Thelwell** and began relating the stories that would become *Ready for Revolution: The Life and Struggles of Stokely Carmichael* (2003). Carmichael was in the last stages of prostate cancer, and he died in 1998 shortly after recording the last story (Wolfe).

Carmichael is best remembered for the radical philosophy advocated in his writings and speeches as well as his participation in civil rights organizations.

Resources: Stokely Carmichael: speech at Seattle, Washington, Apr. 19, 1967, University of Washington Instructional Resource Center Page, http://courses. washington.edu/spcmu/carmichael/transcript/htm; *Stokely Speaks: Black Power Back to Pan-Africanism* (New York: Random House, 1971); "We Are Going to Use the Term Black Power and We Are Going to Define It Because Black Power Speaks to Us," in *Black Nationalism in America*, ed. John A. Bracey, Jr., et al. (Indianapolis: Bobbs-Merrill, 1970); Stokely Carmichael and Charles V. Hamilton, *Black Power: The Politics of Liberation in America* (New York: Random House, 1967); Stokely Carmichael with Ekwueme Michael Thelwell, *Ready for Revolution: The Life and Struggles of Stokely Carmichael* (New York: Scribner's, 2003); Charlie Cobb, "From Stokley Carmichael to Kwame Ture," All Africa News Service (Durham, NC), Nov. 11, 1998, http://fr. allafrica.com/stories/200101050369.html; Gail M. Gerhart, *Black Power in South Africa: The Evolution of an Ideology* (Berkeley: University of California Press, 1978); James Haskins, *Profiles in Black Power* (Garden City, NY: Doubleday, 1972); "Items Attributed to Kwame Ture's Authorship," Kwame Nkrumah Information and Resource Site, www.nkrumah.net/kt2001/bio-biblio.html; Jacqueline Johnson, *Stokely Carmichael: The Story of Black Power* (Englewood Cliffs, NJ: Silver Burdett, 1990); *A Literary Tribute to Sterling A. Brown*, Howard University Libraries, http://www.howard.edu/library/Development/SterlingBrown.htm; John T. McCartney, *Black Power Ideologies: An Essay in African-American Political Thought* (Philadelphia: Temple University Press, 1992); Benjamin Muse, *The American Negro Revolution: From Nonviolence to Black Power, 1963–1967* (Bloomington: Indiana University Press, 1968); Jeffrey Ogbonna Green Ogbar, *Black Power: Radical Politics and African American Identity* (Baltimore: Johns Hopkins University Press, 2005); "Stokely Carmichael," *The National Archives Learning Curve*, www.spartacus.schoolnet.co.uk/USAcarmichael.htm; Timothy B. Tyson, *Radio Free Dixie: Robert F. Williams and the Roots of Black Power* (Chapel Hill: University of North Carolina Press, 1999); William L. Van Deburg, *New Day in Babylon: The Black Power Movement and American Culture, 1965–1975* (Chicago: University of Chicago Press, 1992); Leslie Wolfe, "Finding Peace Through One Final Revolution," *UMassMag Online*, Spring 2004, www.umassmag.com/Spring_2004/Finding_Peace_Through_One_Final_Revolution_607.html.

Patricia L T Camp

Carroll, Vinnette (1922–2003). Director, actress, and playwright. Carroll specialized in bringing Black musical productions to the theater and was one of the first African American women to direct a play on Broadway. She was born in New York City and lived there until the age of three, when she moved with her family to Jamaica, West Indies. The family returned to New York when Carroll was eleven years old, and she earned a B.A. degree from Long

Island University in 1944. She received a M.A. degree in psychology from New York University in 1946, and attended Columbia University, where she completed all requirements for the Ph.D. degree except the dissertation. Carroll worked for a while as a clinical psychologist in the New York City school system. Her interest in drama and theater became apparent in 1948 when she enrolled in Edwin Piscator's dramatic workshop at the New School for Social Research, and when, during the 1950s, she taught drama at the High School for the Performing Arts. In 1967, she founded the Urban Arts Corps, an organization dedicated to helping African American and Latino theater and actors.

Carroll's theatrical roles included parts in *Caesar and Cleopatra* (1955), *Small War on Murray Hill* (1956), *The Octoroon* (1961), and *Moon on a Rainbow Shawl* (1962). Her movie roles include parts in *One Potato, Two Potato* (1964), *Up the Down Staircase* (1967), and *Alice's Restaurant* (1969). It was as a director, however, that Carroll is best known. She adapted **James Weldon Johnson**'s *God's Trombones* for the stage in a 1963 production titled *Trumpets of the Lord*. She also directed the original off-Broadway productions of **Langston Hughes**'s *Black Nativity* and *Prodigal Son* in 1969 (Ostrom). Carroll also directed productions of Joseph White's *Old Judge Mose Is Dead* (1969) and Peter DeAnda's *Ladies in Waiting* (1970). Carroll's most famous directorial work included the musical *Don't Bother Me, I Can't Cope* (1971), which won two Obies and two Drama Desk Awards, and *Your Arms Too Short to Box with God* (1975), both of which Carroll wrote with actress/songwriter Micki Grant. In 1979, Carroll conceived and directed the musical *When Hell Freezes Over, I'll Skate*, which played at the Kennedy Center in Washington and was televised on PBS. Carroll received a Tony nomination for directing *Don't Bother Me, I Can't Cope* in 1973, making her the first African American woman to be nominated in the director category. She was nominated for the same award in 1977, as well as for the best book for a musical in 1976 for *Your Arms Too Short to Box with God*. Carroll won an Obie for her acting in *Moon on a Rainbow Shawl* (1962), and an Emmy for conceptualizing and supervising the television program *Beyond the Blues* in 1964. In 1986, Carroll moved to Fort Lauderdale, Florida, where she founded and served as artistic director of the Vinnette Carroll Repertory Company. She resided in Florida until her death in 2003.

Resources: Darlene Hine Clark, ed., *Black Women in America: An Historical Encyclopedia* (Brooklyn, NY: Carlson, 1993); Christine L. Lunardini, "Vinnette Carroll," in *Encyclopedia of African American Culture and History*, vol. 1, ed. Jack Saltzman, David Lionel Smith, and Cornel West (New York: Macmillan Library Reference, 1996); Calvin A. McClinton, *The Work of Vinnette Carroll: An African American Theatre Artist* (Lewiston, NY: Edwin Mellen Press, 2000); Hans Ostrom, *A Langston Hughes Encyclopedia* (Westport, CT: Greenwood Press, 2002), 42–43, 316; Bernard L. Peterson, Jr., *Contemporary Black American Playwrights and Their Plays: A Biographical Directory and Dramatic Index* (Westport, CT: Greenwood Press, 1988); Jessie Carney Smith, ed., *Notable Black American Women*, vol. 2 (Detroit: Gale, 1996).

Ama S. Wattley

Carter, Charlotte (born 1943). Novelist. Carter grew up in **Chicago, Illinois**. She has traveled extensively and lived abroad; many of her novels deal with African American characters living in or visiting Paris and other locations. She has worked as an editor and freelance writer. Carter currently lives in New York; she also has lived in France, Canada, and North Africa.

Carter has written three mystery novels featuring amateur detective Nanette Hayes, who supports herself by playing **jazz** on the streets of New York. She has an advanced degree in French, but left her career in academia. (She has yet to inform her mother of this fact.) The novels are imbued with jazz and other music. In *Rhode Island Red* (1997), Nanette becomes involved in solving the murder of a man she finds dead in her apartment. In *Coq au Vin* (1999), she travels to Paris to search for her aunt, who has been reported missing. She returns to New York in *Drumsticks* (2000), and solves the murder of a **rap** musician.

Additional works include a love story titled *Walking Bones* (2002), which explores the relationship between an African American woman and a White man who insults her during their first chance encounter in a bar. Carter has recently begun a second mystery series, set in 1968 in Chicago.

Resources: Charlotte Carter: *Coq au Vin* (New York: Mysterious Press, 1999); *Drumsticks* (New York: Mysterious Press, 2000); *Jackson Park* (New York: One World, 2003); *Rhode Island Red* (London: Mask Noir/Serpent's Tail, 1997); *Walking Bones* (London: Serpent's Tail, 2002); Web site, Sept. 9, 2002, http://www.twbooks.co.uk/authors/charlottecarter.html; "Charlotte Carter," in *Contemporary Authors*, vol. 172 (Detroit: Gale, 2000), 55; Bob Cornwell, "Sophisticated Lady," *Tangled Web*, 2001, http://www.twbooks.co.uk/crimescene/ccarterintervbc.htm; Chris Wiegand, "Red Hot and Blue," *Spike*, June 2002, http://www.spikemagazine.com/0602carter.htm.

Elizabeth Blakesley Lindsay

Carter, Rubin "Hurricane" (born 1937). Prison writer, professional boxer, and activist. Hailing from Paterson, New Jersey, Carter was the top contender for the middleweight championship in professional boxing in the 1960s. Then he was imprisoned for a horrendous crime he did not commit. In 1974, while at Rahway State Prison, he wrote his acclaimed firsthand account, *The Sixteenth Round: From Number 1 Contender to #45472*, composed to provoke a retrial and to reveal the circumstances surrounding his arrest and incarceration. The book was also designed to expose the overtly racist climate during the 1960s that led Carter and countless other African Americans to be falsely arrested, convicted, and sent to prison. As Carter would explain: "This book is my life's blood spilled out on the fifteen rounds of these pages. The sixteenth round is still being fought" (336).

Upon its release, *The Sixteenth Round* appealed to a wide variety of North American audiences. Carter received the support of such celebrities as **Muhammad Ali**, Joan Baez, and Bob Dylan. Dylan's 1975 song "Hurricane" recounts Carter's unmerited fall from greatness within a system blinded by innate racist leanings. Although briefly released in 1976 and deemed a folk hero, Carter was sent back to prison after a retrial and subsequently was forgotten about as he sank deeper into the obscurity of prison. However, as the 1980s approached, an African American teenager named Lesra Martin read a copy of *The Sixteenth Round*, and it became a life-altering experience for him. Lesra started corresponding with Carter, who, despite his lack of faith, was touched by the boy's intelligence and compassion. Both Carter and Martin had come from difficult, poverty-stricken backgrounds. Their relationship would eventually prompt Martin's adoptive Canadian family and Carter's team of defense attorneys to work together to help set Carter free. They accomplished their goal in 1985 after a federal judge ruled that overt racist practices contributed to an unfair trial and sentencing (Hirsch, 312).

Carter would achieve fame again after the release of the film *The Hurricane* (1999), directed by Norman Jewison and starring Denzel Washington as Carter. A documentary film, *The Journey of Lesra Martin*, was released by the National Film Board of Canada. Inspired by his own trials and tribulations, Carter, at this writing, works for justice-minded groups dedicated to overturning wrongful criminal convictions. (*See* **Prison Literature**.)

Resources: Rubin Carter, *The Sixteenth Round: From Number 1 Contender to #45472* (New York: Viking Press, 1974); James Hirsch, *Hurricane: The Miraculous Journey of Rubin Carter* (Boston: Houghton Mifflin, 2000); Norman Jewison, director, *The Hurricane* (Universal/MCA, 1999; DVD released 2000).

Stephen M. Steck

Carter, Stephen L. (born 1954). Novelist, essayist, and scholar. Stephen Carter published seven works of nonfiction on legal, political, cultural, and religious topics before publishing his first novel in 2002. His distinctive voice generates debate because his work often subjects established cultural and intellectual norms to an intense critical scrutiny. As a widely respected and controversial African American author and professor of law at Yale University, he has been called "one of America's leading public intellectuals" by the *New York Times*, to which he has regularly contributed. He has also contributed to the *Wall Street Journal*, *The New Yorker*, *The New Republic*, and *Christianity Today*.

Carter was born in 1954 in **Washington, D.C.** After graduating from Stanford University, where as a senior he was managing editor of the student newspaper, he went on to law school at Yale. He served as a law clerk to Justice Thurgood Marshall in 1980 and 1981, and began teaching law at Yale in 1982. In an interview, Carter claimed that his decisions about what and where to study and whether to teach were grounded in his love of writing: "I knew whatever I did, I was going to write. . . . I have always loved putting words on a page. More almost than any other intellectual activity" (Birnbaum). Carter is a self-professed Christian, and many of his works discuss Christian themes, but each utilizes arguments that are anchored in broad philosophical, legal, and social contexts and are intended to be relevant to readers of any religious tradition and to readers with no religious affiliation (Carter, *Civility*, xii).

Carter's first book was *Reflections of an Affirmative-Action Baby* (1991). Next he wrote *The Culture of Disbelief: How American Law and Politics Trivialize*

Religious Devotion (1993), which argues that religion is valuable to democracy when it serves to question the status quo. *The Confirmation Mess: Cleaning up the Federal Appointments Process* (1994) examined the inconsistencies in America's judicial confirmation process. In *Integrity* (1996), Carter analyzes the pervasive and embedded corruption within American society. *The Dissent of the Governed: A Meditation on Law, Religion, and Loyalty* (1998) asserts that dissent does not indicate disloyalty; rather, it is essential to American democracy. In *Civility: Manners, Morals, and the Etiquette of Democracy* (1998), Carter calls for an American citizenry founded on the ideals of respect and love for others. His most recent nonfiction is *God's Name in Vain: The Rights and Wrongs of Religion in Politics* (2000).

Carter's novel, *The Emperor of Ocean Park* (2002), tells the story of Talcott Garland, an African American law professor at Yale, and of his quest to find answers to questions raised by the death of his father, a rejected nominee to the Supreme Court. The novel incorporates many of Carter's previous literary preoccupations, but it is simultaneously a gripping mystery; a family saga; a satirical analysis of academia, politics, and the judicial confirmation process; a revealing investigation of race relations; and a meditation on how religious faith informs personal and political identities. It was both critically and popularly acclaimed. Carter is currently working on his second novel. (*See* **Affirmative Action**.)

Resources: Robert Birnbaum, "Stephen Carter," July 14, 2002, http://identitytheory.com/people/birnbaum52.html; Stephen L. Carter: *Civility: Manners, Morals, and the Etiquette of Democracy* (New York: Basic Books, 1998); *The Confirmation Mess: Cleaning up the Federal Appointments Process* (New York: Basic Books, 1994); *The Culture of Disbelief: How American Law and Politics Trivialize Religious Devotion* (New York: Basic Books, 1993); *The Dissent of the Governed: A Meditation on Law, Religion, and Loyalty* (Cambridge, MA: Harvard University Press, 1998); *The Emperor of Ocean Park* (New York: Alfred A. Knopf, 2002); *God's Name in Vain: The Rights and Wrongs of Religion in Politics* (New York: Basic Books, 2000); *Integrity* (New York: Basic Books, 1996); *Reflections of an Affirmative Action Baby* (New York: Basic Books, 1991).

Windy Counsell Petrie

Cartiér, Xam Wilson (born 1949). Novelist. Cartiér's experimental style is heavily imbued with a musical aesthetic that positions her firmly within an avant-garde African American literary movement. Born in **St. Louis**, Xam Wilson Cartiér was a playwright and television scriptwriter who received a National Endowment for the Arts creative writing fellowship, a California Arts Council grant, and a Millay Colony residency, and exhibited her work at the 1984 San Francisco Fair and Exposition, before publishing her debut novel, *Be-Bop, Re-Bop* (1987).

Be-Bop, Re-Bop is the first-person narrative of an unnamed African American woman's life, opening with funeral of the young girl's father and closing with the adult protagonist as she sets off to begin a new life with her daughter. Told in a loosely chronological order, and interspersed with flashbacks, dreamscapes, journal entries, and fantastical episodes, the text resists conventional linearity, adopting instead a jazzlike organizing principle as it tells of the girl's close relationship with her father and then of her growing alienation from her surroundings as she matures. Overtly signaling her engagement with **jazz** through the novel's title and the numerous musical references, Cartiér's plot is further linked to music as it develops not through structures of disclosure but through processes of repetition and gradual accumulation reminiscent both of bebop and of John Coltrane's later "sheets of sound" style. Cartiér uses this narrative technique to portray the diversity of African American experiences, depicting rural, urban, and suburban life through **slavery**, segregation, integration, and contemporary times.

In *Muse-Echo Blues* (1991), Cartiér similarly demonstrates the literary possibilities of jazz. In this second novel, she depicts three generations of African American women struggling to realize their creative impulses and assert their independence in a predominantly patriarchal society. Kat is a jazz composer in the 1990s, struggling with a creative block, who fabricates Lena and Kitty, the mother and lover, respectively, of Chicago, an archetypal jazz musician. By conjuring these characters, Kat explores African American experiences in the 1930s and 1940s for sources of inspiration, as Cartiér self-consciously problematizes the role of history and tradition. With a cast of characters that includes the jazz musicians Sonny Stitt, Lester Young, and Sarah Vaughan, and directly inspired by Cecil Taylor, the novel is explicitly aligned with a jazz aesthetic that, through the structure, language, and imagery of the text, blurs generic boundaries.

Through her use of first-person narrative and her complex narrative structure, one that shifts between tenses, registers, and narrative moments, Cartiér engages with and effectively subverts various literary traditions. The confessional story of maturation in, and final escape from, alienating environments, related in *Be-Bop, Re-Bop*, articulates the central themes of the **slave narrative**. Furthermore, Cartiér offers a postmodern rewriting of the traditional **romance novel**, manifested in *Muse-Echo Blues*, for example, in the recurring themes of alienation and disorientation, and in rapidly changing perspectives elaborating on the different relationships described in the novel. Finally, through the musical poetry of her prose, Cartiér specifically participates in an African American creative project, evoking, in her innovative jazz style, such writers as **Jayne Cortez, Langston Hughes, Nathaniel Mackey,** and **Ishmael Reed**.

Resources: Xam Wilson Cartiér, *Be-Bop, Re-Bop* (New York: Available Press, 1987); *Muse-Echo Blues* (New York: Harmony Books, 1991); Valerie Smith, "Dancing to Daddy's Favorite Jam," *New York Times*, Dec. 13, 1987, sec. 7, p. 12; Rayfield Allen Waller, "'Sheets of Sound': A Woman's Bop Prosody," *Black American Literature Forum* 24, no. 4 (Winter 1990), 791–802.

Keren Omry

Cary, Lorene (born 1956). Novelist and memoirist. Tackling such themes as the **Underground Railroad**, a young woman's coming of age, the struggle to discover identity at midlife, and Blackness in a quintessentially White world,

Cary's work strives to break stereotypes of Black culture and show that there are many possibilities of success for African American women and men.

Born to John and Carole Hamilton Cary, she grew up and attended school in **Philadelphia, Pennsylvania**. In 1972 she became the first Black female student, and later teacher, at St. Paul's School in New Hampshire. This experience would be the subject of her first book, a memoir titled *Black Ice* (1991). Perhaps her most widely known book, *Black Ice* recounts the struggle of a young Black woman to understand herself and the standards to which she must hold and exceed to be successful in a traditionally White, male school. Her coming of age story was also critically acclaimed. *Black Ice* was named a Notable Book by the American Library Association in 1992. It has been called a "remarkable story with grace and eloquence" (Ott, 264).

In 1995, Cary published her first novel, *The Price of a Child*, which was chosen by her hometown as the One Book, One Philadelphia selection. This novel is the story of Ginny Pryor, an escaped slave who must leave her child behind in order to seek freedom. Cary deals not only with the issues of **slavery** and the **abolitionist movement**, but also with a mother's love for a child and the healing that comes from helping others. In the end, the price of Ginny's child is paid by the numerous men and women she is able to help out of slavery. A dramatically different narrative, Cary's second novel, *Pride* (1998), is the story of four Black women who are about to turn forty. Friends since high school, Cary's characters—an Episcopal priest, a politician's wife, a college professor, and an on-and-off recovering alcoholic—break down stereotypes of Black culture and the role of women in society. In the end, her characters find pride in both their sisterhood as Black women and the unique qualities and heritage of Black culture.

Cary currently teaches creative writing at the University of Pennsylvania, where she received her bachelor's and master's degrees, and has been awarded the Provost's Award for Distinguished Teaching. She has received Doctorates of Human Letters from Colby College, Keene State College, and Chestnut Hill College. Before her career in academia, Cary worked for *Time* magazine and was an associate editor for *TV Guide*. She has written freelance pieces for *Essence, Mirabella, American Visions* and the *Philadelphia Inquirer Sunday Magazine*, and has been a contributing editor for *Newsweek*.

In 1998, Cary founded Art Sanctuary, a nonprofit organization dedicated to bringing Black thinkers and artists to speak and perform as part of a lecture and performance series at Church of the Advocate, a historical landmark in North Philadelphia. Her work with Art Sanctuary has won numerous awards on both the local and the national levels. For her writing, she has received a Pew fellowship and the Leeway Award for Achievement, and has been a fellow at Civitella Ranieri and Yaddo. Cary is a member of PEN and the Authors Guild. She is also on the usage panel for the *American Heritage Dictionary*. She lives in Philadelphia.

Resources: Lorene Cary: *Black Ice* (New York: Knopf, 1991); *The Price of a Child* (New York: Knopf, 1995); *Pride* (New York: Doubleday, 1998); P. Lopate, in *New*

York Times Book Review, Mar. 31, 1991, p. 7; Marcus Mabry, "The Bounds of Blackness," *Newsweek*, June 24, 1991, p. 65; Hans Ostrom, "Prep-School Outsider Spins Painful Tale" (interview with Cary/review of *Black Ice*), *Soundlife* (Sunday supplement), *Morning News Tribune* (Tacoma, Washington), Mar. 8, 1992, p. 8; Bill Ott, "Peculiar Lives," *American Libraries* 23, no. 3 (1992), 264.

Melissa Hamilton Hayes

Cary, Mary Ann Camberton Shadd (1823–1893). Journalist, editor, educator, and activist. A lifelong advocate of racial integration, Shadd was one of the first Black women to lecture, to write pamphlets, to found a newspaper, and to receive a law degree. She also founded schools, recruited Black troops for the Union Army, and raised two children and three stepchildren.

Born into Delaware's Black elite, Shadd was introduced to activism by her father, Abraham Doras Shadd, a prosperous mixed-race shoemaker active in the **abolitionist movement**. After being educated by Quakers, Shadd taught in Pennsylvania, Delaware, and New York, and then wrote *Hints to the Colored People of the North* (1849), a pamphlet advocating racial uplift through education.

Joining the African American exodus following the Fugitive Slave Law in 1850, Shadd emigrated to Canada, where she set up a school in Windsor, Ontario, with support from the American Missionary Association (AMA). A pioneering educator among Canada's Black community, Shadd quickly became an outspoken advocate for integration, thus beginning a feud with **Henry Bibb**, who favored a separatist approach. Her letters to the abolitionist press and the pamphlet *A Plea for Emigration; or, Notes of Canada West, in Its Moral, Social, and Political Aspect* (1852) presented her stance to a growing audience, but led to vituperative attacks in Bibb's paper. Combined with Shadd's outspoken nature, this conflict arguably led to the AMA's withdrawal of support from her school.

In 1853, Shadd, with the aid of abolitionist Samuel Ringgold Ward, founded the *Provincial Freeman*, a newspaper for Canada's Blacks that appeared irregularly out of Toronto and Chatham until 1859. While Ward—and, later, William P. Newman—were named as editors, it was common knowledge that the men were simply a front to maintain social acceptability and that Shadd was the actual editor. Her journalism gained a reputation for its stinging directness, and items from the paper regularly appeared in the U.S. abolitionist press.

In 1856, Shadd married a Toronto barber, Thomas F. Cary. He seems to have been supportive of her work, and, though she helped raise his three children as well as two of the couple's own (a daughter born in 1857 and a son, in 1860) throughout this period, Shadd continued writing. Her editorial work on Osborne Anderson's account of John Brown, *A Voice from Harper's Ferry* (1861), is most notable. She also lectured on both sides of the border and opened significant opportunities for women in the mainly male venues for public discussion of abolition, temperance, colonization, and Black empowerment. While they often disagreed with her, she won the respect of figures ranging from **Frederick Douglass** to **Martin Delany**.

The death of her husband sometime prior to 1863 and the outbreak of the **Civil War** led Shadd to return to the United States, where she secured a commission as a recruiter for the Union Army. Though she thought seriously about returning to Canada after the war, she decided to stay in the United States. In her later years, she remained an active lecturer and writer, though she turned her attention more and more to questions of **gender**. She settled in **Washington, D.C.**, where she continued to teach, work as a community activist, and, intermittently, attend Howard University's law school. In 1883, she became the first woman to receive a law degree from Howard. She was an invited speaker at the 1878 National Women's Suffrage Association conference. She also continued writing—including a series of essays for Douglass's *New National Era*.

Resources: Jason H. Silverman: "Mary Ann Shadd and the Search for Equality," in *Black Leaders of the Nineteenth Century*, ed. Leon Litwack and August Meier (Urbana: University of Illinois Press, 1988), 87–100; *Unwelcome Guests: Canada West's Response to American Fugitive Slaves* (Millwood, NY: Associated Faculty Press, 1985); Jessie Carney Smith, "Mary Ann Shadd," in *Notable Black American Women*, ed. Smith, vol. 1 (Detroit: Gale, 1992), 998–1003.

Eric Gardner

Cassells, Cyrus (born 1957). Poet. Cyrus Cassells is an African American poet who also works as a professor, actor, and translator. He is the author of four volumes of poetry: *Beautiful Signor* (1997), which won the Lambda Literary Award; *Soul Make a Path Through Shouting* (1994), which won the Poetry Society of America's William Carlos Williams Award and was a finalist for the Associated Writing Program Series Award and the Lenore Marshall Prize for outstanding book of the year; and *The Mud Actor* (1982), which was a National Poetry Series selection. His newest book, *More Than Peace and Cypresses*, was published in 2004.

Cassells's numerous awards include a Pushcart Prize received in 1995 for his poem "Sung from a Hospice," and the Peter I. B. Lavan Younger Poets Award from the Academy of American Poets, as well as fellowships from the Lannan Foundation, the Rockefeller Foundation, and the National Endowment for the Arts.

Cassells was a creative writing fellow at the Fine Arts Work Center in Provincetown, Massachusetts (1982–1983) and then served as poet-in-resident at the College of the Holy Cross from 1989 to 1992. He has also taught at Emerson College in **Boston** (1992), Northeastern University in Boston (1990), Assumption College in Worcester, Massachusetts (1990), and George Mason University in Fairfax, Virginia. From 1991 to 1997 he lived in Florence and Rome, where he worked as an actor. He is currently associate professor of English in the M.F.A. program at Southwest Texas State University.

Cassells's literary accomplishments include a play, *Doctor Free*, which is about the **Underground Railroad**. He also has translated the work of the Catalan poet Salvador Espriu. Known for using rich, vivid language and writing in the lyric tradition, Cassells focuses on subjects that range from racial tension surrounding the 1957 integration of a Little Rock public school to the Holocaust, AIDS, Afghan refugee camps, and the Spanish Civil War. He often finds beauty alongside tragedy as he draws upon traditions that range from Greek mythology to the African American oral tradition, seeking to affirm the human spirit. His more recent work explores erotic love and the union of souls alongside human connection.

Resources: Cyrus Cassells: *Beautiful Signor* (Port Townsend, WA: Copper Canyon Press, 1997); *More Than Peace and Cypresses* (Port Townsend, WA: Copper Canyon Press, 2004); *The Mud Actor* (New York: Holt, Rinehart and Winston, 1982); *Soul Make a Path Through Shouting* (Port Townsend, WA: Copper Canyon Press, 1994); Malin Pereira, "An Interview with Cyrus Cassells," *Contemporary Literature* 44, no. 3 (Fall 2003), 381–398.

Elline Lipkin

Censorship. Censorship is defined as the attempt to control the flow of ideas and of new and untried opinions. Throughout history, censorship has been used as a tool to impede new knowledge, new science, new political ideas, new religious beliefs, and new social norms. It generally can take one of four forms: banning, destruction, licensure, or prior restraint. Governmental and religious authorities, social organizations, and academic institutions throughout the world have practiced censorship.

The First Amendment of the U.S. Constitution states: "Congress shall make no law respecting an establishment of religion, or prohibiting the free exercise thereof; or abridging the freedom of speech, or of the press; or the right of the people peaceably to assemble, and to petition the Government for a redress of grievances." While the Constitution arguably created the absolute right of freedom and the written word, there have been numerous attempts to rescind that right for writers who have promoted, subjectively speaking, "dangerous" thoughts and ideas.

The initial subjugation of African American writing can arguably be traced back to **slavery**. Statutes in several states made it illegal for slaves to read or write, thereby putting a stranglehold on Black creative thought. There were no schools in Southern states that would admit Black children, whether they were enslaved or free. The very act of becoming literate was an act of resistance for slaves. The African Americans who did learn to read and write had to rely upon ingenuity and persistence. Some slaves were taught to read by their masters; others taught each other; and many Blacks learned to read using the Bible. A handful of White teachers ran night schools; when they were caught, they faced being forced out of town and/or convicted and imprisoned. In 1860, **Frederick Douglass** eloquently spoke against the suppression of Black literacy: "To suppress free speech is a double wrong. It violates the rights of the hearer as well as those of the speaker. It is just as criminal to rob a man of his right to speak and hear as it would be to rob him of his money" (Douglass).

As slavery came to an end, Black literacy slowly increased until the height of African American creative expression during the **Harlem Renaissance** in the early twentieth century. Since then, Black literature has evolved into a diverse field with African American writers reflecting the spectrum of the Black experience. There have been difficulties, however, and African American writers have struggled to be heard. "The Negro artist works against an undertow of sharp criticism and misunderstanding from his own group and unintentional bribes from the whites," wrote **Langston Hughes** in "The Negro Artist and the Racial Mountain" (1926). Black writers who chronicled racial injustices were often subjected to violence. In 1892, **Ida B. Wells** wrote an editorial defending several Black men accused of raping white women. After it was printed, the office of the *Memphis Free Speech*, the paper Wells wrote for, was attacked and equipment was destroyed.

In the years between then and now, Black writers have experienced numerous threats to their physical well-being and their ideas. Beyond overt violence and legislation designed to keep an entire people illiterate, certain groups have undertaken the task of having books challenged or banned. The American Library Association defines a challenge as an attempt to remove or restrict materials, based upon the objections of a person or group. A banning is the removal of those materials. Challenges do not simply involve a person expressing a point of view; rather, they are an attempt to remove material from the curriculum or library, thereby restricting the access of others. Generally, books are challenged or banned for explicit content, offensive language, or age-inappropriate content. In the year 2000, 6,364 challenges were reported to the Office of Intellectual Freedom. Since 1990, **Maya Angelou** has been the eighth most challenged author, for her book *I Know Why the Caged Bird Sings*, because of anti-White sentiment, offensive language, and sexual content.

There are countless examples of Black books being banned or censored. Five of **James Baldwin**'s books have been banned or challenged for alleged obscenity, allegedly tearing down Christian principles, and/or alleged sexual content. Excerpts of **Ralph Ellison**'s novel *Invisible Man* were banned in Pennsylvania, Wisconsin, and Washington because of offensive language, violence, and sexual content. **Eldridge Cleaver**'s *Soul on Ice* was banned from California public schools because of anti-American sentiment. The list goes on: *The Autobiography of Miss Jane Pittman* by **Ernest Gaines**; *My House* by **Nikki Giovanni**; *The Autobiography of Malcolm X*; *Raisin in the Sun* by **Lorraine Hansberry**; *Their Eyes Were Watching God* by **Zora Neale Hurston**; *Coffee Will Make You Black* by **April Sinclair**; and *Native Son* by **Richard Wright** have also been banned or challenged (Heins). The winners of the Pulitzer Prize, the National Book Award, and the American Fiction Award have not been immune. **Alice Walker** and **Toni Morrison** have had several of their books challenged on the basis of content (Heins; Walker).

Banned Books Week was established in 1982 by the American Library Association to celebrate literature and examine the roots of intolerance that seek to censor self-expression. The events of the week celebrate the freedom to choose and the freedom to express one's opinion even if that opinion might be considered unorthodox or unpopular, and stresses the importance of ensuring the availability of unorthodox or unpopular viewpoints to all who wish to read them. Libraries throughout the country feature historically banned books, organize readings and discussions, hold film festivals and sponsor essay contests to increase awareness of the issues surrounding censorship and challenging and banning books. The American Civil Liberties Union fights censorship by intervening when books are inappropriately banned or challenged.

Resources: Maya Angelou, *I Know Why The Caged Bird Sings* (New York: Bantam, 1983); James Baldwin, *Go Tell It on the Mountain* (New York: Laurel, 1985); Janet D. Cornelius, *"When I Can Read My Title Clear": Literacy, Slavery, and Religion in the Antebellum South* (Columbia: University of South Carolina Press, 1991); Frederick Douglass, "A Plea for Free Speech in Boston" (1860), National Coalition Against Censorship, http://www.ncac.org/issues/blackhistory.html; Ralph Ellison, *Invisible Man* (New York: Vintage, 1995); Nikki Giovanni, *My House* (New York: Perennial, 1974); Marjorie Heins, *Sex, Sin and Blasphemy: A Guide to America's Censorship Wars* (New York: New Press, 1993); Langston Hughes, "The Negro Artist and the Racial Mountain," in *The Portable Harlem Renaissance Reader*, ed. David Levering Lewis (New York: Viking, 1994), 91–95; Louise Robins, *The Dismissal of Miss Ruth Brown: Civil Rights, Censorship and the Amrican Library* (Norman: University of Oklahoma Press, 2000); Alice Walker, *Banned* (San Francisco: Aunt Lute Press, 1996).

Roxane Gay

Chambers, Veronica (born 1971). Screenwriter, editor, journalist, and writer. Veronica Chambers is an award-winning Black Latina author of *Mamma's Girl* (1996), an American Library Association Best Book of 1996. Her writing focuses on her African and Latina heritages. Veronica Chambers was born in Panama. She left Panama at age two and spent the next three years in England before coming to the United States at age five. She grew up in **Brooklyn, New York**. An excellent student, she graduated summa cum laude from Simon's Rock College.

Chambers began her career as an intern at *Sassy* magazine, then became a columnist for *Seventeen*. She has been senior editor for *Premiere* magazine, executive editor of *Savoy*, and senior editor of the *New York Times Magazine*. She has also been a culture writer for and associate editor of *Newsweek*. Chambers has written numerous articles for magazines and newspapers, including *Essence*, the *Village Voice, Utne, Travel and Leisure, USA Weekend, Food and Wine*, and *Vogue*. At this writing she is a staff writer for the UPN hit comedy *Girlfriends*.

Chambers has received numerous awards, including a grant from the National Endowment for the Arts, and the prestigious 2001–2002 Hodder fellowship for emerging novelists from Princeton University. She was a Freedom Forum fellow at Columbia University. *Mamma's Girl* was a selection of the Book-of-the-Month Club.

Chambers's books include *Poetic Justice: Filmmaking South Central Style* (1993), which she wrote with filmmaker John Singleton; *The Harlem Renaissance* (1997); *Amistad Rising: A Story of Freedom* (1998), a picture book; *Marisol and Magdalena: The Sound of Our Sisterhood* (1998); *Quinceañera Means Sweet Fifteen* (2001); *Double Dutch: A Celebration of Jump Rope, Rhyme, and*

Sisterhood (2002); *Having It All? Black Women and Success* (2003); and *When Did You Stop Loving Me?* (New York: Doubleday, 2004). Chambers also has contributed to several anthologies, including *The Bitch in the House* (2003); *Growing Up Ethnic in America* (1999); *Black Hair: Art, Style and Culture* (2001); *Becoming American* (2000); and *Body* (2000).

Resources: Veronica Chambers: *Amistad Rising: A Story of Freedom* (San Diego: Harcourt Brace, 1998); *Double Dutch: A Celebration of Jump Rope, Rhyme, and Sisterhood* (New York: Jump at the Sun/Hyperion, 2002); "Dreadlocked: You See My Hair, but Do You See Me?," *Utne Reader*, Sept./Oct. 1999, http://www.utne.com/pub/1999_95/features/579-1.html; "Driving: Baja Behind the Wheel," *Travel and Leisure*, Oct. 2000, www.travelandleisure.com/invoke.cfm?page=2&ObjectID=C2C8DB24-CF46-4B1F-AC2BF081A7431A29; *The Harlem Renaissance* (Broomall, PA: Chelsea House, 1997); *Having It All? Black Women and Success* (New York: Doubleday, 2003); *Mama's Girl* (New York: Riverhead Books, 1996); *Marisol and Magdalena: The Sound of Our Sisterhood* (New York: Jump at the Sun, 1998); *Quinceañera Means Sweet Fifteen* (New York: Hyperion, 2001); "The Secret Latina," *Essence*, July 2000, 102, 152; Web site, www.veronicachambers.com; *When Did You Stop Loving Me* (New York: Doubleday, 2004); Veronica Chambers and John Singleton, *Poetic Justice: Filmmaking South Central Style* (New York: Delta, 1993); Meri Nana-Ama Danquah, ed., *Becoming American: Personal Essays by First Generation Immigrant Women* (New York: Hyperion, 2000); Ima Ebong, ed., *Black Hair: Art, Style, and Culture* (New York: Universe Publishing, 2001); *Family Literacy Author Residencies*, "Veronica Chambers," 2000, http://www.nationalbook.org/famlit2000vchambers.html; Sharon S. Fiffer and Steve Fiffer, eds., *Body* (New York: Perennial, 2000); Maria Mazziotti Gillam et al., eds., *Growing Up Ethnic in America: Contemporary Fiction About Learning to Be American* (New York: Penguin, 1999); Cathy Hanauer, ed., *The Bitch in the House: 26 Women Tell the Truth About Sex, Solitude, Work, Motherhood, and Marriage* (New York: Perennial Currents, 2003).

Patricia L T Camp

Chancy, Myriam J. A. (born 1970). Writer and professor. Chancy was born in Port-au-Prince, **Haiti**, in 1970, a year that marked the end of the first Duvalier dictatorship and the start of the "Baby Doc" Duvalier regime. She grew up in the cities of Quebec and Winnipeg in Canada after her family left Haiti. After completing studies in English literature at the universities of Manitoba and Halifax, she became a translator as well as a writer. Her first work appeared in a publication for young writers, *proemCanada* (1989), and was a short story titled "Andrew's Universe." In the same magazine she published her first essay, "Soul Searching," and her first photograph, "Osborne Village." At the same time, Chancy became involved in a program for aboriginal women and in a research project concerning women and cross-generational experiences. In 1997 the result of that research was a book, *Searching for Safe Spaces*.

Chancy's career was also becoming an academic one. She received her Ph.D. in English at the University of Iowa (1994) and published two influential essays, "Sin Fronteras/Sans Frontières: Women of Color Writing for Empowerment" and "Black Women Writing; or, How to Tell It Like It Is." During her sabbatical leave in the fall of 1995, while she was an assistant professor at Vanderbilt University, she wrote her first published book, *Framing Silence: Revolutionary Novels by Haitian Women* (1997), on the U.S. occupation of Haiti in the first part of the twentieth century. She discovered that Haitian women writers had preceded her in writing personal and polemical essays and fiction on the American occupation. By 1994, Chancy and two other women writers of Haitian descent, **Edwidge Danticat** and Anne-Christine D'Adesky, were assuming the existence of a Haitian female literary tradition. After her appointment as an associate professor at the University of Arizona, Chancy was produced *Spirit of Haiti* (1998) and was involved in conferences around the world. She has been a member of the editorial boards of **Callaloo** and *Journal of Haitian Studies*. After her resignation from her position at the University of Arizona, she decided to pursue her career as a freelance writer/teacher and consultant. From 2002 to 2004, she was editor in chief of *Meridians* and taught at Smith College. In 2004 she published the novel *The Scorpion's Claw*, set in Haiti.

Resources: Myriam J. A. Chancy: "Black Woman Writing; or, How to Tell It Like It Is," in *Canadian Woman Studies: An Introductory Reader*, ed. Nuzhat Amin et al. (Toronto: Inanna Publications and Education, 1999), 45–52; "Brother/Outsider: In Search of a Black Gay Legacy in James Baldwin's *Giovanni's Room*," in *The Gay '90's: Disciplinary and Interdisciplinary Formations in Queer Studies*, ed. Thomas Foster et al. (New York: New York University Press, 1997), 155–190; *Framing Silence: Revolutionary Novels by Haitian Women* (New Brunswick, NJ: Rutgers University Press, 1997); *The Scorpion's Claw* (London: Peepal Tree Press, 2004); *Searching for Safe Spaces: Afro-Caribbean Women Writers in Exile* (Philadelphia: Temple University Press, 1997); "Sin Fronteras/Sans Frontières: Women of Color Writing for Empowerment," *Frontiers: A Journal of Women Studies* 13, no. 2 (1993), 153–167; *Spirit of Haiti* (1998; repr. New York: Mango Publishing, 2004).

Jérôme Ceccon

Charles, Kraal (Kayo) Y. (born 1975). Actor, poet, writer, and producer. Born in **Brooklyn**, Kayo Charles was raised listening to **rap**'s finest poets, and soon developed a talent for writing biting, acerbic rhymes that criticized the state of the society in which he found himself. Although he claims that he was initially unaware that **hip-hop** was a form of poetry and social commentary, Charles later stated that he realized that if he became a "good rhymester it would innately lead him on a journey to become a better poet." Charles was heavily influenced by the work of **Amiri Baraka**, **Langston Hughes** and **Sonia Sanchez**. Accepting a dare from friends landed Charles on the open-mike stage at the renowned **Nuyorican Poets Café** in New York City. Charles went on to become Nuyorican's youngest Grand Slam Champion in 1998 and has since been featured on *Russell Simon's Def Poetry*, *Hughes Dreams Harlem*, and *Bone Bristle—A Spoken Word Documentary*. Charles studied at the Medgar Evers College of the City University of New York, obtaining his bachelor's degree in marketing. Now a full-time poet and dramatist, Charles has traveled throughout Europe and North America, and took part in the first European

Poetry Exposition, where he performed his unique brand of poetry in his inimitable, deliberately monotone voice. He has published a book of poetry titled *Bridges to Build, Rivers to Cross, Mountains to Move* (2000). His uncompromising commentary on life, politics, and love has made Charles a favorite on the poetry scene and on radio stations, and at colleges and universities across North America. His critically acclaimed one-person show had its off-Broadway debut in 2001. The show, *Lessons I Have Learned as a Man That I Will Tell My Son*, highlights the problematic process of trying to raise a moral, law-abiding son in an irresponsible, dissolute society. Charles has produced one-person shows for Def Poets such as Helena D. Lewis, Daniel Beaty, Regie Cabico, and Yolanda Wilkinson, and has performed in and produced an off-Broadway show titled *Snippets: Which Way to Broadway* (2003). Charles has completed a two-act poetical play titled *The Tragedy of Brooklyn*, which will be produced in April 2005, and has set up PAGA Communications, an Internet-based company dedicated to promoting the spoken word.

Resources: Kraal Y. Charles: *Bridges to Build, Rivers to Cross, Mountains to Move* (New York: PAGA Communications, 2000); www.kayospeaks.com; J. Victoria Sanders, "Moving Mountains in a Literary Landscape," www.horizonmag.com.

Sarah Lynsey Williams

Chase-Riboud, Barbara (born 1939). Poet and novelist. Chase-Riboud is best known for the best-selling novel *Sally Hemings*, in which she depicts a lifelong relationship between Thomas Jefferson and his slave, **Sally Hemings**. Drawing attention to "folklore" that turned out to contain more truth than the official narrative of American history (as subsequent DNA tests have shown), her novel changed the way Jefferson's residence, Monticello, was perceived (Mesa), and it changed U.S. copyright law concerning creative material in historical fiction (Cohen). Her writing has brought attention to other significant historical events in African American history. Trained in the visual arts, music, dance, and poetry, Chase-Riboud first received recognition at the age of fifteen when the Museum of Modern Art in New York purchased her print-work. Born in **Philadelphia, Pennsylvania**, Chase-Riboud had established herself in **Paris, France**, as a sculptor by her twenties. She began to write poetry in 1974, published in *From Memphis and Peking*, and wrote her first novel in 1979. For Chase-Riboud, "writing isn't [a] second choice. Writing is a parallel vocation" (Munsch and Wilmer).

In her work Chase-Riboud writes about, among other things, a kidnapped White **Creole**, Valide, who became Queen Mother of the Ottoman Empire; the triumph of kidnapped Africans over the crew of the *Amistad*; a portrait of a nude Cleopatra; life as she imagines it might have been for Sally Hemings's fair-skinned daughter, Harriet, who was allowed to "stroll" away from **slavery** to live in the North; and a fictionalized set of memoirs of Sshura, the Khosian girl kidnapped in South Africa, renamed the Hottentot Venus, and put on display in England and France in the early nineteenth century (2003).

Chase-Riboud has won a John Hay Whitney fellowship, a National Endowment for the Arts fellowship, the Janet Heidinger Kafka Prize (*Sally Hemings*), and the American Library Association's Black Caucus Award for best novel of 2003 (*Hottentot Venus*). She divides her time between Paris and Rome.

Resources: B. J. Bolden, "Chase-Riboud, Barbara Dewayne (D'Ashnash Tosi)," in *Black Women in America: An Historical Encyclopedia*, ed. Darlene Clark Hine (Brooklyn, NY: Carlson, 1993); Barbara Chase-Riboud: *Echo of Lions* (New York: William Morrow, 1989); *From Memphis & Peking* (New York: Random House, 1974); *Hottentot Venus* (New York: Doubleday, 2003); *Portrait of a Nude Woman as Cleopatra* (New York: William Morrow, 1987); *The President's Daughter* (New York: Crown, 1994); *Sally Hemings* (New York: Viking, 1979); *Valide: A Novel of the Harem* (New York: Random House, 1986); Roger Cohen, "Judge Says Copyright Covers Writer's Ideas of a Jefferson Affair," *New York Times*, Aug. 15, 1991, pp. C1, C17; Vanessa F. Johnson, "*Hottentot Venus: A Novel*," Copperfield Review. www.copperfieldreview .com/reviews/hottentot_venus.html; Christina Mesa, personal interview with Barbara Chase-Riboud, June 1993; Andrew Munsch and Gregg Wilmer, "Barbara Chase-Riboud," *Voices from the Gaps: Women Writers of Color*, http://voices.cla.umn.edu/ newsite/authors/CHASERIBOUDbarbara.htm; Lisa Clayton Robinson, "Chase-Riboud, Barbara Dewayne," in *Africana: The Encyclopedia of African and African American Experience*, ed. Kwame Anthony Appiah and Henry Louis Gates, Jr. (New York: BasicCivitas Books, 1999); Virago, "Barbara Chase-Riboud: Interview," www .virago.co.uk/virago/meet/chase-riboud_interview.

Christina Mesa

Chennault, Stephen D. (born 1940). Poet, essayist, short story writer, and professor. Born, raised, and educated in **Detroit, Michigan**, Chennault earned his master's and doctorate of arts in English and sociolinguistics from the University of Michigan. The author of several articles and books dealing with black idiom, he has held a joint position as national coordinator of Teachers Recruitment Projects for the National Council of Teachers of English and as associate professor of English at the University of Illinois in Champaign.

From 1995 to 2002, Chennault appeared as a guest analyst on "Polishing Ideas: The Canon of Style," one of twenty-two segments of a videotaped freshman composition telecourse titled *A Writers' Exchange*. This production was the first telecourse produced to interact with computer software in providing collaboration among students and instructors.

A senior Fulbright scholar at the Universities of Florence and Pisa in Italy, Chennault is the author of "*Re'lize Whut Ahm Talkin' 'Bout?*" (1997), a collection of tales and short stories written in Ebonics. Linguist James Sledd, professor emeritus of English at the University of Texas in Austin, stated: "Chennault's book . . . is one of the attempts by black writers in the U.S.A. to demonstrate the potentialities of the Black English Vernacular for literary use. . . .Better than anyone else I've read, Steve makes the component reader *hear* the speech of his characters."

Chennault's most recent publication is *Jump at de Sun* (2002), an anthology of personal experience essays, short stories, biographical profiles, poetry, and a play. His essays on Black English inform the reader about the essence of the language spoken by African Americans. The stories express various aspects of urban life, such as the language of the streets of Detroit, in homes or nightclubs.

Presently, Chennault is writing a novel and completing an anthology of short stories. The anthology will include the works of his creative writing students at Wayne County Community College in Detroit.

Resources: Stephen D. Chennault: "Black Dialect: A Cultural Shock," in *Minority Language and Literature: Retrospective and Perspective*, ed. Dexter Fisher (New York: Modern Language Association, 1977), 71–79; *"Re'lize Whut Ahm Talkin' 'Bout?"* (Needham Heights, MA: Simon and Schuster, 1997); "Ways to Approach Dialect Study in the Junior High School English Classroom," in *Questions English Teachers Ask*, ed. R. Baird Shuman (Rochelle Park, NJ: Hayden Books, 1977), 107–109; Stephen D. Chennault, ed., *Jump at de Sun* (New York: McGraw-Hill, 2002).

Ella Davis

Chesnutt, Charles Waddell (1858–1932). Short story writer and novelist. Widely regarded as the most influential African American writer of the late nineteenth and early twentieth centuries, Charles W. Chesnutt voiced the experiences and concerns of mixed-race, middle-class African Americans as well as those of the working-class Blacks of the rural **South**. His stated objective was "not so much the elevation of the colored people as the elevation of the whites" (Broadhead, 139). In other words, he believed that greater social equality for African Americans could be accomplished by a reformation of White social perceptions. Chesnutt envisioned himself as a writer from a young age, and though he earned substantial (if sporadic) critical praise as well as unprecedented acceptance from a White-controlled publishing industry, he would never become successful enough to support himself by his writing alone. Late twentieth-century criticism, however, has recognized Chesnutt as a significant contributor to the development of African American short fiction, an innovator of novel forms, an enabler of the **Harlem Renaissance** of the 1920s, and a figure of indisputable importance in the canon of American literature.

Born in Cleveland, Ohio, in 1858, Chesnutt was the son of free, mixed-race African Americans who were both illegitimate children of White fathers. In 1866 the family moved to Fayetteville, North Carolina, where Charles's father established a grocery store. Chesnutt worked in the store and attended school until 1871, when the death of his mother forced him to seek full-time employment. At the age of fourteen he began working as a teacher, and by 1880 he was principal of a Fayetteville normal school for Blacks. He spent much of his free time in these years studying European literary classics. In 1878 Chesnutt married and began establishing a family, but these professional and domestic responsibilities were unable to quell the literary ambitions of his youth, and he resigned from the normal school in 1883 to pursue a life of letters. By 1887 he had moved his family back to Cleveland, passed the Ohio bar examination, and established his own court reporting business. Chesnutt also began to hone his talents as a writer, publishing short sketches with the S. S. McClure newspaper organization throughout the late 1880s. This gained him the attention and friendship of George Washington Cable, a prominent figure on the Southern literary scene, and through this connection he began writing essays for the Open Letter Club, a group that sought solutions for the socioeconomic difficulties of the postwar South.

Chesnutt's first major success as a writer occurred when "The Goophered Grapevine" (1887) was accepted for publication by *The Atlantic Monthly*. On the surface, this short story seems to operate in the tradition of Southern plantation fiction popularized by Joel Chandler Harris and Thomas Nelson Page, as it featured an ex-slave storyteller named Uncle Julius McAdoo, a **trickster** figure similar to the storyteller of Harris's Uncle Remus tales. Chesnutt manipulated this convention, however, to contradict the typically romanticized view of Southern plantation life and to introduce elements of Black folk culture, such as conjuration lore and hoodoo beliefs. *The Atlantic Monthly* printed two more of Chesnutt's Uncle Julius stories over the next two years, and in 1898 the prestigious Houghton Mifflin publishing house in **Boston, Massachusetts**, agreed to publish several of the stories as a collection. The following year, this collection was issued under the title *The Conjure Woman* (1899). Considered as a whole, these stories represent one of the first literary validations of the African American plantation experience by an African American author, and they did much to debunk the mythology of a plantation-era golden age and the notion that former slaves yearned in any way for its revival. (*See* **Conjuring**.)

Promising sales and a favorable critical reception prompted Houghton Mifflin to publish a second collection of stories. *The Wife of His Youth and Other Stories of the Color Line* (1899) represented a different direction in Chesnutt's writing, but one that was much closer to his own lived experience. Chesnutt had published a story in *The Independent* titled "The Sheriff's Children" (1889), which proved to be the seed of a major literary theme in his career. Eight more stories dealing with similar topics were written over the next decade, including the title story of the collection, which appeared in *The Atlantic Monthly* just months before the publication of *The Conjure Woman*. These stories addressed such sensitive social issues as segregation, racial violence in the era of **Reconstruction**, and, predominantly, the repercussions and complications of miscegenation. Chesnutt sought to express in these tales the conflicts and the dehumanization inherent in the mixed-race African American's search for identity along the color line, the ethnically ambiguous intersection between White and Black.

Several contemporary literary figures, William Dean Howells among them, heralded *The Wife of His Youth* as a triumph of realist fiction. The critical reception and the public's reaction were decidedly less enthusiastic, but this did not prevent Chesnutt from turning his energy completely to writing. Having established a name for himself, he felt he would be able to compensate for irregular sales by taking on the odd literary job. Small, Maynard, and Company of Boston, for instance, commissioned him to write a high school-level biography of **Frederick Douglass** (1899), which appeared in the Beacon

Biographies series. In late 1899, Chesnutt closed the doors of his business and submitted to Houghton Mifflin a novel-length version of an unpublished short story that had originally been titled "Rena Walden." In March 1900 the novel was published as *The House Behind the Cedars*. Again taking up the theme of miscegenation, the novel portrays the social and psychological tribulations of a **mulatto** heroine, Rena Walden, as she attempts to pass as White in order to attain a level of prosperity that is forbidden to her as a woman of mixed race. In keeping with Chesnutt's general literary objective, *The House Behind the Cedars* questioned a White-dominated society that offered promises of the American dream but enforced an unspoken racial caste system that imposed limits on an individual's ability to succeed.

The House Behind the Cedars was well received by critics as a sensible depiction of a legitimate social problem. The sales, however, were moderate at best. Still, Houghton Mifflin was confident enough in Chesnutt to solicit another novel, which he readily provided. This second novel, *The Marrow of Tradition* (1901), is a fictionalized rendering of the Wilmington, North Carolina, massacre of 1898, in which several Blacks were killed during a white supremacist uprising. The book extends Chesnutt's exploration of the color line, depicting the tense interactions between an aristocratic White family and a mixed-race family who have both been drawn into the town's violent events. The novel's characterizations, along with its intricate scheme of subplots, allow it to comment on a variety of Southern cultural issues from a variety of perspectives and mark it as Chesnutt's most complex work. Sales and reviews were disappointing , however, and Chesnutt was faced with the reality of his family's needs. In 1902 he resumed his court stenography business.

Writing on the side, Chesnutt produced *The Colonel's Dream* (1905), the last novel to be published in his lifetime. Though this novel deals with race issues, Chesnutt attempted to secure the empathy of White readers by using a White protagonist, Col. Henry French, an ex-Confederate officer who returns to his Southern homeland after acquiring substantial wealth in the North. He attempts to alleviate the socioeconomic depression he finds there, but the depravity and unwillingness of the community, along with unchecked acts of racial violence, convince him of the futility of his efforts. In a larger sense, the novel can be read as an expression of Chesnutt's own sense of failure in his efforts to change White attitudes. Chesnutt continued to work as an essayist and activist until his death in 1932.

Chesnutt's impact on the development of African American literature was unquestionably deep. He has come to be regarded as the initiator of the first truly definable African American short story tradition, and the inclusiveness of Black perspectives present in his works prompted the **NAACP** to present him with Spingarn Medal in 1928. His entry into the White publishing world set an irrevocable precedent, and his tireless efforts to expose the social conventions that bolstered racial disharmony paved a road upon which the **New Negro** authors were able to step forward. Ironically, Chesnutt united briefly with **W.E.B Du Bois** and **William Stanley Braithwaite** in the late

1920s to criticize the experimentations of the Harlem Renaissance. In his essay "Post-Bellum—Pre-Harlem" (1931), however, he expressed a realization that he belonged to a bygone era and that the continued progression of the African American literary voice was positive evidence of the strength and resonance it had achieved in American culture.

Resources: William L. Andrews, *The Literary Career of Charles W. Chesnutt* (Baton Rouge: Louisiana State University Press, 1980); Bernard W. Bell, *The Afro-American Novel and Its Tradition* (Amherst: University of Massachusetts Press, 1987); Robert Bone, *Down Home: Origins of the Afro-American Short Story* (New York: Columbia University Press, 1975; Richard Brodhead, ed., *The Journals of Charles W. Chesnutt* (Durham, NC: Duke University Press, 1993); Charles Waddell Chesnutt: *The Colonel's Dream* (New York: Doubleday, Page, 1905); *The Conjure Woman* (Boston: Houghton Mifflin, 1899); *The House Behind the Cedars* (Boston: Houghton Mifflin, 1900); *Mandy Oxendine*, ed. Charles Hackenberry (Urbana: University of Illinois Press, 1997); *The Marrow of Tradition* (Boston: Houghton Mifflin, 1901); *The Wife of His Youth and Other Stories of the Color Line* (Boston: Houghton Mifflin, 1899); Helen Chesnutt, *Charles W. Chesnutt: Pioneer of the Color Line* (Chapel Hill: University of North Carolina Press, 1993); J. Noel Heermance, *Charles W. Chesnutt: America's First Great Black Novelist* (Hamden, CT: Archon, 1974); Frances Richardson Keller, *An American Crusade: The Life of Charles Waddell Chesnutt* (Provo, UT: Brigham Young University Press, 1978); Ernestine Williams Pickens, *Charles W. Chesnutt and the Progressive Movement* (New York: Pace University Press, 1994); Sylvia Lyons Render, *Charles W. Chesnutt* (Boston: Twayne, 1980); Eric Sundquist, *To Wake the Nations: Race in the Making of American Literature* (Cambridge, MA: Harvard University Press, 1993); Henry B. Wonham, *Charles W. Chesnutt: A Study of the Short Fiction* (New York: Twayne, 1998).

Lewis T. LeNaire

Chicago, Illinois. A creative center of African American cultural expression, Chicago is the birthplace and home of numerous authors. The city is also portrayed in and provides the setting for important works of literature. In addition, Chicago institutions have actively promoted literary creativity and encouraged public awareness of the resulting works.

Chicago's African American history began in the 1780s, when Jean Baptiste Pointe du Sable, an immigrant from **Haiti** who was of African ancestry, became the area's first non-American Indian resident. By 1850, Chicago had established itself as an important economic center in the trade of grain and livestock. The burgeoning city's African American population remained small, approximately 300 in a city of 30,000. While some Black residents were free, others were fugitives who had escaped **slavery**. Chicago was a stop along the network of escape routes that comprised the **Underground Railroad**, which transported slaves to freedom in the North and Canada. The black population of Chicago steadily increased in the years following the **Civil War** as the city became increasingly industrialized. A Black neighborhood on the city's South Side, the "Black Belt," began to take shape. The city's first Black official was elected in 1871, and Chicago's first African American newspaper, the *Conservator*, was established in 1878. In the 1890s, Chicago journalist and activist **Ida B. Wells-Barnett** made international headlines for speaking out against racial injustice and **lynching**.

At the turn of the century, Chicago's Black residents numbered 30,000, less than 2 percent of the total population. They had created a community with its own leadership, institutions, and services. This community was created largely out of necessity, since the city remained highly segregated. African Americans worked largely in the service industry until the outbreak of **World War I**. The resulting labor shortages provided new employment opportunities for Black workers, who took jobs in the steel mills and stockyards. At the same time, economic conditions in the Southern states had deteriorated. Northern industrial cities became the destination for almost 1 million African Americans, who desired greater social, economic, and political freedoms. Despite increased access to employment, schools, and other resources in the North, African Americans continued to experience racism and discrimination, intensified by competition for jobs and housing. Nevertheless, the **Great Migration** continued, urged on by institutions such as the Black newspaper the ***Chicago Defender***. Founded in 1905 by Robert S. Abbott, the newspaper provided advice and encouragement to those considering and planning the move north. In 1919, racial tensions came to a head and **race riots** erupted in Chicago and other Northern cities. These riots emphasized the reality that racism and discrimination were not simply Southern problems, but American problems.

In 1930, more than 230,000 African Americans lived in Chicago. Chicago had already shaped the literary works of the poet **Fenton Johnson** and the novelist **Nella Larsen**, whose *Quicksand* (1928) was set in the city of her birth. That year, the essayist and short story writer **Marita Bonner** moved to Chicago from the East Coast. The city's largest Black community was Bronzeville, the South Side neighborhood that became the center of Black Chicago's literary activity. Bronzeville was home to the South Side Writers' Group, a network of aspiring Black authors who met weekly to discuss their work. The group included **Richard Wright, Margaret Walker**, the poet **Frank Marshall Davis**, and the playwright **Theodore Ward**. Writers were also drawn together through the Works Progress Administration (WPA). In 1935, the WPA was established by President Franklin Roosevelt to provide jobs for the growing number of Americans left unemployed by the **Great Depression**. Among the cultural projects supported by the WPA, the **Federal Writers' Project** hired both Black and White authors to collect local history and folklore in each state. These histories were compiled to create the series Guide to America. In Chicago, the Illinois Writers' Project hired numerous African American authors. WPA projects also supported writers in other genres, including sociological and historical studies by **Katherine Dunham**, St. Clair Drake, Horace Cayton, and **E. Franklin Frazier**.

Government-supported employment allowed these novelists, poets, playwrights, and scholars to concentrate on their own writings. In a 1950 essay,

Arna Bontemps wrote that the WPA assemblage of Black authors and their creative output made Chicago "the center of the second phase of Negro literary awakening" (46). (The first phase was the work from New York's **Harlem Renaissance** of the 1920s and 1930s.) Thirty-six years later, scholar Robert Bone agreed that a distinct "literary generation"—a "Chicago School" of Black writers—had emerged between 1935 and 1950 (448). This period is also referred to as the **Chicago Renaissance**. In 1935, Richard Wright wrote *Lawd Today!* (not published until 1963), followed by *Native Son* (1940). Arna Bontemps's *Black Thunder* (1936), **William Attaway**'s *Blood on the Forge* (1941), and **Margaret Walker**'s *For My People* (1942) were notable works of this period, as were **Frank Yerby**'s historical novel *The Foxes of Harrow* (1946) and **Willard Motley**'s *Knock on Any Door* (1947).

Chicago's Black press actively promoted the work of its community's authors. The *Chicago Defender* published many works, including early poems by **Gwendolyn Brooks** and a series of short stories by **Langston Hughes** featuring his well-known character "Simple." In the early 1940s, John H. Johnson launched the magazine **Negro Digest**, which regularly featured short stories and poems, as well as commentary about books, music, the visual and performing arts, and their creators. Black authors also received support from the philanthropy of the Chicago-based Julius Rosenwald Fund, which awarded grants to advance Black scholarship and creative works.

Fictional works by or about the experiences of Black Chicagoans gained national attention during the 1940s and 1950s. Wright's *Native Son* (1940) was the first work by an African American author to be chosen as a Book-of-the-Month Club selection. Gwendolyn Brooks became the first African American to be awarded the Pulitzer Price for her second book of poetry, *Annie Allen* (1949). **Lorraine Hansberry**'s play *A Raisin in the Sun* (1959) was the first by a black female playwright to be produced on Broadway, where it earned the New York Drama Critics' Circle Award. Lesser known authors who wrote about Chicago include Waters E. Turpin (*O Canaan!*, 1939), Alden Bland (*Behold a Cry*, 1947), and **Frank London Brown** (*Trumbull Park*, 1959).

By the mid-1960s, the civil rights message of integration through nonviolent protest was increasingly challenged. In Chicago the Black population was nearing 1 million, approximately one-fifth of all residents. Yet segregation was still prevalent, especially in housing. The **Black Power** movement argued that African Americans needed to take pride in their difference and assert their political influence "by any means necessary." The **Black Arts Movement** sprang from this philosophy. Across the country, communities with sizable African American populations experienced a renewed energy to create uniquely Black works of literature and drama, as well as works in the visual arts, music, and dance. Black Arts literary works were published by magazines such as the *Negro Digest*, revived in 1965 and renamed *Black World*, and two Black Arts presses, **Detroit's Broadside Press** and Chicago's **Third World Press**. The latter was founded by the poets **Haki R. Madhubuti** (Don L. Lee) and **Carolyn Rodgers**. In 1967, the Organization of Black American Culture

A street in the African American section of Chicago, Illinois, 1941. Courtesy of the Library of Congress.

(**OBAC**) was founded in Chicago to promote cultural activity in the arts. The OBAC Writers' Workshop brought poets together, including Gwendolyn Brooks and such new voices as Madhubuti, Rodgers, Johari Amini and Eugene Perkins. In 1969, Chicago-born **Sam Greenlee** published his Black Nationalist thriller, *The Spook Who Sat by the Door*.

Following the Black Arts movement, Chicago's literary community discovered new voices. **Cyrus Colter** published a collection of short stories featuring African American Chicagoans (*The Beach Umbrella*, 1970). **Leon Forrest** wrote *There Is a Tree More Ancient Than Eden* (1973) and *The Bloodworth Orphans* (1977), both of which were edited for Random House by **Toni Morrison**. More recently, **April Sinclair**'s novel *Coffee Will Make You Black* (1994) and **Dawn Turner Trice**'s *Only Twice I've Wished for Heaven* (1997) have explored the female perspective of coming of age in Chicago.

Resources: Robert Bone, "Richard Wright and the Chicago Renaissance," *Callaloo* 28 (Summer 1986), 446–468; Arna Bontemps, "Famous WPA Authors," *Negro Digest*, June 1950, pp. 43–47; St. Clair Drake and Horace R. Cayton, *Black Metropolis: A Study of Negro Life in a Northern City* (New York: Harcourt, Brace, 1945); Robert E. Fleming, "Overshadowed by Richard Wright: Three Black Chicago Novelists," *Negro American Literature Forum* 7, no. 3 (Autumn 1973), 75–79; James R. Grossman, *Land of Hope: Chicago, Black Southerners and the Great Migration* (Chicago: University of Chicago Press, 1989); Jim Mendelsohn, "Chicago, Illinois," in *Africana: The Encyclopedia of the African and African American Experience*, ed. Kwame Anthony Appiah and Henry Louis Gates, Jr. (New York: Basic Civitas Books, 1999); Emmanuel S.

Nelson, ed., *Contemporary African American Novelists: A Bio-Bibliographical Critical Sourcebook* (Westport, CT: Greenwood Press, 1999); Phillip M. Richards and Neil Schlager, *Best Literature by and About Blacks* (Detroit: Gale, 2000); Lisa Woolley, *American Voices of the Chicago Renaissance* (DeKalb: Northern Illinois University Press, 2000).

Dana C. Wright

Chicago Defender (1905–present). Newspaper. The *Chicago Defender* is one of the most prominent and influential African American **newspapers** in the United States. It utilizes the written word to reflect the concerns of African Americans, to expose the atrocities of racism, and to provoke social change. Robert S. Abbott (1868–1940) founded the *Defender* on May 5, 1905. He "began [with] a press run of 300 copies, and worked out of a small kitchen in his landlord's apartment" ("*Chicago Defender*"). The first several weekly issues consisted of local news, "gathered by Abbott and clippings from other newspapers" ("*Chicago Defender*"). By 1915, the paper, according to Juliet E. K. Walker, sold 16,000 copies weekly, developed its sections and feature articles, opened branch offices in New York and London, and expanded across the United States (Walker, 25). It made its "greatest impact" in Southern states including Louisiana, Mississippi, Alabama, Tennessee, South Carolina, and Georgia (Walker, 25). Much of its growth is attributed to the countless porters, waiters, and visiting celebrities who circulated copies throughout various communities (Walker, 24).

The *Chicago Defender* played a vital role in the **Great Migration** of African Americans from **the South** to the North during **World War I**. The *Defender* "ran a series of articles emphasizing the social, economic, and political advantages southern blacks would find if they moved North" (Walker, 25–26). Ostrom speculates that the *Defender* may have been responsible for causing "as many as 50,000 African Americans to migrate north in 1915 alone" (Ostrom, *Langston Hughes Encyclopedia*, 72). The increased migration contributed to the *Defender's* growth. The circulation of the paper increased "from 50,000 in 1916 at the beginning of the movement . . . to 125,000 in 1918" (Walker, 26). The federal government, recognizing the power and influence of Abbott's paper, appealed to him to seek African American support in the war. Abbott consented. After all, "if blacks as soldiers could give their lives to make the world safe for democracy, then the government had an obligation to promote full democracy and freedom for blacks" (Walker, 28). Despite the overwhelming African American support for the war, African Americans were victims of racial tension in cities across the nation. The *Defender*, like many other Black papers, reported on the **race riots**. It not only condemned them but "[adamantly denounced] the nation's hypocrisy as defenders of world peace while at the same time tolerating white violence against blacks in this country" (Walker, 30).

By 1920, the *Defender's* competition among Black newspapers included *The Whip* (1919–1939) and *The Search Light* (1910–1932). Later rivals included

The World, the *American Eagle* (1921–1925), the *Metropolitan Post*, the *News Ledger*, the *Chicago Enterprise*, the *Chicago Globe*, *The Idea* (1926), and the *Chicago Bee* (1925) (Walker, 33). The *Defender* retained its preeminence, and Abbot continued to make improvements, including new facilities. The paper offered greater variety of sections and articles: music reviews, women's issues, "Police Court Doings," "Club and Society Notes," a "Foreign Section," and more (Walker, 35). During this same period **Marcus Garvey** and **Carter G. Woodson** helped arouse a collective Black consciousness. In this spirit, Abbott "launched a special full-page features section" of articles about Africa and the "historic contributions of blacks" (Walker, 35).

The *Defender* continued to report on major news affecting its African American readership through the **Great Depression** and **World War II**. When Abbott died in 1940, his nephew John Sengstacke became owner and publisher. Sengstacke turned the *Defender* into a daily paper and introduced five new columnists: **Walter White**, **Langston Hughes**, Dr. U. G. Dailey, S. I. Hayakawa, and John Robert Badger. The previous staff regulars included Lucius C. Harper, Enoc P. Waters, Jr., and "Charley Cherokee" (Doreski, 165). The *Defender* also published poems by the young **Gwendolyn Brooks**. Langston Hughes, a pivotal poet, playwright, and writer during the **Harlem Renaissance**, published his column, "Here to Yonder," for twenty-three years (Ostrom, *Langston Hughes Encyclopedia*, 72). In the column he developed the character Jesse B. Simple, and later published several volumes of stories featuring Simple that had first appeared in the column (Harper). Alfred E. Smith, a.k.a. "Charley Cherokee," published a gossip column that focused "on reporting the actions of public figures or law enforcers [both Black and White] that [hindered] the growth of the African American community" (Gourgey, 114–115).

Sengstacke "continued to champion for full equality" through the **Civil Rights Movement** and beyond ("*Chicago Defender*"). He also "became the first president of the National Negro Publishers Association," and headed the merger of "African American newspapers across the country" ("*Chicago Defender*"). In 1973, Ethel L. Payne became the first African American woman war correspondent. Nearly 100 years after its first issue, the *Chicago Defender* maintains its powerful position as a voice for the African American people.

Resources: "The *Chicago Defender*," *Newspapers*, PBS Online, http://www.pbs.org/ blackpress/news_bios/defender.html; Christopher C. De Santis, ed., *Langston Hughes and the Chicago Defender: Essays on Race, Politics, and Culture, 1942–62* (Urbana: University of Illinois Press, 1995); C. K. Doreski. "Kin in Some Way": The *Chicago Defender* Reads the Japanese Internment, 1942–1945," in *The Black Press*, ed. Todd Vogel (New Brunswick, NJ: Rutgers University Press, 2001); Hannah Gourgey, "Poetics of Memory and Marginality: Images of the Native American in African-American Newspapers, 1870–1899 and 1970–1990," in *The Black Press*, ed. Todd Vogel (New Brunswick, NJ: Rutgers University Press, 2001); Donna Akiba Sullivan Harper, *Not So Simple: The "Simple" Stories by Langston Hughes* (Columbia: University of Missouri Press, 1995); Hans Ostrom: "The Jesse B. Simple Stories and *Something in Common*," in his *Langston Hughes: A Study of the Short Fiction* (New York: Twayne, 1993), 31–50; A

Linotype operators of the *Chicago Defender*, 1941. Courtesy of the Library of Congress.

Langston Hughes Encyclopedia (Westport, CT: Greenwood Press, 2002), 72–73; Roi Ottley, *The Lonely Warrior: The Life and Times of Robert S. Abbott* (Chicago: Regnery, 1955); Juliet E. K. Walker, "The Promised Land: The *Chicago Defender* and the Black Press in Illinois, 1862–1970," in *The Black Press in the Middle West, 1865–1985*, ed. Henry Lewis Suggs (Westport, CT: Greenwood Press, 1996), 9–50.

Gladys L. Knight

Chicago Renaissance (c. 1930–1950). Literary and cultural movement and era. The term Chicago Renaissance refers to a period during which there was an outpouring of African American literary works by writers mainly based in **Chicago, Illinois**. However, it remains an obscure term to the general public compared with the **Harlem Renaissance** and began to be recognized as a major cultural movement only after Robert Bone published his influential article "Richard Wright and the Chicago Renaissance" in the scholarly journal **Callaloo** in 1986. The Chicago Renaissance produced numerous works by artists, musicians, sociologists, and journalists, but most notable was the amount of literature produced. Although **Richard Wright**'s towering achievement has overshadowed other writers of the period, there were many important works published. Some examples include *Blood on the Forge* (1941) by **William Attaway**, *Knock on Any Door* (1947) by **Willard Motley**, and *Black Thunder* (1936) by **Arna Bontemps** (a story of slave revolt set in Virginia). **Frank Marshall Davis** published many volumes of poetry, and **Margaret**

Walker won the Yale Younger Poet's Award for her volume *For My People* (1942). Perhaps the most notable work to come out of the Chicago Renaissance is, however, the poetry of **Gwendolyn Brooks**. Brooks is less recognized than Wright for her involvement in the Renaissance, but she stands as a true Chicago poet. Her first book of poems, *A Street in Bronzeville* (1945), which is about the lives of ordinary Black Chicagoans living in the ghetto and its "kitchenette" buildings, is a lasting portrayal of Bronzeville. *Annie Allen* (1949), her second book of poetry, won the Pulitzer Prize. *Maud Martha* (1953), a novella, is a bildungsroman of a girl named Maud living in the segregated South Side (*see* **Coming-of-Age Fiction**). The most famous play written during this period is *Big White Fog* (1939) by **Theodore Ward**, produced by the Federal Theatre Project (*see* **Federal Writers' Project**). *Abbott's Monthly*, founded in 1929, was an influential periodical that published many short stories and poems.

Understanding the history and geography of the city of Chicago is central to understanding the Chicago Renaissance. As James Grossman writes in *Land of Hope: Chicago, Black Southerners, and the Great Migration*, Chicago was considered to be a city of hope in the early twentieth century, attracting black migrants seeking to escape the Jim Crow of **the South**. Many Black Southerners migrated in anticipation of more opportunities and generally a marked improvement in their lives. As the **Great Migration** progressed, the ***Chicago Defender***, which was founded by Robert Abbott in 1905, played a vital role in disseminating news about migratory experiences. Understandably, the racial makeup of the city went through a drastic change. In the famous study *Black Metropolis* (1945), St. Clair Drake and Horace Cayton tell the story of the formation of the "Black Metropolis" from the Great Migration through the 1940s, explaining that Chicago's South Side became "a persisting city within a city, reflecting in itself the cross-currents of life in Midwest Metropolis, but isolated from the mainstream" (17). As Ernest Burgess demonstrated, Chicago was divided into concentric zones spiraling out from the center, with the poorest people living in a congested area close to the central business district. As the influx of migrants continued, middle-class Blacks who had enjoyed relative mobility and lived in White neighborhoods were forced to move into segregated "Black" neighborhoods. The formation of the "Black ghetto" and residential segregation were integral to the experience of urbanization for Black Chicagoans; the stifling confinement of the ghetto became the backdrop of many important works by writers of this period.

Several key factors overlapped and helped shape the Chicago Renaissance. The first major factor was the influence of communism within the African American intellectual community. With the stock market crash in 1929 and the onset of the **Great Depression**, many African American intellectuals began to take interest in class issues and turned to communism as a solution to the inequalities they saw around them. Many of Richard Wright's stories were published in *Left Front* (John Reed Club's magazine) and *New Masses* (an organ of the Communist Party). In February 1936, the National Negro

Congress (under the influence of the Communist Party) was attended by some of the writers of the Chicago Renaissance, such as Frank Marshall Davis, Theodore Ward, and Richard Wright, and by Arna Bontemps and **Langston Hughes**. Hughes later became a mentor to Gwendolyn Brooks. These writers were part of the Harlem Renaissance as well. Such meetings among the writers based in Chicago contributed to the formation of the South Side Writers' Group in May 1936, which proved to be pivotal in creating a spirit of renaissance. According to Bone, "They met weekly at the Lincoln Center on Oakwood Boulevard to read aloud their work-in-progress, discuss each effort as a work of art, and explore its broader implications for a theory of Negro writing" (447). The members of this group included Richard Wright, Theodore Ward, Frank Marshall Davis, Edward Bland, Russell Marshall, Fern Hayden, Dorothy Sutton, Marian Minus, Theodore Bland, Julius Weil, Banfield Gordon, and Arna Bontemps (Walker, 77).

Another factor that contributed to the close interaction of Black writers was the Federal Writer's Project under the Works Progress Administration (part of the broad New Deal initiative under President Franklin Delano Roosevelt). Writers who worked for the WPA at different times included Theodore Ward, William Attaway, Willard Motley, **Robert Hayden**, Frank Marshall Davis, **Frank Yerby**, and Margaret Walker. Although the South Side Group fell apart in the fall of 1938, federally funded programs such as the Illinois Writers' Project continued to bring the writers together.

Coincidentally, Louis Wirth, who was a professor of sociology at the University of Chicago, became the first director of the Chicago Writers' Project. This led to the third most important factor in the Chicago Renaissance, the Chicago School of Sociology. As Carla Capetti has noted, "the theories and methodologies developed by the Chicago urban sociologists played a central role in the overall shape and specific content of Wright's autobiography" (13). Capetti goes so far as to say that "these social scientists were among the first systematizers of the literatures of the U.S." (31). Although this assessment of their output might be a bit exaggerated, the Chicago Renaissance cannot be discussed without reference to the rise and influence of these sociologists. Robert Park, Ernest Burgess, and Louis Wirth all had a tremendous influence over the sociological vision of the writers in Chicago. Most notably, Richard Wright's *Native Son* (1940); *Twelve Million Black Voices* (1941), a documentary book of essays and photos on the lives of black Chicagoans; and his autobiographical novel, *Black Boy* (1945) all reflect the sociological vision of the Chicago School of Sociology. Wright's involvement with the sociologists culminated in his famous introduction to Drake and Cayton's *Black Metropolis* (1945). The black sociologists **E. Franklin Frazier** (*The Negro Family in the United States*, 1939) and **Charles S. Johnson** trained under Robert Park during the 1920s.

Robert Bone draws interesting distinctions between the Chicago Renaissance and the Harlem Renaissance: "What these two literary outpourings have in common is that both are at bottom responses to the Great Migration.

What differentiates them is the nature of the two responses to the basic phenomenon of urbanization" (467). In characterizing the movement, Bone suggests that the Harlem Renaissance was a "separatist" movement, while the Chicago Renaissance was an "integrationist" movement. By "separatist," he means the tendency in the Harlem Renaissance to emphasize racial pride inspired by the success of **Marcus Garvey** and by "integrationist," he means the way the Chicago Renaissance was predominantly influenced by the Chicago school of sociology. If the writers of the Harlem Renaissance celebrated the "folk," racial pride and Blackness, the writers of Chicago put more emphasis on a Black person's encounter with the new urban environment, exploring themes such as class consciousness and social protest. However, it should be noted that despite the strong influence of the left and that of the Chicago sociologists, the Chicago writers' voices do not uniformly fit into this distinction. Brooks's work, for instance, does not explicitly project a sociological vision or portray class struggle. Seeing the Chicago Renaissance as a movement separate and distinct from the Harlem Renaissance is the most predominant view in the current studies of African American literature. However, some scholars argue that we should think about African American literary history in the early twentieth century in terms of continuous migrations rather than renaissances.

Resources: Richard Bone, "Richard Wright and the Chicago Renaissance," *Callaloo* 3, no. 9 (Summer 1986), 446–468; Carla Cappetti, *Writing Chicago: Modernism, Ethnography, and the Novel* (New York: Columbia University Press, 1993); Chicago Public Library Digital Collections, www.chipublib.org/digital/chiren/introduction.html; St. Clair Drake and Horace R. Cayton, *Black Metropolis: A Study of Negro Life in a Northern City*, rev. and enl. ed. (New York: Harper & Row, 1962); James R. Grossman, *Land of Hope: Chicago, Black Southerners, and the Great Migration* (Chicago: University of Chicago Press, 1989); Margaret Walker, *Richard Wright, Daemonic Genius* (New York: Warner Books, 1988).

Jee Hyun An

Children's Literature. Although children have always enjoyed and used narratives, oral and written, for their entertainment, children's literature emerged as a distinct and independent form only in the late eighteenth century. The genre encompasses a wide range of work, including acknowledged classics of world literature, picture books and easy-to-read stories, poetry, novels, and short fiction, as well as lullabies, fairy tales, fables, folk songs, and folk narratives from oral traditions. Children's literature as a broad category blossomed in England and the United States in the nineteenth century. Since the 1960s, the genre has been studied and taught as two distinct but overlapping categories: children's literature meant for preschool and elementary school children, and young-adult literature designed for readers approximately ten to eighteen years of age. However, preadolescents often read young-adult titles, and adults often enjoy picture books. Just as the boundaries between children's and young-adult literatures are blurred, so are the features that constitute African American literature for young people. Historically, when writing about African American children's literature, most critics tended to dwell on literature by White American authors and illustrators that represents African Americans. These critics assumed that African American children's literature is a matter of audience rather than one of authorship. However, African American children's literature as a category more accurately describes a body of work for children and young adults produced by African American authors and illustrators and appreciated by a multiethnic audience from many age groups.

The late nineteenth century, often referred to as the golden age of children's literature, witnessed a profusion of books designed specifically for a young audience. Despite their abundance, however, these works represented only a portion of the literate youth in America. There were few depictions of African American children in textbooks, periodicals, stories, and poems, and very few of the depictions that did exist were unbiased or avoided stereotypes. African American children would have been exposed mainly to racist stories such as Helen Bannerman's *The Story of Little Black Sambo* (1899), which was reprinted frequently into the 1930s. As late as 1920, the prevailing popular magazine for children, *St. Nicholas* (1873–1945), featured a poem titled "Ten Little Niggers." These texts reinforced popular racist sentiment toward African Americans and perpetuated the ignorance of the White community, the children of which were offered no other literary portrayal of their Black counterparts. Further, *Little Black Sambo* and literature like it threatened to devastate a slowly growing sense of self-worth among a new generation of African Americans (*see* **Sambo**).

However, African Americans began to publish for children during the so-called golden age and thereby present an alternative tradition of literature for young people. Beginning in 1887, Mrs. A. E. (Amelia) Johnson, an African American woman, printed a number of religious tracts for children, including an eight-page magazine, *Joy*. She later published novels, including *Clarence and Corinne; or, God's Way* (1890), which, for whatever reasons, largely featured White characters. Also published in the early era of African American children's literature, **Paul Laurence Dunbar**'s *Little Brown Baby* (1895) is a seminal text in the genre. A collection of **dialect poetry** that celebrates African American folk culture, *Little Brown Baby* is neither didactic nor religious. Intending to delight his young readers, Dunbar depicts African American people and culture in a positive light. Other early pieces have only recently been recovered, among them Leila A. Pendleton's *An Alphabet for Negro Children* (date unknown).

After the turn of the century, this alternative tradition of children's literature expanded with the development of an educated African American middle class that both demanded and could financially support such an endeavor. Readers containing poetry, essays, short stories, folklore, and artwork became available, such as Silas X. Floyd's *Floyd's Flowers, or Duty and Beauty for Colored Children* (1905). **W.E.B. Du Bois**'s visionary magazine **The Brownies' Book** offered African American children an alternative to

St. Nicholas. Recognizing the urgent need for characters Black children could respect and emulate, DuBois, the only Black founder of the **NAACP** and the editor of that organization's magazine, **The Crisis**, experimented with "Children's Numbers," an annual children's issue of *The Crisis.* These issues were so successful that in 1920, Du Bois, along with business manager Augustus Granville Dill and literary editor **Jessie Redmon Fauset**, established a new magazine aimed specifically at children aged six to sixteen. Incorporating a variety of popular forms, such as fiction, **folktales** and fairy tales, poetry, drama, biography, and photography and illustrations by African American artists, *The Brownies' Book* offered nonreligious, nondidactic entertainment that attempted to infuse Black youth with a sense of self-worth and impress upon them the importance of education. The result was often too idealistic in its portrayal of childhood and American society. *The Brownies' Book* effectively inspired self-esteem, confidence, and racial pride.

Du Bois and Dill also published two biographies for children, Elizabeth Ross Haynes's *Unsung Heroes* (1921) and Julia Henderson's *A Child's Story of Dunbar* (1913), thereby pioneering another important form of African American children's literature. Haynes published twenty-two biographies, and many of them introduced children to African Americans rarely depicted in their school texts, figures who are now well-known, including **Frederick Douglass** and **Harriet Tubman**.

Known best for their writing for adults, **Langston Hughes** and **Arna Bontemps** also created large bodies of work for children. Hughes's *The Dream Keeper* (1932) is a classic collection of poetry for children, and his *Black Misery* (1969) remains a popular children's book. His nonfiction titles, among them *The First Book of Jazz* (1955), the *First Book of the West Indies* (1956), and *The First Book of Negroes* (1952), made important contributions, and several have been reprinted. Bontemps also created an extensive body of work, including biography, fiction, and poetry, that helped African American children's literature gain widespread acceptance. The poetry anthology Bontemps edited, *Golden Slippers* (1941), includes poetry by such respected authors as Dunbar, **Countee Cullen, Claude McKay**, Langston Hughes, and **James Weldon Johnson**. Through this and other anthologies, his novels, and his biographies, Bontemps offered children many positive African American role models. In novels such as *You Can't Pet a Possum* (1934) and *Lonesome Boy* (1955), he celebrates African American folk culture and language patterns. One of his collaborations with Hughes, *Popo and Fifina* (1932), remains popular with children. Further, Bontemps's work has gained wide popularity in part because of its literary quality and in part because he offers authentic portrayals of African Americans engaged in daily activities.

While publishers seemed to shy away from African American fiction for children through the 1940s and early 1950s, several African American writers, among them Hughes, **Shirley Graham**, and **Carter G. Woodson**, followed Bontemps in publishing biographies of notable African Americans. Woodson, a noted scholar, writer, and educator, worked toward a new kind of pedagogy that was unfettered by racist ideology, offered new purposes and goals, and used new texts in order to educate African American youth in critical thinking and commitment to the advancement of their race. As the founder of the Associated Press, Woodson achieved many of his objectives; he published a significant number of collections of poetry and folklore, readers, biographies, and histories.

Like Woodson, librarians, classroom teachers, and postsecondary educators and administrators have worked to ensure that African American children's literature flourishes and reaches an audience. In 1939, the librarian Mary McLeod Bethune argued that "the ideals, character and attitudes of races are born within the minds of children; most prejudices are born with youth and it is our duty to see that the great researchers of Negro History are placed in the language and story of the child" (10). When Augusta Baker started work as a young librarian in the **Harlem** branch of the New York City Public Library, she found few children's books portraying Black people in a realistic manner. During the next thirty-seven years Baker corrected this situation, not only by adding appropriate books to the library's collections but also by meeting with authors and publishers to get more African American stories written. She also edited anthologies of African American literature for young readers. A renowned storyteller, Baker started the James Weldon Johnson Memorial Collection in 1939. To promote the project, she met with a number of children's authors, publishers, and editors. When the bibliography of the collection was published under the title *Books About Negro Life for Children* (1961), Baker had assembled hundreds of titles. In 1953, she became the first Black librarian to hold an administrative position in the New York Public Library, and by 1961 she was in charge of children's policies and programs in all eighty-two branches.

Baker's influence spread beyond the library itself: she involved schools and community groups, was a consultant for the television program *Sesame Street*, moderated television and radio programs, and taught courses on storytelling and children's literature. Following Baker, African American members of the American Library Association became concerned that African American children's literature was not being recognized for its artistry and range. In 1969, Glyndon Greer, with the support of Mabel McKissack, established the Coretta Scott King Award for African American authors and illustrators of books for children. It has been the mechanism through which several African American writers and artists have gained professional and public recognition. Also in the late 1960s, the Council on Interracial Books for Children began holding contests in order to identify and support promising young artists. Their first winner, Kristin Hunter Lattany's *The Soul Brothers and Sister Lou* (1968), sold over a million copies.

With such encouragement from educators and librarians, and with the 1954 Supreme Court decision to desegregate schools, African American children's literature became an established and expanding tradition that reflected contemporary social and cultural consciousness. Some of these texts offered an integrationist approach to racial difference and the problems of bigotry. The work of Bontemps's later contemporaries—**Jesse Jackson**'s *Call Me Charley* (1945) and **Lorenz Bell Graham**'s *South Town* (1958) and *North Town* (1965)—are some of the many books about African American experiences written for children of all races. These novels tried to instill in all children a social conscience that afforded awareness and tolerance of racial difference without taking into account social and cultural difference. This "social conscience" literature promoting an ideology of **assimilation** and integration quickly gave way to African American children's literature that is more culturally conscious. Rudine Sims describes culturally conscious children's literature as "books that reflect, with varying degrees of success, the social and cultural traditions associated with growing up Black in the United States" (49).

Since the late 1960s, African American children's literature has most often been "culturally conscious," its focus on African American perspective and setting. Since the mid-1970s, dozens of African American writers have gained wide popularity through works that present the range of African American experiences. They offer historically accurate portrayals of African American lives, and a tradition of resistance to racism and discrimination. They provide aesthetic experience, and they entertain and educate even as they engender racial pride. These books cover multiple forms and genres, and are joined by magazines, such as *Ebony Jr.* (1973–1985), which offered positive representations of African Americans in art and literature and provided a forum for young writers to publish their work, and *Footsteps*, which has been published since 1999, and has included reprints of **Jacob Lawrence**'s work, an interview with baseball great Hank Aaron, and articles on celebrities such as **Ossie Davis**. Today, African American children's literature includes illustrated texts for young children that offer a visual schema that will inform identity formation, and texts for older readers that provide rich literary material for exploring the issues and dilemmas of human experience as perceived by the young.

No literary genre is more dependent on illustrations than literature for children, and African American children's literature is particularly reliant on the ability of illustrations to depict African Americans as individuals with a rich and diverse culture. While children are especially sensitive to illustrations, illustrated texts are read by a wide audience, and it is important that African Americans and their culture and history be accurately depicted. Picture book author **Eloise Greenfield** recognizes the importance of illustrations by stipulating in her book contracts that her work be illustrated by African American artists. Books such as artist Tom Feelings's *The Middle Passage* (1995) rely on pictures alone to tell a story. *The Middle Passage*, which relates the painful story of Africans taken across the Atlantic Ocean and sold into **slavery** in the Americas, is one of many picture books that make clear the African roots of African American culture and identity. (*See* **Middle Passage**.) **Ashley Bryan**'s linecut illustrations for his four volumes of African folktales; Muriel Feelings's Swahili abcediary and counting book, *Jambo Means Hello* (1974) and *Moja Means One* (1971), illustrated by Tom Feelings; Leo and

Diane Dillon's illustrations for Verna Aardema's editions of African fables, such as *Why Mosquitoes Buzz in People's Ears* (1975); and **John Steptoe**'s African Cinderella story, *Mufaro's Beautiful Daughters* (1987) are other notable examples of texts based in African culture and history. The last three of these were the first three texts by African American illustrators to win Caldecott Prizes.

African motifs, particularly patterns and colors of cloth, appear in many picture books that tell African American stories. For example, kente cloth is the predominant pattern of Carole Byard's illustrations in Phil Mendez's *The Black Snowman* (1989), African masks and sculptures inform Byard's work in **Camille Yarbrough**'s *Cornrows* (1979), and **Faith Ringgold**'s African-inspired quilts and tankas (fabric sculptures) are predominant in her *Tar Beach* (1991) and *Dinner at Aunt Connie's House* (1993). In this latter book, Ringgold relies on the African American history that informs many picture books, as her young protagonist imagines historical figures such as Harriet Tubman and Mary McLeod Bethune coming to dinner with her extended family. Ashley Bryan's illustrated collections of African American spirituals, *I'm Going to Sing* (1976) and *Walk Together Children* (2 vols., 1974, 1982), and Brian Pinkney's illustrations for **Patricia McKissack**'s collection of African American folktales, *The Dark Thirty* (1992) are other notable examples.

Illustrated collections of African American poetry are also important in this genre, such as **Romare Bearden**'s collages of poems by Langston Hughes in *The Block* (1995), Ashley Bryan's illustrated collection of Hughes's nativity poems in *Carol of the Brown King* (1998), and the many titles by **Arnold Adoff**, among them *All the Colors of the Race* (1982), illustrated by Steptoe. Illustrated books provide young children, and readers of all ages, with positive images of African Americans and the rich diversity of their history and culture, and offer a literary experience that can aid in the understanding and interpretation of life experiences.

African American literature for young adults plays important educational and cultural roles. The adolescent years are a period for dealing with issues of discrimination, prejudice, and cultural differences because adolescents often perceive themselves as a "culture" apart from the mainstream. Authors of young-adult fiction who deal with themes of diversity in race, religion, **gender**, or class can touch young readers in a profound way. Since the 1960s, African American young-adult fiction has grown into a vast body of work that has achieved recognition and popularity among wide audiences. Again, themes and genres are diverse. These writers offer stories of the inner city and rural America, such as **Walter Dean Myers**'s stories about Harlem in *Fallen Angels* (1988) or **June Jordan**'s urban landscape in *His Own Where* (1971), and **Mildred D. Taylor**'s continuing saga of the Logans, set in rural Mississippi. African American young-adult writers set their fiction in the past, the present, and the future, such as **Julius Lester**'s **slave narrative** *To Be a Slave* (1968), **Virginia Hamilton**'s realistic novel *M. C. Higgins, the Great* (1974), or **Octavia Butler**'s futuristic fantasy *The Parable of the Sower* (1993). These writers deal with themes about and alongside racism, such as **Rosa Guy**'s exploration of a lesbian relationship between two Black teenagers in *Ruby* (1976); **Sharon Bell Mathis**'s *Listen for the Fig Tree* (1974), about the experience of a blind girl, or **Joyce Carol Thomas**'s short stories representing the African American teenager in the midst of various ethnic groups in *A Gathering of Flowers* (1990). Further, poets and novelists who write mainly for adults are widely read by young adults and are taught in their classrooms, among them **Maya Angelou, Alice Walker, Toni Cade Bambara, Lorraine Hansberry, James Baldwin, Lucille Clifton,** and **Zora Neale Hurston**.

Now more than a century old, African American children's literature performs essential functions in the growth and development of its readers, and its benefits go far past simply making visible in texts for children the formerly absent African American, or countering negative portrayals of African Americans with positive ones. Generally, it enables them to define themselves in terms of their cultural heritage as well as their national heritage. Both text and illustration develop the young reader's self-perception, comprehension of the world and personal experience, and ability to form relationships with others.

Resources: Primary Sources: Verna Aardema, *Why Mosquitoes Buzz in People's Ears: An African Folktale,* illus. Leo and Diane Dillon (New York: Dial Press, 1975); Arnold Adoff, *All the Colors of the Race,* illus. John Steptoe (New York: Lothrop, Lee & Shepard, 1982); Helen Bannerman, *The Story of Little Black Sambo* (New York: F. A. Stokes, 1899); Arna Bontemps: *Lonesome Boy* (Boston: Houghton Mifflin, 1955); *You Can't Pet a Possum* (New York: Morrow, 1934); Arna Bontemps, ed., *Golden Slippers: An Anthology of Negro Poetry for Young Readers* (New York: Harper & Row, 1941); Ashley Bryan: *I'm Going to Sing: African American Spirituals* (New York: Atheneum, 1976); *Lion and the Ostrich Chicks, and Other African Folk Tales* (New York: Atheneum, 1986); *The Ox of the Wonderful Horns, and Other African Folktales* (New York: Atheneum, 1971); *Walk Together, Children: Black American Spirituals,* 2 vols. (New York: Atheneum, 1974–1982); Octavia Butler, *The Parable of the Sower* (New York: Four Walls Eight Windows, 1993); Paul Laurence Dunbar, *Little Brown Baby* (1895; repr. New York: Dodd, Mead, 1940); Muriel Swahili Feelings: *Jambo Means Hello,* illus. Tom Feelings (New York: Dial, 1974); *Moja Means One,* illus. Tom Feelings (New York: Dial, 1971); Tom Feelings, *The Middle Passage: White Ships, Black Cargo* (New York: Dial, 1995); Silas X. Floyd, *Floyd's Flowers, or Duty and Beauty for Colored Children* (Atlanta: Hertl, Jenkins, 1905); Lorenz Bell Graham: *North Town* (New York: Crowell, 1965); *South Town* (Chicago: Follett, 1958); Eloise Greenfield, *Africa Dream,* illus. Carole Byard (New York: John Day, 1977); Rosa Guy, *Ruby* (New York: Viking, 1976); Virginia Hamilton, *M. C. Higgins, the Great* (New York: Macmillan, 1974); Elizabeth Ross Haynes, *Unsung Heroes* (New York: Dubois and Dill, 1921); Julia Henderson, *A Child's Story of Dunbar* (Chicago: Conkey, 1913, 1921); Langston Hughes: *Black Misery* (New York: P. S. Eriksson, 1969); *The Block,* illus. Romare Bearden (New York: Viking, 1995); *Carol of the Brown King,* illus. Ashley Bryan (New York: Atheneum, 1998); *The Dream Keeper* (New York: Knopf, 1932); *The First Book of Jazz* (New York: Franklin Watts, 1955); *The First Book of Negroes* (New York: Franklin Watts, 1952); *The First Book of Rhythms* (New York: Franklin Watts, 1954); *The First*

Book of the West Indies (New York: Franklin Watts, 1956); Langston Hughes and Arna Bontemps, *Popo and Fifina: Children of Haiti* (New York: Macmillan, 1932); Jesse Jackson, *Call Me Charley* (New York: Harper & Bros., 1945); A. E. Johnson, *Clarence and Corinne; or, God's Way* (Philadelphia: American Baptist Publication Society, 1890); June Jordan, *His Own Where* (New York: Crowell, 1971); Kristin Hunter Lattany, *The Soul Brothers and Sister Lou* (New York: Scribner's, 1968); Julius Lester, *To Be a Slave*, illus. Tom Feelings (New York: Dial, 1968); Sharon Bell Mathis, *Listen for the Fig Tree* (New York: Viking, 1974); Patricia McKissack, *The Dark Thirty*, illus. Brian Pinkney (New York: Knopf, 1992); Phil Mendez, *The Black Snowman*, illus. Carole Byard (New York: Scholastic, 1989); Walter Dean Myers, *Fallen Angels* (Austin, TX: Holt, Rinehart and Winston, 1988); Leila A. Pendleton, *An Alphabet for Negro Children* (publisher and date unknown); Faith Ringgold: *Dinner at Aunt Connie's House* (New York: Hyperion, 1993); *Tar Beach* (New York: Crown, 1991); John Steptoe, *Mufaro's Beautiful Daughters* (New York: Lothrop, Lee & Shephard, 1987); Joyce Carol Thomas, *A Gathering of Flowers* (New York: Harper & Row, 1990); Camille Yarbrough, *Cornrows*, illus. Carole Byard (New York: Coward, McCann and Geoghegan, 1979). **Secondary Sources:** Augusta Baker, "The Changing Image of the Black in Children's Literature," *Horn Book* 51 (Feb. 1975), 79–88; Mary McLeod Bethune, "The Adaptation of the History of the Negro to the Capacity of the Child," *Journal of Negro History* 24 (Jan. 1939), 9–13; Rudine Sims Bishop, *Shadow and Substance: Afro-American Experience in Contemporary Children's Fiction* (Urbana, IL: National Council of Teachers of English, 1982); Arna Bontemps, "Special Collections of Negroana," *Library Quarterly* 14 (July 1944), 187–206; Violet J. Harris, "African American Children's Literature: The First One Hundred Years," *Journal of Negro Education* 59, no. 4 (1990), 540–555; Dianne Johnson-Feelings, ed., *The Best of The Brownies' Book* (New York: Oxford University Press, 1996); Eleanor Weakley Nolen, "The Colored Child in Contemporary Literature," *Horn Book* 18, no. 5 (1942), 348–355; Carole A. Park, "Goodby, Black Sambo: Black Writers Forge New Images in Children's Literature," *Ebony*, Nov. 1972, pp. 60–70; Jacque Roethler, "Reading in Color: Children's Book Illustrations and Identity Formation for Black Children in the United States," *African American Review* 32, no. 1 (1998), 95–105; Charlemae Rollins, "Promoting Racial Understanding Through Books," *Negro American Literature Forum* 2 (1968), 71–76; Barbara Rollock, *Black Authors and Illustrators of Children's Books* (New York: Garland, 1988); Nancy Tolson, "Making Books Available: The Role of Early Libraries, Librarians, and Booksellers in the Promotion of African American Children's Literature," *African American Review* 32, no. 1 (1998), 9–16.

Roxanne Harde

Childress, Alice (1916–1994). Playwright, actress, stage director, novelist, and children's author. A prolific and polemical writer, Childress often depicted in her work ordinary characters whose lives and choices are limited by the social forces of racism, sexism, and classism.

Childress was born on October 12, 1916, in Charleston, South Carolina; at the age of five, she moved to **Harlem, New York**, to live with her grandmother, Eliza Campbell. Under the guardianship of her grandmother,

Childress learned to appreciate the arts, often visiting museums, concert halls, and theaters. She also became aware of the plight of the urban poor through Wednesday night visits to the Salem Church, where poor people would offer testimonials about their troubles and concerns. As a child and young adult, Childress attended Public School 81, Julia Ward Howe Junior High School, and Wadleigh High School. She dropped out of high school after only three years when her grandmother and mother died in the late 1930s.

After dropping out of high school, Childress soon married, gave birth to a daughter, Jean (who died in 1990), and then divorced. As a single mother in the 1940s, Childress accepted a number of menial jobs (domestic worker, assistant machinist, and salesperson) to support herself and her daughter. On July 17, 1957, she married Nathan Woodard, a professional musician and music instructor with whom she lived on Long Island until her death from cancer on August 14, 1994.

Childress's literary and theatrical career began in the early 1940s when she helped to found the American Negro Theater (ANT). At ANT, Childress learned and held various jobs associated with theatrical production. At first, she pursued acting—and earned a Tony nomination for her role in the Broadway play *Anna Lucasta*—but soon she realized that **race** limited her options for roles. She also wrote and directed her first play at ANT—*Florence* (1949), a one-act play about a Black mother who learns to accept her daughter's decision to become an actress.

For three decades following the production of *Florence*, Childress continued to write for the stage, focusing her realistic plays on how racism, sexism, and classism impact the choices of ordinary African American characters. Childress' major plays include *Just a Little Simple* (1950), which was based on longtime friend **Langston Hughes**'s *Simple Speaks His Mind* and the character Hughes created, Jesse B. Simple; *Trouble in Mind*, a satire of racial stereotyping, a play that earned Childress the honor of being the first woman to receive an Obie; *Wedding Band: A Love/Hate Story in Black and White* (1966); *Wine in the Wilderness: A Comedy-Drama* (1969); *Mojo: A Black Love Story* (1970); *When the Rattlesnake Sounds* (1975); and *Moms* (1987).

Although Childress is widely known and acclaimed for her theatrical work, she also wrote juvenile fiction. In 1973, she penned *A Hero Ain't Nothin' but a Sandwich*, a novel about teenage drug addiction. The novel was adapted for film in 1978; however, the book and the film *Hero* have subsequently been banned in many school districts (as have many of Childress's plays) (*see* **Censorship**). In addition to *Hero*, Childress also wrote another juvenile fiction book titled *Rainbow Jordan* (1981), and several works of adult fiction, including *Like One of the Family: Conversations from a Domestic's Life* (1956) and *A Short Walk* (1979), for which Childress was nominated for the Pulitzer Prize.

Resources: Kathleen Betsko and Rachel Koenig, "Alice Childress," in *Interviews with Contemporary Women Playwrights*, ed. Betsko and Koenig (New York: Beech Tree Books, 1987); Elizabeth Brown-Guillory, "Childress, Alice," in *Black Women in America: An Historical Encyclopedia*, ed. Darlene Clark Hine (Brooklyn, NY: Carlson, 1993), 233–235;

Alice Childress: *A Hero Ain't Nothin' but a Sandwich* (New York: Puffin, 2000); *Like One of the Family: Conversations from a Domestic's Life* (Boston: Beacon, 1986); *Rainbow Jordan* (New York: HarperTrophy, 1982); *Those Other People* (New York: Putnam, 1989); *Wedding Band*, in *9 Plays by Black Women*, ed. Margaret B. Wilkerson (New York: New American Library, 1986); *Wine in the Wilderness* (New York: Dramatists Play Service, 1998); "Childress, Alice," in *Merriam-Webster's Encyclopedia of Literature* (Springfield, MA: Merriam-Webster, 1995), 237–238; "Childress, Alice," in *Modern Black Writers*, 2nd ed., ed. Manitou Wordworks (Detroit: St. James Press, 2000), 169–171; Anne Commire et al., eds., *Women in World History: A Biographical Encyclopedia*, vol. 1 (Detroit: Yorkin/Gale, 1999); Rosemary Curb, "Alice Childress," in *Dictionary of Literary Biography*, vol. 7 (Detroit: Gale, 1981), 118–124; Trudier Harris, "Alice Childress," in *Dictionary of Literary Biography*, vol. 38 (Detroit: Gale, 1985), 66–79; Shari Dorantes Hatch and Michael R. Strickland, "Childress, Alice," in *African-American Writers: A Dictionary*, ed. Hatch and Strickland (Santa Barbara, CA: ABC-CLIO, 2000), 53–54; Jane House, "Childress, Alice," in *The Continuum Companion to Twentieth Century Theatre*, ed. Colin Chambers (London: Continuum, 2002), 154; La Vinia Delois Jennings, *Alice Childress* (New York: Twayne, 1995); Beth Schneider, "Childress, Alice," in *African American Women: A Biographical Dictionary*, ed. Dorothy C. Salem (New York: Garland, 1993), 101–104; Catherine Wiley, "Whose Name, Whose Protection: Reading Alice Childress's *Wedding Band*," in *Modern American Drama: The Female Canon*, ed. June Schlueter (Rutherford, NJ: Fairleigh Dickinson University Press, 1990), 185–186; Kari Winter, "Childress, Alice," in *Notable Black American Women*, ed. Jessie Carney Smith, vol. 1 (Detroit: Gale, 1992), 181–183.

Heath A. Diehl

Chisholm, Shirley Anita St. Hill (1924–2005). Politician, educator, and autobiographical writer. Chisholm was born in **Brooklyn, New York**, and spent most of her youth there and with her grandmother in Barbados. After graduating cum laude from Brooklyn College in 1946, she taught nursery school and pursued her master's degree in early childhood education at Columbia University. Chisholm married Conrad Chisholm in 1949 and graduated in 1952. She first became involved in politics while campaigning to get African American lawyer Lewis S. Flagg elected as a district court judge in 1953. Her interest continued as she helped form the Unity Democratic Club in 1960 to increase the numbers of African Americans elected to the New York State Legislature. Four years later, Chisholm ran for the 17th District seat and won by a large margin. She served in the New York State Assembly until 1968 and introduced more than fifty bills, eight of which passed. In Chisholm's autobiography, *Unbought and Unbossed* (1970), she discussed the passed legislation. One significant bill developed a program named SEEK, which helped disadvantaged youth to receive a higher education. Another notable bill introduced the state's first unemployment insurance program for personal and domestic employees. Chisholm advocated for the rights of minorities, greater educational opportunities for the impoverished, and improvements in urban areas.

In 1969, Chisholm was elected to the U.S. House of Representatives and became the first African American woman elected to Congress. She served on numerous committees: Agriculture, Veterans' Affairs, Education and Labor, and Rules. As Chisholm's reputation grew as an influential figure in Congress, she campaigned for the Democratic presidential nomination in 1972. In her second autobiographical book, *The Good Fight* (1973), she wrote of her courage to run for president and her desire to provide an example to other nontraditional presidential candidates. She also stated the need to change the male-dominated power structure in politics. Although George McGovern received the presidential nomination at the Democratic National Convention, Chisholm won 10 percent of the delegates' votes and admiration for her political endeavor. She stayed in the U.S. House of Representatives until her retirement from Congress in 1982. From 1983 to 1987, Chisholm was Purington professor at Mount Holyoke College and taught political science and women's studies. She also was the visiting scholar at Spelman College in 1985. Even though Chisholm was away from Congress, she continued her political interest by cofounding the National Political Congress of Black Women in 1984. She

Congresswoman Shirley Chisholm announcing her candidacy for presidential nomination, 1972. Courtesy of the Library of Congress.

campaigned for the African American presidential candidate Jesse Jackson in 1984 and 1988. In 1993, President Bill Clinton selected Chisholm as ambassador to Jamaica, but she declined because of ill health. She died on January 3, 2005.

Resources: Susan Brownmiller, *Shirley Chisholm: A Biography* (Garden City, NY: Doubleday, 1970); Shirley Chisholm: *The Good Fight* (New York: Harper & Row, 1973); *Unbought and Unbossed* (Boston: Houghton Mifflin, 1970); Eleanor Marshall-White, *Women: Catalysts for Change: Interpretive Biographies of Shirley St. Hill Chisholm, Sandra Day O'Connor, and Nancy Landon Kassebaum* (New York: Vantage Press, 1991); Jill S. Pollack, *Shirley Chisholm* (New York: Franklin Watts, 1994).

Dorsía Smith Silva

Christian, Barbara T. (1943–2000). Activist, scholar, and literary critic. Christian was a feminist thinker and scholar who wrote criticism on nineteenth- and twentieth-century African American women's literature. An activist scholar, she produced work that brought critical, scholarly attention to the creative works of African American women, helping to secure a space for them in the American literary canon.

Christian was born in St. Thomas, U.S. Virgin Islands, in 1943. She was one of the six children of Judge Alphonso A. Christian and Ruth Christian. A precocious student, she received her A.B. from Marquette University in 1963 (where she was admitted at fifteen years of age), her M.A. from Columbia University in 1964, and her Ph.D. from Columbia University in contemporary British and American literature in 1970. She married and later divorced the poet **David Henderson** and had one daughter, Najuma.

Christian had a long, fruitful career in academia. She was an instructor at Hunter College (1963–1964) and a lecturer and later assistant professor at the City College of New York (1965–Spring 1971). She spent the bulk of her career at the University of California at Berkeley, where she began as a lecturer in English (Fall 1971) and then in African American Studies (1972). At Berkeley, she was the first African American woman to earn tenure (1978), the first African American woman to become full professor (1986), and the first African American woman to receive a Distinguished Teaching Award. At Berkeley, Christian helped to establish, and then served as chairperson of, the African American Studies Department (1978–1983) and later served as chair of the ethnic studies doctoral program (1986–1989); she also helped to found the African-American Studies Ph.D. program and assisted with the establishment of the Women Studies Department.

Christian's first critical text, *Black Women Novelists*, provides a historical survey of literature by key African American women writers. In contrast to the earlier practice of treating such texts as anomalies, Christian insisted that there was an intellectual tradition of African American women's writing and provided a framework for it. Her second major text, *Black Feminist Criticism*, is a collection of seventeen essays written from 1975 through 1984. These essays focused on the works of such writers as **Frances E. W. Harper, Toni Morrison, Alice Walker, Paule Marshall, Gloria Naylor**, and **Audre Lorde**. By presenting critical responses to the literature, she ensured that the literature would continue in public memory and would be taken seriously in academia. Christian wrote many influential essays and was the author of more than 100 articles and reviews. In one of her most cited essays, "The Race for Theory," she asserts the importance of understanding the political nature of literary criticism and decries the way theory is privileged in the academy, often at the expense of the promotion and understanding of the literature itself.

Christian died of complications from lung cancer in 2000.

Resources: Barbara Christian: *Black Feminist Criticism: Perspectives on Black Women Writers* (New York: Pergamon, 1985); *Black Women Novelists: The Development of a Tradition, 1892–1976* (Westport, CT: Greenwood Press, 1980); *From the Inside Out: Afro-American Women's Literary Tradition and the State* (Minneapolis: University of Minnesota Center for Humanistic Studies, 1987); "The Race for Theory" (1988), in *The Norton Anthology of Theory and Criticism*, Vincent B. Leitch, gen. ed. (New York: W. W. Norton, 2001), 2257–2266; Barbara Christian, ed., *Everyday Use*, by Alice Walker (New Brunswick, NJ: Rutgers University Press, 1994); Barbara Christian, Elizabeth Abel, and Helen Moglen, eds., *Female Subjects in Black and White: Race,*

Psychoanalysis, Feminism (Berkeley: University of California Press, 1997); "Barbara Christian," in *Feminist Writers*, ed. Pamela Kester-Shelton (Detroit: St. James Press, 1996), 100–101; "Barbara T. Christian," in *Contemporary Black Biography*, vol. 44 (Detroit: Gale, 2004).

Kimberly Black-Parker

Christian, Marcus Bruce (1900–1976). Poet, printer, historian, and labor organizer. Christian is known as both an important **New Orleans, Louisiana**, poet and a historian of African Americans in Louisiana. He was born in Houma (LaFourche Parish), Louisiana, the son of Emanuel and Rebecca Harris Christian. At Houma Academy, Emmanuel was a schoolmaster for thirty years, and also worked with the Knights of Labor to organize sugarcane factory workers.

There was thus a tradition of resistance in Christian's family as well as of tragedy. When he was three, Marcus's mother died. His father read his children Longfellow, Stevenson, and Whittier as a means of structuring their loss. When he was seven, Marcus's twin sister died, and when he was thirteen, his father died. At thirteen, he left school to earn money and lived with family and friends of family. At nineteen, Christian moved to New Orleans. He found a job as a chauffer and attended night school, and by 1926 had saved enough money to found Bluebird Cleaners.

In 1922, Christian tried to publish his manuscript "Ethiopia Triumphant and Other Poems." Ten years later, he convinced the *Louisiana Weekly* to create a "Poet's Corner." By 1935, Christian had established himself as the Black poet and folklorist of New Orleans. In that year, Lyle Saxon, a writer of popular histories including *Old Louisiana* (1929), befriended Christian. Saxon appealed unsuccessfully to Houghton Mifflin for the publication of Christian's manuscript "The Clothes Doctor and Other Poems."

As head of the Louisiana chapter of the **Federal Writers' Project**, Saxon appointed Christian in 1936 to the Dillard Project, the Black unit, and in 1939 named him the unit supervisor (*see* **Negro Units**). Christian remained with the project until 1942. The result of its research was the manuscript "The History of the Negro in Louisiana." Christian received a Rosenwald fellowship (1943–1944) to continue work on the manuscript, which was revised under the title "A Black History of Louisiana." Neither version was ever published.

Between 1933 and 1946, **Opportunity** showcased Christian's poetry, including the long and moving "Dark Heritage" (1946). In the early 1970s *Negro History Bulletin* published seven of his poems, including "Southern Share-Cropper." In 1945, **Phylon** published "The Theory of the Poisoning of Oscar J. Dunn," and *Negro History Journal* (1972), "Men of Worth in Louisiana." In 1948 Christian published *Common People's Manifesto of World War II*.

Christian's poems are in *The Poetry of the Negro, 1746–1949: An Anthology*, edited by **Langston Hughes** and **Arna Bontemps** (1949), and in **Jerry Ward's** *Trouble the Water* (1997). Christian appears in a number of biographical dictionaries, including Shockley's *Living Black American Authors* (1973) and *Black American Writers Past and Present* (1991), edited by Rush et al.

In 1958, Christian self-published *High Ground*, which commemorated the 1954 Supreme Court school desegregation decision. In 1972, his *Negro Ironworkers of Louisiana* was published. In 1999, Xavier Review Press published *I Am New Orleans and Other Poems*, edited by Rudolph Lewis and Amin Sharif. This fifty-poem book was the first collection of Christian's poems to be published.

As writer-in-residence at the University of New Orleans from 1969 to 1976, Christian taught Louisiana Negro history and directed the poetry workshop. He collapsed in a classroom there and died days later at Charity Hospital. His archive is housed at the University of New Orleans, and of his poems, diary notes, and letters are available on the Web site *ChickenBones: A Journal* (www.nathanielturner.com).

Resources: Marcus Bruce Christian: *Common People's Manifesto of World War II* (New Orleans: Les Cenelles Society of Arts and Letters, 1948); *High Ground* ([self-published], 1954); *I Am New Orleans and Other Poems by Marcus Bruce Christian*, ed. Rudolph Lewis and Amin Sharif (New Orleans: Xavier Review Press, 1999); *Negro Ironworkers of Louisiana 1718–1900* (Gretna, LA: Pelican Publishers, 1972); Langston Hughes and Arna Bontemps, eds., *The Poetry of the Negro, 1746–1949: An Anthology* (Garden City, NY: Doubleday, 1949); Theressa Gunnels Rush, Carol Fairbanks Myers, and Esther Spring Arata, eds., *Black American Writers Past and Present* (New York: Rowman & Littlefield, 1991); Ann Allen Shockley and Sue P. Chandler, eds., *Living Black American Authors: A Biographical Directory* (New York: R. R. Bowker, 1973); Jerry Ward, ed., *Trouble the Water: 250 Years of African American Poetry* (New York: Mentor, 1997).

Rudolph Lewis

Civil Rights Movement. A nationwide, mass campaign in the 1950s and 1960s to gain equal legal, social, and economic rights for African Americans. Led primarily by Blacks but also supported by White sympathizers, the movement focused mostly on desegregating public facilities and schools; eliminating barriers to Black voter registration; abolishing racially discriminatory practices in housing; improving conditions for impoverished urban communities; and enhancing Black economic power. Until the rise of radical, militant **Black Power** groups in 1966, civil rights movement leaders advocated peaceful means for protest, such as boycotts, sit-ins, mass street demonstrations, freedom rides, and picketing. The movement was a joint effort by such organizations as the **NAACP**, the Southern Christian Leadership Conference (SCLC), the Student Nonviolent Coordinating Committee (SNCC), and the Congress of Racial Equality (CORE).

The modern civil rights movement was sparked by the 1954 *Brown v. Board of Education* lawsuit and by the 1955–1956 Montgomery bus boycott, wherein African Americans refused to ride on segregated municipal buses and thereby put economic pressure on the city. However, Black struggles for equal rights began during the **Reconstruction** era, when bills were enacted to guarantee fundamental citizenship rights to Blacks, including the Thirteenth (1865),

Fourteenth (1868), and Fifteenth amendments (1875) to the Constitution. The Civil Rights Act of 1875 also protected civil and legal rights for all citizens.

With the withdrawal of the last federal troops from **the South** in 1877, Southern White supremacists regained control of their state and local governments and began to overturn legislation from the Reconstruction period. In 1883, the U.S. Supreme Court declared the Civil Rights Act of 1875 unconstitutional. In *Plessy v. Ferguson* case (1896), the Supreme Court upheld the 1890 Louisiana law providing "separate but equal" railway carriages for Whites and Blacks, thus legitimizing the Jim Crow system. Moreover, by 1900, all Southern states had passed laws hindering Blacks from voting.

To protest racial segregation and discrimination, Black leaders created new national organizations. The National Afro-American League was organized in 1890, the Niagara Movement in 1905, the NAACP in 1909, and the National League on Urban Conditions Among Negroes (or National Urban League) in 1910. During the 1940s and 1950s, the NAACP won a series of political and legal victories. In 1941, for example, it pressured President Franklin Roosevelt to declare a nondiscrimination policy in war-related industries and federal employment. The lawyers for the NAACP won the 1946 *Morgan v. Virginia* case, in which the Supreme Court banned state laws that sanctioned racially segregated facilities in interstate travel by train and bus. In 1948, the NAACP forced President Harry Truman to sign an executive order banning discrimination by the federal government. Under the leadership of Special Counsel Thurgood Marshall, the NAACP won *Brown v. Board of Education* in the Supreme Court, which unanimously declared the "separate but equal" mandate in *Plessy v. Ferguson* unconstitutional. Energized by this landmark decision, civil rights activists launched a mass movement to end all forms of racial segregation in public life.

On December 1, 1955, Rosa Parks, an African American woman and NAACP member, was arrested and fined for refusing to surrender her seat to a White passenger on a city bus in Montgomery, Alabama. The local NAACP, led by Edgar D. Nixon, rallied local Blacks to a citywide protest; 50,000 Blacks responded to the call. The yearlong boycott was met by harassments, arrests, attacks, and intimidation by police and White supremacists. Finally, as a result of a U.S. Supreme Court ruling declaring segregation of public buses unconstitutional, Montgomery buses were desegregated on December 21, 1956. The bus boycott represented the first large-scale use of nonviolent resistance against racial discrimination in American history.

The bus boycott made **Martin Luther King, Jr.**, a national hero for the oppressed—a moral voice, seasoned with Christian love, fighting for social justice. As president of the Montgomery Improvement Association, he organized the boycott on the principles of Christian charity and nonviolent, direct action. In January 1957, King and other Black leaders formed the Southern Christian Leadership Conference (SCLC), a ministerial organization aimed at coordinating and assisting local civil rights groups in the South. By using highly publicized peaceful resistance, the SCLC played a significant

In Atlanta, Georgia, A Toddle House had the distinction of being occupied during a sit-in by some of America's most effective organizers. In the room are Taylor Washington, Ivanhoe Donaldson, Joyce Ladner, John Lewis (behind Judy Richardson), George Green, and Chico Neblett. Danny Lyon/Library of Congress.

role in pressuring the federal government and Congress to pass the Civil Rights Act and the Voting Rights Act.

The struggle for racial desegregation met much resistance in the Deep South. Alabama passed a law ordering the NAACP to disclose its membership lists. South Carolina barred NAACP members from seeking state employment; after Septima Poinsette Clark Long was named vice president of the Charleston branch of the NAACP, she was not allowed to teach in public schools. Meanwhile, in 1956, the White Citizens' Council—aimed at maintaining the Southern way of life—was established in Greenwood, Mississippi. This segregationist organization used economic and political means to perpetuate White supremacy.

In 1957, civil rights activists won a major victory in their fight against school desegregation in Little Rock, Arkansas. Under the guidance of NAACP leader Daisy Bates, nine Black students won a court order mandating their admission to all-White Central High School. Resisting the court order and the advice of President Dwight Eisenhower, Governor Orval Faubus called out 1,000 Arkansas National Guard paratroopers to prevent the students from entering the school; Eisenhower sent federal troops into the city so that the court order could be implemented.

Sit-in protests to integrate lunch counters began in Greensboro, North Carolina, on February 1, 1960. Four black students from North Carolina A&T University sat down at a "White-only" lunch counter at Woolworth's, demanding to be served. This sparked a wave of sit-ins across the Deep South and then nationwide. In April, Shaw University students in Raleigh, North Carolina, created the Student Nonviolent Coordinating Committee to orchestrate these sit-ins, support their leaders, and publicize their activities. The sit-ins forced the desegregation not only of lunch counters but also of stores, supermarkets, libraries, and movie theaters.

Starting in May 1961, "freedom riders" made bus trips to Southern states to protest segregation in interstate travel facilities. Dispatched by the Congress of Racial Equality, more than 7,000 activists from CORE and SNCC participated in the movement. Among the riders were such prominent civil rights leaders as James L. Farmer, John Lewis, and Frederick Leonard. The riders encountered harassment, mass arrests, imprisonment, and shootings from White supremacists, especially in Alabama. The Kennedy administration finally interceded, providing protection to the riders. In the same year, the SCLC campaigned in Albany, Georgia, for voter registration, desegregation in public places, and equal employment opportunities, among other causes.

The early 1960s also saw Black protests against racial segregation of universities. In 1962, James Meredith, a Black man from Mississippi, applied for admission to the all-White University of Mississippi, which refused to allow him to enroll. With legal assistance from the NAACP, he filed suit in federal court, which ordered the university to desegregate. His enrollment, opposed by Governor Ross Barnett as well as university administrators, incited riots. Federal troops clashed with White students, resulting in two deaths and hundreds of injuries. A similar incident took place on the campus of the University of Alabama the following year. Governor George C. Wallace repeatedly defied federal mandates to desegregate the university on the pretext of "states' rights" on racial issues. In September 1963, the controversy over admission of six Black students ended as President Kennedy ordered the U.S. Army to ensure the students' safe entry into the university.

The spring of 1963 saw a large-scale civil rights campaign in Birmingham, an uprising featuring peaceful marches by thousands of Blacks. More than 4,000 demonstrators were jailed. As 2,500 more Blacks, many of whom were schoolchildren, marched through the streets, they were brutally suppressed by Police Commissioner Eugene "Bull" Connor; he ordered the use of fire hoses, German shepherds, tear gas, and clubs against the marchers. Police brutality, televised all over the world, led President Kennedy to propose an extensive civil rights bill in Congress. In August, King and other civil rights leaders orchestrated a march on **Washington, D.C.**—the largest civil rights protest in U.S. history—to draw national and international attention to racial problems in the United States and to support passage of civil rights legislation pending in Congress. It was at this march that King delivered the famed "I Have a Dream" speech to more than 200,000 civil rights supporters gathered around the Lincoln Memorial: "I have a dream that my four little children will one day live in a nation where they will not be judged by the color of their skin, but by the content of their character."

Photograph showing civil rights leaders, including Martin Luther King, Jr., marching on Washington, 1963. Courtesy of the Library of Congress.

Despite significant achievements in civil rights struggles, the year 1963 was marred by high-profile murders of Blacks in the South. On June 11, **Medgar Evers,** an NAACP field secretary in Jackson, Mississippi, was assassinated in front of his house. Byron de la Beckwith, a member of the White Citizens' Council, was arrested and tried twice for the killing. After two hung juries, he was acquitted and was not convicted until 1994. On the early Sunday morning of September 15, the Ku Klux Klan bombed Birmingham's Sixteenth Street Baptist Church, killing four young Black girls and injuring twenty people. Riots erupted in Birmingham, resulting in the deaths of two more Black youths. Local authorities and then FBI agents investigated the bombing but failed to file charges by 1968. The case was closed, and it was not until 1977 that one of the bombers was finally convicted.

In the summer of 1964, the Council of Federated Organizations—a coalition of civil rights groups including SCLC, CORE, SNCC, and NAACP—launched the Freedom Summer Campaign, designed to end the political disenfranchisement of Blacks in the Deep South. Directed by Robert Moses, it established the Mississippi Freedom Democratic Party; more than 80,000 people joined the party, and sixty-eight delegates attended the Democratic National Convention to protest the presence of the all-White Mississippi contingent. On June 21, a day after the Freedom Summer began, three civil rights workers—James E. Cheney, Andrew Goodman, and Michael Schwerner—disappeared in Mississippi. Their bodies were discovered six weeks later. Finally, on July 2, the Civil Rights Act was signed by President Lyndon Johnson. Considered the most comprehensive civil rights legislation since Reconstruction, the act outlawed segregation in public facilities and guaranteed equal opportunity in employment, education, and federal programs, regardless of race, color, religion, or national origin. It also gave the executive branch of government the power to enforce desegregation.

The following year was turbulent but victorious for civil rights activists. On February 21, **Malcolm X**—a member of the **Nation of Islam** and founder of the Organization of Afro-American Unity (1964)—was shot and killed in a **Harlem, New York**, auditorium. In February and March, a march was held in support of Blacks' voting rights at the Dallas County Courthouse in Selma, Alabama. After a Black man named Jimmy Lee Jackson was killed by a state trooper, hundreds of protesters, including Catholic priests and nuns, Protestant clergymen, and rabbis, marched in the streets. On March 7, state troopers responded with whips, clubs, and tear gas, fatally injuring Rev. James Reeb. Fifty marchers were hospitalized. After "Bloody Sunday," the day when police brutality reached its peak, more than 3,000 protesters marched from Selma to Montgomery. The violence in Selma forced President Johnson to seek passage of the Voting Rights Act, which protected Blacks' constitutional right to vote. It suspended literacy tests and other such voting obstacles for Southern Blacks. Approved by Congress, the Voting Rights Act was signed into law on August 6. On September 24, President Johnson issued Executive Order 11246, designed to improve the economic and education opportunities of minority groups and women.

After the 1964 and 1965 legal victories, the civil rights movement increasingly lost its popular appeal as some Blacks, especially those in Northern cities, turned to violence in protest against inner-city poverty. The August 1965 rioting in the Watts district of Los Angeles served as a prime example. The black area exploded into violence after two young Black males were arrested by White police officers for reckless driving. In the clash between Black youths and police, thirty-four people died, more than 1,000 were injured, and almost 4,000 were arrested. Looting and firebombings resulted in significant property damage, estimated at around $40 million. In October 1966, in Oakland, California, **Huey P. Newton** and Bobby Seale founded the **Black Panther Party** for Self-Defense. Inspired by Maosim and **Marxism**, the party embraced militant socialism in its struggle to bring about tangible economic, social, and political improvements for women and racial minorities.

Despite the rising voices of militant Black civil rights leaders, Martin Luther King, Jr., continued his crusade for social justice through peaceful means. At the beginning of 1966, he launched a massive protest in **Chicago**—the first major civil rights campaign outside the South. Marchers demanded abolition of racially discriminatory practices in housing, employment, and schooling. King also established Operation Breadbasket to promote job opportunities for Blacks. Except for Operation Breadbasket, however, King's Chicago campaign resulted largely in unfulfilled promises made by government. On November 27, 1967, King announced the "Poor People's Campaign," a multiracial, nonviolent mass march to be held in Washington. Its aim was to demand elimination of all forms of barriers to economic freedom for the impoverished. It also called for the funding of a $12 billion "Economic Bill of Rights."

In the spring of 1968, King accepted a request by sanitation workers in **Memphis, Tennessee,** to support their strike. On April 4, while standing on the balcony of the Lorraine Motel, he was assassinated by a sniper. More than 10,000 people gathered outside the Ebenezer Baptist Church in Atlanta, where his funeral was held. On April 11, the Civil Rights Act of 1968 was passed, which made it illegal to discriminate in the sale, rental, and financing of housing. The Fair Housing Act, prohibiting racial discrimination in housing, was passed in 1968.

King's death was a closing chapter for the modern civil rights movement. The movement had achieved legal and moral victories for Blacks whose constitutional rights had been violated for decades. It brought freedom and equality to Blacks as well as other racial minorities. The movement also inspired feminist activists who were beginning to assert their civil rights.

Important African American authors of the period whose poetry, fiction, nonfiction, and drama mirror issues central to the movement include **James Baldwin, Amiri Baraka, Melba Patillo Beals, Julian Bond, Elaine Brown, Eldridge Cleaver, Angela Davis, Mari Evans, Langston Hughes, Haki R. Madhubuti**, and **Dudley Randall**.

Resources: Henry Julian Abraham and Barbara A. Perry, *Freedom and the Court: Civil Rights and Liberties in the United States*, 8th ed. (Lawrence: University Press of Kansas, 2003); Lucius J. Barker, Jr., and Twiley W. Barker, Jr., *Civil Liberties and the Constitution: Cases and Commentaries*, 5th ed. (Englewood Cliffs, NJ: Prentice-Hall, 1986); Taylor Branch, *Parting the Waters: America in the King Years, 1954–1963* (New York: Simon and Schuster, 1988); James H. Cone, *Martin & Malcolm & America: A Dream or a Nightmare* (Maryknoll, NY: Orbis, 1991); Kermit L. Hall, ed., *Civil Liberties in American History: Major Historical Interpretations* (New York: Garland, 1987); Henry Hampton, Steve Fayer, and Sarah Flynn, comps., *Voices of Freedom: An Oral History of the Civil Rights Movement from the 1950s Through the 1980s* (New York: Bantam, 1990); Richard H. King, *Civil Rights and the Idea of Freedom* (New York: Oxford University Press, 1992); Robert Weisbrot, *Freedom Bound: A History of America's Civil Rights Movement* (New York: Norton, 1990); Juan Williams, *Eyes on the Prize: America's Civil Rights Years, 1954–1965* (New York: Penguin, 2002).

John J. Han

Civil War, American (1861–1865). Except for the American Revolution, which led to the establishment of the United States, the Civil War, which could have led to the dissolution of the United States, is arguably the most important event in the nation's history. For approximately 3.5 million African Americans living in **the South**, the war ultimately meant the difference between freedom and **slavery**. The war officially began in mid-April 1861, when Confederate artillery fired on Fort Sumter in South Carolina. In December 1860, however, South Carolina had already seceded from the Union, and tensions between Northern "free" states and Southern slaveholding states had been mounting for years, partly because of the pressure applied by the **Abolitionist Movement** and the **Underground Railroad**. By the time the war ended with the final surrender of Confederate troops in May 1865 (General Robert E. Lee had surrendered a month earlier), 65,000 Union troops had been killed in action, and 43,000 had died from their wounds or from disease; 80,000 Confederate troops had been killed in action, and at least 160,000 had died from their wounds or from disease; and President Abraham Lincoln, who had issued the Emancipation Proclamation on January 1, 1863, had been assassinated (Morison et al., 292–384). The United States remained intact, and the horrific institution of slavery had ended, even if the realization of full citizenship for African Americans faced implacable obstacles for nearly 100 more years. At least 186,000 Black troops fought on the Union side in the war, meaning tens of thousands men went, almost instantaneously, from being slaves to officially serving the nation that had allowed their slavery. Company E, an all-African American company, was deployed to defend **Washington, D.C.** (Franklin, 238-240). Some black soldiers held commissions, and several, including Decatur Dorsey and James Gardner, were decorated for valor (Franklin and Moss, 242). Arguably the most famous group of Black soldiers in the war was the Fifty-Fourth Massachusetts Infantry, led by a White officer, Robert Gould Shaw. Their exploits have been dramatized in the motion picture *Glory*, and the group of soldiers is meditated upon in Robert Lowell's famous poem "For the Union Dead." A monument commemorating Shaw and his men is located in **Boston, Massachusetts**.

The effect of the Civil War on African American literature is incalculable. Even before the Emancipation Proclamation was issued and the Confederate armies were defeated, former slaves began leaving plantations and streaming into the North. At the war's end, more African Americans went North, and after **Reconstruction** failed, the **Great Migration** truly began. This migration had been set in motion, however, by the Underground Railroad before the war and with the outbreak of armed conflict in 1861. In the North, African Americans found not just freedom and employment but also education and literacy, which had been forbidden in the South. Countless writers emerged from this expansion of literacy; moreover, a vast new African American audience for literature began to take shape. As one by-product of freedom, then, education translated into literacy, which translated in innumerable ways into the production and consumption of journalism and literature. Immediately after the Civil War, numerous educational institutions for African Americans were founded, including Howard University, the Hampton Institute, Atlanta University, and Fisk University, providing an academic foundation for future readers and writers, scholars and teachers. **Charlotte Forten Grimké**, a native of **Philadelphia, Pennsylvania**, and born free, began teaching in South Carolina in 1862. Her poem "The Grand Army of the Republic" concerns the war (Lee, 758).

Concerning the Civil War itself, **Susie King Taylor** produced *Reminiscences of My Life in Camp* (1902), a chronicle of her experience as a nurse and

District of Columbia. Company E, 4th U.S. Colored Infantry, at Fort Lincoln, undated. Courtesy of the Library of Congress.

therefore a unique work of African American literature. A collection of letters written by African American soldiers during the Civil War appeared in 1992 (Redkey). **Paul Laurence Dunbar**'s best-known poem on the Civil War is "The Colored Soldiers."

Frances E. W. Harper's novel *Iola Leroy* (1892) is set in the Civil War era. **Alex Haley**'s saga, *Roots* (1976), includes episodes set during the Civil War, and **Margaret Walker**'s acclaimed novel *Jubilee* (1966) is set during the war. So, too, are **Ishmael Reed**'s novel *Flight to Canada* (1976), **Leon Forrest**'s novel *The Bloodworth Orphans* (1977), and **Edward P. Jones**'s novel *The Known World* (2003). **Ernest J. Gaines**'s best-known novel, *The Autobiography of Miss Jane Pittman* (1971), contains reminiscences by the protagonist concerning secession and war. **Connie Rose Porter**'s *Meet Addy: An American Girl* (1993) is a children's book about a young African American girl living during the Civil War. *The Wind Done Gone* (2001), the controversial novel by Alice Randall, is in part a **parody** of the most famous, most popular novel of the American Civil War, Margaret Mitchell's *Gone with the Wind* (1936). A federal district court in Atlanta temporarily, but ultimately unsuccessfully, blocked distribution of Randall's novel. That Mitchell's depiction of the Civil War would, as late as 2001, be considered sacred indicates the depth of feeling the Civil War still inspires in the United States, and Randall's counternarrative indicates the extent to which the Civil War remains a fruitful topic for African American writers. (*See* **Chesnutt, Charles Waddell**; **Douglass, Frederick**; **Jacobs, Harriet Ann**; **Stowe, Harriet Beecher**; **Tubman, Harriet Ross**; **Wilson, Harriet E.**)

Resources: Leon Forrest, *The Bloodworth Orphans* (New York: Random House, 1977); John Hope Franklin and Alfred A. Moss, Jr., *From Slavery to Freedom: A History of African Americans*, 8th ed. (Boston: McGraw-Hill, 2000); Ernest J. Gaines, *The Autobiography of Miss Jane Pittman* (1971; repr. New York: Bantam, 1982); Alex Haley, *Roots* (Garden City, NY: Doubleday, 1976); Edward P. Jones, *The Known World* (New York: Amistad, 2003); A. Robert Lee, "War Experience," in *The Oxford Companion to African American Literature*, ed. William L. Andrews, Frances Smith Foster, and Trudier Harris (New York: Oxford University Press, 1997), 758–759; Robert Lowell, "For the Union Dead," in *The Norton Anthology of Poetry*, 3rd ed., ed. Alexander W. Allison et al. (New York: Norton, 1983), 1198; Samuel Eliot Morison, Henry Steele Commager, and William E. Leuchtenburg, *A Concise History of the American Republic*, rev. ed. (New York: Oxford University Press, 1977), 276–384; Connie Rose Porter, *Meet Addy: An American Girl* (Middleton, WI: Pleasant, 1993); Alice Randall, *The Wind Done Gone* (Boston: Houghton Mifflin, 2001); Edwin S. Redkey, ed., *A Grand Army of Black Men: Letters from the African-American Soldiers in the Union Army, 1861–1865* (New York: Cambridge University Press, 1992); Ishmael Reed, *Flight to Canada* (New York: Random House, 1976); Susie King Taylor, *A Black Woman's Civil War Memoirs: Reminiscences of My Life in Camp with the 33rd U.S. Colored Troops, Late 1st South Volunteers*, ed. Patricia W. Romero (1902; repr. New York: Wiener, 1988); Margaret Walker, *Jubilee* (Boston: Houghton Mifflin, 1966); Edward Zwick, director, *Glory* (Columbia Pictures, 1989; DVD, Columbia/Tri-Star, 2001).

Hans Ostrom

Clair, Maxine (born 1939). Novelist, poet, and educator. A native of Kansas City, Kansas, Maxine Clair graduated from the University of Kansas at Lawrence. She worked as a medical technologist for several years, and then earned an M.F.A. in 1984 at American University. She has received multiple awards, including the **Chicago Tribune**'s Heartland Prize for fiction for *Rattlebone* (1994), a collection of short stories set in Kansas City in the 1950s. *Rattlebone* also won the Friends of American Literature Fiction Award and the American Library Association's Black Caucus Award. *Rattlebone* was the basis for the chapbook *October Brown*, which received Baltimore's Artscape Prize for Maryland Writers in 1992, and for the full-length novel *October Suite*, published in 2001. *October Suite* examines a young woman's dilemma as she bucks 1950s middle-class tradition, and it explores the consequences that affect her family. The novel was written as a tribute to African American women teachers of the 1950s, who suffered as a result of sexism. Clair's writing was strongly influenced by her childhood community and the music played by her mother, a pianist. Clair has also written a collection of poems, *Coping with Gravity* (1988). She received the Edgar Wolfe Literary Award in 1996 and was a Langston Hughes Visiting Professor of Literature at the University of Kansas in 2001. Clair is a professor of English at George Washington University.

Resources: Maxine Clair: *Coping with Gravity* (Washington, DC: Washington Writers Publishing House, 1988); *October Suite* (New York: Random House, 2001); *Rattlebone* (New York: Farrar, Straus and Giroux, 1994); press release information: BayPath College, Oct. 9, 2003; Friends of the Library in Kansas City, Kansas, 2001; University of Kansas, *Oread*, Feb. 16, 2001.

Dera R. Williams

Clarke, Breena. Novelist, playwright, actress, and journalist. Clarke, the daughter of Edna Higgins Payne Clarke and James Sheridan Clarke, grew up in **Washington, D.C.**, and attended Webster College and Howard University. Her debut novel, *River, Cross My Heart*, brings to life the Georgetown community during the 1920s. The story is based on the community in which her parents lived and stories told to her by her mother. Clarke portrays an African American community struggling with the effects of segregation. However, in her portrait of a community that supports and depends on each other, Clarke shows that this form of racism does not supplant the function, need, and thriving of familial and communal relationships. The novel revolves around the Bynum family, recent migrants from rural North Carolina. As they adjust to the big city, where they moved to in search of new and improved opportunities for themselves and children, they experience the death of their youngest daughter, Clara, who drowns in the Potomac River and the coming of age of Johnnie Mae, their eldest daughter.

Clarke has achieved acclaim as an actress and playwright. In 1980, she made her Broadway acting debut in *Reggae*. The play *Re/Membering Aunt Jemima: A Menstrual Show*, written with Glenda Dickerson, which is included in the anthology *Contemporary Plays by Women of Color*, seeks to dismantle the myth of the stereotypical Aunt Jemima icon. Currently, Clarke administers the Editorial Diversity Program at Time, Inc. in New York City.

Resources: Breena Clarke: *Re/Membering Aunt Jemima: A Menstrual Show*, in *Contemporary Plays by Women of Color*, ed. Kathy A. Perkins and Roberta Uno (New York: Routledge, 1996), 32–45; *River, Cross My Heart* (Boston: Little, Brown, 1999).

Brandon L. A. Hutchinson

Cleage [Lomax], Pearl Michelle (born 1948). Playwright, novelist, essayist, and educator. Pearl Cleage's work focuses on the social problems of Black women and Black communities. It also concerns the difficulty of familial relationships, the rising rate of HIV-infected Black women, domestic violence, and the devastating impact of drug addiction and chronic illness. In 2003, **Oprah Winfrey** placed Cleage squarely in the public eye by choosing her novel *What Looks Like Crazy on an Ordinary Day* for the Oprah Winfrey Book Club. Subsequent novels are *I Wish I Had a Red Dress* (2001) and *Some Things I Thought I'd Never Do* (2003). Her latest novel is *Babylon Sisters* (2005). *Deals with the Devil* (1994) is a book of her essays, and *The Brass Bed and Other Stories* (1991) is a collection of her short fiction.

Cleage began writing plays while an undergraduate at Howard University in the late 1960s. Her piece *puppetplay* achieved widespread recognition following its premier by the Negro Ensemble Company in 1983. Cleage's plays *Hospice* (1983), *Flyin' West* (1992), *Blues for an Alabama Sky* (1995), and *Bourbon at the Border* (1997) (the latter three commissioned for Atlanta's Alliance Theatre) have also met with critical acclaim. Cleage has been a frequent contributor of essays and short stories to magazines and anthologies. For ten years, she wrote the popular column "Stop Making Sense" that ran in the *Atlanta Tribune*. She is the cofounder and editor of *Catalyst*, a literary magazine; has served as the playwright-in-residence and artistic director for the Just Us Theater Company; has taught creative writing at Spelman College in **Atlanta, Georgia**, and has conducted interviews for WETV television, Atlanta. Cleage has received grants from the Georgia Council for the Arts, the National Endowment for the Arts, the Atlanta Bureau of Cultural Affairs, the Coordinating Council of Literary Magazines, AT&T, the Coca-Cola Company, the Coca-Cola Foundation, and the Whitter-Bynner Foundation for Poetry.

Resources: Samiya A. Bashir, "Pearl Cleage's Idlewild Idylls (Interview)," *Black Issues Book Review* 3, no. 4 (July 2001), 16; Pearl Cleage: *Babylon Sisters* (New York: Ballantine/One World, 2005); *The Brass Bed and Other Stories* (Chicago: Third World Press, 1991); *Deals with the Devil, and Other Reasons Not to Riot* (New York: Ballantine, 1994); *Flyin' West and Other Plays* (New York: Theatre Communications Group, 1999); *I Wish I Had a Red Dress* (New York: William Morrow, 2001); *Some Things I Never Thought I'd Do* (New York: Ballantine/One World, 2003); *What Looks like Crazy on an Ordinary Day* (New York: William Morrow, 1997); Freda Scott Giles, "The Motion of Herstory: Three Plays by Pearl Cleage," *African American Review*, Winter 1997, 709–712; Gwendolyn Glenn, "Home Time and Island Time: Novelist Pearl Cleage Finds Inspiration Just Outside Her Window in Southwest Atlanta, While Paule Marshall Has Twice Drawn on a Long Ago Trip to Grenada," *Black Issues Book Review*, Mar.–Apr. 2004, 30–34.

Michelle LaFrance

Cleaver, Eldridge (1935–1998). Essayist, prison writer, spokesperson, and political activist. Born in Wabbaseka, Arkansas but raised in **Los Angeles, California**, Cleaver gained fame after publishing the nonfiction book *Soul on Ice* (1968), one of the best-selling works of **prison literature** in American history. He changed his political views in the 1970s after embracing religion and rejecting communism.

In 1957, Cleaver was convicted of assault and served nine years in two of California's most dangerous prisons, San Quentin and Folsom. While incarcerated, he developed theories on revolution, **race**, and violence, subsequently creating a philosophical doctrine that served as motivational fuel for the **Black Power** movement (Rout, 32). Inspired by **Malcolm X**, Cleaver warned his Black compatriots, "We are engaged in the deepest, the most fundamental revolution and reconstruction which men have ever been called upon to make in their lives, and which they absolutely cannot escape or avoid except at the peril of the very continued existence of human life on this planet" (*Post-Prison Writings and Speeches*, 136).

Beyond provocative rhetoric, Cleaver's collection of autobiographical essays (*Soul on Ice*) also provided literary theorists with ideas they could apply to the work of major African American authors, including **James Baldwin** and **Richard Wright**. Most of these ideas had to do with what African Americans should do politically to change their situation in the United States.

Upon being released from prison in 1966, Cleaver became the minister of information for the **Black Panther Party** and a regular contributor to *Ramparts* magazine. As Maxwell Geismar first observed in 1967, "In a literary epoch marked by a prevailing mediocrity of expression, a lack of substantial new talent, a kind of spiritual slough after the great wave of American writing from the 1920s to the 1940s, Eldridge Cleaver is one of the distinctive new literary voices to be heard" (13). Cleaver married Kathleen Neal in 1967; they were both committed to the ideals of the Black Panther Party at the time. **Kathleen Cleaver** went on to develop her own voice as an activist and writer.

In 1968 his writing brought national acclaim, and Cleaver became a candidate for the American presidency on the Peace and Freedom Party ticket. That same year he was wounded in a shoot-out with police and sent back to prison for parole violation. Released within months, he was on the run after refusing to serve additional prison time related to his 1957 convictions. A fugitive, Cleaver nonetheless managed to publish *Post-Prison Writings and Speeches* (1969), *Conversations with Eldridge Cleaver* (1970), and *Revolution in the Congo* (1971), an idealistic manifesto backed by the Revolutionary Peoples' Communications Network.

On the run in Algeria, he found himself at serious odds with the Black Panther Party's vanguard, specifically with high-ranking members such as **Huey Newton** and Bobby Seale. As a result, irreconcilable differences led Cleaver to work with other revolutionary groups, most notably the Black Liberation Army. However, upon returning to the United States in 1975, he not only broke with the Black Panther Party but also cut theoretical ties with former allies and activists such as **Angela Y. Davis**. *Soul on Ice* remains a controversial book, not only because of its political theories but also because of views toward women that it expresses. Cleaver's final work of nonfiction, *Soul on Fire* (1978), was published twenty years before his death and documents his departure from **Marxism** (and ultimate conversion to Christianity) after living in exile. (*See* **Black Nationalism; Brown, Elaine; Feminism/Black Feminism; Feminist/Black Feminist Literary Criticism**.)

Resources: Eldridge Cleaver: *Post-Prison Writings and Speeches*, ed. Robert Scheer (London: Jonathan Cape, 1969); *Revolution in the Congo* (London: Stage One for the Revolutionary Peoples' Communication Network, 1971); *Soul on Fire* (New York: Thomas Nelson, 1995); *Soul on Ice* (1968; repr. New York: Delta Books, 1999); Maxwell

Geismar, "Introduction to *Soul on Ice*" (1967), in *Soul on Ice* by Eldridge Cleaver (New York: Delta Books, 1999); Kathleen Rout, *Eldridge Cleaver* (Boston: Twayne, 1991).

Stephen M. Steck

Cleaver, Kathleen Neal (born 1946). Scholar, essayist, editor, foundation director, and activist. Cleaver is the former communications secretary of the **Black Panther Party** and wife of **Eldridge Cleaver**. She was born in Tuskegee Institute, Alabama. **Martin Luther King, Jr.**, inspired her to join the Student NonViolent Coordinating Committee prior to her membership in the Black Panthers. Because her father worked for the Agency for International Development, Cleaver grew up in colonized countries, living in India and the Philippines during the 1950s. She is the first female to have served as spokesperson for the Panthers, and in 1967 she became the first female to organize and sit on the Panther's Central Committee. Her oratory and her prominent afro hairstyle influenced young Black women across the country to join the Panthers. She edited *The Black Panther* newspaper and assisted in putting together the national and international "Free Huey" (Newton) campaign. With her husband forced underground, Kathleen Cleaver joined him in exile in North Africa during the 1970s. They started the first international unit of the Black Panther Party, and her observations about this experience are included in *The Black Panther Party Reconsidered* (1998), by Charles Jones.

After returning from exile, Cleaver studied law and now teaches at Emory University. With George Katsiaficas she edited *Liberation, Imagination, and the Black Panther Party* (2001), and with Jamal Joseph she founded the Panther Film Festival (2000) that travels annually to universities. In the film *Public Enemy* (1999) she appears with Bobby Seale. Her scholarly essays appear in *Critical White Studies*, *The Promise of Multiculturalism*, *Yale Journal of Law and Humanities*, *A Turbulent Voyage*, *Black Renaissance*, and *Human Rights in the U.S.* Currently, she is director of the Human Rights Research Fund. (*See* **Black Nationalism**; **Brown, Elaine**; **Newton, Huey Percy**.)

Resources: *The Black Panther Newspaper* (1967–1970); Kathleen Cleaver, personal interview with Regina Jennings (2000); Kathleen Cleaver and George Katsiaficas, eds., *Liberation, Imagination, and the Black Panther Party* (New York: Routledge, 2001); Richard Delgado and Jean Stefanic, eds., *Critical White Studies: Looking behind the Mirror* (Philadelphia: Temple University Press, 1997); Floyd W. Hayes, ed., *A Turbulent Voyage: Readings in African American Studies* (San Diego, CA: Collegiate, 1992); Charles Jones, *The Black Panther Party Reconsidered* (Washington, DC: Black Classic Press, 1998); George Katsiaficas and Teodros Kiros, eds., *The Promise of Multiculturalism: Education and Autonomy in the 21st Century* (New York: Routledge, 1998).

Regina Jennings

Cliff, Michelle (born 1946). Novelist, poet, and critic. Cliff's attention to the difficult intersections between **race**, class, **gender**, sexuality, and nation gives her works a powerful voice in Black literature. Born in Jamaica in 1946, when it was still a British colony, raised largely in the United States in a Caribbean neighborhood in New York City, and educated in the United Kingdom, Michelle Cliff now lives and teaches in the United States. She earned her Ph.D. at the Warburg Institute of the University of London, studying the Italian Renaissance. Cliff is primarily recognized as a novelist, but has also published poetry, short fiction, and scholarly criticism. Her novels include *Abeng* (1985), in which she introduces the reader to Clare Savage, a Creole Jamaican girl who moves from the island to the United States in the 1960s, London in the 1970s, and then back to Jamaica. That character returns in *No Telephone to Heaven* (1987), Cliff's second novel, which deals more explicitly with both state-sponsored violence in Jamaica and the devastating effects of globalization. Her other works include *Free Enterprise* (a novel, 1993), *Bodies of Water* and *The Store of a Million Items* (short stories, 1990 and 1998) and two collections of poetry, *The Land of Look Behind* (1985) and *Claiming an Identity They Taught Me to Despise* (1980). Cliff remains an activist, often publishing political essays in publications such as *Ms.* and the *Village Voice*, as well as in the influential feminist anthology *Making Face, Making Soul* (1990), edited by Gloria Anzaldúa. She served as editor of a collection of writings by Lillian Smith, a social reformer from **the South**, titled *The Winner Names the Age* (1978). Cliff currently teaches at Trinity College in Connecticut and lives part of the time in Santa Cruz, California.

As a Caribbean-born Black woman, Cliff has brought attention to the complex lineages that make up Black subjects living in the United States. Her work is often set in Jamaica and engages politically with issues such as globalization, miscegenation, and colonial and contemporary histories of Jamaica. Her semiautobiographical texts in particular deal with intraracial conflict over skin tone and sexuality. A light-skinned woman herself, Cliff often talks about the complex negotiation between claiming Blackness, being stigmatized for being too White and upper-class, and a family history that attempts to deny that link and encourages "**passing.**" She has also been an influential critic of homophobia in the Black **diaspora**, critiquing the view from the Caribbean that queerness is a "White" or "upper-class" luxury.

Resources: Michelle Cliff: *Abeng* (New York: Plume, 1985); *Bodies of Water* (New York: Dutton, 1990); *Claiming an Identity They Taught Me to Despise* (Watertown, MA: Persephone Press, 1980); *Free Enterprise* (New York: Dutton, 1993); *The Land of Look Behind: Prose and Poetry* (New York: Firebrand Books, 1985); *No Telephone to Heaven* (New York: Dutton, 1987); "Object into Subject: Some Thoughts on the Work of Black Women Artists," in *Making Face, Making Soul/Haciendo Caras: Creative and Critical Perspectives by Women of Color*, ed. Gloria Anzaldúa (San Francisco: Aunt Lute, 1990), 271–290; *The Store of a Million Items* (Boston: Houghton Mifflin, 1998); Michelle Cliff, ed., *The Winner Names the Age*, by Lillian Smith (New York: W. W. Norton, 1978); Judith Raiskin, "The Art of History: An Interview with Michelle Cliff," *Kenyon Review*, Winter 1993, 57–71; Meryl F. Schwartz, "An Interview with Michelle Cliff," *Contemporary Literature* 34, no. 4 (1993), 595–619; *Voices from the Gaps: Women Writers of Color*, http://voices.cla.umn.edu/newsite/authors/CLIFFmichelle.htm.

Samantha Pinto

Clifton, Lucille (born 1936). Poet and children's author. Along with her accomplishments as a poet, Clifton is known for her work in bringing cultural diversity to **children's literature**. Born Thelma Louise Sayles on June 27, 1936, in Depew, New York, Clifton is the child of Samuel and Thelma Sayles, who were both laborers. Her father worked in the steel mills, and her mother was a laundress (Moody, 157). In addition to her work and her own house-keeping, Clifton's mother wrote poetry for enjoyment (Moody, 157). Clifton's mother recited poetry to her, and her father was an avid storyteller, a griot who taught his children the history of their ancestors and those ancestors' journeys to America (Hatch and Strickland, 60). Although neither parent had been formally educated, both encouraged Clifton to attempt whatever she wanted to do, even though her father was against the idea of her mother trying to publish her own work (Glaser, 313–314).

Clifton attended Howard University on a drama scholarship; there she met **Sterling A. Brown**, **A. B. Spellman**, LeRoi Jones (**Amiri Baraka**), and Chloe Wofford (now known as **Toni Morrison**) and acted in the first performance of **James Baldwin**'s play *The Amen Corner* (Draper, 458). She left Howard to attend Fredonia State Teachers College. She met her husband, Fred James Clifton, during that time.

Clifton worked for the U.S. Department of Education as a literature assistant for the Central Atlantic Regional Educational Laboratory from 1969 to 1971 ("Lucille Clifton," 56). Clifton notes that the position involved locating books to be used in schools. As she describes it, "I had to find books that had characters in them that looked like my children, which is why I started writing children's books" (Davis, 1060). Clifton asserts that "American children's literature ought to mirror American children" (Davis, 1061). Clifton has written a number of children's books, many of which feature a boy named Everett Anderson who experiences a number of life events, such as a new stepparent and death of a relative. One of the books in this series won the Coretta Scott King Award in 1984.

Although she did not complete her college degree because she became engrossed in her writing and "forgot to study," education was and remains important to her (Draper, 458). She has received honorary doctorates from Colby College, the University of Maryland, Towson State University, Washington College, and Albright College ("Lucille Clifton," 57), and has held several visiting professorships. She has been distinguished professor of humanities at St. Mary's College of Maryland since 1991 ("Lucille Clifton," 56). A well-received teacher of poetry and creative writing, she has had interesting experiences while teaching, including an occasion at Duke University when her students did not know who Paul Robeson was. In telling the story Clifton says, "Well, I thought, 'Okay, he's dead,' but when they said they had never heard of Julian Bond," she became more concerned, and has made it her practice to "teach about the things people don't know about" (Davis, 1061). In her own experiences growing up, Clifton says she became a "nosy kind of curious person" when she realized that teachers were "only going to teach me what they thought I could learn or what they wished me to know" (Davis, 1064).

In her 1976 work *Generations*, Clifton writes about her family history. Each segment is written in the first person, giving an individual voice to each particular ancestor (Moody, 157). The collection has received greater critical attention in recent years for its narrative structure, her use of lines from Walt Whitman's "Song of Myself" as epigraphs for each segment, and its importance not just for African America, but as American genealogy, history, and literature (Holladay; Wall; Whitley). Among the ancestors who tell their stories are her great-great-grandmother, Caroline Sale Donald, born in 1822 or 1823, who was taken from Dahomey to **New Orleans** as a slave (Peppers, 57; Moody, 157). During and after her time in **slavery**, Caroline was a strong woman who was viewed as a leader among her community. Caroline's daughter Lucille, who was the first Black woman legally hanged in Virginia (for killing the White man who was the father of her son) is also given a voice in *Generations* (Peppers, 57). The poems in *An Ordinary Woman* (1974) also feature the lives of Caroline and other family members, based upon the stories that Clifton's father told her.

Clifton's earlier works are often associated with the **Black Arts Movement**, which promoted the arts as a means to overcome racism and oppression (Draper, 458). Her subsequent works, as one critic put it, were "a poetry not of race but of revelation, in the manner of Denise Levertov" (Cooper, 94). Many of her poems deal with politics; some, for example, concern events in Soweto, South Africa; Nagasaki, Japan; Kent State; and Gettysburg. Other poems deal with religion, in both Eastern and Western traditions. Her works of family history mentioned above are also remarkable; many of her writings are elegies or poems of mourning for dead friends and family members, particularly for her mother, who died at age forty-four. Clifton's poetry has been nominated for the Pulitzer Prize three times; she has also been nominated for the National Book Award. Clifton was poet laureate of Maryland from 1974 to 1985 and received three National Endowment for the Arts awards. She has received a number of awards and prizes, including induction into the National Literature Hall of Fame for African American Writers in 1998 and a Lila Wallace Readers Digest Award in 1999.

Writing for Clifton is about bearing witness and being connected to the world intellectually and emotionally. When asked why she continues to write, Clifton replied that "writing is a way of continuing to hope" and "a way of remembering" that she is not alone (Glaser, 311).

Resources: Primary Works: Lucille Clifton: *The Black BC's* (New York: Dutton, 1970); *Blessing the Boats: New and Selected Poems 1988–2000* (Brockport, NY: BOA Editions, 2000); *Everett Anderson's Goodbye* (New York: Holt, Rinehart and Winston, 1983); *Everett Anderson's 1-2-3* (New York: Holt, Rinehart and Winston, 1977); *Everett Anderson's Year* (New York: Holt, Rinehart and Winston, 1974); *Generations* (New York: Random House, 1976); *Good News About the Earth: New Poems* (New York: Random House, 1972); *Good Times: Poems* (New York: Random House, 1969);

Good Woman: Poems and a Memoir, 1969–1980 (Brockport, NY: BOA Editions, 1987); *An Ordinary Woman* (New York: Random House, 1974); *Quilting: Poems, 1987–1990* (Brockport, NY: BOA Editions, 1991); *Some of the Days of Everett Anderson* (New York: Holt, Rinehart and Winston, 1970); *Sonora Beautiful* (New York: Dutton, 1981); *The Terrible Stories: Poems* (Brockport, NY: BOA Editions, 1996); *Three Wishes* (New York: Viking, 1976); *The Times They Used to Be* (New York: Holt, Rinehart and Winston, 1974); *Two-Headed Woman* (Amherst: University of Massachusetts Press, 1980). **Secondary Works:** Jane Todd Cooper, "Lucille Clifton," in *The Oxford Companion to Twentieth-Century Poetry in English*, ed. Ian Hamilton (New York: Oxford University Press, 1994), 94–95; Eisa Davis, "Lucille Clifton and Sonia Sanchez: A Conversation," *Callaloo* 25, no. 4 (2002), 1038–1074; Michael S. Glaser, "I'd Like Not to Be a Stranger in the World: A Conversation/Interview with Lucille Clifton," *Antioch Review* 58, no. 3 (2000), 310–328; Shari Dorantes Hatch and Michael R. Strickland, eds., *African-American Writers: A Dictionary*, ed. Shanti Dorantes Hatch and Michael R. Strickland (Santa Barbara, CA: ABC-CLIO, 2000); "Lucille Clifton," in *Black Literature Criticism*, ed. James P. Draper (Detroit: Gale, 1992), 458–469; "Lucille Clifton," in *Contemporary Authors*, new rev. ser., vol. 97 (Detroit: Gale, 2001), 56–62; Jocelyn K. Moody, "Lucille Clifton," in *The Oxford Companion to African American Literature*, ed. William L. Andrews, Frances Smith Foster, and Trudier Harris (New York: Oxford University Press, 1997), 157–158; Wallace R. Peppers, "Lucille Clifton," in *Dictionary of Literary Biography*, vol. 41, *Afro-American Poets Since 1955* (Detroit: Gale, 1985), 55–60.

Elizabeth Blakesley Lindsay

Clinton, Michelle T. (born 1954). Poet. Born in Bridgeport, Connecticut, Clinton grew up primarily in southern California and continued to live there into adulthood. She has more recently relocated to Berkeley. Although she has not formally studied writing in a university setting, Clinton has received a grant supporting her creative work from the National Endowment for the Arts. A spoken-word poet whose identity as an African American lesbian represents a doubled marginalization, Clinton has asserted her right to be heard in poems with such unambiguous titles as "History as Trash" and "Manifesting the Girl Hero." One of her anthologized stories bears the title "Free Your Mind and Your Ass Will Follow."

Clinton's poems have been collected in the volumes *High Blood Pressure* (1987) and *Good Sense and the Faithless* (1994). With Sesshu Foster and Naomi Quinonez, Clinton has edited the anthology *Invocation L.A.: Urban Multicultural Poetry* (1989), which was nominated for an American Book Award. Her own poems, stories, and essays have been included in *Grand Passion: The Poets of Los Angeles and Beyond* (1995), *Home Girls: A Black Feminist Anthology* (2000), *L.A. Shorts* (2000), and *Bisexual Politics: Theories, Queries, and Visions* (1995), as well as in such periodicals as *Bridges* and ZYZZYVA.

Clinton's poem "Tantrum Girl Responds to Death" was selected for inclusion in *Best American Poetry 1994*. Originally published in the *Kenyon Review* and republished in *Good Sense and the Faithless*, the poem consists of eleven sections presented as paragraphs but containing conventional lines marked by slashes. In a narrative with somewhat scrambled elements, the lesbian speaker of the poem describes her flirtations with Cookie, a lesbian as deliberately mannish in appearance and manner as the speaker is exaggeratedly feminine. The focus of the poem is, however, on Cookie's wasting away from breast cancer and on her family's refusal to accept her lesbianism even when she is dead and prepared for burial. The speaker is enraged but has channeled her rage into the poem. If Cookie's surviving family members are capable of having their "bull-dyke" daughter and sister laid out in a hairstyle, makeup, and clothing that suggests she were a suburban matron, no outrage is going to penetrate their denial. The poem is representative of Clinton's work in its synthesis of emotional intensity and a pragmatic recognition of some enduring obstacles to social progress.

Named one of the best performance poets by *High Performance* magazine, Clinton has recorded the spoken-word CDs *Black Angels* (1992) and *Blood as a Bright Color* (1994). Her work has also been featured in the audiovideo anthology *The United States of Poetry*. (*See* **Los Angeles, California**.)

Resources: "Authors Without Borders," *L.A. Weekly*, Sept. 26, 2003, p. 59; Michelle T. Clinton: *Good Sense and the Faithless* (Albuquerque, NM: West End Press and University of New Mexico Press, 1994); *High Blood Pressure* (Albuquerque, NM: West End Press, 1987); Robert Dassanowsky, "Book Review Desk: Review of *Grand Passion: The Poets of Los Angeles and Beyond*," *Los Angeles Times*, Oct. 19, 1997, p. 6; Patricia Holt, "Remarkable Books of 1990," *San Francisco Chronicle*, June 17, 1990, p. 2.

Martin Kich

Cobb, Ned (1885–1973). Autobiographer. Ned Cobb's **autobiography**, *All God's Dangers: The Life of Nate Shaw*, represents a narrative literary tradition that began in the eighteenth century and continues to evolve today. An illiterate man with a gift for storytelling, Cobb told the story of his life to Theodore Rosengarten, who would capture Cobb's narrative in *All God's Dangers*. In this manner, Cobb's autobiography exemplifies the "as-told-to" tradition of African American autobiography.

All God's Dangers was published in 1974 and won a National Book Award in the same year. The novel presents the oral history of Ned Cobb, a folk hero in his rural home community of Tallapoosa County, Alabama. Hoping to protect his privacy, Cobb chose the name Nate Shaw as his pseudonym. Beginning his account during the nineteenth century, Shaw captures the disappointment he and his family members experienced because they were treated like slaves, despite their freedom. In particular, Shaw recounts his experience as a tenant farmer sentenced to jail for twelve years for defending a neighbor's property from being unjustly confiscated by four White deputy sheriffs.

In the spirit of **slave narratives** written by **Olaudah Equiano, Frederick Douglass**, and **Harriet Jacobs**, Cobb's story represents the concept of learning through struggle as a source of freedom. Moreover, because Cobb's is an oral history written by a third party, it is comparable with *The Confessions of Nat Turner* (1931) and *The Autobiography of Malcolm X* (1965).

Resources: Ned Cobb and Theodore Rosengarten, *All God's Dangers: The Life of Nate Shaw* (New York: Knopf, 1974); Theodore Rosengarten, "Stepping over Cockleburs: Conversations with Ned Cobb," in *Telling Lives: The Biographer's Art*, ed. Marc Pachter (Washington, DC: New Republic Books, 1979), 104–131; Roland L. Williams, Jr., "Ned Cobb," in *The Oxford Companion to African American Literature*, ed. William L. Andrews, Frances Smith Foster, and Trudier Harris (New York: Oxford University Press, 1977), 159–160.

Ondra K. Thomas-Krouse

Cobb, William Jelani (born c. 1972). Essayist, cultural critic, author, and scholar. Born and raised in Queens, New York, Cobb exhibited an early admiration and penchant for the written word. A graduate of Jamaica High School, he earned his bachelor's degree from Howard University. Cobb, a prolific writer, has published in a number of popular and scholarly venues, including the online journal *Africana.com*, in which he writes a bimonthly column titled "Past Imperfect." He has been a contributor to *Essence* magazine, *The Progressive*, the *Washington Post*, the book *In Defense of Mumia*, and the anthology *Mending the World*. In his work published in the anthology *My Daughter, Once Removed*, Cobb explores the meaning and breadth of fatherhood as he relates a moving personal account of his love and dedication to a friend's young daughter. In his short story "The Comeback," Cobb deftly crafts a battle between the old and the young on a basketball court. The older, worn, but wiser contender rises to the occasion and teaches the younger a life lesson.

Cobb is one of the leading essayists exploring **hip-hop** culture and contemporary Black music. Many of his works attack the sexual exploitation, **misogyny**, and racial buffoonery Cobb observes in some current music videos and lyrics. His most important scholarly work to date is *The Essential Harold Cruse: A Reader* (2002), which he edited. This is a collection of cultural critic and theorist **Harold Cruse**'s essays, letters, and speeches with an extensive introduction, emphasizing the import of Cruse's work, written by Cobb. Cobb joined the Department of History at Spelman College in 2001 and completed his doctorate at Rutgers University in 2003. His dissertation was supervised by Pulitzer Prize-winning historian David Levering Lewis and is titled "Antidote to Revolution: African American Anticommunism and the Struggle for Civil Rights 1931–1954." In this work, Cobb explores whether communism was an aid or a hindrance to the African American quest for freedom during this time period. A forthcoming monograph that extends the boundaries of his doctoral research is scheduled to be published by the Columbia University Press. He continues to write about his areas of expertise—the post–**Civil War** period and African Americans, the **Cold War**, and twentieth-century issues and politics. Cobb currently resides in **Atlanta, Georgia**.

Resources: S. E. Anderson and Tony Medina, *In Defense of Mumia* (New York: Writers & Readers, 1996); William Jelani Cobb, "The Comeback," *William Jelani Cobb*, http://www.jelanicobb.com; William Jelani Cobb, ed., *The Essential Harold Cruse: A Reader* (New York: Palgrave, 2002); Rosemarie Robotham, ed., *Mending the*

World: Stories of Family by Contemporary Black Writers (New York: BasicCivitas Books, 2002).

Joan F. McCarty

Coffin, Frank B[arbour] (1871–1951). Poet. Coffin was the author of two collections of poetry, published fifty years apart: *Coffin's Poems with Ajax' [sic] Ordeals* (1897) and *Factum Factorum* (1947). Many of his poems have religious themes. Coffin was born in Holly Springs, Mississippi (Foster). Several of his poems are held in the electronic database *African American Poetry, 1760–1900*, at Stanford University.

Resources: *African-American Poetry, 1760–1900*, http://library.stanford.edu/depts/hasrg/hdis/afroampo.html; Frank B. Coffin, *Coffin's Poems with Ajax' Ordeals* (Little Rock, AK: The Colored Advocate, 1897); *Factum Factorum* (New York: The Haven Press, 1947); Mamie Marie Booth Foster, *Southern Black Creative Writers, 1829–1953: Bio-bibliographies* (Westport, CT: Greenwood Press, 1988).

Hans Ostrom

Cold War, The (c. 1947–1960). The Cold War occurred between the end of **World War II** and the beginning of the **Black Arts Movement**. The Cold War itself consisted of constant political animosity, combined with the chronic threat of military conflict and even nuclear war, between the United States and its allies and the Soviet Union and its allies following World War II; one result of World War II was the partitioning of Europe into "West bloc" and "East bloc" nations. The Cold War was widely perceived to be a conflict between capitalist-democratic and Communist systems of government (*see* **Marxism; McCarthyism**), with global implications. Some scholars argue that all artists were influenced by the mainstream conformist culture of the period in the United States (Schaub, Whitfield). However, more recent scholarship suggests that there was a younger generation of African American writers who rebelled against this culture (Wald, Washington).

The increase in African American people migrating north in the 1930s had a tremendous impact on the literature that was written during that period. Writers were prone to discuss the conditions of the communities and services awaiting this largely unskilled, undereducated population. The poverty, displacement, unhealthy living conditions, and discrimination that African American workers faced was in stark contrast to the images of the North as a liberal place of opportunity for anyone who wanted a job. The shifting political and social culture in the late 1940s did not do much to change the landscape for African Americans, but it did force certain restrictions on how artists should discuss these conditions. In the political climate of the late 1940s and early 1950s, one that arguably encouraged an encroachment on the civil rights of all Americans, especially in the era of McCarthyism, African American citizens were particularly vulnerable.

The restrictive atmosphere of the Cold War made African American literature generally unpopular with the White mainstream audience, and a strong Black readership would take at least another decade to develop fully. During the 1940s, a support system for writers did not exist in the same way that it had in the 1920s. There were some publishers who offered advances for the completion of manuscripts, but most African American writers had to find other work to support themselves. Periodicals such as **Phylon** and the **Negro Digest** emerged, but they were more interested in politics and civil rights issues. There were articles that introduced new writers and critiqued their work, but there were no longer coveted literary prizes.

Blacks and Whites lived largely segregated lives in the 1940s and 1950s. Through their vivid portraits of Black life, African American writers often attempted to educate mainstream America about the poverty and despair that Blacks suffered at a disproportionate rate. At the same time, the country was experiencing a tremendous change in the complexities of racial politics. The end of the war brought new challenges. The decision to integrate the armed forces in the early 1950s raised questions about racial equality that had never been tested before on a national scale. Increasingly, there were conversations in every segment of the population about the inevitability and consequences of race mixing or integration (*see* **Civil Rights Movement**).

By the late 1940s, talks about race relations in America took on a decisively more significant role in the country's relation to other parts of the world. During this period, the mood of the country shifted to suspicion and surveillance. This climate had a huge impact particularly on African Americans and the way they questioned policies that limited their access to opportunity and advocacy. The struggle for civil rights became a high-stakes enterprise. The fact that America's treatment of its minority citizens was being highly scrutinized by its enemies abroad placed governmental officials and agencies under tremendous pressure to suppress all forms of protest.

The reality for many African American artists was that the themes they chose to write about in their literature could make them the subject of an FBI investigation in the 1940s and 1950s. The infamous trials of Hollywood figures and the blacklisting of the Hollywood Ten proved that fame and popularity could not protect those accused. Art that was perceived to address political issues or push an agenda that fought for social justice was, by some, considered too political, and thus dangerous. Many had watched great artists and intellectuals, including **Paul Robeson** and **W.E.B. Du Bois**, suffer both professionally and personally for speaking out against racial injustice.

As a result, some artists avoided writing novels with all Black characters or working-class themes. Examples are **Chester Himes**'s *If He Hollers Let Him Go* (1945), **Ann Petry**'s *Country Place* (1947), and **Willard Motley**'s *Knock on Any Door* (1947). In some cases, however, this perceived compromise provided them an opportunity to strategically raise many of the same issues (poverty, discrimination, etc.) that had been discussed in earlier fiction. Many prominent African American writers left the United States to avoid the increasingly hostile climate (Fabre). An interesting consequence of this phenomenon was that their presence overseas extended the discussion of Blacks beyond America. The treatment of American Blacks became a part of a larger international forum. Subsequently, the liberation of colonially ruled countries such as Ghana also raised important opportunities for African American writers to understand their situation from a more global perspective. As a result, many of them found allies in the countrymen of these newly independent states and, more important, inspiration. Writers such as Le Roi Jones (**Amiri Baraka**), who wrote "Cuba Libre" (1961), talked about the transformative power of witnessing the liberation struggles of other minority nations.

Back home, the fight for civil rights continued (Marable, Dudziak, Biondi). **Houston Baker, Jr.**, explores the significance of certain key moments in the late 1950s that brought about a Black Nationalist perspective that would later influence the 1960s Black Arts Movement (*see* **Black Nationalism**). The two *Brown v. Board of Education* decisions from the U.S. Supreme Court (1954), the 1959 American Society of African Culture's first Conference of Negro Writers, and a growing Black readership were significant developments of this period. While **Ralph Ellison**'s *Invisible Man* (1952), which questioned the significance of Black leadership and participation in leftist organizations such as the American Communist Party, is one of the most discussed novels from this period, there were "lesser known" African American artists who continued to push a more radical social agenda (John Henrik Clarke, **Julian Mayfield, Lloyd Brown**, and **John O. Killens**). Another group that has not received much attention is African American women writers who wrote during the 1940s and 1950s. **Lorraine Hansberry, Alice Childress**, and **Paule Marshall** wrote female-centered fiction that questioned masculinist constructions of identity and social protest. These writers talked about women from their communities who challenged traditional stereotypes and expectations for women. (*See* **Feminism; Protest Literature**.)

Resources: Houston A. Baker, Jr., "Generational Shifts and the Recent Criticism of Afro-American Literature," *Black American Literature Forum* 15, no. 1 (Spring 1981), 3–21; Martha Biondi, *To Stand and Fight: The Struggle for Civil Rights in Postwar New York City* (Cambridge, MA: Harvard University Press, 2003); Alice Childress, *Like One of the Family: Conversations from a Domestic's Life* (Brooklyn, NY: Independence, 1956); Mary Dudziak, *Cold War Civil Rights: Race and the Image of American Democracy* (Princeton, NJ: Princeton University Press, 2000); Michel Fabre, *Black American Writers in France, 1840–1980: From Harlem to Paris* (Urbana: University of Illinois Press, 1991); Carl Hughes, *The Negro Novelist* (New York: Carol Publishing Group, 1990); Leroi Jones, "Cuba Libre" (New York: Fair Play for Cuba Committee, 1961); John O. Killens, *Youngblood* (New York: Dial, 1954); Manning Marable, *Race, Reform and Rebellion: The Second Reconstruction in Black America, 1945–1990*, 2nd ed. (Jackson: University Press of Mississippi, 1991); Paule Marshall, *Brown Girl, Brownstones* (New York: Random House, 1959); Ann Petry: "The Novel as Social Criticism," in *The Writer's Book*, ed. Helen Hull (New York: Harper, 1950); *The Street* (Boston: Houghton Mifflin, 1946); Thomas Schaub, *American Fiction in the Cold War* (Madison: University of Wisconsin Press, 1991); Alan Wald, *Revising the Barricades: Scholarship About the U.S. Cultural Left in the Post-Cold War Era*, Working Papers

Series in Cultural Studies, Ethnicity and Race Relations (Pullman: Washington State University, 2000); Mary Helen Washington, "Desegregating the 1950s: The Case of Frank London Brown," *Japanese Journal of American Studies* no. 10 (1999), 15–32; Stephen Whitfield, *The Culture of the Cold War* (Baltimore: John Hopkins University Press, 1991).

Katrina Caldwell

Cole, Harriette (born c. 1963). Author, syndicated columnist, etiquette expert, and entrepreneur. In the long history of American advice and style mavens, Harriette Cole offers a new perspective on manners and self-representation. Following in the tradition of Ophelia Devore and Charlotte Hawkins Brown, Cole presents a contemporary twist on solving the age-old dilemmas of home training and how to be. A best-selling author, entrepreneur, editor, events planner, and etiquette expert, Cole grew up with her two sisters in an affluent **Baltimore, Maryland**, household; her father, Harry Augustus Cole, was the first Black judge on the Maryland Court of Appeals, and her mother, Doris Irene Freeland Cole, was a homemaker. A Phi Beta Kappa, summa cum laude alumna of Howard University, Cole felt that her life calling was to find a profession that blended her passions for media relations, communication, journalism, and self-empowerment.

Working as a professional runway model, Cole gained access to the world of trendy fashions and classic style. Later, she parlayed her experiences and skills into her career as the lifestyle editor and fashion director at *Essence* magazine, the most widely circulated periodical for African American women. She wrote the best-selling bible for African American brides, *Jumping the Broom: The African-American Wedding Planner* (1993), and followed this accomplishment with the practical companion guide, *Jumping the Broom Wedding Workbook* (1996).

In 1995, after ending her eleven-year career at *Essence*, Cole launched profundities, inc., a life-coaching, style, and literary production company of which she is the president and creative director. Cole coaches entertainers, recording artists, other public figures, and the general public in presentation and speaking skills, to help develop their careers and enhance their image. In 1999, she penned *How to Be*. The purpose of this book was to help African American readers live life with grace, style, and fulfillment. Her most recent advice book, *Choosing Truth: Living an Authentic Life* (2003) is directed at a more general audience. She has published two other texts, *Coming Together* (Jump at the Sun/Hyperion, 2003), a children's activity book that provides resources for meaningful planned activities that will enrich African American families, and *Vows* (Simon and Schuster, 2004), a guide to help African American couples personalize their wedding ceremony. These books further solidify her dedication to researching and recording important aspects of African American familial integrity, courtship, celebrations, and ceremonial practices. She has maintained her connections with periodicals, applying her expertise as the editor in chief of *American Legacy Woman*, a lifestyle magazine targeted toward African American women, and as the editorial director of *UPTOWN*, a magazine that highlights the trends and tastes of **Harlem, New York**, and upper-class African American urbanites.

In addition to writing monographs and editing popular magazines, Cole provides advice three times each week in her column *Sense & Sensitivity*, which began in the *New York Daily News* and now appears in twenty-five newspapers nationwide.

Resources: Harriette Cole: *Choosing Truth: Living an Authentic Life* (New York: Simon and Schuster, 2003); *How to Be* (New York: Simon and Schuster, 1999); *Jumping the Broom: The African American Wedding Planner* (New York: Henry Holt, 1993); *Jumping the Broom Wedding Workbook* (New York: Henry Holt, 1996); Web site, http://www.harriettecole.com.

Aisha X. L. Francis

Coleman, Anita Scott (1890–1960). Short story writer, poet, and essayist. Born in Guaymas, Mexico, to a Cuban father and an African mother, Coleman published stories, poems, and essays in the African American periodicals **The Crisis, Opportunity, The Messenger**, and *Half-Century* magazine.

Little is known about Coleman other than that she received her degree from New Mexico Teachers College and later taught in **Los Angeles, California**. After her marriage, she kept a boardinghouse and continued to write. She is also reported to have written for Pathé films, a British company that produced prefilm features for movie theaters (Young, 271). Under the pseudonym Elizabeth Stapleton Stokes, she published *Small Wisdom* in 1937.

Coleman's short stories, mostly published between 1919 and 1930, address many of the topics found in the work of her **Harlem Renaissance** contemporaries. Along with Prohibition and birth control, women's rights and racism are frequent themes in her work.

"Rich Man, Poor Man" (1920) and "Cross Crossings Cautiously" (1930) address the inability of Black males to find jobs while there was a constant market for Black female domestic workers. In these stories, being denied the luxury of mothering her own children is exchanged for the power of being the family breadwinner. Coleman's female characters are often independent thinkers.

"Cross Crossings Cautiously" is also an example of Coleman's examination of interracial themes. An African American man is lynched when he accompanies a young White girl to the circus. Another story, "G'long, Old White Man's Girl" (1928), shows the destructive power of gossip when a White man leaves money to a Black family that helped take care of him.

Love and the perils of the northward migration is the theme of a trilogy of stories published in 1919–1920: "Phoebe and Peter up North," "Phoebe Goes to a Lecture," and "The Nettleby's New Year." The length of the trilogy allowed Coleman to develop the character of Phoebe, showing her growth from a backward rural girl to a mature urban woman. Mary E. Young compares Coleman's slice-of-life fiction with Chekhov's (286) in its objectivity.

Little is written about Coleman's poetry. *Reason for Singing*, published in 1948, declares its purpose is "to ponder many aspects of life and death . . . , and most of all, to declare an optimism for the future of humanity" (Roses and Randolph, 61). *Singing Bells* was published posthumously in 1961.

Resources: Anita Scott Coleman: *Reason for Singing* (Prairie City, IL: Decker Press, 1948); *Singing Bells* (Nashville, TN: Broadman, 1961); Lorraine Elena Roses and Ruth Elizabeth Randolph, eds., *Harlem Renaissance and Beyond* (Boston: G. K. Hall, 1990), 59–62; Elizabeth Stapleton Stokes (pseud.), *Small Wisdom* (New York: H. Harrison, 1937); Mary E. Young, "Anita Scott Coleman: A Neglected Harlem Renaissance Writer," *CLA Journal* 40, no. 3 (Mar. 1997), 271–287.

Patricia Kennedy Bostian

Coleman, Evelyn (born 1948). Fiction author and children's writer. Evelyn Coleman has published books for children and adults that present African American protagonists and themes. Among her children's books are *The Glass Bottle Tree* (the title refers to the African American custom of leaving colorful bottles on a tree to keep the spirits of ancestors), *The Foot Warmer and the Crow* (which tells the triumphant story of the slave Hezekiah), and *White Socks Only*, which she turned into a screenplay. Within her writing, Coleman consistently explores themes of race. *White Socks Only* recounts a grandmother's remembrance about a sign above a drinking fountain that leads to a confrontation. The story has been adapted for film. *Smithsonian* magazine named *White Socks Only* the Most Outstanding Children's Book Title for 1996. It was also selected by the Anti-Defamation League and Barnes & Noble's national campaign Close the Book on Hate, and was featured on the television program *Entertainment Tonight* in 2001.

Circle of Fire draws on Coleman's own childhood in **the South** during the 1950s and firsthand experiences of racism. *To Be a Drum* takes its title from Coleman's father's instruction to put an ear to the ground and listen to the beat of the earth. In *The Riches of Osceola McCarty*, Coleman writes the story of a washerwoman who gave her life savings to the University of Southern Mississippi. This book has received numerous awards, among them inclusion on the Children's Literature Top Choice List for 1999. It was also chosen as a Society of School Librarians International Honor Book in 1999. Both educational and entertaining, Coleman's books reveal African American traditions and realities to a new generation of readers.

What a Woman's Gotta Do is a mystery novel. In it Coleman combines science writing, **folklore**, African culture, and martial arts into a story that explores issues of **race** and **gender** as protagonist Patricia Conley must uncover what happened to her fiancé.

Coleman has published articles in *Essence*, *Black Enterprise*, *Southern Exposure*, *Quarterly Black Review*, and many newspapers, including the *Atlanta Journal and Constitution*. She has also had a career as a psychotherapist. In 1987, she was the first African American recipient of a $5,000 North Carolina Fiction

Fellowship. Coleman received the Atlanta Mayor's Fellowship for Literary Achievement in 1999.

Coleman frequently lectures at writers' conferences, schools, universities, and churches, and has given talks for the American Library Association and the National Council of Teachers of English. In 2002–2003 Coleman was named Georgia Author of the Year for Children's Literature, and in 2002 she was awarded the King Baudouin Cultural Exchange Fellowship.

Resources: Evelyn Coleman: *Born in Sin* (New York: Atheneum, 2001); *Circle of Fire* (Middleton, WI: Pleasant Company, 2002); *The Flight of Kites* (New York: McGraw-Hill, 1999); *The Foot Warmer and the Crow* (New York: Simon and Schuster, 1994); *The Glass Bottle Tree* (New York: Orchard Books, 1995); *Mystery of the Dark Tower* (Middleton, WI: Pleasant Company, 2000); *The Riches of Oseola McCarty* (Morton Grove, IL: Albert Whitman, 1998); *To Be a Drum* (Morton Grove, IL: Albert Whitman, 1998); *What a Woman's Gotta Do* (New York: Simon and Schuster, 1998); *What If* (New York: Celebration Press, 1997); *White Socks Only* (Morton Grove, IL: Albert Whitman, 1996); Web site, http://www.evelyncoleman.com.

Elline Lipkin

Coleman, Wanda (born 1946). Poet and fiction writer. Coleman, who was born in the Watts neighborhood of **Los Angeles, California**, began writing as an adolescent. Although a substantial number of other young writers in the neighborhood participated in the Watts Writers Workshop that was founded after the rebellious protests in the summer of 1965, Coleman for the most part gravitated toward other communities. The first poet she met, for instance, was John Thomas, one of the members of the Venice West Beat scene (*see* **Beat Movement**). In the late 1960s and early 1970s she was an intermittent member of the Beyond Baroque poetry workshop in Venice. She began sending her poems out to magazines, and her work appeared in several magazines in the Los Angeles area, most notably *BACHY*, edited by Leland Hickman. Her first chapbook, *Art in the Court of the Blue Fag*, appeared in 1977, and her first full-length collection, *Mad Dog Black Lady*, in 1979. *Mad Dog, Black Lady* was reviewed on both the East and the West coasts. Coleman, without a college degree, often found herself restricted to jobs such as medical-billing transcription; she also worked as a scriptwriter, winning an Emmy, and as a freelance journalist.

Even at this early point, Coleman classified herself as an intransigent oppositional figure. In an interview with the novelist Kate Braverman shortly after her first book came out, Coleman emphasized that the poet's task was to be an outlaw, "pointing his finger at something that someone doesn't want to see. . . . [A poet] takes up the slack that psychoanalysts can't handle because they refuse to recognize certain truths." Coleman frequently points to racism as the most insidious repercussion of Euro-American history, but she is one of the rare writers who also consistently acknowledges the influence that cultural capital in the form of class has on social development.

Coleman had over a dozen titles published by Black Sparrow Press between 1977 and 1998 (when Black Sparrow Press folded). These books include *Imagoes* (1983), *Heavy Daughter Blues: Poems & Stories 1968–1986* (1987), *The Dicksboro Hotel* (1989), *African Sleeping Sickness* (1993), *American Sonnets* (1994), and *Bathwater Wine* (1998). She is also a fiction writer, and her stories and other prose pieces have appeared in several collections. She has received major awards and honors, including a Guggenheim and a National Endowment for the Arts creative writing fellowship. In 1999 the Academy of American Poets awarded her the Lenore Marshall Poetry Prize.

Like many of the Los Angeles poets in the last quarter-century, Coleman has had a long-standing interest in the long poem or the serial poem (*see* **Epic Poetry/The Long Poem**). In her books, she often breaks up these longer sequences, separating them with other, completely unrelated poems. Regardless of the length, Coleman writes with an eye for the detail that has been freshly ripped from its sources and still has its cut lines visible. If much modern and postmodern poetry flaunts its idiosyncratic difficulty and hermetic nuances, Coleman leans toward accessibility, favoring a poetics of urban immediacy in which her hometown is both reviled and admired. Although little of the humor of the Stand-Up School associated with Southern California surfaces in her work, her work deserves consideration as part of that growing school because of its contribution to the ultimate seriousness of craft and theme that underlies the best work of the Stand-Up School. Coleman's work also merits substantial appreciation for its influence on writers outside of, as well within, the African American canon. Very little critical attention has been devoted, however, to annotating the potential contexts of her artistic visions. Although Coleman's writing pulsates with a distinct voice within the huge choir of contemporary poetry, criticism of her work rarely correlates the thoughtful, if understated, pivots of her line breaks with the dramatic power of her narratives. Her poetry constitutes an insurgency that traverses the indefatigable memory of the personal with defiant accounts of public events.

Resources: Kate Braverman, "The Outrage of Wanda Coleman" (Interview), *L.A. Weekly*, Nov. 14–20, 1980; Wanda Coleman: *African Sleeping Sickness* (Santa Barbara, CA: Black Sparrow Press, 1993); *American Sonnets* (Santa Barbara, CA: Black Sparrow Press, 1994); *Art in the Court of the Blue Fag* (Santa Barbara, CA: Black Sparrow Press, 1977); *Bathwater Wine* (Santa Barbara, CA: Black Sparrow Press, 1998); *The Dicksboro Hotel* (Santa Barbara, CA: Black Sparrow Press, 1989); *Heavy Daughter Blues: Poems and Stories 1968–1986* (Santa Barbara, CA: Black Sparrow Press,1987); *Imagoes* (Santa Barbara, CA: Black Sparrow Press, 1983); *Mad Dog, Black Lady* (Santa Barbara, CA: Black Sparrow Press, 1979); Wanda Coleman and Leland Hickman, correspondence, Archive for New Poetry, Library of the University of California, San Diego; Julian Murphet, *Literature and Race in Los Angeles* (Cambridge: Cambridge Press, 2001); Joyce Pettis, *African American Poets* (Westport, CT: Greenwood Press, 2002).

Bill Mohr

College Language Association. The College Language Association (CLA) is the nation's foremost organization of primarily African American scholars of languages and literature. It was founded as the Association of Teachers of English in Negro Colleges (ATENC) at LeMoyne College in **Memphis, Tennessee,** on April 23, 1937. Integrated at its beginning, ten scholars (nine Black and one White) founded ATENC in response to the historic exclusion of Blacks from membership in learned societies, especially by their Southern affiliates.

The goal of the ATENC was, in the words of founder and first president, Dr. Hugh Morris Gloster, "to end Jim Crow in American letters," to enhance English proficiency among African American students, to serve the academic and professional interests of its members, and to help showcase the work of Black scholars.

Following **World War II**, during which the organization canceled its national meetings (1943–48), the ATENC began to attract a considerable amount of interest from teachers in the nation's historically Black colleges and universities, including foreign language teachers. In 1949, in response to this outpouring of interest among foreign language teachers, the ATENC changed its name to CLA to reflect its broadening membership and scope.

The CLA has led the way in redrawing the boundaries of literary scholarship in the Americas and beyond through publications by its members and in the pages of *The College Language Association Journal*. In 1938, Velaurez Spratlin published *Juan Latino, Slave and Humanist*, a groundbreaking work exploring the role of Africans in European culture. In 1941, the publication of the monumental *The Negro Caravan*, edited by **Sterling A. Brown, Arthur P. Davis**, and Ulysses P. Lee, established the canon of African American literature. In 1944, *The Haitian-American Anthology*, edited by Mercer Cook and Dantes Bellegarde, prompted American scholars to investigate critically the comparative aspects of Black literatures of the Americas (*see* **Haiti**).

Ecumenical in its approach to publishing articles in both the English and foreign language areas, the *CLA Journal*, founded in 1957, evolved from the *News Bulletin* (1941–1944) and the *CLA Bulletin* (1949–1957), a digest of conference papers and the president's address. From its inception the *Journal* reflected a special concern with race-related aspects of language and literature. It contains a treasure trove of articles on the Black **diaspora**.

CLA members provided much of the energy and muscle that led to the founding of Black special-interest sections in the major professional organizations, including the National Council of Teachers of English (1970) and the Modern Language Association (1981). The CLA traditionally holds its annual convention on the third weekend in April. The CLA papers are in the Robert W. Woodruff Library in the Atlanta University Center, the official archival repository. (For more information, see http://www.clascholars.org.)

Resources: A. Russell Brooks: "CLA Journal," in *The Oxford Companion to African American Literature*, ed. William L. Andrews, Frances Smith Foster, and Trudier Harris

(New York: Oxford University Press, 1997), 152; "The *CLA Journal* as a Mirror of Changing Ethnic and Academic Perspectives," *CLA Journal* 26, no. 3 (Mar. 1983), 265–276; James J. Davis and Dolan Hubbard, "College Language Association," in *Organizing Black America: An Encyclopedia of African American Associations*, ed. Nina Mjagkij (New York: Garland, 2001), 159–162; Carolyn Fowler, *The College Association: A Social History* [microfilm] (Ann Arbor, MI: University Microfilms, 1988), (800) 521–0600; Dolan Hubbard, "Slipping into Darkness: CLA and Black Intellectual Formation," President's Address Delivered at the Fifty-sixth Annual CLA Convention, Winston-Salem, NC, 11 April 1996, *CLA Journal* 40, no. 1 (Sept. 1996), 1–20; Therman B. O'Daniel, *A Twenty-five-Year Author-Title Cumulative Index to the CLA Journal (1957-1982)* (Baltimore: J. H. Furst, 1985); John W. Parker, "The Origin and Development of the College Language Association," *Quarterly Review of Higher Education Among Negroes* 27 (1959), 35–37.

James J. Davis and Dolan Hubbard

Collier, Eugenia (born 1928). Short story writer, playwright, poet, literary critic, and professor. Eugenia Collier, best known for her short stories and an anthology of African American literature, was born in **Baltimore, Maryland**. Her father, Harry M. Williams, was a physician who became the first African American director of a health center; and her mother, Eugenia (Jackson) Williams, was an elementary school teacher who was principal of a school she founded. Collier received a B.A. from Howard University (1948), an M.A. from Columbia University (1950), and a Ph.D. from the University of Maryland (1976). Her dissertation was "Steps Toward a Black Aesthetic: A Study of Black American Literary Criticism." From 1950 to 1955, prior to pursuing a career as an educator, she was a social worker for the Baltimore City Department of Public Welfare and Crownsville State Hospital. Collier taught English at Morgan State University (1955–1966); the Community College of Baltimore (1966–1974); Southern Illinois University (summer of 1970); Atlanta University (summers of 1973 and 1974); University of Maryland Baltimore County (1974–1977); Howard University (1977–1987); Coppin State College (1987–1992), where she was chair of the Department of Languages, Literature, and Journalism; and Morgan State University (1992–1996), where she was chair of the Department of English and Language Arts until her retirement.

Collier is the author of *Breeder and Other Stories* (1993); in addition to the title story, the other narratives include "Marigolds," which won the Gwendolyn Brooks Award for Fiction (1969) and was first published in **Negro Digest** (November 1969). Since then, "Marigolds," Collier's best-known short story, has been reprinted in anthologies such as *Brothers and Sisters: Modern Stories by Black Americans* (1970), edited by **Arnold Adoff**; *The New Cavalcade: African American Writing from 1760 to the Present*, volume 2 (1992), edited by **Arthur P. Davis**, **J. Saunders Redding**, and **Joyce Anne Joyce**; and *Centers of the Self: Short Stories by Black American Women from the Nineteenth Century to the Present* (1994), edited by Judith A. Hamer and Martin J. Hamer. In addition to the tales included in *Breeder*, among Collier's other published short stories are

"Sinbad the Cat," first published in *Black World* (July 1971); "Sweet Potato Pie," first published in *Black World* (August 1972); and "The Caregiver," first published in the *African American Review* (Spring 2002). Her poems have appeared in *Black World* and other publications. Collier's plays include *Ricky*, based on her short story by the same title that is published in *Breeder*, which was produced by the Kuumba Workshop at Chicago's Eugene Perkins Theatre in October 1976. Collier's other theatrical contributions include serving as a dramaturge at Baltimore's Arena Players, the longest continuously running African American community theater in the United States.

Collier's collaborations with her colleagues at institutions of higher learning have resulted in the publication of *Impressions in Asphalt: Images of Urban America in Literature* (1969), edited with **Ruthe T. Sheffey**; *A Bridge to Saying It Well: Grammar and Form for Today's Students* (1970), with Joel Glasser, Edward Meyers, George Steele, and Thomas Wolf; and *Afro-American Writing: An Anthology of Prose and Poetry* (1972; enlarged edition, 1985), with Richard A. Long. Collier's critical essays have been published in *Langston Hughes, Black Genius: A Critical Evaluation* (1971), edited by **Therman B. O'Daniel**; and *Black Women Writers (1950–1980): A Critical Evaluation*, edited by **Mari Evans**; as well as in periodicals such as *Black World*, *CLA Journal*, *MAWA Review*, and **Phylon**. Among Collier's many honors are her selection as an Outstanding Educator of America (1972–1975) and the Distinguished Writers Award from the Middle-Atlantic Writers Association (1984).

Resources: Eugenia Collier, *Breeder and Other Stories* (Washington, DC: Black Classics Press, 1993); Arthur P. Davis, J. Saunders Redding, and Joyce A. Joyce, eds., *The New Cavalcade: African American Writing from 1760 to the Present*, vol. 2 (Washington, DC: Howard University Press, 1992), 198–199; Sharon Malinowski, ed., *Black Writers: A Selection of Sketches from Contemporary Authors*, 2nd ed. (Detroit: Gale, 1994), 141–142; Ann Allen Shockley and Sue P. Chandler, *Living Black American Authors: A Biographical Directory* (New York: Bowker, 1973), 32.

Linda M. Carter

Colonialism. Colonialism is the process of one country settling in and taking over the governance of a foreign land. Proponents of colonialism often believe that such governance benefits those colonized because it can develop the economy and systems of the area so that the area can be modernized and attain democratic forms of government. Those opposed to colonialism believe that this system permits the colonizers to take the wealth of the colonized land and exploit the labor of those who inhabit it. Colonialism is also understood to involve the colonizers' attempting to change the behavior and beliefs of the original inhabitants of the place colonized.

Concepts of colonialism apply to African Americans and African American literature in part because African Americans have suffered oppression parallel to that suffered by colonized peoples.

The word "colonialism" derives from the Latin *colonia*, from *colonus* (cultivator, settler), from *colere* (cultivate, till, inhabit; cognate with Sanskrit *karsú-s*, furrow) (*Oxford English Dictionary*). This etymology connects colonialism to a furrowing of the earth, then. Furrowing implies the cultivation of certain plants and the elimination of others as "weeds," and it suggests laying claim to ownership. More symbolically, "furrowing" can be interpreted as a process that cuts through and divides ethnic groups and demands arbitrary coalitions, as was the case in colonial Africa, for example. Also, that the words "culture" and "colonialism" derive from the same etymological root points to an association of colonialism with attempts to control the cultures of those colonized, including native definitions of "self." In many of his essays, **James Baldwin** explores questions of colonialism, culture, and identity ("Stranger in the Village").

Colonialism has impacted African Americans in many ways. In the most obvious ways, Africans were kidnapped from their homelands; most were taken to lands colonized by Europeans; and nearly all existed under "colonial" conditions of physical exploitation and domination. More than merely suffering physical brutality and spatial imprisonment, African Americans also labored under repeated attempts at cultural deracination. They were uprooted from Africa, their families were divided, and their language groups were mixed to prevent communication and the passing on of knowledge. Defiant individuals were "weeded out" through torture and death. The imposition of foreign systems of knowledge and spirituality worked to colonize not only the body but also the mind.

That colonialism usually turns to greed and exploitation is obvious. But to understand both European colonialism and African American responses to that colonialism, it is also necessary to realize the importance of Eurocentrism, which is characterized by a belief not just in a Christian and an Enlightenment worldview but also in the universal applicability of that worldview. Eurocentrism also involves a binary view of race, such as White vs. Black, light vs. dark. These four elements—greed, Eurocentrism, universalism, racism—interpenetrated and supported each other, with the latter three working to "hide" greed by inculcating the idea that colonialism wasn't about exploiting foreign lands and peoples but about bringing the superiority of things "European" to non-European cultures. These non-European cultures were depicted as in need of a European presence, and this need (according to the Europeans' logic) morally obligated Europeans to engage in what the British eventually called their "civilizing mission" and the French called *la mission civilisatrice*. Ironically, even **slavery** was portrayed as an enterprise that would both Christianize and cultivate in Africans such needed "European virtues" as a strong work ethic, moral restraint, and rationality.

Not all Europeans supported the colonization of Africa and other parts of the world. This lack of support, however, typically stemmed not from disagreement with the ideas supporting colonization but from European's inability to hold true to those ideas. The consensus was not to abandon but to improve the mission to civilize. And because Europeans remained the sole messengers of such supposedly universal—and therefore irrefutable—truths as Christianity, science, and laissez-faire capitalism, there was no need for true dialogue. Europe, especially insofar as it was imagined to be a White, male, and implicitly heterosexual continent, saw itself as a "parental" presence speaking down to the "immature," and often "feminine," peoples of the world—especially to the "childish race" of the "dark continent." Furthermore, as exploitation increased Europe's wealth, this wealth was seen as confirming Europe's superiority, which then justified a greater European presence in foreign lands. This confluence of ideas and growing material wealth fueled a colonialism of unprecedented confidence and proportions.

Such early critics of Europe's presence in Africa as **Olaudah Equiano** necessarily incorporated Europe's "absolute truths" of Christianity, science, **race**, culture, and capitalism in their pleas to end slavery. Because the arguments Europeans used to justify slavery were similar to the arguments used to justify colonialism, Olaudah Equiano's *Interesting Narrative* (1789) can be read as a response to colonialism, as can other African American **slave narratives**. But because colonialism has become intertwined with political divisions of space, especially the division called "nation," African American responses to colonialism most clearly begin after the parceling out of Africa among European nations at the Berlin Conference of 1884–1885. Before this, Liberia's independence in 1847, the settling of freed slaves in Sierra Leone, and especially **Haiti**'s independence in 1804 promoted African American awareness of colonialism as a racist ideology intertwined with nationalism. But it was only some three decades after Europe's division of Africa, beginning just before the **Harlem Renaissance**, that defined responses to colonialism appear. One significant response was **Marcus Garvey**'s version of **black nationalism**, which featured a **Back-to-Africa movement**.

During the Harlem Renaissance an admiration of Africa and its cultural heritage developed. This admiration was also part of the **Négritude** movement some years later. The most influential precursor to this "elevation" of Africa was the work of **W.E.B. Du Bois**. Du Bois and Harlem Renaissance writers responded to racist presumptions (which are also colonialism's presumptions) of African inferiority not by proposing that Africans can equal Europeans in their own activities (although this "nineteenth-century position" is not rejected), but by proposing that Africans and people of African ancestry offer unique and vital contributions to the world. Concomitant with this cultural focus on Africa, the United Negro Improvement Association (UNIA) of Marcus Garvey (founded 1914) developed a more political focus on African peoples and the economics of colonialism; Garvey promoted a global and political perspective on what it meant to be African American, an essential ingredient in expanding African American critiques of racism to include the critique of colonialism.

The intent of this critique was to change (even eliminate) colonialism and thereby change the conditions under which Blacks in the United States, with its internal colonial system featuring "Jim Crow" laws, and elsewhere labored. Garvey's major significance was his call for people of Africa and African ancestry to adopt the political and economic strategies of the colonizer, the strategies of Western nations. Garvey called for "Negro people" everywhere to trade, sell, and buy among themselves. Thus Garvey responded to the "furrowing" of colonialism not with the traditional response of equality and integration, but with the colonizer's logic of separation and competition.

Not surprisingly, Garvey's "back to Africa" philosophy sustained such "colonial" ideas as racial separation (he argued against interracial alliances based on class), a monolithic sense of the peoples of Africa, and the need for a more militaristic tone. Many Black intellectuals chastised Garvey's ideas, but the tremendous popularity of UNIA among African Americans indicates their frustration with a system that showed little interest in self-decolonization.

The hardships of the **Great Depression** and then **World War II** obscured the importance of colonialism until the 1950s. But following the war, the movement for ending European colonial rule in Africa and the Caribbean revived the issue. The work of Frantz Fanon (1925–1961) and other intellectuals conveyed the psychological violence of the binary logic of racism and colonialism, and integration was seen as politically incapable of eliminating America's de facto colonialism of segregation. This resulted in a UNIA-like philosophy of liberation through segregation expressed, to differing degrees, in the **Black Arts Movement**, **Afrocentricity**, Black Nationalism, and the rallying cry of **"Black Power"** during the 1960s.

Fed up with centuries of White America's "do as I say, not as I do" rhetoric, Black nationalists wanted to take the "furrowing" of colonialism to mark out their own separate "Black nation" within the nation of America. An increasing unwillingness to acquiesce to America's "colonial demands" cultivated the violence and militarization evident, for instance, in the 1966 creation of the **Black Panther Party (for Self-Defense)**. Anticolonial writers and politicians throughout the world promoted understanding African Americans as part of a global colonialism and struggle that often included violence.

The binary "Black–White" logic of colonialism, however, promotes a homogenization of *both* groups, and the Black nationalism of the 1960s largely equated "Black" with African American, heterosexual men. By the late 1960s African American women, homosexuals, and people of decidedly multicultural backgrounds demanded that their voices become part of the African American "conversation." (*See* **Feminism**; **Gay Literature**; **Lesbian Literature**; **Queer Theory**.)

Also important to African American responses to colonialism from the late 1960s to the present is that the independence of colonized African and Caribbean nations has resulted not in true independence but in a neocolonial subjugation that has maintained Western domination and exploitation through multinational companies and, some say, by such financial institutions as the World Bank and International Monetary Fund. Because of this, the increasing diversity of African American perspectives on colonialism since the 1960s has also become increasingly international in scope.

To be sure, such organizations as the U.S. Congressional Black Caucus and the African Union remain as important countercolonial voices even though they largely maintain the spatial "furrowings" of state and nation inherited from colonialism. But peoples of the African **diaspora** are also responding to the legacy of colonialism with **gender**, sexuality, environmental, cultural, class, and religious alliances that cross borders and thereby call the validity of those borders into question. If it is agreed that European colonialism developed to promote global exploitation, then the increasingly global response of African American writers to today's neocolonialism indicates a growing refusal to remain trapped within the divisions, both physical and mental, that have caused untold suffering.

Resources: James Baldwin, "Stranger in the Village" (1953), in his *Collected Essays* (New York: Library of America, 1998); Simon Gikandi, *Maps of Englishness* (New York: Columbia University Press, 1996); Anne McClintock, Aamir Mufti, and Ella Shohat, eds., *Dangerous Liaisons* (Minneapolis: University of Minnesota Press, 1997); Amritjit Singh and Peter Schmidt, eds., *Postcolonial Theory and the United States* (Jackson: University Press of Mississippi, 2000).

Kevin M. Hickey

Color of Skin. African American literature contains countless representations of skin color. From the beginning, writers drew attention to the symbolic value of the terms "Black" and **"White"** that divided two so-called races (*see* **Race**). These terms created a binary opposition between Black and White, superior and inferior, that allegedly explained and justified the enslavement of people of African origin. Skin-color terms increased in number over time and adapted to the historical conditions and numerous incarnations of the African American population. Eventually, the descriptors no longer simply divided into Black and White, but they also diversified and lightened, reflecting the changing complexion of the people. Authors have mirrored, reclaimed, reversed, reinterpreted, and invented new names for skin color, responding to the demands of their particular historical moment—in **slave narratives**, **spirituals**, abolitionist works, **Reconstruction** novels, and **science fiction**, as well as in literary periods such as the **Harlem Renaissance**, the era of the **Civil Rights Movement**, and the era of **Modernism**.

The literature captures the changing conditions of African Americans as well as the trends and traditions that society created in response to the changing population. **Phillis Wheatley**'s poetry proved that African Americans could be educated and deserved respect. In "On Being Brought from Africa to America" (1773), the elegant word "sable" describes Africans. When the poem depicts her people as "stained with a diabolic dye" (Wheatley, 250), quotation marks challenge readers to acknowledge their own racial bias in associating dark skin with the devil. Eventually, the mixing of "the races" gave birth to a "mixed" population that caused a variation in the terms of Black and White. **Mulatto**, quadroon, octoroon, fancy, and white Negro came into frequent use. Later in the nineteenth century, literacy spread among free African Americans. Once the privilege of only White Americans, reading and writing began to spread among the slaves, some of whom were members of the master's own family. The changing complexion of the slaves made it difficult to distinguish the skin color of the master from that of the slave. As African Americans began to write, some, such as **Frederick Douglass** and **William Wells Brown**, brought this paradox to the page. In *Clotel* (1864), a novel by the fugitive slave William Wells Brown, a little slave girl must have her hair shorn and be put out into the fields to "roast" because her skin is too white. *Clotel* also shows the quadroon balls, where young men could meet fair-skinned young women, and "placage," where a man established a household for the quadroon he could not marry, and the "shadow families" that resulted from such relationships. Later descriptions of skin color were accompanied by clues to divine a drop of Black blood in the person who is seemingly White, as in *Iola Leroy* by **Frances E. W. Harper** (1893).

Representation of skin color charts the identity, emotions, and increasing authority of African American writers. Terms have been taken up and discarded as they have come under scrutiny. Skin-color terminology may also register the imagined "authenticity" of so-called Black and White races. The literature sometimes reproduces the stereotypes of racial purity and impurity; those very stereotypes, from the pure black African to the fair-skinned traitor to the race, often are reversed. Certain literary tropes can be found in African American literature: discovery of a drop of Black blood, being taken for White, crossing into the North as White for survival (what critics have traditionally called **"passing"**), and the tragic mulatto. The relative lightness or darkness of skin color is in the eye of the beholder, and changes according to context and condition. Such "prejudicial or preferential treatment of same-race people based solely on their color" is called colorism (Walker, 291). This anxiety about dark skin, colorism, or colorphobia, may be seen in paper bag clubs and blue vein societies, where the skin must be light as a paper bag, or light enough to reveal veins, and the act of skin bleaching. **Dorothy West**'s *The Living Is Easy* (1948) describes a light-skinned elite. Dael Orlandersmith, a Pulitzer Prize finalist, captures skin color prejudice fifty years later in her play *Yellowface* (2003).

In **Wallace Thurman**'s *The Blacker the Berry* (1929), a "luscious black complexion was somewhat of a liability." And it "was a decided curse... dipped, as it were, in indigo ink when there were so many other pleasing colors on nature's palette" (Thurman, 9). **Nella Larsen**'s *Quicksand* (1928) lists myriad skin colors: "sooty black, shiny black, taupe, mahogany, bronze, copper, gold, orange, yellow, peach, ivory, pinky white, pastry white... black eyes in white faces, brown eyes in yellow faces, gray eyes in brown faces, blue eyes in tan faces" (Larsen, 59). **Malcolm X** disdained his own "mariny" skin. According to his *Autobiography* (1965) Americans, both Black and White, still tend toward prejudice in their reaction to skin color; but lighter skin may or may not afford privilege, depending upon the context. Malcolm X's depiction of pilgrims in Mecca gave the variety of skin color a different, transnational meaning: "They were of all colors, from blue-eyed blonds to black-skinned Africans...all participating in the same ritual, displaying a spirit of unity and brotherhood that my experiences in America had led me to believe never could exist between the white and the non-white" (Haley, 346). Color in **Toni Morrison**'s *The Bluest Eye* varies from soft brown, to pale, cheerless yellow, to pretty milk-brown, and living, breathing silk of Black skin.

Quoting **James Baldwin**'s declaration that "[t]his world is white no longer, and it never will be white again" in *Black Looks* (1992), **bell hooks** insists that everyone must rethink skin color and its associations. "Critically examining the association of whiteness as terror in the black imagination, deconstructing it, we both name racism's impact and help to break its mold" (hooks, 178). **ZZ Packer** does just that in "Brownies" (2003), where the complexions of "White" girls are "a blend of ice cream: strawberry, vanilla" (Packer, 1), and never mentions the skin color of the other girls. Illustrations of skin color by the twenty-first century are remarkable for their eloquence and sometimes for their absence. (*See* **Negro**; **Race**.)

Resources: William Wells Brown, *Clotel, a Tale of the Southern States* (1864; Philadelphia: Albert Saifer, 1955); Willard B. Gatewood, "Skin Color," in *Encyclopedia of African-American Culture and History*, ed. Jack Salzman et al. (New York: Simon and Schuster, 1996); Marita Golden, *Don't Play in the Sun: One Woman's Journey Through the Color Complex* (New York: Doubleday, 2004); Alex Haley, Malcolm X, and Betty Shabazz, *The Autobiography of Malcolm X* (1965; New York: Ballantine Books, 1999); Frances Ellen Watkins Harper, *Iola Leroy, or Shadows Uplifted* (1893; repr. New York: Oxford University Press, 1988); bell hooks, *Black Looks* (Boston: South End Press, 1992); Clemora Hudson-Weems, "The African American Literary Tradition," in *The African-American Experience: An Historiographical and Bibliographical Guide*, ed. Arvarh E. Strickland and Robert E. Weems, Jr. (Westport, CT: Greenwood Press, 2000); Nella Larsen, *Quicksand and Passing*, ed. Deborah McDowell (1928; New Brunsick, NJ: Rutgers University Press, 1986); Eric Lott, *Love and Theft: Blackface Minstrelsy and the American Working Class* (New York: Oxford University Press, 1993); Toni Morrison, *The Bluest Eye* (1970; New York: Penguin, 1994); Dael Orandersmith, *Yellowman; My Red Hand, My Black Hand: Two Plays* (New York: Vintage, 2002); Z. Z. Packer, "Brownies," in Packer's *Drinking Coffee Elsewhere* (New York: Riverhead Books, 2003); Kathleen Pfeiffer, *Race Passing and American Individualism* (Amherst: University of Massachusetts Press, 2003); Kathy Russell, Midge Wilson, and Ronald Hall, *The Color Complex: The Politics of Skin Color Among African Americans* (New York: Harcourt Brace Jovanovich, 1992); Wallace Thurman, *The Blacker the Berry: A Novel of Negro Life* (New York: Macanly Co., 1929); Alice Walker, *In Search of Our Mothers' Gardens* (San Diego: Harcourt Brace Jovanavich, 1983); Phillis Wheatley, "On Being Brought from Africa to America," in *Norton Anthology of American Literature* (1979; 2nd ed., abbrev., New York: W. W. Norton, 1986).

Christina Mesa

Colter, Cyrus (1910–2002). Poet, novelist, and short story writer. A distinguished African American writer and educator, Colter worked briefly for the Internal Revenue Service. He then served in **World War II** as a field artillery captain and saw combat in Europe before returning home in 1946 to practice law in **Chicago, Illinois**. Born in Noblesville, Indiana, to James Alexander and Ethel Marietta Basset Colter, Cryus graduated from Rayan Academy, received his undergraduate degree from Ohio State University, and earned his law degree in 1940 from the Chicago-Kent College of Law. In 1950 Governor Adlai Stevenson appointed Colter to the Illinois Commerce Commission (ICC). His twenty-three-year tenure was the longest in ICC history. In 1960, Colter began an accelerated reading program that focused on Russian literature. Once he recognized that African American literature was not regarded as highly as European literature, and his wife encouraged him to address the problem, he began his writing career. In 1973, after resigning from the ICC, he joined the faculty of Northwestern University as a professor of African American Studies and English. In 1975, he was named chair of the African-American Studies Department, the first Black person to hold an endowed chair. In 1976, Colter was named the first Chester D. Tripp Professor of Humanities. He remained in this post until his retirement in 1978. His other honors include an honorary Doctor of Letters from the University of Illinois (Chicago) and having his name engraved on the frieze of the new Illinois State Public Library in 1990. Colter's biographical information, speeches, drafts of publications, publications, and correspondence, dating from 1935 to 1995, are held at the Northwestern University Archives in Evanston, Illinois.

Colter began writing at age fifty and published his first novel at the age of sixty. His first collection of short stories, *The Beach Umbrella*, won first prize from the University of Iowa School of Letters in 1970. Colter's first short story, "A Chance Meeting," appeared in *Threshold* in 1960. He wrote short stories, poems, and six novels. *The Rivers of Eros* (1972) explores the Black working-class society and the representation of place in Chicago. *The Hippodrome* (1973) is a psychological tale about a man's mental, physical, and spiritual demise after the murder of his wife and her White lover. *Night Studies* (1979) makes a social commentary on the influence of the African American past on present-day America. A *Chocolate Soldier* (1988) explores Black social history during the **Civil Rights Movement**. *The Amoralists and Other Tales* (1988) is Colter's second collection of short fiction, and *City of Light* (1993) explores political and class themes in an attempt to expose the racial issues in economic and social relationships. His stories focus mainly on the Black working class and middle class.

Resources: Robert M. Bender, "The Fiction of Cyrus Colter," *New Letters* 48 (Fall 1981), 92–103; Cyrus Colter: *The Amoralists and Other Tales* (New York: Thunder's Mouth Press, 1988); *The Beach Umbrella and Other Stories* (Iowa City: University of Iowa Press, 1970); *A Chocolate Soldier* (New York: Thunder's Mouth Press, 1988); *City of Light* (1993; Evanston, IL: Northwestern University Press, 1998); *The Hippodrome* (Chicago: Swallow Press, 1973); *Night Studies* (1979; Athens: Ohio University Press, 1980); *The Rivers of Eros* (1972; Urbana: University of Illinois Press, 1991); Gilton Gregory Cross et al., "Fought for It and Paid Taxes Too: Four Interviews with Cyrus

Colter," *Callaloo* 14 (Fall 1991), 855–897; Robert M. Farnsworth, "Conversations with Cyrus Colter," *New Letters* 39 (Spring 1973), 16–39; Reginald Gibbons: "Colter's Novelistic Contradictions," *Callaloo* 14 (Fall 1991), 898–905; "Remarks on the Passing of Cyrus Colter," *Context: A Forum for Literary Arts and Culture* 11 (Online Edition); James Robert Payne, "Cyrus Colter," in *The Oxford Companion to African American Literature*, ed. William Andrews, Frances Smith Foster, and Trudier Harris (New York: Oxford University Press, 1997), 164.

Sharon D. Raynor

Columbian Orator, The (c. 1797). Anthology and oratory textbook. As editor Caleb Bingham explains, *The Orator* contained "a variety of original and selected pieces together with rules calculated to improve youth and others in the ornamental and useful art of eloquence" (iii) selected to "inspire the pupil with the ardour of eloquence and love of virtue" (3). Bingham, a Dartmouth-educated **Boston, Massachusetts**, schoolteacher and bookseller, first published the book in 1797. By 1800, it was a best-seller and so widely used as a textbook that printers in other East Coast cities began issuing pirated versions. By the time J. B. Lippincott published the final regular edition of the book in 1860, *The Orator* had sold an estimated 200,000 copies (Blight, xvii). As schoolbooks, *The Orator* and Bingham's companion volume, *The American Preceptor*, were second in popularity only to Noah Webster's reading and spelling texts. Several historians claim that a Bible and one of Bingham's texts were the only two books in many American homes.

The *Orator* stands as an important and representative vision of what Bingham and others saw as the essential ideals of early postcolonial American republicanism. The book is a wide-ranging anthology of short selections from speeches, essays, poems, sermons, dialogues, and dramas that praise virtues such as tolerance while condemning personal vices and **slavery**. The virtues are not limited to qualities such as public speaking ability, honesty, integrity, temperance, and diligence. According to Bingham's vision, a young American would be unabashedly patriotic, pious, tolerant, egalitarian, democratic, opposed to any form of tyranny, and fiercely anti-aristocratic. *The Orator's* brand of egalitarianism even goes so far as championing Native Americans and strongly espousing abolitionism. Several selections roundly denounce slavery as patently immoral and non-Christian. Unsurprisingly, many Southerners condemned and blacklisted *The Orator* as a schoolbook.

Abraham Lincoln read *The Columbian Orator* at about the age of twenty-two, and **Frederick Douglass** praised it in his well-known personal literacy story within *The Narrative of the Life of Frederick Douglass*. Douglass purchased a used copy as part of his efforts to learn to read. The book had a profound effect on him, one that would be difficult to overstate. He explains, "[e]very opportunity I got, I used to read this book. . . . The reading of these [selections] enabled me to utter my thoughts, and to meet the arguments brought forward to sustain slavery. . . . The more I read, the more I was led to abhor and detest my enslavers" (52–53). Douglass's comments about *The Columbian Orator* raise the intriguing possibility that it not only had an ideological impact on him, but also may have provided some rudimentary oratorical skills long before he met William Lloyd Garrison.

Resources: David W. Blight, "Introduction," in *The Columbian Orator*, ed. Caleb Bingham (1797; repr. New York: New York University Press, 1998); Charles Carpenter, *History of American Schoolbooks* (Philadelphia: University of Pennsylvania Press, 1963); Frederick Douglass, *The Narrative and Selected Writings*, ed. Michael Meyer (1845; repr. New York: Modern Library, 1984); George E. Littlefield, *Early Schools and School-Books of New England* (1904; repr. New York: Russell & Russell, 1965); Stephen B. Oates, *With Malice Toward None: The Life of Abraham Lincoln* (1977; repr. New York: Mentor/New American Library, 1978).

David M. Owens

Combahee River Collective (c. 1974–1980). Social and political activist community group. Based in **Boston, Massachusetts**, the Combahee River Collective was a loose-knit group of Black feminists who organized African American women, drafted political statements, protested injustices, and engaged in consciousness-raising sessions. These sessions often focused on events and ideas related to **race**, class, sexuality, **feminism**, and **Black Nationalism**. The Combahee River Collective and its statements, especially those on black feminism, hold a significant place in ideas of representation and visibility that have had vast implications not only for Black feminism, but also for who is valued and how persons are valued in African American literary traditions. Many scholars, feminists, and African American writers acknowledge the role played by the Combahee River Collective and its central document, "A Black Feminist Statement," which functioned as a conceptual foundation in shaping the identity politics of the 1980s, in demanding African American lesbian visibility and in valuing the public work and voices of women of color. Along with the rise of **Black Studies** in the 1980s, the Combahee River Collective and its publications helped to bring both attention and financial support to many African American women writers who otherwise might have remained relatively unknown, unpublished, or disregarded except in specialized circles. In her 1986 assessment of the legacy of the Combahee River Collective, founding member **Barabara Smith** notes, "The fact that some non-Lesbian Black persons are now able to value and respect the work of Black Lesbians is a 'miracle' that our integrity made possible" (Smith, 1986, 5).

The Combahee River Collective began in 1974 as the local Boston chapter of the National Black Feminist Organization (NBFO), an influential organization that brought to national debates about race issues of sexism that were otherwise often ignored or rendered secondary in male-dominated movements such as the **Black Panther Party**, and its predecessors the Student Nonviolent Coordinating Committee and the Congress of Racial Equality. The group took its name from an antislavery guerrilla campaign of June 2, 1863, led by **Harriet Tubman**, that freed about 750 slaves in the Port Royal region of South Carolina. Smith reports that the core group of the Combahee River Collective was often quite small, but that hundreds of women were in some way involved during its six-year existence (Smith, 1986, 3). Even more than the NBFO, the Combahee River Collective was crucial in placing the diverse concerns of black women at the center of political analysis, national debates, and community organizing. The group convened numerous retreats for Black feminists during which activists and intellectuals from all over the East Coast both formed networks among disparate local groups and honed a Black feminism that addressed the diversity of concerns and identities among African American women. The Combahee River Collective's insistence on lesbian visibility and socialist politics within Black feminism challenged existing homophobia in African American movements, and also shaped the direction of Black feminist thought toward identity politics, critiques of capitalism, and inclusive understandings of sexuality.

The Combahee River Collective also influenced the direction of both the national feminist movement and emerging feminist scholarship. The stated mission of the Combahee River Collective was primarily to raise the consciousness of African American women. By the mid-1970s, the modern feminist movement had gained national prominence with a diverse network of consciousness-raising groups that variously focused on local organizing, advocated policy and legal changes to benefit all women, staged local protests to make the public aware of everyday sexism, or empowered women as participants in all sectors of society. As a consciousness-raising group, the Combahee River Collective joined many other prominent women's liberation groups including Boston's Cell 16, Bread and Roses, the Chicago Women's Liberation Union, DC Women's Liberation, The Feminists, The Furies, New York Radical Women, Redstockings, Seattle Radical Women, and Women's International Conspiracy from Hell (WITCH), as well as the national network of chapters of the National Organization for Women (NOW). Many feminists and feminist historians point to the Combahee River Collective as an important group that helped bring race consciousness, class analysis, and lesbian visibility to a movement that some considered to be dominated largely by middle-class White women. With a focus on the intersections and simultaneity of various oppressions, the Combahee River Collective is seen as a pivotal group that determined the direction of feminist theory in the 1980s toward examinations of the differences among women.

Black feminist literary criticism also has deep roots in the Combahee River Collective, especially since Barbara Smith wrote the influential literary essay "Toward a Black Feminist Criticism" (1977), which echoes many of the collective's key beliefs. Along with **Toni Cade Bambara**'s groundbreaking anthology *The Black Woman* (1970) and **Barbara Christian**'s foundational literary study *Black Women Novelists: The Development of a Tradition* (1980), the Combahee River Collective helped usher in a movement of serious consideration of representations of African American women in literary studies, as well as in political life. In the wake of the Combahee River Collective's emphasis on Black lesbian visibility and on an autonomous sisterhood among

African American women, much of Black feminist literary criticism focused on the representation of Black women characters and advocated studies of distinct literary traditions with Black women writers, including especially lesbians, at the center. More so than other proximate political or scholarly projects, the Combahee River Collective demonstrated the connection between political analysis and daily life, thereby helping to bridge the divisions between activists and scholars, or between theory and practice.

The Combahee River Collective's most important contribution to women's liberation, black feminism and literary study is the influential position paper "A Black Feminist Statement" (1977). The statement was written primarily by Barbara Smith, her twin sister Beverly Smith, and Demita Frazier, who sought to represent the diverse input and interests of the fluctuating membership. The statement is the manifesto of the Combahee River Collective, and it serves as an early articulation of identity politics by demanding that African American women speak for themselves, and that they determine their own issues of concern. The statement explains, "Above all else, our politics initially sprang from the shared belief that Black women are inherently valuable, that our liberation is a necessity not as an adjunct to somebody else's but because of our need as human persons for autonomy." The statement marked a new era in feminism and other liberation movements by demanding a coalitional politics among groups of different identities. The statement criticizes separatist movements by advocating that autonomous political groups and identities work together: "Although we are feminists and Lesbians, we feel solidarity with progressive Black men and do not advocate the fractionalization that white women who are separatists demand."

"A Black Feminist Statement" was composed in April 1977, widely reprinted in diverse feminist publications throughout the 1970s and 1980s, and continues to be included in a wide variety of documentary anthologies. Though position papers, manifestos, and other political writings are generally considered ephemeral documents specific to their time and place (Armstrong, 2002, esp. 16), the publication history of the statement demonstrates an influence well beyond the immediate membership of the Combahee River Collective. The statement was first published in the radical women's liberation journal *Off Our Backs* in a 1979 special issue "by and about wimmin of color" titled "Ain't I a Woman?," as well as in the collection edited by Zillah Eisenstein, *Capitalist Patriarchy and the Case for Feminist Revolution* (1979). These printings of the statement were photocopied and distributed by Smith and other members of the Collective (Smith, 1986, 3). The statement was included in three influential collections of Third World women's writing: *This Bridge Called My Back: Writings by Radical Women of Color* (1981), *All the Women Are White, All the Blacks Are Men, But Some of Us Are Brave: Black Women's Studies* (1982), and *Homegirls: A Black Feminist Anthology* (1982). In 1986, Smith, through **Kitchen Table: Women of Color Press**, included the statement in a five-part series of organizing pamphlets for women of color. The statement now appears in contemporary anthologies of second wave feminism,

Black feminism, women's history, studies of rhetoric, and feminist journals, including a 1991 issue of Ms.

The Combahee River Collective was an important participant in the re-birth of African American women's writing in the 1970s and 1980s, as well as in the valuation of African American women, including especially Black lesbians, as important political agents and thinkers. *The Reader's Companion to U.S. History*, edited by Smith and other founding members of the feminist movement and scholars, states simply: "The Combahee River Collective Statement inspired Black women's mobilizations during the 1980s and 1990s" (17). (*See* **Feminism/Black Feminism; Feminist/Black Feminist Literary Criticism; Lesbian Literature.**)

Resources: Elizabeth Armstrong, *The Retreat from Organization: U.S. Feminism Reconceptualized* (Albany: State University of New York Press, 2002); Wini Breines, "What's Love Got to Do with It? White Women, Black Women, and Feminism in the Movement Years," *Signs* 27, no. 4 (2002), 1095–1134; Joy James and T. Denean Sharpley-Whiting, eds., *The Black Feminist Reader* (Malden, MA: Blackwell, 2000); Wilma Mankiller, Gwendolyn Mink, Marysa Navarro, Barbara Smith, and Gloria Steinem, eds., *The Reader's Companion to U.S. Women's History* (Boston: Houghton Mifflin, 1998); Cherríe Moraga and Gloria Anzaldúa, eds., *This Bridge Called My Back: Writings by Radical Women of Color* (1981; repr. New York: Kitchen Table: Women of Color Press, 1983); Linda Nicholson, ed., *The Second Wave: A Reader in Feminist Theory* (New York: Routledge, 1997); Barbara Smith, Foreword, "The Combahee River Collective Statement: Black Feminist Organizing in the Seventies and Eighties," *Freedom Organizing Series #1* (New York: Kitchen Table: Women of Color Press, 1986); Barbara Smith, ed., *Home Girls: A Black Feminist Anthology* (New York: Kitchen Table: Women of Color Press, 1983).

Brian J. Norman

Comic Books. *See* **CQ Comics Group; Graphic Novels; Milestone Comics/ Milestone Media.**

Coming-of-Age Fiction. The coming-of-age story has had a long and varied history in African American literature, including nineteenth-century **slave narratives**, early twentieth-century novels of social protest or social uplift, and intimate and powerful late twentieth-century stories of suffering and en-durance. Often semiautobiographical, these stories encompass many themes common to African American literature, such as family heritage, the power of education, racism, race relations, violence, poverty, **passing**, sexual identity, community, and religious tradition. They often follow the narrative pattern of a journey from innocence to experience, from self-rejection to self-acceptance, from bondage to freedom, or from silence to speech, although sometimes the journeys are reversed, with tragic consequences. At the heart of the African American coming-of-age story is the quest for a self-determined identity, one that frees itself from stereotypes or other environmental forces while cele-brating the innate beauty of being African American.

African American coming-of-age literature in the nineteenth century often expressed clear sociopolitical purposes. For instance, **William Wells Brown**'s *Clotel* (1853) focuses on the title character's journey in search of peace, personhood, and family. From being sold by her biological father, and then by her lover, from whom she had demanded a sanctified marriage, to passing as a White man to search for her daughter, her quest for self-determination and dignity meets with obstacles at every turn. At the novel's end, Clotel ends her own life rather than live as a slave. In the same decade, **Harriet Wilson**'s *Our Nig* (1859) describes the misadventures of Wilson's autobiographical **mulatto** heroine, Frado. Abandoned by her Caucasian mother after her Black father dies, Frado works for a Massachusetts family who treat her like a slave although she is nominally free. The narrative focuses on her experiences as a sensitive but strong-willed girl and her growing realizations about Northern racism and hypocrisy. It also asserts the value of literacy as both sanctuary and practical skill: the story explains that, abandoned by her husband, Frado/Wilson turned to writing her story as her means of support. At the end of the nineteenth century, **Frances Ellen Watkins Harper**'s *Iola Leroy; or Shadows Uplifted* (1892) tells the story of another mixed-race heroine. The novel retrospectively depicts Iola's childhood, in which she was raised passing for White, her search for her mother, her role as a **Civil War** nurse, her encounters with discrimination in the North, her work as a spokesperson in postbellum African American movements, her rejection of a White suitor and her marriage to a mulatto, and her return to the South. Aimed in part at inspiring social and political reforms, the novel affirms the intellect, ability, valor, and moral courage of African Americans. Similarly, **James Weldon Johnson**'s *Autobiography of an Ex-Colored Man* (1912), which concerns the protagonist's experiences passing, is a socially focused work.

Coming-of-age novels written by African Americans became even more common in the context of the **Harlem Renaissance**, and they often focused on redefining African American identity against cultural stereotypes. For instance, **Langston Hughes**'s semiautobiographical novel, *Not Without Laughter* (1930), served, **Dolan Hubbard** has argued, to counter the sensationalized portrait of African Americans created in popular novels of the period, especially in **Carl Van Vechten**'s *Nigger Heaven* but also in **Claude McKay**'s *Home to Harlem*. Incorporating some of his own childhood experiences, Hughes tells the story of young Sandy Williams's difficult exploration of the roles he might play as an African American in the early twentieth century. Each of his family members models a different response to the racism and poverty Sandy encounters. Sandy's grandmother, a pious, humble woman, dreams that he will become a great leader of the race; his eldest aunt becomes a bourgeois snob; his mother works as a domestic; and his younger aunt rebels against her mother's religious values and becomes an embittered prostitute before she makes it as a **blues** singer. With these various role models before him, and a growing realization of what it means to be Black, Sandy is drawn to either living it up, like his father, a bluesman, or pursuing an education. When his mother decides to remove him from school so that he can begin working, his younger aunt provides the money for him to continue his education. The novel ends on a hopeful note that he will overcome his circumstances and fulfill his grandmother's dream.

Also during the Harlem Renaissance, **Nella Larsen**, **Jesse Redmon Fauset**, and **Zora Neale Hurston** wrote novels exploring their heroines' struggles with their sexual and professional identities. Larsen's *Quicksand* (1928) depicts Helga Crane's search for freedom and acceptance as a mixed-race individual through a series of geographic locales and love affairs in both America and Europe. Fauset's *Plum Bun* (1929) follows the journey of Angela Murray from a comfortable childhood in **Philadelphia, Pennsylvania**, to New York City, tracing her dream of becoming a painter, her desire for upward social mobility, and her experiences passing for a White woman. *Quicksand* and *Plum Bun* depict their characters' painful experiences with interracial romantic relationships: Helga's Danish suitor's gifts to her reveal his exotic, primitive view of her; and Angela's White lover reveals his racism. Both protagonists eventually choose husbands of their own race, among other means of affirming their own ethnic identities. In Hurston's *Their Eyes Were Watching God* (1937), heroine Janie Crawford undergoes a journey not unlike that of the protagonists in Larsen's and Fauset's novels. Not realizing that she was Black, and that it was considered inferior, until she was six, Janie is a high-spirited dreamer. She is taught by her grandmother and her second of three husbands, Joe Starks, that her sexuality is a dangerous thing that must be repressed and controlled, and that her dreaminess is a flaw. However, in the course of the novel, she comes to appreciate and realize her own beauty, and to gain the confidence necessary not to let anyone define her but her own soul. All three novels highlight the passage from silence into speech or vice versa—from the literal silence that occurs when Janie is subordinate to her husbands, the silent lie of passing for White that Angela finally repudiates, or the once fiery Helga's lapse into silence and lassitude as a housewife and mother.

In the 1940s and 1950s, the struggle to transcend one's environment is foregrounded in several key coming-of-age stories. **Richard Wright**'s, **Ralph Ellison**'s, and **James Baldwin**'s young male protagonists struggle to escape the confines of the societies into which they are born. Wright's *Native Son* (1940) depicts the poverty of his protagonist, Bigger Thomas, a character Wright claimed was an amalgam of about five character types he encountered as a child (Bryant, 64). Bigger grows up in a one-room apartment with his mother and two siblings, and his seething rage, hatred, and need to feel significant result in violence and intimidation that lead him to two murders. Eventually sentenced to death, Bigger declares that, through the unpremeditated, unintentional murder of his White victim, he felt he had finally found himself, and embraces the act rather than blaming it on his circumstances.

In Ellison's *Invisible Man* (1952), the protagonist undergoes a vicious journey from innocence to experience fostered by the racism of **the South**, the corruption he sees at his college, and the failed role models he finds in the North, who are corrupt, persecuted, or isolated. At the end of the novel he crawls into a cellar, unable to find a road to take that does not seem ultimately hopeless.

Baldwin, in *Go Tell it on the Mountain* (1953), writes a coming-of-age story that occurs on protagonist John Grimes's fourteenth birthday. John is the illegitimate child of an affair, and his stepfather is violent and oppressive. The stepfather has channeled his previous violence as a profligate and a thug into religious and moral domination over his sons. John's half brother, at age twelve, is already running with dangerous **Harlem, New York**, gangs, but John finds an alternative to both these paths in a powerful conversion experience, turning to Jesus and an accepting religious community to help him find salvation, self-acceptance, and hope.

All these protagonists grow up with absent, powerless, or abusive father figures, in locales where they see the future only as a dead end. Bryant has argued that as these characters "discover themselves, they escape the psychological and emotional confines of the ghetto, though perhaps not the physical ones," as if "the increased negatives of the ghetto stimulate a compensatory increase in the need to achieve personal identity" (74). During this same era, **Ann Petry**'s *The Street* (1946) and **Gwendolyn Brooks**'s *Maud Martha* (1953) focus on poverty and other environmental factors in the formation of identity.

The dynamics of matriarchal families are central in several African American novels in the mid-twentieth century. **Dorothy West**'s *The Living Is Easy* (1948) and **Paule Marshall**'s *Brown Girl, Brownstones* (1959) portray female protagonists who grow up in the shadow of powerful, dynamic mothers who dominate the household and seek to determine the direction of their daughters' lives. Both girls do not wish to conform to the values and lifestyles for which their mothers are grooming them: Black upper-class **Boston, Massachusetts**, for Judy in *The Living Is Easy* and the bourgeois brownstones of **Brooklyn, New York**, for Selina in *Brown Girl, Brownstones*. Each finds a surrogate mother figure who offers an alternative vision of what it means to be a Black woman in her society. Both novels end with hope that the main character will find herself as an individual at last, not falling into the mold her mother has set for her but with a new respect for her mother's strength and courage.

Since the 1960s, the African-American coming-of-age story has reemerged in the form of the neo-slave narrative—fictional or semifictional reconstructions of the quests for freedom and identity of slaves. The coming-of-age story has also manifested itself in novels for young adults. **Margaret Walker**'s *Jubilee* (1966) and **Ernest Gaines**'s *The Autobiography of Miss Jane Pittman* (1971) are prime examples of neo-slave narratives. They, along with young adult novels such as **Gordon Parks**'s *The Learning Tree* (1963), Kristin Hunter's *God Bless the Child* (1964), or **Louise Meriwether**'s *Daddy Was a Number Runner* (1970), were part of the consciousness-raising movement of that era. In the 1970s and 1980s many of these novels dealt with fatherless young men struggling to keep out of trouble, or young women facing abandonment by one or both parents, poverty, and/or teen pregnancy. In this category of novel is **Alice Childress**'s *Rainbow Jordan* (1981). James Baldwin's *If Beale Street Could Talk* (1974), with the young female protagonist Tish, fits loosely into this category as well. (*See* **Lattany, Kristin Hunter**.)

Many more recent young adult novels focus on the challenges of interracial friendships or families, celebrate the figure of the African American father, emphasize the value of education, or depict Black middle-class life, such as Rita Willliams-Garcia's *Fast Talk on a Slow Track* (1991).

In the later twentieth century, works such as **Toni Morrison**'s *The Bluest Eye* (1970), **Alice Walker**'s *The Color Purple* (1982), **Audre Lorde**'s *Zami: A New Spelling of My Name* (1982), and **Gloria Naylor**'s *Mama Day* (1988) continued the coming-of-age tradition in African American literature, with an even more intimate focus on violence, self-rejection, and the power of community. For instance, Pecola Breedlove, the main character of *The Bluest Eye*, and Celie, the heroine of *The Color Purple*, both endure rape by a father or father figure, and both suffer from a sense of worthlessness and ugliness as a result not only of the abuse, but also of the community around them. For example, the preference Pecola sees for golden-haired, white-skinned, blue-eyed femininity makes her obsessively desire blue eyes—and the love and security they suggest to her. In *The Color Purple*, Celie's stepfather, husband, stepchildren, and, at first, her husband's mistress treat her with contempt. However, while Celie, taught to love and stand up for herself, grows strong and becomes the center of a vital community, Pecola, finding no support anywhere, goes insane and dies.

Relatively recent memoirs also relate powerful, complex coming-of-age stories and complement contemporary coming-of-age fiction. Among these memoirs are **Lorene Cary**'s *Black Ice* (1991), which in part concerns Cary's experiences in an elite, chiefly White private school in New England, and **Patrice Gaines**'s *Laughing in the Dark: From Colored Girl to Woman of Color—A Journey from Prison to Power* (1994).

Coming-of-age stories have exercised an enormous cultural power as they have represented the formation of African American identities across the centuries, in different social settings, and with regard to both genders. (*See* **Children's Literature; Gay Literature; Lesbian Literature**.)

Resources: Primary Sources: James Baldwin: *Go Tell It on the Mountain* (New York: Knopf, 1953); *If Beale Street Could Talk* (New York: Dial, 1974); Gwendolyn Brooks, *Maud Martha* (New York: Harper, 1953); William Wells Brown, *Clotel; or, the President's Daughter: A Narrative of Slave Life in the United States* (Boston: Bedford, 2000); Lorene Cary, *Black Ice* (New York: Knopf, 1991); Alice Childress, *Rainbow Jordan* (New York: Coward, McCann, & Geoghegan, 1981); Ralph Ellison, *Invisible Man* (New York: Random House, 1952); Jesse Redmon Fauset, *Plum Bun* (Boston: Beacon, 1990); Ernest Gaines, *The Autobiography of Miss Jane Pittman* (New York: Dial, 1971); Patrice Gaines, *Laughing in the Dark: From Colored Girl to Woman of Color—A Journey from Prison to Power* (New York: Crown, 1994); Frances Ellen Watkins Harper, *Iola Leroy; or, Shadows Uplifted* (NewYork: Oxford Univeristy Press, 1899); Langston Hughes, *The Novels: Not Without Laughter, and, Tambourines to Glory*, in the *Complete*

Works of Langston Hughes (Columbia: University of Missouri Press, 2001); Kristin Hunter, *God Bless the Child* (New York: Scribner's, 1964); Zora Neale Hurston, *Their Eyes Were Watching God* (New York: Perennial, 1990); James Weldon Johnson, *The Autobiography of an Ex-Colored Man* (New York: Dover, 1995); Nella Larsen, *Quicksand* (New York: Negro University Press, 1969); Audre Lorde, *Zami: A New Spelling of My Name* (Trumansburg, NY: Crossing Press, 1982); Paule Marshall, *Brown Girl, Brownstones* (New York: Feminist Press, 1981); Louise Meriwether, *Daddy Was a Number Runner* (Englewood Cliffs, NJ: Prentice-Hall, 1970); Toni Morrison, *The Bluest Eye* (New York: Holt, Rinehart and Winston, 1970); Gloria Naylor, *Mama Day* (New York: Ticknor & Fields, 1988); Gordon Parks, *Learning Tree* (New York: Harper & Row, 1963); Ann Petry, *The Street* (Boston: Houghton Mifflin, 1946); Alice Walker, *The Color Purple* (New York: Harcourt Brace, 1982); Margaret Abigail Walker, *Jubilee* (Boston: Houghton Mifflin, 1966); Dorothy West, *The Living Is Easy* (New York: Feminist Press, 1975); Rita Williams-Garcia, *Fast Talk on a Slow Track* (New York: Dutton, 1991); Harriet Wilson, *Our Nig; or, Sketches from the Life of a Free Black* (New York: Vintage, 1983); Richard Wright, *Native Son* (New York: Harper & Bros., 1940). **Secondary Sources:** Bernard W. Bell, *The African-American Novel and Its Tradition* (Amherst: University of Massachusetts Press, 1987); Devon Boan, *The Black ''I'': Author and Audience in African-American Literature* (New York: Peter Lang, 2002); Jerry H. Bryant, *Born in a Mighty Bad Land: The Violent Man in African-American Folklore and Fiction* (Bloomington: Indiana University Press, 2003); Pin-chia Feng, *The Female Bildungsroman by Toni Morrison and Maxine Hong Kingston: A Postmodern Reading* (New York: Peter Lang, 1998); Florence Howe and Jean Casella, eds., *Almost Touching the Skies: Women's Coming of Age Stories* (New York: Feminist Press, 2000); Dolan Hubbard, "Introduction," in *The Novels of Langston Hughes* in the *Complete Works of Langston Hughes* (Columbia: University of Missouri Press, 2001); Gunilla Theander Kester, *Writing the Subject: Bildung and the African-American Text* (New York: Peter Lang, 1995); Geta Lesuer, *Ten Is the Age of Darkness: The Black Bildungsroman* (Columbia: University of Missouri Press, 1995); Hans Ostrom, *A Langston Hughes Encyclopedia* (Westport, CT: Greenwood Press, 2002), esp. pp. 277–282; Karen Patricia Smith, ed., *African-American Voices in Young Adult Literature: Tradition, Transition, Transformation* (Metuchen, NJ: Scarecrow, 1994).

Windy Counsell Petrie

Cone, James H. (born 1939). Religious writer, professor, pastor, and activist. Cone is perhaps best known for his role in developing a "Black theology," beginning in the 1960s. He was born in Fordyce, Arkansas, but spent most of his childhood in Bearden, a small African American community on the outskirts of Fordyce. He began attending church at a young age and decided early on to become a minister one day. As a young African Methodist Episcopal pastor in Bearden, Cone faced a reality that challenged his Christian beliefs: racism.

While attending Morehouse College in the mid-1950s, Cone closely monitored events surrounding the bus boycott in Montgomery, Alabama, that was being led by an alumnus of Morehouse, **Martin Luther King, Jr.** After graduating from Morehouse, Cone received his M.A. from Garret Theological

Seminary in Wisconsin. He then earned a Ph.D. from Northwestern University in 1965. He found merit in both the ideas of nonviolence advanced by King and those advanced by **Malcolm X** concerning Black resistance to White violence (*Martin & Malcolm*). The reality of the mistreatment of African Americans was virtually invisible to professors at Northwestern University until Cone brought it to their attention. He wrote to them: "[Y]ou've been talking for weeks now about the wrong doing of Catholics against Protestants in the sixteenth and seventeenth century; but you've said absolutely nothing about the monstrous acts of violence by White Protestants against Negroes in the American South today" (*Risks of Faith*, 38). In June 1969, at the National Conference of Black Churches in **Atlanta, Georgia**, Cone and other Black ministers argued for a "Black theology" that would be one of "liberation" (*Black Theology*; *Risks of Faith*). Since then Cone, like his intellectual predecessors **W.E.B. Du Bois** and **David Walker**, has emphasized the role Christianity must play in addressing social injustice. He insists—in *God of the Oppressed* and *Risks of Faith*, for example—that White Christianity must be consistent in its interpretation of brotherhood or risk losing credibility in a pluralistic society: "The Civil Rights Movements [*sic*] of the 1960's awakened me from my mythological slumber. As I became actively involved in the black freedom movement that was exploding in the streets all over America, I soon discovered how limited my seminary education was" (*Risks of Faith*, 25). Cone has distinguished himself as a pastor, scholar, professor, activist, and prolific author. At this writing, he is distinguished professor in the Union Theological Seminary in New York.

Resources: James H. Cone: *A Black Theology* (1970; repr. Maryknoll, NY: Orbis Books, 1990); *Black Theology and Black Power* (San Francisco: HarperSanFrancisco, 1989); *God of the Oppressed*, rev. ed. (Maryknoll, NY: Orbis Books, 1997); *Martin & Malcolm in America: A Dream or a Nightmare* (Maryknoll, NY: Orbis Books, 1991); *Risks of Faith: The Emergence of a Black Theology of Liberation, 1968–1998* (Boston: Beacon Press, 2000).

Robert H. Miller

Conjuring. In general, "conjuring" refers to the practices of magic, casting spells, and/or summoning spirits. Conjuring, sometimes called "conjuration," in African American **folklore** is connected to a complex multitude of ideas, traditions, and practices belonging to African American slaves. Many of these ideas, traditions, and practices spring from or are connected to the cultures of Africa (especially West Africa) and/or the Caribbean. Traditions of conjuring subsequently found form in modern African American literary works and helped sustain a continuation of regional customs and cultural ideologies that were sometimes threatened with extinction when their preservation depended solely on oral tradition. A variety of terms has been used to refer to the practitioner and practice of conjuring; among these are "root doctor," "hoodoo," **"voodoo/vodoun,"** "goopher," and the West Indian "obeah." Traditions of conjuring are found on the west coast of Africa and in the Caribbean, especially **Haiti**. An eclectic belief system was passed down from generation to generation in an oral tradition. Parts of it were later portrayed in literature that mirrored the African American experience in a new territory.

African American slaves were forced into dependence on their owners even though the slaves were indispensable partners in the taming of the wilderness of the New World and, subsequently, maintaining farms and plantations. The slaves' knowledge was essential to the survival of White immigrants, explorers, and settlers who owned them, and yet the slaves had almost no control over their own lives, current or future, or over the lives of those they loved; families were torn apart. The folk art of conjuring helped to build a sense of family and community in an otherwise hostile environment, for conjuring was a supernatural means of controlling experience. The magical powers of conjuring took on a central role in the lives of many African American slaves. Conjure doctors or "root-doctors" preserved and protected the health and welfare of those who came to them and requested help. This gave slaves the ability to exert their will and aid in establishing a semblance of control in a way that was in keeping with their customs (Bacon).

Later, conjuring practices in literature reflected the power of folk traditions. **Charles Waddell Chesnutt** was one of the first African Americans whose works were known for their use of conjuring. *The Conjure Woman* (1899), a collection of short stories, many of which had previously appeared in *The Atlantic Monthly*, is famous for its accurate representation of slave life. Chesnutt's work makes use of the idea that magical powers, in the form of two conjurers, Aunt Peggy and Uncle Jube, give authority to those whose independence is threatened or nonexistent. Uncle Julius, an ex-slave, has told stories to John and Annie, the new owners of Uncle Julius' old plantation home. In the *Conjure Woman*, John narrates these stories and, as the work unfolds, the reader becomes aware of the intelligence and clever wit of Uncle Julius, the source of the stories. In some of Chesnutt's stories, even slave owners use the conjure doctors to deal with slave problems, suggesting the social function and power of conjuring. This social function gave credibility to the folk tradition and also showed the interdependent relationship that was developing, if not always acknowledged, between slave and slave owner.

More recent uses in literature give sufficient evidence that conjuring is still part of African American and American culture. One of the more remarkable novels of the **Harlem Renaissance** was **Rudolph Fisher**'s *The Conjure-Man Dies: A Mystery Tale of Dark Harlem* (1932), which is arguably the first African American mystery novel as well as an interesting treatment of a contemporary "conjure man." And, as Pryce and Spillers suggest, aspects of conjuring inform works by **Toni Cade Bambara**, **Frances Smith Foster**, **Zora Neale Hurston**, **Toni Morrison**, **Alice Walker**, and **Ann Petry**, and literary creation itself can be interpreted as a form of conjuring, of summoning spirits from memory and imagination. The novel *Mumbo Jumbo* (1972), by **Ishmael Reed**, improvises on aspects of conjuring in its complicated, very playful narrative; one of the novel's main settings is **New Orleans, Louisiana**. In John Berendt's *Midnight in the Garden of Good and Evil* (1994), also set in **the South**, supernatural forces are summoned by a conjure woman to aid an alleged murderer; thus, conjuring is by no means limited to African American literature.

Both physical and spiritual healers, conjure doctors have been characterized as medicinal practitioners who used materials found in the natural world to aid those who requested assistance with either physical ills or emotional desires. The potions and remedies concocted by conjure doctors could ward off evil spirits or invoke the bonds of love and desire. Various roots, herbs, plants, and animal parts were used to summon the spirits of both good and evil, inviting death to some and postponing death for others. A charm or amulet, also known as a fetish, may be worn by its owner or set out in the home. It can either guard against evil or be instrumental in bringing good fortune to its owner. Unseen forces moved inside and outside the lives of those who relied on the conjure doctor to protect and cure them from such forces (Bacon).

Secret rituals and voodoo, or hoodoo, practices were prevalent in New Orleans. In her book *Mules and Men* (1935), Zora Neale Hurston relates detailed information pertaining to sacred hoodoo practices, information she acquired after gaining the confidence of practitioners in New Orleans. Conjuring is also found in some of the tales anthologized by Roger D. Abrahams in *African American Folktales: Stories from Black Traditions in the New World* (1999).

Conjuring practices mix traditional folk arts with religion (Puckett; Smith). Within this mix there are African, Anglo-Christian, and African American elements. African-derived and Anglo-Christian spiritual concepts might, for example, continue under the guise of magical practices in conjuring. The church and voodoo are not entirely separate, that is. *The Interesting Narrative of the Life of Olaudah Equiano, or Gustavus Vassa, the African* (1789), a **slave narrative**, relates the difficulties inherent in assimilating various aspects of the life of an African native's spiritual traditions with an English version of Christianity. Spirits from the Bible are used to confirm the spirit world of the conjurer. In her novel *Moses, Man of the Mountain* (1939), Zora Neale Hurston relates the Christian Moses to the African Moses of folktales.

Sometimes labeled superstitions by scientists trying to understand a deceptively complicated system of beliefs, most conjuring practices were an integral part of the everyday religion of the African culture. "Superstition" evokes a sense of unreality about a real, powerful influence in the lives of those who continued this folk tradition; many of the beliefs that accompany the folk traditions of conjuring were credible in their specific context, but they lost much of this credibility when they mixed with Anglo-American ideas of ghosts and witchcraft.

Conjure-magic as part of a folk tradition is often a way to retaliate against those in power and give voice to the politically and socially disenfranchised. From medicine to religion to literature, conjuring can function as a kind of equalizer in a socially and economically stratified system. Conjuring incorporates the idea of supernatural forces literally and figuratively at play in a wide variety of African American experiences, past and present.

Resources: Roger D. Abrahams, ed., *African American Folktales: Stories from Black Traditions in the New World* (New York: Pantheon, 1999); A. M. Bacon, "Folklore and Ethnology: Conjuring and Conjure-Doctors," in *The Negro and His Folklore in Nineteenth Century Periodicals*, ed. Bruce Jackson (1895; repr. Austin: American Folklore Society/University of Texas Press, 1967); John Berendt, *Midnight in the Garden of Good and Evil: A Savannah Story* (New York: Random House, 1994); Charles W. Chesnutt, *The Conjure Woman* (New York: Houghton, Mifflin, 1899); Alan Dundes, ed., *Mother Wit from the Laughing Barrel: Readings in the Interpretation of Afro-American Folklore* (Englewood Cliffs, NJ: Prentice-Hall, 1973); Olaudah Equiano, *The Interesting Narrative of the Life of Olaudah Equiano, or Gustavus Vassa, the African* (London, 1789); Rudolph Fisher, *The Conjure Man Dies: A Mystery of Dark Harlem* (1932; Ann Arbor: University of Michigan Press, 1992); Zora Neale Hurston: *Moses, Man of the Mountain* (Philadelphia: Lippincott, 1939); *Mules and Men* (Philadelphia: Lippincott, 1935); Harry M. Hyatt, ed., *Hoodoo—Conjuration—Witchcraft—Rootwork*, 2 vols. (Hannibal, MO: Western Press, 1970); Lawrence W. Levine, *Black Culture and Black Consciousness: Afro-American Folk Thought from Slavery to Freedom* (New York: Oxford University Press, 1977); David G. Nicholls, *Conjuring the Folk: Forms of Modernity in African America* (Ann Arbor: University of Michigan Press, 2000); Mary Alicia Owen, *Voodoo Tales: As Told Among the Negroes of the Southwest* (New York: Putnam, 1893); Marjorie Pryse and Hortense J. Spillers, eds., *Conjuring: Black Women, Fiction, and Literary Tradition* (Bloomington: Indiana University Press, 1985); Newbell Niles Puckett, *Folk Beliefs of the Southern Negro* (Westport, CT: Greenwood Press, 1968); Theophus H. Smith, *Conjuring Culture: Biblical Formations of Black America* (New York: Oxford University Press, 1994).

Kathy Hawthorne Olson

Cook, William W. (born 1933). Poet, playwright, literary critic, and teacher. Born in Trenton, New Jersey, Cook taught public school in New Jersey from 1954 to 1973. In l973, he joined the Dartmouth College English Department, and in l993 was named Israel Evans Professor of Oratory and Belles Lettres there. Cook holds a B.A. from the College of New Jersey and an M.A. in English and language from the University of Chicago. At Dartmouth, Cook teaches American poetry and drama, African American literature, and oratory and oral interpretation. In 1993, Cook was named New Hampshire Professor of the Year, an award given by the Council for the Advancement and Support of Education. In 1996, the *Dartmouth Review* named Cook "One of Dartmouth's Best Professors" for his charismatic reading of poetry, his sense of humor, and his in-depth analysis of literature. He served on the Executive Committee of the National Council of Teachers of English from 1971 to 1973 and in l992 became chair of the Conference on College Composition and Communication. In 1994, he received an honorary Doctor of Humane Letters from Rivier College. Cook's first volume of poetry, *Hudson Hornet and Other Poems*, was published in l989; it was followed by *Spiritual: Poems by William W. Cook* in 1999. Cook's poetry has also appeared in numerous journals, including *New England Review*, *Breadloaf Quarterly*, and *International Poetry Review*.

He has written one play, *Flight to Canada*. Cook is also known for his contributions to literary criticism and has had articles published about African American literature and theater in journals and anthologies. In March 1998, Cook chaired the National Black Theatre Summit, "On Golden Pond," convened by playwright **August Wilson**. Held at Dartmouth's Minary Center in Ashland, New Hampshire, the summit brought together people from disparate fields—scholars, actors, producers, directors, representatives of public and private funding agencies, activists, and members of the business community—to discuss the future and survival of Black theater in a era when all theaters are becoming more multicultural.

Resources: William W. Cook: *Hudson Hornet: Poems by William W. Cook* (Berkeley, CA: Ishmael Reed Publishing, 1989); "Members and Lames: Language in the Theater of August Wilson," in *Black Theatre: Ritual Performance in the African Diaspora*, ed. Paul Carter Harrison, Victor Leo Walker II, and Gus Edwards (Philadelphia: Temple University Press, 2001), 388–396; "The New Negro Renaissance," in *A Companion to Twentieth Century Poetry*, ed. Neil Roberts (Malden, MA: Blackwell, 2001), 138–152; *Spiritual: Poems by William W. Cook* (Berkeley, CA: Ishmael Reed Publishing, 1999).

Julie Neff-Lippman

Cooking. Cooking has been integral to African American culture partly because the evolution of "soul food," as African American cuisine is often referred to, mirrors the history of African Americans in America. The foundation of African American cooking can be found in the traditional foods of Africa. Grains, legumes, yams, leafy greens, and similar foods can all be found as early as 4000 B.C.E. on the African continent. As explorers began discovering the African continent, new foodstuffs were introduced to the continent, such as cabbage from Spain.

The African diet was predominantly vegetarian. Cooking techniques were simple. Utensils and dishes were often fashioned out of natural resources such as gourds and other squashes. Food was boiled, with leaves used as a natural steamer. Fried foods were made with palm oil or butters strained from vegetable oils. Certain foods were roasted in open fires or baked beneath hot ashes. Meals were mostly eaten communally, and oral histories and stories would be exchanged during these mealtimes—creating a tradition, early on, that combined repast with reflection.

The slave trade forced many African culinary traditions to change. During the long **middle passage**, Africans were fed small portions of rice and beans. It was rare for them to receive fresh fruit or vegetables, and often they were fed a gruel made from rotten and salted beef products and fish. Once in the New World, slaves had to make do with the food their masters didn't want to eat—the undesirable parts of animals; cast-off vegetables; weekly rations; wild game (generally possum); fish; and other foods slaves were able to acquire independently. Weekly rations could include cornmeal, molasses, a few pounds of meat, and greens such as collards, kale, mustard greens, and dandelions. Cooking was generally done in one pot over an open fire. When cooking for their masters, slaves prepared fried chicken, sweet potatoes, boiled white potatoes, roasted pork, and pies, and puddings containing fruits and berries. Because slaves had been transplanted from their homeland, their dishes acquired the local nuances of the states the slaves resided in. In Louisiana, in particular, African American cuisine became marked by rich, sauce-based dishes.

As early as the late 1800s, African American women began writing down their recipes for family collections or to share with friends. The first published cookbook written by an African American woman was *What Mrs. Fisher Knows About Old Southern Cooking*, by Abby Fisher. Though little is known about Fisher, records have shown that she was a woman of mixed ethnicity, born a slave in 1832, who reached **San Francisco California**, by the age of forty-eight. She married Alexander C. Fisher, bore eleven children, and in 1879 was awarded a diploma at the Sacramento State Fair of 1879, as well as two medals at the San Francisco Mechanic's Institute Fair. Fisher's work was supported by prominent San Franciscans who helped her write and publish her cookbook. The book had a folkloric tone and included recipes for succotash, jambalaya, oyster gumbo, crullers, biscuits, and several meat dishes. It was intended, as Fisher wrote, "to be found a complete instructor, so that a child can understand it and learn the art of cooking."

African American cooking in general did not rely upon exact measurements and quantities because slaves so often prepared meals based upon whatever was at hand. Dishes were named more for the nature of the dish than for the ingredients. Hush puppies were named for catfish that would have otherwise been discarded. Slaves would add milk, egg, onion, and fry the concoction. The name arose when women would tell dogs to hush as the food was transported between the frying pan and the dining table. Hoecakes were named for cornbread batter held in the fire on a hoe to make a quick batch of bread, and ashcakes were cornmeal batter baked in an open fire.

When the slaves were emancipated in 1863, African American cuisine followed the **Great Migration** of African Americans northward. African Americans were cooks on trains, in the homes of Whites, and in restaurants across the country—spreading the influence of their unique cuisine through the dishes they prepared. Because families were so busy during the week, members often working more than one job, Sunday dinners became a time for African American families to reconnect both to each other and to their heritage. The term "soul food" became part of the African American lexicon during the turbulent 1960s, at the height of the **Civil Rights Movement**—a time when African Americans were reaffirming their authentic Black selves.

Traditionally, African American cuisine is characterized by using pork products, and fried dishes are made with animal fat or lard. While these techniques add flavor to African American dishes, they also lead to health problems including hypertension, diabetes, and obesity. New approaches to cooking soul food are emerging that include healthier alternatives to frying and use vegetable or canola oil.

Signature soul food dishes include cornbread, barbecued ribs, candied yams, hush puppies, red beans and rice, fried chicken, fried catfish, grits, black-eyed peas, chitterlings, liver and onions, greens, smothered pork chops, peach cobbler, salmon croquettes, pig's feet, bread pudding, neck–bone soup, and sweet potato pie. These dishes reflect the regional diversity within African American cuisine and are only a fraction of the dishes that comprise the whole of African American cuisine.

In 1997, the movie *Soul Food* was released, starring Vanessa Williams, Nia Long, Vivica Fox, Mekhi Phifer, and Michael Beach. The movie followed the trials and tribulations of an African American family in **Chicago, Illinois**, but, more important, it reflected the importance of cooking to African American culture, with the family's Sunday dinners as the focal point of the movie.

In addition to being a staple in many African American homes, soul food has become a part of the larger American culture through soul food restaurants. In California, Aunt Kizzy's Back Porch is popular with locals and tourists alike. In **Harlem, New York**, the world-renowned Sylvia's Restaurant of Harlem serves more than 3,000 people each day, has been featured in **Spike Lee**'s film *Jungle Fever*, and appears in the novels of **E. Lynn Harris**. Countless other restaurants, large and small, across the United States exemplify the diversity of soul food and its place within African American history. Tracy Poe, Charles P. Toombs, and Doris Witt are among the scholars who have studied cooking and food in relation to African American literature.

Resources: Pearl Bowner and Jean Eckstein, *A Pinch of Soul* (New York: Avon, 1970); Carol Counihan and Penny Van Esterik, eds., *Food and Culture: A Reader* (New York: Routledge, 1997); Abby Fisher, *What Mrs. Fisher Knows About Old Southern Cooking* (Bedford, MA: Applewood Books, 1995); Jessica Harris, *The Welcome Table: African American Heritage Cooking* (New York: Simon and Schuster, 1996); National Council of Negro Women, *The Black Family Reunion Cookbook: Recipes and Food Memories* (New York: Fireside Books, 1993); Tracy N. Poe, "The Origins of Soul Food in Black Urban Identity: Chicago, 1915–1947," *American Studies International* 37, no. 1 (Feb. 1999), 4–33; Charles P. Toombs, "The Confluence of Food and Identity in Gloria Naylor's *Linden Hills*: 'What We Eat Is Who We Is'," *College Language Association Journal* 37, no. 1 (Sept. 1993), 1–18; Doris Witt: "Soul Food: Where the Chitterling Hits the (Primal) Pan," in *Eating Culture*, ed. Ron Scapp and Brian Seitz (Albany: State University of New York Press, 1998), 258–287; "What (N)ever Happened to Aunt Jemima: Eating Disorders, Fetal Rights, and Black Female Appetite in Contemporary American Culture," *Discourse: Journal for Theoretical Studies in Media and Culture* 17, no. 2 (Winter 1994–1995), 98–122.

Roxane Gay

Cooper, Anna Julia Haywood (1858/1859–1964). Essayist and lecturer. An activist and pioneer in education, Cooper devoted her life to scholarship and the improvement of conditions for African Americans, particularly women.

Born in 1858 or 1859 in Raleigh, North Carolina, to Hannah Stanley, a slave, and George Washington Haywood, her White owner, Cooper early demonstrated her intellect, tutoring fellow students at St. Augustine's Normal and Collegiate Institute when she was only nine. In 1877, she married George A. C. Cooper, who died unexpectedly in 1879.

Shortly thereafter, Cooper enrolled at Oberlin College, where she took the "gentlemen's courses" and earned a B.A. and an M.A. in mathematics. As principal at the "M" Street School (later known as Dunbar High School) in **Washington, D.C.**, Cooper's support of a rigorous academic curriculum angered officials of the school system, who revoked her principalship when she refused to implement **Booker T. Washington**'s vocational model of education. Cooper chaired the Language Department at Lincoln Institute in Jefferson City, Missouri, from 1906 until 1910, returned to "M" Street as a Latin teacher in 1910, and, in 1929, became president of Frelinghuysen University, an evening school for working people. She remained with this institution, despite its loss of accreditation, until it closed in the 1950s.

Cooper's studies reflected her belief that education must be varied and challenging. In the summer of 1911, she began studying at the Guilde International in Paris; in 1925, when she was sixty-six, she became the fourth known African American woman to earn a doctorate when the Sorbonne (University of Paris) awarded her the degree. Cooper completed two dissertations: *Le Pèlerinage de Charlemagne: Voyage à Jérusalem et à Constantinople* (1925), a translation of a medieval tale, and *L'Attitude de la France à l'Égard de l'Esclavage Pendant la Révolution* (1925), a historical study of French racial attitudes. As the work of an African American who had herself been a slave, *L'Attitude* (published in English as *Slavery and the French Revolutionists*) is a significant text. Although concerned with French **slavery** on both sides of the Atlantic, it situates slavery within a global and historical framework and suggests that slavery everywhere could have been abolished if there had been a will to do so.

Cooper's other major work, a collection of essays titled *A Voice from the South, by a Black Woman of the South* (1892), addresses social issues from a Black female's perspective, insisting that even though they are generally denied access to higher education, African American women are the key to improving social conditions for their race. She cites as evidence her own experiences at St. Augustine and Oberlin, where males with only "a floating intention to study" were encouraged, while females had to struggle "against positive discouragements." As to the race problem, Cooper suggests that the solution lies in the hands of God and will be resolved when America becomes more concerned with capabilities than with color. While acknowledging that the African American experience has encouraged oratory, Cooper argues for a written African American literary tradition crafted by African Americans. She describes African American **folklore** as a "native growth" that "could claim the attention and charm the ear of the outside world" and wishes for a "painter-poet" to depict "a black man honestly and appreciatively" and "the white man, occasionally, as seen from the Negro's standpoint."

Cooper's extensive activist career expounded her theme of uplift for African American women. It began in 1886 with "Womanhood a Vital Element in the Regeneration and Progress of a Race," a presentation at the Convocation of Clergy of the Protestant Episcopal Church, and included such important addresses as "The Needs and Status of Black Women" (Congress of Representative Women, 1893) and "The Negro Problem in America" (first Pan-African Conference in London, 1900). Cooper helped found the Colored Women's League (1892) and the Colored Women's YWCA in Washington (1905). She was the only woman elected to the prestigious American Negro Academy and was active in numerous organizations. Cooper's later works include *Legislative Measures Concerning Slavery in the United States* (1942), *Equality of Races and the Democratic Movement* (1945), *The Life and Writings of the Grimké Family* (1951), and an autobiography, *The Third Step* (c. 1950). Her long life validated her commitment to social and intellectual equality, her feminist stance, and her racial pride.

Resources: Karen Baker-Fletcher, *A Singing Something: Womanist Reflections on Anna Julia Cooper* (New York: Crossroad Publishing, 1994); Anna Julia Cooper: *Slavery and the French Revolution*, trans. Frances Richardson Keller (Lewiston, NY: Mellen, 1988); *A Voice from the South, by a Black Woman of the South* (1892; New York: Oxford University Press, 1988); Leona C. Gable, *From Slavery to the Sorbonne and Beyond: The Life and Writings of Anna J. Cooper* (Northampton, MA: Dept. of History, Smith College, 1982); Karen A. Johnson, *Uplifting the Women and the Race: The Educational Philosophies and Social Activism of Anna Julia Cooper and Nannie Helen Burroughs* (New York: Garland, 2000); Charles Lemert and Esme Bhan, eds., *The Voice of Anna Julia Cooper* (Lanham, MD: Rowman & Littlefield, 1998); Shirley Wilson Logan, ed., *With Pen and Voice: A Critical Anthology of Nineteenth-Century African-American Women* (Carbondale: Southern Illinois University Press, 1995).

Gloria A. Shearin

Cooper, Clarence, Jr. (1934–1978). Novelist. Cooper is known for realistic novels about urban African American life and is sometimes compared with **Chester Himes.** Originally trained as a journalist, Cooper was born in **Detroit, Michigan,** in 1934. He became an editor of the Black newspaper *Chicago Messenger,* but his journalistic career was cut short by his drug use and the amount of time he spent incarcerated. Cooper wrote seven novels, most of which did not attract the critical attention they deserved. Embittered at the string of literary failures, Cooper stopped writing entirely in 1967 and died eleven years later, penniless, alone, and in almost complete obscurity in the 23rd Street YMCA in New York City. None of his books were in print at that time.

This fate hardly seemed likely in 1960, however, when the twenty-six-year-old Cooper published his first novel, *The Scene,* to nearly universal acclaim. Unfortunately, he could not bask in his literary spotlight, for at the time he was languishing in a federal prison. Ultimately, his life came to be punctuated by incarceration and drug addiction. Cooper's editor at Regency House (a publisher of pulp fiction) was Harlan Ellison, who often celebrated Cooper's talent, despite his lack of readers. Cooper's best-known work is arguably *The Scene*, which blends genres and moves from highly stylized poetics to pseudo-documentary passages, as the narrative weaves through flashbacks and "flash-forwards," all the while examining the lives of pimps, prostitutes, cops, and junkies who are all connected by "junk" (heroin).

Cooper's other 1960 novel, *The Syndicate*, follows hit man Andy Sorrel as he attempts to locate the freelancers who pulled off a New Jersey bank robbery. *Weed* (1961) is a matter-of-fact account of a community plagued by drugs and abject poverty. Cooper's final novel, also an acknowledged masterpiece, was *The Farm* (1967), a meditation on prison, addiction, love, and, ultimately, the interrelationship among the three. It is arguably the most experimental of Cooper's books. *The Scene* was rereleased in the 1990s, as was *Black!*, a collection featuring the short novel *The Dark Messenger* (1962) and the sardonic novellas *Yet Princes Follow* (1963) and *Not We Many* (1963).

The life and works of Cooper, along with those of Chester Himes, **Iceberg Slim**, and **Donald Goines**, may be seen as a metaphor for the constant struggle of African Americans in the world and in the literary world. This situation may have been best described in a brief foreword by Harlan Ellison in 1963: "Clarence Cooper, Jr. is black and can not get along with this world. No special star shone at his birth to tell anyone that another dark face or a special talent had come to stare at us and wonder what place it could find for itself. He had to find his own voice for his own message and that message is here."

Resources: Clarence Cooper, Jr.: *Black: The Dark Messenger/Yet Princes Follow/Not We Many* (London: Canongate, 1997); *The Farm* (1967; repr. New York: W. W. Norton, 1998); *The Scene* (1960; repr. New York: W. W. Norton, 1996); *The Weed* and *The Syndicate* (London: Canongate Books, 1998); Harlan Ellison, "Foreword," in *Black! Two Short Novels* (Evanston, IL: Regency Books, 1963).

Marc Leverette

Cooper, J[oan] California (born 193?). Short story writer, novelist, and playwright. Since the early 1970s, Cooper has written six collections of short stories, three novels, and seventeen plays. Her play *Strangers*, also known as *Ahhh, Strangers* (1978), won the Black Playwright of the Year Award, and her second collection of short stories, *Homemade Love* (1986), won an American Book Award. Cooper's works are late twentieth-century manifestations of the folk tradition of African American literature, displaying a unique mix of oral-tradition immediacy, **feminism**, Christianity, the importance of family, critique of class inequalities that doesn't deny personal responsibility, and a "blues sensibility" of optimism under hardship.

It is this unusual, and sometimes quirky, mix of elements conveyed in a quiet intimacy—an intimacy similar to that created by listening to a story told by a friend—that has most attracted many readers. Through intentional misspellings, malapropisms, fragments, and other devices, Cooper connects an oral intimacy to the **vernacular** tradition of providing an insider's view of communities whose "non-standard" languages indicate educational, economic, and political marginalization, yet also a resilience and insightful "folk wisdom" that calls the imputed "superiority" of "standard" into question. In this regard, her writing is like that of **Zora Neale Hurston**. Cooper manifests the African American vernacular tradition of telling seemingly simple stories that show how disenfranchised communities not only survive but can inspire and educate those willing to pay attention.

These characteristics situate Cooper's work as descending from the **spirituals**, work songs, and **folktales** that promote African American vitality and coherence while countering the rhetoric of racism. To this tradition, Cooper adds both a consistent feminist critique of patriarchy and occasional graphic depictions of sexuality. These depictions range from celebrations of women's sexuality to scenes of degradation. The tone Cooper takes toward women in degrading scenes, however, remains matter-of-fact, maintaining a sort of documentary "distance" that refrains from judging these actions. This reticence to judge acknowledges that poverty, racism, and patriarchy sometime leave women with few socially admirable options. What Cooper's stories do not refrain from judging, however, are people's motives, and this sometimes results in a rather old-fashioned moralizing that some critics find heavy-handed.

Another criticism is that Cooper's optimism and belief in the agency of the individual situates her in the **Booker T. Washington** tradition of unduly minimizing the effects of the racism and poverty into which many African Americans have been—and continue to be—born. From this point of view, Cooper's emphasis on hard work, frugality, honesty, and belief in God lets the dominant "White" society off too easily. However, her characters are not blind to class and racial injustices, and the "successes" of her characters are often limited. In many ways, Cooper expresses the **blues** tradition of turning hardship and loss into success, but it is a success that never leaves sorrow behind.

Cooper's work argues that although African Americans struggle under the injustices of racism, and although women struggle under the injustices of patriarchy, individuals cannot be reduced to categories, and the complexities and possibilities of individuals are beyond capture. From this comes an appreciation of others *as individuals*, an appreciation of their quirks and their potentials, and a connecting with others as part of an empathy that Cooper calls "love."

Love in Cooper's work intertwines with Christian faith while sympathizing with those disregarded or rejected by society. This is apparent in her earliest works. The plot, for instance, of Cooper's *How Now?* (produced in 1973 by the Black Repertory Group of Berkeley, which produced most of Cooper's early plays) details the conflict between a disabled girl who wants to continue her education and the girl's mother, who wants her daughter to become pregnant to qualify for welfare benefits. *The Unintended* (c. 1983) tells about the love that unexpectedly results when a thirty-five-year-old virgin's need for money leads to her sexual involvement with a hunchback.

Cooper's work shows not only the value of paying attention to—and ultimately empathizing with—those ignored by society but also how things are often not as they seem. These themes appear in the short story version of Cooper's play *Loved to Death* (date unknown), which appeared under the same title in Cooper's first collection of short stories, *A Piece of Mine* (1984). This ten-page short story, quintessential Cooper, is conveyed in a modified oral tradition of a narrator speaking to "Mr. Notebook." The narrator is an "all crooked" woman whose sister, Zalina, has the apparent luck of great beauty. But the father tries to rape Zalina; Zalina leaves home and marries; and then the White boss of the husband rapes her and kills the husband. Zalina returns home and dies of alcoholism. The narrator raises Zalina's children and also experiences sex with a local man who had initially come to visit Zalina but then switched to the narrator. In this "oral" story Cooper packs class, **race**, **gender**, **feminist criticism**, oral sex, the Bible, the importance of education, a counterintuitive understanding of beauty, and physical disability that ends with the "blues optimism" of the narrator going outside to run with one of Zalina's children.

Although Cooper has spent much of her adult life in California, many of her stories seem to take place in rural **Texas** (Marshall), where she lived for a year as a child and for eight years as an adult. Cooper refuses to divulge her age, is vague about how many times she has been married, and is generally reticent with personal information. The broad arc of her work has tended toward increasing "Christian moralizing," but this predominates only in her second novel, *In Search of Satisfaction* (1994).

Cooper's short stories have received more acclaim than her novels, but her more extended analyses of people and motives in, for instance, the novels *Family* (1991) and especially *The Wake of the Wind* (1998) are historically grounded studies of the horror and complexity of **slavery** and its aftereffects. Both novels could productively companion such **slave narratives** as those by **Harriet Jacobs** and **Frederick Douglass**. With her sixth short story collection, *The Future Has a Past: Stories* (2000) Cooper remains a most unique, engaging, and underappreciated African American voice.

Resources: J. California Cooper: *Family* (New York: Doubleday, 1991); *The Future Has a Past: Stories* (New York: Doubleday, 2000); *Homemade Love* (New York: St. Martin's, 1986); *In Search of Satisfaction* (New York: Doubleday, 1994); *The Matter Is Life* (New York: Doubleday, 1991); *A Piece of Mine* (1984; New York: Doubleday, 1992); *Some Love, Some Pain, Sometime* (New York: Doubleday/Anchor, 1995); *The Wake of the Wind* (New York: Anchor, 1998); Keith Lawrence, "J. California Cooper," in *Dictionary of Literary Biography*, vol. 212 (Detroit: Gale, 1998); Hans Ostrom, "Author's Feeling Flourishes in Texas" (review of *The Matter Is Life* and interview with Cooper), *Soundlife*, Sunday supp., *Morning News Tribune* (Tacoma, WA), Oct. 6, 1991, p. 11.

Kevin M. Hickey

Coppin, Fanny Marion Jackson (c. 1837–1913). Educator and activist. Though primarily known for her distinguished career as a pioneering African

American educator, Coppin produced some literary work—most notably her autobiographical *Reminiscences of School Life, and Hints on Teaching.*

Born a slave in **Washington, D.C.,** Coppin's grandfather, a prominent Black caterer named John Orr, purchased freedom for himself and five children, but he refused to purchase the freedom of Coppin's mother because she had given birth to Fanny. One of Coppin's aunts, Sarah Orr Clark, purchased Coppin's freedom and sent her north to live with an uncle, John Orr. When the Orrs moved to Newport, Rhode Island, Coppin found domestic work in the home of the wealthy George and Mary Calvert. The Calverts had no children of there own, were well connected to the **Boston, Massachusetts,** literati, and took an interest in Coppin's education. Coppin eventually spent a year at the Rhode Island State Normal School and then attended Oberlin College, beginning in the preparatory program in 1860.

At Oberlin, Coppin distinguished herself not only as a scholar but also as a citizen: she tutored other students, gave night classes for free Blacks, and was elected class poet. She took an A.B. degree in 1865—one of the first African American women to do so. She soon found work as a teacher at the Institute for Colored Youth, in **Philadelphia, Pennsylvania**, where she gained the respect of both colleagues and students. In 1869, she was named principal of the school.

Over the next three decades, Coppin raised funds, established a curriculum for training teachers and an Industrial Department, and made the Institute one of the most respected Black schools in the North. She worked tirelessly for women's education and, later, for suffrage. She also became an active voice in the African Methodist Episcopal Church and is credited with saving the church's paper, the *Christian Recorder*, when it fell on financial hard times in the late 1870s. She married to Rev. Levi Coppin in 1881 and, rather than leave her position, convinced her Baltimore-based husband to transfer to Philadelphia. Only in the 1890s, when her health began to suffer, did she slow her pace. Coppin retired in 1902, when her husband accepted a missionary assignment in South Africa. After a year of work in and around Cape Town, the Coppins toured Europe and returned home. Coppin lived most of the rest of her life in Philadelphia, where, though seriously ill, she composed most of her *Reminiscences.*

Coppin State University in Baltimore is named for her.

Resources: Fanny Jackson Coppin, *Reminiscences of School Life* (1913; repr. New York: G. K. Hall, 1995); Levi Coppin, *Unwritten History* (1919; repr. New York: Negro Universities Press, 1968); Leslie H. Fishel, Jr., "Fanny Jackson Coppin," in *Notable American Women*, ed. Edward T. James (Cambridge, MA: Harvard University Press, 1971), vol. 1, 383–384; Linda M. Perkins, *Fanny Jackson Coppin and the Institute for Colored Youth, 1865–1902* (New York: Garland, 1987).

Eric Gardner

Corbin, Steven (1953–1995). Novelist and short story writer. Corbin's work is recognized in part for raising issues of racism, sexism, and homophobia.

Steven Corbin was born October 3, 1953, in Jersey City, New Jersey, to Warren Corbin and Yvonne O'Hare. He attended Essex County College from 1973 to 1975, then pursued a degree in film at the University of Southern California from 1975 through 1977 but did not complete his degree. He held various odd jobs, including secretary and taxi driver, while pursuing a writing career. Corbin was an instructor in fiction writing at the University of California at Los Angeles and served as the fiction editor for the *Southern California Anthology* in 1985.

Though he was influenced by **Toni Morrison**, **Alice Walker**, and **Richard Wright**, the greatest influence upon Corbin appears to have been **James Baldwin**. "Reading the works of James Baldwin convinced him that he should write about being black and gay" (McGovern, 108). Corbin takes issues that are well established in the Black community and makes them public knowledge. In 1989 Corbin published his first novel, *No Easy Place to Be*, in which he uses historical facts to cement his depiction of the tensions faced by his characters. Situated during the **Harlem Renaissance**, *No Easy Place to Be* features a party thrown by **Carl Van Vechten**, rallies for **Marcus Garvey**, and the famous Cotton Club in **Harlem, New York**, as settings in this novel. Like the period it depicts, *No Easy Place to Be* ends with the stock market crash of 1929. Alyson Publications published his second novel, *Fragments That Remain* (1993). In *Fragments*, Corbin illuminates the intercultural issue of discrimination based upon the lightness or darkness of one's skin tone. In his final work *A Hundred Days from Now* (1994), Corbin tackles the personal issue of the HIV-positive gay male. The title of the book refers to the duration of one of the main characters (Sergio's) treatment, or protocol, for the life-threatening complications of AIDS.

Corbin also published several short stories: "Upward Bound," in *Breaking Ice: An Anthology of Contemporary African-American Fiction*, edited by **Terry McMillan** (1990); "Coming Full Circle," in *More Like Minds*, edited by Ben Goldstein (1991); and the posthumously published "Jazz," in *Sundays at Seven: Choice Words from a Different Light's Gay Writer Series*, edited by R. Mieczkowski (1996). He was nominated for a 1994 Lambda Literary Award in the category of gay male fiction.

Corbin died August 31, 1995, at the age of forty-one, from complications of AIDS. (*See* **Gay Literature**; **Queer Theory**.)

Resources: Michael Bronski, "Review of *A Hundred Days from Now* by Steven Corbin," *Lambda Book Report* 4, no. 5 (July–Aug. 1994), 20; Steven Corbin: *Fragments That Remain* (New York: Alyson Publications, 1993); *A Hundred Days from Now* (Berkeley, CA: Consortium Books, 1994); *No Easy Place to Be* (New York: Simon and Schuster, 1989); Terence McGovern, "Steven Corbin," in *Contemporary African American Novelists: A Bio-Bibliographical Critical Sourcebook*, ed. Emmanuel S. Nelson (Westport, CT: Greenwood Press, 1999); "Review of *Fragments That Remain*," *Publishers Weekly*, Jan. 3, 1993, p. 295.

Denisa Chatman-Riley

Cornish, Sam[uel] James (born 1935). Poet and children's writer. Cornish was a significant participant in the **Black Arts Movement**. Born in **Baltimore, Maryland**, at a time when segregation determined much of a young African American boy's fate, Cornish grew up primarily under the influence and care of his mother and grandmother, his father having died when he was young. He dropped out of high school during the first semester of his freshman year and decided instead to pursue his education on his own. After serving in the Medical Corps of the U.S. Army from the ages of twenty-three to twenty-five, Cornish took classes at Goddard College and Northwestern University.

Cornish began publishing his verse in the mid-1960s, his collection *Generations* (1964, Beanbag Press) garnering the most attention. When several of his poems were anthologized in *Black Fire: An Anthology of Afro-American Writing* (1968, Morrow), edited by LeRoi Jones (**Amiri Baraka**) and **Larry Neal**, he became associated with the revolutionary writers of the Black Arts Movement. Much of his writing embraces the Black aesthetic of this time, charged with political energy and acerbic in its delivery. Cornish reveals the hypocrisy of American democracy with a simplicity and directness that appealed to a popular Black audience of the late 1960s and early 1970s. Though many of his poems deal with famous civil rights activists from **Marcus Garvey** to **Malcolm X**, Cornish also wrestles with the hardships of common Black folk, employing the **vernacular** of his urban childhood. Additionally, his family members find their way into much of his poetry, his older brother taking particular prominence above noted authors **Richard Wright** and **James Baldwin**.

In his autobiographical work *1935: A Memoir*, published in 1990, Cornish blends the prose and poetry to tell his life story, a story that actually moves beyond the boundaries of his own life. Though he was a mere child in the 1930s, he writes of **Harlem Renaissance** players and musicians with an intimacy that belies his age. He catalogs the tragedies of the **Great Depression** as if he had witnessed them himself.

Throughout his life Cornish has demonstrated a devotion to Black youth. In 1969 he edited an anthology of poetry and prose, *Chicory: Young Voices from the Black Ghetto*, written by urban youth attending his creative writing classes. In 1970 he published his first juvenile literature, *Your Hand in Mine*, with Harcourt.

Resources: Sam Cornish: *Cross a Parted Sea: Poems* (Cambridge, MA: Zoland Books, 1996); *Folks Like Me* (Cambridge, MA: Zoland Books, 1993); *Generations: Poems* (1964; Boston: Beacon Press, 1971); *Grandmother's Pictures* (New York: Simon and Schuster, 1976); *1935* (Boston: Ploughshares Press, 1990); *Songs of Jubilee: New and Selected Poems* (1969–1983) (Greensboro, NC: Unicorn Press, 1986); *Your Hand in Mine* (New York: Harcourt, Brace & World, 1970); Sam Cornish and Lucian W. Dixon, eds., *Chicory: Young Voices from the Black Ghetto* (New York: Association Press, 1969); LeRoi Jones and Larry Neal, eds., *Black Fire: An Anthology of African American Writing* (New York: Morrow, 1968); "Sam Cornish," in *Afro-American Poets Since 1955*, vol. 41 of *Dictionary of Literary Biography*, ed. Trudier Harris and Thadious M. Davis

(Detroit: Gale, 1985); Afaa M. Weaver, ed., *Obsidian III: Literature in the African Diaspora* 1, no. 2 (Fall–Winter 2000), special Sam Cornish issue.

Theresa L. Burriss

Cornish, Samuel Eli (c. 1790–1858). Editor and activist. Cornish helped found and edit the first African American newspaper and was a major force in antebellum Black journalism.

Born to free Black parents in Delaware, Cornish moved to **Philadelphia, Pennsylvania**, as a young man and studied with Rev. John Gloucester of the First African Presbyterian Church; he received a probationary license to preach in 1819. After preaching in Pennsylvania and Maryland, he moved in 1821 to New York, where he founded the New Demeter Street Presbyterian Church. Ordained in 1822, he married Jane Livingston and became active in the community, especially the African free schools.

Cornish's desire to further Black education and civil rights led him to found, with John Russwurm, the first African American newspaper, *Freedom's Journal*, in March 1827. The weekly boldly listed Cornish and Russwurm on the masthead as "Editors and Proprietors," and the initial issue proclaimed that, as African Americans, "We wish to plead our own cause." In addition to printing items of local interest, the paper was consciously designed to reach out to Blacks across the North, and agents from Philadelphia to **Boston, Massachusetts** (including radical **David Walker**) actively solicited support. In addition to current news, *Freedom's Journal* published biography, history, and poetry, but it focused on writing that considered a range of political questions. Cornish's writing against colonization was especially noteworthy—and scathing. When he stepped down from the editor's post in September 1827, citing health and career demands, some thought that he had challenged powerful colonizationists too much. Russwurm, who stayed, was more friendly to colonization; indeed, the paper folded in 1829 because he moved to Liberia.

Soon after, Cornish left New Demeter to preach across New York and New Jersey. When *Freedom's Journal* folded, he attempted to publish a monthly, *Rights of All*, but it lasted only six months. The *Colored American* represented his last venture into newspaper publishing; he helped found the paper and edited it from 1837 to 1839. Taken together, founding these **newspapers** represents a central early achievement in African American journalism.

A major African American voice, Cornish was involved in both local and national societies—from the New York Vigilance Committee to the American Anti-Slavery Society to the American Missionary Society. Outspoken and blunt, however, he was often a lightning rod for controversy, withdrawing from some organizations because he believed they were not radical enough and fighting with others because he found them to be too radical. By 1850, Cornish had disagreed vociferously with William Lloyd Garrison, David Ruggles, the Tappan brothers, several African Americans who favored all-Black conventions, and a growing number of prominent Presbyterian ministers who supported colonization.

Cornish gradually lost his early position as a leader among African Americans in the North. His ministerial career and his family life after he left New Demeter were also difficult. He served briefly at churches in Philadelphia (Gloucester's), Newark, and New York. Cornish also settled for a time in Belleville, New Jersey. By 1850, his wife and three of his four children had died. While the 1850 census taker estimated his property to be worth $12,000, other records suggest that he was often in financial trouble. (*See* **Abolitionist Movement; Back-to-Africa Movement.**)

Resources: James Oliver Horton and Lois E. Horton, *In Hope of Liberty: Culture, Community, and Protest Among Northern Free Blacks, 1790–1860* (New York: Oxford University Press, 1997); C. Peter Ripley, ed., *The Black Abolitionist Papers*, vol. 1 (Chapel Hill: University of North Carolina Press, 1985); David Everett Swift, *Black Prophets of Justice: Activist Clergy Before the Civil War* (Baton Rouge: Louisiana State University Press, 1989).

Eric Gardner

Corrothers, James (1869–1917). Poet, novelist, journalist, autobiographer, and minister. Born in Cass County, Michigan, and raised by his staunchly religious grandfather (of Cherokee, Irish, and Scottish descent) in predominantly White South Haven, Michigan, Corrothers was exposed to the harshness of racism at an early age. Yet despite this early discrimination, and the poverty and frequent hardships that he experienced throughout his life, Corrothers remained an optimistic voice in African American literature. After high school, he supported himself with odd jobs while educating himself by reading the works of his favorite authors, the poets Alfred, Lord Tennyson, Oliver Goldsmith, Robert Burns, Henry Wadsworth Longfellow, and James Whitcomb Riley. His career as a writer started when the author Henry Demarest Lloyd met the promising youth while he was working as a bootblack, and arranged for the publication of Corrothers' poem "The Soldier's Excuse" in the *Chicago Tribune*. He quickly became a reporter for the *Chicago Tribune* but was fired after publication of his first story, when he protested the editorial changes made by a White reporter in order to maintain preconceived racial stereotypes.

Carrothers entered Northwestern University, but he never completed his degree. At the Columbian Exposition in **Chicago, Illinois**, in 1893, he was greatly impressed by the orator **Frederick Douglass** and was befriended by the poets **Paul Laurence Dunbar** and **James E. Campbell**, who influenced and supported his writing throughout the rest of his career. In 1896, after the success of the publication of "De Carvin," a dialect sketch, in the *Chicago Evening Journal*, Corrothers entered, despite deep misgivings, into the brief but profitable tradition of dialect writing made popular by contempories such as Dunbar. (He rejected the form entirely in 1910 for more verse and nondialect writing.) He never was able to support himself solely through his writing, and did manual labor to supplement his income and support his families from three marriages. Always a man of faith, he later became a Methodist minister and, after a falling out with that church, a Baptist minister. Because of his participation in the dialect tradition (ironically, the middle-class Corrothers was raised speaking Standard or "White" English and had to consult a book to write in dialect), he has historically been seen as a problematic figure in African American literature. Thus, he fell out of the literary canon shortly after his death, despite his popularity at the time.

Carrothers' only novel, *The Black Cat Club*, a narrative that centers on the meetings of uneducated Black men who have as their leader Sandy Jenkins, a dialect poet nicknamed "Doc," has been largely dismissed because of its "characterizations that owe more to minstrelsy than to African-American life, creating images of ignorance and vulgarity that caricature as much as they represent 'Negro Life'" (Bruce, 665). Only recently have critics such as Bruce and Gaines called for a reassessment of his work, revealing its important ambivalence: "Portraying his understanding of the problems of literary creation and reputation, Corrothers made *Black Cat Club* highly complex and reflexive . . . deforming the form, Corrothers gave concrete shape to his own discomfort with the bases upon which a growing number of literary reputations, including his own, appeared to rest" (Bruce, 670). Abandoning his ties to the dialect tradition, Carrothers went on to write poetry that focused on the sharp division between the American dream and the reality of Black oppression, and consequently was printed only in Black publications such as **The Crisis**, *Century*, and *Colored American*. In 1916, he released a well-received **autobiography**, *In Spite of Handicap*, which remained hopeful about Blacks' ability to triumph over adversity through fortitude and hard work.

Though he does not match Dunbar and Campbell in talent, Corrothers has historical significance, as Yarborough points out: "his career vividly reveals how black writers striving for a broad audience in the late-nineteenth and early-twentieth century America had to cope with the racial stereotypes which shaped the expectations of white editors and readers alike" (52). He died of a stroke at age forty-seven. (*See* **Vernacular**.)

Resources: Dickson D. Bruce, "James Corrothers Reads a Book; or, the Lives of Sandy Jenkins," *African American Review* 26, no. 4 (Winter 1992), 665–673; James Corrothers: *The Black Cat Club* (New York: Funk and Wagnalls, 1902); *In Spite of Handicap* (New York: Doran, 1916); Kevin Gaines, "Assimilationist Minstrelsy as Racial Uplift Ideology: James D. Corrothers's Literary Quest for Black Leadership," *American Quarterly* 45, no. 3 (Sept. 1993), 341–369; Richard Yarborough, "James Corrothers," in *Dictionary of Literary Biography*, vol. 50, *Afro-American Writers Before the Harlem Renaissance*, ed. Trudier Harris (Detroit: Gale, 1986).

Alicia D. Williamson

Cortez, Jayne (born 1936). Poet, visual artist, and performance artist. Cortez, a poet and performance artist, combines elements of **jazz** and **blues** in her work, in which she promotes humanitarian themes of social justice and empowerment.

Cortez was born in Fort Huachuca, Arizona, on May 19, 1936. Her family moved to California, where she grew up in the Watts section of **Los Angeles,**

California. Her parents loved jazz, so Cortez developed a profound admiration for the musical form, citing artists such as **Duke Ellington**, Charlie Parker, **Billie Holliday**, Lena Horne, Thelonious Monk, **Count Basie**, and Jimmy Lunceford as inspiring her. (*See* **Gillespie, Dizzy, Charlie Parker, and Thelonius Monk**.) She attended Manual Arts High School, an art/music high school, and Compton Junior College, where she began painting and drawing. She studied drama at Ebony Showcase in Watts, where she also participated in writers' workshops. She became active in the **Civil Rights Movement** in the 1960s. Cortez worked a wide assortment of jobs, having experiences and gaining insights that later informed her work: she worked in a shirt factory and a belt factory, as a waitress and as a telephone operator, and performed clerical work. Cortez moved to New York City. She taught at Rutgers University from 1977 to 1983 and has lectured at many colleges.

In 1954 Cortez married jazz saxophone legend Ornette Coleman, whom she divorced in 1964. They had a son, Denardo, who is an accomplished drummer. Subsequently, Cortez married sculptor Melvin Edwards in 1975; he has created illustrations for some of her books.

Cortez has traveled to many countries in Latin America and Africa. Influences from travel are evident in her work. Cortez still performs readings and gives lectures and appears at jazz festivals around the world.

Cortez has founded and promoted several organizations and institutions. She cofounded the Watts Repertory Theater in 1964 and serves as its artistic director. She founded Bola Press in 1972 and helped to establish the Organization of Women Writers of Africa in 1991.

Cortez received a National Endowment for the Arts Fellowship in Poetry in 1979, a New York Foundation for the Arts Award in 1973 and 1981, a Before Columbus Foundation American Book Award for Excellence in Literature in 1980, an award from the Afrikan Poetry Theatre in 1994, and a Fannie Lou Hamer Award in 1994.

Cortez's work is an artful combination of several distinct expressive modes; it also encapsulates her life's experience, ideals, and passions. A singular intellectual coherence in content and expressive style characterizes her poetic art. Cortez's poetry is an amalgamation of visual art, dance, music, poetry, orature, and performance. She enacts the idioms of both jazz and blues music; her poetry is the transformation of experience, feeling, mood, and process into words. Cortez assumes a Pan-Africanist stance and deftly integrates African cosmology and iconography into her work. She is overtly political and often polemical; she engages in all of the weighty social issues of the time; ultimately her work maintains a hopefulness about the future and leaves room for the possibility of positive change.

Cortez's first collection of poems, *Pissstained Stairs and the Monkey Man's Wares* (1969), describes ghetto life, provides social protest, and expresses solidarity with the urban working class. Other poems express a love of blues and jazz; there are tributes to **Bessie Smith**, **Billie Holiday**, **Leadbelly**, Charlie Parker, and other jazz and blues icons. Her second collection of poems, *Festivals* *and Funerals*, published in 1971, presents the fusion between African American and African influences along with the element of the surreal and an invocation of ritual. The collection includes a critique of **colonialism** and tributes to **Malcom X** and Patrice Lumumba. In *Scarifications* (1973), there is a strong anti–**Vietnam War** message. Other poems explore urban life and culture and criticize U.S. imperialism. *Mouth on Paper* (1977) incorporates forms from traditional African "praise poems" and elements of Yoruba cosmology. There are tributes to **Martin Luther King, Jr.**, Miles Davis and Duke Ellington. Her poems of this era evoke orature and appeal to sound. In *Firespitter* (1982) the poems are highly surrealistic and impressionistic in imagery. Cortez challenges the abuse and rape of women and writes about the Miami **race riots**. *Coagulations* (1984) contains old and new poems in which Cortez confronts militarism, globalization, and environmental issues. *Poetic Magnetic* (1991) contains poems that Cortez recorded earlier; in some of them the words take a visual structure on the page. Her latest collections include *Somewhere in Advance of Nowhere* (1996) and *Jazz Fan Looks Back* (2002).

Cortez is both a writer and a performer—she has recorded and published readings of her work and has given performances of her poetry with musical accompaniment.

Resources: Fahamisha Patricia Brown, "Jayne Cortez," *American Women Writers*, vol. 5, supp., ed. Carol Hurd Green and Mary Grimley Mason (New York: Continuum, 1994), 233–234; Jayne Cortez: *Coagulations: New and Selected Poems* (New York: Thunder's Mouth Press, 1984); *Festivals and Funerals* (New York: Cortez, 1971); *Firespitter: Poems* (New York: Bola Press, 1982); *Jazz Fan Looks Back* (Brooklyn, NY: Hanging Loose Press, 2002); *Mouth on Paper* (New York: Bola Press, 1977); *Pissstained Stairs and the Monkey Man's Wares* (New York: Phrase Text, 1969); *Poetic Magnetic* (New York: Bola Press, 1991); *Scarifications* (New York: Cortez, 1973); *Somewhere in Advance of Nowhere* (London: Serpent's Tail, 1996); Tom Lavazzi, "Cortez, Jayne," in *Encyclopedia of World Literature in the 20th Century*, ed. Steven R. Serafin, 3rd ed. (Detroit: St. James Press, 1999), 537–538; D. H. Melham, "A MELUS Profile and Interview: Jayne Cortez," MELUS 21, no. 1 (Spring 1996), 71; D. H. Melham, ed., *Heroism in the New Black Poetry* (Lexington: University Press of Kentucky, 1990).

Kimberly Black-Parker

Cosby, William (Bill) (born 1937). Comedian, actor, writer, television producer, and product spokesperson. Cosby is one of the most successful comedians and storytellers in American history. His presence on stage and screen and in books has appealed to audiences partly because of themes in his comedy that examine African American culture but also transcend it. Cosby was born in **Philadelphia, Pennsylvania**. He served in the Navy from 1956 to 1960, briefly attended Temple University, became a professional standup comedian in 1963, and appeared on television and released recordings of his comedy in the 1960s.

Although Cosby is a popular entertainer and not primarily a literary figure, his work continues the tradition of **James Weldon Johnson** and **Langston**

Hughes, exploring African American culture through narrated experiences and situating it in the larger American literary mosaic. His mode of storytelling—criticism through verbal and situational satire—echoes that of Mark Twain. Cosby has been critical of artists whose appeal is based upon personal attacks or profanity. In a 1993 *Newsweek* interview he said, "Getting people to laugh without being vulgar and cruel is the creative process at its best." He manages to discuss Black life not merely as a reproduction of White life, nor as a repudiation of society, but as a unique and important part of the American mosaic.

Cosby's stories introduced White America to positive and negative issues of African American life. His first prominent acting role was in the television series *I Spy* (1965–1968). *The Bill Cosby Show* followed in 1969–1971. However, it was as a producer and comedian that Cosby's storytelling skills became clear.

The Cosby Show (1984–1992) established Cosby as one of America's great narrators. The series and its spin-off, *A Different World* (1987–1993), used its plots, settings, and characters to present aspects of African American culture, including artwork, music, historical events, and historically Black colleges and universities. At the same time that his shows projected racial pride, they also managed to convey that many of these issues were important regardless of race, such as sustaining the family unit when both parents work outside of the home. This universal appeal is also evident in Cosby's books, such as *Fatherhood* (1986) and *Time Flies* (1988), whose themes include parenting and aging.

Cosby's critics have complained that his work is not confrontational or edgy enough. In the 1990s, television shows such as *In Living Color* criticized Cosby's portrayals as bland and unrealistic. In 2004, Cosby received significant public attention when he candidly voiced many of the observations he had been making in his works, including lack of emphasis on education in some Black households, misplaced emphasis on material goods, and the failure to rear children properly as some of the issues Black America needed to address.

Resources: Bill Adler, *The Cosby Wit: His Life and Humor* (New York: Carroll and Graf, 1986); "Black Is Bountiful: Fox Focuses on African-American Shows, but at What Cost?" (interview with Cosby), *Newsweek*, Dec. 6, 1993, p. 59; Donna Brett-Gibson, "Cover Story: The Cos, Family Man for the 80's," *USA Today*, Dec. 23, 1986; Bill Cosby: *Fatherhood* (Garden City, NY: Doubleday, 1986); *Love and Marriage* (New York: Doubleday, 1989); *Time Flies* (New York: Doubleday, 1987); Brad Darrrach, "Cosby!" *Life*, June 1985, 35–42; Linda K. Fuller, *"The Cosby Show": Audiences, Impact, and Implications* (Westport, CT: Greenwood Press, 1992); Dan Goodgame, "'I Do Believe in Control'; Cosby Is a Man Who Gets Laughs and Results—By Doing Things His Way," *Time*, Sept. 28, 1987, pp. 56–57; Cynthia Griffin and George Hill, "Bill Cosby: In Our Living Rooms for 20 Years," in *Ebony Images: Black Americans and Televisions* (Los Angeles: Daystar Publications, 1986); Sut Jhally and Justin Lewis, *Enlightened Racism: "The Cosby Show," Audiences, and the Myth of the American Dream* (Boulder, CO: Westview Press, 1992).

Gregory W. Fowler

Cose, Ellis (born 1950). Journalist, essayist, and novelist. In the last decade of the twentieth century, Ellis Cose became a leading articulator of the African American aesthetic in the popular media. He has published several important books, and he is a contributing editor of *Newsweek*. A native of **Chicago, Illinois**, he has published his books on racial views in America in a steady stream since the early 1990s. *The Press* (1989) presents an early history of the media. *A Nation of Strangers* (1992) is a history of immigration in America. His best-selling work, *The Rage of a Privileged Class* (1993), revealed the complexities in the sources of anger among African Americans who were thought to have achieved the American dream. *A Man's World* (1995) took on the complexities of **gender** relationships. *Color-Blind: Seeing Beyond Race in a Race-Obsessed World* (1997) discussed how Americans might best begin to work toward **Martin Luther King, Jr.**'s dream of a united county. The *New York Times Book Review* called it "a book this country desperately needs, one with genuine healing potential," and included *Color-Blind* among its recommendations for 1997. That same year Cose edited an essay collection entitled *The Darden Dilemma* (1997). (*See* **Darden, Christopher.**) In the midst of this most prolific output, Cose wrote a courtroom drama titled *The Best Defense* (1998). He resumed his reflections on African American life in 2002 with his intriguingly titled *The Envy of the World*, a study of and advice guide for African American men. In 2004, Cose published two non-fiction studies: *A Bone to Pick: Of Forgiveness, Reconciliation, Reparation, and Revenge* and *Beyond Brown v. Board: The Final Battle for Excellence in American Education*.

Given his prodigious output, it is not surprising that Cose has been honored with grants and/or fellowships from the Ford Foundation, the Andrew Mellon Foundation, the Rockefeller Foundation, and the Aspen Institute for Humanistic Studies, and has received many journalism awards, including the University of Missouri Medal for Career Excellence and Distinguished Service in Journalism, four National Association of Black Journalists first-place awards (for commentary and for magazine writing), and two Clarion awards (for commentary and writings on the incarceration crisis). Cose was named the 2002 winner of the New York Association of Black Journalists lifetime achievement award, winner of the 2003 award for best magazine feature from the National Association of Black Journalists, and winner of two New York Association of Black Journalists first-place awards in 2003 for commentary and magazine features. He currently lives in New York.

Resources: Ellis Cose: *The Best Defense* (New York: HarperCollins, 1998); *Bone to Pick: Of Forgiveness, Reconciliation, Reparation, and Revenge* (New York: Atria, 2004); *Color-Blind* (New York: HarperCollins, 1997); *The Envy of the World* (New York: Atria, 2002); *A Man's World* (New York: HarperCollins, 1995); *The Rage of a Privileged Class* (New York: HarperCollins, 1993); Ellis Cose, ed., *The Darden Dilemma: 12 Black Writers on Justice, Race, and Conflicting Loyalties* (New York: HarperPerennial, 1997).

Piper G. Huguley-Riggins

Cotter, Joseph Seamon, Jr. (1895–1919). Poet. Though he published only one book of poetry during his short life, Cotter is recognized as an important voice in early twentieth-century Black poetry.

Cotter was born to poet and educator Joseph Seamon Cotter, Sr., and Maria Cox Cotter, in Louisville, Kentucky—supposedly in the room where **Paul Laurence Dunbar**, visiting the elder Cotter the year before, had given his first poetry reading in **the South**. While Cotter's father had struggled for both education and economic stability, Cotter and his older sister, Florence, were raised in a solidly middle-class home. Cotter attended schools in the same system in which his father had taught and become a well-respected principal, and he grew up in a house focused on literacy. With Florence, who taught him to read early in life, he explored the Cotters' large library and read widely—especially poetry.

Cotter graduated from Louisville's Central High School in 1911 (second in his class) and followed his sister to Fisk University in **Nashville, Tennessee**. Fisk, already recognized as one of the most important historically Black colleges, was still reeling from student protests held in response to the dismissal of six Black teachers by White university president George Gates. It was amidst this environment of growing race consciousness by the youth whom **W.E.B. Du Bois** would see as the **"Talented Tenth"** that Cotter's worldview began to mature.

In his second year at Fisk, Cotter was diagnosed with tuberculosis and returned home. His sister soon followed, and she died of tuberculosis on December 16, 1914. Florence Cotter's death—and probably a recognition of his own limited time—led Cotter to focus his remaining years on writing; indeed, his "To Florence" is generally recognized as his first serious poem. His only book, *The Band of Gideon and Other Lyrics*, was published in 1918—less than a year before his death.

Though Cotter's literary production was cut short, some late twentieth-century critics have argued that he is a notable figure, especially given his roots in the **dialect poetry** of Dunbar and his father, and his place on the cusp of the **Harlem Renaissance**'s rethinking of Black aesthetics. While *The Band of Gideon* contains masterful poems in traditional forms, it also holds significant technical experimentation. Its consciousness of **race** and rich frame of reference also move significantly beyond much nineteenth-century Black poetry. The title figure—the Gideon of the Old Testament who fiercely defended the Israelites—is placed in dialogue with both complex poems on race and artistry (most notably, "The Mulatto to His Critics") and reminders, as in "Sonnet to Negro Soldiers," of the debate over Black troops in **World War I**. This last poem was featured in the June 1918 special issue of Du Bois's **The Crisis** devoted to issues surrounding African American soldiers; its subject matter was also played out in Cotter's posthumously published one-act play, *On the Fields of France*.

Resources: Joseph Seamon Cotter, Jr., *Complete Poems of Joseph Seamon Cotter, Jr.*, ed. James Robert Payne (Athens: University of Georgia Press, 1990); Joseph Seamon Cotter, Sr., "Joseph Seamon Cotter, Jr.," in *Caroling Dusk: An Anthology of Verse by*

Negro Poets, ed. Countee Cullen (New York: Harper & Brothers, 1927), 99–100; James Robert Payne, "Joseph Seamon Cotter, Jr.," *Dictionary of Literary Biography*, vol. 50 (Detroit: Gale, 1986), 70–73.

Eric Gardner

Cotter, Joseph Seamon, Sr. (1861–1949). Educator, storyteller, and poet. Cotter is generally remembered today as a disciple of **Paul Laurence Dunbar**, though this characterization significantly oversimplifies his career.

Born to a White father and a free Black mother outside of Bardstown, Kentucky, Cotter was raised by his mother in Louisville. Poverty forced him to leave school at age eight, and his early work—picking rags and then working in a brickyard—exposed him to violence and racism. Still, buoyed by his mother's storytelling and his own love of language (he had learned to read at four), he left a succession of jobs—from teamster to prizefighter—to attend night school in 1883. Cotter began teaching in 1885 even as he continued his own studies. In 1889, he took a teaching position at Louisville's Western Colored School and was eventually named principal at the Paul Laurence Dunbar School, a position he held until 1911.

Cotter married Maria F. Cox in 1891, and the couple had three children: Florence Olivia in 1893, Joseph, Jr., in 1895, and Leonidas in 1899. Cotter worked tirelessly in the community, helping to organize "Little Africa," an all-Black section in Parkland on the edge of Louisville, and promoting Black education.

Cotter's early poems appeared in the *Louisville Courier-Journal* and the *National Baptist Magazine*, and his first collection, *A Rhyming*, was published locally in 1895. While these poems—formal verse, with emphasis on the **ballad**—are notable neither for technique nor for content, they nonetheless gained Cotter some prominence and aided the publication of his second collection, *Links of Friendship* (1898). Reprinting some of the poems from his initial book, *Links* added additional formal pieces, children's verse, and poems that considered **race** more explicitly. Cotter had hosted Dunbar in 1894—he later bragged that his son was born in the room where Dunbar gave a reading—and increasingly experimented with **dialect poetry**.

In both his poetry and his public life, Cotter revealed himself to be a supporter of **Booker T. Washington**, and his work implicitly embraces Washington's sense of uplift. It also, through Cotter's growing prominence as an oral storyteller, embraced specific components of the Black community and evinced his lifelong love of children. His poetic career arguably reached its apex with the 1909 publication of *A White Song and a Black One*, which treats race in much more depth, offers a fuller range of poetic forms, and shows more tonal variation (from serious to humorous). During this period, Cotter also made his most significant experimentation with other forms—writing a **blank verse** play, *Caleb, the Degenerate* (1903), one of the first plays published by an African American, and a collection of fiction, *Negro Tales*, which was published by a New York firm (Cosmopolitan Press) in 1912.

The early twentieth century brought both great promise and great tragedy to the Cotters. In 1911, he became principal of the Samuel Coleridge Taylor School, an appointment he held for thirty-one years. His economic status allowed him to raise two children (Leonidas died in infancy) in relative comfort and to send them to Fisk University. Both, though, contracted tuberculosis. Florence died in 1914, and Joseph, Jr., on the edge of his own career as a poet, died in 1919. (*See* **Cotter, Joseph Seamon, Jr.**)

Though he never stopped writing, Cotter did not return to publishing actively until 1934, four years after his wife's death. Over the next decade, his *Collected Poems* (1938) and his *Sequel to the Pied Piper of Hamelin and Other Poems* (1939) were published and distributed nationally. While they maintained Cotter's pattern of including previously published poems, they added some new work—most notably his "The Tragedy of Pete," a ballad that had won the 1926 **Opportunity** contest. His final book, a collection of short stories and proverbs, *Negroes and Others at Work and Play*, appeared in 1947.

Resources: A. Russell Brooks, "Joseph Seamon Cotter," in *Dictionary of Literary Biography*, vol. 50 (Detroit: Gale, 1986), 62–70; Joseph Seamon Cotter [Sr.]: *Caleb, the Degenerate: A Play in Four Acts* (Louisville, KY: Bradley & Gilbert, 1903); *Collected Poems* (1938; repr. Freeport, NY: Books for Libraries, 1971); *Links of Friendship* (1898; repr. Lousiville, KY: Bradley & Gilbert, 1938); *Negro Tales* (New York: Cosmopolitan Press, 1912); *A Rhyming* (Louisville, KY: North South Publishers, 1895); *Sequel to the the Pied Piper of Hamlin and Other Poems* (New York: H. Harrison, 1939); *A White Song and a Black One* (Louisville, KY: Bradley & Gilbert, 1909); Joan R. Sherman, "Joseph Seamon Cotter, Sr.," in her *Invisible Poets* (Urbana: University of Illinois Press, 1989), 164–171; Ann Allen Shockley, "Joseph Seamon Cotter," *CLA Journal* 18 (1974): 327–340.

Eric Gardner

Cowdery, Mae V. (1909–1953). Poet. Cowdery's work often addressed issues of **race**, femininity, and sexuality. Her poetry attempted to reveal the essence of Black womanhood as related to such themes as racial protest, beauty, nature, and passion. Like her contemporary **Angelina Weld Grimké**, Cowdery expressed women's romantic love for women in "Insatiate" and "Poem . . . for a Lover."

Born to middle-class parents in the Germantown area of **Philadelphia, Pennsylvania** (her mother was a social worker and her father a caterer), Cowdery cultivated her scholastic and artistic gifts at the Philadelphia High School for Girls. She became a published poet during her senior year; three of her poems were included in the spring 1927 issue of *Black Opals*, which showcased the work of Black Philadelphia writers.

After graduation, Cowdery ventured to New York City to pursue her interest in visual arts at Pratt Institute. There she met such **Harlem Renaissance** notables as **Langston Hughes** and **Alain Locke**. Locke encouraged her to submit her work to *The Crisis* and *Opportunity*, and her poetry appeared in both publications from 1927 through 1930. Cowdery was featured on the cover of the January 1928 issue of *The Crisis* after winning both the magazine's poetry contest and the Krigwa Poetry Prize in 1927. Her short hair and tailored suit in the portrait reflect the influence of the poet Edna St. Vincent Millay, whose writing and carefree lifestyle Cowdery admired.

Although her poems appeared in Black periodicals and in **Charles S. Johnson**'s anthology *Ebony and Topaz* in 1927, Cowdery did not achieve the level of public recognition held by many Harlem Renaissance writers. Her only volume of poetry, *We Lift Our Voices and Other Poems* (1936), was published later than much of the period's celebrated work. Cowdery's literary career came to a premature end when she took her life in 1953. Her work has since been resurrected in anthologies of African American women's writing, including Erlene Stetson's *Black Sister* (1981) and Maureen Honey's *Shadowed Dreams* (1989). The latter text is dedicated to Cowdery's memory and features seventeen of her poems.

Her poem "The Young Voice Cries," dedicated to **Alice Dunbar-Nelson**, is included in *The Portable Harlem Renaissance Reader*. (*See* **Lesbian Literature.**)

Resources: Mae Cowdery, *We Lift Our Voices and Other Poems* (Philadelphia: Alpress, 1936); Maureen Honey, ed., *Shadowed Dreams: Women's Poetry of the Harlem Renaissance* (New Brunswick, NJ: Rutgers University Press, 1989); David Levering Lewis, ed., *The Portable Harlem Renaissance Reader* (New York: Viking, 1994), 238–240; Lorraine E. Roses and Ruth E. Randolph, *Harlem Renaissance and Beyond: Literary Biographies of 100 Black Women Writers* (Boston: G. K. Hall, 1990); Erlene Stetson, ed., *Black Sister: Poetry by Black American Women, 1746–1980* (Bloomington: Indiana University Press, 1981).

Janaka N. Bowman

CQ Comics Group (1997–present). Publisher. CQ Comics, a small publisher of comic books, originated in **Atlanta, Georgia**, as the brainchild of Shawn Askew. Blackman, the company's flagship character, evolved from a Batman-inspired character in the newspaper *Imprint* (1993), published at Grissom High School in Huntsville, Alabama (Cavendar). By 1997 Blackman, in Askew's view, became "the first *truly* African-American [comic-book] super hero" (CQ Comics Web site). Popular Black heroes had existed since the 1960s, such as Marvel Comics' Black Panther and the Falcon, but by the 1990s, Askew felt that none fully captured a realistic representation of the modern Black experience. Often Black superheroes in comics were portrayed as sidekicks, as with the Falcon's relationship to Captain America, or as offshoots or knockoffs of established, more dominant, and more popular White heroes, such as DC Comics' Superman and Steel, or Marvel's Iron Man and War Machine. Askew attempted to change this situation, finding it important to suggest, by means of his protagonist's name and character, aspects of African American society in the 1990s. Blackman was intended, in Askew's words, to "bridge the gap between pride in his African heritage and hope in his future as an American" (CQ Comics Web site). Wearing a costume with the multicolored African nation flag and toting a bullwhip and Zulu spear as weapons, the hero displayed a connection to his African roots but was also a modern African American hero.

Craig Johnson, the alter ego of Blackman, is portrayed as an ordinary college student at Terminus Polytechnic Institute in Terminus, Georgia. Terminus alludes to Askew's alma mater, the Georgia Institute of Technology. Because Johnson is part of a a top-secret government plan to create a line of ultra soldiers, he becomes aware of his own "heightened senses, increased physical stamina, strength, and muscle mass, and vastly superior intelligence & quick reasoning abilities" (CQ Comics Web site). Here Askew is drawing on conventions of popular comic books, insofar as Blackman's origins parallel those of Captain America. However, Blackman's origins may also be taken as a reference to the Tuskegee experiment, wherein African American men were unwitting subjects in governmental experiments on the effects of venereal diseases.

The goal of CQ was both to integrate a contemporary African American presence into the world of comic books and to establish an original comic book hero. *Blackman #0*, an eight-page story, was apparently a free offering at a handful of Atlanta and Huntsville bookshops, and Askew planned to debut Blackman #1 in the fall of 2001. However, the *Blackman* series did not succeed. Like **Milestone Comics** (1993), an earlier imprint supported by DC Comics that featured several titles about African American superheroes, Blackman nonetheless represented an effort to bring African American issues to popular American comic books. Traces of the ideas present in CQ comics are obvious in recent comics, such as Marvel's 2003 miniseries *Truth*, in which it is revealed that African Americans were the "guinea pigs" through which the American government honed the experimental process of creating Captain America.

Resources: Shawn Askew, CQ Comics Web site, http://www.geocities.com/cqcomics/; "Black Proteges: Is There a Superheroic Plantation System?" *The Museum of Black Superheroes*, http://www.fortunecity.com/tatooine/niven/142/profiles/pro13 .html; Emily Cavendar, "Up, Up, and Away with Black-Man," *Campus Life* (June 29, 2001), http://cyberbuzz.gatech.edu/technique/issues/summer2001/2001-06-29/11.html.

James Bucky Carter

Craft, William (1824–1900) and Ellen Smith Craft (1826–1891). Abolitionists and activists. Important figures in the **abolitionist movement**, the Crafts are most famous today for their **slave narrative** *Running a Thousand Miles for Freedom; or, the Escape of William and Ellen Craft from Slavery* (1860).

Both were born into slavery in Georgia. William's parents' names are unknown. He may have been the slave of George W. Craft, of Bibb County, Georgia. William gained a rudimentary knowledge of carpentry before he and his sister Sarah were mortgaged in 1841 and eventually sold. His new master, a slaveholder living in Macon, Georgia, allowed him to work for hire as a carpenter/cabinetmaker and keep some of his earnings.

Ellen was born in Clinton, Georgia, to a slave named Maria and her master, Maj. James Smith. Her extremely cruel mistress, Eliza Smith, gave Ellen to her namesake daughter (and Ellen's half sister) on the daughter's marriage to wealthy speculator Robert Collins in 1837. The younger Eliza seems to have been kinder, and Ellen became both a personal servant and a seamstress in her household. Collins kept a home in Macon, and while there, Ellen met William around 1842. They married in 1846 but recognized that they ran continuous risk of separation. Given this and the violence both had experienced in **slavery**, they planned to escape. In late 1848, they obtained passes for the Christmas holidays, and, on December 21, 1848, the couple left Macon.

Their escape became one of the most celebrated in the abolitionist movement. The light-skinned Ellen dressed as an invalid planter (with poultices on her face and spectacles hiding her eyes) and kept her right arm in a sling so that she, being illiterate, would not have to sign her name. The darker-skinned William posed as her valet. Using funds William had saved, "Mr. William Johnson" and his "slave" traveled to Savannah, Charleston, and eventually **Baltimore, Maryland**, before arriving in **Philadelphia, Pennsylvania**, on Christmas Day. In rich irony, they met a friend of Ellen's former master who did not see through her disguise, planters' daughters who were attracted to the soft-spoken and sickly "Mr. Johnson," and Southerners who were consistently concerned that abolitionists might "make off" with William.

An engraving of Ellen Craft, disguised as "Mr. William Johnson," as published in *The Illustrated London News*, April 19, 1851. Photographs and Prints Division, Schomburg Center for Research in Black Culture, The New York Public Library, Astor, Lenox and Tilden Foundations.

In Philadelphia, Robert Purvis and **William Still**, who would later recount their story in *The Underground Rail Road* (1872), aided them, as did Quakers in the area. **William Wells Brown**, who would also invoke the Crafts in his writing (in *Clotel; or, The President's Daughter* [1853]), accompanied them to **Boston, Massachusetts**, a few weeks later. There, the Crafts became important figures at antislavery events. Brown and the Crafts began lecturing together as early as 1849; generally, the more experienced Brown would begin and, after telling his story, introduce William, who would speak and, on most occasions, introduce Ellen. Initially, contemporary historians questioned how active Ellen's role in such lectures was, but recent research shows that she spoke more often than initially assumed (McCaskill).

Abolitionist Theodore Parker performed a marriage ceremony for the Crafts on November 7, 1850. Already harrassed by the passage of the Fugitive Slave Law, though, they decided to go to Great Britain when agents of their master successfully appealed to President Millard Fillmore to help secure their capture.

The Crafts were already recognized as celebrities among British abolitionists. Befriended by, among others, Lady Byron, the Crafts lived, studied, and taught at the experimental Ockham School before moving to London. There, Brown and the Crafts continued to lecture; prints of Ellen in her disguise became popular souvenirs. Active in the formation of the London Emancipation Society, they published their narrative on the eve of the American **Civil War**. Arguably more fragmented than most slave narratives, it appeared too late to have significant impact on the U.S. abolitionist movement. Still, it is regularly read today because of the richness of the Crafts' escape story, which has been adapted by writers ranging from Thomas Wentworth Higginson to **Georgia Douglas Johnson**. While the narrative is told in William's voice, some contemporary critics have begun to assert that Ellen may have made some contributions to its writing. Both William and Ellen contributed to the abolitionist press.

Active in a variety of reform causes, the Crafts evinced a growing interest in Africa during this period; eventually, William made two trips to Dahomey as an agent for the African Aid Society. During their time in Britain, they had five children: Charles, Brougham, William, Ellen, and Alfred; in 1865 Ellen, with the aid of British friends, brought her mother to live in London.

The Crafts returned to the United States in 1869 and, after a stay in Boston, moved to South Carolina. While historians have claimed that only two or three of their children accompanied them, evidence shows that at least four of the children settled and raised families in the United States. Using the principles they learned at Ockham, the Crafts bought a plantation close to the Georgia line called Hickory Hill and opened an industrial school for African Americans in the area. Racist "night riders" burned the school down within a year, and the Crafts moved to Savannah, where their sons Charles and Brougham worked as rental agents. The elder Crafts reportedly incurred substantial losses when an attempt at running a boardinghouse failed in 1871, but they saved enough money to buy another plantation—Woodville, in Bryan County, Georgia—where they again set up a school.

Ellen seems to have managed both the school and the farm while William divided his time between fund-raising (often in the North) and participating in local Republican politics; he was a candidate for the Georgia State Senate in 1874. They were able to maintain the school—and a working farm—for several years, but eventually financial problems and the opposition of Whites in the area forced the school's closure in or soon after 1878. While William attempted to keep the farm going, Ellen moved to Charleston, where she lived with her daughter, who had married a physician named William Demos Crum (an advocate of **Booker T. Washington**'s ideas who served as collector of the port of Charleston and, later, Minister to Liberia). Eventually, William joined his wife in Charleston. When she died, she reportedly was buried under her favorite oak tree at Woodville; William continued to live with their daughter until his death.

Resources: R.J.M. Blackett, *Beating Against the Barriers: Biographical Essays in Nineteenth-Century Afro-American History* (Baton Rouge: Louisiana State University Press, 1986); Barbara McCaskill, "Introduction," in *Running a Thousand Miles for Freedom* (Athens: University of Georgia Press, 1999); Dorothy Sterling, *Black Foremothers: Three Lives* (New York: Feminist Press of CUNY, 1988).

Eric Gardner

Crafts, Hannah. Fugitive slave and novelist. In April 2002, **Henry Louis Gates, Jr.**, published Hannah Crafts's novel *The Bondwoman's Narrative* to acclaim and controversy. Almost as fascinating as the author's identity and the novel's provenance is Gates's purchase of the previously unpublished manuscript at the Swann Galleries' auction of "Printed and Manuscript African-Americana" in New York City for $8,000 two years earlier. The manuscript had been in the library of the noted Howard University librarian and historian **Dorothy Porter Wesley**. Gates then embarked on a diligent and long-from-completed search for Crafts's identity; Wesley had surmised she was Black and a fugitive slave. If this proves to be true, *The Bondwoman's Narrative* is "a major discovery, possibly the first novel written by a Black woman and definitely the first novel written by a woman who had been a slave" (Gates, xii). Indeed, Gates argues that the authentication of Crafts's narrative and identity would be of "great historical importance: to be able to study a manuscript written by a black woman or man, unedited . . . would help a new generation of scholars to gain access to the mind of a slave in an unmediated fashion heretofore not possible" (Gates, xxxiii).

At issue in determining Crafts's identity is the degree to which the *Narrative* is a purely fictionalized **slave narrative** or a thinly disguised **autobiography** (the protagonist's name is Hannah). Proceeding under the assumption that the narrative is at least partly autobiographical, Gates searched through census records and databases trying to locate Hannah Crafts. So far, he has identified several possible candidates but has been unable to secure many hard facts. Crafts probably was born in Virginia and was a slave on plantations in Virginia and North Carolina. She was likely purchased by John Hill Wheeler (a Wheeler is also mentioned in the novel) in 1855. Based on expert manuscript historians' investigations, Crafts's use of polysyllabic words, coupled with frequent misspellings, suggests she was self-educated and may have had access to Wheeler's sizable library (Gates, xxxiii). She most likely escaped to freedom in the North between March 21 and May 4, 1857 (Gates, lvi). Since she was a fugitive slave and subject to the provisions of the Fugitive Slave Act, Gates guesses Crafts may have settled in a free Black community in New Jersey as Hannah Vincent, married to a Methodist clergyman (lxi–lxiii).

The Bondwoman's Narrative relates the story of a young educated house slave who escapes to freedom in the North with her mistress, who has been passing and has just been betrayed by the appropriately named Mr. Trappe. Like **Harriet Wilson**'s *Our Nig*, *The Bondwoman's Narrative* combines the conventions of several genres, including spiritual narratives, slave narratives, gothic novels, and sentimental novels (Gates, xxi). It is one of the earliest narratives to chronicle the tension between house slaves and field slaves. Also significant, according to Gates, is Crafts's resistance to using distinctive racial markers to identify her characters, instead suggesting racial identity by context (Gates xxiv–xxv). Her plot device of switching a **"mulatto"** and White child at birth presages **Mark Twain**'s use of the device in *Pudd'nhead Wilson*. It is not clear why Crafts failed to publish her novel. Gates argues that publishing in the nineteenth century was especially difficult for African American women, and that Crafts may have wanted to conceal her identity if she was passing in the North. She also may not have wanted the veracity of her story challenged. In any case, scholars' interest in *The Bondwoman's Narrative* is considerable, as demonstrated in a new collection of twenty-seven essays edited by Gates and Hollis Robbins covering the novel's place in the canon and the literary marketplace, its relationship to African American **gothic literature**, and the search for her identity.

Resources: Henry Louis Gates, Jr., "Introduction," in *The Bondwoman's Narrative* (New York: Warner Books, 2002), ix–lxxiv; Henry Louis Gates, Jr., and Hollis Robbins, eds., *In Search of Hannah Crafts: Critical Essays on The Bondwoman's Narrative* (New York: BasicCivitas Books, 2004).

Rebecca R. Saulsbury

Creole. Generally, "Creole," as a linguistic term, refers to the product of cultural contacts between the peoples of Africa and western Europe. Derek Bickerton, in his study of Creole languages around the world, has shown that the majority of Creole languages are based on English and other Indo-European languages, which he calls their superstrate language, combined with local or immigrant languages as substrate languages. Today's Creole languages (whether in West Africa or in the Americas) are one clear and direct consequence of the contacts between Europe and Africa through **slavery** and colonization.

Creole is the new, hybrid language that results when the speakers of a dominant culture (in this case European slave traders and colonizers) are more powerful—technologically or politically—and the speakers of the other language or languages are illiterate. The language of the dominant group undergoes gradual modification through regular usage by members of different groups within the community. This process usually takes many years, even centuries. The new language assumes a broader national or ethnic role as the lingua franca. It is spoken by a majority of all the diverse groups in order to facilitate all forms of interaction. In its most simplified forms this new language is a pidgin. However, over time, as this lingua franca becomes the standard or native language of the community, usually of the less dominant group, it becomes a Creole. Linguists use the lowercase "creole" to describe this new language. Historians and literary theorists tend to adopt the uppercase "Creole."

As a term in African American literature, "creole" specifically denotes two fundamental concepts. First, it refers to the presence of African, European, and native cultures in the Americas, especially in the Caribbean, since Christopher Columbus's first voyage to the New World in 1492. Second, it refers to the blending of these cultures to produce a new, unique, and hybrid culture that is as dynamic as it is diverse. Creole, as a culture, embraces a wide variety of subjects and fields such as history, identity, language, literature, and music. As a language in the Americas, Creole has regional varieties—English, French, Portuguese, and Spanish. Historically, however, the term has been controversial. According to Eric Bennett:

> The word carries political as much as racial meaning, having denoted, at various times, people of both African and European descent, as well as their racially mixed offspring. The word creole derives from the Spanish *criollo*, meaning "native to the locality." In the sixteenth, seventeenth, and eighteenth centuries, it referred to American-born children of Spanish parents. With the settling of North America and the onset of the slave trade, *créole*, a French cognate, became in many places a name for all non-indigenous but locally reared inhabitants— including the descendants of both African slaves and European colonialists, and even, in some cases, new breeds of plants and livestock. In most Caribbean communities, where ethnicity shaped social relations, "Creole" also became a loaded and divisive term. (*Encarta Africana*, 1999)

In the United States "creole" refers to two distinct linguistic and cultural communities, both of which reflect aspects of African, or Black, identity and ethnicity. In the nineteenth century the term was used to denote all Black, White and, mixed-race Louisianans in order to distinguish them from foreign-born and Anglo-American settlers. At the time mixed-race Creoles of color (or *gens de couleur libres*, "free persons of color") came into their own as an ethnic group. They had access to many of the legal rights and privileges of Whites. As a hybrid group they occupied the middle ground between Whites and enslaved Blacks. They often owned property and had formal education. After the **Civil War**, most Creoles of color lost their privileged status and became part of a subclass that included impoverished former Black slaves. All the while, however, "creole" persisted as a term. It also described white Louisianans, usually of upper-class, non-Cajun origin. The term "Cajun" was often conflated with Creole, mainly by outsiders unfamiliar with local ethnic labels. Like the Creoles of color, these white Creoles, also called French Creoles, suffered major decline in social and economic status after the Civil War. Impoverished White Creoles often intermarried with the predominantly lower-class Cajuns and were largely assimilated into Cajun culture.

Historically, Cajuns are the descendants of Acadians, French settlers who were deported, in 1755, from Nova Scotia by British Governor Charles Lawrence as a result of their refusal to swear allegiance to the British Crown. Lawrence's army destroyed thousands of Acadian houses and dispersed the

Acadians to the American colonies, from Massachusetts to Georgia. Some of these colonies refused to take in any refugees. For example, Virginia deported the Acadians to England and France. Many settled in Louisiana, which was then subject to the French Crown. The term "Cajun" is a corruption of the French pronunciation of the word *acadien*, after Acadia, the name of their ancestral home in Nova Scotia. The name "Cajun" was applied to them by English-speaking colonists when they settled in Louisiana. As a category of identity and culture, Cajuns are, like French and Black Creoles, products of colonization and dispersal—a **diaspora**. (*See* **Colonialism**.)

Today "Creole" is most often used in Louisiana to refer to persons of full or mixed African heritage. It is generally understood among these Creoles that "Creole of color" still refers to Creoles of mixed-race heritage, while the term "Black Creole" refers to Creoles of more or less pure African descent. Thus, in Louisiana, "Creole" seems to have become interchangeable with Cajun. For example, many names of French Creole origin are now widely considered Cajun. It is also now accepted that Creole is a broad cultural group of people of all races who share a French or Spanish background. Louisianans who identify themselves as "Creole" are most commonly from historically French-speaking communities and have ancestors who came to Louisiana either directly from France or through the French colonies in the Caribbean:

A French Creole family is one that arrived in Louisiana directly from France or via the West Indies, West Florida, . . . before 1803, the year Louisiana ceased to be a colony and became a territory of the United States; this includes the handfull [*sic*] of non-Acadian French Catholic families who . . . ended up in the English colonies of North America and moved on to Louisiana before 1803. The term "creole" . . . is a generic one . . . meaning simply a European born in the New World; these French Creole families should not to be confused with the Afro-Caribbean Creoles of present-day south Louisiana who descended from free blacks and slaves of the area and speak their own patios [*sic*] of the French language. (http://www.acadiansingray.com)

In the nineteenth century, Creole was a feature in African American literature. Creole language and culture were portrayed by Kate Chopin, herself married to a Creole, in her short stories, the most famous of which, "The Awakening," was published in 1899. Her fiction was well received as an example of "local color" literature and helped establish Chopin's reputation as a major contributor to Southern regional literature. In the 1930s **Négritude**, the Francophone literary and cultural movement, and its Latino counterpart, Negrismo, became major forces in the promotion of Afro-Caribbean Creole culture and identity. Chief among the promoters of the latter movement were the Generación del Treinta, a group of Creole intellectuals who situated themselves as the voice of a new cultural nationalism in Puerto Rico. Initially, both movements were political in their focus and aspirations. They devoted their energies to the fight against colonization, oppression, and the dehumanization of Africans and Caribbean Africans, which paralleled the enslavement and dehumanization of Caribbean and Latino Black people. Among the major intellectual forces for these movements were **W.E.B. Du Bois** and **Alain Locke**. Both these men were also leaders of the **Harlem Renaissance**, another Black consciousness movement of the same era. Authors of this period infused their works with creole speech patterns, mannerisms, color, and rhythmic tones. All these movements, artistic, literary, cultural, and political have a common root in Social Realism, a 1930s, Marxist-leaning, sociopolitical movement dedicated to social justice through portrayal of colored peoples' daily experiences in the arts.

Since 1960 conditions have favored the expansion of African American literature to include works produced by writers of Caribbean origin who have settled or were born in the United States. This is due largely to the influence of both postcolonial and area studies in American colleges and universities. The works of these writers, their styles, and their thematic preoccupations have become part of the literary curriculum and discourse. Thus the presence of Caribbean Creoles, linguistically and culturally, remains a defining feature of this type of modern African American literature. Indeed, creolization, an adjacent term, has gained currency in American literary circles. It encompasses most Afro-Caribbean literature with Creole culture and identity—not necessarily languages—as the defining feature. Thus a multiplicity of creole voices—Latino, Haitian, and French—exists within the corpus of African American literature and cultural experience. Notable figures include Edouard Glissant, **Edwidge Danticat**, and Junot Díaz. They have helped to promote the influence of creole in African American literature. For Junot Díaz, who was born in the Dominican Republic, bordering **Haiti**, Danticat is the "quintessential American writer, tackling the new world's hidden history of apocalypse and how one survives it." Another U.S. writer from the Caribbean, Robert Antoni, says Danticat is "doing for Haiti's history of violence and vengeance what **Toni Morrison** did for the US in tackling the horrors of slavery and its aftermath."

An adjacent term, *Créolité*, is currently being used to denote African American literature produced not only in the Caribbean but also in the United States, by African Americans of francophone Caribbean origin. Its major exponents include Jean Bernabé, Patrick Chamoiseau, Raphael Confiant, and Edouard Glissant. Glissant, in both his literary and his theoretical works, has focused in an unprecedented way on the Caribbean in terms of the diverse and hybrid culture of the region. His ideas on a cross-cultural politics have been a major force in the francophone Caribbean *Créolité* movement. Its themes express the main social and political concerns of the Caribbean diaspora for the respective Caribbean nations, while still retaining the African element as its underlying and defining historical identity. However, *Créolité* has not been without its critics. Maryse Condé, another francophone Caribbean writer living in the United States, argues that "*Créolité* should not be transformed into a cultural terrorism within which writers are confined. . . . To each his or her own *Créolité* that is to say, to each his or her own relationship with oral materials and the oral tradition, to each his or her own way of expressing it in written literature."

Haitian creole is one of the newest American languages, due to the efforts of the Creole Institute at Indiana University. The institute has a Web site and is recognized as the only center of its kind in the United States. Equipped to tackle linguistic and related educational matters in Haiti and for the burgeoning Haitian American population of the United States, the institute has also provided language training for the U.S. Army. It specializes in research and training in applied linguistics. The focus is on French-based Creoles. In 1964 Indiana University was the first institution of higher learning to offer instruction in Haitian creole, and it has developed the basic materials for learning that language. It has also prepared the most authoritative dictionary for Haitian creole, as well as a bilingual English-creole dictionary. With universities in Louisiana, it also completed a major research project that resulted in a glossary and historical dictionary for Louisiana creole (http://www.indiana.edu/~creole/history.html).

Resources: "Acadians in Gray," http://www.acadiansingray.com/progress_report .htm; Eric Bennett, "Creoles," *Encarta Africana*, ed. Kwame Anthony Appiah and Henry Louis Gates, Jr. (Microsoft, 1999); Derek Bickerton, *Roots of Language* (Ann Arbor, MI: Karoma, 1985); Carl A. Brasseaux, Keith P. Fontenot, and Claude F. Oubre, *Creoles of Color in the Bayou Country* (Jackson: University Press of Mississippi, 1994); Edward Kamau Brathwaite, "Creolization in Jamaica," in *The Post-Colonial Studies Reader*, ed. Bill Ashcroft et al. (New York: Routledge, 1995); Keith Cartwright, *Reading Africa into American Literature* (Lexington: University Press of Kentucky, 2004); Daryl Dance, ed., *Fifty Caribbean Writers: A Bio-Bibliographical Critical Sourcebook* (Westport, CT: Greenwood Press, 1986); J. Michael Dash, *Edouard Glissant* (New York: Cambridge University Press, 1995); James H. Dormon, ed., *Creoles of Color of the Gulf South* (Knoxville: University of Tennessee Press, 1996); "Haitian Creole," *Encyclopaedia Britannica Online*, http://search.eb.com/eb/article?tocId=9038824; Gwendolyn Midlo Hall, *Africans in Colonial Louisiana: The Development of Afro-Creole Culture in the Eighteenth Century* (Baton Rouge: Louisiana State University Press, 1995); Indiana University Creole Institute, "History and Mission," http://www.indiana.edu/~creole/ history.html; Peter Manuel, *Caribbean Currents: Caribbean Music from Rumba to Reggae* (Philadelphia: Temple University Press, 1995); Lizabeth Paravisini-Gebert and Olga Torres-Seda, *Caribbean Women Novelists: An Annotated Critical Bibliography* (Westport, CT: Greenwood Press, 1993); Francoise Pfaff, ed., *Conversations with Maryse Condé* (Lincoln: University of Nebraska Press, 1996); John Shelton Reed and Dale Volberg Reed, eds., *1001 Things Everyone Should Know about the South* (New York: Doubleday, 1996); Emily Toth, *Unveiling Kate Chopin* (Jackson: University Press of Mississippi, 1999); Albert Valdman, ed., *Pidgin and Creole Linguistics* (Bloomington: Indiana University Press, 1977); Charles Reagan Wilson and William Ferris, eds., *Encyclopedia of Southern Culture* (Chapel Hill: University of North Carolina Press, 1989), preface.

'BioDun J. Ogundayo

Crime and Mystery Fiction. Fashioned in the nineteenth century out of gothic literary forms, sensationalistic journalism, and discourses of scientific rationalism by the American writer Edgar Allan Poe, the English novelist Sir Arthur Conan Doyle, and others, crime and mystery writing seeks to sort out the tangle of modern social relations by way of recognizable narrative conventions and an especially clever and determined protagonist. The rise of crime fiction has also been connected to urbanization and industrialization, to the growth of psychology, and to the ever increasing influence of science, among other social forces (Kalikoff; Thomas). Ultimately crime fiction came to feature three primary kinds of detectives: the amateur, the independent professional (private investigator), and the police detective employed by a city or state (Mansfield-Kelley and Marchino). Themes of detection and intrigue have preoccupied African American novelists since the turn of the twentieth century, but it was not until the early to mid-twentieth century that Black writers took up crime–mystery as a precise mode of genre writing. Contemporary African American crime novelists have moved beyond the genre's historically White, masculinist, and sometimes patently racist imaginaries to constitute a rich tradition of Black literary critique on questions of culture, justice, and the law.

As the critics Frankie Y. Bailey, Maureen T. Reddy, and Stephen F. Soitos have extensively and instructively documented, the hard-boiled crime fiction made popular by early twentieth-century American writers such as Dashiell Hammett and Raymond Chandler feature non-White characters—Blacks, "Mexicans," Asians—in stereotyped roles that alternate among domestic servants, obsequious hired hands, "taboo women," and shifty buffoons. Chandler is even self-reflexive about such stereotypes; for example, in *Farewell, My Lovely* (1940), he has a police detective admit that a homicide involving a Black victim is much less important than one involving a White person, and Chandler's detective, Philip Marlowe, becomes interested in a murder in spite of the fact that the victim is Black. These characterizations should not be surprising, however, given the ideological valences of hard-boiled crime fiction. The development of the genre between the 1920s and 1940s, through a variety of pulps (a term that refers to inexpensive, widely circulating magazines) but particularly in the magazine *Black Mask*, popularized the all-important persona of the detective protagonist as a quick-witted and determined White man, a maverick who lives and plays by his own rules. Hammett's Sam Spade and Chandler's Marlowe work outside or barely within the bounds of the law in order to solve their cases. This narrative gesture grants them a certain mobility of social positioning in performing the duties of the police more effectively than the police themselves. It also infuses the detectives with a rugged individualism that serves as a device of compensatory masculine heroism in the midst of feminizing bureaucracy, consumerism, and mass culture. Scholars have pointed out the historical irony of this individualist fantasy being packaged and distributed through the very institutions of modern society it deemed stultifying. Whether ironic or not, Spade and Marlowe remain larger-than-life icons of White heterosexual masculinity whose crime-solving capacities are unmarked by **race**, **gender**, or sexual difference.

In her study of hard-boiled crime fiction's fascination with racial tropes, *Traces, Codes, and Clues* (2003), Reddy argues that the detective protagonist's typically first-person narrative voice is both the primary agent of racist ideology in the genre and the primary target for critical revision by non-White and female mystery writers. She notes, "The centrality of voice distinguishes the hard-boiled from the classical detective story [by Poe or Doyle] and I think is the element that most attracts writers interested in challenging hard-boiled racial and sexual codes—because the voice is everything. To change the voice, to let the Other speak, is to transform the genre by replacing the traditional central consciousness with another that does not share the ideology or the racial (or sexual or gender) identity around which the genre formed" (9). Soitos's pathbreaking genealogy of African American crime fiction, outlined in *The Blues Detective* (1996), seems to confirm this thesis. Black writers have generally given non-White "Others" fuller "speaking" or agential roles in their detective stories, but they have done so mainly in the process of articulating alternate narrative consciousnesses whose relation to the law is already conditioned by racial discrimination and gender exclusion. One might say, then, that the history of African American crime fiction has been the history of radical **deconstruction** and then reconstruction of this popular genre's most alluring and entertaining element, the detective protagonist.

The earliest prototypes of African American crime fiction are serial novels: **Pauline E. Hopkins**'s *Hagar's Daughter*, published in the *Colored American* magazine in 1901–1902, and John E. Bruce's *The Black Sleuth*, published in *McGirt's* magazine in 1907–1909. These texts have more in common with the classical detective story than with the hard-boiled tradition, which had yet to come into existence. Still, Hopkins and Bruce construct narratives that go a long way in displacing stereotypes about Black intellectual and cultural inferiority that were circulating at the time. The central conceit of intrigue in *Hagar's Daughter* is racial **passing**. The buildup of suspense in this tragic saga about racial prejudice in antebellum and postbellum society rests upon Hagar and her daughter, Jewel's, capacity to pass as White members of aristocratic families. Despite the sprawling narrative, the mystery of the Enson, Sumner, and Bowen families' bloodlines is neatly left to be sorted out by Detective Henson; his Black assistant, Henry Smith; and, most notably, Venus Johnson, a Black maid who uses her intuition and connections in the Black community to locate the kidnapped Jewel. Technically a minor character in the novel, Venus becomes the crux of narrative resolution thanks to her keen and attentive participation in the case.

The Black Sleuth is notable for its Yoruba protagonist, Sadipe Okukenu, and the narrative's internationalist scope, with scenes set in Africa, the United States, and England. In the employ of the private International Detective Agency, Sadipe is charged with recovering American Capt. George De Forrest's African diamond, which was stolen from him by White robbers. Combining sharp intellect with playful masquerade, Sadipe tracks down the bandits by putting on a repertoire of "blackface" disguises that conceal his true identity. Here Bruce invokes stereotypes about the African persona in order to use them parodically against the perpetrators of those stereotypes, including the decidedly supremacist Captain De Forrest. This critical inversion of racist thought and practice is common among Sadipe, his brother Mojola, and their father, the elder Okukenu. In its emphasis on the family's collective pride and resistance to White domination, the novel is one of the most fascinating precursors to the Pan-Africanist ideals of **Black Nationalism** in the 1960s. In terms of the emergence of African American crime fiction, *The Black Sleuth* shares with *Hagar's Daughter* the early counterdiscursive portrayal of Blacks thinking critically and creatively in solving problems to which White characters are largely color-blind.

A product of the **Harlem Renaissance**, **Rudolph Fisher'**s *The Conjure Man Dies* (1932) is the first Black detective novel originally published in book form. According to Soitos, Fisher's story takes up the country-house mystery mode made famous by Agatha Christie and the locked-room mystery mode characteristic of Poe's "The Murders in the Rue Morgue" (1841). The seven suspects in the murder of **Harlem, New York**, conjure man N'Gana Frimbo are "confined to one locale," and "red herrings are scattered through the text" (101, 102). It is up to two African American detectives—Perry Dart of the New York Police Department and amateur sleuth John Archer, a physician by trade—to piece together the suspects' testimonies and analyze their motives for wanting N'Gana dead. The intimate setting of this jigsaw puzzle of a mystery ultimately points to marital infidelity as the primary motive for N'Gana's eventual murder, "eventual" because his body is not the one that turns up at the beginning of the tale. Aside from its entertaining narrative qualities, *The Conjure-Man Dies* establishes in Dart and Archer the paradigmatic Black male crime-solving duo: the streetwise, pragmatic, and physically intimidating Dart complementing the lighter-complexioned abstract thinker Archer, and vice versa.

Undoubtedly the preeminent African American crime writer of the twentieth century was **Chester Himes**. With the benefit of hard-boiled hindsight and the capital to support his writing for a living, Himes was the first African American to pen a full series of crime novels, all of which are set in Harlem and feature the memorable partnering of police detectives Grave Digger Jones and Coffin Ed Johnson. Interestingly, Himes was living in **Paris, France**, by 1953, and so it was Marcel Duhamel, editor of the publisher Gallimard's "Série Noire" and translator of Himes's novel *If He Hollers Let Him Go* (1945), who invited him to write detective stories on commission. Thus most of the eight novels that constitute the Harlem series were written in Europe explicitly for future translation into French: *For Love of Imabelle* (1957), retitled *A Rage in Harlem* (1965); *The Crazy Kill* (1959); *The Real Cool Killers* (1959); *All Shot Up* (1960); *Big Gold Dream* (1960); *Cotton Comes to Harlem* (1965); *The Heat's On* (1966); and *Blind Man with a Pistol* (1969). Grave Digger and Coffin Ed are a striking pair; though the former tends to be the more reasonable of the two, they both regularly flout standard police procedure to extract information from witnesses and informants. Yet despite their bullying practices and identification with a mostly White police force, the people of Harlem look up to Grave Digger and Coffin Ed as protectors of their neighborhood and, indeed, racial community. Himes's detectives may be mavericks, but their actions, even when extravagantly violent, are almost always rooted in sympathy for the common folk, the real victims of particular acts of crime as well as of structural state racism in the form of police brutality and urban blight. In the trenchant satire *Cotton Comes to Harlem*, Grave Digger and Coffin Ed almost single-handedly foil Rev. Deke O'Malley's scheme to swindle Harlemites out of their life savings after they sign up for his **back-to-Africa** steamship cruise.

Ishmael Reed's *Mumbo Jumbo* (1972) and *The Last Days of Louisiana Red* (1974) signal African American **postmodernism**'s somewhat limited engagement with the genre. It is difficult to situate Reed's work within the crime fiction tradition because his story lines defy most narrative conventions and generic categories. But his "HooDoo" detective Papa LaBas might be said to explode the Eurocentric valences of Spade's and Marlowe's characters in the carnivalesque way he unearths the mysteries of Black social and cultural Being. At stake in these mysteries is the course of global history itself: whether it will recognize the life-giving properties of creolization or deny them through the clash of Western and non-Western civilizations. LaBas is a sleuth of hybrid origins, then, and Reed's hyperreferential prose saturates his plots with a fullness of detail that questions the stylistic economy of most other modes of crime writing.

In the 1990s a number of African American male crime novelists flourished in the wake of the **Terry McMillan**–led renaissance of Black popular writing in the United States. Robert O. Greer, **Gar Anthony Haywood**, **Hugh Holton**, and **Blair S. Walker** are notable examples. But **Walter Mosley** has easily been the most celebrated Black crime and mystery writer since Himes's Harlem series ended in 1969. The first African American to become president of the influential Mystery Writers of America (1995), Mosley has created a series of detective novels set in **Los Angeles, California**, and featuring the working-class private eye Ezekiel "Easy" Rawlins: *Devil in a Blue Dress* (1990), *Red Death* (1991), *White Butterfly* (1992), *Black Betty* (1994), *A Little Yellow Dog* (1996), *Gone Fishin'* (1997), *Bad Boy Brawly Brown* (2002), and *Little Scarlet* (2004); *Six Easy Pieces* (2003) is a collection of Easy Rawlins stories. In post–**World War II** Los Angeles, amid abstract promises of racial progress and upward mobility, Easy struggles not only as a sleuth prone to errors in judgment but also as a divorced single father of two adopted kids. But insofar as these struggles are characteristic of the Black community in this city and of this era more generally, the reader is able to imagine Easy's immersion in his work as a matter-of-fact way of life. *Devil in a Blue Dress* is the most compelling of Mosley's narratives; in it he revisits Hopkins's trope of passing by way of the mysterious and seductive Daphne Monet and deliberately rewrites the opening scene of Chandler's *Farewell, My Lovely*, one might say, from the previously degraded Black character's point of view. Amazingly, while developing the essential narrative thread of his Easy Rawlins mysteries, Mosley has found the time to initiate another series set in Los Angeles, this one focused on U.S. Army veteran Fearless Jones, who is much more of an unpredictable loose cannon than Easy. The two novels in this emerging series are *Fearless Jones* (2001) and *Fear Itself* (2003).

In recent years, however, African American women have come to problematize the hard-boiled Harlem and Los Angeles imaginaries of Himes and Mosley, not because their writing is lacking but because their writing is so adept at continuing to stifle or degrade female characters in the genre. At the core of Black feminist crime fiction is a radically different conception of the roles and functions of the detective protagonist. **Eleanor Taylor Bland**'s trailblazing Marti MacAlister series—*Dead Time* (1992), *Slow Burn* (1993), *Gone Quiet* (1994), and *Done Wrong* (1995), to name only the first four volumes—is set in Lincoln Prairie, Illinois, a suburb of **Chicago, Illinois**, where the veteran investigator tackles cases that are shrugged off by the police department because they involve the socially disadvantaged, including endangered children and the mentally ill. **Barbara Neely**'s remarkable Blanche White series—*Blanche on the Lam* (1992), *Blanche among the Talented Tenth* (1994), *Blanche Cleans Up* (1998), and *Blanche Passes Go* (2001)—is set in Farleigh (Raleigh), North Carolina, and **Boston, Massachusetts**, where a domestic-turned-sleuth keeps her ear to the ground to solve murders in aristocratic Southern and New England families. With sharp wit and penetrating insight, Neely has Blanche uncover more than secret plots; she also addresses issues from class and color politics to sexual violence and rape. In a similar vein, **Valerie Wilson Wesley**'s Tamara Hayle is a Newark, New Jersey, private eye and single mother whose relation to her clients is always mediated by concerns about her immediate family and the surrounding Black community. Crucially, although Marti, Blanche, and Tamara share with Easy a fundamental connection with Black working-class concerns, the women detectives are persistently reminded of their **gender** and sexual difference in ways that Easy, even as a single father, cannot experience. Other well-known Black female detectives include **Nikki Baker**'s Virginia Kelly, **Charlotte Carter**'s Nanette Hayes, **Grace F. Edwards**'s Mali Anderson, **Pamela Thomas-Graham**'s Veronica "Nikki" Chase, and **Paula L. Woods**'s Charlotte Justice. These characters, among others, count cops, professors, journalists, and businesswomen among their ranks, and they highlight the extent to which successful Black females utilize their professional expertise to solve crime cases.

As these contemporary examples demonstrate, African American crime fiction continues to develop in new and unexpected ways as more and more publishers distribute this type of popular literature. Black women writers have critiqued the patriarchal and sexist elements of both the hard-boiled and the Black male crime traditions in order to tease out the most progressive potential of the genre's appeal. Furthermore, African American crime fiction's narrative strategy of situating "law and order" within social structures of dominance has influenced revisionary cultural production in a variety of media, from **blaxploitation** cinema and gangsta **rap** to the ghetto realism of **Donald Goines** and **Iceberg Slim**, and the **prison literature** of **Eldridge Cleaver** and

Angela Y. Davis. In this regard, the genre merits further attention by literary and cultural critics who continue to labor to produce responses to the seemingly indefinite criminalization of the Black underclass and young, urban Black males in particular. Rather than posit "real world" policy solutions to this procedure of state control, authors such as Mosley, Neely, and Wesley offer ways to reimagine the precise history of racial discrimination within dominant conceptions of justice and the law. Their literary output also suggests that changing these conceptions requires not an absolute ideal of narrative consciousness but a narrator who is himself or herself grounded in family and community, the trials and struggles of everyday Black life. (*See* **Davis, Thulani.**)

Resources: Primary Sources: Nikki Baker, *The Lavender House Murder* (New York: Naiad Press, 1992); Eleanor Taylor Bland: *Dead Time* (New York: St. Martin's Press, 1992); *Done Wrong* (New York: St. Martin's Press, 1995); *Gone Quiet* (New York: Signet, 1994); *Slow Burn* (New York: St. Martin's Press, 1993); John Edward Bruce, *The Black Sleuth* (Boston: Northeastern University Press, 2002); Charlotte Carter, *Walking Bones* (London: Serpent's Tale, 2002); Raymond Chandler, *Farewell, My Lovely* (1940; repr. New York: Vintage, 1988); Grace F. Edwards, *The Viaduct* (New York: Doubleday, 2003); Rudolph Fisher, *The Conjure-Man Dies: A Mystery Tale of Dark Harlem* (Ann Arbor: University of Michigan Press, 1992); Gar Anthony Haywood, *Bad News Travels Fast* (New York: Putnam, 1995); Chester Himes: *All Shot Up* (1960; repr. New York: Thunder's Mouth Press, 1996); *Big Gold Dream* (London: Chatham Bookseller, 1960); *Blind Man with a Pistol* (1969; repr. New York: Vintage, 1989); *Cotton Comes to Harlem* (1965; repr. New York: Vintage, 1988); *The Crazy Kill* (1959; repr. New York: Vintage, 1989); *For Love of Imabelle* (1957; repr. London: Chatham Bookseller, 1973); *The Heat's On* (1966; repr. New York: Vintage, 1988); *If He Hollers Let Him Go* (1945; repr. New York: Thunder's Mouth Press, 2002); *The Real Cool Killers* (1959; repr. New York: Vintage, 1989); Hugh Holton, *The Thin Black Line* (New York: St. Martin's Press, 2005); Pauline E. Hopkins, *The Magazine Novels of Pauline Hopkins* (New York: Oxford University Press, 1987); Walter Mosley: *Bad Boy Brawly Brown* (Boston: Little, Brown, 2002); *Black Betty* (New York: W. W. Norton, 1994); *Devil in a Blue Dress* (New York: W. W. Norton, 1990); *Fear Itself* (Boston: Little, Brown, 2003); *Fearless Jones* (Boston: Little, Brown, 2001); *Gone Fishin'* (Washington, DC: Black Classic Press, 1997); *Little Scarlet* (Boston: Little, Brown, 2004); *A Little Yellow Dog* (New York: W. W. Norton, 1996); *Red Death* (New York: W. W. Norton, 1991); *Six Easy Pieces* (New York: Atria, 2003); *White Butterfly* (New York: W. W. Norton, 1992); Barbara Neely: *Blanche among the Talented Tenth* (New York: St. Martin's Press, 1994); *Blanche Cleans Up* (New York: Penguin, 1998); *Blanche on the Lam* (New York: St. Martin's Press, 1992); *Blanche Passes Go* (New York: Penguin, 2001); Ishmael Reed: *The Last Days of Louisiana Red* (New York: Random House, 1974); *Mumbo Jumbo* (1972; repr. New York: Scribner's, 1996); Pamela Taylor-Graham, *Orange Crush: An Ivy League Mystery* (New York: Simon and Schuster, 2004); Blair S. Walker, *Up Jumped the Devil* (New York: William Morrow, 1997); Paula L. Woods, *Dirty Laundry* (New York: One World/Ballantine, 2003). **Secondary Sources:** Frankie Y. Bailey, *Out of the Woodpile: Black Characters in Crime and Detective Fiction* (Westport, CT: Greenwood Press, 1991); Eleanor Taylor

Bland, ed., *Shades of Black: Crime and Mystery Stories by African-American Authors* (New York: Berkley, 2004); Michel Fabre and Robert E. Skinner, eds., *Conversations with Chester Himes* (Jackson: University Press of Mississippi, 1995); Adrienne Johnson Gosselin, ed., *Multicultural Detective Fiction: Murder from the "Other" Side* (New York: Garland, 1999); Beth Kalikoff, *Murder and Moral Decay in Victorian Popular Literature* (Ann Arbor: UMI Research Press, 1986); Kathleen Gregory Klein, ed., *Diversity and Detective Fiction* (Bowling Green, OH: Bowling Green State University Popular Press, 1999); Helen Lock, *A Case of Mis-Taken Identity: Detective Undercurrents in Recent African American Fiction* (New York: Peter Lang, 1994); Deane Mansfield-Kelley and Lois A. Marchino, eds., *The Longman Anthology of Detective Fiction* (New York: Pearson-Longman, 2005); Maureen T. Reddy, *Traces, Codes, and Clues: Reading Race in Crime Fiction* (New Brunswick, NJ: Rutgers University Press, 2003); Charles L. P. Silet, ed., *The Critical Response to Chester Himes* (Westport, CT: Greenwood Press, 1999); Robert E. Skinner, *Two Guns from Harlem: The Detective Fiction of Chester Himes* (Bowling Green, OH: Bowling Green State University Popular Press, 1989); Stephen F. Soitos, *The Blues Detective: A Study of African American Detective Fiction* (Amherst: University of Massachusetts Press, 1996); Ronald R. Thomas, *Detective Fiction and the Rise of Forensic Science* (Cambridge: Cambridge University Press, 1999); Charles E. Wilson, Jr., *Walter Mosley: A Critical Companion* (Westport, CT: Greenwood Press, 2003); Paula L. Woods, ed., *Spooks, Spies, and Private Eyes: Black Mystery, Crime, and Suspense Fiction of the Twentieth Century* (New York: Doubleday, 1995).

Kinohi Nishikawa

Crisis, The (1910–present). The magazine of the National Association for the Advancement of Colored People (**NAACP**), it was established to serve as its official organ. Its original full name was *The Crisis: A Record of the Dark Races*. The magazine's name came from a poem titled "The Present Crisis," by James Russell. **W.E.B. Du Bois**, a founding member of the NAACP, was the primary creator and first editor. Only 1,000 copies were published of the first, sixteen-page issue. Throughout its first year, the circulation rose by nearly 1,000 each month. By the end of 1911, total monthly circulation was approximately 10,000.

The stated goal of *The Crisis* was to serve as a magazine that would "set forth those facts and arguments which show the danger of race prejudice, particularly as manifested today toward colored people" (Kellogg; *Crisis* online). It reported on domestic race relations as well as worldwide events having an impact on the lives of African Americans. It also included editorials and essays and reviews of African American literature. In this way, *The Crisis* was an important medium not only of information but also of exposure to new African American writers and artists of the time. It held a literary competition each year through 1928. Although Du Bois was a supporter and promoter of African American artists of the time, he was selective in his choices, viewing art as another means of propaganda to force social change (Du Bois, "Criteria"; Lewis).

The Crisis was critical to spreading news about the NAACP's activities and priorities. In the early years of the organization, outreach had been done through lectures at meetings or at commemorative gatherings. Because circulation of the magazine far outpaced membership in NAACP, Du Bois also used it as a recruiting tool. Once the NAACP grew and opened branch offices, the continued growth in circulation for *The Crisis* meant the association could continue to spread its message and recruit members through the print medium, while using its manpower to focus on other aspects of its mission.

From the beginning, critics attacked the opinions set forth in *The Crisis*. Despite his reputation, Du Bois was one of a few African Americans in the organization's leadership. Some African American newspapers and periodicals charged that the White leadership of the NAACP was suppressing any true expression by African Americans in the pages of *The Crisis*.

In addition, the magazine faced the challenge of increasing its circulation through a nontraditional method of distribution. Initially, subscriptions were sold by NAACP staff members while they were in the field. Although circulation numbers rose rapidly, *The Crisis* faced a new challenge: rising costs as the staff expanded to meet the demands of the magazine's growth. Advertisers posed an obstacle as well. White businesses were reluctant to buy space for advertising because they did not recognize the buying power of the 80 percent African American readership of the magazine, and African American businesses did not have enough prominence at either the regional or the national level to make advertising in *The Crisis* a cost-effective tool for them (Kellogg, 150–153).

Not all of the difficulties were related to circulation and economics. Du Bois saw *The Crisis* as a representation of his personal opinion, believing that competing personalities and agendas within any organization could not lead to a consensus of opinion (Du Bois, *Autobiography*, 261). He saw the purpose of the NAACP and *The Crisis* as being to "place consistently and continuously before the country clear-cut statement of the legitimate aims" of African Americans, as well as details of how they were being treated throughout American society (Du Bois, *Autobiography*, 260). Du Bois did not limit his views to America, however. In addition to a strong opposition to **colonialism** in Asia and Africa, he was a strong supporter of Pan-Africanism. He was well traveled and saw the struggle in America as part of a larger global picture, with events happening outside of the United States affecting and reinforcing events domestically. The other members of the NAACP's leadership, however, wanted to limit the content of *The Crisis* to domestic issues, with a focus on NAACP activities.

Despite these growing pains and differences of opinion, by 1912, circulation of *The Crisis* had grown to 24,000 per month, and by 1916 it was up to 37,000. Subscriptions seemed to be concentrated in the East, North Central, Mid-Atlantic, and South Atlantic states, in towns with populations over 5,000. To address this situation, the staff of the magazine began a four-month circulation drive in **the South** in 1917. However, nothing helped with the increase in circulation as much as the growing acts of violence against African Americans (Kellogg, 153).

The Crisis regularly reported on acts of police brutality, and sometimes included special pull-out sections such as "The Waco Horror," an account of the **lynching** and burning of an eighteen-year-old boy before a crowd of 15,000 spectators in May 1916. Antagonism and violence against African Americans seemed to hit a peak in the "Red Summer" of 1919. Southerners were agitated by the loss of laborers to the war, African American soldiers returned home from **World War I** to find their social standing had not improved, and tensions erupted in a wave of lynchings and riots across the Midwest, parts of the South, and in **Washington, D.C.**

In May 1919, *The Crisis* published "Documents of the War"—copies of documents revealing prejudice in the military and American attempts to influence French attitudes toward African American soldiers. The year before, Du Bois had encouraged a show of solidarity in "Close Ranks," an essay emphasizing the need to fight against a common enemy. African Americans now felt betrayed, and the results of Du Bois's exposé were immediate. In June 1919, *The Crisis* hit a peak circulation of 104,000 (Kellogg, 153).

Domestic unrest following a war was disquieting to the U.S. government. Local and federal government initiatives designed to dampen the influence of anyone perceived to be a government critic and/or socialist sympathizer began to appear. As a registered member of the Socialist Party, Du Bois, and by extension *The Crisis*, were under suspicion. Two congressional bills were proposed in 1920 that would deny postal privileges to publications thought to be appealing to prejudice in order to incite rioting and violence. Through the increased power of its membership, informed readership, and burgeoning legal efforts, the NAACP was able to rally enough opposition to defeat both bills (Kellogg, 289–290).

Du Bois was credited with making *The Crisis* self-sustaining; however, the onset of the **Great Depression** meant the magazine would need financial support from the NAACP. In 1933, a wholly owned subsidiary of the NAACP, Crisis Publishing Company, took over publication of the magazine. By this time, internal disputes had caused numerous structural changes within the NAACP and in how *The Crisis* was run. Du Bois continued to publish controversial editorials, sometimes without presenting them to the advisory board for review. The final straw came in 1934 when Du Bois published a series of six editorials advocating that African Americans begin "fighting segregation with segregation." The editorials were contrary to the principles and views of the NAACP, and Du Bois resigned as editor.

After **World War II**, the focus of the NAACP turned to gaining full equality for African Americans. The organization had become a savvy and powerful legal force, both in the defense of African Americans and in waging legal battles against discrimination. *Crisis* began to publish more human-interest articles, success stories, and a new feature: an annotated list of books by domestic and foreign black authors. Although the book listing was discontinued in 1968, it is still considered to be an excellent resource of African American and African **diaspora** literature of the time (*Crisis* Online).

Circulation of *The Crisis* has fluctuated with economics, NAACP membership, and domestic and world events. The **Civil Rights Movement** of the 1960s brought another era of increased influence for both *The Crisis* and the NAACP. In 1964, the year of the highest NAACP membership (534,710), circulation of *The Crisis* also reached a new high (122,289) (*Crisis* Online). The victories of the Civil Rights era, subsequent advances in technology, and the increase in the number of specialized social-reform organizations and publications have changed the impact and influence that *The Crisis* had in its early history.

Today, *The Crisis* is published bimonthly, and the most recent figures for its circulation average around 100,000. The Crisis Publishing Company is a for-profit company and legally separate from the NAACP. Although the magazine includes a disclaimer that the views expressed in its articles may not necessarily represent those of the NAACP, the magazine contains a regular news section titled "The NAACP Today" and is still advertised as the magazine of the NAACP (*Crisis* Online).

Throughout its history, *The Crisis* has confronted the controversial issues of its time, as well as reporting on topics as diverse as literacy, children's education, **Marxism**, color lines in Russia, Gandhi's work in India, and the relationships among ethnic minorities in modern America. It has been a significant tool in education and has had a significant impact in shaping ideas and opinions about the social state of African Americans; in doing so, it has served as a catalyst for change. With such magazines as ***Opportunity***, ***Negro Digest***, and ***The Messenger***, it ranks as one of the most important magazines in African American history.

Particularly during and immediately after the **Harlem Renaissance**, *The Crisis* published the work of many significant African American writers, including **Jessie Redmon Fauset** (a literary editor for the magazine in the 1920s), **Marita Bonner, Rudolph Fisher, Claude McKay, Sterling A. Brown, Countee Cullen, Arna Bontemps, James Weldon Johnson, Walter White, E. Franklin Frazier**, and **Charles Waddell Chesnutt**. Over the course of his career, **Langston Hughes** published more than eighty poems in *The Crisis*, beginning with "The Negro Speaks of Rivers" in 1921 (Ostrom). In 1999, an anthology of short stories, poems, and essays from *The Crisis* was published (Wilson).

Resources: Arna Bontemps, *The Harlem Renaissance Remembered: Essays, Edited, with a Memoir* (New York: Dodd, Mead, 1972); *The Crisis* Magazine Online, http://www.thecrisismagazine.com; W.E.B. Du Bois: *The Autobiography of W.E.B. Du Bois* (New York: International Publishers, 1968); "Criteria of Negro Art," in *The Portable Harlem Renaissance Reader*, ed. David Levering Lewis (New York: Viking/Penguin, 1994), 100–105; Charles Flint Kellogg, *NAACP: A History of the National Association for the Advancement of Colored People*, vol. 1, *1909–1920* (Baltimore: Johns Hopkins Press, 1967); David Levering Lewis, *When Harlem Was in Vogue* (New York: Oxford University Press, 1989); Hans Ostrom, *A Langston Hughes Encyclopedia* (Westport, CT: Greenwood Press, 2002), 85–86; Jeffrey C. Stewart, *1001 Things Everyone Should*

Know About African American History (New York: Doubleday, 1996); Sondra Kathryn Wilson, ed., *The Crisis Reader: Stories, Poetry, and Essays from the N.A.A.C.P.'s "Crisis" Magazine* (New York: Modern Library, 1999).

Michelle Mellon

Cross-Dressing. Cross-dressing, a practice in which a person of one **gender** wears clothes customarily associated with the other gender, when used in literature often signifies the crossing of geographical boundaries and cultural categories other than that of gender. Cross-dressing is often a plot device, a mode of character exposition, or both in African American literature, reaching back from the twentieth-century novel all the way to **slave narratives** and the **trickster** tales of African and early African American culture. Scholars, including **Henry Louis Gates, Jr.**, have traced the trickster **folktales** of slave culture back to the mythologies and **folklore** of several African cultures. These stories often depict gods and other mythic figures whose gender and sexual orientation are fluid or ambiguous. According to Gates, for example, the trickster figure of the dually sexed Esu Elegba of Yoruba culture survived the **middle passage** from Africa and was imported to the United States, taking root in slave culture. Esu's gender ambiguity is observable in African American trickster folklore, including John-the-Slave cycles and tales featuring Br'er Rabbit. An illustration of gender ambiguity can be observed, for example, in the tale wherein Br'er Rabbit tricks Old Grinny Granny Wolf into climbing into a stew pot, and then puts on her frock and cap and passes himself off as Granny to Br'er Wolf; Adolf Gerber traces this story back to a Kaffir folktale about the trickster Hlakanyana. The pervasive motif of masquerade and escape in African American trickster tales often finds expression in gender-crossed dress.

The trickster elements of slave folklore were incorporated, both thematically and historically, into the tradition of slave narratives, which depicted the escape to freedom in the North, with disguise—including gender-crossed disguise—as a frequent strategy for escape. The most influential early instance of cross-dressing in African American slave narrative is the story of **William and Ellen Craft**, originally told in African American newspaper accounts starting in 1849. Ellen, light-skinned enough to pass for White, made herself a gentleman's suit of clothes and cut her hair; she and her darker-skinned husband then escaped to the North by **passing** as an ailing gentleman slaveholder and his slave valet. Although it took them until 1860 to publish a narrative of their experience, *Running a Thousand Miles for Freedom*, under William's name, the details of their escape were widely known among abolitionists almost immediately upon their arrival in **Boston, Massachusetts**. The Crafts then traveled as speakers on the abolitionist circuit with **William Wells Brown**, who posted bulletins about their tour in *The Liberator*. By the summer of 1849, the Crafts' story had become a fixture in the abolitionist and mainstream press, and their story was to prove deeply influential on the African American literary tradition.

The first use of the Craft narrative in fiction appeared in *Uncle Tom's Cabin* (1852); **Harriet Beecher Stowe** drew on the Craft narrative to create the fictional journey of the Harrises northward to Canada. The parallels between the Crafts' story and Stowe's are apparent: Eliza, a light-skinned **mulatto**, escapes with her husband after cutting her hair short and donning a man's suit; Stowe doubled the device by dressing the Harrises' son, Harry, as a girl. By the time Stowe's novel had been established as a blockbuster, William Wells Brown was coming out with the first African American novel: *Clotel; or, the President's Daughter* (1853). Brown, like Stowe, drew on the Craft narrative for one of his subplots: he related the story of Clotel's cross-dressing to escape on a stagecoach, traveling with a Connecticut Yankee and his two daughters. Here Brown put to use a portion of Ellen Craft's story, perhaps unknown to Stowe, with which Brown had no doubt become familiar while on tour with William and Ellen: the infatuation of Ellen's White, female travel companions with her cross-dressed persona. Brown also complicated the cross-dressing device by having the characters of George and Mary exchange clothes to facilitate George's escape from prison and execution.

The cross-dressing device illustrated in the Crafts' story of escape and in the novels of Stowe and Brown was put to use in the work of many nineteenth-century African American novelists and slave narrative authors. **Frank J. Webb** used the device briefly in *The Garies and Their Friends* (1857) when he had the trickster character, Kinch, cross-dress to entertain his friend Charlie. In a narrative that went unpublished until 2002 (*The Bondwoman's Narrative*, c. 1857), **Hannah Crafts** passes as a White, orphaned boy in order gain to freedom in the North. A year after William and Ellen Craft finally published their narrative, **Harriet Ann Jacobs** published her book-length narrative of trickster cross-dressing and escape, *Incidents in the Life of a Slave Girl* (1861). After the **Civil War**, **Mark Twain** continued to use the device in fictionalized slave narratives within such novels as *The Adventures of Huckleberry Finn* (1883, wherein Huck and Jim, among others, cross-dress) and *Pudd'nhead Wilson* (1894, wherein Tom and Roxana cross-dress).

By the time of Twain's novels, cross-dressing was already a common feature of **minstrelsy**. By the time **Sutton E. Griggs** wrote his dystopian novel, *Imperium in Imperio* (1899), the influence of fictionalized slave narrative had begun to evolve into narratives of passing. In Griggs's novel, the main character, Belton, after months of searching for a job without success, finally determines he will cross-dress and pass as a Black woman nurse—both as a means of finding employment and of spying on the White folks in power, to see what they are up to. Twentieth-century novelists have continued to put the cross-dressing device to work, but more as a means of character self-expression rather than a form of disguise or masquerade. This trend is observable with such fictional figures as the title character of *Winona* (1902), by **Pauline E. Hopkins**; Janie in *Their Eyes Were Watching God* (1937), by **Zora Neale Hurston**; the bar princess in *Giovanni's Room* (1956), by **James Baldwin**; Celie in *The Color Purple*

(1982), by **Alice Walker**; and Chino in *The Men of Brewster Place* (1998), by **Gloria Naylor**. (*See* **Dystopian Literature**; **Myth**.)

Resources: William and Ellen Craft, *Running a Thousand Miles for Freedom: The Escape of William and Ellen Craft from Slavery* (Athens: University of Georgia Press, 1999); Hannah Crafts, *The Bondwoman's Narrative: A Novel*, ed. Henry Louis Gates, Jr. (New York: Warner Books, 2002); Marjorie Garber, *Vested Interests: Cross-Dressing and Cultural Anxiety* (New York: Routledge, 1992); Henry Louis Gates, Jr., *The Signifying Monkey: A Theory of African-American Literary Criticism* (New York: Oxford University Press, 1988); Adolf Gerber, "Uncle Remus Traced to the Old World," *Journal of American Folklore*, Oct.–Dec. 1893, pp. 245–257; Lawrence W. Levine, *Black Culture and Black Consciousness: Afro-American Folk Thought from Slavery to Freedom* (New York: Oxford University Press, 1977); Mary Lamb Shelden, *Novel Habits for a New World: Cross-Dressing in the Nineteenth-Century American Novel* (Ann Arbor: UMI, 2003).

Mary Lamb Shelden

Crouch, Stanley (born 1945). Essayist, novelist, poet, and social critic. Stanley Crouch is a multifaceted writer, jazz musician, and social commentator concerned with issues facing the African American community. With a career that spans almost four decades, Crouch is currently a columnist for the *New York Daily News* and writes about such topics as rapper gangsters, the MTV Video Music Awards, Islamic terrorists, and other current cultural and political events and their negative, or positive, influence on American society. Of **rap** gangsters, Crouch has said, "I dislike the side of rap that encourages violence over trivia, theft, drive-by shootings, misogyny, the side of rap that gives young women the impression that in order to rebel, they should become sluts.... These things have had a very destructive influence on our society" (Broder, 23). Such straightforward commentary is characteristic of Crouch's writings, including his numerous published collections of essays. David Futrelle, in a review of Crouch's 1998 collection *Always in Pursuit: Fresh American Perspectives, 1995–1997*, states that Crouch is known for his "assaults on celebrities... particularly those African-Americans who... take too seriously the pieties of political correctness and multiculturalism."

Crouch's first novel, *Don't the Moon Look Lonesome: A Novel in Blues and Swing* (2000), deals with equally conflict-ridden issues. The plot involves a White South Dakota-born **jazz** singer and the Black musician whom she loves. In an interview with *The American Enterprise*, Crouch's reply to the question of what he thinks of interracial romance is revealing of his attitude that race shouldn't be a divisive issue: "you have an ethnic heritage and you have a human heritage. Your human heritage includes everything of human value. So I don't think that black kids or white kids... should only judge the significance of things by whether or not the people who put them together look like them" (Walter, 12). Along with his work as a newspaper columnist, Crouch is an artistic consultant at Lincoln Center in New York City.

Resources: Primary Sources: Jonathan Broder, "The *Salon* Interview: Stanley Crouch: White/Black...Men/Women. Get Over It—We're All American," *Salon*, Feb. 1998, http://archive.salon.com/books/int/1998/02/cov_si_25int.html; Stanley Crouch: *Ain't No Ambulances for No Nigguhs Tonight* (New York: R. W. Baron, 1972); *The All-American Skin Game; or, The Decoy of Race: The Long and the Short of It, 1990–1994* (New York: Pantheon, 1995); *Always in Pursuit: Fresh American Perspectives, 1995–1997* (New York: Pantheon, 1998); *Don't the Moon Look Lonesome: A Novel in Blues and Swing* (New York: Pantheon, 2000); *Notes of a Hanging Judge: Essays and Reviews, 1979–1989* (New York: Oxford University Press, 1990); *One Shot Harris: The Photographs of Charles "Teenie" Harris* (New York: Abrams, 2002); Stanley Crouch and Playthell Benjamin, *Reconsidering "The Souls of Black Folk"* (Philadelphia: Running Press, 2002); Scott Walter, "'Live' with *The American Enterprise*: Stanley Crouch," *The American Enterprise*, Mar. 2001, 12+. **Secondary Sources:** Jabari Asim, "Hasty Consideration of Du Bois' Seminal Essays," *The Crisis*, Mar./Apr. 2003, 44+; David Futrelle, "Review of *Always in Pursuit: Fresh American Perspectives, 1995–1997*, by Stanley Crouch," *Salon*, Feb. 25, 1998, http://archive.salon.com/books/sneaks/1998/02/25review.html; Sarah F. Gold, Emily Chernoweth, and Jeff Zaleski, "Review of *Reconsidering 'The Souls of Black Folk,'* by Stanley Crouch," *Publishers Weekly*, Mar. 10, 2003, p. 69; Elisabeth Lasch-Quinn, "Radical Chic and the Rise of a Therapeutics of Race," *Salmagundi*, Fall 1996, 8+; Sanford Pinsker, "Climbing over the Ethnic Fence: Reflections on Stanley Crouch and Philip Roth," *Virginia Quarterly Review*, Summer 2002, 472+; Clarence V. Reynolds, "Review of *One Shot Harris*, by Stanley Crouch," *Black Issues Book Review*, Jan./Feb. 2003, 17.

Judith M. Schmitt

Crummell, Alexander (1819–1898). Minister, scholar, and nonfiction writer. Though often overlooked in the annals of black American history, Alexander Crummell made a significant impact throughout his lifetime as a tireless advocate for the rights of African peoples throughout the world. As a writer, Crummell is known primarily for his published sermons and speeches and his commentary on African American life.

Crummell was born in 1819, to an African prince who demanded his freedom and a free Black mother, in New York City. At a time when there were few educational opportunities for Black Americans, Crummell was able to attend an interracial school in New Canaan, New Hampshire, that had a curriculum combining manual labor and classical education. In 1839, Crummell intended to attend the General Theological Seminary of the Episcopal Church, but was denied admission because of his **race**. Undeterred, Crummell studied theology on his own, and in 1844 he became an Episcopal minister, defying expectation and circumstance. Nonetheless, being denied educational opportunity would influence his life's work of promoting literacy for Black Americans.

In 1848, Crummell traveled to England with the goal of raising funds to build a church for indigent Blacks in America. While abroad, he attended Cambridge, where he continued his studies in theology. Wishing to spread Christianity throughout the world, Crummell headed for Liberia upon graduation from Cambridge. At the time, Liberia was a unique country in that it was established as a colony, in 1822, for freed slaves. Crummell had originally argued against colonization, but after being subjected to the indignities of discrimination from his White peers, he began to foster the belief that Africa was the true cradle of civilization. In his treatise *The Regeneration of Africa*, Crummell states, "What nobler plan could the great Baptist denomination fall upon, than just this providential movement to effect that which is dear to their hearts, and to the hearts of all Christians—the redemption of Africa! And what a living thing would not their work be, if perchance, they could plant some half dozen compact, intelligent enterprising villagers of such Christian people, amid the heathen populations of West Africa!" Crummell would spend the next twenty years in Africa as the leader of a congregation and a professor at Liberia College (*see* **Colonialism**).

In 1873, Crummell returned to the United States and founded St. Luke's Episcopal Church in **Washington, D.C.**, and assumed the task of increasing the visibility of Blacks in the Episcopal Church. He was pastor of his congregation for twenty-one years, serving as spiritual leader and also fighting for rights for Black Americans and for the education of his people. After retiring from the ministry, Crummell went on to found the American Negro Academy in 1897. The Academy endeavored to improve the lives of Black people through promoting the science, literature, art, and philosophy of Black intellectuals, and in turn foster the ideal of higher education for Blacks. It also sought to show White intellectuals that the contributions of Black intellectuals were equal to theirs. Prominent members included **Paul Laurence Dunbar**; **W.E.B. Du Bois**, who writes of Crummell in *The Souls of Black Folk*; and **Francis James Grimké**. Though the Academy remained intact for thirty-one years, it ultimately served the needs of the few over the many and never achieved its ambition as a significant intellectual force.

Resources: Alexander Crummell: *Africa and America: Addresses and Discourses* (Miami, FL: Mnemosyne, 1969); *The Black Woman of the South: Her Neglects and Her Needs* (Cincinnati, OH: Woman's Home Missionary Society of the Methodist Episcopal Church, 1883); *The Future of Africa; Being Addresses, Sermons, etc., etc., Delivered in the Republic of Liberia* (New York: Negro Universities Press, 1969); *The Greatness of Christ and Other Sermons* (New York: Thomas Whittaker, 1882); *The Relations and Duties of Free Colored Men in America to Africa: A Letter to Charles B. Dunbar* (Hartford, CT: Case, Lockwood, 1861); Wilson J. Moses, *Alexander Crummell: A Study of Civilization and Discontent* (New York: Oxford University Press, 1989); J. R. Oldfield, *Alexander Crummell (1819–1898) and the Creation of an African American-Church in Liberia* (Lewiston, NY: E. Mellen Press, 1990); Gregory Rigsby, *Alexander Crummell: Pioneer in Nineteenth-Century Pan-African Thought* (Westport, CT: Greenwood Press, 1987).

Roxane Gay

Cruse, Harold Wright (born 1916). Scholar, essayist, intellectual, and political activist. Cruse's work was influential during the 1960s. He was born March 18, 1916, in Petersburg, Virginia, and his parents separated when he was young. He and his father moved to New York City, where the elder Cruse was a supervisor for the Long Island Rail Road. After graduating from public high school in New York City, Cruse served in the Quartermaster Corps of the Army during **World War II**. Following the war, Cruse attended City College of New York but dropped out of school after a year.

After attending a lecture by **Richard Wright** in **Harlem, New York**, Cruse was increasingly drawn into New York leftist politics and intellectual life. Although often associated with the Communist Party during the 1950s, he was an outspoken anticommunist by the early 1960s. He pursued a variety of interests and employment opportunities in the New York City area during the postwar years, including office clerk for the Veterans Administration, film and drama critic for the *New York Labor Press*, teacher of Black history, and cofounder of LeRoi Jones's **(Amiri Baraka) Black Arts Repertory Theatre/ School**.

Cruse received considerable attention and notoriety for his 1967 publication *The Crisis of the Negro Intellectual*, on which he had been working for four years. The book caused a stir because of its criticism of the Black establishment. In his lengthy historical overview, Cruse argues that Black leadership, due to its affiliation with White political groups such as the Communist Party, are elitists who have little to offer the Black masses other than assimilation into White America. He concludes that it is the duty of Black intellectuals to develop a sense of cultural identity and nationalism that will provide a meaningful alternative to integration. Cruse's book was less than well received by the Black liberal establishment, but his ideas connected well with the developing **Black Power** movement. His call for an enhanced public and political role for intellectuals elicited favorable reviews in such publications as the *New York Review of Books*.

In 1968, Cruse published a collection of essays on black nationalism titled *Rebellion or Revolution?*, and he was hired by the University of Michigan, where he founded the university's Center for Afro-American and African Studies. He was named a full professor in 1978, although he had never earned a college degree. While teaching, he contributed to numerous anthologies, and in 1987 he published *Plural but Equal*, in which the Black intellectual criticized the impact of integration upon African American life and culture. In 1987 Cruse was named professor emeritus at the University of Michigan. His more radical work on **Black Nationalism** pioneered the concepts of pluralism and multiculturalism that would enjoy considerable acceptance within the intellectual and academic communities during the late twentieth century. **William Jelani Cobb** edited an anthology of Cruse's writing, and it was published in 2002.

Resources: William Jelani Cobb, ed., *The Essential Harold Cruse: A Reader* (New York: Palgrave, 2002); Harold Cruse: *The Crisis of the Negro Intellectual* (New York: Morrow, 1967); *Plural but Equal: A Critical Study of Blacks and Minorities and America's Plural Society* (New York: Morrow, 1987); *Rebellion or Revolution?* (New York: Morrow, 1968); Arthur P. Davis and J. Saunders Redding, eds., *Cavalcade: Negro American*

Writing from 1760 to the Present (Boston: Houghton Mifflin, 1971); LeRoi Jones and Larry Neal, eds., *Black Fire: An Anthology of Afro-American Writing* (New York: Morrow, 1968); William H. Robinson, ed., *Nommo: An Anthology of Modern Black African and Black American Literature* (New York: Macmillan, 1972).

Ron Briley

Cullen, Countee (1903–1946). Poet and novelist. Apart from an obligatory inclusion in **Harlem Renaissance** anthologies, relatively little attention is today paid to Countee Cullen, who was one of the most celebrated young Harlem Renaissance stars, the movement's poet laureate, and an extremely accomplished writer of formal verse. Personal information extant about him is somewhat confusing. Starting with his place of birth and continuing with his childhood, Cullen's personal life seems shrouded in mystery. For instance, it remains unclear exactly where Cullen was born on May 30, 1903—Kentucky; **Baltimore, Maryland**; or New York City—he gave different information at various times during his career. Cullen, who was adopted by Rev. Frederick Asbury Cullen and his wife in 1914 or 1918, apparently had had an unhappy childhood and was highly sensitive regarding his personal life. He was still in high school when he entered the limelight by winning a citywide poetry contest, but he quickly realized the significance of a public image. Consequently, it seems, he invented an "appropriate" family background: Claiming to be born in New York, he could uphold the fiction that he was the Cullens' natural son. To some extent, the poet laureate Cullen was thus a public construct.

Cullen's resolve to cover up blemishes in his personal history indicates the extent to which he was willing to guard his reputation and the importance he attributed to his public image. He focused on a literary career and sought a leading position among the **"Talented Tenth,"** the educated African American elite. Cullen worked hard to attain the academic merits required and succeeded. He excelled in his studies of English and French at New York University, received numerous awards, graduated Phi Beta Kappa, and went on to receive an M.A. from Harvard in 1926. At the same time, the young poet successfully followed his literary ambitions. His poems were published in all the leading magazines from *Vanity Fair* to *The Bookman*, **Opportunity**, and **The Crisis**; his works were recited in Harlem's churches; he was invited to poetry readings; and his first volume of poetry, *Color*, was published in 1925, while Cullen was still in graduate school. At the age of twenty-two, Cullen had already taken a major career step—he was a Harlem Renaissance star, a celebrity whose every accomplishment was followed by the media and whose works were critically appraised. It seemed only natural that Cullen's career flourished further during the 1920s. Within a span of five years, he not only published the tale *The Ballad of the Brown Girl* (1927) and two more poetry volumes, *Copper Sun* (1927) and *The Black Christ* (1929), but his poems were included in **Alain Locke's** *The New Negro* (1925), he edited a volume of young Renaissance writers' works (*Caroling Dusk*, 1927), and from December 1926 to September 1928 contributed a monthly literary column, "The Dark

Tower," to *Opportunity*, one of the best-known African American journals of the era. In addition, Cullen won several literary awards and prestigious fellowships, including a Guggenheim fellowship (1928).

Among the large group of young writers and artists who gathered in **Harlem, New York**, in the early-to-mid-1920s Cullen stood out. Within the **New Negro** movement, he represented an "old-school" writer whose choice of a strict, formal Romanticism and adherence to traditional measures and rhymes separated him from, for instance, **Langston Hughes**, who experimented with form and created his popular **blues poetry**. Whereas many younger Renaissance writers celebrated blackness, intending to, as Hughes put it, "express [their] individual dark-skinned selves without fear or shame," Cullen declared that he was "POET and not NEGRO POET," and bemoaned in "Yet Do I Marvel" (1925) the seeming irony of a God who decided to "make a poet black and bid him sing." Similar to scholars of the Harlem Renaissance, many of whom felt unable to deal with the extremely popular but at the same time curiously old-fashioned poet, who seems out of place in an era generally identified more with raunchy **blues** songs than with decorous Romanticism, many of the younger

Countee Cullen in Central Park, 1941. Courtesy of the Library of Congress.

Renaissance writers were highly critical of Cullen. An artistic gulf separated them—a fact that was demonstrated in the publication of the provocative journal *Fire!!* (1926), to which Cullen contributed the strictly metered **sonnet** "From the Dark Tower," which contrasted harshly with the majority of other contributions, such as tales about prostitution and homoerotic fantasies.

While many of the younger writers of the Harlem Renaissance—the "Niggeratti," a satiric term made popular by **Wallace Thurman** and **Zora Neale Hurston**—rebelled against the Renaissance establishment, represented by figures such as **W.E.B. Du Bois** and Alain Locke, Cullen proved a model Renaissance artist who willingly accepted what could be termed a "burden of representation"—the responsibility of African American artists as interpreters and representatives of the whole "race." When the Niggeratti thus proclaimed their artistic freedom, Cullen admonished them that "whether they relish the situation or not, Negroes should be concerned with making good impressions." He was willing and able to contribute fully to the aim of the Harlem Renaissance as defined by its leaders: the artistic creation of new and "representative" (meaning positive) images of African Americans was to convince White Americans of Black Americans' equality and to end racial discrimination. Unsurprisingly, Cullen, following in the footsteps of his literary idols John Keats, Alfred Tennyson, and A. E. Housman, was highly acclaimed by genteel critics and Renaissance leaders alike.

In order to attain and then to keep this prominent and respected position within the Harlem Renaissance, Cullen continued to work hard to present an acceptable public persona. Far more significant at the time than a dubious family background, Cullen's same-sex desire could have provided a significant obstacle on the path to fame and popular approval. Describing himself as "Puritanical" in taste, the conservative Cullen felt unable to follow, for instance, the path traveled by the openly gay bohemian writer and artist **Richard Bruce Nugent**. Instead, Cullen opted for a strenuous division of his private and public sexual personas. He thus publicly presented himself as a shy yet clearly heterosexual young man. One can conclude from his private correspondence that his interest in women mainly rested on their representative function as potential wives. In 1928, he married Nina Yolande Du Bois, the daughter of the leading African American intellectual. The public display of heterosexual bliss was extravagant—1,300 invited guests and numerous spectators were at the ceremony—yet the marriage did not endure. On his "honeymoon," Cullen was accompanied not by his wife but by his intimate friend Harold Jackman, a young, attractive bisexual African American teacher who belonged to the Harlem Renaissance network. By 1930, the unhappily married couple was divorced.

While some critics claim that there is no "proof" of Cullen's homosexuality, his intimate correspondence with Locke, a closeted gay Harlem Renaissance intellectual, clearly indicates Cullen's love interest in and sexual desire for men. Locke introduced the young man to a gay literary heritage and to a special type of gay discourse that fused terms from the Greek discourse of homosexuality such as "perfect friendship" with Whitmanesque expressions such as "comraderie"—terms that one encounters in Cullen's poetry. Locke's interpretations of homosexuality as a "perfect friendship," as Cullen commented, "threw a noble and evident light on what [he] had begun to believe, because of what the world believes, ignoble and unnatural," thereby sparing him from internalizing homophobia. However, he still retained doubts and feared detection. But while Cullen exercised self-censorship even in his private correspondence, he did not exclude the topic of homosexuality from his literary works, in which his gay voice, ranging from sombre depictions of same-sex love to the expression of hope, is audible to varying degrees. His preference for Romanticism served him well as a veil for references to same-sex love, yet sometimes, as in "Tableau" (1925), which was dedicated to Donald Duff, a White male lover of Cullen's, Cullen proved more courageous: Here, Cullen depicts a White boy and a Black boy who, walking arm in arm, publicly transgress racial and sexual boundaries.

Despite claims to the contrary by a number of Harlem Renaissance scholars who focus on Cullen's alleged unwillingness to discuss racial issues, Cullen masterfully blended a multitude of topics in his works, ranging from moods of desperation and gloom in poems such as "Saturday's Child" (1925) and "Suicide Chant" (1925), to hope and courage, as evident in "Tableau." While Cullen refused to be viewed solely as a racial poet, he did not shy away from the topic, either, as two of his most famous poems—"Heritage," in which the question "What is Africa to me?" is explored in sensuous detail, and "The Black Christ," in which Cullen transforms Christ into a deity suitable to the needs of African Americans—clearly show. Cullen's most successful works contain exquisite layerings of themes. He interweaves religion, paganism, love, desire, (homo)sexuality, and race, thereby appealing to overlapping audiences consisting of genteel critics who applauded his application of traditional poetic forms, a black readership focusing on racial readings, and gay readers accustomed to the sounds of his specific gay voice.

In 1930, Cullen returned from a two-year stay in France that had been sponsored by a Guggenheim fellowship. In France, Cullen had felt liberated, embracing an environment he perceived to be less racist and homophobic than the United States. After Cullen's return, his steep climb up the career ladder slowed perceptibly. It seems, in fact, that by the time he was twenty-six, Cullen's literary career had already passed its climax. The Harlem he encountered on his return had changed; the **Great Depression** had left its marks, calling in the end of a decade of splendor. It seems that Cullen adapted to this new sense of reality. The boy wonder had grown up, and Cullen the man now decided on a career as a public school teacher in New York City and eventually gave marriage another try; in 1940, Cullen married Ida Roberson. Though this marriage lasted for the rest of his life, Cullen proved incapable of dedicating himself solely to a heterosexual relationship and was involved in a long-lasting secret love affair with the younger Edward Atkinson. Significantly, Cullen continued his literary efforts and started exploring different literary genres, writing *One Way to Heaven* (1932), a Harlem-based novel that barely received critical attention, juvenile fiction with *The Lost Zoo* (1940), and *My Lives and How I Lost Them* (1942), a choreo-musical with **Owen Dodson**, as well as dramatic adaptations of his own novel and **Arna Bontemps**'s *God Sends Sunday*. Additionally, he published one more volume of verse—*The Medea and Some Poems* (1935), arguably the weakest of his poetry collections. His career was slowing down, and Cullen, who suffered from serious heart problems, seems to have sensed, if not his life's nearing end, at least his creative period's passing. In 1945, he started to prepare a collection of his poems, thereby determining his own literary heritage. He died on January 9, 1946, and thus did not live to see the publication of *On These I Stand* (1947).

Cullen's works remain outstanding examples of Harlem Renaissance writing, indicating the great variety of work produced during the era and the divergent ideologies of the writers and artists involved. In contrast to many of his younger colleagues, Cullen proved a fully committed Harlem Renaissance artist whose efforts to contribute to the aim of racial uplift and an end of racial discrimination were rewarded with praise by his readers who, as Dodson summarized, found in Cullen's poetry "all … dilemmas … the hurt pride, the indignation, the satirical thrusts, the agony of being black in America." (*See* **Gay Literature**.)

Resources: Primary Sources: Countee Cullen: *Color* (New York: Harper & Bros., 1925); *Copper Sun* (New York: Harper & Bros., 1927); "Countee Cullen," in *Caroling Dusk: An Anthology of Verse by Negro Poets*, ed. Countee Cullen (New York: Harper & Bros., 1927), 179; "The Dark Tower," *Opportunity*, Mar. 1928, p. 90; *The Lost Zoo (A Rhyme for the Young, but Not Too Young)* (New York: Harper & Bros., 1940), published as by Christopher Cat and Countee Cullen; *The Medea and Some Poems* (New York: Harper & Bros., 1935); *My Lives and How I Lost Them* (New York: Harper & Bros., 1942), published as by Christopher Cat and Countee Cullen; *My Soul's High Song: The Collected Writings of Countee Cullen, Voice of the Harlem Renaissance*, ed. Gerald Early (New York: Doubleday, 1991); *On These I Stand: An Anthology of the Best Poems of Countee Cullen* (New York: Harper & Bros., 1947); *One Way to Heaven* (New York: Harper & Bros., 1932); Countee Cullen, ed., *Caroling Dusk: An Anthology of Verse by Negro Poets* (New York: Harper & Bros., 1927); Countee Cullen Papers, Amistad Research Center, Tulane University, New Orleans; Countee Cullen, letter to Harold Jackman (n.d.), Countee Cullen Papers, box 1, Beinecke Rare Book and Manuscript Library, Yale University. **Secondary Sources:** Houston A. Baker, Jr., *Afro-American Poetics: Revisions of Harlem and the Black Aesthetic* (Madison: University of Wisconsin Press, 1988); Nicholas Canaday, Jr., "Major Themes in the Poetry of Countee Cullen," in *The Harlem Renaissance Remembered*, ed. Arna Bontemps (New York: Dodd, Mead, 1972), 103–125; Owen Dodson, "Countee Cullen (1903–1946)," *Phylon* 7 (1946), 20; Gerald Early: "Introduction," in *My Soul's High Song: The Collected Writings of Countee Cullen, Voice of the Harlem Renaissance*, ed. Early (New York: Doubleday, 1991), 3–73; "Three Notes Toward a Cultural Definition of the Harlem Renaissance," *Callaloo* 14 (1991), 136–149; Michel Fabre, *From Harlem to Paris: Black American Writers in France, 1840–1980* (Urbana: University of Illinois Press, 1991); Blanche E. Ferguson, *Countee Cullen and the Negro Renaissance* (New York: Dodd, Mead, 1966); Michael L. Lomax, "Countee Cullen: A Key to the Puzzle," in *The Harlem Renaissance Re-examined*, ed. Victor A. Kramer (New York: AMS, 1987), 213–222; Hans Ostrom, "Countee Cullen: How Teaching Re-Writes the Genre of 'Writer,'" in *Genre and Writing: Issues, Arguments, Alternatives*, ed. Wendy Bishop and Hans Ostrom (Portsmouth, NH: Heinemann, 1997), 93–104; Margaret Perry, *A Bio-Bibliography of Countée P. Cullen, 1903–1946* (Westport, CT: Greenwood Press, 1971); Alden Reimonenq, "Countee Cullen's Uranian 'Soul Windows,'" in *Critical Essays: Gay and Lesbian Writers of Color*, ed. Emmanuel S. Nelson (New York: Haworth Press, 1993), 143–166; D. Dean Shackleford, "The Poetry of Countée Cullen," in *Masterpieces of African-American Literature*, ed. Frank N. Magill (New York: HarperCollins, 1992), 382–386; Alan Shucard, *Countee Cullen* (Boston: Twayne, 1984); Margaret Sperry, "Countee P. Cullen, Negro Boy Poet, Tells His Story," *Brooklyn Daily Eagle*, Feb. 10, 1924, n.p.; James W. Tuttleton, "Countee Cullen at 'The Heights,'" in *The Harlem Renaissance: Revaluations*, ed. Amritjit Singh, William S. Shiver, and Stanley Brodwin (New York: Garland, 1989), 101–137; Jean

Wagner, *Black Poets of the United States: From Paul Laurence Dunbar to Langston Hughes*, trans. Kenneth Douglas (Urbana: University of Illinois Press, 1973).

A. B. Christa Schwarz

Cuney-Hare, Maud (1874–1936). Composer, pianist, music historian, biographer, and teacher. Cuney-Hare is well known as a translator of lyrics in **Creole** folk songs and as the author of *Negro Musicians and Their Music* (1936), an ambitious survey of the topic. Maud Cuney was born in Galveston, **Texas**, the daughter of Adelina and Norris Wright Cuney. Norris Wright Cuney was the son of a slave, also born in Texas but educated in Pennsylvania. He later returned to his home state and became a prominent participant in Republican Party politics there, as well as a labor organizer of stevedores in Galveston. Cuney-Hare wrote a biography of her father: *Norris Wright Cuney: A Tribune of the Black People* (1913). *Six Creole Songs*, the lyrics of which Cuney-Hare translated into English, was published in 1921. For many years, Cuney-Hare lived in **Boston, Massachusetts**, in the historical section of the city known as Jamaica Plain (*Boston Women's Heritage Trail*). Her papers, the Maud Cuney-Hare Collection, 1900–1936, are in the Archives and Special Collections section of Woodruff Library, Atlanta University Center, **Atlanta, Georgia**.

Resources: Maud Cuney-Hare: *Negro Musicians and Their Music* (Washington, DC: Associated Publishers, 1936); *Norris Wright Cuney: A Tribune of the Black People* (New York: Crisis Publishing, 1913); *Six Creole Folk-Songs, with Original Creole and Translated English Text* (New York: Carl Fischer, 1921); "Jamaica Plain," *Boston Women's Heritage Trail*, http://www.bwht.org/jp2.html.

Hans Ostrom